PSYCHOLOGICAL TESTING

Design, Analysis, and Use

LISA FRIEDENBERG
The University of North Carolina at Asheville

Allyn and Bacon
Boston • London • Toronto • Sydney • Tokyo • Singapore

Vice President, Publisher: Social Science: Susan Badger
Marketing Manager: Joyce Nilsen
Production Administrator: Marjorie Payne
Editorial Assistant: Susan Hutchinson
Cover Administrator: Linda Knowles
Composition/Prepress Buyer: Linda Cox
Manufacturing Buyer: Megan Cochran
Editorial-Production Service: Raeia Maes

Copyright © 1995 by Allyn & Bacon
A Simon & Schuster Company
Needham Heights, Massachusetts 02194

Library of Congress Cataloging-in-Publication Data

Friedenberg, Lisa.
   Psychological testing : Design, analysis, and use / Lisa
Friedenberg.
     p.   cm.
   Includes bibliographical references and index.
   ISBN 0-205-14214-1
   1. Psychological tests. 2. Psychometrics. I. Title.
BF176.F784 1995
150′.28′7—dc20   94-34623
                                 CIP

REVIEW COPY
ISBN: 0-205-16911-2

Printed in the United States of America

10 9 8 7 6 5 4 3 2   99 98 97 96

To Michael
The best there is!

Contents

Preface

Psychological Testing is designed for courses that emphasize an understanding of testing as an assessment technique and the development of test writing and evaluation skills. It differs significantly from other testing or assessment books in several critical ways. First, the book provides a detailed explanation of how tests are developed, including a description of different types of test scores, different types of test items, and the construction of scales to measure ability, personality, attitudes, and behavior. Most students are interested in learning about test development; they like the idea of learning how to write a good survey or test and of learning skills that they can apply in their research or jobs. Even if they will never write tests of their own, students can become educated test consumers if they understand something about the advantages and problems associated with different types of tests.

Second, the book is written specifically for students with minimal background in statistics. Although most students do not have a sophisticated grasp of statistical concepts after a single statistics course, these concepts are critical to understanding how we evaluate the usefulness of a test. To help students develop evaluation skills, the text includes a review of concepts such as scales of measurement, descriptive statistics, and score transformations. These concepts are used as a point of departure for in-depth discussions of reliability, validity, and item analysis.

Third, the book provides a detailed account of how tests are used to make decisions in educational, psychological, and employment settings. Although many other texts discuss the use of psychological tests, their chapters often are organized to focus on either single tests or on particular categories of tests. In contrast to this approach, *Psychological Testing* organizes its discussion of test use by settings. Within each setting, the reasons for administering tests are described and examples of the tests used for these purposes are presented. In this way, the text focuses directly on the applications of testing and the issues raised by using tests. Because specific tests are used to illustrate these points, the same test may be discussed in more than one chapter, with each chapter detailing its application in that particular setting. Such a presentation reinforces an appreciation of the diversity of ways in which a single test can be used.

Psychological Testing grew (literally) out of the extensive supplementary handouts I wrote to make other textbooks more intelligible and interesting to students. Most of the decisions I made about what to cover and how to do it were based on my own experiences with other texts and on feedback from my students. For example, I found it difficult to cover 16 or more chapters in a one-semester course and equally difficult to select chapters to delete without omitting important course concepts. I therefore decided to reorganize the traditional material into a smaller number of chapters, leaving it to individual instructors to add material according to the design of their particular courses.

When studying chapters on the analysis of test data, students expressed frustration at the lack of opportunities to practice statistical analysis and interpretation. Although some texts do provide optional student workbooks, the design and expense of these supplements reduced their usefulness. I therefore decided to insert practice problems directly after discussion of each statistical concept or analysis, providing students with opportunities for immediate feedback about their understanding of statistical procedures without having to purchase separate student workbooks. Since so many statistical concepts are interrelated, it is useful for students to test themselves right away to see if they are ready to move on to the next concept.

Psychological Testing contains 12 chapters divided into three parts. Part I, Principles of Test Design, contains four chapters devoted to the process of test development. Chapter 1 discusses the principles of testing and measurement and identifies the characteristics of a good measurement instrument. Chapter 2 introduces the planning process, including questions about the purpose of a test and how it will be used. Chapter 3 describes the construction of ability tests, and Chapter 4 describes the development of tests of personality, attitudes, and interests and the development of evaluation scales. Students completing these four chapters should understand the advantages and disadvantages of different types of tests, item formats, and scoring systems; they should be well prepared for either designing or selecting psychological tests.

Part II, Principles of Test Analysis, is devoted to a variety of analytical procedures. Chapter 5 begins with a review of basic statistical concepts and moves on to more sophisticated issues, such as linear and nonlinear transformations and linear regression. Chapter 6 discusses the various reliability analyses, including discussions of standard error and confidence intervals. Chapter 7 covers criterion, content, and construct validity; Chapter 8 is devoted to item analysis. The level of detail in these sections is designed to facilitate both a better understanding of analytical concepts and the development of analytical skills. Practice problems are incorporated into each chapter to encourage self-testing as each concept is introduced.

Part III, Principles of Test Use, is organized according to the settings in which tests are used. Chapter 9 discusses the use of tests in educational settings. Chapters 10 and 11 present tests used in personality and clinical assessment. Chapter 12 is devoted to testing in the workplace: the use of tests in business and industry. The chapters are designed to educate students about both the diversity of standardized tests and the variety of ways in which these tests are used.

In addition, the text contains a glossary of highlighted terms, a reference list, and appendixes covering the normal distribution table and sources of information about psychological tests. I have tried to maintain an informative but informal writing style to make the book not only easier to read but also more enjoyable to read. In general, I have tried to incorporate into the book all the lessons I learned from my students while teaching this course. I hope I listened well and wrote the book they wanted.

ACKNOWLEDGMENTS

There are more people to thank for their help with this project than I can possibly hope to remember. First come my students: for encouraging, prodding, and otherwise convincing me to turn all those outlines and handouts into a finished product. Second, my department: for helping me to find the time to do this. Third, all those people who read and commented on various drafts: Without you this book would not exist. Fourth, the reviewers: Paul Blaney, University of Miami; Jack Conboy, Southeastern Massachusetts University; Robert E. Dear, California State University/Northridge; Robert Dihoff, Rowan College of New Jersey; George Domino, University of Arizona; Frances Haemmerlie, University of Missouri/Rolla; James Hennessey, Fordham University; Linda Hynan, Baylor University; B. L. Klintz, Western Washington University; V. Krishna Kumar, West Chester University; William Lancaster, Georgia College; Judi Leslak, Central Michigan University; Jody Newan, Fordham University; Robert Reeves, Augusta College; and Tony Vernon, University of Western Ontario. And, finally, to my publisher: my thanks for being willing to take a chance on a somewhat unorthodox text.

L.F.

Using This Book

1. The book is organized into three four-chapter parts: test design, test analysis, and test use. Each part begins with an **Overview** of the major issues discussed in the subsequent chapters. Use these overviews to locate specific topics within each section.

2. Each chapter begins with a **Chapter Outline** listing the major topics and subtopics covered in the chapter. Use these outlines to locate topics within each chapter and to organize your notes for studying.

3. Each chapter also contains a list of **Chapter Goals and Objectives** detailing what you should know and be able to do after reading the chapter. Use these lists to identify topics needing further study.

4. Within each chapter, **Key Concepts** are highlighted in boldface type. These concepts are discussed in the chapter and defined in the **Glossary** at the end of the book. Use the Glossary as you read the chapters to make sure you understand each key concept.

5. In Part II, each important element of test analysis is followed by a **Practice Box** containing questions about that concept. Use these questions to make sure that you can apply each concept before reading the next section.

6. Each chapter closes with a **Chapter Summary** reviewing all important concepts and issues. The Chapter Summary contains each of the key concepts highlighted in the chapter. Use the Chapter Summary to test your familiarity with the major points of that chapter.

7. At the end of each chapter is a set of **Questions** covering the important concepts in the chapter. The information needed to answer these questions is contained in the chapters themselves. Use these questions to test yourself and identify topics that you need to review.

PRINCIPLES OF TEST DESIGN

OVERVIEW

Understanding the principles of testing and test design is critical to both the development of good tests and the evaluation of existing tests. Although some of you may have occasion to write tests, many more of you will be in a position to use a published test in your teaching or research. The information in this section describes the different purposes and uses of tests, their administration formats, the types of items they use, and the ways they can be scored.

Chapter 1 discusses testing as an assessment technique, identifying the defining features of a test, the way tests are used, and the characteristics of a good test. Emphasis is placed on the measurement function of tests and the difference between measuring physical and psychological characteristics. Chapter 2 presents a system for identifying the type of test best suited to a particular situation. Although a wide variety of test types is available, not all types are equally compatible with all testing scenarios. This chapter focuses on three features of tests: purpose, administration format, and content.

Chapters 3 and 4 are devoted to constructing specific types of tests. Chapter 3 covers the various items formats and scoring systems available for ability tests. The chapter compares and contrasts two aspects of test construction: alternate-choice and free-response item formats and norm-referenced and criterion-referenced scoring systems. Chapter 4 describes item formats and scoring procedures for personality and interest tests and attitude and evaluation scales. The personality section discusses the process of writing items and constructing scales for objective (self-report) and projective tests. The sections on scales detail the procedures for constructing scales to measure attitudes, to record behavioral observations, and to evaluate job performance.

Introduction to Psychological Testing

CHAPTER OUTLINE

CHAPTER GOALS AND OBJECTIVES

After completing this chapter you should be able to:

- Differentiate between testing and other assessment techniques.
- List and describe the three characteristics defining a test.
- Describe how tests can be used for rating, placement, selection, competency and proficiency, diagnosis, and evaluation.
- List and describe the characteristics of a good test.
- Differentiate between (1) objective and subjective scoring rules and (2) reliability and validity.
- Define and give examples of nominal, ordinal, interval, and ratio scales of measurement.
- Explain why scale of measurement is important in testing.
- Explain why the measurement of psychological characteristics is (1) less precise and (2) less direct than the measurement of physical characteristics.
- Identify some of the major criticisms and advantages of testing as an assessment technique.
- Identify source books for locating information about tests.
- Identify professional and legal mechanisms for regulating the use of tests.

The 20th century has seen a steadily increasing emphasis on the evaluation and classification of people. It seems that more and more often the decisions we must make require us to know something about the characteristics of people and, specifically, the ways in which they differ. Psychological tests have become an increasingly important part of this decision-making process. Today, psychological tests are used in schools and colleges, business and industry, hospitals and counseling centers, and a wide variety of research projects. The purpose of this chapter is to give you a better understanding of testing as an assessment tool and a measurement process. Perhaps the best place to start our discussion of testing is with the most basic question: What is a test?

TESTING AND ASSESSMENT

Any procedure used to gather information about people can be called **assessment**. A **test** is a type of assessment that uses specific procedures to obtain information and convert that information to numbers or scores. Testing can be contrasted with other more subjective assessment techniques such as observation or interview. The most significant difference between testing and these more subjective techniques is in the degree of control exerted over the information-gathering process. In testing there are specific questions to answer or tasks to perform, a standard administration procedure, and a specific mechanism to score responses. Subjective techniques may also use specific questions or tasks, but there is more flexibility in the information-gathering process and more reliance on judgment and interpretation of responses. Rather than attempting to cover the broad area of psychological assessment, this text focuses specifically on psychological testing.

A More Precise Definition of "Test"

From the preceding description, we can infer that a test has at least two defining features: (1) the use of specific or systematic procedures and (2) the scoring of responses. Let's examine these one at a time. The *systematic procedures* involved in testing include mechanisms for (a) selecting a set of items or test questions, (b) specifying the conditions under which the test is administered, and (c) developing a system of scoring and interpreting responses. It might seem that developing test items simply requires being knowledgeable about the attributes being measured; however, an obvious, logical relationship between the content of an item and the attribute under study is not enough. Test developers must select items based on scientific study of an item pool. Only then can they be sure that the test items really measure what they are intended to measure.

Our need for systematic procedures extends to the administration and scoring of test items. Our goal is to use the same administration procedures and scoring criteria for all test takers. It is important to keep constant across test takers such factors as amount of time allowed or number of points earned for a question. By doing so, it is easier to conclude that differences among people in test scores reflect real differences in their knowledge, skills, and characteristics. Systematic procedures may be easier to create in some contexts than in others. For example, tests given individually may vary more in administration conditions than tests given to a group of people. The scoring of open-ended questions, such as essay questions, may vary more than the scoring of multiple-choice questions.

We also said that a test *quantifies responses* by converting them to numbers or scores. Tests are designed to *measure* attributes of the test taker, and measurement implies the assignment of numerical values. All tests have a set of rules or procedures for describing the test taker's responses in numerical terms. Tests vary considerably in the precision and detail of their scoring rules. Some tests use **objective scoring**, a process in which responses are converted to numbers by comparing them to lists of possible answers. Standardized achievement tests such as the SAT are a good example of this type of scoring. Each test question has a specific correct answer. Test takers receive points according to the number of correct answers selected. A key feature of objective scoring is that different people grading the test arrive at the same total score.

Other tests use **subjective scoring**, a process in which answers are evaluated relative to a set of scoring guidelines. An inkblot test, in which test takers describe what they see in each inkblot card, is a good example of subjective scoring. There are many possible descriptions of each inkblot, too many to code in a list of possible answers. Instead, the answer key would include a list of guidelines that specifies the points to be awarded for different *types* of answers. Because subjective scoring requires evaluation or interpretation of answers, clear and precise guidelines are needed to ensure that everyone scoring a particular answer awards it the same number of points.

There is, however, a third defining feature of a test. Each test must be viewed as a *sample of behavior*. All tests have a finite number of questions; therefore, tests provide a *sample* of our knowledge, skills, and characteristics. Because tests typically are used to make inferences from this sample of behavior, the selection of questions is crucial to the quality of a test. A good test generates a representative sample of behavior by including a well-balanced selection of questions. Imagine taking a test on world geography that included only questions about North America! Test developers must be able to balance practical constraints, such as amount of time available for testing, with the need to adequately sample the attribute under study.

Comparing Testing to Other Assessments

Given that a test has the specific features described, how does the information gained by testing differ from the information obtained through other assessments? Let's illustrate some of these differences by contrasting the use of testing with the use of interview, a more subjective assessment technique, in a familiar scenario: evaluating applicants for a job.

Exactly what happens when candidates are interviewed for a job? Most job interviews begin with a specific set of questions covering relevant experiences, skills, and attitudes. However, the interviewer may decide to pursue different lines of questioning with different candidates. In the judgment of the interviewer, it may be important to know more about the educational background of candidate A and the previous work experience of candidate B. Furthermore, the interviewer may adopt different postures with different candidates. It might be important, in the interviewer's opinion, to determine how candidate A reacts to pressure situations. Therefore, the interviewer may adopt a more neutral tone with one candidate and a more confrontative tone with the other.

Because of this flexibility, interviews can produce a richer variety of information about the people under study. However, there are three consequences of this flexibility. First, the nature of the information gathered may vary from person to person. If the interviewer pursues different lines of questions with different candidates, we may not end up with the same set of data for all applicants. Second, interview is less likely to collect these data under the same conditions. If candidates are evaluated under the different conditions, it may be difficult to compare their performance to determine how they are similar and different. Finally, because the process of interview does not necessarily translate information into numbers or scores, it may be difficult to compare people objectively, even when the same information is available and the same conditions are used.

In testing, all candidates would respond to the same questions or perform the same tasks under identical conditions; furthermore, their responses would be analyzed using the specific scoring procedures. The use of such systematic procedures maximizes the likelihood that we obtain similar data about each applicant. Furthermore, it may be easier to compare candidates objectively because their responses have been converted to numbers on relevant scales. However, we must ensure that the tests we use tap knowledge and skills that are *relevant* to job performance. If inappropriate tests are used, the information obtained is useless.

Clearly, testing and interview both have strengths and limitations. This brings us to an important point about the evaluation of people: In general, the best decisions are made when a variety of data is collected using a variety of techniques. In the course of diagnosis and treatment, psychologists typically interview and observe clients as well as test them. School systems decide on placements for children based on test scores and more subjective data, such as teacher observations and ratings. Testing is an important component of these processes because it facilitates the direct comparison of one person to another. This is the source of its dominance as an assessment technique: Testing's systematic approach to information gathering makes it well suited to the study of individual differences.

USE OF PSYCHOLOGICAL TESTS

Testing has become an everyday occurrence. Many people view testing as a recent invention and the emphasis on testing as an American phenomenon. In reality, both assumptions are false. According to historians, the ancient Chinese used written tests to select people for civil service positions over 4000 years ago (DuBois, 1966, 1970). The use of a **test battery**, a set of two or more tests, and the use of national testing programs can be traced to early Chinese dynasties. Furthermore, the British government implemented its nation-wide system of civil service testing in 1855, almost 30 years before the U.S. government established the American Civil Service Commission.

Interest in individual differences during the late 19th and early 20th century led to an increase in the use of tests. Introductory psychology classes often cite the work of Sir Francis Galton as an early example of using tests to study individual differences. A relative of Charles Darwin, Galton theorized that genius in the human animal was hereditary, resulting from a process of natural selection (Galton, 1869). He attempted to prove his theory by devising and administering tests of sensory-motor functions such as visual acuity and reaction time. Galton's work became the basis of later research by James Cattell, an early American psychologist who coined the term "mental test" (Cattell, 1890).

Although individual difference research was important to the growth of testing, the prevalence and diversity of modern tests result directly from the more practical need to evaluate people. The two most notable examples are rather strange bedfellows: the education of the mentally retarded and the classification of military recruits. The first systematic tests of general intelligence were developed by Binet and Simon (1905) to assist the French Ministry of Public Instruction in evaluating mentally retarded students. These were individual tests, forerunners of the Stanford–Binet intelligence tests developed in this country (Terman, 1916; Terman & Merrill, 1937). Since the mentally retarded were only a small segment of the population of school children, individual intelligence tests were a reasonable option. But World War I made it clear that occasions arise when group testing is necessary. America's entry into the war brought thousands of recruits and thousands of decisions as to the placement of these men. Individual testing was neither practical nor efficient. With the assistance of the American Psychological Association, a group of psychologists was assembled to develop a group test of mental abilities (Yerkes, Bridges, & Hardwick, 1915). Interestingly, this first group test came in two forms: the Army Alpha, for recruits who could read, and the Army Beta, for illiterate recruits. World War I also made clear the need for structured personality tests, especially tests for the identification of psychopathology. The first such test, the Woodworth Personal Data Sheet (Woodworth, 1917), was developed during World War I, although it was not completed in time to screen recruits.

Throughout the 20th century, tests and testing techniques have developed in response to both theoretical concerns and practical needs. The area of personality testing contains many examples of the *role* of theory in test development. For example, Freud's theory of personality is reflected in tests such as the Rorschach Inkblot Test (Rorschach, 1921), which assumes that personality can be measured by analyzing the pattern an individual perceives in an ambiguous stimulus. The Minnesota Multiphasic Personality Inventory or MMPI (Hathaway & McKinley, 1943) comes from an alternative perspective, the belief that accurate assessment of personality requires empirical comparisons of how different types of people answer a given set of questions. The influence of practical needs is evident in the development of ability tests. The tremendous increase in number of students applying to college created a need for admissions tests such as the SAT. As the workplace increased in complexity, business and industry saw a need for more testing of both general ability and specific skills. And the need for more flexible testing, in which the test is tailored to the individual respondent, has led to the development of computerized testing techniques.

Although tests are used to obtain information about people, in most cases we use that information in an evaluative way. For example, tests provide the data we use to make decisions about people, such as whom to admit to a program or which grade to assign to a person. Tests are also used to make decisions in research, such as which hypothesis to support or which community program to fund. Across these various scenarios, tests typically are used to make one of the following types of decisions.

Rating

We use tests to rate people when test data help determine where they fall relative to either (1) their peers or (2) some standard of performance. Rating, therefore, involves using test scores to represent an individual's level of performance. For example, in most educational settings, grades are used as a measure of student performance. When tests are used in the process of assigning grades, the test scores serve to rate student performance. In the workplace, tests can be used to rate worker productivity for comparison either to some standard of performance or to the performance of co-workers.

Placement

Placement involves the evaluation of people so that they can be matched with the appropriate services or environments. For example, tests can be used in the process of determining optimal learning setting. Should the student receive academic assistance, be placed in an accelerated program, be enrolled in vocational courses? What math course will be best for this college freshman? Military recruits are placed in training programs based on test performance, and business and industry use tests to decide where to place new employees.

Selection

Tests are frequently used for selection of a group of people from a larger pool of applicants or candidates. Private schools, colleges, graduate schools, and professional schools use performance on standardized tests as one criterion for admission to their academic programs. Business and industry also use test scores as one measure of the applicant's suitability for a particular job. In these cases, tests are used as screening devices to help identify the individuals who are most likely to be successful.

Competency and Proficiency

Tests can be used to indicate whether or not an examinee's performance meets a preselected criterion. Many school systems require students to pass competency exams prior to receiving a high school diploma. These tests certify that students have met the minimal requirements necessary for graduation. Many professions require individuals to pass licensing exams after completion of their training. Rather than demonstrating minimal competency, these tests are used to determine the candidates' level of proficiency. Both instances use tests to decide whether or not an individual is performing at an acceptable level.

Diagnosis

Diagnosis is probably one of the more familiar areas of test use. In diagnosis, tests are used to determine the nature and typicality of an individual's underlying characteristics. Tests designed for diagnosis often provide a multidimensional picture of an attribute, such as reading or self-concept, by incorporating a set of subscales. A reading test could yield scores on vocabulary, grammatical knowledge, and reading comprehension. A self-concept test could produce scores indicating test-taker perceptions of self in social situations and academic situations. Schools use tests to identify potential learning problems in children and suggest areas of strength useful in planning remediation. Clinicians use tests to identify areas of pathology or adjustment problems and to plan treatment approaches.

Outcome Evaluation

The preceding categories all involve making decisions about individuals. Tests also can be used to make decisions by evaluating an outcome, such as the value of a program, a product, or a course of action. Standardized tests can be used to compare the effectiveness of alternative teaching techniques, to determine the effects of a drug, or to assess the efficacy of different types of therapies. Tests can be used for outcome evaluation both in the course of basic science research and in the process of deciding which course of action to choose in applied settings. For example, sets of different tests could be compared to determine which is the best predictor of job performance and thus the best to use for screening job applicants.

CHARACTERISTICS OF A GOOD TEST

Although we have discussed the defining features of a test and the ways tests are used, we must acknowledge an obvious point: Not all tests—even among those that are published—are good tests. A good test is designed carefully and evaluated empirically to ensure that it generates accurate, useful information. The design phase consists of decisions about test purpose, content, administration, and scoring; the evaluation phase consists of collecting and analyzing data from pilot administrations of the test; these data are then used to identify the psychometric properties of the test.

Design Properties

In terms of its design, we can identify four basic properties of a good test: (1) a clearly defined purpose, (2) a specific and standard content, (3) a standardized administration procedure, and (4) a set of scoring rules. Let's consider each of these.

Property 1.   A good test has a clearly defined purpose. To define the purpose of a test, the test developer must answer three questions:

1.   What is the test supposed to measure?
2.   Who will take the test?
3.   How will the test scores be used?

   The first question is one of domain. The **domain** of a test is the knowledge, skills, or characteristics assessed by the test items. Tests can be designed to measure elements of academic knowledge or skill, personality characteristics, personal attitudes—almost anything you can name. A domain could be a single attribute, such as piano-playing skill, or a set of attributes, such as the central dimensions of personality. Specifying the domain of a test is like outlining the information to be covered in a term paper. When writing a term paper, you begin by selecting a topic and then proceed to decide on a set of specific points or issues to cover. When designing a test, you begin by selecting a domain and then proceed to specify the kinds of knowledge, skills, behaviors, and attitudes that comprise the domain.

The second question is one of audience. A test for adults must necessarily be different from a test for grade-school children, regardless of the test domain. The audience may dictate practical concerns such as whether the questions should be presented orally or in writing or whether the answers should be in pictures or in words.

The third question deals with the appropriateness of different types of test items and test scores. Some tests are designed to compare the performance of test takers to each other. Other tests are designed to determine each person's level of performance independently. Some tests measure current level of ability or skill, whereas others are used to predict how well the test taker is likely to perform in the future. Different types of items and scores are used for these different types of comparisons.

Property 2.   A good test has a specific and standard content. The content is *specific* to the domain the test is designed to cover. Questions are selected to cover that domain as comprehensively as possible, taking into account the nature of the test takers and the constraints implied by that audience. The content also is *standard*, meaning that all test takers are tested on the same attributes or knowledge. This may seem obvious—but there are situations in which examinees may answer different but comparable questions. For example, many tests are available in more than one form. These alternate forms are useful when people must be tested repeatedly or when test takers will be in close quarters and cheating is a concern. Sometimes these alternate forms contain the same questions in different orders; other times, each form contains different questions. In the latter case, the questions on the various forms must require equivalent levels of knowledge or skill. If they do not, your score might differ according to which form you take.

Property 3.   A good test has a set of standard administration procedures. Some tests are self-administered; others require the use of a proctor, who administers the test, or an **examiner**, who both administers the test and records your responses. In each case, it is critical that all test takers receive the same instructions and materials and have the same amount of time to complete the test. You no doubt have experience with the effort devoted to creating standard conditions during achievement tests or entrance exams such as the SAT or ACT: large black letters in boldface type on the bottom of a page saying, "Stop. Do not go on." Proctors looking at their watches while you eagerly hold your pencil, waiting to hear the words, "You may turn over your test booklet and begin."

Standard conditions are necessary to minimize the effects of irrelevant variables, factors other than the test taker's knowledge, skills, and characteristics. Standard conditions help ensure that the test score is an accurate representation of test-taker characteristics. Sometimes, however, standard conditions are difficult to create. Some tests are designed to be administered individually by an examiner. With these tests it is crucial that the test developer specify the precise rules to follow during each test administration. Sometimes a student may miss a classroom test and take an individual makeup exam. It is necessary for the teacher to make sure that this student receives the same amount of time and assistance as the group received, no more, no less. Without standard conditions it is impossible to be sure what a given test score means or to compare the scores of different test takers.

Property 4. A good test has a standard scoring procedure. This procedure must be applied the same way to all individuals who take the test. Objective tests, such as multiple-choice tests, are relatively easy to score in a standard and consistent way. Answers can be coded as right or wrong for knowledge or skill tests or as representing certain attitudes or characteristics for personality tests. It is more difficult to ensure consistency in the scoring of essay tests or projective personality tests like the Rorschach Inkblot Test (Rorschach, 1921). Both of these types of tests use open-ended questions, and there is often great variety in the types of answers given by test takers. Effective grading of essay tests requires the development and use of a detailed answer key. Without such a key, it is difficult to be confident that examinees earning different scores differ in knowledge or skill. The same is true for projective tests like the Rorschach. Since the range of possible descriptions of an inkblot is almost infinite, the test requires a scoring system that can be applied consistently to a wide variety of descriptions.

Psychometric Properties

A good test is one that measures what it is designed to measure in as accurate a way as possible. The measurement characteristics of a test are called **psychometric properties**. They are determined by analyzing responses to test items during pilot administrations of the test. There are three important psychometric properties of a good test.

Property 1. A good test is reliable. A synonym for **reliability** is "consistency." Just as a reliable person will be consistent in his or her actions and reactions, a reliable test will provide a consistent measure of current knowledge, skills, or characteristics. Without changes in knowledge, skills, or characteristics, an individual taking a reliable test can expect to obtain about the same score on another administration of the test or on another form of the test. Why is this important? When test scores change, we would like to be able to conclude that the test taker has learned more or has changed somehow. Without a reliable test, we cannot determine what a change in scores really means. Some examples will clarify the point.

Let's say you take the SAT and are displeased with your scores. You decide to enroll in a study course for the SAT and to retake the exam. Six months later you retake the exam and your total score is 100 points higher. What does the 100-point increase mean? The SAT is a reliable exam. If you keep retaking it without brushing up on your math and English, reducing your test anxiety, or becoming a better guesser, you will earn about the same score each time. Since we know that the SAT is a reliable exam, we can conclude that you in fact performed better on the second testing.

Let's say that you do not study for a class exam and receive a low grade. The instructor offers you the chance to retake the exam and raise your grade. If the exam is not reliable, your grade may go up or down just by chance. A higher score may not indicate that you in fact have learned more material. But if the test is reliable and you do improve, the instructor can be confident that you have in fact learned more material.

Property 2. A good test is valid. Reliability analysis indicates whether the test provides a consistent measure, but does not tell us *what* the test measures. The second property, **validity**, indicates whether the test measures what it was designed to measure. When you make a valid point in the course of a discussion, you make a point that is relevant to the issue being discussed. When a test is valid, it measures test-taker characteristics that are relevant to the purpose of the test. For example, suppose you are developing a math placement exam containing a large number of word problems. If this test is designed to measure math skills, performance should not be affected by the test taker's level of reading comprehension. Therefore, although you must write word problems tapping a variety of math skills, you must make sure that the grammar and vocabulary of the word problems are understandable to all test takers. The test is only valid as a math placement test if scores reflect math skills rather than reading skills.

Although validity sometimes is viewed as the most important characteristic of a test, we always evaluate the reliability of a test first. Reliability is a prerequisite to validity, a *necessary but not sufficient condition* for validity. If the test does not provide a consistent measure of performance, it really does not matter what the test is measuring. On the other hand, if the test does provide a consistent measure of performance, we must be sure that it is measuring characteristics that are relevant to the purpose of the test. I could "measure" your intelligence by counting the number of inches you can walk heel to toe in a straight line. This would be a relatively reliable measure—you would earn about the same score each time—but an obviously invalid one.

Property 3.   A good test contains items with good item statistics. In addition to determining the reliability and validity of a test, test developers also analyze the pattern of responses to individual test items. This **item analysis** is important for the identification of items in need of revision. It is a rare test that cannot be improved by the addition, deletion, or rewriting of test items. In fact, identifying and revising poor items can improve the overall reliability and validity of a test.

The organization of this textbook is designed to take you through the process of designing and selecting good tests. The first four chapters are devoted to issues of test design, including defining test purpose, specifying test domain, and selecting administration and scoring procedures. The second four chapters cover issues of test analysis, including reliability, validity, and item analysis.

TESTING AND SCALES OF MEASUREMENT

When a test is administered, the characteristics of people are represented numerically as test scores. A key issue in testing is identifying the scale of measurement represented by these scores. Different scales of measurement provide different types of information and make it easier or more difficult to compare people to each other. The following sections discuss the properties of each scale of measurement and the relevance of measurement scale to psychological testing.

Scales of Measurement

In the language of measurement, a characteristic under study is called a **variable**. A variable is simply a dimension along which people or objects differ. It can be a physical dimension, such as length or weight, or a psychological dimension, such as intelligence or self-concept. Measurement tools, such as tests, are designed to locate objects or people on these variables. All measurement tools do so using one of four scales of measurement: nominal, ordinal, interval, or ratio.

Nominal Scales

When we classify people or objects according to category labels, we use a **nominal** scale of measurement. For example, when we "measure" the variable of sex, we assign people to the categories of "male" or "female." When we "measure" the variable "color," we assign labels such as "red," "blue," "green," or "yellow" to the object being measured.

A test that is graded "pass" or "fail" uses a nominal scale of measurement. Test takers are placed into one of two categories based on their test performance. Competency and proficiency tests may use this type of measurement. Nominal scales, however, are limited in their usefulness because they do not provide very precise information about individual differences, a primary focus of psychological tests.[1] Nominal measures indicate the presence or absence of a property or the nature of a property, but not the extent or amount of a property. Nominal scales, therefore, do not really quantify test-taker performance. When we *do* use numbers as nominal measures, the numbers merely serve as category labels, not indexes of the extent of a property. For example, when studying gender differences, we can choose to give all females a "score" of 1 and all males a "score" of 2. Although their characteristics are being scored numerically, the numbers only represent membership in a category. The fact that males receive a "2" does not imply that they possess "more gender" than females.

Certain variables, such as sex, race, and geographic region, can be measured only nominally. We can, however, choose to measure other variables with a nominal scale. For example, we can administer an IQ test to a group of people and reclassify their scores as "below average," "average," or "above average." We can record the ages of a group of people and reclassify them as "20 to 29 years old," "30 to 39 years old," "40 to 49 years old," and so on. Note that when we transform scores to a nominal scale of measurement our information becomes more general and less precise. When we reclassify the people in the preceding examples using a nominal scale, we no longer know the specific IQ score or age of the people under study.

---

[1]There are times, however, when we use a nominal measurement scale in the *analysis* of test data. Once we define a set of categories, a nominal scale, we can count the number of people who fall into each category. We can then compare the number of people in different categories to make inferences about properties of the test. When validating a new intelligence test, we could administer our new test along with an existing intelligence test. We then could count the number of people who score (1) similarly on both tests (i.e., above average on both tests or below average on both tests) and (2) differently on both tests (i.e., above average on one, below average on another). If our test is valid, most people should fall into the category of similar scores on both tests.

Ordinal Scales

When we classify people or objects by ranking them on some dimension, we use an **ordinal** scale of measurement. The actual number given to each person or object measured is called a *rank*. For example, we can put a group of 10 objects in order according to their size and rank them from largest to smallest with the numbers 1 to 10. We could line up a group of children and rank them according to height. Usually, we use the number 1 to represent the best example of the variable under study. If we are interested in height or "bigness," the tallest or largest group member receives a 1. Conversely, if our focus is on "smallness," the shortest or smallest group member would receive a 1. Sometimes group members will be tied on the variable being measured. Two objects could be the same size; three children could be the same height. When ties occur, the group members who are tied each receive the *average* of the ranks in question. If two objects are tied for ranks 5 and 6, each object receives a rank of 5.5 (the average of 5 + 6), and none of the objects receives either a rank of 5 or a rank of 6. If three children are tied for ranks 6, 7, and 8, each child receives a rank of 7 (the average of 6 + 7 + 8). Ranks of 6, 7, and 8 are not used.

An ordinal scale provides information about where group members fall relative to each other. It does not, however, indicate the precise extent by which the group members differ. The children ranked 1 and 2 on height could differ by $\frac{1}{4}$ inch, 1 inch, or 6 inches. Furthermore, we cannot say that the difference in height between ranks 1 and 2, a rank difference of 1, is equivalent to the difference in height between ranks 2 and 3, also a rank difference of 1. The ranks simply tell us that one child is taller than the other. Sometimes this is enough information. If we are interested in the top five students, we do not need to know by exactly how much they outperformed their classmates. It is rare, however, that we design psychological tests to produce ordinal scales of measurement. Ordinal scales do not provide the type of individual difference information we typically want to obtain by using a test.

Note that we can choose to use an ordinal scale with variables that could be measured more precisely. We can choose to ignore exact height or IQ or age and simply assign numbers to represent the relative heights or IQ scores or ages of the group members. As with the case of reclassifying measurements to a nominal scale, the use of an ordinal scale results in some loss of precision.

Interval Scales

When we classify people or objects by ranking them with an equal-unit scale, we use an **interval** scale of measurement. To qualify as an interval scale, we must be able to establish that a difference of 1 or 3 or 5 units is equivalent at any place along the scale. Height is a good example of an interval scale. The difference between 60 and 65 inches, a 5-unit difference, is exactly the same as the difference between 40 and 45 inches. Scores on most psychological tests are designed to represent interval scales of measurement. Assume that three people, A, B, and C, receive scores of 65, 55, and 45, respectively, on a standardized test of anxiety. If this is an interval-level test, we can draw three conclusions about the relationships among these people. First, person A demonstrates a higher level of anxiety than person B, who in turn is more anxious than person C. The scores permit us to determine the relative extent of anxiety in these three people. Second, we can conclude that the difference between a score of 55 and a score of 65 for persons A and B is equivalent to the difference between 45 and 55 for persons B and C. Each pair represents a difference of 10 units. Third, we can say that the difference in extent of anxiety between persons A and C (20 units) is twice as great as the difference between persons A and B (10 units).

Although scores on most tests are treated as interval scales, there is much debate as to the accuracy of this assumption. Consider the classroom test. Is it true that all questions are of equal difficulty? If not, moving from a grade of 60 to a grade of 70 may require correct answers to some relatively easy items, whereas moving from 80 to 90 may require correct answers to more difficult items. Although in both cases scores change by 10 units, the change may reflect different changes in extent of knowledge at the lower and higher scale values. A similar problem exists on standardized tests such as IQ tests. Raising a low score may require less increase in intelligence than raising a high score. Critics claim that scores on these tests should be treated as an ordinal scale of measurement. In practice, however, we assume that a test uses an interval scale unless it is otherwise stated in the test manual.

Ratio Scales

When we rank people or objects with an equal-interval scale that has a true zero point, we use a **ratio** scale of measurement. A *true zero point* indicates the absence of the characteristic being measured; the other points on a ratio scale represent equal increments of the characteristic. Miles per hour is an example of a ratio scale. Miles per hour measures the extent of speed attained by a moving object. At 0 miles per hour, the object is not moving. Each mile per hour increment above 0 indicates the increase in speed on an equal-interval scale. The presence of a true zero point enables us to establish ratios between scores, making it accurate to define 10 miles per hour as twice as fast as 5 miles per hour.

Ratio scales are rare in psychological measurement because it is virtually impossible to define a true zero point for most psychological characteristics. Could a person ever be classified as possessing no intelligence, no aggression, no self-concept? Even when a person receives a score of 0 on an algebra test, is it accurate to say that the person knows no algebra? In reality, that score of 0 means the person earned no points on the test. But the test includes only a sample of algebra questions. With a different sample, the person might perform differently. The zero point on most psychological tests, therefore, is really an *arbitrary zero point*.

Why Scale of Measurement Matters

There are two reasons why the scale of measurement used by a test is important. First, the scale of measurement determines the nature of the information it provides about test takers. Specifically, scale of measurement influences our ability to use the test to compare people, to assess individual differences. As we move from a nominal scale to interval and ratio scales, we increase the precision of the measurement process. Nominal scales indicate which test takers fall into each category. Even if the categories represent relative amounts of a property, such as "below average," "average," and "above average" IQ scores, we can only compare people in very broad, general ways. Ordinal scales allow for more specific comparisons of where people fall on different variables, but the lack of an equal-unit scale makes it difficult to compare people at different points on the scale. Clearly, interval and ratio scales, with their equal units, are most appropriate for comparing people, for the study of "individual differences."

Second, the scale of measurement used affects our ability to apply statistical techniques to the study of test scores. Many common statistical procedures can only be used with scores at an interval or ratio level of measurement. For example, the statistical procedures commonly used to determine a test's reliability and validity require either interval or ratio scales. Likewise, the statistical analyses conducted when tests are used in research projects frequently assume scores are at the interval or ratio level. Although there are statistics for analyzing nominal and ordinal data, they are not as powerful [2] and therefore not as useful as higher-level analyses. Just as the information conveyed by simpler scales is less precise, the statistical techniques available to analyze them are not capable of identifying subtle differences between people. Once again, it appears that test scores based on the higher scales of measurement are more useful for assessing individual differences.

---

[2]All statistical analyses are designed to evaluate the relative likelihood of two hypotheses: H_0, the null hypothesis, and H_1, the alternative hypothesis. The power of a statistical test is the probability of rejecting the null hypothesis (H_0) given that the alternative hypothesis (H_1) is true. A more powerful test is better because it is more likely to lead to a correct decision about the data being analyzed.

MEASURING PSYCHOLOGICAL VERSUS PHYSICAL CHARACTERISTICS

The measurement of psychological characteristics is quite different from the measurement of physical characteristics. As long as our measuring tools are calibrated accurately, we can measure physical characteristics as height and weight using very precise units such as millionths of an inch or millionths of a pound. Physical characteristics like height and weight also have clear physical manifestations that can be measured directly. The measurement of psychological characteristics, in contrast, is both less precise and less direct.

Why Psychological Measurement Is Less Precise

There are three reasons for this lack of preciseness in the measurement of psychological characteristics. First, psychological tests measure only a sample of the property under study. When we determine a person's height or weight, we measure the complete person. We typically do not measure the length of a person's leg and use that to infer overall height. In psychological testing, however, we measure only a sample of the overall test domain. We do not measure the complete property. We obtain responses to a subset of questions and use these responses to *infer* the extent of a particular property. For example, answers to items on classroom tests are used to draw conclusions about overall mastery of course material. Responses to items on a test of depression are used to infer the extent of depression. It is not practical, and in many cases not even possible, to "measure" the entire property under study. We instead make inferences from a limited measurement.

Second, psychological measurement uses a more limited scale. Psychological tests contain a specific number of items worth a specific number of points. Remember that we often cannot measure the complete property; therefore, even those test takers with "perfect" scores cannot be viewed as possessing the highest possible extent of a property. (Even if we could design a test to measure a complete property, it probably would be too long to provide an accurate measure. After all, test takers only can concentrate for so long!) Thus, although we can measure the length of an object to a millionth of an inch, our measures of psychological characteristics use a much more limited scale.

Third, psychological measurement is more easily affected by extraneous variables. The attitude of the test taker, the temperature of the room, the behavior of the test administrator—and a myriad of other variables—can affect performance on a psychological test. None of these factors significantly affects physical measurement. You probably have taken tests under less than optimal conditions—on days you felt poorly or when the lawn was being mowed outside your classroom. As psychologists, we know it is possible that your test score would have been different if you had taken the test under different conditions.

Why Psychological Measurement Is Less Direct

There are two reasons why the measurement of psychological characteristics is less direct. First, many psychological tests are designed to draw inferences about underlying attributes or characteristics. The actual behavior being measured is how test takers respond to the test items, but our intent is to do more than simply monitor item responses. We use those responses to infer about an aspect of knowledge, personality, etc. Consider the SAT. When college officials require applicants to take the SAT, they are looking for a way to draw inferences about the likelihood of succeeding in college. Performance on the test is a vehicle for learning about applicant knowledge and skills that are relevant to college success. Similarly, a psychologist uses client responses on a test of neuropsychological functioning to infer the nature and extent of brain dysfunction.

Second, many psychological tests are designed to measure constructs, hypothetical dimensions on which individuals differ. Basically, a **construct** is a label given to a hypothetical characteristic, such as assertiveness or intelligence. Constructs usually are conceptualized as dimensions along which people can be located according to their patterns of behavior. The presence of a construct is suggested when research indicates that people seem to show consistent differences in sets of related behaviors.

Intelligence is a good example of a psychological construct. Studies of human behavior indicate that people differ in their problem-solving skills, their ability to learn, and their ability to adapt by applying information in new ways and in new settings. The levels of ability in these areas are usually related; people skillful in one area are usually skillful in the others. These abilities have come to be referred to as elements of the construct "intelligence." Similar processes have resulted in the labeling of other sets of behaviors as elements of constructs such as aggression, achievement motivation, dependency, and self-concept. In fact, most of the dimensions we use to describe people are psychological constructs.

Because psychological constructs are really theoretical abstractions, they cannot be measured directly. Instead, we must infer their presence from measurements of specific behaviors. We cannot measure your intelligence or aggressiveness or self-concept per se. Instead, we identify a set of behaviors believed to reflect the construct under study, measure these behaviors, and use this information to decide where to locate people along the construct or dimension. For example, an intelligence test measures the number of different types of problems that you can solve. We use this number to draw a conclusion about your level of intelligence and to assign you a location on this hypothetical dimension.

Clearly, the measurement of constructs is an indirect process. But, in fact, the process is even more complicated. First, psychologists do not always agree on the behaviors to use for measuring a construct. Consider intelligence once again. Hundreds of different behaviors can be used to demonstrate level of intelligence. Which do we choose and which do we exclude? To some extent the choices are based on theoretical orientation and research findings. To some extent the choices are arbitrary. The result of this dilemma is the development of multiple tests for popular constructs like intelligence and personality traits that do not necessarily sample the same behaviors or qualities. Second, different psychological tests use different scoring systems, and sometimes even different scales of measurement.

Because measurement of a construct can involve different behaviors or scoring systems, we must always specify how a construct is measured. An **operational definition** is a statement that describes the technique used to measure a construct. When a published test is used to measure a construct, the name of the test can be used as an operational definition. For example, intelligence could be operationally defined as a test taker's score on intelligence test A or intelligence test B. Although we expect people to be described in similar ways by these two tests, we do not necessarily expect them to receive identical scores. It is possible, for example, that two tests sample different aspects of behavior or use different scoring systems. In those cases, the same score on the two tests would correspond to (1) measurement of different elements of intelligence or (2) different locations on the dimension, "intelligence." Knowing how the construct was measured, therefore, is critical to the accurate interpretation of a test score.

Intelligence tests are an excellent example of the importance of operational definitions. One important use of intelligence tests is to identify the presence and extent of mental retardation. A person's eligibility for certain services may depend on the extent of retardation as determined by such a test. In their earlier editions, two of most popular tests, the Stanford–Binet and the Wechsler, used slightly different intervals to define the extent of mental retardation. As a result, the category "mild retardation" on the Stanford–Binet included scores between 52 and 68, whereas the "mild retardation" category on the Wechsler was defined as scores between 55 and 69. Without knowing how intelligence was measured, it would be impossible to interpret a score of 52.

SOURCES OF INFORMATION ABOUT TESTS

Literally thousands of psychological and educational tests are available today, so many that obtaining information about published tests could be a problem. Fortunately, several references volumes are available to help you to locate and learn about tests. *Tests in Print II* (Buros, 1974) and *Tests in Print III* (Mitchell, 1983) contain descriptive information for most currently available tests. Organized by topic, these books list the tests available alphabetically by test name. Each entry describes the features of the test and the test publisher. Entries are cross-referenced to *The Mental Measurements Yearbook*, or MMY, a series of volumes first published by Oscar K. Buros in 1938 and now published by psychologists at the Buros Institute of Mental Measurement. Published every few years, each volume of the MMY contains comprehensive critical reviews of tests. In 1990, the reviews also became available on *Mental Measurement Database*, an on-line computer service.

To give you an idea of the variety of tests available, Table 1.1 presents a summary of the number and percentage of entries devoted to different categories of tests in a recent edition of the MMY (Conoley & Kramer, 1989). Almost 400 tests are reviewed in this one volume! To simplify somewhat the process of learning about a particular test, you can consult one of Buros's smaller volumes devoted to specific categories of tests: *Intelligence Tests and Reviews*, *Personality Tests and Reviews*, *Reading Tests and Reviews II*, and *Vocational Tests and Reviews*.

A second comprehensive reference series was begun by Sweetland and Keyser. *Tests: A Comprehensive Reference for Assessment in Psychology, Education, and Business* (Sweetland & Keyser, 1983, 1986) provides descriptive information on more than 3500 tests. Critical reviews of these tests are contained in the accompanying volumes of *Test Critiques* (Keyser & Sweetland, 1984–1988). Other useful source books are described in Appendix A.

One final and important caveat: A test "in print" is just that—a test that has been published and is available for use. No other criteria are required for a test to be listed in one of the preceding sources. There is no guarantee that a published test is a good-quality test. That's why it is so important to read published reviews of tests. You can only determine the quality of a test and its appropriateness for your purpose by reading as much as you can about the test and talking to other individuals who have used it.

REGULATIONS GOVERNING THE USE OF TESTS

Given both the diversity of tests and their widespread use, an important development has been the creation of professional and legal standards for their

TABLE 1.1 Types of Tests by Major Classifications

Category	Number	Percentage
Vocations	100	25.3
Personality	72	18.2
Miscellaneous	43	10.9
Developmental	31	7.8
Intelligence and scholastic aptitude	28	7.1
Reading	24	6.1
English	24	6.1
Speech and hearing	22	5.6
Education	20	5.1
Achievement	12	3.0
Mathematics	9	2.2
Social studies	3	0.8
Fine arts	2	0.5
Foreign languages	2	0.5
Neuropsychological	2	0.5
Total	396	100.0

From J. C. Conoley and J. J. Kramer (eds.) (1989). *The Tenth Mental Measurements Yearbook*, Reprinted with permission of The Buros Institute of Mental Measurements.

use. More than 30 years ago, the American Psychological Association began publishing documents relevant to the use of testing. In its most recent form, the *Ethical Principles of Psychologists* (1992) contains a section devoted exclusively to issues of assessment. Principle 8, Assessment Techniques, emphasizes the importance of selecting appropriate tests and using those tests in ways that protect client rights and promote client welfare. Likewise, the *Standards for Educational and Psychological Testing* (American Education Research Association, et al., 1985) details the standards to follow in the construction, evaluation, interpretation, and use of psychological tests. In addition, all 50 states and the District of Columbia have legal statutes regulating the administration and use of psychological assessment techniques.

PROS AND CONS OF TESTING

Testing is an important but highly controversial activity. Many problems encountered in the use of tests come from misunderstandings about or misuse of psychological tests. For example, some people regard test scores as precise measures, assuming that a person with an IQ score of 125 will always perform better than a person with an IQ score of 120. When their prediction is not supported, these critics charge that tests are inaccurate measures that create misleading pictures of individual differences. Unfortunately, these critics have missed an important point about test scores. Tests are not precise measures of characteristics and should never be used as precise measures. Remember that a test is a sample of behavior and as such can only estimate the nature and level of psychological attributes. In addition, performance on tests can be affected by variables such as test-taker attitude and testing conditions. Test scores generate the most accurate predictions when converted to ranges within which we believe the person's real characteristics fall. Viewing test scores as precise measures leads to misinterpretation of both individual test scores and the differences between test scores. That fact that tests are not perfect measures leads psychologists themselves to caution that test scores should never be the only factor used to make predictions or decisions about people. In Part II of this book you will learn how to determine the extent of error in test scores and how to use this information to construct test score ranges. These procedures enable us to obtain a better estimate of the level of an attribute measured by a test.

Other critics readily acknowledge that tests are imprecise measures. In fact, they assert that *because* tests are imprecise measures they are ineffective assessment tools. These people fail to recognize that all tools and techniques of psychological measurement are indirect and therefore to some extent imprecise. If we believe it is important and necessary to measure psychological attributes, we have an obligation to use the most accurate measurement tools available. Remember that tests have one important advantage over other assessment techniques: They can be studied to determine their degree of accuracy and improved to become even more accurate. Although tests will never be perfect measures, we can at least identify their degree of accuracy and consider that when deciding what a particular test score means. Part II discusses techniques for determining the measurement characteristics tests and identifying strategies for improving them.

Other people criticize tests as being biased against women and minority groups, dehumanizing, and as invasions of personal privacy. These are important issues that must be addressed by those who develop and use tests. There is no doubt that some tests are in fact unfair and that sometimes tests are used in inappropriate and even illegal ways. However, recent court rulings and legislation have increased regulation of the testing industry. Federal agencies such as the Equal Employment Opportunity Commission and the Departments of Justice and Labor have adopted guidelines for the evaluation of personnel testing programs. At the state level, licensing laws regulate the practice of psychology and the use of psychological testing. Additional oversight is available from professional organizations such as the American Psychological Association (APA). As mentioned previously, the APA's *Standards for Educational and Psychological Testing* (1985) and *Ethical Principles of Psychologists* (1992) contain regulations for the construction and use of tests and the interpretation of test scores. Taken together, these rulings and regulations comprise part of an ongoing national effort to protect individuals from testing abuse, an effort clearly warranting our support. Part III of this book will discuss issues such as test bias and invasion of privacy in more detail.

SUMMARY AND KEY CONCEPTS

The evaluation and classification of people have become an integral part of modern society. A **test** is an **assessment** technique that uses systematic procedures to quantify a sample of behavior. Whether tests use **objective scoring** or **subjective scoring**, they are designed to generate numbers that enable us to identify the characteristics of people and make decisions based on those attributes. Although we associate testing with the 20th century, the use of a **test battery** to evaluate people can be traced back thousands of years. The diversity and prevalence of tests today reflect an attempt to address both theoretical concerns and practical needs. The diversification of tests has led to the publication of numerous source books for information about tests. The prevalence of testing has led to the development of both professional and legal standards regulating their use.

Tests often are used to make decisions about people. Common examples include rating the performance of people, the placement or selection of people, determining an individual's competency or level of proficiency, and diagnosis of individual characteristics. Tests can also be used for evaluating the outcome of a program, a product, or a research hypothesis. Tests are used today in educational settings, by counselors and clinicians, and in business and industry.

The process of developing a good test is long and complex. A good test has a clearly defined purpose and a specific content determined by the test **domain**. The test must be administered under a set of standard conditions, sometimes by an **examiner**, who also scores test performance. Responses to test items must be quantified using a specific set of scoring rules. Test developers must also evaluate the **psychometric properties** of tests and revise them according to the results of their evaluations. Important analyses include determining test **reliability** and **validity** and conducting a thorough **item analysis**.

Tests are designed to measure and quantify performance on **variables**. Like other measurement tools, psychological tests can be designed to produce **nominal**, **ordinal** (rank), or **interval** level measures. It is extremely difficult, however, to design **ratio** measures of psychological characteristics because they require a true zero point, rather than an arbitrary zero point. In most cases, psychological tests are assumed to represent an interval scale of measurement.

There are several important differences between measuring physical characteristics and measuring psychological characteristics. The measurement of psychological characteristics typically involves making inferences from measurement of only a sample of behavior. Furthermore, many psychological characteristics are **constructs**, which cannot be measured directly. In these cases, we can use a test as an **operational definition** of a construct, defining a domain and a scale that we can use to measure the characteristic. Because psychological tests use a limited scale and because performance may be influenced by extraneous variables, scores are best viewed as estimates, rather than as precise measures. Although many people dislike using tests to make decisions about people, steps can be taken to ensure that tests are developed, evaluated, and applied in appropriate ways.

QUESTIONS

1.1 How does testing differ from other assessment techniques? What are the three defining features of a test?

1.2 Give an example of using a test in each of the following ways: rating, placement, selection, determining competency or proficiency, diagnosis, and outcome evaluation.

1.3 List the characteristics of a good test.

1.4 How do objective scoring and subjective scoring differ? Give an example of a test item using each type of scoring.

1.5 What are reliability and validity? Why are they referred to as psychometric properties?

1.6 You administer a test of self-concept to a group of people that uses an interval scale of measurement. A high score indicates a positive self-concept. Explain the differences among scores of 60, 50, and 40.

1.7 How could you change the scores obtained in Question 6 to reflect (a) ordinal and (b) nominal measurement? How would the information conveyed by the scores differ in each case?

1.8 What are the advantages and problems associated with designing a test using an interval scale of measurement?

1.9 List three reasons why the measurement of psychological characteristics is less precise than the measurement of physical characteristics.

1.10   List two reasons why the measurement of psychological characteristics is less direct than the measurement of physical characteristics.

1.11   What is a construct and an operational definition? Why must constructs be operationally defined? Give an example of an operational definition of a construct.

1.12   List three common criticisms of tests. How would you address each?

Issues in Test Design

CHAPTER OUTLINE

CHAPTER GOALS AND OBJECTIVES

After completing this chapter you should be able to:

- Explain how test purpose influences test design.
- Describe the features and design issues for maximal-performance and typical-performance tests and give examples of each.
- Describe the difference between alternate-choice and free-response items.
- Discriminate between (1) aptitude and achievement tests and (2) speed and power tests.
- Describe the difference between projective and objective items.

- Describe the features of (1) norm- and criterion-referenced scores and (2) normative and ipsative scores.
- Explain why audience issues are important.
- Explain the importance of specifying test content.
- Distinguish among scenarios requiring test plans, construct explication, and task analysis.
- Distinguish between content and behavioral objectives and identify the importance of each.
- Write a test plan for a familiar topic, an explication of a familiar construct, and a task analysis for a familiar job.
- Explain the importance of standardized administration procedures.
- Describe the advantages and limitations of individual testing, group testing, and computer-assisted testing.

Although Chapter 1 described the general properties of tests, it did not discuss the variety of types of tests available and how they differ in their design. An understanding of these issues is critical if you are to select an appropriate test to use in some project or to write a test of your own. Our discussion of test design is structured around the characteristics of a "good test" previously cited: a clearly defined purpose, a specific and standard content, a standard administration format, a set of scoring rules, and good psychometric properties. This chapter contrasts tests in terms of first three properties—purpose, content, and administration—and describes how the design of each type differs. The following two chapters will discuss two additional issues—item construction and test scoring—in more detail. Psychometric properties will be covered in Part 2.

TESTS DIFFERING IN PURPOSE

The first design issue in the construction or selection of a test is identifying the purpose of the test. According to Chapter 1 (p. 11), the purpose of a test is defined by answers to the following three questions:[1]

---

[1] Often the name of a test contains some information about its purpose. The Wechsler Adult Intelligence Scale clearly is designed to (1) measure intelligence and (2) be administered to adults. The Peabody Individual Achievement Test is (1) an individual test (2) to measure achievement. Be careful, though, about overreliance on titles as indexes of test characteristics. Just as the publication of a test does not guarantee a quality product, the title of a test does not guarantee its content. There is no substitute for careful reading of research on published tests!

1. What is the test supposed to measure?   (domain)
2. Who will take the test?   (audience)
3. How will the test be used?   (types of scores)

As we describe tests differing in purpose, we also will consider some basic contrasts among item formats. Test purpose affects the appropriateness of item formats two ways. First, different types of items are appropriate for different test domains. A test measuring knowledge of chemistry needs direct questions having specific correct answers. A test to elicit information about unconscious conflicts with parents, however, can use ambiguous stimuli that the test taker must interpret.

Second, different types of items are needed to generate different types of test scores. A test designed to assess a person's level of sociability and leadership can use separate items tapping each of these attributes. A person could demonstrate high levels of both characteristics, low levels of both characteristics, or any other combination. On the other hand, a test to determine whether a person exhibits more sociability or more leadership—a question of relative strength—can use items requiring the test taker to choose between statements endorsing the two attributes. Since the goal of the test is to determine which characteristic is stronger, items should require test takers to consider whether they see themselves more as sociable people or as leaders.

Test Domain

The test domain is the focus of the test. The domain determines the content of the test and, to some extent, the appropriateness of certain item formats. There are a variety of ways to categorize tests according to domain. One of the simplest systems categorizes tests either as maximal performance or typical performance.

Maximal-performance Tests

A **maximal-performance test** determines the upper limits of test-taker knowledge or skill. Instructions emphasize the goal of answering as many questions correctly as possible, thereby earning the highest possible score. Maximal-performance tests can be designed to cover a variety of contents, including knowledge, skill, and performance of tasks. Tests of statistical knowledge, typing ability, or job performance can all be classified as maximal-performance tests. Because these tests are designed to measure how well test takers perform, questions must be designed so that responses can be identified as right or wrong and performance as good or poor. The tests must be scored so that more accomplished people receive higher scores. Because score on a maximal-performance test indicates the highest level of performance to be expected, it is unlikely that a test taker will perform consistently at that level on a day-to-day basis.

Because maximal-performance tests assess level of knowledge and skill, they are commonly referred to as **ability tests**. Ability tests traditionally use interval scales of measurement. Points are awarded on the basis of the accuracy or desirability of a response. There may be a graded scoring system in which responses are coded as best, adequate, and poor, with different numbers of points awarded in each category. Some ability tests also award points according to the speed of response. The Wechsler intelligence tests (Wechsler, 1974, 1981), familiar to Introductory Psychology students, are a good example. In several subtests of the Wechsler subtests, additional points are earned for producing a correct answer within certain time limits. Another example of a test scoring speed and accuracy is a typing test. The difference between a score of 90 wpm (words per minute) and 80 wpm reflects both typing speed and number of words typed correctly.

Ability tests can include alternate-choice items, free-response items, or both types of items. An **alternate-choice item** presents a question and a set of possible answers to the question. The test taker is instructed to select the best answer from the set. Multiple choice, matching, and true/false are common types of alternate-choice items. Table 2.1 presents examples of each type. A **free-response item** presents a question without a set of possible answers. The test taker is instructed to generate an answer within a specific set of guidelines. Essay, short answer, and fill-in-the-blank are familiar types of free-response items. Examples of these item types are presented in Table 2.2.[2]

Achievement and Aptitude Tests.   Sometimes ability tests are further divided into tests of achievement and tests of aptitude. Traditionally, an **achievement test** is designed to measure what you already have learned, whereas an **aptitude test** is designed to determine your potential for learning new information or skills. Your score on an achievement test represents your *current* level of performance. In contrast, your score on an aptitude test is designed to predict your *future* level of performance. We could not, for example, give you an achievement test assessing your ability to play the piano unless you had been taught to play the piano. We could, however, give you an aptitude test

---

[2]Not all free-response items use written questions and written answers. For example, the items on the Bender Visual Motor Gestalt Test also meet the criteria for free-response items. The Bender assesses visual-motor skills by requiring test takers to produce copies of a set of line drawings. The test items are the individual line drawings to be copied. The test taker must produce the "answer"—a copy of the drawing. The items must be free-response items because the test taker is not given a set of answers to consider.

TABLE 2.1   Sample Items for Alternate-Choice Ability Tests

Multiple choice

Select the best answer to complete the following statement:

The first country to use tests to select people for civil service positions was
(a)   the United States.
(b)   Great Britain.
(c)   China.

Matching

Match the appropriate country to each of the following statements.

_____   The first country to use tests to select people for civil service positions.
_____   The country that instituted a nation-wide system of civil service testing in 1855.

(a)   the United States.
(b)   Great Britain.
(c)   China.

True/false

Decide if the following sentence is true or false:

T   F   China was the first country to use tests to select people for civil service positions.

TABLE 2.2   Sample Items for Free-response Ability Tests

Essay

In two to three paragraphs, describe the significance of China, Great Britain, and the United States in the history of psychological testing.

Short answer

List one important event in the history of psychological testing associated with each of the following three countries: China, Great Britain, the United States.

Fill-in-the-blank

_____   was the first country to use tests to select people for civil service positions.

---

assessing the likelihood that you will learn to play the piano if you start piano lessons.

Although the distinction between achievement and aptitude tests appears quite clear, in reality it is often quite hazy. The SAT or Scholastic *Aptitude* Test is designed to predict the likelihood that you will succeed in college. However, we make that prediction by measuring your verbal and math abilities, abilities that obviously reflect your previous learning. In many cases, aptitude and achievement are highly related, and it is difficult to separate prior learning from potential to learn. This issue will be discussed in more detail in Chapter 9, on the use of tests in educational settings.

Speed and Power Tests.   Ability tests can also be designed to focus on either speed or power. On a **speed test**, our interest is the number of items a test taker can answer correctly in a specific period of time. The items are of relatively equal difficulty and the time limit is stringent. We do not expect all test takers to complete all items. In fact, the difference between a more competent and less competent test taker is the number of items completed. Both aptitude and achievement tests can focus on speed. A test designed to screen good candidates for stenographer training, in which test takers are given a limited amount of time to record a series of symbols as accurately as possible, is a speed-based aptitude test. A typing test used to select competent typists is a speed-based achievement test. Each test taker must type a page of text accurately within a specific time limit. The test score is the number of words typed correctly.

On a **power test**, we are interested both in the number and nature of items a test taker answers correctly. The test includes items of varying difficulty and may or may not have a time limit. If a time limit is imposed, it is set so that most test takers have sufficient time to complete all items. In contrast to a speed test, score on a power test reflects the level of difficulty of items the test taker answers correctly. There are power varieties of aptitude and achievement tests. The typical classroom test is a power-based achievement test. An intelligence test, designed to predict performance in future grades, is a power-based aptitude test. Table 2.3 summarizes the different types of ability tests.

Typical-Performance Tests

A **typical-performance test** measures usual or habitual thoughts, feelings, and behavior. The focus is on everyday characteristics and behaviors, rather than on the best performance possible. Performance on these tests, therefore, *should* indicate how test takers think and act on a daily basis. Typical-performance tests can be designed to measure constructs, such as personality characteristics and attitudes, or patterns of behavior. These tests do not use questions with right or wrong answers. Instead, items are designed so that answers can sort test takers into groups based on their particular characteristics.[3] Most typical performance tests use interval scales of measurement.

Personality Tests.   A **personality test** measures individual dispositions and preferences. Questions on these tests are designed to *identify* characteristics and therefore do not have right or wrong answers. Instead, answers are coded

---

[3]It is possible, though unusual, to assess knowledge or skill using a typical-performance test. In this case, items would have right and wrong answers.

TABLE 2.3   Types of Ability Tests

Achievement Current level of skills and knowledge based on previous learning and experience	*Speed: A typing test* selecting best candidate for secretarial position (how fast candidates can use their existing skills to accurately type a page of text)
	Power: A classroom test identifying current level of mastery of course material (how well students can use existing knowledge and skills to answer questions on material they were taught)
Aptitude Ability to use existing skills and knowledge to learn new skills and knowledge	*Speed: A screening test* selecting best candidates for stenographer training (how fast candidates can use visual-motor discrimination skills to copy unfamiliar symbols)
	Power: An intelligence test identifying likely level of future school success (how well students can use their existing knowledge and skills to solve new or unfamiliar problems)

according to the characteristics they represent and, sometimes, the degree to which a response typifies a characteristic. Some tests assess where people fall relative to each other on personality dimensions such as depression, achievement motivation, or sociability. Others explore the structure of an attribute, such as a test tapping into the elements of self-concept.

Like ability tests, personality tests can use different item formats. The basic distinction in personality testing is between projective and objective items. In contrast to ability tests, which may use both alternate-choice and free-response items, personality tests rarely include both types of items. On a personality test using **projective items**, the test taker is presented with a series of ambiguous stimuli and must respond to each item according to the instructions given. Common types of projective items are visual images, such as the Rorschach inkblots, and incomplete sentences. Table 2.4 presents examples of projective test items. On a personality test using **objective items**, each question is presented along with a set of possible responses, much like the items on an alternate-choice ability test. Tests using objective items also are called *self-report tests*, a label that draws our attention to the processes involved in responding to the items. Since these tests use direct questions with specific answers, test takers "report" on the behaviors, feelings, and interests of which they are aware. Common formats for objective or self-report tests, illustrated in Table 2.5, include rating

TABLE 2.4   Sample Items for Projective Personality Tests

Visual image

A simulated Rorschach inkblot

Incomplete sentences

When I am with my family I want to _____..

Spending time with people makes me feel _____..

statements, forced choice, and true/false. Item formats for personality tests will be discussed in more detail in Chapter 4.

Attitude Tests.   An **attitude test** is a related type of test used to elicit personal beliefs and opinions. An attitude is a tendency to react positively or negatively to a specific type of object, person, or situation. Although attitudes can be considered an element of personality, the assessment of attitudes uses somewhat different techniques. Like other aspects of personality, attitudes are constructs that cannot be measured directly. The presence and nature of an attitude must be inferred from observable behaviors, including such behaviors as responses to a set of questions. Attitude tests traditionally use objective items such as true/false statements or statements that are rated on a several-point scale (e.g., strongly agree to strongly disagree).[4]

[4]Psychologists sometimes distinguish among attitudes, beliefs, and opinions, but the distinctions are often unclear (e.g., Aiken, 1991; Anastasi, 1988).

TABLE 2.5 Sample Items for Objective Personality Tests

Rating statements

How often does this statement apply to you?
On my day off I like to take a walk. _____

1	2	3	4	5
never		sometimes		always

Forced choice

Select an answer to complete the following sentence:
On my day off I like to
(a) repair a radio
(b) take a walk

True/false

Decide if the following statement is true or false:
On my day off I like to take a walk.   T   F

Interest Tests.   An **interest test** is designed to identify patterns of likes and dislikes useful for making decisions about future careers and job training. Interest tests use objective items such as true/false statements or statements to be rated on a several-point scale. The statements are keyed to scales reflecting different areas of interest, and the points earned on each scale are used to construct a profile of test-taker interests. Because interests may be related to personality, some interest tests also include scales designed to assess personality characteristics.

A key issue in the development of interest tests is the use of groups of people in different occupations during the standardization process. Items are administered to these groups to determine their characteristic patterns of response. When you take a standardized interest test, your scores on different scales are compared to the scores of people in the standardization group. Parallel patterns of interest are used to identify the occupations, and sometimes academic majors, that you might enjoy.

Test Audience

Specifying the purpose of a test also requires decisions about the test audience. Tests can be used with a wide variety of audiences, and the design or selection a good test requires careful consideration of the characteristics of that audience. Age of audience is a good example. A test to be used with children must be shorter and contain simpler items than a test to be used with adults. Similarly, the abilities of audience members must be considered. A test using visual stimuli is not appropriate when the test audience may include blind individuals. A test requiring assembly of puzzles is not appropriate when the test audience may include people with limited use of their hands. A test in English is not appropriate for an audience that might include nonspeakers of English. Consideration of audience characteristics is vital to the validity of test data. A valid test measures what it was intended to measure. If performance on the test is influenced by characteristics other than those we wish to measure, such as vision, physical skill, or knowledge of a language, the validity of the test data is compromised.

Test Score Type

The final element of test purpose is deciding how the test scores will be used. Tests can be designed to produce different types of scores. The appropriate type of score depends on *how* the test will be used to evaluate test takers. To keep things simple, we will focus on two basic issues. First, will the test be used to compare the performance of test takers to each other or to evaluate each test taker separately? Second, will the test measure a single characteristic or a set of characteristics? If it is to measure a set of characteristics, should it provide a set of independent measures of these characteristics or a ranking of the relative strength of each characteristic?

This feature of tests may be a bit trickier to grasp than it seems. We are focusing on the *type of score* used to describe test performance. We could, for example, decide to represent your performance on a particular test as percent correct or as rank within a group. It is important to distinguish the issue of type of score from other scoring issues. First, we are not discussing *scoring system*. Scoring system refers to the process used to evaluate the responses to individual test items. Chapter 1 identified two basic types of scoring systems: objective scoring rules and subjective scoring rules. The type of score used by a test is independent of the scoring system. The scores described in this section can be used on tests with objective scoring rules, such as multiple-choice tests, or subjective scoring rules, such as essay tests.

Second, we are not discussing the choice of *measurement scale*. Chapter 1 described four types of measurement scales—nominal, ordinal, interval, and ratio—and identified interval scales as the type used most often in psychological testing. The various scores discussed in this section traditionally are used with tests at an interval or ratio level of measurement.

Norm-referenced versus Criterion-referenced Scores
The first test score question posed was, Will the test be used to compare the performance of test takers to each other or to evaluate each test taker

separately? The answer to this question enables us to choose between using norm- and criterion-referenced scores. **Norm-referenced scoring** indicates where members of a group of test takers fall relative to each other; it is used on both maximal and typical performance tests. **Criterion-referenced scoring** indicates where test takers fall relative to the content of the test. It is used primarily on maximal performance tests.

Norm-referenced Scores.　Norm-referenced scores are produced by a two-stage process. First, we determine people's total scores on the test using the test's scoring criteria. Next, we convert or transform these total scores to a new form that includes information about the performance of other people who took the test. For example, suppose you are told that you performed better than 75% of the students in your class on a particular test. You have not been told what your actual total score is. Instead, your performance has been described using a type of norm-referenced score called *percentile rank*, determined by comparing the number of correct answers you produced to the number of correct answers produced by the other members of your class. Although your original total score is based on the questions *you* answered correctly, your score has been converted to a new scale based on the performance of the entire group. Your norm-referenced score, therefore, depends on the performance of others, as well as on your own performance. If you answered many questions correctly and others did too, your norm-referenced score will not be very high. On the other hand, if you answered many questions correctly and others did not, your norm-referenced score will be high.

Most standardized tests (intelligence tests, achievement tests, skills tests, personality tests) produce norm-referenced scores. Norm-referenced scores are the appropriate choice when our goal is to sort test takers into groups according to how much they know or what they are like *relative to each other*. Scenarios in which norm-referenced scores are most useful include tests designed for rating, selection, placement, or diagnosis.

The group to which you are compared with a norm-referenced score is called the **norm group**. The term *norm-referenced score* actually means that test-taker performance is compared to or *referenced to* a particular norm group. In classroom testing, the norm group simply is the set of people in the class—in fact, we usually don't even bother calling this a norm group. With a standardized test, we administer the test to a group called the **standardization sample** and use the responses of those test takers to develop the scale for our norm-referenced scores. The standardization sample, therefore, becomes the norm group. When the test is administered to new test takers, their total scores are converted to norm-referenced scores according to data from the standardization sample. To receive a percentile rank of 75 on a standardized test, your total score would have to equal the total score falling at the 75th percentile in the norm group.

There is a critical distinction in the design of maximal- versus typical-performance tests that are used to generate norm-referenced scores. Maximal-performance tests identify the upper limits of test-taker ability. When a maximal-performance test is designed to produce norm-referenced scores, it is being used to sort test takers into groups based on their relative levels of ability. The test cannot do so unless it contains some very difficult items, items that will be answered correctly only by the most knowledgeable or skillful test takers. On these tests, it is important to evaluate items in terms of their **item difficulty**, the proportion of people who answer an item correctly. The calculation of item difficulty will be discussed in Chapter 8.

When a typical-performance test is designed to produce norm-referenced scores, our goal is somewhat different. Now the test is designed to sort people into groups according to personal characteristics, not level of ability. The norm groups, therefore, differ in terms of qualities such as personality dimensions, attitudes, or interests. To determine where test takers fall relative to these groups, we must include items that differentiate or discriminate among different types of people. In a test of depression, for example, we need items that a depressed person answers differently from a person who is not depressed. In these scenarios, we focus on a different characteristic of items—their item-discrimination properties. **Item discrimination** refers to the way different types of people respond to an item. The calculation of several item-discrimination indexes will be discussed in Chapter 8.

Criterion-referenced Scores. Criterion-referenced scores, sometimes referred to as content-referenced (Brown, 1983), are designed to evaluate the performance of each test taker independently. The word *criterion* refers to a particular level of performance on the test domain to which your performance is compared. If you were told that you answered 75% of the items on a test correctly, the test used criterion-referenced scores. Rather than comparing your performance to the performance of others, you were evaluated relative to the domain of test items using the criterion of *perfect performance*—correct answers to all questions. Your score indicates where you fall relative to that criterion. It makes no difference how many questions other people answered correctly. You, and they, are evaluated independently.

The goal of criterion-referenced scoring is to represent the extent to which test takers have mastered the test domain. In general, criterion-referenced scores are used with maximal-performance tests. Criterion-referenced scores are found most often in classroom testing, where the purpose of the test is to determine how much of the required material each student learned. Some diagnostic tests and competency/proficiency tests are criterion referenced. A high school competency test, for example, may be graded pass/fail using a criterion of 70% correct. All students receiving scores at or above the criterion pass the exam, whereas those scoring below the criterion fail.

Not all maximal-performance tests, however, are suitable for criterion-referenced scoring. Criterion-referenced scores are most appropriate when there is a clearly defined specific content to be tested. Within these settings it is possible to design a test that covers the domain comprehensively and to set a meaningful criterion for evaluating performance. It is more difficult, how-ever, to develop criterion-referenced systems for large-scale standardized tests that are designed for examinees with widely varying backgrounds and experi-ences. At the present time, most standardized ability tests are norm referenced. Table 2.6 summarizes the properties of norm- and criterion-referenced scores.

Normative versus Ipsative Scores

The second test score question posed contained two parts: Will the test measure a single characteristic or a set of characteristics? If it is to measure a set of

TABLE 2.6   Properties of Norm- and Criterion-referenced Scores

Norm-referenced scores

1. May be used with **either** maximal performance (aptitude or achievement) tests **or** typical performance (personality or attitude or interest) tests.
2. Used **both** with tests of a single domain **and** tests covering several differ-ent domains; in the latter case, separate scores are produced for each domain measured.
3. For each domain measured, the norm-referenced score compares your perfor-mance to the performance of others in a specified norm group; it indicates where your score falls relative to the scores of the others in that group.
4. *Example*: Percentile rank. Earning a percentile rank of 75 means that your score was as good or better than 75% of the scores earned by people in the norm group.

Criterion-referenced scores

1. Used **primarily** with maximal performance (aptitude or achievement) tests.
2. Used **primarily** with tests of a single domain.
3. Compares your performance to a criterion (a specific level of performance); indicates how much of the domain you have mastered.
4. *Example*: Percent correct. Earning 75% correct means that you correctly an-swered 75% of the test questions. The criterion is perfect performance (i.e., **all** correct answers); you reached 75% of that criterion.

characteristics, should it provide an independent measure of each characteristic or a ranking of the relative strength of each characteristic? The first part is relevant to both maximal- and typical-performance tests. Both types can be designed to measure a single attribute, such as vocabulary or anxiety, or a set of attributes, such as language skills or the elements of self-concept. In the former cases, the tests are each designed to produce a single test score. In the latter cases, the tests generate separate scores for each attribute tested. However, the second part of the question is most relevant to the design of typical performance tests. When tests of personality, interests, or attitudes measure a *set* of attributes, we can choose between independent measures of each characteristic or rankings of the relative strength of each characteristic. Typical performance tests of single attributes are designed to produce normative scores; tests of several characteristics can generate either normative or ipsative scores.

A **normative score** represents the absolute strength of a particular characteristic, the extent to which the test taker possesses that attribute. If you received a score of 22 on a 25-item test of assertiveness, we can conclude that you are a pretty assertive person! By comparing the scores earned by you and another person on our assertiveness test, we can determine if you differ in overall level of assertiveness. A test measuring a single personality characteristic or attitude *must* produce a normative score—all we can do in this case is measure the extent of that property in the people we test. However, normative scores can also be used in tests of several characteristics.

For example, a test could include some items measuring assertiveness and some items measuring leadership. In this case, the test will produce separate scores for each characteristic, and each score indicates the overall strength of the characteristic measured. In other words, tests of several attributes using normative scores measure each characteristic independently. Test takers can earn all high scores, all low scores, or any other pattern. By comparing your normative scores on our test of assertiveness and leadership, we could determine whether or not you differ in the extent of these properties. By comparing your scores to another person's scores, we can determine whether or not you differ in the extent of *each* characteristic.

An **ipsative score** presents personality characteristics in relative rather than absolute terms and is used *only* when tests measure several different attributes. Ipsative scoring is designed specifically so that you *cannot* earn all high or all low scores on the characteristics measured. Instead of determining the strength of each characteristic independently, ipsative measures in essence rank a person's needs, feelings, and tendencies relative to each other. By comparing your ipsative scores on a test of assertiveness and leadership, we could determine which property is stronger within you. By comparing your ipsative scores to the scores of another person, we could determine whether or not you show the same personality pattern rather than whether you are similar in overall extent of each attribute. For each person we would know whether assertiveness or leadership is a stronger property.

Normative and ipsative scores are tied to different item formats. Specifically, tests to produce ipsative scores must use items requiring test takers to consider characteristics *relative to each other*. If the goal is to determine the relative strength of different characteristics, the test must be designed so that the resulting scores serve to rank characteristics in terms of strength. The most common item format for ipsative scoring is a variation on alternate-choice items called **forced-choice**. In a forced-choice item, test takers must select the alternative from a set of alternatives that best characterizes their thoughts, feelings, or behavior.

A test of assertiveness and leadership could, for example, present 25 pairs of statements, each pair including an assertiveness-oriented *and* a leadership-oriented statement. Test takers would be instructed to select the statement (a or b) from each item that best describes them. Although a total of 50 statements are presented, they are presented within only 25 items and each test taker would select only 25 statements—one per item. In essence, selection of any assertiveness statement prevents selection of a leadership statement, and vice versa. Since one choice is made for each item, the total number of "assertiveness points" plus the total number of "leadership points" equals the total number of test items (25 in our example). If you chose 14 assertiveness statements, you could only have chosen 11 leadership statements. The resulting scores, therefore, indicate which property is more characteristic of you.

Both normative and ipsative scores can be converted to *norm-referenced* scores. Before you panic, think about this. A normative or ipsative score on a personality test basically is a *total score*. It indicates the extent to which a person possesses a characteristic—in absolute or relative terms—just as total score on an ability test indicates the extent of a person's knowledge. Your normative score of 22 on our 25-item assertiveness test means you answered 22 items the way assertive people answer them. If we administered our test to a norm group and calculated the score earned by each person, we then could determine the number of times each score was earned and convert your score of 22 out of 25 to a percentile rank. The percentile rank would indicate the proportion of norm group members earning 22 or fewer points on our test.

The same procedure could be used for our ipsative test of assertiveness and leadership. Your ipsative scores of 14 (assertiveness) and 11 (leadership) indicate how often you selected each type of statement. If we administered our test to a norm group, we could calculate how many of these people selected 14 assertiveness statements and convert your score to a percentile rank. We could do the same with a leadership score of 11 and give you a percentile rank on each personality characteristic.

Remember that the choice between using normative and ipsative scores depends on the type of information desired. If the purpose of the test is to determine the relative strength of different characteristics, the test should be designed to produce ipsative scores. If relative strength of properties is not important, the test should use normative scores. Table 2.7 summarizes the properties of normative and ipsative test scores.

TESTS DIFFERING IN CONTENT

A clearly defined purpose is an important feature of a good test, but a good test must also have a specific and standard content. Before you can write a test or select an existing one to use in some scenario, you must specify or outline the content to be covered. In other words, you must identify exactly what knowledge, skills, or characteristics the items should cover. People often underestimate the importance of this step to the testing process. It may seem that once you have a clear purpose in mind you can proceed directly to write your test or pick one from the various reference volumes. But how many items should the test include? What are the really central elements of content that

TABLE 2.7   Properties of Normative and Ipsative Scores

Normative scores

1. Used **either with** typical performance (personality or attitude or interest) or maximal performance (aptitude or achievement) tests.
2. Used **both** with tests of a single domain **and** a test covering more than one domain. For a test of more than one domain, each characteristic is assessed independently; you can earn all high scores, all low scores, or any other score pattern.
3. Typically are transformed to norm-referenced scores for each domain measured (see Table 2.6). Once they are norm referenced, each new score compares your performance to the performance of others in a specified norm group.

Ipsative scores

1. Used **only with** typical performance (personality or attitude or interest) tests.
2. Used **only** with tests of more than one domain. Characteristics are assessed relative to each other to determine which is strongest, next strongest, and so on. You **cannot**, therefore, earn all high or all low scores.
3. Often are transformed to norm-referenced scores for each domain measured (see Table 2.6). Once they are norm referenced, each new score compares your performance to the performance of others in a specified norm group.

should be tapped by several test items? What kinds of items should be used? Without a blueprint for your test, these questions are impossible to answer. Furthermore, without prior specification of test content, it is extremely difficult to determine the validity of a newly constructed test. Remember that a good test is valid; it measures what it was intended to measure. By specifying the content of the test before writing the items, the test developer has a definite outline of what the test should measure, something to which the final test can be compared to determine its validity.

Tests can be designed to cover many types of domains. Ability tests measure knowledge or skill domains; personality and attitude tests focus on construct domains. Still other tests, such as job performance tests, assess behavioral domains. The following sections discuss the process of specifying test content for each of these domains.

Knowledge or Skill Domains: Test Plans

When a test is intended to measure knowledge and/or skills, the content can be specified in a test plan. A **test plan** is a written list of the information to be covered by the test items and the behaviors required to answer the questions correctly. Test plans are used most often in the development of classroom and standardized achievement tests.

The two components of a test plan are called content objectives and behavioral objectives (e.g., Carlson, 1985). *Content objectives* define the "what" of testing, the information (e.g., vocabulary) and/or skills (e.g., addition) to be covered by the test. Writing content objectives is much like writing an outline of domain, identifying the topics and subtopics. *Behavioral objectives* define the "how" of testing. They translate the content objectives into statements that specify the types of responses to be required of test takers.

Consider the development of a vocabulary test. The content objectives determine the level at which vocabulary will be tested and thus the types of words to include on the test. But content objectives alone are not enough. Should test takers be able to define words, identify synonyms and antonyms or produce sentences using the words correctly? Each of these is a different behavior that could be used to measure vocabulary. The test developer must decide which of these behaviors to elicit by the test.

One of the most popular systems for identifying behavioral objectives was developed by Benjamin Bloom (Bloom, 1956; Krathwohl, Bloom, & Masia, 1964). Table 2.8 lists some behavioral objectives useful for planning ability tests. Listed in order of increasing cognitive complexity, the objectives range from simple recognition and recall of facts or principles to evaluation of how facts or principles are used. Perhaps now you can see why these are called

TABLE 2.8 Popular Behavioral Objectives

Objective	Explanation
Knowledge	Remembers previously learned material, including specific facts and terms.
Comprehension	Grasps the meaning of learned material and can explain, summarize, or translate it.
Application	Can use information in concrete situations.
Analysis	Can break material down into its parts, identifying both the parts and their relationships to each other.
Synthesis	Can put parts together to produce a unique entity, generate a plan, or derive new relationships.
Evaluation	Can use internal evidence and external criteria to judge the value of a thing for a given purpose.

Adapted from B. S. Bloom (ed.), *Taxonomy of Educational Objectives*, Longman, Green, and Co., New York, 1956.

behavioral objectives. Each lists one or more observable behaviors. When content objectives are translated into behavioral form, the test developer specifies the type of action to be performed for each element of the domain.

Let's demonstrate how content and behavioral objectives can be used to develop a test plan for an achievement test. Table 2.9 identifies some content objectives to be used in the construction of a test on the topic of "test administration" and translates each content objective into a behavioral form. Note that the rewritten behavioral objectives actually suggest possible test items and test item formats. For example, behavioral objective 1 lists a number of specific definitions to be tested. Since it calls for recognition or recall of these definitions, the objective will not be met by a broadly written essay question asking test takers to compare and contrast the administration types. It suggests the need for a set of shorter, more specific items. Now consider behavioral objective 3b, which identifies several important dimensions on which test administrations differ. Since this objective calls for explanation of these differences, it is a good choice for essay or short-answer questions.

There is one more element of writing test plans to discuss. In many cases, some aspects of the test domain are more central or important than others. In other words, the test domain has not only a content but a *structure*. The resulting test should match both the content and structure of that domain. The test plan must contain information about the relative emphasis or weight

TABLE 2.9   Sample Objectives for a Test on "Test Administration"

Content objectives

1.   Knows terms and vocabulary used in the area of test administration.
2.   Knows relationship of item format to administration format.
3.   Knows advantages and disadvantages of each type of test administration.

Content objectives translated into behavioral objectives

1.   Recognizes or recalls the definitions of

individual testing	subjective scoring
group testing	objective scoring
computer-assisted testing	tailored testing

2.   Produces examples of situations in which the same item format (e.g., multiple choice) requires different types of administration.
3a. Describes the type of information about the test taker that can or cannot be obtained through each administration format.
3b. Explains how the three types of administration differ in terms of role of examiner, scoring, and cost/efficiency.

to be given to each test objective. This weighting information can be used to decide how many items are needed to cover each objective and/or how many points to award to items devoted to different objectives.

The weight given to each content area and objective should correspond to their relative importance within the domain. To some extent, decisions about relative importance are subjective, based on the perspective of the test developer. But subjective does not mean arbitrary. There always is some way to determine both the content areas to be covered by the test and the relative importance of each content area. For a classroom achievement test, the test content is defined by the material covered during instruction. The test writer can use the relative emphasis placed on material in required readings, classroom lectures, and assignments to determine the weight to give to each content area. For a standardized achievement test, the test developer can consult curricular guides published by state education departments to determine both the content and structure of the domain. Such a process ensures that test takers have had an opportunity to learn the material covered by the test. Only then can we interpret differences between people in test scores as reflecting differences in their level of achievement.

Table 2.10 applies this procedure to outlining the structure of the domain "test administration," based on the material presented later in this chapter. If we operationally define "importance" as the number of pages devoted to the topics in this book, we can rank the topics in terms of the weight each should be

TABLE 2.10   Sample Analysis of the Structure of the Domain for a Test on "Test Administration"

Topic	No. of Pages[a]	Focus[b]
Item–administration relationships	3	Gives examples of test items requiring a specific administration format
Standardization	0.5	Explains relationship between test administration and test reliability
Individual administration	3.33	Identifies defining features of an individual test Describes approaches to presenting items of varying difficulty Describes advantages Identifies problems associated with examiner and scoring
Group administration	2.5	Identifies defining features of a group test Describes approaches to presenting items of varying difficulty Describes advantages Identifies and addresses frequently raised criticisms
Computer-assisted administration	2	Describes important features Identifies advantages

[a]Used as a measure of the relative emphasis given to each topic.
[b]Used to represent level of analysis and extent of detail.

given in the completed exam. For example, in decreasing order of emphasis, the three administration formats are individual, group, and computer-assisted. For the test to be an accurate representation of the domain, the number of questions and/or number of points assigned to each administration format should parallel this structure.

Remember that there is an important advantage to taking this rather long approach to specifying test content. After the test is written it must be analyzed to determine its validity. A detailed test plan provides the data necessary to evaluate the adequacy of the test. The use of test plans to determine test validity will be discussed in Chapter 7.

Behavioral Domains: Task Analysis

A second type of content outline is appropriate when tests are used to measure or predict patterns of behavior. For example, a business may want a test to determine how effectively supervisors monitor the workers on their shifts or a test to identify shift workers who would be good candidates for supervisor positions. You probably have some experience with this type of testing. It is likely that you have completed forms evaluating the performance of your instructors during the course of your college career.

Our concern, again, is the validity of the test to be written or selected. For the test to be valid, the items on the test must match up with relevant performance variables. The development of valid tests begins with an outline of the tasks on which the person must be rated. The process of specifying test content in these cases is through **task** or **job analysis**. In task/job analysis, the job or task is broken down into specific components. These components define the content of the test. Each component is translated into a set of behaviors for use in generating individual test items. Just as the content domain of an achievement test has a particular structure, the components of the job under analysis have a structure. Central elements of the job are defined as high-priority activities or activities engaged in on a frequent basis. The selection of items and the scoring system should reflect this structure. Important activities should be tapped by more items and should be linked to earning more points than less important activities. By using this analytic approach, we are more likely to produce a test that is a valid measure of performance.

Let's use a familiar job to illustrate the process. Assume you are to design an instrument to rate the effectiveness of your college instructors. You begin by analyzing the job into components. What tasks must an instructor perform to be effective? These terms define the content of the scale to be developed. For example, the effectiveness of an instructor probably depends on activities relative to organization, preparation, communication, availability, and grading. Although we could simply write items asking students if the instructor is well organized, well prepared, and so on, it is difficult to tell what these items measure. What defines being "well organized"? How can we be sure that all students rating an instructor as "well organized" are basing their opinions on the same set of behaviors? A better approach would be to translate these task components into behavioral statements. The behavioral statements could then be used to write the actual items for the instrument. For example, items tapping opinions about the instructor's organizational skills could ask about the instructor's use of handouts to structure course material or the instructor's use of the blackboard as an organizational tool.

A possible outline for a scale to rate teacher effectiveness is presented in Table 2.11. Note that by translating the objectives into behaviors we direct student attention to specific, observable activities. The process removes the ambiguity associated with blanket statements about being "well organized" and increases the likelihood that all raters will base their evaluations on the same characteristics of teacher behavior.

The same approach can be used to develop or select a screening test for a particular job. For a screening test to be a valid predictor of job performance,

---

TABLE 2.11   Possible Test Plan for an Instrument to Rate Teacher Effectiveness

---

Organization

The instructor outlines material to be covered on the blackboard at the beginning of class.
The instructor distributes handouts summarizing important course material at regular intervals throughout the course.
The instructor's class presentations have a clear theme and goal.
The instructor provides links between the material covered during adjacent class periods.

Preparation

The instructor can answer specific questions about assigned readings.
The instructor can elaborate on topics and issues covered in assigned readings.
The instructor begins each class period at a point in the material consistent with where the last class ended.

Communication

The instructor recites or distributes specific course objectives.
The instructor informs the class of assigned readings, deadlines, exam or homework dates, and course policies.
The instructor speaks clearly and is easy to understand.

Availability

The instructor recites or distributes a set of office hours during which students may seek help.
The instructor is available during stated office hours.
The instructor will make appointments with students who are not available during office hours.

Grading

The instructor recites or distributes a grading scale for assignments, exams, and final grades.
The instructor uses the same criteria to grade the work of all students in the course.
The instructor will meet with students to answer questions about the grading of assignments or exams.

---

the test must generate an accurate measure of job-relevant knowledge and skills. Although it may seem expedient to assemble a collection of existing tests to screen applicants, the best predictions are produced by tests that tap behaviors directly relevant to job success. The use of performance-based tests will be discussed further in Chapter 12.

Construct Domains: Construct Explication

Not all tests cover knowledge, skill, or behavioral domains. Some tests are designed to measure constructs, those hypothetical dimensions on which individuals differ. Constructs cannot be measured directly. The presence of a construct must be inferred from measurements of specific behaviors. In **construct explication** (Murphy & Davidshofer, 1988), the test developer compiles a list of specific behaviors, beliefs, and attitudes that demonstrate the presence of the construct and specific behaviors, beliefs, and attitudes inconsistent with its presence. The lists are then used to determine the nature and content of the actual test items.

Table 2.12 illustrates a possible analysis of the construct "friendliness." First, the table lists behaviors related to the presence of friendliness. Test items tapping these behaviors should be endorsed only by test takers who are friendly. For example, people who are friendly are more likely to mark as "true" statements about frequently spending time with other people and initiating conversations with new people. Next, the table lists behaviors inconsistent with the presence of friendliness. Test items covering these behaviors should be endorsed only by test takers who are not friendly. People who are not friendly are more likely to mark as "true" statements about preferring to spend time alone.

The process of defining the construct to be tested is complex and important. It is complex because constructs are theoretical abstractions. There are no concrete, specific domains to outline. Instead, the test developer must consult previous theoretical analyses and research studies of the construct to generate ideas about the behaviors to be measured. The process is important because it influences later evaluation of test validity. Without a detailed analysis of what the test is supposed to measure, it is difficult to determine the validity of the completed test. The use of construct explication to determine test validity will be discussed in detail in Chapter 7.

TABLE 2.12   Possible Analysis of the Construct "Friendliness"

Behaviors consistent with the presence of "friendliness"

Initiating contact with other people
Frequently spending time with other people
Choosing to spend time with other people rather than spending time alone
Initiating conversations with new people
Smiling, talking, and laughing in the company of other people
Making frequent eye contact with other people

Behaviors inconsistent with the presence of "friendliness"

Avoiding contact with other people
Rarely spending time with other people
Choosing to spend time alone rather than spending time with other people
Engaging in conversations with other people only when others initiate the
   conversations
Demonstrating physiological and behavioral signs of distress when in the company
   of other people
Rarely making eye contact with other people

TESTS DIFFERING IN ADMINISTRATION FORMAT

A good test also has a standard administration procedure. The three popular formats for psychological tests are individual administration, group administration, and computer-assisted administration. The following sections discuss the strengths and weaknesses of each administration format. Remember, however, that the choice of an administration format occurs within the context of designing a test to fit a particular purpose. Although any test can be administered individually, not all tests are suitable for group or computer-assisted administration.

As an example, consider the Thematic Apperception Test or TAT (Murray, 1943), a projective personality test using ambiguous visual images as test items. Test takers tell stories about these images, in theory projecting unconscious elements of personality into their descriptions. It would be difficult to design a test like the TAT that could be administered to a group of people. It is technically possible to require test takers to write out their responses, just as students write answers to free-response items like essay questions. But, in practice, examiners often must ask test takers to clarify and expand on their stories. If the test were administered to a group of people, examiners could not follow up on individual responses.

Likewise, it would be difficult to develop a test like the Wechsler Adult Intelligence Scale–Revised or WAIS–R (Wechsler, 1981) that could be administered by a computer. The WAIS–R is a free-response ability test tapping a variety of mental abilities. Several of the subtests in the WAIS–R require test takers to perform tasks, to physically manipulate objects such as puzzle pieces and blocks. It is technically possible to design computer software that presents images of objects that can be manipulated through either a keyboard or a "mouse." But it is difficult to say whether the abilities tested through this computer-simulated task are the same as the ones tested through direct manipulation of objects.

A few interesting points emerge on test administration. First, not all alternate-choice tests are suitable for group administration. The Peabody Picture Vocabulary Test or PPVT (Dunn & Dunn, 1981) is an alternate-choice achievement test requiring individual administration. The reason for this is that in the PPVT the test taker defines each word by pointing to one of four pictures. The use of pointing as a response requires that the test be administered individually, even though it is technically an alternate-choice test. Second, not all projective tests require individual administration. Sentence-completion blanks are technically projective tests, but since these are written tests in which test takers write phrases to complete sentences, they can be administered to a group of people. The point of this discussion is to underscore the interrelatedness of test purpose, item format, and administration format. Just as there is no one-to-one correspondence between test purpose and item format, there is no one-to-one-correspondence between item format and administration format.

People often underestimate the importance of considering different administration formats. In fact, this decision is very important to producing a good test. A good test has a carefully standardized administration procedure, one that ensures that the test will be presented in the same way to all test takers every time it is given. Standardization of test administration is critical to test reliability. If the test administration varies, test takers may earn different scores on two administrations because of the change in administration. A test cannot be reliable unless people earn similar scores on all administrations until their actual knowledge or characteristics change. Furthermore, if the administration varies, the resulting test scores may reflect different characteristics of test takers. A reliable test taps the same test-taker characteristics each time it is given.

Individual Administration

Individual administration requires an examiner to work with a single test taker. The examiner provides the instructions according to the procedures stated in the test manual. The examiner then presents an item to the test taker, who makes the required response. The examiner records that response and proceeds to the next item according to the directions in the test manual. Most individual tests use free-response or projective items.

Many individual ability tests contain items of varying difficulty. One approach is to group items by content and arrange them in increasing order of difficulty. Items are administered until the test taker no longer answers items correctly. The Wechsler intelligence tests use this format. In other cases the examiner selects the items to be administered on the basis of test taker performance, establishing a basal and a ceiling level of performance. The *basal* is the level at which the test taker answers all items correctly. The *ceiling* is the level at which the test taker no longer answers items correctly. Item difficulty, therefore, is matched specifically to the test taker's ability. The Stanford–Binet intelligence test (Thorndike, Hagen & Sattler, 1986) uses the basal/ceiling approach.

The examiner plays a major role in the administration of individual tests. In the case of maximal-performance tests, such as intelligence tests, the examiner takes responsibility for eliciting the test taker's best performance. If the test taker is anxious or uncooperative, the examiner is supportive and encourages the test taker to try hard. The examiner even may encourage guessing. For some typical-performance tests, such as projective personality tests, the examiner takes responsibility for recording the test-taker's response in a complete and detailed manner. If the test taker is describing an inkblot, the examiner requests an explanation of exactly how and why the image appears as it does.

Individual testing also provides an opportunity for the examiner to observe test-taker behavior. In addition to recording test-taker responses, the examiner can note whether the test taker is cooperative, on-task, and calm. Since these factors can influence test performance, the examiner's observations can help explain the resulting test scores. Because items are presented individually, the examiner can also record response time to individual items. Items, therefore, can be scored on both speed and accuracy. Finally, the examiner can note how the test taker responds to different test items. Test takers can reveal a lot about themselves by their different reactions to items they know they can answer and items that they find quite difficult. Furthermore, experienced examiners know how people usually react to certain tasks or situations and can identify unusual reactions in test takers.

Although individual testing may sound ideal, it does present some problems. It is not a practical or efficient technique when large numbers of people need to be screened. Also, the role of the examiner may make individual administration difficult to standardize, and standardized administration is critical to developing a reliable test. Finally, the one-to-one administration format is an intimate setting. Research suggests that examiner behavior can influence test-taker performance on individual tests. Test scores have been shown to vary as a function of examiner rapport (Feldman & Sullivan, 1960), approving/disapproving examiner comments (Witmer, Bornstein, & Dunham, 1971), and the familiarity of the examiner with the test taker (Fuchs & Fuchs, 1986).

Unfortunately, even if examiners behave in a professional manner, it is possible that test takers *perceive* one examiner more positively than another and that their performance is affected accordingly. Standardizing the administration of individual tests and reducing the degree to which test scores reflect examiner behavior requires specific, explicit test instructions and careful training of examiners.

Since many individual tests use either free-response or projective items, they also must use subjective scoring rules, guidelines for the evaluation of answers. It is not possible to anticipate all the answers test takers could generate to an open-ended question, so it is not possible to create a test manual that scores each potential answer. Instead, the manuals for individual tests outline rules for assigning points based on the characteristics of the answers. The process is subjective in that it relies on the judgment of the examiner, and there is no guarantee that two different examiners would award the same number of points to a particular answer. Such variation threatens the reliability of individual tests. Detailed scoring rules and careful training of examiners are needed to ensure standardized scoring of individual tests.

Group Administration

Group administration is a cost-efficient way to evaluate people. Group tests minimize the amount of time needed to test a large number of people, which in turn lowers cost by reducing the amount of professional administration time. Most standardized group tests are paper-and-pencil, using an alternate-choice format, which reduces the cost of test materials and the amount of training necessary for administration and scoring. Alternate-choice items can be scored using objective scoring rules; two examiners will always score a particular response the same way. In fact, many group tests are scored mechanically. Some group tests, however, do use free-response items requiring subjective scoring rules. Examples include classroom tests and certain standardized aptitude and achievement tests including short-answer or essay questions. Because they are fast and easy to administer, group tests can quickly generate large data sets. Large samples are important in the development of norm-referenced tests. Group tests may include standardization samples of 100,000 to 200,000 people, a sharp contrast to the 1000 to 8000 characteristic of individual tests (Anastasi, 1988).

Group ability tests often contain items of varying difficulty. Because the test is administered to several people at once, group tests cannot use the basal/ceiling approach. Instead, items of similar content can be grouped together in order of increasing difficulty within separately timed subtests. Test takers have an opportunity to answer items in each content area and to answer easier items before tackling difficult items that might require more time to complete.

It is fashionable to criticize group tests for their frequent use of alternate-choice questions and to accuse them of being strongly influenced by test takers' language skills. Critics charge that alternate-choice questions focus on rote learning and do not assess more sophisticated cognitive skills, such as ability to apply or analyze information. Because group tests often adopt a paper-and-pencil format, critics complain that scores are contaminated with measures of reading skill and therefore likely to be culturally biased. These concerns should not be dismissed, but they must be placed in perspective. Research comparing performance on individual and group ability tests, to be discussed in Chapter 9, indicates that most people perform similarly on both types of tests. As with any category of tests, some group tests are poorly designed. It is possible, however, to design alternate-choice items to assess application and analytic skills. And group tests need not rely heavily on reading skills. Group tests can use pictures, mazes, and other types of nonverbal items. On the other hand, even a well-designed test, with sophisticated verbal or nonverbal items, can produce dismal validity and culturally biased scores.

There is, however, a critical difference between group and individual tests. When a test is administered to a group of people, it is not possible for the examiner to observe and record features of test-taker behavior, including response time to individual items. Group tests cannot be designed to incorporate the interviewlike features of individual testing. Information about the attitudes and reactions of test takers is simply unavailable. Group tests can only reveal how test takers respond to the different test items.

Computer-assisted Administration

In computer-assisted administration, a personal computer or computer terminal is used to present test items and record test-taker responses. The computer can be programmed to provide instructions to the test taker at the beginning of testing, and help menus can be written to provide additional instructions during testing. Many of the major group tests are available today in computerized form. In fact, computer-assisted testing has become so popular that the American Psychological Association has published policies for its development and use, the *Guidelines for Computer-Based Tests and Interpretations* (APA, 1986).

Computer-assisted testing combines many of the advantages of individual testing with the advantages of group testing and adds a few unique features, too. Using a computer to present test items and record responses is the ultimate in standardized administration and scoring. The computer can also be used to record the time taken to respond to each test item, data unavailable in group testing. Although only one test taker is tested at each computer terminal, computer-assisted administration is more cost effective than individual administration. The use of a computer frees examiners for other activities. Computerized testing is not only efficient—it is fast. Use of a computer enables us to obtain information about test takers in less time than either of the other administration formats.

A unique feature of computer-assisted testing is the opportunity for **tailored testing**, an adaptive administration format in which the items presented are determined by the test taker's performance. If the test taker is correct on several items at one level of difficulty, the program advances to items at the next level of difficulty. Tailored testing can be used to mirror the basal/ceiling method employed in individual tests like the Stanford–Binet. First, data about the test taker are entered to estimate level of ability. The program then selects and presents items at that level of difficulty. If the test taker is correct on these items, a basal is established and the program advances to the next level. If the test taker has problems with these items, the program backs up to progressively easier items until a basal level is established. By selecting items on the basis of test-taker responses, the program can continually revise its estimate of the person's ability (Recase, 1977; Weiss & Davidson, 1981).

Before we rush to design more computer-assisted tests, we need more research on the effects of this type of test administration. For example, do people receive similar scores on the computer-assisted and paper-and-pencil versions of psychological tests? There are few studies on this issue, and most of them use very small samples. Comparisons thus far suggest that scores generally are quite similar (Elwood, 1969; Ward et al., 1989) and that cultural differences may be smaller when tests are administered by computer (Johnson & Mihal, 1973). In addition, several studies suggest that test takers view computerized tests more positively than paper-and-pencil tests (Rosenfeld et al., 1989) and that they are willing to divulge more personal information to a computer than to a human interviewer! It appears that computer-assisted administration may be a useful alternative to traditional group testing.

SUMMARY AND KEY CONCEPTS

The selection or construction of a good test requires understanding the properties, advantages, and limitations of different types of tests. The design of a test depends on its purpose, content, and administration format. The purpose of a test is determined by test domain, test audience, and the type of test score it produces. The domain of a test can be either **maximal performance** or **typical performance**. Maximal-performance or ability tests can be subdivided into tests of **aptitude** or **achievement** and tests of **speed** or **power**. Typical-performance tests include tests of **personality**, **interests** and **attitudes**.

The domain of a test also influences the selection of item formats and test instructions. Ability tests can use **alternate-choice items** and/or **free-response items**. Personality tests use either **projective items** or **objective items**, whereas interest and attitude tests use objective items. Maximal-performance tests must include instructions encouraging test takers to try their hardest; typical-performance test instructions request answers based on everyday feelings and behaviors.

Depending on the purpose of the test, different types of test scores can be used. **Norm-referenced scoring** provides a relative evaluation of test takers, comparing them to each other or to a specific **norm group** or **standardization sample**. When maximal-performance tests use norm-referenced scores, **item difficulty** is an important concern. When typical-performance tests use norm-referenced scores, **item discrimination** is an important concern. **Criterion-referenced scoring** evaluates test-taker performance relative to the test domain, determining where test takers fall relative to some standard of performance or criterion. Criterion-referenced scores are only found in maximal-performance tests.

Tests can also be designed to use either normative or ipsative scores. **Normative scores** present the absolute strength of each characteristic tested. **Ipsative scores** compare the relative strengths of different characteristics within a test taker and therefore often used **forced-choice** test items. Both normative and ipsative scores can later be converted to norm-referenced scores through the use of a norm group. Because ipsative scores are only used in typical performance testing, this distinction is most relevant to tests of personality, attitudes, and interests.

The purpose of a test is also defined by test audience and test content. The design of a test, including length and types of items to be used, must be appropriate for the intended audience. The content of the test must be specified clearly using one of three procedures. Tests designed to assess a knowledge or skill domain are outlined using a **test plan**, including a set of content and behavioral objectives. Tests designed to measure behavioral domains are outlined through **task** or **job analysis**. The content of a test designed to measure a construct is outlined through **construct explication**, a process in which behaviors indicating the presence and absence of the construct are specified.

Tests also differ in administration format. In individual administration, a test is administered to a single test taker by an examiner. This one-to-one approach allows for some flexibility in test organization, such as the use of a basal and ceiling to identify test-taker ability level. In group administration, an examiner administers a test to several people at the same time. Because many people can be tested at once, group tests can quickly generate large data sets during the standardization process. Computer-assisted administration combines many of the advantages of individual and group testing. In addition, computer software can be designed to adapt to the responses of the test taker, presenting different sets of questions to different people. Such **tailored testing** can be an effective way to accurately estimate a person's ability level.

Many aspects of the test-planning process are important to the development of a reliable and valid test. Ensuring a standardized administration format and scoring procedure are critical to producing a reliable test. Likewise, careful consideration of test audience characteristics and specification of test content increase the probability that the test is valid.

QUESTIONS

2.1 What is the difference between a maximal-performance test and a typical-performance test? Give an example of each.

2.2 How do aptitude tests differ from achievement tests? How easy is it to classify a test as "aptitude" or "achievement"? Explain.

2.3 How do speed and power tests differ in their measurement of test-taker ability?

2.4 Why are tests using objective items sometimes called "self-report" tests? Why is this label not used for tests containing projective items?

2.5 Describe how a norm-referenced test on American history would differ from a criterion-referenced test on American history.

2.6 Why is item difficulty important on norm-referenced tests of maximal performance and item discrimination on norm-referenced tests of typical performance?

2.7 Describe how the information generated by ipsative scores differs from the information generated by normative scores.

2.8 How are consideration of test audience and specification of test content important to the validity of a test?

2.9 How is the role of the examiner both a potential asset and a potential liability in individual testing?

2.10 What specific advantages does group administration present compared to individual administration?

2.11 Why do many people identify computer-assisted administration as a technique with the advantages of both individual and group testing?

2.12 List the test design issues that can affect (a) the potential reliability and (b) the potential validity of a test.

Design of Ability Tests

CHAPTER OUTLINE

CHAPTER GOALS AND OBJECTIVES

After completing this chapter you should be able to:

- Give examples of how the purpose, audience, and administration format of a test influence decisions about test items.
- List the requirements for writing good ability test items.
- Contrast the basic features of alternate-choice format with the features of free-response format.
- Identify the characteristics of well-written items for each type of alternate-choice and free-response item.
- Calculate scores corrected for guessing and identify the issues surrounding the use of guessing correction formulas.
- Explain how the choice of type of test score is related to the purpose of the test.
- Describe the general procedure used to generate a norm-referenced score.
- Contrast the features and problems associated with each type of norm-referenced score.
- Contrast criterion-referenced scoring with norm-referenced scoring.
- Identify the issues raised about development of effective criterion-referenced scores and the procedures suggested to address these issues.
- Describe how norm- and criterion-referenced tests currently are used and explain why the patterns of use are unlikely to change.

Chapter 2 dealt with three central issues in test design: test purpose, administration format, and content. Our attention now turns to the two other design features: how test content is translated into test items and how test scores are generated. The present chapter explores these issues in the development of maximal-performance (i.e., ability) tests. Chapter 4 covers typical-performance (e.g., personality) tests.

BASIC DESIGN ISSUES

Let's begin by reiterating some points about this type of testing from Chapter 2:

1. Ability tests are maximal-performance tests designed to determine the upper limits of test takers' knowledge and/or skills.

2. They must use items with right and wrong answers.
3. They may be used to measure aptitude or achievement.
4. Their focus can be power or speed.
5. They can be designed to generate norm-referenced or criterion-referenced scores.

Each type of test must be written in a slightly different way. Consider a test designed to be a maximal-performance, norm-referenced, power test. It must contain items of varying difficulty but must be designed so that most people can attempt all the items (power focus). It must contain some very difficult items that challenge even the most competent test takers (maximal performance). But items of lesser difficulty are needed, too, since the goal is to determine *all* test takers' relative ability levels (norm referenced).

Let's change one dimension of the test at a time to see what happens. If our power test becomes *criterion-referenced* instead of norm-referenced, item difficulty becomes less important. Criterion-referenced tests focus on what test takers know or can do, rather than their relative status. Item difficulty is less of an issue than the match between items and objectives. And time limits may not even be necessary.

If we switch from a power test to a *speed* test, we must ensure that the items represent a consistent level of item difficulty and we must use a stringent time limit, regardless of whether the test will produce norm- or criterion-referenced scores. Speed tests focus on the number of items completed. When they produce norm-referenced scores, the number of items you complete is compared to the number completed by people in the norm group to see where you fall relative to your peers. When they generate criterion-referenced scores, the number of items you complete is compared to a preselected criterion to see if you have reached that level of performance.

Three other factors must be considered when designing an ability test: the nature of the domain, the test audience, and the test's administration format. Different types of domains may require different types of stimuli (test items) and responses. A test of color vision should require visual stimuli (test items). A test of piano-playing skill should require a psychomotor (action) response. Different audiences also require different types of items. A test for preschool children, for example, should not require extensive reading skill. And, although standardized administration is necessary in all cases, the feasibility of different item types is influenced by the administration format. Separately timed items, for example, are suitable for individual or computer-assisted administration. Other administration features influence decisions about test length. Must the test fit within a 50-minute class period? Even if you can set the time limit for the test, how long can people be expected to work effectively on test items?

Before beginning to write items for a test or before selecting an existing test to use in some scenario, you should reflect on the issues raised by the purpose, audience, and planned administration format for that test. Table 3.1 presents some of the factors to consider when making decisions about item difficulty, item features, and time limits.

The basic contrast in maximal performance testing is between alternate-choice and free-response items. The following sections discuss the writing of different types of alternate-choice and free-response questions. Students interested in more information about item writing should consult one of the following references: Ebel, 1979; Sax, 1980; Wesman, 1971.

ALTERNATE-CHOICE FORMATS

An **alternate-choice item** presents a question and a set of possible answers. Because test takers select an answer from this set, alternate-choice items are sometimes called *selection type items* (e.g., Thorndike et al., 1991). Alternate-choice items are scored using objective rules, leading some psychologists to refer to them as *objective items* (e.g., Aiken, 1991).

Alternate-choice items differ primarily in the number of alternatives or answers provided. On true/false items, the test taker must choose between two answers: Is the statement presented true, or is it false? Other item types present more than two possible answers. Multiple-choice items typically include between three and five possible alternatives for each question. Matching items

TABLE 3.1   Factors to Consider Before Writing Test Items

Item difficulty

Is item difficulty a meaningful construct for this test?
If yes:
    Does the test need items of varying difficulty?
    Does the test need some extremely challenging items?

Stimulus and response features of items

Is there a theoretical reason either to select or avoid certain item types?
What types of items have been used successfully on similar tests?
How does the intended test audience affect selecting item types?

Time limits

Will the test be administered in a setting with a time limit?
Does the test need a stringent time limit?
How does the intended test audience affect setting time limits?

present a list of to-be-matched items and a list of matching answers, and therefore may include 5, 10, or as many alternatives as you'd like.

True/False Items

True/false items are useful for assessing knowledge of categorical, factual information. It is difficult to write true/false items that tap more sophisticated behavioral objectives. True/false is a popular format for classroom testing but rarely is used in standardized ability tests. It is appealing because these items seem relatively simple to write, administer, and score. Furthermore, each item takes less time to answer because only one decision is required: Is it true or is it false? If each item takes less time, more items can be presented within the time allowed. In theory, more items could produce a more representative sample of the content domain.

In reality, good true/false items are harder to write than most people think, and the interpretation of scores on true/false tests is difficult. On any true/false item, a test taker has a 50% chance of being correct simply by guessing. On a 50-item test, a test taker theoretically can earn a score of 25 by randomly selecting true or false for each item. Given the high probability of a correct guess, it is difficult to generate accurate information about individual differences in knowledge or skills unless many items are used. Unfortunately, it is difficult to write a large number of items without violating any of the following guidelines for producing good items:

1. True/false items should avoid qualifiers like "always," "sometimes," or "never." The use of qualifiers can give test takers clues to the correct response or, worse yet, predispose test takers to answer in a particular way. For example, most of us perceive statements using "always" or "never" as likely to be false and statements using "sometimes" as likely to be true.
2. Good test items are drawn from important elements of the test domain. But important facts and concepts may not translate easily into simple true/false statements. Trying to write simple, unambiguous statements may lead to the creation of items on trivial points.
3. True/false questions should use short, simple statements covering a single point. Long statements often end up including more than one idea and therefore may contain both true and false elements.
4. True/false items should use simple grammatical structures. Grammatically complex sentences are more difficult to read and understand and take more time to answer. Negative statements, such as "True/false is not a free-response item format," are the worst offenders. These statements are easy to misread or misinterpret.

Matching Items

Matching questions include a set of items to be matched and a list of alternatives. For each item, the test taker selects the appropriate alternative from the accompanying list. In this sense, matching items are like a series of multiple-choice questions combined into a single set. The format is rather flexible; items can be purely verbal or can incorporate graphs, maps, or diagrams. Although most people recognize that matching is an effective technique for assessing knowledge of facts and principles, it can also be used to determine ability to understand or apply information. For example, matching items can be constructed in which test takers apply their knowledge by matching terminology with examples of the different phenomena. It is difficult, however, to assess more sophisticated operations, such as the ability to analyze or synthesize information, with matching items. There are several guidelines for writing good matching items:

1. Each set of matching items should be drawn from a specific area of the domain. If the items are drawn from different areas, test takers can eliminate obviously irrelevant alternatives and increase their chances of guessing at the correct answer. In practical terms this means limiting the number of items within a set. Long matching sets are less likely to be homogeneous.
2. The items to be matched are similar to the stems of multiple-choice questions. They should define a clear and specific topic for the test taker to consider. The alternatives should be brief and written using simple grammatical structures.
3. It is best to include at least one incorrect alternative that does not match to any of the items. This reduces the likelihood of correctly answering an item through the process of elimination.
4. The directions for a matching set must specify whether the alternatives can be used in more than one match.

Multiple-choice Items

Of the alternate-choice formats, multiple-choice questions are the most popular type for both classroom and standardized ability tests. Multiple-choice items are composed of a stem (the question part) and a set of alternatives (the answers), including a correct answer and a set of distractors or incorrect answers.

Different Types of Multiple-choice Items
The popularity of multiple-choice items is directly related to their flexibility. For example, multiple-choice items can be verbal or pictorial or can include

a combination of the two. Although classroom tests and familiar standardized achievement tests use verbal items, there are many examples of other types of multiple-choice items.

The Federal Aviation Administration has developed a multiple-choice aptitude test to determine an applicant's ability to handle the job of air traffic controller (Turner, 1986). One subtest, the symbol classification subtest, uses completely nonverbal (pictorial) items. Figure 3.1 presents a hypothetical item from this subtest. Each of the 76 items presents two sets of symbols that differ but still share a common characteristic. The first set contains three symbols, the second two symbols followed by a question mark. These two sets of symbols comprise the *stem* of the question. The *alternatives* are a set of five new symbols, only one of which can correctly be substituted for the question mark in the stem. There are no words, beyond the instructions, in this subtest. Although the format is multiple choice, all the questions and all the alternatives are pictures (symbols).

The Peabody Picture Vocabulary Test–Revised, or PPVT–R (Dunn & Dunn, 1981), is an individual test combining verbal stimuli (words) and pictorial alternatives in a multiple-choice format. Designed for use with ages 2½ to adulthood, the 175 items in the test consist of vocabulary words and corresponding pictorial cards called plates. Each plate is divided into four sections, with a different line drawing in each quadrant. Figure 3.2 presents a

FIGURE 3.1   A hypothetical symbol classification item

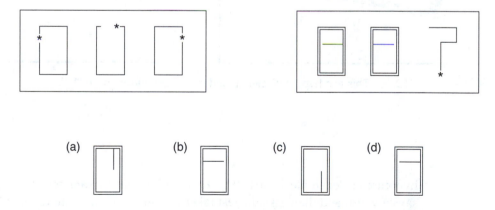

Note: This is a hypothetical item and is not taken from the FAA test.

FIGURE 3.2   A hypothetical pictorial vocabulary item

NOTE: This is a hypothetical item and is not taken from the PPVT.

hypothetical example of a PPVT–R test item. The examiner shows a plate, says a word, and then asks the test taker to point to the picture on the plate that best illustrates the meaning of the word. The test items clearly are multiple choice, but they do not require a verbal response. The test, therefore, can be used successfully with people who have speech impairments or reading problems.

Manipulating Alternatives in Multiple Choice

There are other advantages to the multiple-choice format. For example, the distractors in a multiple-choice question can be manipulated to adjust item difficulty or to address different behavioral objectives. In fact, writing different types of distractors is one of the best ways to make items more or less difficult. It clearly is preferable to creating a difficult item by drawing on an obscure element of the test domain or creating an easy item by tapping a trivial element.

Multiple-choice items can also be written to provide feedback about instructional effectiveness and errors in learning. The distractors for an item can be written to include likely misconceptions and misunderstandings about the relevant concept or fact. By studying the pattern of errors on the test, an instructor can identify material in need of further discussion and students in need of assistance.

Multiple-choice items typically have from three to five alternatives, one of which is the correct answer. There is no particular rule for selecting the number of alternatives; in fact, there is no reason why all multiple-choice questions in a particular test must have the same number of alternatives. Decisions about the number of alternatives to use are based on three factors: (1) the need to reduce the effects of guessing, (2) the need to sample the domain adequately, and (3) the feasibility of writing good distractors.

The number of alternatives used affects the likelihood that test takers can earn points by guessing. The greater the number of alternatives, the lower is the probability of guessing the correct answer. On a three-alternative item, the probability of a correct guess is one out of three, or 33%. With four alternatives the probability drops to one out of four, or 25%. The probability on a five-alternative item is lower still: 20%, or one out of five. Using items with four or five alternatives reduces the likelihood that a test score reflects extensive correct guessing.

The need for items to sample the domain adequately also influences decisions about the number of alternatives to use. If the test covers a large domain, the test writer may want to include a large number of items. But the number of items it is feasible to use varies according to the number of alternatives in each item. Since it takes less time to answer a three-alternative question than a five-alternative question, a 1-hour test using three-alternative items can include more questions than a 1-hour test using five-alternative items.

The feasibility of writing good distractors is another important concern. The increase in number of alternatives actually is an increase in number of distractors. Sufficient information must be available in the domain to produce good distractors. Distractors that are obviously wrong do not contribute to the measurement of individual differences in knowledge and skill. Test takers can eliminate these distractors immediately, reducing the actual number of alternatives under consideration. By eliminating an obviously wrong distractor, the test taker can increase the likelihood of guessing the correct answer. On the other hand, distractors that are too similar to the correct answer also undermine the ability of the test to measure individual differences accurately. These distractors may be selected by people who possess the appropriate information but are confused by the contrast between the correct answer and the distractor.

Measuring Different Levels of Thinking

Although critics charge that multiple-choice items simply measure rote learning, good item writers can construct items to measure any behavioral objective except those relating to written expression and creativity, including application, analysis, and synthesis of information. Table 3.2 presents examples of multiple-choice questions tapping different behavioral objectives.

Guidelines for Good Written Items

Written items probably are the most frequently encountered form of multiple choice. The following are some general rules for evaluating written multiple-choice items:

1. The stem of each item should identify the focus of the question. Test takers should be able to identify the problem or question to be answered before reading any of the alternatives. Most of the item should be contained in the stem itself; the alternatives should be as short as possible.
2. The stem should not include unnecessary information. Items including introductory sentences in the stem increase the time needed to read the item and reduce the time available for evaluating alternatives and completing the test.

TABLE 3.2   Sample Multiple-choice Items

An item tapping *application* of information

Which of the following demonstrates negative reinforcement of a behavior?
(a) A teenager stays out past curfew and loses a week of TV time.
(b) An adult takes Valium and a migraine headache disappears.
(c) A child rakes leaves in the yard and is paid.
(d) A child bites a playmate and is spanked.

An item tapping *analysis* of information

If $2x$ is an even number, then x is
(a) an even number.
(b) an odd number.
(c) an even or an odd number.

---

3. There should be only one correct alternative. The distractors should be plausible but clearly incorrect and compatible grammatically with the question stem. Good test takers will exclude alternatives on the basis of grammatical inconsistency.

4. Avoid complex grammar, negative sentence structures, and items using "all of the above" or "none of the above" alternatives. The problem with the latter structures is similar to the qualifier problem in true/false tests: It is difficult to create several alternatives that are unambiguously correct or incorrect.

FREE-RESPONSE FORMATS

A **free-response item** presents a question without a set of possible answers. The test taker must generate an answer within the guidelines provided by the test directions. Free-response items are sometimes called *supply-type items* because the answer is "supplied" by the test taker (e.g., Aiken, 1991; Thorndike et al., 1991). The answers to free-response items are evaluated through subjective scoring, a process in which scoring guidelines are used to award points. As such, scoring is a more lengthy process, and different graders may not award answers the same number of points. However, free-response items do have a unique advantage over alternate-choice items: Test takers have no a priori basis on which to guess the correct answer.

The most familiar types of free-response items are fill-in-the-blank or completion items, short answer, and essay. These labels traditionally are used for written items requiring written responses. The difference between them is the extent of response required, from a word or phrase in fill-ins to several pages for an essay. However, free-response items in fact may present written, oral, or visual stimuli and may require written, oral, or psychomotor responses.

The Wechsler Adult Intelligence Scale–Revised, or WAIS–R (Wechsler, 1981), is an individual intelligence test that provides good examples of these other types of free-response items. In the Comprehension subtest, the examiner asks a question designed to assess the test taker's basic reasoning skills. For example, the examiner might ask, "Why is it a good idea for people to wear shoes?" The test taker then provides a response. This clearly is a free-response item, but it uses both an oral item stimulus and an oral response.

Figure 3.3 presents an example of a hypothetical item from the WAIS–R picture arrangement subtest. In this subtest, the examiner places a series of pictures in a predetermined order on the table in front of the test taker. The test taker is instructed to put the pictures in order so that they tell a story. Again, this is a free-response item, but the item stimulus is visual and the response is psychomotor.

FIGURE 3.3   A hypothetical picture arrangement item

Put these three cards in order so that they tell a story.

The preceding free-response items would be categorized as variations on the traditional short-answer item. The point of this discussion is to make you aware of the variety of ways free-response items can be constructed. Just as the Peabody Picture Vocabulary Test (PPVT) presents a unique adaptation of the alternate-choice format, tests like the WAIS–R present unique adaptations of the free-response format. Although the following sections focus on the construction of written items, it is important to remember that other modalities can be used.

Completion Items

Completion items consist of a sentence with one or more blanks. The format is not very flexible. It is designed for use on written or oral tests and is most appropriate for assessing knowledge of facts, such as names, dates, and vocabulary or terminology, and comprehension of simple concepts. Most completion items are found on classroom achievement tests.

Several problems are inherent to the completion format. As was the case with true/false items, it is difficult to generate many completion items without resorting to questions on trivial points. Also, scoring answers can present some unique challenges. If the items omit key words and concepts, test takers must complete them by writing technical terms or specialized vocabulary. Does spelling count? What if the written answer is difficult to read but has the general appearance of the desired term? Does a partial answer deserve partial credit? And what does one do when the test taker produces an unanticipated but technically correct response?

Good completion items have the following features:

1. Items focus on important facts and concepts from the test domain. A good item requires the test taker to supply a word or phrase for a key concept or term in the domain.
2. Accurate completion of the sentence produces a correct statement.
3. The sentence identifies the focus of the item before presenting the blank. It is better, therefore, to design items with blanks near the end than items with blanks near the beginning. It is also better to avoid items with multiple blanks. As more words are omitted, the focus of the item becomes obscured.

Short Answer

Short answer probably is the most flexible of the free-response formats. It can be adapted to use written, oral, or pictorial items and written, oral, or psychomotor responses. This format is popular for individual ability tests, such as intelligence tests and tests of visual-motor skill, and classroom achievement tests. In their oral and written forms, short-answer questions typically require no more than two or three sentences to answer. In fact, these questions may require only a word, a date, or a number. On achievement tests, short-answer questions can be used to assess knowledge, comprehension, or application objectives. They are not particularly useful for measuring analysis, synthesis, or evaluation skills.

Short-answer items are popular because of their ease of construction and adaptable format. Remember, however, that they are scored using subjective rules. As was the case with completion items, there is always the possibility that test takers will produce unanticipated but technically correct answers. Many short-answer items are graded using systems for awarding partial to full credit.

Good short-answer questions have the following features:

1. Each item should have a very specific focus and cover a very limited area of the content or skill domain.
2. When answers must contain a few sentences, rather than a single word or number, the wording of the item should specify the structure of the response. Terms such as "list," "define," and "identify" are useful determiners.

Essay

Essay questions are written questions that require one or more paragraphs to answer. Essay items are uniquely suited to measuring ability to organize and communicate information. Questions can be written to tap sophisticated skills, such as the ability to analyze, synthesize, or evaluate information. Essay items also provide an opportunity to assess originality or creativity in organization, application, or integration of material. Writing essay questions that incorporate these features, however, takes considerably more time than most people realize. Many essay questions end up simply measuring mastery of basic factual information. If the test plan calls for factually oriented items, it is better to abandon the essay format and use alternate-choice items instead.

There are other important considerations in the preparation of essay items. Because test takers must construct and write out their answers, essay tests must contain fewer items than alternate-choice tests. Essay tests may not, therefore, be an efficient way to sample a large content domain. And although it is difficult for test takers to "guess" the correct answers, essay items are susceptible to bluffing. Finally, it may be difficult to interpret the meaning of differences among answers to essay questions. For example, when questions are written to tap sophisticated skills such as evaluation or analysis, differences among answers may reflect differences in knowledge of the material—not differences in evaluative or analytic skill. Likewise, when essays are used for in-class tests, differences among answers may reflect different reactions to time constraints. And essays are the ultimate challenge in terms of scoring, even when sample answers are prepared in advance. Essay items invariably will produce some responses that are difficult to evaluate with the preplanned system.

Here are some guidelines for identifying good essay items, including items that are easier to score:

1. Although essay questions should require the test taker to draw on many areas of knowledge and skill, the best essay questions have a specific focus and are written in precise, objective terms.
2. Keep the test objectives in mind when considering essay items. You must know exactly what the item should measure in order to make the desired response clear to the test taker.
3. The test taker's task should be defined in a clear and unambiguous way. Use words such as "contrast," "explain," and "illustrate," rather than words like "discuss" or "describe."
4. Avoid giving test takers choices among essays; choices may produce test scores that do not measure comparable knowledge or skills.

COMPARING ALTERNATE-CHOICE AND FREE-RESPONSE ITEMS

Throughout the preceding sections you may have noticed an emphasis on the strengths of alternate-choice items and the problems associated with free-response items. The emphasis is deliberate. Most students seem biased against multiple-choice items in particular, viewing short-answer and essay questions as better measures of knowledge or skill. Nationwide, many parents and educators voice similar concerns. There has been extensive media criticism of the use of multiple-choice questions in standardized aptitude and achievement tests. Critics repeatedly charge that such tests do not provide accurate measures of knowledge or abilities. Although it is true that writing good multiple-choice items is difficult, it is not true that the format per se is an ineffective way to measure knowledge or skill. The decision to use one or the other format does involve trade-offs, but not necessarily the trade-offs critics charge.

Table 3.3 summarizes the important contrasts between these item types.

TABLE 3.3   Comparing Different Item Formats

Factor	Essay	Multiple Choice
Focus of items		
Can measure knowledge and understanding of information	Y	Y
Can measure ability to apply information	Y	Y
Can measure ability to analyze, synthesize, or evaluate information	Y	M
Can identify original or innovative uses of information	Y	N
Features of items		
A time-efficient technique to sample objectives	M	Y
Takes little time to write	Y	N
Is free from opportunities for guessing	Y	N
Produces consistent scores from one scorer to another	N	Y
Can be scored by machine	N	Y

Y = Yes, this generally is true.
M = Maybe, depending on the situation.
N = No, this generally is not true.

Note that each item type has advantages and disadvantages. Two obvious examples are item writing and response scoring. Multiple choice items are more difficult to write but offer distinct scoring advantages. On the other hand, essay items may be easier to write but are more challenging to score. Most importantly, note that with a skillful writer *either* item type can be used to measure a variety of sophisticated abilities and skills.

SELECTING A SCORING SYSTEM

Once the items are written and the test is organized into its final form, one decision remains: How will the test be scored? Obviously, there will be a key for identifying answers as correct or incorrect. But will the test use a correction for guessing? And what type of score, norm or criterion referenced, will be used to describe test-taker performance?

Correction for Guessing

Alternate-choice items present both the question and the possible answers. It is possible, therefore, that test takers can earn points by randomly selecting an answer to each question. Random guessing contaminates test scores as measures of what people know or can do. To generate a purer measure of ability, scores on alternate-choice tests can be adjusted by a *correction for guessing* formula. The basic formula is

$$\text{corrected score} = R - \frac{W}{A-1}$$

in which

R = the number of *right* (correct) answers

W = the number of *wrong* (incorrect) answers

A = the number of *alternatives* for each item

Items that are omitted are not included in the formula.

Although the formula may appear strange, it does in fact adjust test score according to the probability of correct guessing. Consider a 100-item test using five-alternative multiple-choice questions. A test taker has a 20% chance of guessing correctly the answer to each item. A test taker who randomly selected answers for each item in theory would earn a score of 20. Look what happens when the above formula is used to correct a score of 20 on this test:

$R = 20$, the number of right answers

$W = 80$, the number of wrong answers

$A = 5$, the number of alternatives per item

$$\text{corrected score} = 20 - \frac{80}{5-1} = 20 - \frac{80}{4} = 20 - 20 = 0$$

Once the correction for guessing is used, the test taker receives a score of 0, an accurate representation of the knowledge and skills used to answer the questions in this example.

There is much controversy surrounding correction for guessing. For the formula to be statistically sound, two events must occur. First, all guesses must be *random* guesses, with each alternative having an equal probability of selection. Second, *all* incorrect answers must be the result of guessing. Neither of these conditions is likely to be met in most testing scenarios. Let's examine each assumption separately. Test takers often have enough information to eliminate at least one alternative. If an alternative is eliminated immediately, the probabilities of selection are not equal across all alternatives. Even if this occurs on only one test item, it means that all "guessing answers" are not random guesses.

The second assumption requires that guessing be the source of all wrong answers. As someone who has taken tests before, you know quite well that many incorrect answers result from misunderstanding the facts or principles tapped in the question or, worse still, misreading the question. In both of these cases, wrong answers result from factors other than random guessing. If either of these events occurs, even for only one test item, all wrong answers do not result from random guesses.

Although once quite popular, correction for guessing is used less often today. Random guessing is most likely to be a problem on true/false tests and tests with stringent time limits. It is unlikely to be a significant problem on multiple-choice tests and tests with more reasonable time limits. In the latter cases, most experts agree that the number of correct answers is a reasonable measure of test-taker knowledge and skills.

Norm-referenced Scores

Norm-referenced scoring typically is used on standardized aptitude and achievement tests and is designed specifically to provide information about individual differences in performance. The process of producing norm-referenced scores has several stages and can result in any one of a variety of types of norm-referenced scores. Let's examine these issues one at a time.

Process of Norm Referencing

Two decisions must be made in the process of norm referencing. First, the test developer must define the reference group (norm group) to which test takers will be compared. Second, the test developer decides which type of norm-referenced score to use. After making these decisions, the test developer administers the test to the reference group and uses the resulting data to develop a set of norm-referenced scores.

In the case of a classroom test, the norm group typically is defined as the group of the people in a particular class. After grading all the tests, the instructor uses the performance of the group to develop a scale for translating test scores into grade categories such as A, B, and C. Instead of awarding an A for a score of 90, the instructor may give A grades only to those students who perform significantly above the class average. If your classmates perform well, you might need a score of 93 to earn an A. On the other hand, if your classmates perform poorly, you might receive an A with a test score of 86. This procedure, often called *grading on a curve*, is a type of norm-referenced scoring.

In the case of a standardized test, the scoring system is developed during the standardization process and then is used to assign norm-referenced scores during all future administrations. The norm group is the standardization sample, the group of people who took the test while it was in development. When you take the test at a later date, your score is determined by comparing your performance to the performance of people in the standardization group. For example, your score on an intelligence test is determined by comparing the number of questions you answer correctly to the number answered correctly by standardization sample members of your age.

The preceding examples illustrate an important point about the use of norm groups in testing. If we are to compare you to a reference group, we must have some rationale for selecting that group. For a norm-group comparison to be meaningful, the characteristics of the people in the norm group must be similar to the characteristics of the people being evaluated. In the classroom test example, you were compared to the other people in your class. All of you participated in the same course, and comparing you to each other is a reasonable way to measure individual differences in what you learned. In standardized testing, we often compare you to other people of your age or your level of education. Intelligence tests, for example, define norm groups on the basis of age, whereas such tests as the SAT define norm groups on the basis of educational level.

There may be additional concerns, however, about the composition of a norm group. In standardized testing, it is important to define clearly the composition of the norm group and to ensure that the norm group is a representative sample of the population to be tested. Imagine for a moment a standardized test of spatial aptitude for which the norm group contained only boys. Would it be reasonable to administer this test to children of both sexes? Probably not. Most psychological research indicates that boys perform better on tests of spatial skills. Girls would likely receive low scores on this test. If the norm group contained both boys and girls, the comparison would be more meaningful. It might even be useful to develop separate grading scales for the two genders.

When test scores are used to compare people from different areas of the country, national norms are necessary. However, in some cases it may be valuable to construct **local norms**. Local norms are generated by analyzing the performance of a subgroup of people, such as individuals within a particular state or students within a particular school system. Many states use standardized achievement tests to evaluate the performance of grade-school children. These tests are standardized using national samples of school children. However, some states base evaluation of their own students on local norms derived by analyzing the performance only of children living within the respective states. By using local norms, the states increase the match between the children on whom the grading scale was based and the children now taking the test. Local norms can be developed for a state, a county, or even a particular school system.

Types of Norm-referenced Scores

In addition to defining a norm group, the test developer must select a type of norm-referenced score to use. The process of norm referencing involves changing or transforming the total points you earn on the test, your **raw score**, to a new scale of measurement. There are two basic categories of norm-referenced scores: (1) scores using an ordinal (rank) scale of measurement and (2) scores using an interval scale of measurement. The basic type of ordinal score is percentile rank, briefly discussed in Chapter 2 (see p. 39). The other norm-referenced ordinal scores are transformations of percentile rank, alternative labels for different sets of percentiles.

The basic type of interval score is the z-score you probably encountered in your statistics class, usually referred to as a standard score. The other norm-referenced interval scores are transformation of z-scores to a different *unit* of measurement. Although this may sound confusing, it's really pretty simple. Changing a z-score to another unit of measurement is no more complicated than converting a measurement in inches to a measurement in centimeters.

Ordinal Scale Scores.   **Percentile rank** is probably the most familiar type of ordinal scale score. Percentile rank indicates the test taker's ranking relative to the other people in the norm group. It is defined as the proportion or percentage of people in the norm group who earned lower scores. For example, a percentile rank of 80 means that 80% of the people in the norm group earned lower test scores. Alternatively, 20% of the people in the norm group earned test scores at or above this level. Percentile ranks usually are presented as tables in which each raw score is listed next to its corresponding percentile rank. The table is referred to as a table of **percentile norms**.

Table 3.4 presents a table of percentile norms for a fictional classroom test and can be used to illustrate several important points about percentile ranks. First, percentile ranks are based on the *number of people* earning each possible test score. A percentile rank of 75 is not the same as a score of 75% correct. By itself, a percentile rank says nothing about the actual test score earned. Only through the table can we link a percentile rank to an actual test score. In Table 3.4, a percentile rank of 75 corresponds to a test score of 40. Since the table indicates that the test had a total of 50 points, the *percentage correct* corresponding to a test score of 40 is 40/50 or 80% correct.

Second, percentile rank is an ordinal scale of measurement (see Chapter 1). The difference between two percentile ranks must be interpreted as an ordinal difference, a difference in rank. It does not indicate anything about the degree of difference between the test scores corresponding to those ranks. In Table 3.4, test scores of 45 and 50 differ by 5 points. The corresponding percentile ranks, 92.5 and 99, differ by 6.5 units. On the test score scale we are measuring differences in the number of points earned. On the percentile rank scale we are measuring differences in the number of people earning different test scores.

Third, as an ordinal scale, percentile rank does not represent scores on a scale with equal intervals. When people are ranked in height from tallest to shortest, we cannot say that the difference in height for the people ranked 1

TABLE 3.4   Sample Table of Percentile Norms (Fictional Data)

Raw Score	Number of People Earning the Score[a]	Percentile Rank
50	3	99
45	7	92.5
40	5	75
35	5	62.5
30	6	50
25	4	35
20	5	25
15	4	12.5
10	1	2.5

[a]A total of 40 people took this test. You can tell by adding the number of people who earned each score.

and 2 is the same as the difference in height for the people ranked 2 and 3. The same problem exists with percentile ranks. In Table 3.4, test scores of 45 and 50 differ by 5 units, just like test scores of 20 and 25. But their respective percentile ranks do not differ by equivalent amounts. The ranks for scores of 45 and 50 differ by 7.5 units, but the ranks for scores of 20 and 25 differ by 10 units! Again, the distinction is between number of points earned (raw score scale) and number of people earning different scores (percentile rank scale).

Percentile rank is a popular norm-referenced score because it is easy to calculate and understand. Percentile ranks can be used with any type of norm group, including people differing in age, grade level, sex, or occupation. Percentile ranks are used on both ability tests and normative personality tests. The calculation of percentile ranks will be discussed in Chapter 5.

When we create percentile ranks, we typically convert each raw score to its corresponding percentile. The number of percentile rank scores produced, therefore, depends on the number of raw scores available. If each possible test score was earned by the same number of people, a 100-point test would produce up to 100 different percentile rank scores, a 200-point test up to 200 different percentile rank scores, and so on. Sometimes, it is not necessary to have such a detailed picture of individual differences. In these cases the test developer can select a type of percentile-based score that divides the complete set of percentile ranks into a smaller number of categories.

Two popular systems are **quartiles** and **deciles**. To create quartiles, the test developer identifies the raw scores at four specific percentile points. The score at the first quartile, Q_1, is the score at the 25th percentile, meaning that one quarter or 25% of the scores fall below this point. Anyone with a raw score at or below this point is simply described as falling within the first quartile. The second quartile, Q_2, is defined by the raw score at the 50th percentile. Anyone with a raw score between the Q_1 cutoff and this point is identified as falling within the second quartile. The third quartile, Q_3, corresponds to the 75th mark; the fourth, Q_4, is the top percentile. Sometimes test developers identify the *interquartile range* for a test, the set of scores falling between the 25th and 75th percentiles. Deciles are similar to quartiles except that points are marked by 10%, rather than 25%, intervals. The top decile, D_{10}, is defined by the top raw score, and the bottom decile, D_1, by the raw score at the 10th percentile point. Like percentile ranks, quartiles and deciles can be used with any type of norm group and any type of test.

Refer back to Table 3.4. If we were to transform these percentile ranks to quartiles, what would we get? The first quartile range, Q_1, would be defined as scores between 0 and 20. Why? Because a score of 20 falls at the 25th percentile. How about Q_2? In this case, the score at the 50th percentile is 30. The second quartile, then, is scores between 21 and 30. See if you can figure out the next two quartile ranges on your own.

Tests designed for use with children often use **age-equivalent** or **grade-equivalent scores,** two other norm-referenced scores derived from percentile ranks. The norm group in these cases contains children of many different ages, and the test includes many items at increasing levels of difficulty. The assumption is that level of ability increases in a fairly steady and continuous way as children get older. Therefore, younger children are expected to earn fewer points than older children. Age-equivalent scores are computed based on the raw scores at the 50th percentile in each age group. Imagine that the data in Table 3.4 represent the performance of 5-year-olds on a 100-item test. The highest score a 5-year-old earned was 50. A score of 30 fell at the 50th percentile. That means a score of 30 becomes an age-equivalent score of 5. A 7-year-old would be expected to earn more than 30 points. A 7-year-old who *did* earn only 30 points, however, would in fact receive an age-equivalent score of 5. Age-equivalent scores usually are presented in years and months. An age-equivalent score of 7;3 means that the test score matches the score earned by the average child of 7 years, 3 months old.

Grade-equivalent scores have a parallel meaning based on the performance of children in different school grades. In this case, the raw scores at the 50th percentile for each *grade level* are used to determine the grade-equivalent score. For example, if the 50th percentile for children in the second grade is 15, a test score of 15 becomes a grade-equivalent score of 2. The scales for grade-equivalent scores usually are broken down into number of months within each grade. A grade-equivalent score of 2.3 translates to the third month of second grade.

Although the process of determining age and grade equivalents is rather complex, remember that they simply are transformations of percentile ranks. In essence, we define the "average" child at each age or grade point based on the raw score at the 50th percentile. Age and grade equivalents, therefore, are also related to quartiles—the raw score at the 50th percentile is the raw score defining the second quartile range, Q_2. You may not have realized it, but age-equivalent scores were used by Binet and Simon (1905) in their first individual intelligence test. The test identified intellectual ability on the basis of "mental age," which was simply a translation of the number of questions answered correctly into an age-equivalent score.

Although age-equivalent scores seem easy to understand, interpreting score differences can be difficult. Remember the assumption underlying these scores: that ability increases in a steady and continuous way with increasing age. Because rate of development often varies from year to year, age-equivalent scores really do not represent an equal-unit scale. The additional number of correct answers needed to move from an age-equivalent score of 6 to an age-equivalent score of 7 is not necessarily the same as the number needed to move from 16 to 17. For example, most intellectual abilities develop at a fairly constant rate throughout childhood, but rate of growth begins to slow somewhat during adolescence. Consequently, the raw score difference between age-equivalent scores of 6 and 7 is greater than the difference between age-equivalent scores of 16 and 17.

Grade-equivalent scores suffer from similar interpretive problems. For example, it is tempting to recommend remedial help for a student in the second month of fifth grade with a grade-equivalent score of 4.8. In reality, the score is probably within the average range for beginning fifth graders. The process used to construct of grade-equivalent scores dictates that half the children being tested will score below average for their grade. Remember that the test score translating to 5.2 is the score at Q_2, the 50th percentile. Fifty percent of the children in the norm sample who were in the second month of fifth grade fell below this level!

In addition, many people interpret grade-equivalent scores as though they were *criterion referenced*, an obviously inappropriate move. Consider a child beginning fourth grade who earns a grade-equivalent score of 5.2 on an achievement test. It is tempting to recommend acceleration for this child. After all, the child already has the knowledge and skills of a beginning fifth grader. No! Grade-equivalent scores are referenced to the performance of peers, not to the content or curriculum of different grades. The child has answered as many *questions* correctly as the average beginning fifth grader. Obviously, this is more than the number of questions answered correctly by average fourth graders. But there is no way to know *which* questions were answered correctly. In fact, the child may lack many of the skills and facts needed for successful performance in fifth grade.

Knowing that a child received an age-equivalent score of 6;3 is meaningless without also knowing the child's chronological age. **Quotients** provide a mechanism to represent the relationship between a person's actual age and age-equivalent performance with a single number. The most familiar example is the intelligence quotient or IQ score used on older versions of the Stanford-Binet Intelligence Scale:

$$IQ = \frac{MA}{CA} \times 100$$

The test taker received an age-equivalent score (mental age or MA) based on the number of questions answered correctly. MA was divided by the test taker's chronological age (CA) and then multiplied by 100 to produce the IQ score. If the test taker's actual performance matched what was expected on the basis of age, the quotient would equal 100. The extent to which actual performance was above or below the level of age-mates was reflected in the distance of the IQ score from 100.

Quotients are derived, then, from age-equivalent scores, making them also a type of percentile-based score. Although the use of multipliers, like the 100 in the old IQ formula, may make them *look* like interval scales of measurement, quotients suffer from the same problem as age-equivalent scores. The difference between IQ scores of 110 and 115, using the quotient formula, does not necessarily parallel the difference between scores of 115 and 120. Quotients are rarely used in modern tests. In fact, the actual determination of modern IQ uses a totally different procedure.

Interval Scale Scores.   In all the preceding cases, raw scores were transformed to an ordinal scale of measurement. There is another category of norm-referenced scores, however, that uses an *interval* scale instead. These are referred to as **standard scores**, and the basic type of score in this category is the *z*-score familiar from statistics classes. Basically, standard scores create an interval scale of measurement based on the extent to which people differ from each other.

The creation of standard scores, like all norm-referenced scores, begins with administering the test to the norm groups and determining each person's raw score. Next, the test developer calculates the test score **mean**, or arithmetic average, and the test **standard deviation**, the average number of points by which scores in the set differ. An equal-interval scale is created by determining the number of standard deviations between the mean and each test score.

Consider the **z-score**, which converts raw scores to a new scale with an average or mean of 0. Raw scores above the average or mean become positive numbers; raw scores below the average become negative numbers. Let's say the mean (average) on a test is 70, and the standard deviation (the average amount by which scores differ) is 10. A score of 85 is $1\frac{1}{2}$ standard deviations above the mean (70 + 15) and therefore becomes a *z*-score of 1.5. A score of 65 is $\frac{1}{2}$ a standard deviation (5 points) below the mean and becomes a *z*-score of −0.5. And anyone earning a test score of 70 would receive a *z*-score of 0! Why? Go back and re-read this paragraph—you'll find the answer several lines back.

Just as there are many types of percentile-based scores, there are a variety of standard score formats. One you've probably encountered is the **T-score**, used in tests like the SAT. Although they look very different, T-scores are simply *z*-scores changed to a new unit of measurement. It's like changing inches to centimeters. First, we calculate the *z*-scores for a set of test scores. Then we change the *z*-scores to a new scale with a mean of 500. Test takers who score above the mean earn T-scores above 500; test takers scoring below the mean earn scores below 500. The T-score transformation, therefore, eliminates the presence of positive and negative scores.

For example, if the average number of questions answered correctly were 70, anyone earning a score of 70 would earn a *z*-score of 0 and an SAT score of 500. Units of 100 points are used to represent the number of standard deviation between the average and another test score. For example, a test score falling 1 standard deviation above the mean becomes a score of 500 + 100 or 600. A score $\frac{1}{2}$ a standard deviation below the mean becomes a score of 450 (e.g., $500 - [\frac{1}{2}(100)]$).

Don't worry about the calculation of standard scores at this point. Focus instead on the concept. There are important reasons why standard scores are preferred over percentiles, age or grade equivalents, and quotients. First, standard scores create an equal-unit scale. The unit of measure is the standard deviation—the average number of points by which the test scores in a particular group differ. Second, standard scores reflect the extent to which people are expected to differ. To be 1 standard deviation above the mean at any age, for example, requires you to answer correctly (1) the average number of questions answered correctly at your age and (2) an additional number of questions based on the pattern of score differences observed in the norm group. If people your age earn very similar scores, being "above average" will require a relatively small number of additional correct answers. If people your age earn a wide variety of scores, being "above average" will require a much larger number of additional correct answers. Like all norm-referenced scores, standard scores compare people to each other. But unlike the other varieties, the comparison process is more statistically sound. To help you to see the similarities and differences across these score types, Table 3.5 summarizes both the ordinal scale and interval scale scores usually used in norm referencing.

Criterion-referenced Scores

Unlike norm-referenced scoring, **criterion-referenced scoring** does not represent performance as a comparison of your performance to the performance of other people. Instead, criterion-referenced scores represent each person's performance independently. There is, however, a comparison or frame of reference. Each person's performance is compared to a standard of performance called a *criterion*. The criterion is used both to produce the scores and to guide interpretation of those scores. For example, the content of the test can be used as a frame of reference for scoring test performance. The criterion can be set as mastery of the test content (i.e., answering the items correctly). A person who produces correct answers to half the test questions indicates mastery of half the test content. The appropriate criterion-referenced score in this case is 50%. A second person demonstrating knowledge of three-quarters of the content would earn a score of 75%. This should be a familiar type of criterion-referenced score—it is frequently used in classroom testing.

Although criterion-referenced testing is used most often in educational settings, other notable applications have emerged. Criterion-referenced tests

TABLE 3.5   Types of Norm-referenced Scores (Transformations of Raw Scores)

Ordinal scale scores

Percentile rank: Converts raw score to a percentile based on the frequency with which each test score was earned.

Quartiles/deciles: Transformation of percentile rank; divides the percentile distribution into either fourths (quartiles) or tenths (deciles); each raw score is assigned to a quartile or decile based on the raw score's percentile rank.

Age and grade equivalents: Transformation of percentile rank; divides age or grade levels into a set of month-by-month scores; each raw score is converted to an age or grade equivalent based on the score at the 50th percentile for each month.

Quotients: Transformation of percentile rank; creates a ratio of age-equivalent score to actual chronological age.

Interval scale scores

z-scores: Converts raw score to a standard score based on the mean and standard deviation of the distribution.

T-scores: Transformation of *z*-scores; converts *z*-scores to a new interval scale that removes negative numbers.

---

were used in the National Assessment of Educational Progress (Womer, 1970) and have been adapted for determining competency in specific skill areas, such as in qualifying for a driver's license, or for testing proficiency in a skill or knowledge domain. A recent change in the North Carolina licensing law for practicing psychologists mandated the use of a criterion-referenced approach to scoring performance on the national licensing exam. In switching from the previous norm-referenced procedure, the North Carolina Psychology Board noted a need to ensure that licenses were issued only to those psychologists who possessed the knowledge and skills necessary for effective practice. By using a criterion-referenced approach, score on the exam could be tied to mastery of specific content and skills.

Process of Criterion Referencing

Developing criterion-referenced scores begins with the identification of a criterion—something to which your performance will be compared. Once the criterion is selected, the test is administered, and the total points earned or raw scores are converted to a criterion-referenced form. The criterion could be something simple like mastery of the content of the test. In this case, your score would reflect the number of test items answered correctly. Alternatively, the criterion could be mastery of a list of specific facts, principles, and/or skills that test takers must master. In this case, your score would reflect the number of facts, principles, and skills that you had mastered.

Generating criterion-referenced scores is quite different from producing norm-referenced scores. The criterion selected determines both the nature of the referencing process and the type of criterion-referenced score to be generated. Because the process depends on the criterion used, we will discuss the production of each type of score separately.

Types of Criterion-referenced Scores

When first proposed by Glaser (1963), the term *criterion-referenced* was used specifically for scenarios in which test score reflected knowledge of the domain represented by the test. Unfortunately, terminology in this area has become increasingly muddled. Currently, the term is used both to describe a specific type of score and a category of scores. Furthermore, even those psychologists who discuss different types of criterion-referenced scores do not agree on which scores to include in the broader category. The following sections are written using a broad interpretation of the concept of criterion referenced and include discussions of current controversies regarding criterion-referenced scores. Excellent discussions of the construction and evaluation of criterion-referenced tests are available in Berk (1984) and Ebel (1972).

Content-referenced Scores. In **content-referenced scoring** (Brown, 1983), the frame of reference is the test content, and the criterion is mastery of that content (i.e., all correct answers). The simplest type of content-referenced score is percent correct, calculated as

$$\text{percent correct} = \frac{\text{total number of points earned}}{\text{total number of points possible}} \times 100$$

These scores are appealing because they are simple to compute and seem simple to interpret. However, the true meaning of percent correct scores is somewhat uncertain. Remember that any test includes only a subset of items from the larger set of possible test items. Although our intent is to use percent correct to infer about knowledge of the underlying domain being tested, the interpretation of these scores is confounded by the nature of the items selected. In reality, percent correct indicates how test takers perform relative only to the *test items*. If the test items are not a representative sample of the content domain, a percent correct score tells us only about knowledge of the content elements included on the test.

Interpretation also is confounded with item difficulty. Any element of the content domain can be assessed through items at a variety of levels of difficulty. Receiving a score of 80% correct on a test with simple items is quite different from receiving a score of 80% on a test with difficult items. If a test includes items of equal point values but varying levels of difficulty, two test takers could earn the same score based on very different sets of knowledge and skills.

Objective-referenced Scores.   One way to avoid the preceding problems is to define the frame of reference in a slightly different way. Rather than using test content, **objective-referenced scoring** (Thorndike et al., 1991) uses the test *objectives* as the frame of reference. Our criterion, then, becomes mastery of those objectives, and our scoring system indicates the number or percent of objectives mastered by each test taker.

This approach arose from concerns regarding our ability to make inferences from test scores. After all, our goal is to determine mastery of an underlying domain, not simply ability to answer this one set of questions. If test items are selected in an arbitrary way or if item difficulty is not manipulated appropriately, it is difficult to use test performance as the basis for such inferences. This problem can be avoided if items are written to address specific content and behavioral objectives.

In this procedure, each objective is identified and linked to a specific set of test items. The test taker indicates mastery of the objective by correctly answering a predetermined number of these items. Although the process is more complex, an objective-referenced score in theory is a better measure of mastery of the test domain. In practical terms, however, the problems of item difficulty and score interpretation remain. If item difficulty is not carefully controlled, objective-referenced scores are no easier to interpret than content-referenced scores. In fact, some testing experts object to identifying *either* of these as "criterion-referenced" unless objectives are written in a way that specifies the behavior to be measured. Under these circumstances, the objectives actually identify the appropriate level of difficulty for each potential item. Item difficulty no longer confounds the interpretation of test score, and test score becomes a direct measure of mastery of test objectives.

Pass/Fail or Mastery Scores.   It is possible to transform either content-referenced or objective-referenced scores into other types of scores. Sometimes criterion-referenced tests are used to sort test takers into two categories: those whose test performance meets a particular criterion (pass) and those whose performance does not (fail). The institution or group administering the test selects a test score defining an acceptable level of performance. Only test takers who reach that level pass the test. In this case a specific test score itself becomes the test criterion. Although the test initially is scored using a scale such as percent correct, scores then are transformed into nominal (category) measures using the preset criterion. If the criterion score is 80% correct, scores of 80% are treated no differently than scores of 99%. Likewise, scores of 79% are treated no differently than scores of 30%.

This type of scoring is used in several scenarios. Scores on competency exams, such as the minimal competency exams administered in many high schools or the state tests to qualify for a driver's license, often are reported simply as pass or fail. A similar procedure can be used for proficiency tests, such as professional licensing exams. There is some disagreement, however, as to whether such tests truly qualify as instances of criterion-referenced scoring (e.g., Thorndike et al., 1991). To be criterion referenced, these tests must link the scoring procedure to the content of the test. The setting of a cutoff score as a criterion for successful performance does not by itself define the test as criterion referenced.

Perhaps the best example of this approach is the mastery testing used in some educational settings. The basic philosophy in mastery learning is that almost all students can learn if given sufficient time and instruction (e.g., Block, 1971). Individual differences, therefore, are reflected in *rate* of learning rather than in extent of learning. Mastery testing traditionally is used with more individualized approaches to education. Material to be learned is divided into small units, each with its own behavioral objectives. Separate tests covering these objectives are written for each unit, and a **mastery score** indicating successful completion of each unit is identified. Students study the unit and take the test. Those reaching the mastery score pass the unit and move to the next unit. Those who do not continue to work on the unit and later retake the original test or take an alternate form of the test. Mastery testing is most suitable for testing basic skills and structured domains. With complex skills and less structured domains, learning is more variable and true "mastery" may be undefined.

The critical issue in these approaches is identification of the criterion or cutoff score. In the past the process was based primarily on professional judgment. For example, mastery testing usually used cutoff scores in the 80% to 85% range (e.g., Glass, 1978). At present, a variety of empirical techniques is under study in an effort to define a more objective criterion-setting process (see Berk, 1984).

Comparing Norm- and Criterion-referenced Scores

Although norm- and criterion-referenced scores were compared in Chapter 2, it is useful to consider again their different applications. Norm-referenced scores are designed to indicate the *relative extent* of knowledge and skills each test taker possesses. Criterion-referenced tests are designed to identify the *absolute extent* of knowledge and skills each test taker possesses. Most standardized ability tests are norm referenced. Tests used for selection and placement decisions usually are norm referenced. Most criterion-referenced tests are found in educational settings. These tests are used primarily for rating students and identifying strengths and weaknesses (a diagnostic function). The difference in purpose explains why the two types of tests are used in different circumstances.

The key to criterion-referenced testing is thorough sampling of all test objectives. It is difficult to develop a criterion-referenced score for a test of a broad domain or a construct-based domain. Imagine trying to develop criterion-referenced scores for a test on "American literature" or "human intelligence." It is easier, however, to develop criterion-referenced scores for tests of a classroom unit or the skills identified as necessary for entering first grade. Criterion-referenced testing is an inefficient approach to testing broad domains or constructs, and it is unlikely to replace norm-referenced testing as the technique for assessing such areas.

There is a second feature of criterion-referenced scores that limits their popularity among many testing experts. Criterion-referenced scores determine each test taker's knowledge and skills independently. Although criterion-referenced scores can reveal individual differences, it is quite possible that all test takers will earn very similar scores. In fact, our goal in mastery testing it to *ensure* that all students pass all units.

Because norm-referenced scores are designed to sort test takers relative to each other, tests using norm-referenced scores traditionally produce a wider variety of test scores. In the language of statistics, this set of test scores has greater variability. As you will see in Part II, many statistical techniques used to evaluate test reliability and validity only work when used with a wide variety of test scores. Many of these techniques cannot be applied to tests generating criterion-referenced scores. Other ways of evaluating criterion-referenced tests are being explored (e.g., Ferguson & Novick, 1973; Hambleton & Novick, 1973). Until rigorous techniques are developed, however, it is unlikely that criterion-referenced scores will be used more widely.

SUMMARY AND KEY CONCEPTS

The two final considerations in the development or selection of an ability test are the nature of the test items and the scoring of the test. Both topics must be considered within the context of the purpose of the test, its audience, and its administration format. Ability tests can include **alternate-choice** and/or **free-response** items. Alternate-choice formats include items such as true/false, matching, and multiple choice. Free-response formats include completion items, short answer, and essays.

Good items are defined by certain specific features that to some extent vary by item type. For example, good multiple-choice items have a clearly written and focused stem followed by a set of distinct alternatives. Various factors must be considered when deciding the number of alternatives to use, including the composition and function of the item distractors. Good items also use a format appropriate to the objective being tested. For example, although multiple-choice questions can test knowledge and ability to apply information, they cannot be used to assess written expression or originality in thinking. Sometimes an objective can be met by a variety of test items. In these cases the decision may be based on such considerations as test length and efficiency of scoring.

Because the test taker is given answers to alternate-choice items, the final test score may be inflated by successful random guessing. Some alternate-choice tests are scored using a correction for guessing, although the technique has become less popular over time.

Depending on their purpose, ability tests use either **norm-referenced** or **criterion-referenced scoring**. In standardized testing, the norm group is the **standardization sample,** people who took the test expressly for the purpose of developing its scoring system. Sometimes a smaller norm group is used, such as the members of a single class or people within a particular state. The latter type of group is used in the development of **local norms**. Since norm-referenced scores compare test takers to each other, the selection of the comparison group is critical to the usefulness of the scores.

All norm-referenced scores represent some way of changing **raw scores** to a new scale that incorporates information about the performance of other people. Norm-referenced scores include percentile-based scores, such as **percentile ranks**, **quartiles** and **deciles**, **age-** and **grade-equivalent scores**, **quotients**, and **standard scores**, such as *z*-scores and **T-scores**. Some norm-referenced scores are simple to determine; others require more statistical sophistication. For example, standard scores are based on the **mean** and **standard deviation** of the raw scores earned by norm group members. The actual calculation of norm-referenced scores will be presented in Chapter 5.

The relationship between raw scores and norm-referenced scores is usually presented in summary tables, such as the **percentile norms** used for percentile ranks. Norm-referenced scores can be used to identify subgroups of test takers, such as the people whose scores fall within the interquartile range.

Although criterion-referenced testing is an identifiable genre, there is some dissension about what constitutes a criterion-referenced score. A criterion-referenced score compares each test taker to a standard of performance, rather than to the performance of other people. The simplest type is percent correct, a **content-referenced score**. When test items are selected to address specific objectives, tests can be designed to product **objective-referenced scores**. When tests are used to sort test takers into those meeting and not meeting the criterion, **pass/fail** or **mastery scores** can be used. Criterion-referenced tests are popular in educational settings, where they are used in such scenarios as mastery testing. However, the purpose and design of criterion-referenced tests tends to limit the variability of their test scores, making it difficult to evaluate these tests through traditional reliability and validity analyses. Until alternative analyses are developed, it is likely that most standardized tests will continue to use a norm-referenced format.

QUESTIONS

3.1 Using item difficulty as your example, explain how the purpose of a test affects the process of writing ability test items.

3.2 Rule 5 for writing good test items says that items should "tap relevant aspects of the test domain." For which type(s) of items is this likely to be a problem? Why?

3.3 Under what circumstances is it reasonable to use a correction for guessing? Why?

3.4 Give an example of a situation in which it is better to use national test norms and a situation in which it is better to use local test norms.

3.5 What common feature of percentile ranks, age-equivalent scores, and grade-equivalent scores makes them difficult to interpret accurately?

3.6 Why have standard scores become such a popular type of norm-referenced score?

3.7 Why do some testing experts object to using percent correct as a criterion-referenced score? How do their alternative proposals attempt to address their objections?

3.8 Why is it unlikely that the majority of standardized tests will become criterion referenced in the near future?

Design of Typical Performance Tests

CHAPTER OUTLINE

CHAPTER GOALS AND OBJECTIVES

After completing this chapter you should be able to:

- Describe the difference between objective and projective tests in terms of both item format and philosophy.
- Contrast the features of item formats for objective tests, including problems of interpretation.
- Explain the relationship between ipsative and normative scores and different item formats.
- Identify different types of response biases and techniques to reduce their impact.
- Contrast the item formats and scoring procedures for different objective tests.
- Contrast the item formats and scoring procedures for different projective tests.
- Describe the different techniques for constructing attitude scales.
- Compare and contrast different types of standard and comparative rating scales.
- Identify common types of rater errors and techniques to reduce their impact.

Chapter 3 described the construction of items and scoring systems for ability tests; the present chapter outlines these procedures in a sample of typical performance domains: personality and interests, attitudes, and patterns of behavior. Because of their focus, typical performance tests differ from ability tests in several specific ways:

1. Items on typical performance tests do not have right and wrong answers.
2. Because we are not testing the upper limits of ability or skill, time limits are not a concern.
3. Tests can be designed to measure a single characteristic or a set of characteristics.
4. When designed to measure a single characteristic, the measurement is normative (absolute). When designed to measure a set of characteristics, the measurement can be *either* ipsative (relative) or normative (absolute).
5. These tests do not use criterion-referencing scoring. However, both ipsative and normative scores are often further transformed into a norm-referenced form.

As we discuss the design of typical performance tests, popular tests will be used to illustrate different principles of test construction. Don't worry if the presentation of these tests seems brief. The features and uses of these tests will be discussed in more detail in Part 3.

OBJECTIVE TESTS: PERSONALITY AND INTERESTS

In terms of item structure, objective tests are the typical performance equivalent of alternate-choice ability tests. Objective tests present test takers with words or statements (stimulus items) and a set of possible responses. Test takers select the responses that best reflect their attitudes, feelings, and patterns of behavior. These tests may be designed to measure personality and/or interests and may cover a single attribute or several attributes. In the latter case, the test contains items that are keyed to different scales, each scale representing a different aspect of personality or interest. Most objective tests are suitable for individual or group administration.

Because our focus is the *writing* and *scoring* of objective test items, we will discuss personality and interest tests together. Remember, however, that personality tests and interest tests often cover very different domains. Personality tests measure individual dispositions and preferences and often focus on constructs such as leadership, anxiety, or self-control. Objective personality tests are also called self-report tests (e.g., Thorndike et al., 1991), personality inventories (e.g., Aiken, 1991), or structured personality tests (e.g., Kaplan & Saccuzzo, 1993). Interest tests measure individual patterns of likes and dislikes, typically by having test takers report preferences for activities, settings, and academic subjects. They may also include measures of personality traits.

Item Formats

Objective tests use either **independent** or **forced-choice** formats, illustrated in Table 4.1. The independent format generates normative measures representing the absolute or overall strength of characteristics. It can be used on tests of a single characteristic, such as extroversion, or tests tapping several different characteristics, such as extroversion, leadership, and autonomy. In the latter case, different items are needed for each characteristic to be measured; test takers must be able to answer separate items about each dimension of the domain.

The forced-choice format generates ipsative measures representing the *relative* strength of each characteristic. It is used *only* on tests of more than

TABLE 4.1   Item Formats for Typical Performance Tests

Independent items

Read each statement carefully. Select "T" (true) if the statement describes how you act or feel most of the time. Select "F" (false) if the statement does not describe how you usually act or feel.

T   F   1.   I enjoy spending time with other people.
                 (a sociability item)
T   F   2.   People say I am good at making decisions.
                 (a leadership item)
Note: Selecting "T" for an item adds points to its underlying scale. By selecting "T" for both items, a point is added to *each* scale.

Forced-choice items

Read each statement and pair of alternatives carefully. Select the alternative that best describes how you act or feel most of the time.

1.   When I am with other people
     (a)   I enjoy myself. (a sociability answer)
     (b)   I make the decisions about what we will do.
           (a leadership answer)
Note: The answer selected determines to which scale a point is added. Selecting (a) adds a point to the sociability scale; selecting (b) adds a point to the leadership scale.

---

one characteristic. Forced-choice items require test takers to choose between statements or phrases representing different characteristics; test takers must choose one statement at the expense of another. Selecting a statement adds points to the scale it represents; by doing so, however, the test taker loses the opportunity to add points to the scale represented by the other statement. The task, then, is for test takers to identify the statement that is more "like me" *relative to* the one with which it is paired.

Independent Items

Independent items differ primarily in the number of response options. The simplest item is a *dichotomous* item, which presents two possible responses. The common dichotomous responses are yes/no and true/false. Checklists are good examples of the dichotomous approach. The adjective checklist by Gough (1960) presents a series of words or statements that are checked if they describe the test taker (the "yes" response) or left blank if they do not (the "no" response). Although the approach seems straightforward, there is a hidden interpretative problem in the dichotomous format. What if test takers cannot decide whether a word truly describes them? Or, alternatively, what if they decide that a word neither applies nor does not apply, falling instead into a "neutral" response category? Although the adjective checklist has a truly dichotomous structure—items are checked if they apply and not checked if they don't—the categories created in the test taker's mind while checking the items may not be dichotomous. It is possible that items not checked represent up to three different categories: (1) some that do not apply to the test taker, (2) some about which the test taker is neutral, and (3) some about which the test taker is unsure—a "cannot say" category.

The Minnesota Multiphasic Personality Inventory–2 (MMPI–2), the recent revision of the popular self-report test, uses a modified dichotomous structure to determine the presence of clinical syndromes such as depression and psychopathic deviancy. The MMPI–2 (Hathaway & McKinley, 1989) contains 567 statements to be rated as either true or false. Each true or false response to a statement translates into points added to a personality scale. However, the MMPI–2 provides an additional response option: "cannot say." Although test takers are encouraged to identify all statements as true (applies to me) or false (does not apply to me), the test directions state that they may omit items that they truly cannot rate. The response options, therefore, are really statement "applies to me," "does not apply," and "cannot say."

Even with its modified dichotomous format, however, the MMPI–2 cannot distinguish between the "cannot say" and "neutral" categories. The Strong Campbell Interest Inventory[1] (SCII), a popular interest test, provides *four* response options per item. The SCII determines the strength of different interests and compares them to the patterns observed in people with different occupations. The instructions require test takers to sort a series of school subjects and activities into "like," "dislike," and "indifferent" categories and permit test takers to omit items about which they are uncertain (Hansen & Campbell, 1985). Each decision awards a specific number of points to the appropriate interest scale. A "like" response is worth more points than "indifferent," which is worth more than "dislike." Since test takers can omit items about which they are uncertain, the format separates the "dislike," "neutral" (i.e., "indifferent"), and "cannot say" categories.

The number of response options can be extended further through the use of Likert items (Likert, 1932). Items using the Likert format typically include five or more alternatives. For example, test takers might be given a series of statements and asked to rate each on a 5-point scale corresponding to "strongly disagree," "disagree," "neutral," "agree," and "strongly agree." Items can be

[1]The original version of this test was called the Strong Vocational Interest Blank (SVIB). In the 1974 revision, the name was changed to the Strong–Campbell Interest Inventory (SCII). The name of the newest version, published in 1985, is the Strong Interest Inventory. However, many people still refer to the test as the SCII, and most of the literature published on this test refers to the SCII. For purpose of convenience, the test will be referred to here also as the SCII.

scored a variety of ways. The five response options then could be linked to the numbers, such as 1 to 5. Selecting a particular option would add between 1 and 5 points to the corresponding underlying scale. (The five options could be linked to *any* set of numbers. For example, we could use the numbers −2 to +2, with a "neutral" response equal to 0 points, a "strongly disagree" equal to −2 points, and a "strongly agree" equal to +2.)

Two often-asked questions in the development of such items are the following: What is the optimal number of response categories, and should an even or odd number of categories be used? The optimal number of categories varies as a function of the test audience and test content. A greater number of categories requires that test takers make finer discriminations. Tests for children, therefore, should use a smaller number of categories than tests for adults. When used with adults, there is often a relationship between the number of categories and the reliability or consistency of test-taker response (Thorndike et al., 1991). As the number of categories increases up to 7, the reliability increases. As the number increases from 7 up to 20, the reliability of the measure declines. In other words, people are less likely to select the same response consistently when they are tested repeatedly.

Most existing Likert items use an odd number of categories. Test takers generally prefer an odd number of categories because it presents a clear midpoint for the neutral response. The danger is that people will overuse that category. The neutral category provides an easy out for those who are unwilling to take the task seriously or who are defensive about revealing their personal characteristics. Using an even number of categories removes the midpoint. However, with this format there is the chance that test takers will omit more items because they are denied the option of a clear neutral response.

Forced-choice Items

The most common forced-choice format is *paired statements*, which require test takers to choose between two attributes presented as words, phrases, or statements. The Edwards Personal Preference Schedule (EPPS) uses forced-choice items to examine the relative strength of 15 needs, such as the need to achieve and the need to conform (Edwards, 1959). Each item presents two statements reflecting two different needs; across the different items each statement is paired with every other statement. To illustrate this format, consider the following hypothetical item:

1. (A) I feel good when I receive good grades.
   (B) I feel good when I fit into the crowd.

In the hypothetical item, option A reflects the need to achieve, whereas option B reflects the need to conform. By selecting one of these statements, the test taker expresses a *relative* preference for that need over the other. When all the items are completed, the test taker actually has expressed the same number of "likes" as "dislikes"—one of each for each item. What varies is the number of times statements tapping different needs are placed in the like or dislike category and thus the number of points added to each underlying scale. The resulting scores on each scale rank the 15 needs in terms of relative strength. The need with the highest score corresponds to the one whose statements were selected most often.

The Kuder Occupational Interest Survey (KOIS) illustrates a more complicated paired-statements format (Kuder, 1979). Each item presents *three* activities. Test takers select one as the "most preferred" and a second one as the "least preferred." The format creates a three-way ranking of activities, with different numbers of points awarded for each of the three possible ranks. Points are awarded on the interest scales according to the number of times relevant activities are assigned to each of the three ranks. The interest with the highest score corresponds to the one whose activities received the most ranking points. Scores are used to create a profile of interests, which is compared to the profiles obtained in different occupational groups during the standardization process. Similar profiles indicate occupations the test taker should consider.

The *Q-sort* is a flexible procedure whose number of response categories can be adapted to the wishes of the test developer (Stephenson, 1953). The Q-sort requires test takers to sort a set of cards into a series of piles. Cards may contain words (e.g., adjectives) or statements. In a nine-pile Q-sort, a common structure, those that truly describe the test taker are placed in pile 9, and those that do not are placed in pile 1. Other items are placed in piles 2 through 8 according to the extent to which they are accurate descriptions. The potential to increase the number of scale points or categories is limitless. Some psychologists have suggested using scales with as many as 20 points (e.g., Champney & Marshall, 1939)!

Although it may seem that the Q-sort format involves independent evaluation of statements, it is a forced-choice task that generates ipsative measures. The Q-sort categories define the relative fit of each statement to the test taker. In other words, the sorting task ranks the descriptions from "most like me" to "least like me." While it is possible theoretically for a test taker to put all statements into the "most like me" category, test takers typically are required to place a specific number of statements into each pile.

Response Bias and Item Format

So far we have distinguished between independent and forced-choice formats on the basis of measurement scheme—normative or ipsative. The formats also differ in their approach to the problem of response bias. Because objective tests ask direct questions, test takers potentially can bias or distort their responses. Test takers may try to figure out how a particular type of person would answer the question and respond accordingly. In addition, because objective tests ask test takers to select a response from a set of options, they can produce answers to test items without ever considering item content. They can randomly select answers, always pick "true" for even-numbered questions—engage in all sorts of bizarre answer-generating strategies. Any type of systematic distortion or bias of responses threatens the validity of test results because responses would not reflect true test-taker characteristics (e.g., Cronbach, 1946). The ability of the test to control or identify such distortion varies as a function of item format (e.g., Cronbach, 1950).

Two types of response bias or **dissimulation** are possible. Test takers could demonstrate a *response set*, systematically selecting answers in an effort to present themselves in a particular light. For example, test takers could be concerned about social desirability and attempt to present very positive pictures of themselves (Edwards, 1957). To bias responses in this way, the test taker tries to imagine how a well-liked person would answer each item and selects alternatives accordingly. Response set, therefore, is a content-dependent bias. Test takers distort their responses systematically according to the content of each item.

A second type of distortion is *response style*. In this case, test takers adopt systematic strategies for answering items about which they are unsure. The strategy "When in doubt, pick C" on multiple-choice achievement tests is a response style. Similarly, the tendency to agree with statements regardless of their content (acquiescence) and to avoid the use of extreme categories when rating statements (central tendency) are response styles used on personality tests. In contrast to response set, a response style is a content-free bias.

The use of forced-choice items or independent items presents different options for test developers concerned about response sets. The contrast is clearly seen when the design of the Edwards Personal Preference Schedule (EPPS) and the Minnesota Multiphasic Personality Inventory (MMPI—2) are compared.

Edwards was particularly concerned about social desirability because research indicated that people were significantly more likely to select socially desirable statements whenever a choice was available (Edwards, 1957). The design of the EPPS attempts to use the forced-choice format to *control* this bias. First, statements were written to represent the different needs being measured. Next, a large sample of people was used to assign a social desirability rating to each statement. The forced-choice pairs were constructed so that each pair contained statements representing different needs *equated* for degree of social desirability. Each item, therefore, requires test takers to choose between two equally desirable or equally undesirable alternatives. The construction of items makes it impossible for a test taker to select only statements expressing socially desirable characteristics.

Although the forced-choice format of the EPPS reduces the social desirability response set, research indicates that it is not eliminated (e.g., Feldman & Corah, 1960). It is difficult to write a large number of items that are truly equated on a response set dimension. Furthermore, most objective personality tests do not use the forced-choice format. Many examinees are uncomfortable with the forced-choice format. With independent items, however, test takers rate each statement independently. There is no way to prevent people from selecting socially desirable answers—or from engaging in any other response set. Tests using independent formats can, however, use other techniques to *identify* the presence of response sets.

The MMPI–2 uses a set of special validity scales to identify possible response biases. These validity scales are summarized in Table 4.2. Note that these scales let us identify a variety of possible biases in test-taker responses. For example, a high "lie" (L scale) score suggests a need to present oneself as a good person, whereas a high "fake bad" (F scale) implies possible exaggeration of symptoms. Since the "fake good" (K) scale covers several issues, either a high *or* a low K score leads us to question the validity of the test results. In fact, K scores are used to adjust the scoring of the personality scales themselves to produce a more accurate overall profile.

TABLE 4.2   Validity Scales of the MMPI–2

Scale	Measures:	By Noting:
? or cannot say	willingness to disclose information	Number of items not answered
L or "lie" scale	Presentation of self as "ideal" or "perfect"	Number of false responses to statements describing ordinary "bad" behavior (e.g., not always telling the truth)
F or "fake bad" scale	Presentation of self as pathological; random responding; failure to understand questions	Responses to items describing unusual or pathological events (e.g., hearing voices, out-of-body experiences)
K or "fake good" scale	Overly favorable presentation of self; defensiveness (high K); willingness to present self in socially undesirable way (low K)	Similarities between your answers and those given by clinical versus nonclinical samples who produced otherwise normal profiles

The comparison of the EPPS and the MMPI–2 illustrates how the problem of response set can be addressed when forced-choice or independent formats are selected. But what of the problem of response style or content-free biases? Again, a variety of strategies is available. To check on possible random responding, items can be repeated within a test and the pattern of answers evaluated to determine the consistency of response. Both the EPPS and the MMPI–2 use this procedure. For example, the EPPS repeats 15 items in random locations throughout the test. Research during test development indicated that most individuals answer at least 9 of these items consistently. Therefore, test takers who answer less than 9 of these items consistently are suspected of random responding.

To identify the tendency to acquiesce on a true/false or yes/no test, statements tapping a particular attribute can be written in forms that require different responses. A particular behavior or attitude could be presented twice, once stated positively and once stated negatively. If the process is repeated for several behaviors or attitudes, the consistency of content-based responding could be determined. Inconsistent responding in this case would indicate either acquiescence (too many "true" or "yes" answers) or negativism (too many "false" or "no" answers).

Another possibility is to write items so that points are earned on half of them by a true/yes response and on half by a false/no response. Test takers responding independently of content would earn test scores close to 0. Research during the test development stage can identify the average range of scores on such a scale. Later, test takers scoring outside this range would be suspected of a response bias. This procedure is similar to the one used in the development of the MMPI–2's F scale.

Item Selection and Scale Construction

The last step in constructing an objective personality test is to select the actual test items and, if the test is multidimensional, key the items to the attributes being measured. If we began by specifying the content of the test (Chapter 2), we know what the items should cover. But how do we know whether the items we write successfully tap these characteristics? On what do we base our decision to include or exclude a particular item?

Historically, psychologists have taken several approaches to item selection and scale development. The approach used on early personality tests, such as the Woodworth Personal Data Sheet (Woodworth, 1917, 1920), was the *logical-content or rational strategy*. Items were selected and assigned to scales on a rational basis. The focus is on whether the content of the item seems logically related to the characteristic being measured. A test to measure friendliness might include true/false statements such as "I enjoy spending time with people" and "I am uncomfortable around new people."

Although the logical-content approach can be a useful way to begin writing items, it is no longer a popular approach to test construction. The approach leads to selection of items that obviously are related to the characteristics being measured. While we may hope that test takers answer questions honestly, it is easy to distort responses to these items. Furthermore, assuming that an item measures what it is supposed to measure is dangerous. What an item in fact measures is an empirical question!

A second strategy, employed in development of the EPPS, is theoretical. Rather than simply using logic to decide if the content of an item is appropriate, the *theoretical approach* uses psychological theory to determine the content of test items. The EPPS is based on a theory of human needs first proposed by Murray (1938). Edwards selected 15 needs from Murray's list and wrote statements whose content reflected these different needs. The 15 need scales were constructed by keying each statement to the appropriate need. Linking item content to theory is somewhat less subjective than the logical-content approach, but still produces rather obvious items. The EPPS dealt with this problem by using a forced-choice format and attempting to match items on social desirability—with only limited success.

Although more "scientific" than the logical-content strategy, the theoretical approach still emphasizes content relationships between items and attributes they measure. A more rigorous approach uses empirical analysis of responses to items as the basis for selecting items and constructing scales. Two types of empirical analysis have been used: (1) the criterion group method and (2) the factor analysis method.

In the *criterion* or *contrasted group method*, items are presented to various reference groups, and the responses are analyzed to determine how different types of people answer each item. The focus here is item discrimination—we want to select items that are answered differently by different groups of people. The criterion group approach was used in the development of Strong's first interest test, the Strong Vocational Interest Blank (Strong, 1927). Approximately 400 items describing a variety of activities and interests were given to criterion groups representing different occupations and professions. Items were assigned to occupational scales according to their responses. For example, if most architects placed the activity "drawing" in the "like" category, that response would be keyed to the architect occupational scale. A test taker selecting "like" for "drawing" would earn points on the architect scale.

The MMPI–2 is a good example of a more refined criterion group method. For its original version (MMPI), Hathaway and McKinley (1940, 1943) selected a set of over 500 personal statements taken from case histories, psychological reports, other tests, and textbooks. The items were administered to a control group drawn from the general population and eight criterion groups drawn from psychiatric inpatients at the University of Minnesota Hospital. Each criterion group was composed of inpatients with a particular diagnosis, such as depression, and was used to determine items for the corresponding clinical scale. For each diagnosis, the procedure identified the items that discriminated between the normal (control) and inpatient (criterion) groups. Only these items were keyed to the personality scale representing that diagnostic category.

The 1989 revision of the MMPI, which produced the MMPI–2, maintains this emphasis on empirical process (e.g., Butcher et al., 1990). Items using dated content, sexist language, or difficult vocabulary were dropped or rewritten. Other items that no longer discriminated between criterion groups were eliminated, and items were written for a set of new scales (e.g., suicide, eating disorders) relevant to today's population.

The criterion group approach produces scales composed of items that are answered differently by different criterion groups. In other words, it guarantees selection of items that discriminate between different types of people. It does not ensure, however, that the items on a scale make any theoretical sense. In fact, it does not even assume that test takers answer the items truthfully. The critical issue is *how* different types of people answer the items. If depressed individuals are the only ones to endorse the statement, "I hate the color green," it does not matter whether depressed people really dislike green. What is important is that depressed people mark the item true and other people do not.

There are, however, several problems with the criterion group method. First, the procedure produces scales that are keyed to the particular criterion groups used. Using a different sample of people might result in selecting a different set of items for the scale. Furthermore, it is possible that these scales only apply to people whose demographic characteristics match those of the criterion groups. Scales that cannot be generalized across demographic variables are not particularly useful. Finally, the criterion group method may result in the same items being used in several scales. This would produce scales that were not independent—a score on one scale would be related to a score on another if the same items occur on both scales. If the attributes being measured are viewed as distinct characteristics, the scores on these attributes should be independent.

A second empirical procedure, the *factor analysis method*, can be used to reduce the extent of relationships between scales. Factor analysis is a complicated statistical procedure for analyzing the patterns in answers to test items, but the basic principle can be described simply. The responses produced by a group of people are analyzed statistically to identify the test items that are highly related to (i.e., correlated with) each other. If people who answer true to item 1 always answer false to item 11, performance on item 1 predicts performance on item 11. The two items are related somehow and should be keyed to the same dimension or scale. A small set of scales or factors should emerge, with each item keyed to only one of them.

The procedure can be illustrated with the 16 Personality Factor Questionnaire or 16PF (Cattell, 1949; Cattell, Eber, & Tatsuoka, 1970). Cattell began with a list of 171 adjectives that could be used to describe people. College students rated their friends on these items and the results were factor analyzed. The procedure indicated that the pattern of ratings could be accounted for by 16 factors or personality dimensions. Items strongly correlated with each of these factors were keyed to their respective scales. Items with weak relationships to the 16 factors were eliminated.

There is, however, a significant drawback to this procedure. Factor analysis can identify the items that are related to each other statistically, but it cannot identify what these items represent. In other words, the test developer must examine the identified items and try to "name" the characteristic that they tap. Although the resulting scale is coherent statistically, there is no way to predict whether it will correspond to a theoretically coherent construct.

In fact, a major criticism of *both* empirical approaches is their lack of theoretical coherence. Just as a theoretically determined scale may have little statistical validity, a statistically determined scale may have little theoretical validity. Recently, test developers have attempted to combine the theoretical and empirical approaches to item selection and scale construction, with rather notable success. Two examples of this process follow.

The Personality Research Form or PRF (Jackson, 1967), like the EPPS, is based on Murray's (1938) theory of needs. Before writing items, a specific definition of each need was generated. This additional step was taken to ensure that (1) the items for each scale would be as independent as possible and (2) the resulting scales would be homogeneous, each composed of items tapping the same specific need. Items were administered to over 1000 college students and their responses analyzed to identify the items most clearly related (statistically) to each proposed scale. The resulting scales are both theoretically and statistically coherent.

Although the early form of Strong's interest test (SVIB) was developed through the criterion group method, the most recent form uses a combined approach. Strong's criterion group research demonstrated that different interests were associated with different occupations. But the SVIB lacked a theoretical justification for why people in different occupations had different interests. When the test was revised and renamed the SCII (Hansen & Campbell, 1985), the test developers provided a theoretical rationale for these relationships based on Holland's (1973) theory of vocational choice. Holland proposed that personality shaped an individual's interests and therefore would be an important predictor of vocational choice. Holland's research identified six personality factors that were associated with particular patterns of interests. For example, someone high on the "social" factor would be interested in activities involving people and helping, whereas someone high on the "investigative" factor would be interested in facts and exploration. By integrating Holland's theory with Strong's criterion group research, the SCII was able to link personality, interests, and occupations. Scores now identify *general themes* characterizing test takers' answers. Each theme corresponds to one of Holland's personality types. The resulting *theme profiles* are used to suggest possible occupations.

Now that the strategies for selecting items and constructing scales have been presented, we have covered all the basic issues in the development of objective personality tests. Although our discussion has been quite extensive, it really only introduces the issues in objective test construction. Students interested in more information about item writing and scale construction can check some classic references (e.g., Guilford, 1954; Edwards, 1957; Torgerson, 1958) and some current suggestions (e.g., Sax, 1989; Wesman, 1971).

Generating Norm-referenced Scores

Note that all the tests described in this section compare test takers to reference groups. In other words, these tests are designed to generate norm-referenced scores such as percentile rank or standard scores (Chapter 3, p. 79). The process of producing these scores, however, differs widely. The development of a normative test like the MMPI–2 parallels the development of a norm-referenced ability test. Items are administered to reference groups (criterion groups) during the test development stage. The performance of these standardization groups is used to develop a system for translating raw scores into norm-referenced scores (standard scores, to be specific). After the test is developed, the scoring system is used to compare the characteristics of new test takers to the characteristics of the reference groups.

Reference groups are used differently in the development of ipsative tests. In fact, the EPPS and KOIS each use a different technique for comparing test takers to reference groups. In the development of the KOIS, groups of people in different occupations were used to develop *typical* profiles for each occupational group. When a person takes the KOIS, the profile generated is compared to the occupational group profiles to identify possible matches.

The EPPS, on the other hand, attempts to convert ipsative measures to percentile rank, a norm-referenced score. The test was administered and scored during the test development stage and the results used to determine how many people earned each score for each characteristic. The frequencies were used to create a scoring system that converts total scores for each characteristic to percentile ranks or standard scores. The scores of people tested later are converted to percentile ranks that compare their personality profiles to the patterns in the reference group.

Some psychologists criticize this procedure (e.g., Anastasi, 1988). It is confusing to interpret scores produced by combining ipsative measures with a normative frame of reference. If a test generates ipsative measures, its scores should rank the relative strength of a person's qualities. A percentile rank of 85 on a particular characteristic technically means that only 15% of the standardization sample had higher scores on this attribute. But how meaningful is that score if our focus is the structure of personality *within* an individual?

There is an additional, more general concern about ipsative measures. It is important to be able to assess the relationship between test scores and other variables, such as test-taker behavior. Such analyses are part of the process of determining the validity of a construct-based test and will be discussed in detail in Chapter 7. With ipsative measures, score on any one scale is not independent of score on the other scales. Remember that, by choosing one statement in a forced-choice pair and adding points to the scale it represents, the test taker forfeits an opportunity to select the other statement and add points to its underlying scale. Score on one scale, therefore, increases at the expense of score on another scale. This interrelatedness violates some of the assumptions necessary to use conventional statistical procedures to evaluate the test (Anastasi, 1988). As was the case with criterion-referenced ability tests, it is difficult to determine the adequacy of ipsative personality tests.

PROJECTIVE TESTS: PERSONALITY

As discussed in Chapter 2 (see p. 35), projective test items are ambiguous stimuli to be interpreted by the test taker. Most projective tests are administered individually. Projective items can use oral, written, or pictorial stimuli and require oral, written, or drawing responses. In terms of structure, the contrast between objective and projective personality tests is similar to the contrast between alternate-choice and free-response ability tests. In both cases, the first type of test presents test items (stimuli) and possible responses. Test takers select a response for each item. In both cases, the second type of test presents only test items (stimuli). Test takers must produce a response for each item.

In terms of rationale, however, the contrast between objective and projective tests reflects more fundamental differences. Objective tests come from the same tradition as ability tests. There is an emphasis on measurement of specific characteristics, on standardized administration and scoring, and on the use of empirical procedures to select items and construct scales. Although some psychologists see these as the strengths of objective tests, others cite these as problems. Critics charge that this emphasis on empiricism has led to development of tests without any theoretical framework and tests that present personality as a set of discrete, separate characteristics. Furthermore, the direct questions put forth by objective tests measure only what test takers consciously can or want to reveal. There is much more to personality, critics say, than objective tests can measure.

Projective tests attempt to address these concerns. Although projective tests may generate scores on different personality dimensions, the goal is to present a more integrated, holistic picture of personality. There is more emphasis on evaluating personality within a theoretical framework and on eliciting information from different levels of consciousness.

Logic of Projective Testing

The original theoretical rationale for projective testing was the **projective hypothesis** (e.g., Frank, 1939). According to this hypothesis, interpretation of an ambiguous stimulus elicits projection, a process in which needs, feelings, and experiences are reflected in the way a person perceives and describes the stimulus. Through projection a person may reveal unconscious or latent aspects of personality unlikely to be tapped by objective test items. The key to eliciting projection is (1) presenting an ambiguous stimulus or unstructured task, such as describing an inkblot or drawing a person, and (2) requiring test takers to produce, rather than select, responses.

There is extensive controversy over the validity and usefulness of projective tests and over whether test-taker responses truly involve projection. Even their proponents agree that interpretation of projective responses is difficult. For example, two people might produce the same response for very different reasons. How, then, can we link different responses to different personality characteristics? A single individual may produce different responses at different times. Does this mean personality characteristics have changed between testings? A test taker may produce a totally unique response. Is it possible to develop a reliable scoring system that adapts to unique responses? And, finally, is it really possible to determine whether a particular response is a projection of an underlying unconscious need, wish, or fear? Although projective tests remain an important part of personality assessment, many psychologists are not convinced that the test-taker characteristics they measure are different from those measured by objective tests.

Item Formats

Although all projective tests require test takers to respond to ambiguous stimuli, they can be grouped into categories according to (1) the type of stimuli presented and (2) the response required of test takers. The three most popular projective item formats are verbal techniques, drawing tasks, and pictorial techniques.

Verbal Techniques

Verbal techniques use verbal stimuli and verbal responses. The underlying assumption is that our thinking is revealed by our choice of words. Verbal tests can be either oral or written and can be adapted for group administration. The two most popular verbal techniques are *word association* and *incomplete sentences*.

Word association is usually an individual oral test, although it can be adapted for written presentation. In its oral form, the examiner reads a list of words, one at a time, to a test taker, who responds with the first word that comes to mind. Sometimes called *free association*, word association was first used diagnostically by Jung (1910) as a technique to study neurotic symptoms. Word association tests can be designed to use either theoretically relevant stimuli (e.g., Jung, 1910) or common, neutral words (e.g., Kent & Rosanoff, 1910).

Incomplete-sentence tasks present sentence fragments, such as "My mother ...," which test takers complete using their own words. These usually are written tests, although they can be presented orally. The fragments can be designed to assess overall level of adjustment or to sample specific personality characteristics, such as characteristics relevant to a particular age or diagnosis. In fact, it is the flexibility of the format that makes it so attractive to clinicians. The Rotter Incomplete Sentences Blank (RISB) is an example of a global approach (Rotter & Rafferty, 1950). The RISB is designed to identify the overall extent of emotional maladjustment. The Incomplete Sentences Task (IST) was designed to provide a more differentiated profile of test-taker characteristics (Lanyon & Lanyon, 1980). Used with junior high through college age students, the IST generates specific measures of hostility, anxiety, and dependence.

Drawing Tasks

Although verbal techniques present ambiguous stimuli, the tasks themselves are quite structured and the type of response required is quite specific. Many psychologists view verbal techniques as *too* structured, limiting the test taker's opportunities for self-expression. Drawing tasks are less structured, requiring test takers to draw pictures of people and, sometimes, other objects with minimal direction from the examiner. Drawing tests reflect psychoanalytic assumptions about the way characteristics and conflicts are expressed in creative activities. Popular examples are the Draw-A-Person Test (Machover, 1971), the

House–Tree–Person Technique (Buck, 1948, 1966), and the Draw-A-Family Test (Harris, 1963). Features of the drawing process and the drawings themselves are analyzed to reveal global descriptions of personality.

Pictorial Techniques

Pictorial techniques present ambiguous visual images to test takers. Two distinct types have emerged. *Inkblot tests* require test takers to describe what they see when they look at a series of black and white or colored inkblots. *Story tests* require test takers to describe the people and events represented on a series of picture cards.

The Rorschach Inkblot Test (Rorschach, 1921) was the first test to use inkblots to identify psychological disorders and is probably the most popular of the inkblot tests. The Holtzman Inkblot Technique (Holtzman et al., 1961), a popular challenger, is notable for its inclusion of an alternate form—a useful feature when retesting may be necessary. Inkblot tests traditionally are individual tests. Each inkblot is printed on a card, and the cards are shown to the test taker one at a time in a specified sequence. The test taker describes the image, the examiner records the response, and the next card is displayed.

Compared to inkblots, story tests are more structured and less open ended. The stimuli are less ambiguous and the instruction to "tell a story" about each picture requires test takers to produce a much more coherent response. There is also more variety in the types of stimuli. For example, the Thematic Apperception Test or TAT (Murray, 1943) uses pictures of adults and children, whereas the Children's Apperception Test (Bellak, 1954, 1986) uses pictures of animals and the Senior Apperception Test (Bellak & Bellak, 1973; Bellak, 1986) uses pictures only of elderly persons. The selection of characters and scenes in each case reflects assumptions about the stimuli most likely to facilitate a projective response. For example, the use of animals in the Children's Apperception Test reflects the assumption that children project more readily to pictures of animals than pictures of humans. Similarly, the use of elderly people on the senior test is designed to promote test-taker identification with the images on the cards and thereby elicit projective stories.

Item Selection and Scale Construction

Like objective tests, projective tests can be developed using a logical-content, theoretical, or empirical approach. Because of their strong link to psychoanalytic theory, however, many projective tests employ a theoretical strategy. For example, Jung (1910) used the theoretical approach to select items and develop a scoring system for a word-association test. Words were selected based on their psychoanalytic significance (e.g., "mother," "success") and responses were analyzed in terms of reaction time, content, and physical expressions of emotional tension. The interpretation of responses was also psychoanalytic. For example, a long reaction time indicated the presence of an underlying conflict. A bizarre association indicated an attempt to disguise a conflict.

Jung's work was the basis for a more recent word-association test developed at the Menninger Clinic (Rapaport, Gill, & Schafer, 1946, 1968), which uses some criterion group comparisons. In addition to scoring responses on the basis of features like reaction time, the Rapaport test determines proportion of common or popular responses by comparing test-taker answers to those generated by a standardization group.

It is possible, however, to develop a word-association test through empirical analysis. The Kent–Rosanoff Free Association Test (1910), designed as a psychiatric screening instrument, used the criterion group method to develop an objective scoring system. The 100 items are common, emotionally neutral words selected because they frequently elicited the same associations from a standardization group of 1000 ordinary people (a control group), but rarely elicited those associations from clinical groups such as schizophrenics. Although clearly a more empirically rigorous test, the Kent–Rosanoff suffers from the same problem as all criterion-group-based tests: The norms cannot necessarily be generalized to people with different demographic characteristics. Although additional norms have been collected over the years, the Kent–Rosanoff is used today primarily in research on language and personality (Anastasi, 1988).

Empirical approaches have dominated the development of incomplete-sentence tasks. For example, both the Rotter Incomplete Sentences Blank (RISB) and the Incomplete Sentences Task (IST) were developed through study of criterion groups. The RISB (Rotter & Rafferty, 1950) requires test takers to generate complete-sentence responses to 40 sentence fragments. Control and criterion groups were used to determine the structure and content of completions characterizing well-adjusted and maladjusted individuals. Each completion is scored on a 7-point scale (0 to 6), representing degree of adjustment. The empirical approach used to develop the RISB clearly paid off. The RISB demonstrates impressive reliability and validity for a projective test (e.g., Goldberg, 1965).

The IST (Lanyon & Lanyon, 1980) demonstrates the use of combined theoretical and empirical approaches to test construction. Designed for junior high through college age students, the IST measures extent of hostility, anxiety, and dependence. The three characteristics were selected because of their theoretical and diagnostic importance during these ages. Items tapping each dimension were written and administered to a standardization sample of students. Selection and scoring of items for each dimension were determined by comparing the responses of two criterion groups: students rated by their teachers as "high" on the characteristic and students rated by their teachers as "low" on the characteristic. Although item selection and scoring were determined empirically, there is rather limited research on the test's reliability and validity (Anastasi, 1988).

The design and scoring of drawing tests demonstrate the emphasis on theory in projective test development. A popular example is the Draw-A-Person (Machover, 1971). In the Draw-A-Person Test (DAP), test takers are asked simply to draw a person and, after completing the drawing, to draw a person of the opposite sex from the first. The examiner notes features both of the drawing process and the drawings themselves. The drawings are interpreted qualitatively, identifying the characteristics that test takers project. For example, the size of the head may indicate something about intellectual ability, or emphasis on the mouth may suggest eating disorders or substance abuse. Other tests, such as the House–Tree–Person Technique (Buck, 1948, 1966) and the Draw-A-Family Test (Harris, 1963), take the same interpretative approach but analyze a wider variety of drawings.

Although drawing tests base guidelines for interpretation of drawings on the features produced by clinical samples, they reflect a theoretical rather than an empirical approach. There are no specific control–criterion group comparisons and no norms for scoring. As often happens with tests developed through a theoretical approach, many of the relationships between features of the drawings and psychological problems have not been supported by research (e.g., Roback, 1968; Swensen, 1957, 1968).

Probably the most familiar projective tests are the Rorschach Inkblot Test (Rorschach, 1921) and the Thematic Apperception Test (Murray, 1943), two pictorial approaches that demonstrate different purposes and test construction principles. The Rorschach was designed as a diagnostic instrument, a technique to identify emotional disturbance. Rorschach items were developed without a specific theoretical base. Item selection and scoring were based on empirical comparisons of criterion groups. The TAT, in contrast, was not designed as a diagnostic test. Instead, the TAT was presented as a technique for general personality assessment suitable for use with clinical or nonclinical populations. The TAT also had a definite theoretical base—Murray's (1938) theory of human needs. Because both tests are so popular, and so frequently criticized, we'll explore their development in detail.

Rorschach's goal was to develop an empirically based system for scoring descriptions of inkblots. The scoring dimensions were to reflect the response features that discriminated between different criterion and control groups. A set of 10 symmetric inkblots was printed on cards, 5 in black–white–gray, 2 with touches of red, and 3 including several other colors. Cards were presented one at a time, with test takers asked to describe what they saw. Test takers could turn the cards however they wished and take as much time as they desired. Thus, administration was allowed to vary extensively across test takers. Initial norms for scoring the descriptions were developed by noting the characteristic responses of different criterion groups, including a variety of both clinical and nonclinical populations (e.g., artists, scholars). Little attention was paid to symbolic interpretation of the contents of these responses, a primary interest of psychoanalytic theorists (Groth-Marnat, 1990).

Unfortunately, Rorschach died shortly after the publication of *Psychodiagnostik* in 1921, and further development of the test was undertaken by a variety of individuals. By 1957, five Rorschach systems were in use, each employing different administration and scoring procedures (Groth-Marnat, 1990). A survey of Rorschach users by the Exners (Exner & Exner, 1972) indicated that 22% used no specific scoring procedures at all, basing their interpretations instead on subjective analysis of contents! Exner and colleagues began work on a standardized system for administering and scoring the Rorschach that integrated features of the five existing scoring systems. The result was a series of volumes (Exner, 1974, 1978, 1986; Exner & Weiner, 1982) presenting a comprehensive system that is now the most frequently taught system in graduate programs (Ritzler & Alter, 1986). Comprehensive scoring focuses on several aspects of test-taker responses, including the sections of the inkblot described, the features of the inkblot on which the response is based, and the match between features of the inkblot and the description.

The TAT presents an interesting contrast to the Rorschach on several dimensions. Unlike the Rorschach, the TAT was derived from a specific theoretical base. The goal of the TAT was to identify basic themes in personality, themes reflecting the different needs outlined in Murray's (1938) theory of personality. It is not surprising, then, that a theoretical approach was used to select items (pictures) and score responses. Furthermore, analysis of TAT responses was designed specifically to focus on their symbolic content. The test consists of 20 cards to be presented in a standard order. The stories told in response to TAT pictures supposedly express the test taker's unconscious needs, wishes, and fantasies. They are interpreted by examining a test taker's description of the main character (the "hero"), who represents the test taker, and the forces affecting the hero (the types of environmental "press").

Murray did provide examples of the relationships between specific needs and presses and different story themes. However, no formal norms for typical and atypical themes were developed and no quantitative scoring system was presented. As use of the TAT increased, so did variations in administration and scoring procedures. By 1950, there was sufficient variation in administration and scoring to produce an entire book summarizing the systems (Shneidman, 1951)! Even today there is no consensus on TAT administration and scoring; clinicians still vary in number of cards used, order of presentation of cards, and scoring systems (Haynes & Peltier, 1985). Although several quantitative scoring systems have been developed, they are time-consuming and therefore rarely used in clinical practice (Anastasi, 1988).

Personality Testing Revisited

By now you may well have decided never to use, let alone design, a personality test. It might be useful, therefore, to reflect for a minute on the process of personality testing. First, remember the basic rules about using tests and interpreting test scores. Tests are used to provide estimates of test-taker characteristics. Only naive individuals believe that test scores are absolute or perfect measures. Personality tests may have their share of problems, but they do provide some standardized techniques for examining test-taker characteristics. Second, because they are tests, they use systems to evaluate people that can be researched to determine their effectiveness. It *is* possible to identify their technical strengths and weaknesses.

Third, hundreds of personality tests are currently available. Most clinicians use more than one test in an evaluation process. By using several different tests, it is possible to increase the accuracy of inferences about test-taker characteristics. And, finally, personality tests are only one mechanism for exploring personality. The most accurate assessments combine information from tests, behavioral observations, and interviews. No reputable psychologist bases a decision on testing alone.

ATTITUDE SCALES

An *attitude* is a tendency to react positively or negatively to a specific type of object, person, or situation. Although attitudes can be considered an element of personality, the construction of attitude scales involves somewhat different techniques. Like other aspects of personality, attitudes are constructs that cannot be measured directly. The presence and nature of an attitude must be inferred from observable behaviors, including such behaviors as responses to a set of questions. The content of items for attitude scales, therefore, is developed through the process of construct explication. The test outline must include information about the specific types of statements expressing and running counter to the attitude under study.

Item Formats

Attitude scales present specific statements for test takers to rate. As with objective personality tests, the formats vary in number and type of response categories. Items on attitude scales use the same variety of structures discussed in the section on independent items (see p. 96). For example, attitude tests can require true/false ratings of statements or can use a yes/no (dichotomous) checklist format. Thurstone used the checklist format to measure attitudes toward capital punishment (Peterson & Thurstone, 1933). Test takers were instructed to check statements with which they agreed and to use a cross to mark those with which they disagreed.

Many attitude tests use Likert items (Likert, 1932). For example, the Minnesota School Attitude Survey (Ahlgren, 1983), designed to elicit children's attitudes about school experiences, scores items on a 5-point Likert scale. An interesting feature of this instrument is the use of only three response categories on the form designed for grades 1 through 3: a smiling face, scored as 5 points, a neutral face, scored as 3 points, and a frowning face, scored as 1 point. As mentioned in our earlier discussion of Likert items, scales for use with children are more reliable if they include a limited number of units.

Item Selection and Scale Construction

The primary difference between attitude scales and personality tests is the process of item selection and scale construction. A complete discussion of scaling techniques is beyond the scope of this book; entire volumes have been written just on the process of constructing attitude scales. Instead, we will concentrate on construction of two popular types: Thurstone scales and Likert scales.

Thurstone's concern (e.g., Thurstone, 1925) was the creation of attitude tests that truly represented an interval scale of measurement (see Chapter 1, p. 17). **Thurstone scales** (Thurstone & Chave, 1929; Thurstone, 1947, 1959) begin with a large set of statements (often 200 or more) expressing a wide range of positive and negative attitudes on a particular topic and the identification of a large number of "expert judges" (often 40 to 50)—people knowledgeable about the topic being evaluated. Using capital punishment as an example, the item pool might include statements like "Murderers don't deserve to live" and "The Bible says 'Thou shalt not kill'." The expert judges individually sort these statements into 11 categories from most favorable (category 1) to least favorable (category 11). Judges are instructed to treat the 11 categories as an equal-interval scale and to rate statements independent of their personal feelings. Using our example, "Murderers don't deserve to live" probably would get *low* category ratings because this statement reflects a *favorable* view of capital punishment.

Once the judges have finished, the pattern of ratings for each statement is noted. The goal is to identify statements that fall at different positions on the 11-point scale. We begin by looking for consistency in how judges rate the statements. Statements with a wide variety of category ratings are dropped; statements with a narrow range of category ratings are kept.

The statements retained are given point values, called *scale values*, indicating where they fall on this 11-point scale. We do this by listing the judges' category ratings in order for each statement and selecting the middle (median) rating as the scale value. In our example, the statement "Murderers don't deserve to live" may have received several different scale values—some 1s, some 2s, some 3s, even some 4s. Its final scale value (1, 2, 3, or 4) is determined by the pattern of the judges' ratings.

The pool of statements is further reduced by selecting only a few statements with each scale value. The goal is to end up with a set of approximately 20 statements with the widest spread of scale values. The final test presents the statements in random order. When the test is administered, test takers mark the statements that represent their personal attitudes. We score the test in much the same way as we assigned scale values during development of the test. For each test taker, the scale values of the items selected are listed in rank order. The score on the test is the middlemost (median) value of the set of statements endorsed.

Thurstone generated some 30 attitude scales using this process (Thurstone & Chave, 1929; Thurstone, 1959). As you no doubt can see, construction of a Thurstone scale is a long and complicated process. Thurstone scales have been the subject of much criticism in recent years (e.g., Sellitz, Wrightsman, & Cook, 1976). For example, critics charge that it is difficult even for "expert judges" to disregard their personal attitudes when rating statements. Thurstone scales have also been criticized as an ineffective way to measure individual differences in attitudes. Even with such a complex scaling and scoring process, many people can receive the same attitude score. Furthermore, testing experts question whether or not the procedure really produces an interval-level measure (e.g., Petrie, 1969). Is it reasonable to assume that all the judges view the extent of difference between categories 1 and 3, two very favorable categories, as equivalent to the degree of difference between categories 5 and 7, two categories in the middle range?

Perhaps because of the problems associated with Thurstone scales, **Likert scales** (Likert, 1932) have become a more popular format for attitude tests. Likert scales are easier to construct and more reliable. As with Thurstone scales, scale construction begins with a large number of statements (also often 200 or more) expressing a variety of positive and negative attitudes about a topic. The statements are rated on a multipart scale by a large group (100 to 200) of ordinary people. The traditional Likert scale uses five categories from "strongly agree" (1 point) to "strongly disagree" (5 points). The goal is to produce a scale in which *low* scores indicate *favorable* attitudes and high scores indicate unfavorable attitudes. But since the scale includes positive and negative statements, they must be scored separately.

The points earned on positive statements, such as "Murderers don't deserve to live," are simply totaled. Marking "strongly agree" gives you 1 point, and we want low scores to indicate favorable attitudes. The scoring of negative statements, "The Bible says 'Thou shalt not kill'," must be reversed. Marking "strongly agree" indicates an *un*favorable attitude and should earn you 5 points, not 1 point. Now, when all the points earned are added together, high scores will indicate unfavorable attitudes and low scores will indicate favorable attitudes.

Our next step is to identify the statements rated differently by people with extremely favorable and extremely unfavorable attitudes. Two procedures can be used. The contrasted or extreme group approach identifies items answered differently by members of two groups of people with extreme scores. Usually, the two groups compared are people with scores in the upper 25% to 33% and people with scores in the lower 25% to 33% of the standardization group. The item–total correlation approach examines, for each item, the relationship between *all* raters' answers to that item and their total scores. (The execution of both procedures will be described in more detail in Chapter 8.) About 10 positively worded and 10 negatively worded statements are retained and presented in a random order. When the test is administered, the ratings of negatively worded statements again are reversed to obtain test takers total scores. Ratings are totaled to produce a final score. High scores indicate very unfavorable attitudes; low scores indicate favorable attitudes.

The Likert scaling technique has several advantages over the Thurstone technique. First, it does not require the use of expert judges. It also does not require people during the test development process to disregard their personal feelings—these feelings in fact are the basis of the standardization process. Second, the technique allows for more variability in the content of items. Like other techniques based on empirical analysis, item selection is based on statistical properties rather than theoretical coherence. Since the statements selected do not necessarily have obvious relationships to the underlying attitudes, the scale may be less susceptible to response bias. Third, Likert scales generally are more reliable than Thurstone scales with the same number of items (Sellitz, Wrightsman, & Cook, 1976). However, many testing experts view Likert scales as still representing ordinal measurement. They are developed through a process requiring the standardization group to treat a set of categories as equally spaced units, and there are few data to suggest that people really do so.

EVALUATION SCALES

Many contexts require the evaluation of personal characteristics, behaviors, or job performance. Students evaluate their instructors, supervisors evaluate their subordinates, psychologists evaluate their clients—and there are times when people even are asked to evaluate themselves! What these scenarios have in common is an attempt to quantify the results of an observational process. Although the qualities being evaluated and the scale being used may vary from one situation to the next, in each case the scales are used to translate observer perceptions into numbers.

The content of evaluation scales is determined through the procedures described in Chapter 2. If the scale is to evaluate job performance, content is determined through the process of task or job analysis (p. 49). If the scale is to evaluate personality traits, content is determined via construct explication (p. 51). Specification of scale content, however, does not ensure that the evaluation process will yield reliable, valid, or even useful data. The following sections, therefore, discuss both the construction of scale and the structure of evaluation tasks.

Item Formats

The formats for evaluation scales fall into two categories. One set of formats, **standard rating scales**, is designed to evaluate each person independently. Standard rating scales can be used for evaluation of personality and behavior, as well as for evaluation of job performance. The other type, **comparative rating scales**, is designed to rate people relative to each other. Comparative rating scales do not provide information about absolute levels of performance. Instead, these scales rank people in terms of their relative performance. Someone with a low rating relative to the others in the group may in fact be quite good at the task being evaluated. Likewise, the person with the highest rating is defined as the most competent person *within this particular group*. Each individual's status could change if the mix of people in the group being rated changes. Comparative scales are used primarily in evaluation of job performance.

Standard Rating Scales

Two familiar item formats used as standard rating scales are checklist and Q-sort. Although these are popular formats for assessing personality and patterns of behavior, they typically are not used for evaluation of job performance. Checklists may include lists of descriptors (e.g., adjectives) or lists of behaviors. An observer then checks the behaviors that occur or the descriptors that apply. For example, the Adjective Check List (Gough & Heilbrun, 1983) has been used by psychologists to record observations of client personality characteristics (Anastasi, 1988).

In the Q-sort technique, descriptions are sorted into piles according to the degree to which the statements match what has been observed. As mentioned in the section on objective tests (p. 99), Q-sorts are popular because they adopt an ipsative or intrapersonal framework, ranking the individual's characteristics in order of salience or frequency of occurrence. In fact, the California Q-Sort

Deck originally was developed to provide a standard system for personality evaluation by trained observers (Block, 1978).

Rating tasks can use many other types of standard scales. Rating tasks using *continuous scales* require the rater to locate a person along a particular dimension. The construction of continuous scales begins with identifying the characteristics to be rated, such as sociability or oral communication skill. A separate scale is constructed for each characteristic to be rated. The scales can use a graphic or numerical format. Samples of each type are presented in Table 4.3.

In the graphic form, each characteristic is presented along with an unbroken line or a series of boxes. The end points or anchors of the scales are identified with descriptors such as "excellent" and "poor" or "satisfactory" and "unsatisfactory." In some cases, the midpoints are identified too. For each characteristic, raters place a mark on the line or in a box to represent the person's performance or characteristic. Scores are determined by measuring the distances from the end point to the marks or counting the number of boxes

TABLE 4.3 Sample Items for Continuous Rating Scales

Graphic

Linear form

For each item, rate your instructor by making a slash mark (/) at the point corresponding to the instructor's level of performance.

1. Organization of course material

poor   excellent

Box form

For each item, rate your instructor by making an X in the box corresponding to the instructor's level of performance.

1. Organization of course material

poor   excellent

Numerical

For each item, rate your instructor by circling the number corresponding to the instructor's level of performance.

1. Organization of course material

     1   2   3   4   5

     poor   excellent

from the end point to the marks. In the box format, the most reliable ratings are generated by scales using 5 to 10 boxes (Murphy & Davidshofer, 1988; Thorndike et al., 1991).

In the numerical form, each characteristic is presented along with a series of numbers. Reliable ratings can be generated by scales using 5 to 10 categories. As the number of categories increases above 10, however, the reliability of ratings declines (Thorndike et al., 1991). The lowest number, usually 0 or 1, is used to anchor the "poor" or "unsatisfactory" end of the scale; the highest number is used to anchor the "excellent" or "satisfactory" end of the scale. The scale midpoint may or may not be anchored to a term such as "average" or "acceptable."

The continuous-scale format is used in several popular personality evaluation techniques. For example, the semantic differential technique (Osgood, Suci, & Tannenbaum, 1957) uses continuous scales to explore individual differences in the meanings of words. People are asked to rate the meaning of words such as "mother" and "hate" on several 7-point scales. The end points or anchors of the scales are defined by bipolar adjectives, such as "good" and "bad" or "weak" and "strong." The responses to each concept are scored and compared to each other. Similar patterns of responses indicate concepts with similar connotations to the rater.

Although continuous scales are designed to be simple to complete, they are often quite difficult. The first problem is interpreting the meaning of the dimension. Continuous scales traditionally use labels like "organizational skill" or "initiative." These basically are constructs whose presence must be inferred from patterns of behavior. But what behaviors should be used? And how do we know that all raters use the same set of behaviors? Another problem is interpreting the scale anchors. Exactly what does it mean to be "excellent" or "acceptable"? Is "average" really a type of "good" rating or more like a nice way of saying someone is not too bad? A third problem is interpreting the difference between the points along the continuum. If the high end of the continuum is "excellent," how many inches, boxes, or numbers should be used to differentiate "very good" from "excellent" or "good" from "very good"?

Behaviorally anchored rating scales or BARS are one way to address these problems. The goal of BARS is to reduce ambiguity in the meaning of the dimension being rated and the meaning of the scale points. BARS are constructed using concrete, behavioral statements as "anchors" for the various scale points (Smith & Kendall, 1963). The development of BARS begins with assembling a group of people who are very knowledgeable about the property being evaluated. For each dimension to be measured, the group generates a large number of *critical incidents*, behavioral statements that (1) are relevant to property or task being rated, (2) are observable illustrations of the property or task being rated, and (3) correspond to different levels of that property or performance on that task. The statements are discussed thoroughly until the group reaches consensus on the best example of each performance level. Each scale presents a continuum, with the final statements listed in order. Table 4.4 presents an example of BARS.

In addition to being a popular format for evaluating job performance, BARS are also used in psychological evaluation. The Adaptive Behavior Scale of the American Association of Mental Deficiency (AAMD) contains several subtests in which BARS are used for rating the skill level of retardates in such areas as shopping, communication, and social interaction (AAMD, 1981). However, the key to the effectiveness of BARS appears to lie in the use of explicit behavioral statements, rather than the use of a scale with anchor points (e.g., Dickinson & Zellinger, 1980). In other words, other scale formats incorporating behavioral statements typically are as reliable as the behaviorally anchored format. BARS also have some clear disadvantages. They are developed through a long and difficult process that unfortunately does not guarantee success. Even though anchor behaviors are chosen by group consensus, there is no way to guarantee that the behaviors used as scale anchors are the behaviors that raters will observe.

A simpler alternative, retaining the use of behavioral statements, is a *behavioral observation scale* or BOS (Latham & Wexley, 1977). A BOS is composed of a list of behaviors demonstrating various levels of performance. The list is presented along with a system for rating the frequency of each behavior. The rater is asked to indicate how frequently each behavior has occurred within a specified period of time. When used for performance evaluation, the

---

TABLE 4.4   Sample Items for a Behaviorally Anchored Rating Scale

Organization of course material

Circle the number of the statement that best describes your instructor.

5	Consistently provides a creative integration of course concepts that emphasizes important relationships and contrasts.
4	Occasionally integrates material to highlight relationships and contrasts among course concepts.
3	Follows the organization of course material in the textbook and assigned readings.
2	Makes an attempt to present course material in an organized way, but occasionally is difficult to follow.
1	Generally presents course concepts in a way that is difficult to follow or understand.

list includes behaviors representing effective performance and ineffective performance. The ratings on the latter type are rescaled so that high scores indicate frequent demonstrations of effectiveness (e.g., Latham, Fay, & Saari, 1979).

The BOS system is also used for psychological evaluations. For example, the Vineland Adaptive Behavior Scales (Sparrow, Balla, & Cicchetti, 1984), a revision of Doll's Vineland Social Maturity Scale, lists approximately 300 behaviors to be rated as "usually" (2 points), "sometimes" or "partially" (1 point), "never" (0 points), or "no opportunity to observe" and "don't know" (not scored).

The BOS format is often presented as a simpler and more reliable alternative to BARS (e.g., Latham, Saari, & Fay, 1980). Raters only need note the frequency of a behavior; behaviors that they have not observed are identified as such. In addition, raters completing a BOS need not interpret the behaviors they have observed to classify them relative to the behavioral anchors provided on BARS. However, research indicates that raters are not necessarily reliable when recalling the frequency of a behavior. In fact, frequency ratings are often based on inferences that raters make from their overall impressions of the people being rated (e.g., Murphy, Martin, & Garcia, 1982). Furthermore, recent reviews of research on standard scales question whether existing data identify any format as better than the rest (e.g., Landy & Farr, 1980).

Comparative Rating Scales

All the preceding scales are standard scales, designed to evaluate each person independently. It is sometimes useful to rate people by comparing them to each other, especially in job performance situations. To do so, the test developer constructs a comparative rating scale. Comparative scales rank people relative to each other on one or more characteristics and are used most often in situations such as decisions about salary raises or promotions.

Let's examine three types of comparative rating scales. A *full-ranking scale* literally rank orders all the people in a group on a specific dimension. The number of ranks used is equal to the number of people in the group. It provides the maximum information about individual differences, but it requires considerable effort. A *forced-distribution scale* requires the rater to designate a fixed number of people in each rating category. For example, the rater could be required to identify people in the top 25%, middle 50%, and bottom 25% on a particular characteristic. The percentages are used to determine the number of people to locate in each category, based on the total number of people being compared. Although the measure is less precise than a full ranking, the scale is much easier to construct.

The third type of comparative scale is *paired comparison*, also called a *man-to-man scale* (e.g., Brown, 1983). The item format is similar to the forced-choice format used on ipsative tests. The people to be rated are listed in a series of pairs so that each person is paired with every other person. The rater must select, for each pair, the person who is performing best or who best exemplifies a particular characteristic. Although the method may seem odd, it in fact can generate very precise comparative scores. The technique requires analysis of many pairs with even modest-sized groups. [For a group of N people, the number of pairs to be evaluated is $N(N-1)/2$. For 10 people, the number of pairs = $(10 \times 9)/2$ or 45 pairs!] In addition, scaling techniques can be used to transform the resulting data to interval-level measures (e.g., Torgerson, 1958).

Rater Errors and Item Format

For the data from an evaluation task to be valid, the observer must rate or rank people accurately and objectively. Unfortunately, rating tasks are susceptible to a variety of rater errors. Like the response biases found on personality tests, these rater errors undermine the validity of the measurement process. Certain item formats, however, can be used to reduce the frequency of these errors.

One of the most familiar rater errors is the **halo effect**, the tendency of raters to base their ratings on general impressions. Halo effects can be identified by examining the pattern of ratings across the characteristics rated. If the ratings given to a person on different dimensions are similar, a halo effect may have occurred. Although there is no way to eliminate halo effects, they are less likely to occur when rating categories are defined in concrete, behavioral terms.

Another set of errors occurs when raters overuse certain portions of the rating scale. *Central tendency errors* occur when raters overuse the middle portion of the scale, avoiding the use of extreme ratings. *Leniency errors* occur when raters overuse the high categories and avoid using the lower ones; *severity errors* occur when raters overuse the low categories and avoid using the upper ones. One way to reduce these errors is to use comparative scales that force raters to discriminate between the individuals being evaluated. If standard scales are more appropriate, a forced-choice format can be used to require raters to discriminate between different behaviors or characteristics. A forced-choice item presents a set of two or more descriptions. The rater must choose the description from the set that best fits the person being rated. By matching descriptions carefully, raters can be prevented from providing a narrow range of evaluations.

Increasing the Accuracy of Ratings

Although one strategy to reduce rater error is to select a specific type of item format, much research suggests that item formats do not differ significantly in reliability or validity. A better approach is to address the causes of rater error by restructuring the evaluation task itself. The most successful rating scenarios contain the following features (Thorndike et al., 1991):

1. Raters are committed to the evaluation process. Often raters see the process as a nuisance and are unwilling to commit themselves to the careful observation needed to generate accurate data. The evaluation task must be presented as something worthwhile and important.
2. Raters are objective. It is difficult for anyone to prevent personal biases or stereotyped ideas from coloring observations of other people. One way to increase objectivity is to use observers who are unfamiliar with the person being rated. Another is to train raters to be more objective observers and to be able to distinguish between observation and interpretation of behavior.
3. Raters have extensive opportunities to observe the people to be rated. It is difficult to rate people based on a small sample of behavior.
4. Raters are given concrete, behavioral descriptions of the characteristics to be rated. Many of the characteristics to be rated are constructs such as "initiative" or "judgment." Regardless of the type of scale used, the rating task is easier and the ratings are more reliable when characteristics are described in behavioral terms.

SUMMARY AND KEY CONCEPTS

Typical performance tests can be used to assess personality, interests, attitudes, and patterns of behavior. Tests of personality and/or interests often use objective items, words, or statements to be evaluated by the test taker. When objective tests focus specifically on personality, they also are called self-report tests, personality inventories, or structured personality tests. If the goal is to produce normative measures, **independent** items are used. If the goal is to produce ipsative measures, **forced-choice** items are used. Common independent formats include dichotomous items and Likert items. Common forced-choice formats include paired statements and the Q-sort.

An important concern in objective testing is **dissimulation** or distortion of responses. Because objective tests ask direct questions about test-taker characteristics, they are susceptible to problems of response set, such as social desirability. Because they ask test takers to select a response from the options presented, they are susceptible to problems of response style, such as acquiescence and central tendency. Forced-choice tests can try to control for response set; tests using other item types can try to identify response sets through the use of validity scales. Other techniques can be used to limit the effects of response styles.

Once an item format is selected, information from the test outline (see Chapter 2) is used to generate possible test items. Three techniques have been used to select items and construct personality scales. The logical-content or rational strategy focuses on rational relationships between item content and the characteristic to be measured. The theoretical approach stresses correspondence between item content and important constructs or processes. Empirical analysis selects items and constructs scales based on the statistical properties of item responses. Two popular empirical strategies are comparing item responses in different groups, the criterion or contrasted group method, and factor analyzing item responses.

Personality tests can also use projective items. Although the theoretical rationale for projective testing, the **projective hypothesis**, is questioned by some psychologists, projective tests remain a popular form of personality assessment. Projective items require test takers to respond to ambiguous stimuli or tasks with minimal direction from the examiner. A variety of types of stimuli and response are used. Verbal techniques include word (free) association and incomplete-sentence tasks. Drawing tasks use a less structured and more creative activity, requiring test takers to draw pictures in response to examiner instructions. Pictorial techniques require test takers to respond to visual images, as in inkblot tests and story tests.

Attitude scales, another type of self-report test, indicate the strength of positive or negative feeling relative to a particular object or event. Common scale construction techniques include the **Thurstone** and **Likert** methods. Evaluation scales are used to measure personal characteristics or patterns of behaviors. Scales can be designed so that people rate themselves or others and are designed to quantify the results of an observational process. The basic contrast in design is between **standard rating scales**, which rate each person individually, and **comparative rating scales**, which evaluate people relative to each other. In addition to the checklist and Q-sort formats, standard scales include the continuous, BARS, and BOS formats. Standard scales are used both in personality and performance evaluation.

When assessing job performance, it is sometimes useful to evaluate people relative to each other. In this case, the test developer constructs a comparative rating scale. Common formats include a full-ranking scale, a forced-distribution scale, and a paired-comparison or man-to-man scale.

The most serious drawback to the use of rating scales is the problem of rater error. The effect of rater error in evaluation tasks parallels the effect of response bias on personality: Both events undermine the validity of the obtained measures. The most common types of rater error are the **halo effect** and errors of central tendency, leniency, and severity. Although modifications of item format, such as the use of forced-choice items, theoretically can reduce rater error, more effective approaches focus on improving the rating scenario itself.

QUESTIONS

4.1 Why do we say that dichotomous items have a "hidden interpretive problem"? Give examples to illustrate your points.

4.2 Explain why forced-choice items are inappropriate for generating normative scores.

4.3 Why do we say that forced-choice tests attempt to *control* response set, whereas tests using other items attempt to *identify* response set? What's the difference?

4.4 What are the disadvantages of an empirical approach to scale construction?

4.5 Contrast the philosophy of projective testing with the approach taken by objective tests.

4.6 Compare the degree of tasks structure presented by each of the following projective item formats: word-association tasks, drawing tasks, sentence-completion tasks, inkblot tasks, and story tasks.

4.7 Contrast the development of a scale to measure attitudes toward abortion using the Thurstone and the Likert procedures.

4.8 Why do many testing experts criticize the use of continuous rating scales?

4.9 Contrast the way behavioral statements are used in behaviorally anchored rating scales (BARS) and behavioral observation scales (BOS).

4.10 Explain why the problem of rater error in evaluation tasks is similar to the problem of response bias in personality testing.

II

PRINCIPLES OF TEST ANALYSIS

OVERVIEW

Whether or not a test is "good" is an empirical question. As with many other enterprises, even careful planning does not guarantee success. Part II presents a variety of statistical procedures to judge the adequacy of a test and its individual items. Intelligent decisions about the use of a test or the revision of a test under development require an ability to evaluate these statistical measures.

Before discussing the specifics of test analysis, it is useful to review the statistical concepts on which test analysis is based. Chapter 5, on working with scores, begins with the concept of a score distribution and the statistics used to describe score distributions. It continues with techniques for describing the relationship between scores in a single distribution, including a variety of score transformations, and techniques for describing the relationships between scores in two distributions.

Chapters 6, 7, and 8 each focus on a single aspect of test analysis. Chapter 6, on reliability, explains the theory behind reliability analysis and presents several techniques for determining test reliability. The chapter emphasizes the relationship between reliability and measurement error and the importance of considering measurement error when interpreting test scores. Chapter 7, on validity, begins with a discussion of the relationship between reliability and validity and the theory behind validity analysis. Different types of validity are defined and the analysis of each type is described in detail. The chapter emphasizes that the purpose of a test determines the appropriateness of any specific validity analysis. Chapter 8, on item analysis, shifts to analysis of the individual items within a test. The chapter explains how the statistical properties of test items can affect test reliability and validity and illustrates the calculation of different item statistics.

Working with Scores

CHAPTER OUTLINE

CHAPTER GOALS AND OBJECTIVES

After completing this chapter you should be able to:

- Differentiate between raw score and frequency distributions.
- Construct and interpret frequency tables and graphs.
- Calculate and interpret the three measures of central tendency and the three measures of variability.
- Differentiate between symmetric and skewed distributions.
- Describe the characteristics of the normal distribution.
- Calculate and interpret z-scores.
- Construct and interpret scatterplots.
- Calculate and interpret correlation coefficients.
- Calculate a regression equation from correlational data and use it to generate predicted scores.
- Describe the difference between linear and nonlinear transformations.
- Calculate and interpret T-scores, percentile ranks, and stanines.
- Describe the relationship between z-scores and percentiles in normal and nonnormal distributions.

$\mathbf{P}$ractically speaking, people learn about psychological testing so that they can design and/or select scientifically sound tests. These processes require an ability to calculate, in the design case, and interpret various test statistics. These statistics describe the psychometric properties of tests and their items, that is, their measurement characteristics. Although this may sound like a formidable task, these test analyses are based on a small number of statistical concepts and formulas. The purpose of this chapter is to identify the statistical concepts basic to test analysis and to illustrate their calculation using sets of test scores.

DESCRIBING A SET OF SCORES

In testing scenarios we typically work with scores earned by a group of people. They may be the scores on a class exam, a diagnostic test, an aptitude test—any type of test. A set of scores is called a *distribution*, and the characteristics represented by these scores are called *variables*, properties on which people differ (vary). When we test people to measure an attribute such as knowledge or skill, we produce a distribution of scores on that variable.

Raw Score Distributions

The simplest way to represent the performance of a group is in a *raw score distribution*, a table indicating the score earned by each member of the group. Table 5.1 presents two raw score distributions, the scores of a class on two homework assignments. By looking at the distributions, we can see the actual score earned by each group member. However, the format of the distribution makes it difficult to get a sense of the overall performance of the group.

Frequency Distributions

One way to develop a better sense of the performance of the group is by constructing a *frequency distribution*. Frequency distributions can be written as tables or drawn as graphs. There are some conventions for the construction of frequency distributions.

Frequency Tables

A frequency table contains two columns. The first column lists the scores; the second column lists how many times each score was earned. Scores are listed in *descending* order, with the highest score first. You can list only the scores

TABLE 5.1   Scores of 16 Students on Two Homework Assignments

Student	HW 1	HW 2
A	8	20
B	6	20
C	7	20
D	10	19
E	9	20
F	7	15
G	8	19
H	7	20
I	8	20
J	8	19
K	8	17
L	9	20
M	6	12
N	7	19
O	9	20
P	8	14

actually earned or all possible scores. If all scores are listed, those that no one earned receive a frequency of 0.

In statistical formulas, scores are usually represented as X's. In a frequency table, the score column is labeled X. The mathematical symbol for frequency is f. Therefore, the frequency column is labeled $f(X)$, read as "the frequency of score X." When constructing frequency distributions, you can check your work by adding a column for cumulative frequency, labeled $cf(X)$. Beginning at the bottom of the chart, add the frequencies *below* each score to the frequency *at* each score. Enter each total in the cumulative frequency column. The cumulative frequency listed next to the highest score in the distribution should equal the total number of people in the group.

When working with two sets of scores, the second set is usually labeled Y. The frequency column is therefore labeled $f(Y)$. Table 5.2 presents the scores on the two homework assignments in frequency tables. Note how much easier it is to get an idea about the group's performance on each assignment. On Homework 1, there were a few high scores and a few low scores, but most people performed somewhat in the middle. In contrast, on Homework 2, most people received very high scores! Notice also that some information is lost by organizing scores into frequency distributions. We can no longer determine which scores were earned by different group members.

TABLE 5.2   Frequency Tables for Scores on the Two Homeworks

Homework 1				Homework 2		
X	$f(X)$	$cf(X)$		Y	$f(Y)$	$cf(Y)$
10	1	16	$(2+4+6+3+1)$	20	8	16
9	3	15	$(2+4+6+3)$	19	4	8
8	6	12	$(2+4+6)$	18	0	4
7	4	6	$(2+4)$	17	1	4
6	2	2		16	0	3
				15	1	3
				14	1	2
				13	0	1
				12	1	1

Note: You can also check your work by adding the numbers in the frequency column. In the Homework 1 data, the sum of $f(X) = 16$; for Homework 2, the sum of $f(Y) = 16$.

Frequency Graphs

A frequency graph provides a pictorial representation of the frequency of test scores. By convention, scores are listed on the horizontal axis and the frequency of scores on the vertical axis. Scores and frequencies are listed in *ascending* order from the point where the two axes meet. The axes in a graph are number lines, and the points marked on them are like the numbers on a ruler. Once the lowest score and lowest frequency have been marked on the graph, scores and frequencies should be marked in consistent intervals. Graphs may use horizontal bars, individual points, or a line connecting individual points. Figure 5.1 presents the two sets of homework scores as frequency graphs.

Descriptive Statistics

A second way to describe the performance of a group is by the use of **descriptive statistics**, numbers that represent certain characteristics of the distribution. Descriptive statistics are used to summarize features of a set of scores and

FIGURE 5.1   Frequency graphs for scores on the two homeworks

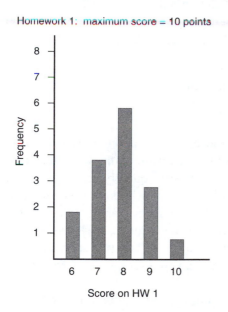

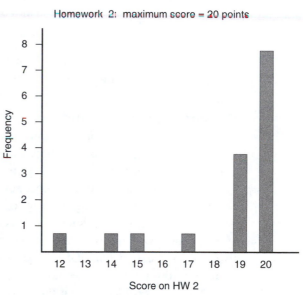

PRACTICE BOX 5.1 Frequency Tables and Frequency Graphs

Construct a frequency table and a frequency graph for each of the following raw score distributions:

Person	Quiz 1	Quiz 2	Quiz 3	Quiz 4
A	8	7	8	8
B	4	6	6	7
C	3	4	4	6
D	6	7	7	8
E	8	7	8	7
F	9	9	10	10
G	6	6	5	8
H	7	7	6	9
I	5	5	6	6
J	7	8	5	9
K	6	6	5	8
L	7	6	7	8
M	8	8	9	10
N	7	8	7	9
O	5	6	6	7

Check your answers against the answers at the end of the book. If you make any mistakes, reread the appropriate sections.

Note: Hold on to your answers to these practice problems. You will use these data sets throughout the chapter, and several exercises begin with the answers from an earlier practice box!

---

are necessary for statistical analysis of the scores. There are two categories of descriptive statistics: measures of central tendency and measures of variability.

Measures of Central Tendency

Measures of central tendency represent the center of a set of scores. This concept of *center* is interpreted three ways in three different measures of central tendency. The **mode** of the distribution is the most frequently occurring score. It is easily determined from a frequency distribution. Although it is simple to identify, it is the least useful measure of central tendency. One problem is that not all distributions are unimodal, that is, have a single mode. It is possible that several scores will tie as modes of the distribution. When two scores tie, the distribution is called *bimodal*.[1] When more than two scores tie in frequency, we usually do not report the mode.

A second problem is that the mode is not necessarily close to the middle score of the distribution. Look at the frequency distributions in Figure 5.1. The

---

[1]We may also call a distribution bimodal when two scores clearly are much more frequent than the other scores, even if their frequencies are unequal.

mode for Homework 1 is 8, which is in fact at the center of the distribution. However, the mode for Homework 2 is 20, which is the highest possible score. The mode is closest to the middle scores or center when the distribution has a bell-like shape, as in the case of Homework 1. A third problem is that the mode can be greatly affected by slight changes in frequencies. Look at the frequency distribution for Homework 1. If only two of the people who earned scores of 8 instead had earned scores of 7, the mode would shift to 7. In general, the mode is a reasonable index of the center of the distribution when the set of scores is symmetric and unimodal.

The second measure of central tendency is the **median** (Md), mentioned in our discussion of norm-referenced scores in Chapter 3. (Age- and grade-equivalent scores are based on the median score at each age or grade level.) The median is the score that divides the distribution into two equal parts so that half the scores are above and half below the median. It corresponds to the score at the 50th percentile of the distribution.

The median is easily determined from a frequency distribution. Divide the total number of scores in half and find the score whose cumulative frequency equals *half* the total number of scores. The score at that halfway point is the median. Look at the frequency distribution for Homework 2 in Table 5.2. A total of 16 people completed the homework. Half that number is 8; the median, therefore, is the score dividing the distribution into two 8-score halves. In terms of cumulative frequency, the median must fall between a cumulative frequency of 8 and a cumulative frequency of 9. Looking at the cumulative frequency column, you will see that a cumulative frequency of 8 occurs at a score of 19. The median of this distribution must fall between a score of 19 and a score of 20. Eight people received scores of 19 or lower, and eight people received scores of 20. In this case, the median is neither 19 nor 20. It is *halfway between* 19 and 20, or 19.5. This illustrates an important property of the median. The median is not always a score that occurs in the distribution. It is the score dividing the distribution in half, regardless of whether that score was earned by any member of the group.

Now look at the frequency distribution for Homework 1 in Table 5.2. There are 16 scores in the set, so the median again must fall between a cumulative frequency of 8 and a cumulative frequency of 9. But if you examine the cumulative frequency column in the table, you will discover that this is an impossible task. A score of 7 has a cumulative frequency of 6, meaning that 10 scores scores fall above 7. A score of 8 has a cumulative frequency of 12, with 4 scores above it. You cannot divide the distribution of Homework 1 scores into two equal parts from the data in the table.

The problem is solved by a mathematical procedure called *interpolation*. Interpolation assumes that the median occurs within an interval containing a subset of the test scores. By determining the limits of this interval and the proportion of scores in the interval that are below the median, we can assign a specific value to the median using the formula

$$Md = X_L + p_b(X_U - X_L)$$

in which

X_L = the lower limit of the median interval

p_b = the proportion of scores in the median interval that are below the median

X_U = the upper limit of the median interval

In the case of Homework 1 (Table 5.2), we want 8 scores to fall above the median and 8 below it. Four scores fall above a score of 8, six fall at a score of 8, and six fall below it. To reach our criterion of 8 above and 8 below the median, we need four of the six scores at 8 to fall above the median and the remaining two scores at 8 to fall below the median. In other words, the median must fall in the interval containing these six scores of 8. Although this may sound ridiculous, remember that all scores are only *estimates* of actual characteristics. We make two important assumptions in interpolation. First, we assume that scores of 8 represent scores within an actual interval of 7.5 to 8.5. Second, we assume that this set of scores is evenly distributed throughout this interval.

Now we have the information necessary to calculate the median of Homework 1. The upper limit of the interval, X_U, is 8.5; the lower limit, X_L, is 7.5. There are 6 scores in the interval, 2 of which must fall below the median. The value of p_b, the proportion of scores in the interval that are below the median, is $\frac{2}{6}$. Substituting into the formula,

$$Md = 7.5 + \tfrac{2}{6}(8.5 - 7.5) = 7.5 + .333(1) = 7.833$$

How good is the median as a measure of the center of the distribution? Remember how the median defines the concept of center. It is the middle of the distribution in terms of score frequencies. Rather than considering the *values* of the scores, the median focuses on how often different scores were earned. It identifies the center of the distribution in terms of score frequencies. It is the score dividing the distribution into two parts, each containing 50% of the scores.

How close is the median to the middle score in terms of score values? That depends on the shape of the distribution. The median is a reasonable representation of the central value in the distribution when the distribution is roughly symmetric. For scores on Homework 1, the median is around 8, which is roughly the center of the distribution. For scores on Homework 2, the median is 19.5. It is closer to the middle score value than the mode (20), yet it is still at the high end of the distribution. Perhaps you now can understand better our concern about age- and grade-equivalent scores. When we define the performance of the "average" child as the median score earned, we are not necessarily identifying a score in the center of the age or grade distribution.

The mode and median are based on the *frequency* with which different scores occur. The third measure of central tendency, the **mean** ($\overline{X}$ or M), focuses instead on score values. The mean is the average of the scores in the distribution. It is calculated by summing the scores and dividing by the number of scores. The process is represented by the formula

$$\overline{X} = \frac{\sum X}{N}$$

in which

$$\overline{X} = \text{the mean}$$
$$\sum X = \text{the sum of scores in the distribution}^2$$

The mean can be calculated from either a raw score or a frequency distribution. When calculating the mean from a raw score distribution, add all the scores and divide by N. When calculating the mean from a frequency distribution, multiply each score by its frequency, add the resulting numbers, and divide by N. Table 5.3 presents the calculation of the means for Homework 1 and Homework 2 using each of these methods.

Since the mean is the average of the scores in the distribution it is affected by the *value* of each score. For Homework 1, mode = 8, Md = 7.833, and $\overline{X} = 7.8125$. The mean is a little lower than both the mode and median because there are slightly more low scores (four 7's and two 6's) than high scores (three 9's and one 10). For Homework 2, mode = 20, Md = 19.5, and $\overline{Y} = 18.375$. The mean is lower than both the mode and the median because there are a few extremely low scores (one 12, one 14, and one 15). When added to the other scores, these scores lower the total points earned by the group and thus lower the mean. Even a single extremely high or low score will affect the value of the mean. The mean, therefore, represents the precise middle or center of the distribution in terms of score *values*. Because it reflects the value of all scores in the distribution, it is a powerful measure of central tendency and an element of many statistical analyses.

---

²*Note:* The Greek capital letter sigma ($\sum$) is the standard statistical notation for the operation of addition. $\sum X$ (read as "sigma X") means that you should add all the X's, all the scores in the distribution.

TABLE 5.3   Calculating the Mean from a Raw Score Distribution

Homework 1	Homework 2
X	Y
8	20
6	20
7	20
10	19
9	20
7	15
8	19
7	20
8	20
8	19
8	17
9	20
6	12
7	19
9	20
8	14
$\sum X = 125$	$\sum Y = 294$
$N = 16$	$N = 16$
$\overline{X} = \dfrac{125}{16} = 7.8125$	$\overline{Y} = \dfrac{294}{16} = 18.375$

Calculating the Mean from a Frequency Distribution

Homework 1			Homework 2		
X	$f(X)$	$X[f(X)]$	Y	$f(Y)$	$Y[f(Y)]$
10	1	10	20	8	160
9	3	27	19	4	76
8	6	48	17	1	17
7	4	28	15	1	15
6	2	12	14	1	14
			12	1	12

$$\sum X[f(X)] = 125 \qquad\qquad \sum Y[f(Y)] = 294$$

$$N = 16 \qquad\qquad\qquad N = 16$$

$$\overline{X} = \frac{125}{16} = 7.8125 \qquad\qquad \overline{Y} = \frac{294}{16} = 18.375$$

PRACTICE BOX 5.2   Measures of Central Tendency

Determine the mode, Md, and $\overline{X}$ for the distributions listed in Practice Box 5.1. Check your answers against the answers at the end of the book. If you make any mistakes, reread the appropriate sections.

Measures of Variability

The other category of descriptive statistics consists of *measures of variability*, statistics that summarize the degree to which scores in the distribution differ from each other. Measures of variability are also called measures of spread or dispersion because they indicate the extent to which scores are close together or spread out (i.e., the degree to which they are dispersed). Variability is a concept of extreme importance in psychological testing. A major use of tests is identification of individual differences (see Chapter 1). Measures of variability enable us to see the extent of individual differences in a set of test scores.

There are three measures of variability. The **range** is the difference between the highest and lowest scores in the distribution. It is the mathematically simplest measure of variability because it involves comparison of only two scores. Looking at the frequency distributions in Figure 5.1, the range for Homework 1 is 10 to 6, or 4 points. The range for Homework 2 is 20 to 12, or 8 points. These values seem reasonable since the scores on Homework 2 were in fact more spread out or dispersed than the Homework 1 scores. However, the range can give a misleading picture of the degree to which scores differ. Consider the graphs of scores of 20 students on three 100-point tests presented in Figure 5.2. In all three cases, the range is 95 to 75, or 20 points. Yet the distributions clearly do not reflect equivalent degrees of spread or dispersion. Students differed greatly from each other in performance on test A, earning a wide variety of scores between 75 and 95. On test B, students differed by a moderate amount, with many students scoring midway between 75 and 95. On test C, students differed little in their performance. In fact, the range of 20 points is due exclusively to the fact that one person earned a grade of 75. The range, then, is best viewed as a very gross or general measure of variability.

The second measure of variability, the **variance** (σ^2), is a more powerful statistic. Like the mean, the variance is affected by the value of every score in the distribution. The variance indicates the degree of spread by comparing every score to the mean of the distribution. Conceptually, the variance is the average squared deviation of scores from the mean. This definition actually generates one of the formulas for calculating variance, sometimes called the derivational formula:

$$\sigma^2 = \frac{\sum(X - \overline{X})^2}{N}$$

FIGURE 5.2 Three distributions with identical ranges

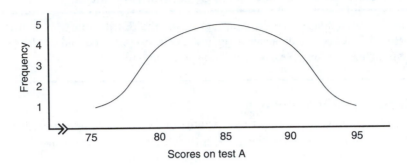

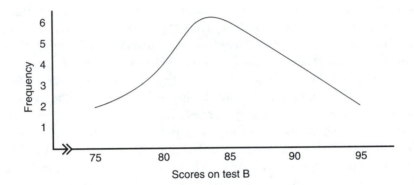

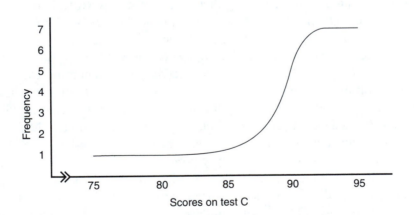

in which

$$\sigma^2 = \text{the variance}$$
$$X - \overline{X} = \text{the difference between each score and the mean}$$
$$(X - \overline{X})^2 = \text{the square of each (score} - \text{mean) difference}$$
$$\sum(X - \overline{X})^2 = \text{the sum of the squared (score} - \text{mean) differences}$$
$$N = \text{the total number of scores in the distribution}[3]$$

Examine the formula. The mean is subtracted from each score, resulting in a value called a *deviation score*. This deviation score reflects how much the raw score differs from or "deviates from" the mean. Each deviation score is squared and the resulting values are summed. The total of the squared deviations from the mean is then divided by the number of scores, producing the average of the squared deviations from the mean.

The variance is an important descriptive statistic, serving as a cornerstone of many statistical analyses. It is our principle measure of individual differences in test scores. However, when describing a set of scores, the variance has a major drawback. It represents the degree to which scores differ from the mean in *squared* units. This means, for example, that on a 100-point test with a mean of 75 the variance might be 225 points! The third measure of variability, the **standard deviation** (σ), compensates for the squaring operation in variance and presents information about dispersion on the same scale as the original raw scores. The standard deviation is calculated in the following way:

$$\sigma = \sqrt{\frac{\sum(X - \overline{X})^2}{N}}$$

or

$$\sigma = \sqrt{\sigma^2}$$

The standard deviation is literally the average deviation of scores from the mean in raw score (unsquared) units. It cannot be determined without going through the process of calculating the variance. You may recall a brief reference to standard deviation in the section on standard scores in Chapter 3 (see p. 84). The standard deviation is a basic component for calculating all standard scores.

Why such a long process to obtain a measure of variability on the same scale as the raw scores themselves? Deviation scores have an interesting feature. Examine Table 5.4, which uses the derivational formula to calculate σ^2 and

---

[3]In many statistical writings we draw a distinction between a complete group of people or population and a subset of people drawn from that group or sample. In such instances, the sample standard deviation is represented by s or SD, and σ refers to the population standard deviation as estimated from the sample data. The formula for s or SD uses $N - 1$ instead of N in the denominator.

σ for Homeworks 1 and 2. Look closely at the columns labeled $(X - \overline{X})$ and $(Y - \overline{Y})$. If you add these deviation scores without first squaring them, they will always total to 0. The 0 sum results from the fact that the mean is the precise middle value in the distribution. There will always be as many deviation points above it as below it. Therefore, the *sum* of the deviation scores cannot be used as a mechanism to develop a measure of variability. This problem is eliminated by summing the *squared* deviation scores to obtain the variance. If a measure in raw score units is needed, we compensate for the squaring operation by taking the square root of the variance. Note also that when deviation scores are squared a score that is below the mean is treated identically to a score that is equally far above the mean. In variance, the critical issue is the score's *distance* from the mean, not its *position* relative to the mean.

TABLE 5.4 Calculating Variance Using the Derivational Formula

Homework 1				Homework 2		
X	$(X - \overline{X})$	$(X - \overline{X})^2$		Y	$(Y - \overline{Y})$	$(Y - \overline{Y})^2$
8	0.1875	0.0351		20	1.625	2.6406
6	−1.812	3.2851		20	1.625	2.6406
7	−0.812	0.6601		20	1.625	2.6406
10	2.1875	4.7851		19	0.625	0.3906
9	1.1875	1.4101		20	1.625	2.6406
7	−0.812	0.6601		15	−3.375	11.390
8	0.1875	0.0351		19	0.625	0.3906
7	−0.812	0.6601		20	1.625	2.6406
8	0.1875	0.0351		20	1.625	2.6406
8	0.1875	0.0351		19	0.625	0.3906
8	0.1875	0.0351		17	−1.375	1.8906
9	1.1875	1.4101		20	1.625	2.6406
6	−1.812	3.2851		12	−6.375	40.640
7	−0.812	0.6601		19	0.625	0.3906
9	1.1875	0.0351		20	1.625	2.6406
8	0.1875	0.0351		14	−4.375	19.140
$\Sigma = 0$		18.437		$\Sigma = 0$		95.75
$N = 16$				$N = 16$		

$$\sigma^2 = \frac{\Sigma(X - \overline{X})^2}{N}$$

$$\sigma_X^2 = \frac{18.437}{16} = 1.1523 \qquad\qquad \sigma_Y^2 = \frac{95.75}{16} = 5.9844$$

$$\sigma_X = \sqrt{1.1523} = 1.0735 \qquad\qquad \sigma_Y = \sqrt{5.9844} = 2.4463$$

Note: Much of the repeated calculation in these tables can be eliminated by the use of frequency tables.

The preceding formula is useful for explaining what variance measures. It is not, however, one we use for actual calculation of variance and standard deviation. The calculations required by this formula would be rather tedious, producing strings of decimals that must then be squared. When we calculate variance and standard deviation, we use the following *computational* formula:

$$\sigma^2 = \frac{\sum X^2 - (\sum X)^2/N}{N}$$

in which

$$\sum X = \text{the sum of the raw scores}$$
$$(\sum X)^2 = \text{the square of the sum of the raw scores}$$
$$X^2 = \text{each raw score squared}$$
$$\sum X^2 = \text{the sum of the squared raw scores}$$
$$N = \text{the total number of scores}$$

As with the previous formula for variance,

$$\sigma = \sqrt{\sigma^2}$$

The computational formula eliminates the need to work with fractional numbers, greatly simplifying the calculations. It requires, however, close attention to the order of operations. The term $(\sum X)^2$ calls first for *adding* the scores and then *squaring* the total. The term $\sum X^2$ calls first for *squaring* each raw score and then *adding* the squared scores. One way to keep the two summation terms straight is to remember that the variance is always a *positive* number. This is to be expected, since it is the average *squared* deviations of scores from the mean. (And, since the standard deviation is the square root of the variance, it too is always a positive number.) If you reverse the two summation terms, it is likely that you will generate a negative variance, alerting you to your error. Table 5.5 presents the calculation of variance and standard deviation for Homeworks 1 and 2 using the computational formula. Note that the values obtained through this procedure are identical to those obtained through the derivational formula.

The variance and standard deviation in essence provide the same type of dispersion information. Both are precise measures of the average amount by which scores differ from the mean. They differ in their unit of measurement. The variance uses a scale of *squared* raw score units, whereas the standard deviation uses the original raw score scale. When describing a set of scores, we typically report standard deviation. For example, a standard deviation of 15 points on a 100-point test means that the average amount by which scores differed from the mean was 15 points. Obviously, some scores may differ by more than 15 points and some by less than 15 points.

TABLE 5.5 Calculating Variance Using the Computational Formula

Homework 1			Homework 2	
X	X^2		Y	Y^2
8	64		20	400
6	36		20	400
7	49		20	400
10	100		19	361
9	81		20	400
7	49		15	225
8	64		19	361
7	49		20	400
8	64		20	400
8	64		19	361
8	64		17	289
9	81		20	400
6	36		12	144
7	49		19	361
9	81		20	400
8	64		14	196
$\sum X = \overline{125}$	$\sum X^2 = \overline{995}$		$\sum Y = \overline{294}$	$\sum Y^2 = \overline{5498}$
$N = 16$			$N = 16$	

$$\sigma^2 = \frac{\sum X^2 - [(\sum X)^2/N]}{N}$$

$$\sigma_X^2 = \frac{995 - [(125)^2/16]}{16} \qquad\qquad \sigma_Y^2 = \frac{5498 - [(294)^2/16]}{16}$$

$$\sigma_X^2 = \frac{995 - 976.5625}{16} = 1.1523 \qquad\qquad \sigma_Y^2 = \frac{5498 - 5402.25}{16} = 5.9844$$

$$\sigma_X = \sqrt{1.1523} = 1.0735 \qquad\qquad \sigma_Y = \sqrt{5.9844} = 2.4463$$

Note: Much of the repeated calculation in these tables can be eliminated by the use of frequency tables.

PRACTICE BOX 5.3 Measures of Variability

Determine the range, σ^2, and σ for the distributions listed in Practice Box 5.1. Check your answers against the answers at the end of the book. If you make any mistakes, reread the appropriate sections.

Shapes of Distributions

The shape of a distribution is determined by the frequency with which different scores occur. The shape is easily seen in a frequency graph. The graphs of homework scores in Figure 5.1 and of test scores in Figure 5.2 illustrate some of the types of score distributions. One obvious difference among the various graphs is in symmetry. If you were to draw lines down the center of each graph, some of the distributions would be divided into two similar looking shapes. Others clearly would not. One basic distinction between the shapes of distributions is between symmetric or skewed.[4]

Symmetric Distributions

Symmetric distributions have parallel patterns of score frequencies at complementary points in the score distribution. When a line is drawn down the center of the graph of a symmetric distribution, the resulting halves are mirror images of each other. The scores on Homework 1 (Figure 5.1) and on test A (Figure 5.2) are roughly symmetric. Figure 5.3 illustrates several other types of symmetric distributions. Notice that the distributions can differ greatly in their absolute shapes and in the extent of variability of scores. However, in symmetric distributions, the mean and median are about equal. The mode is not necessarily related to these other central tendency measures; symmetric distributions can be unimodal, bimodal, or without a mode. The mean, median, and mode are equal only in distributions that are symmetric *and* unimodal.

A symmetric distribution with special characteristics is the **normal distribution** or **normal curve**, illustrated in Figure 5.4. The normal distribution is bell shaped and unimodal, with mode = Md = $\overline{X}$. In addition, specific percentages of scores occur at precise points within the distribution. Look carefully at Figure 5.4. Using the standard deviation (σ) to mark points along the distribution, approximately 34% of the scores fall between the $\overline{X}$ and $\overline{X} + 1\sigma$. Because the distribution is symmetric, approximately 34% of the scores also fall between $\overline{X}$ and $\overline{X} - 1\sigma$. An additional 13.5% fall between $\overline{X} + 1\sigma$ and $\overline{X} + 2\sigma$ and between $\overline{X} + 1\sigma$ and $\overline{X} - 2\sigma$. The remainder of the scores fall at the two extremes. Because of these characteristics, certain predictable relationships exist between different types of scores which will be discussed later in this chapter. Many of the variables studied through psychological testing do in fact produce sets of scores that are close to normally distributed. In these cases we can take advantage of the properties of the normal distribution when transforming scores from one type of score to another.

[4]Not all distributions fit neatly into these two categories. Some distributions have unique shapes that cannot be classified.

FIGURE 5.3   Examples of symmetric distributions

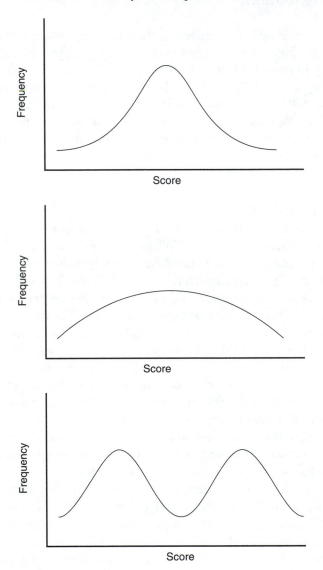

How do we know what percentage of scores falls between different standard deviation marks? The normal distribution is a sampling distribution that
can be generated through a mathematical equation. The equation determines
the probability or frequency of occurrence of different scores, given a specific mean and standard deviation. The normal distribution is important in

FIGURE 5.4 The normal distribution

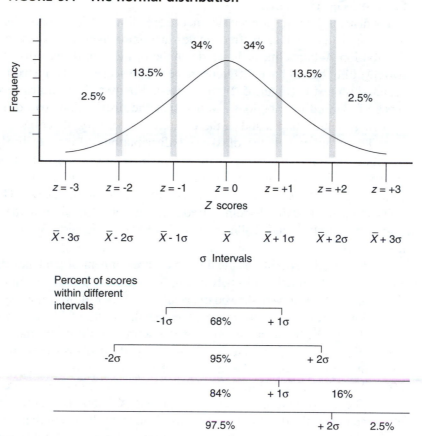

statistical analysis because it represents the theoretical distribution of events as determined by chance. For example, imagine tossing a coin 100 times. In the world of perfectly random events, you would expect 50 tosses to come up heads and 50 tosses to come up tails. But, in reality, it is *possible* that 75 tosses would be heads. It even is possible, although unlikely, that 99 would be heads. The equation generating the normal distribution can be used to determine the probability of each of these outcomes, from 0 heads per 100 tosses to 100 heads per 100 tosses. The symmetric bell shape corresponds to the fact that the most likely outcome is 50 heads per 100 tosses, with numbers approaching 0 or 100 heads per 100 tosses becoming increasingly less likely.

Skewed Distributions

Many distributions that are not symmetric are *skewed*. Skewed distributions have different patterns of score frequencies at complementary points in the score distribution. When a line is drawn down the center of a skewed distribution, the two resulting halves have different shapes. The scores on Homework 2 (Figure 5.1) and on test C (Figure 5.2) are skewed. Figure 5.5 illustrates several other types of skewed distributions. Notice that the distributions can differ greatly in their absolute shapes and in the extent of variability of scores.

There are two types of skewed distributions. In a positively skewed distribution, there are fewer high scores than low scores. In a negatively skewed distribution, there are fewer low scores than high scores. The area containing the *fewest* scores determines the name of the skew. The type of skew is easily identified from a frequency graph. Looking at the graphs in Figure 5.5, tests 1 and 2 illustrate positive skew and tests 3 and 4 illustrate negative skew.

In skewed distributions the three measures of central tendency differ from each other. The relationship between them depends on the type of skew in the distribution. In *positively* skewed distributions, $\overline{X} > \text{Md}$. More of the scores are at the low end of the distribution, lowering the value of Md (the 50% mark). The value of $\overline{X}$, the average value of the scores, is raised by the presence of a few high scores. Conversely, in *negatively* skewed distributions, $\overline{X} < \text{Md}$. More of the scores are at the high end of the distribution, raising the value of Md. The value of $\overline{X}$ is lowered by the presence of a few low scores.

When distributions are seriously skewed, $\overline{X}$ is not as useful as a measure of the center of the distribution. This can lead to problems in the use of certain statistical analyses, which assume that the distribution is roughly symmetric.

RELATIONSHIP BETWEEN SCORES IN A DISTRIBUTION

Once the performance of the group as a whole has been described, the focus moves to comparison of the scores within the distribution. Many testing scenarios focus on the measurement of individual differences (see Chapter 2, norm-referenced scores). In these contexts it is important to know how people performed relative to each other. Although raw scores, such as number of points earned or percentage correct (number of points earned/total number of points possible) differentiate higher scores from lower scores, the *relative* meaning of a particular raw score may vary in different distributions. A grade of 90 on a test with $\overline{X} = 75$ is a very good score; a grade of 90 on a test with $\overline{X} = 92$ is "about average." Thus, the mean of a test can influence the interpretation of a raw score.

FIGURE 5.5   Examples of skewed distributions

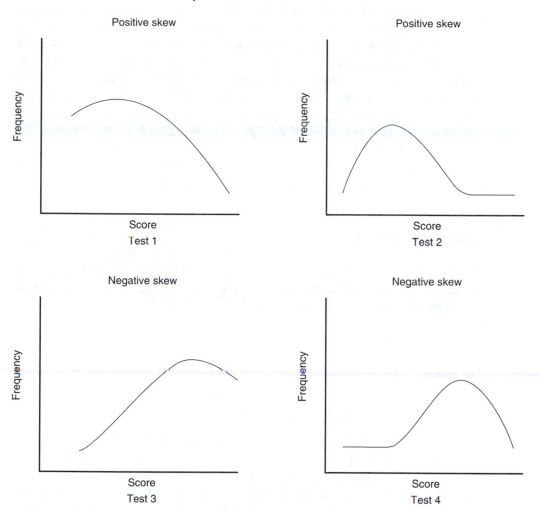

Knowing where a score falls relative to the mean, however, is not really enough. The degree of variability in test scores can also influence the interpretation of a score. Consider a 100-point test with $\overline{X} = 75$ and $\sigma = 15$. Since the standard deviation (σ) is the average amount by which scores differ from the mean, the scores falling at the average distance from the mean are 60 ($\overline{X} + \sigma$) and 90 ($\overline{X} - \sigma$). Now consider a 100-point test with $\overline{X} = 75$ and $\sigma = 7$. There is considerably less variability in this second test. The scores at this "average distance" are 68 and 82. Although a score of 90 is above the mean on both of these tests, it is one standard deviation above the mean on the first test and more than two standard deviations above the mean on the second. To express the relationship between a raw score and the mean and standard deviation of the distribution, the raw score is converted to a **standard score**.

Standard Scores

As we discussed in Chapter 3 (p. 84), the simplest type of standard score is the **z-score**. A z-score indicates the location of a raw score relative to the mean in standard deviation units. The formula for calculating a z-score is

$$z = \frac{X - \overline{X}}{\sigma}$$

in which

X = a raw score in the distribution

$\overline{X}$ = the mean of the distribution

σ = the standard deviation of the distribution

The transformation of a raw score to a z-score uses the mean and standard deviation of the distribution in which the score occurs. The relationship between a raw score value and a z-score, therefore, is specific to a particular distribution. The same raw score might generate very different z-scores if the mean and/or standard deviation was different. Note also that raw scores falling above the mean will always convert to positive z-scores and scores falling below the mean to negative z-scores. Any score in a distribution can be converted to a z-score, even the mean itself. When the mean is converted to a raw score, it is subtracted from itself. Thus, the mean always converts to a z-score of 0.

To interpret z-scores, just remember how they are defined. A raw score converting to a z-score of 1.5 is one and one-half standard deviations above the mean. A raw score converting to a z-score of -1.0 is one standard deviation below the mean. The mean, with a z-score of 0, is 0 standard deviations below the mean, which might sound odd but is mathematically true. When calculating z-scores, the actual values of $\overline{X}$ and σ do not matter. Any score equal to $\overline{X} + 1\sigma$

will convert to a z-score of 1.0, any score equal to $\overline{X} - 2\sigma$ will convert to a z-score of -2.0, and so on. Table 5.6 demonstrates the calculation of z-scores for the grades of Homeworks 1 and 2.

Standard scores such as z-scores are very useful in testing. First, z-scores represent a precise way of indicating position within a distribution using an internal scale of measurement. Second, they can be used to compare the performance of individuals on a single measure or the performance of a specific person on several different measures. Although tests may differ in their raw score means and raw score standard deviations, once test scores are converted to z-scores, all test distributions are on the same scale. A student who earns a z-score of 1.5 on one test and a z-score of 0.5 on the other performed better *relative to his or her* classmates on the first test.

One final point: For all z-score distributions, $\overline{X}_z = 0$ and $\sigma_z = 1$. On a z-score scale a raw score equal to $\overline{X}$ becomes a z of 0. Because there are the same number of deviation points above and below the mean (see Table 5.4),

TABLE 5.6   Computation of z-Scores for Homework 1 and Homework 2

$$z = \frac{X - \overline{X}}{\sigma}$$

Homework 1			Homework 2		
$\overline{X} = 7.8125, \quad \sigma_X = 1.0735$			$\overline{Y} = 18.375, \quad \sigma_Y = 2.4463$		
X	$(X - \overline{X})$	z_X	Y	$(Y - \overline{Y})$	z_Y
8	0.1875	0.174663	20	1.625	0.664287
6	−1.8125	−1.68841	20	1.625	0.664287
7	−0.8125	−0.75687	20	1.625	0.664287
10	2.1875	2.037746	19	0.625	0.255495
9	1.1875	1.106204	20	1.625	0.664287
7	−0.812	−0.75687	15	−3.375	−1.37967
8	0.1875	0.174663	19	0.625	0.255495
7	−0.812	−0.75687	20	1.625	0.664287
8	0.1875	0.174663	20	1.625	0.664287
8	0.1875	0.174663	19	0.625	0.255495
8	0.1875	0.174663	17	−1.375	−0.56208
9	1.1875	1.106204	20	1.625	0.664287
6	−1.812	−1.68841	12	−6.375	−2.60605
7	−0.812	−0.75687	19	0.625	0.255495
9	1.1875	1.106204	20	1.625	0.664287
8	0.1875	0.174663	14	−4.375	−1.78846

Note: Much of the repeated calculation in these tables can be eliminated by the use of frequency tables.

PRACTICE BOX 5.5   Calculating z-Scores

Calculate the z-scores for the scores in the Practice Box 5.1 distributions. Present your answer for each quiz in a summary table including raw scores and z-scores. (Try using frequency distributions to eliminate redundant calculations.) Check your answers against the answers at the end of the book. If you make any mistakes, reread the appropriate sections.

---

the sum of a set of z-scores must equal 0. It follows then that the mean of any z-score distribution must also be 0. And because a raw score distance of one standard deviation converts to a z-score distance of one unit, the standard deviation of any z-score distribution must be 1.

RELATIONSHIP BETWEEN TWO DISTRIBUTIONS

Scatterplots

Often in psychological testing we work with two sets of scores. We might be trying to predict grades from scores on a pretest, examining the relationship between two administrations of the same test, or determining whether two forms of a test are in fact equivalent. The simplest way to see the relationship between two sets of scores is with a graph called a **scatterplot**. The scores could be two tests given to the same group of people, the same test given to two different groups of people, or even two different tests given to a single group. The critical element is to have each score on one variable paired with a score on the other.

To make a scatterplot, the two sets of scores are paired *by person* to reveal, for each member of the group, the scores earned on both variables. Look again at Table 5.1, which lists the grade earned by each person on Homeworks 1 and 2. To make a scatterplot of the relationship between homework grades, one variable is placed along each axis. This relationship is graphed in Figure 5.6. If the two sets of scores were obtained in a particular order, the one obtained *first* (X) is placed on the horizontal axis. In this case, students completed Homework 1 first, so it is placed on the horizontal axis in Figure 5.6. Each point on the graph represents the scores earned by a particular person on the two variables (the two homeworks). Remember that you cannot create a scatterplot unless each score on one variable is paired with its corresponding score on the other.

A graph of the relationship between two sets of scores also has a particular shape. One analysis of the shape of the relationship looks at the ex-

FIGURE 5.6   Scatterplot of the relationship between scores on Homework 1 and Homework 2

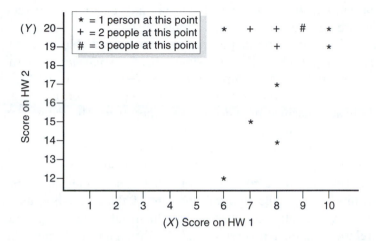

tent to which the points fall on or near a straight line. The presence of a straight line on a scatterplot indicates a *linear relationship* between the two sets of scores. Linear relationships imply that we can make specific predictions about performance on one variable from the person's performance on the other variable. The relationship graphed in Figure 5.6 clearly is not linear. Why? Look closely at Figure 5.6. Quite a few people received perfect scores (20's) on Homework 2. If the relationship between homework grades were linear, we would expect these people to have also received high scores on Homework 1. In fact, people with grades from 6 to 9 on Homework 1 received 20's on Homework 2, and the one person with a perfect Homework 1 score earned a 19 on Homework 2! Can we predict a person's grade on Homework 2 from his or her grade on Homework 1? Obviously not.

Correlation

Correlation is a mathematical measure of the relationship between two variables. Although a scatterplot can visually illustrate the degree of linear relationship between variables, a correlation coefficient indicates the exact degree of linear relationship with a single number. Correlations differ in two parameters: size and sign. The size of a correlation, represented by its distance from 0, indicates the *strength* or degree of linear relationship between two variables. A value close to 1 indicates a strong relationship. The closer to 1 that the value is, the more likely it is that the points will fall close to a straight line in a scatterplot. The sign of a correlation, either + or −, indicates the *pattern* of the relationship. A positive correlation (+) indicates that high scores on one variable are accompanied by high scores on the other. The relationship can be summarized by saying that an increase on one variable is accompanied by an increase on the other. The plus sign indicates a *matching* pattern of change on the two variables. A negative correlation (−) indicates that high scores on one variable are accompanied by low scores on the other; an increase on one variable is accompanied by a decrease on the other. The minus sign indicates an *opposite* pattern of change on the two variables.

There are three important features of correlations. First, a correlation can never be greater than 1 or less than −1. Correlation assesses degree of linear relationship, and a correlation of either 1 or −1 indicates a perfect linear relationship. Second, the sign and the size of the correlation are interpreted separately. A correlation of −.8 is stronger than and indicates a greater degree of linear relationship than a correlation of .6. The sign is irrelevant to interpreting the strength of the correlation. Third, the variables being correlated need not have similar means, variances, or ranges. We can correlate overall SAT scores (values ranging from 400 to 800) with number of math courses taken in high school (values ranging from 1 to 4).

How can we correlate variables with such different values? The key is the procedure correlation uses to determine degree of linear relationship. When variables use an interval scale of measurement, correlation can be represented conceptually as

$$r_{XY} = \frac{\sum z_X z_Y}{N}$$

in which

z_X = the z-scores for scores on variable X

z_Y = the z-scores for scores on variable Y

$z_X z_Y$ = each z_X-score times its corresponding z_Y-score

$\sum z_X z_Y$ = the sum of all z_X-scores times their z_Y-scores

N = the number of pairs of scores (equal to the number of people in the group under study)

Now you can see why we can correlate very different types of scores. The procedure converts the raw scores to z-scores. If raw scores are converted to z-scores, they are changed to a common scale of measurement. Remember that for all z-score distributions $\overline{X}_z = 0$ and $\sigma_z = 1$.

This type of correlation is called the Pearson correlation and it is used only with interval/ratio scale data. The preceding method of representing the correlation, sometimes called the *derivational formula*, illustrates the underlying principle of the Pearson correlation. If a linear relationship exists between the two variables, each pair of scores should produce a pair of similar z-scores. Individuals above the mean on one variable should be above the mean by an equivalent amount on the other variable. Individuals below the mean on one variable should be equivalently below the mean on the other. In essence, correlation examines the degree to which individuals earn precisely the same positions *relative to each other* on the two variables.

As in the case of variance, the derivational formula typically is not used for the actual calculation of correlations. Multiplying, adding, and averaging so many z-scores would be extremely difficult. This process is illustrated in Table 5.7. All raw scores are converted to z-scores, which are then multiplied, added, and divided by N. The resulting correlation is positive and rather low, .36 on a scale that ranges from 0 to 1.0. Look again at the scatterplot of the relationship in Figure 5.6. The points do not fall close to a straight line, indicating that the correlation should be low. Cross-checking a correlation against a scatterplot is a useful way to alert yourself to possible calculation errors.

TABLE 5.7 Calculation of Correlation between Homeworks 1 and 2 Using the z-Score Formula

Homework 1		Homework 2		
X	z_X	Y	z_Y	$z_X z_Y$
8	0.174663	20	0.664287	0.116027
6	−1.68841	20	0.664287	−1.12159
7	−0.75687	20	0.664287	−0.50278
10	2.037746	19	0.255495	0.520634
9	1.106204	20	0.664287	0.734838
7	−0.75687	15	−1.37967	1.044243
8	0.174663	19	0.255495	0.044625
7	−0.75687	20	0.664287	−0.50278
8	0.174663	20	0.664287	0.116027
8	0.174663	19	0.255495	0.044625
8	0.174663	17	−0.56208	−0.09817
9	1.106204	20	0.664287	0.734838
6	−1.68841	12	−2.60605	4.400103
7	−0.75687	19	0.255495	−0.19337
9	1.106204	20	0.664287	0.734838
8	0.174663	14	−1.78846	−0.31238

$$\sum z_X z_Y = 5.759703$$

$$r_{XY} = \frac{\sum z_X z_Y}{N} = .35998 = .36$$

There are a variety of simpler calculation formulas for correlation. The most frequently taught computational formula for correlation is the *raw score formula*:

$$r_{XY} = \frac{N \sum XY - (\sum X)(\sum Y)}{\sqrt{N \sum X^2 - (\sum X)^2} \; \sqrt{N \sum Y^2 - (\sum Y)^2}}$$

in which

XY = each X-score times its corresponding Y-score

$\sum XY$ = the sum of all the XY cross-products

$\sum X$ = the sum of all the X-scores

$\sum Y$ = the sum of all the Y-scores

$\sum X^2$ = the sum of all the squared X-scores

$\sum Y^2$ = the sum of all the squared Y-scores

Table 5.8 presents the calculation of the same correlation using the raw score formula. Note that this formula produces the same value as the derivational one.

On the other hand, one of the simplest versions is the *means and standard deviations* formula:

$$r_{XY} = \frac{[\sum XY / N] - (\overline{X})(\overline{Y})}{(\sigma_X)(\sigma_Y)}$$

in which

$\sum XY$ = the sum of each X-score times its Y-score

N = the total number of pairs of scores

$\overline{X}$ = the mean of the X distribution

$\overline{Y}$ = the mean of the Y distribution

σ_X = the standard deviation of the X distribution

σ_Y = the standard deviation of the Y distribution

This may be a useful shortcut formula if you have already calculated the means and standard deviations of the distributions. You need only calculate $\sum XY / N$ to determine the correlation. However, to avoid introducing error by using rounded off values, the means and standard deviations should be taken to at least 4 decimal places. Table 5.9 illustrates the use of this formula to calculate the correlation between the grades of Homeworks 1 and 2. Notice that the correlation produced by this formula is identical to the correlation resulting from the other two formulas.

There are important similarities in the interpretation of correlations and z-scores. In both cases the size and sign of the measures convey independent

**TABLE 5.8 Calculation of Correlation between Homeworks 1 and 2
Using the Raw Score Formula**

Homework 1		Homework 2		
X	X^2	Y	Y^2	$(X)(Y)$
8	64	20	400	160
6	36	20	400	120
7	49	20	400	140
10	100	19	361	190
9	81	20	400	180
7	49	15	225	105
8	64	19	361	152
7	49	20	400	140
8	64	20	400	160
8	64	19	361	152
8	64	17	289	136
9	81	20	400	180
6	36	12	144	72
7	49	19	361	133
9	81	20	400	180
8	64	14	196	112
$\sum X = 125$	$\sum X^2 = 995$	$\sum Y = 294$	$\sum Y^2 = 5498$	$\sum XY = 2312$
				$N = 16$

$$r_{XY} = \frac{N \sum XY - (\sum X)(\sum Y)}{\sqrt{N \sum X^2 - (\sum X)^2}\sqrt{N \sum Y^2 - (\sum Y)^2}}$$

$$= \frac{16(2312) - (125)(294)}{\sqrt{16(995) - (125)^2}\sqrt{16(5498) - (294)^2}}$$

$$= \frac{36{,}992 - 36{,}750}{\sqrt{15{,}920 - 15{,}625}\sqrt{87{,}968 - 86{,}436}} = \frac{242}{\sqrt{295}\sqrt{1532}}$$

$$= \frac{242}{(17.175564)(39.140772)} = \frac{242}{672.26483} = .3599 = .36$$

pieces of information that can be interpreted separately. The size of a correlation, regardless of its sign, represents the strength of the linear relationship; the size of a z-score, disregarding its sign, represents the score's distance from the mean in standard deviation units. The sign of a correlation, whatever its size, represents the pattern of the relationship, just as the sign of a z-score indicates the score's position as above or below the mean. In other words, the size of both measures represents something about degree or amount, whereas the sign of both measures represents something about pattern or location.

The similarities explain how the size and sign of a correlation are affected by the sizes and signs of the z-scores in the set. The *size* of the correlation reflects the degree to which each person received z-scores of comparable size

TABLE 5.9 Calculation of Correlation between Homeworks 1 and 2 Using the Means and Standard Deviations Formula

Homework 1		Homework 2		
X	X^2	Y	Y^2	$(X)(Y)$
8	64	20	400	160
6	36	20	400	120
7	49	20	400	140
10	100	19	361	190
9	81	20	400	180
7	49	15	225	105
8	64	19	361	152
7	49	20	400	140
8	64	20	400	160
8	64	19	361	152
8	64	17	289	136
9	81	20	400	180
6	36	12	144	72
7	49	19	361	133
9	81	20	400	180
8	64	14	196	112

$$\overline{X} = 7.8125 \qquad \overline{Y} = 18.375 \qquad \sum XY = 2312$$

$$\sigma_X = 1.07349 \qquad \sigma_Y = 2.44623 \qquad N = 16$$

$$r_{XY} = \frac{[\sum XY/N] - (\overline{X})(\overline{Y})}{(\sigma_X)(\sigma_Y)}$$

$$= \frac{(2312/16) - (7.8125)(18.375)}{(1.07349)(2.44623)}$$

$$= \frac{144.5 - 143.5546}{2.626}$$

$$= \frac{.9453}{2.626} = .3599 = .36$$

on the two measures. A high correlation (close to +1 or −1) indicates that each person received z-scores of about the same on both measures. In other words, each member fell about the same distance from the mean, in standard deviation units, on each measure. A low correlation (close to 0) implies that the members of the group did not earn parallel z-scores on the two measures. The *sign* of the correlation reflects the signs of the z-score pairs. If the z-scores on both measures are positive or negative, $(z_X)(z_Y)$ will produce a positive number. If most pairs of z-scores have parallel signs, the correlation will be positive, indicating that people fell either above or below the mean on both measures.

If the z-scores have opposite signs, one positive and one negative, $(z_X)(z_Y)$ will produce a negative number. If most pairs of scores have opposite signs, the correlation will be negative. A negative correlation indicates that people who fell above the mean on one measure fell below the mean on the other, and vice versa.

Correlation is a statistic of great importance in psychological testing. Just as standard scores like z-scores enable us to compare individual scores *within* distributions, correlation enables us to compare score relationships *across* distributions. Correlation is the statistic used in most reliability and validity analyses. In both cases we are interested in whether people earn the same positions relative to each other on two sets of scores.

Correlations can be interpreted qualitatively or quantitatively. Qualitatively, a correlation can be described as high, moderate, or low (size) and as positive or negative (sign). The relationship evaluated by a correlation can be described as strong, moderate, or weak (size) and as positive or inverse (sign). These are rather general statements about the value of the statistic and the nature of the underlying relationship. A more precise quantitative interpretation uses a variance proportion to describe the extent to which scores on one variable can be used to predict scores on the other. The variance proportion equals the square of the correlation. It is represented symbolically as r_{XY}^2 and is called the **coefficient of determination**. The resulting fraction is interpreted as the percent of variance predictable from the relationship between the two measures.

Before you panic, let's use the two sets of homework scores as an example of this process. Suppose we are interested in predicting scores on Homework 2 from scores on Homework 1. The correlation between them is .36, so $r_{XY}^2 = .13$. This means that 13% of the variance on Homework 2 is related to or predictable from Homework 1 scores. Conversely, 87% of the variance on Homework 2 is unrelated to or not predictable from Homework 1 scores. But what does this really mean? The variance on Homework 2 is a number, 5.9844, representing the extent of differences between people in Homework 2 scores. The coefficient of determination value of .13 means that our prediction about Homework 2 variance would be only about 13% accurate. Instead of generating a set of Homework 2 scores with $\sigma^2 = 5.9844$, we would generate a set of Homework 2 scores with $\sigma^2 = 13\%$ of 5.9844 or 0.778. Our predicted set of scores would not vary as much as the actual set of scores because we cannot predict the remaining 87% of Homework 2 variance (5.9844 − .778 or 5.2064 units) from Homework 1 scores. Basically, the coefficient of determination indicates the precise proportion of variance that we can accurately predict.

Students make several common mistakes when interpreting variance estimates. Our .13 does not mean that 13% of the people received similar raw scores or z-scores on the two homeworks. It also does not mean that we can accurately predict 13% of the *scores* on one homework from scores on the

---

PRACTICE BOX 5.6 Calculating Correlations

Using the distributions in Practice Box 5.1, calculate the correlation between performance on Quiz 1 and Quiz 3 and between Quiz 2 and Quiz 4 using (a) the raw score formula and (b) the means and standard deviations formula. Check your answers against the answers at the end of the book. If you make any mistakes, reread the appropriate sections.

---

other homework. It means we can predict 13% of the *variance* or differences between people in scores on one homework from scores on the other.

MAKING PREDICTIONS FROM THE RELATIONSHIP BETWEEN SCORES

Many of the contexts within which we use psychological tests involve making predictions. From correlation we can infer about the accuracy of our predictions. If a correlation is high, whether positive or negative, we know that one set of scores can be predicted reasonably well from the other. Often we are interested in actually taking the next step and predicting that other set of scores. For example, assume we are developing an admissions policy for a college or university. We are interested in whether or not SAT scores are useful predictors of success at our institution. We admit a large group of students who have taken the SAT and monitor their progress. At the end of their freshman year, we correlate SAT with freshman GPA and discover a correlation of .8, a relatively high correlation. From our study of correlation we know that $.8^2$ or 64% of the differences between people (variance) in freshman GPA are predictable from their SAT scores. Considering all the factors that affect grades during the freshman year, a single test being able to predict 64% of these differences is remarkable. Now we want to determine an SAT cutoff score for admitting students in the future, a score dividing prospective students into those likely to succeed during the freshman year and those unlikely to succeed. How can we do this?

Linear Regression

Through **linear regression** we can predict the specific score a person might receive on one variable given a particular score on another variable. Linear regression is usually used after a correlational analysis indicates that a reasonably good relationship exists between two measures. In linear regression we construct an equation called the *regression equation* for predicting one set of scores from the other set. The form of the regression equation is

$$Y' = a + bX$$

in which

Y' = the predicted Y score for this X score

X = the X score used in the prediction

b = the slope, or change in Y score per unit change in X score, calculated as $b = (r)\sigma_Y/\sigma_X$

a = the Y-intercept, which adjusts for the scale change when going from X score to Y score, calculated as $a = \overline{Y} - (b)\overline{X}$

Two points are important to note. First, in linear regression we call the two measures, X and Y, the *predictor* and the *criterion*. In correlation we can label either measure as X or Y. But in linear regression, the predictor is *always* labeled X and the criterion is *always* labeled Y. These labels are important because the formula is designed to predict the scores that are labeled as criterion scores, the Y's. Second, the regression equation always predicts the same Y-score for a particular X-score. Like correlation, linear regression is a measure of linear relationship. It calculates the criterion scores we would expect if the correlation between X and Y were equal to +1 or −1. It in essence puts all the data points on a straight line, as though the relationship between X- and Y-scores were perfect.

Let's go back to predicting Homework 2 scores from Homework 1 scores. Homework 1 is the predictor and should be labeled as X. Homework 2 is the criterion and should be labeled as Y. We have the following values for X (HW 1) and Y (HW 2):

$$\sigma_X = 1.0735, \quad \overline{X} = 7.81, \quad r = .36$$
$$\sigma_Y = 2.4463, \quad \overline{Y} = 18.38,$$

Therefore,

$$b = (.36)\frac{2.4463}{1.0735} = (.36)(2.2788) = .8204$$
$$a = (18.38) - (.8204)(7.81) = 18.38 - 6.407 = 11.9727$$

And the regression formula becomes

$$Y' = 11.9727 + (.8204)(X)$$

Table 5.10 shows the actual and predicted Homework 2 scores for each person. Figure 5.7 illustrates the actual relationship between scores on the two homeworks and the relationship predicted by the regression equation. Notice that the predicted Homework 2 scores are not always similar to the actual scores, underscoring the weak relationship discovered through the correlational analysis. The mean of these predicted scores is accurate ($\overline{Y}' = 18.38$), but the *variance* of the predicted scores is .777, only 13% of the variance in actual Homework 2 score—just what was predicted by the coefficient of determination discussed in the section on correlation. Notice also that the predicted points in Figure 5.7 fall on a straight line, whereas the actual points are quite scattered. Remember that linear regression predicts criterion scores expected from a perfect linear relationship. With such a poor linear relationship between scores on Homeworks 1 and 2, we would not expect linear regression to be very useful in the prediction of these scores.

Linear regression has many applications in the field of testing. For example, admission and placement decisions often involve selecting a cutoff score to sort people into categories. Linear regression will be discussed again in Chapter 7.

TABLE 5.10 Actual and Predicted Scores on Homework 2

Person	X	Y	Y'
1	8	20	18.5359
2	6	20	16.8924
3	7	20	17.7155
4	10	19	20.1767
5	9	20	19.3563
6	7	15	17.7155
7	8	19	18.5359
8	7	20	17.7155
9	8	20	18.5359
10	8	19	18.5359
11	8	17	18.5359
12	9	20	19.3563
13	6	12	16.8924
14	7	19	17.7155
15	9	20	19.3563
16	8	14	18.5359

$$X_{Y'} = 18.38$$
$$\sigma^2_{Y'} = 0.777$$

X = score on HW 1, Y = score on HW 2
Y' = predicted score on HW 2 = $11.9727 + .8204X$

FIGURE 5.7   Actual and predicted scores on Homework 2

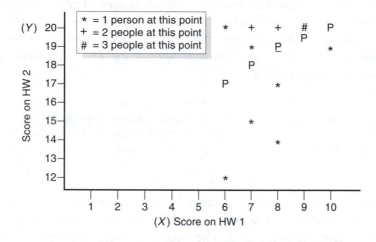

P = Predicted points,   P̲ = Predicted and actual points

PRACTICE BOX 5.7   Using Linear Regression

Using the distributions in Practice Box 5.1, calculate the linear regression equation for predicting performance on Quiz 3 from Quiz 1 and for predicting performance on Quiz 4 and Quiz 2. Then use each equation to predict scores on Quiz 3 and Quiz 4. For each analysis, make a table comparing the predicted scores to the actual scores. Check your answers against the answers at the end of the book. If you make any mistakes, reread the appropriate sections.

TRANSFORMING RAW SCORES

Linear and Area Transformations

Sometimes it is useful to transform raw scores to a different type of score. As noted in Chapter 3, raw scores on psychological tests are often transformed to norm-referenced scores, such as standard scores or percentile ranks. There are two basic categories of raw score transformations, linear transformations and area or nonlinear transformations. A **linear transformation** changes the unit of measurement only; it does not change either the scale of measurement, the relationship between individual raw scores, or the overall shape of the distribution. Standard scores, in all their varieties, are linear score transformations. They maintain an interval *scale* of measurement while changing the *unit* of measurement, similar to the change made when we switch from inches to centimeters. All linear transformation formulas use only operations such as multiplication, division, addition, and subtraction. The basic form of a linear transformation equation is

$$\text{transformed score} = (\text{raw score} \times \text{weight}) + \text{constant}$$

The second type of transformation is a **nonlinear** or **area transformation**. These transformations change not only the unit of measurement, but *also* the scale of measurement, the relationship between the scores and the shape of the distribution. Nonlinear transformations may use other mathematical operations, such as squaring or square root. All varieties of percentile-based scores, including percentile ranks, age and grade equivalents, and quotients, are nonlinear score transformations. The transformation of interval-level raw scores to percentile ranks changes the scale of measurement from interval to ordinal.

Common Linear Transformations

Many psychological tests use norm-referenced scores that are produced through linear transformation of raw scores. The standard scores discussed in Chapter 3 are linear score transformations. The linear transformation used as the basis for generating standard scores is the z-score. Remember that z-scores are a type of standard score that represents raw scores on a scale with $\overline{X} = 0$ and $\sigma = 1$. Raw scores above the mean yield positive z-scores; scores below the mean yield negative z-scores. Z-scores use the standard deviation of the raw score distribution as the unit of measurement. A z-score of 1 means that the raw score fell 1 standard deviation above the mean. A z-score of -1.5 means that the score fell one and a half standard deviations below the mean. The calculation formula for the z-score can be modified through basic math to a format consistent with the linear transformation form:

$$z\text{-score formula:} \quad z = \frac{X - \overline{X}}{\sigma}$$

$$\text{in linear transformation form:} \quad z = (X)\frac{1}{\sigma} - \overline{X}$$

However, there are two features of z-scores that people dislike: z-scores can be negative numbers, and z-scores are often fractional. The popularity of *T-scores*, a linear transformation of z-scores, is due to their elimination of these z-score features. The formula for calculating T-scores is

$$T = 50 + 10(z\text{-score}), \quad \text{then round off to remove the fraction}$$

T-scores have a mean of 50 and a standard deviation of 10. The mean of the raw score distribution, equal to a z-score of 0, becomes a T-score of 50. Raw scores above the mean have T-scores greater than 50 and raw scores below the mean have T-scores less than 50. A T-score of 60 is 1 standard deviation *above* the mean $(50 + 10)$; a T-score of 40 is 1 standard deviation *below* the mean $(50 - 10)$. T-scores are *always* rounded to the nearest whole number.

Table 5.11 presents the z- and T-scores for grades on Homeworks 1 and 2. Note that scores below the mean convert to negative z-scores and to T-scores of less than 50. Scores above the mean convert to positive z-scores and to T-scores greater than 50. Note also that T-scores are *always* rounded to the nearest integer. Fractional values are not reported.

Figure 5.8 is a frequency graph of the raw scores, z-score, and T-scores on the two homeworks. Notice that the shape of the distribution does not change whether we use raw scores, z-scores, or T-scores on the horizontal axis. Standard scores such as z- and T-scores are linear transformations, which do not change the relationship between scores or the shape of the distribution. In the distribution of Homework 1 scores, $\overline{X} = 7.81$ and $\sigma = 1.07$. A raw score

TABLE 5.11 z- and T-scores for Homeworks 1 and 2

HW 1: Score	z-score	T-score[1]
10	2.0378	70.378 = 70
9	1.1062	61.062 = 60
8	0.1747	51.747 = 52
7	-0.7569	42.431 = 42
6	-1.6884	33.116 = 33

HW 2: Score	z-score	T-score
20	0.6643	56.643 = 57
19	0.2555	52.555 = 53
17	-0.5621	44.379 = 44
15	-1.3797	36.203 = 36
14	-1.7885	32.115 = 32
12	-2.6061	23.939 = 24

[1] $T = 50 + 10z$

of 6 is about 1.7 standard deviations below the mean $(7.81 - [1.07 \times 1.7] = 5.9)$. A raw score of 6 corresponds to a z-score of 1.688 and a T-score of 33. It is obvious that 1.688 is almost 1.7 standard deviations below the mean. With a little calculation, we see that a T-score of 33 is also almost 1.7 standard deviations below the mean:

$$\overline{X} = 50, \quad \sigma = 10 \rightarrow 10 \times 1.7 = 17, \quad 50 - 17 = 33$$

Just to underscore the point about linear transformations, let's compare some pairs of scores:

HW 1:	Raw Scores	Raw Score Difference	z-score Difference	T-score Difference
	6, 7	1	.932	9.32
	8, 9	1	.932	9.32

HW 2:	Raw Scores	Raw Score Difference	z-score Difference	T-score Difference
	14, 15	1	.409	4.09
	19, 20	1	.409	4.09

The relationship between scores is unchanged by linear transformations. Raw scores differing by a consistent raw score amount (1 raw score point) differ by a consistent number of z-score points (.932 or .409) and T-score points (9.32 or 4.09). Notice also that the T-score difference equals 10 times the z-score difference. Why? Because z-scores use a unit of 1 to measure distance from the mean and T-scores use a unit of 10.

Many types of psychological tests use some form of standard scores. Modern intelligence test scores, called *deviation IQs*, are standard scores on a scale with $\overline{X} = 100$ and $\sigma = 15$. Scores on the Scholastic Aptitude Test (SAT) and Graduate Record Exam (GRE) are standard scores with $\overline{X} = 500$ and $\sigma = 100$. Scores on many personality tests, such as the Minnesota Multiphasic Personality Inventory (MMPI), are reported as T-scores. Because standard scores represent scores in terms of distance from the mean in standard deviation units and do not change the relationships between scores, they have become an industry standard for tests producing norm-referenced scores.

FIGURE 5.8 Graphs of Homework 1 and Homework 2, z- and T-scores

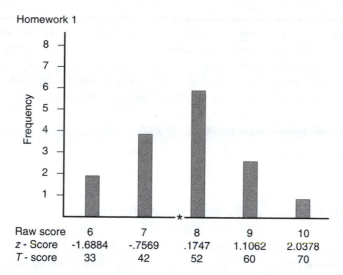

Homework 1

Raw score	6	7	8	9	10
z - Score	-1.6884	-.7569	.1747	1.1062	2.0378
T - score	33	42	52	60	70

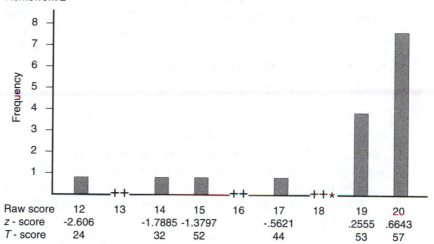

Homework 2

Raw score	12	13	14	15	16	17	18	19	20
z - score	-2.606		-1.7885	-1.3797		-.5621		.2555	.6643
T - score	24		32	52		44		53	57

Note: Since no one earned raw scores of 13, 16, or 18, these scores are represented by "placeholder" +'s. The mean in each distribution is marked by ⋆.

PRACTICE BOX 5.8 Linear Transformations

Transform the z-scores calculated in Practice Box 5.5 to T-scores. Make a table for each quiz showing raw score, z-score, and T-score. Then, for each quiz, compare the z- and T-scores corresponding to raw scores of 6, 7, and 8. Following the example in the text, demonstrate that linear transformations change the scale of measurement, but not the relationship between the scores. Check your answers against the answers at the end of the book. If you make any mistakes, reread the appropriate sections.

Common Nonlinear (Area) Transformations

The section on norm-referenced scores in Chapter 3 also covered several types of percentile-based scores. All percentile-based scores are nonlinear transformations of raw scores. The basic nonlinear score transformation is **percentile rank**, which represents each score according to how frequently the various scores occurred. Because it focuses on the *frequency* of scores rather than their values, the relationships between the scores are changed. Pairs of raw scores near the center of the distribution, near the 50% mark, differ greatly in their percentile ranks, whereas scores at the extremes, near the 10% or 90% marks, tend to have similar percentiles.

The calculation of percentile rank (PR) begins with construction of a frequency table. Three options are available. First, we can calculate percentile ranks that indicate the proportion of people with scores *below* each target score. We begin by calculating the *cumulative frequency below* (cf$_B$) for each score (the total number of scores falling below each score), which we then divide by N, the total number of people, and multiply by 100. The calculations are represented as

$$PR_B = \frac{cf_B}{N} \times 100$$

The problem with this approach is that the person earning the lowest score will receive a percentile rank of 0. There are 0 scores below this point, so the percentile rank is 0/N or 0. Although this is an accurate representation of the person's performance, it is an awkward score to report to a test taker. An alternative is to calculate percentile ranks indicating the proportion of people with scores *at or below* each target score. This calculation is based on the *cumulative frequency* (cf) of each score (the frequency of the score added to the number of scores below it), which is divided by N, the total number of people, and multipled by 100. The procedure can be represented as

$$PR = \frac{cf}{N} \times 100$$

The problem with this approach is that the person earning the highest score receives a percentile rank of 100. Since *all* the scores are either at or below this point, the percentile rank would be $N/N \times 100$ or 100. Although this may be accurate in some theoretical sense, it is confusing to test takers. It is easy to misinterpret as a "perfect score"—correct answers to all questions.

The third approach is a compromise between the first two and uses a new frequency estimate called the cumulative frequency midpoint. The *cumulative frequency midpoint* (cf-mp) for a score is equal to the score's cumulative frequency below (cf_B) plus one-half of the score's frequency:

$$\text{cf-mp for } X = cf_B(X) + \tfrac{1}{2}[f(X)]$$

To calculate percentile rank, we divide cf-mp by N and multiply times 100. The process is represented as

$$PR_{mp} = \frac{\text{cf-mp}}{N} \times 100$$

The midpoint approach is popular in psychological testing because it avoids producing both percentile ranks of 0 and percentile ranks of 100. Table 5.12 presents the calculation of midpoint percentile ranks for the two homeworks. Note that the relationship between a raw score and a particular

TABLE 5.12 Calculation of Percentile Ranks (PR$_{mp}$) for Homeworks 1 and 2

HW 1: Score	$f(X)$	$cf_B(X)$	cf-mp	PR$_{mp}$
10	1	15	15.5	96.875
9	3	12	13.5	84.375
8	6	6	9	56.25
7	4	2	4	25
6	2	0	1	6.25

HW 2: Score	$f(X)$	$cf_B(X)$	cf-mp	PR$_{mp}$
20	8	8	12	75
19	4	4	6	37.5
17	1	3	3.5	21.875
15	1	2	2.5	15.625
14	1	1	1.5	9.375
12	1	0	0.5	0.47

percentile rank is specific to the sample being analyzed. The same raw score would generate a different percentile rank if the distribution of scores changed.

Remember that percentile rank is a nonlinear or area transformation. To illustrate the characteristics of nonlinear transformations, let's compare some pairs of scores from Table 5.12:

HW 1:	Raw Scores	Raw Score Difference	Percentile Difference
	6, 7	1	18.75
	7, 8	1	31.25
	8, 9	1	28.125
HW 2:	**Raw Scores**	**Raw Score Difference**	**Percentile Difference**
	14, 15	1	6.25
	19, 20	1	37.5

Unlike linear transformations, nonlinear transformations such as percentile rank do not preserve the relationship between raw scores. Scores differing by an equal raw score amount (1 raw score point) do not differ by equal numbers of percentile rank points. Scores near the center of the distribution (e.g., 7 and 8, 19 and 20) differ greatly in their percentile ranks, whereas scores near the end of the distribution (e.g., 6 and 7, 14 and 15) have more similar percentile ranks.

Percentile rank is a popular type of score and is easy to interpret, as long as you remember that it is an *ordinal* measure. A percentile rank of 75 means the person performed better than 75% of the people who took the test. But because it is an ordinal measure, the number of points between the raw scores underlying pairs of percentile ranks is not necessarily consistent. The raw scores corresponding to percentile ranks of 75 and 76 could differ by 1 point, 30 points, 50 points—any amount. When interpreting percentile ranks, it is important to remember that they are determined by the frequency of scores and that they only consider score value in an ordinal sense (highest, next highest, and so on, to lowest).

Percentile rank is the basis for the construction of other scores, such as quartiles, deciles, and age or grade equivalents. Percentile ranks may also be transformed to scores called *stanines*, short for "standard nines." In this case, the distribution of percentile ranks is divided into 9 units, and raw scores are transformed to a 1 to 9 scale. Stanine scores were popular when computer data were limited to single-digit numbers. They are used less frequently today. For purpose of illustration, Table 5.13 applies the stanine transformation to the two sets of homework scores. Because converting raw scores to stanines is a nonlinear transformation based on percentile rank, the relationships between raw scores are changed by the stanine transformation. Comparing scores:

TABLE 5.13   Stanine Scores for Homeworks 1 and 2

Homework 1					
Score	6	7	8	9	10
Percentile rank	6.25	25	56.25	84.38	96.88
Stanine	2	4	5	7	9

Homework 2						
Score	12	14	15	17	19	20
Percentile rank	.47	9.38	15.63	21.88	37.5	75
Stanine	1	2	3	3	4	6

FIGURE 5.9   Frequency graphs for two types of homework scores

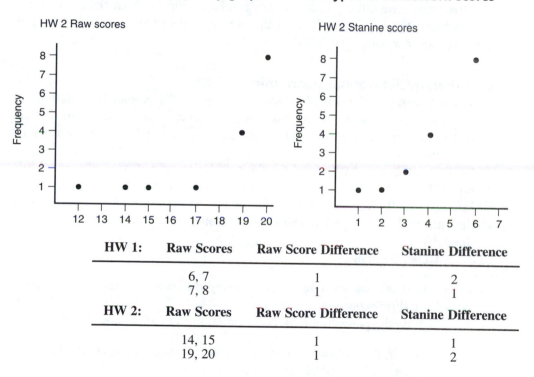

HW 1:	Raw Scores	Raw Score Difference	Stanine Difference
	6, 7	1	2
	7, 8	1	1
HW 2:	Raw Scores	Raw Score Difference	Stanine Difference
	14, 15	1	1
	19, 20	1	2

To illustrate how this nonlinear transformation changes the shape of a distribution, compare the frequency graphs of Homework 2 scores in Figure 5.9. Note also that the stanine transformation provides only general information about the relative magnitude of scores. It again has an ordinal focus, putting scores in order from highest to lowest, but makes even fewer discriminations between scores than the percentile rank system. As such, its potential to convey individual differences is limited.

> **PRACTICE BOX 5.9   Nonlinear Transformations**
>
> Using the frequency tables you created in Practice Box 5.1, transform the raw scores for each quiz into percentile ranks using the PR_{mp} approach. Make a table for each quiz including raw scores and percentile ranks. Then, for each quiz, compare the percentile ranks corresponding to raw scores of 6, 7, and 8. Following the example in the text, demonstrate that nonlinear transformations change both the scale of measurement and the relationship between the scores.

Relationships Between z-Scores and Percentile Ranks

Although z-scores and percentiles are different types of transformations (linear versus nonlinear), there is sometimes a relationship between these two types of scores. The key is the shape of the raw score distribution: whether the raw scores are normally distributed.

A (Relatively) Normal Distribution

When a variable is normally distributed, there is a predictable relationship between a person's raw score and percentile rank. This results from the fact that the normal distribution has a standard and predictable shape, with fixed percentages of scores falling at specific points along the distribution. These fixed percentages can be used for the translation of raw scores to percentile ranks. The table is called the z-score or *normal distribution table* and is available in Appendix B. When the distribution of raw scores is relatively normal, as is the case with scores on Homework 1, we can estimate percentile ranks using this table.

To use the table,

1. Convert the raw score to a z-score using the mean and standard deviation of the distribution.
2. Look up the percentile rank corresponding to that z-score.

Note: If the z-score is *negative*, you will need to subtract the listed percentile from 100 to obtain the percentile.

A Nonnormal Distribution

When a variable is not normally distributed, use of the z-score table will mislead you as to the true percentile rank for each raw score. In these cases, it is necessary to calculate the percentiles. The following chart presents the percentile ranks calculated from Homework 2 raw scores and the percentile ranks you would have obtained from the z-score table.

PRACTICE BOX 5.10   Using the z-Score Table

    For each quiz, make a table with the following columns: Raw Score, z-Score (from Practice Box 5.5), Calculated PR (from Practice Box 5.9), and Estimated PR. Using the z-scores and the normal distribution table, look up the percentile ranks for scores on each quiz and enter in the columns labeled Estimated PR. What conclusions can you draw about the nature of each quiz distribution by comparing the estimated and calculated percentiles? Check your answers against the answers at the end of the book. If you make any mistakes, reread the appropriate sections.

X	f(X)	cf_B(X)	cf-mp	True PR	z-Based PR
20	8	8	12	75	74.7
19	4	4	6	37.5	60.1
17	1	3	3.5	21.875	28.8
15	1	2	2.5	15.625	8.4
14	1	1	1.5	9.375	4.7
12	1	0	0.5	3.125	0.47

    Just in case you were wondering whether all this is really true, here's a chart presenting the raw scores, frequencies, true percentile ranks, and percentile ranks estimated from the z-score table for the scores on Homework 1. Compare this chart to the one for Homework 2. In which case are the percentile ranks estimated from the z-score table reasonable and in which case are they inaccurate? (Note, also, how raw score differences of 1 point convert to *large* percentile rank differences near the center of the distribution, but *small* percentile rank differences at or near the 10% and 90% marks.)

(X)	f(X)	cf_B(X)	cf-mp	True PR	z-based PR
10	1	15	15.5	96.875	97.9
9	3	12	13.5	84.375	85.5
8	6	6	9	56.25	56.9
7	4	2	4	25	22.5
6	2	0	1	6.25	4.6

SUMMARY AND KEY CONCEPTS

    Evaluating the psychometric properties of a test requires understanding some basic statistical concepts. The variables measured by a test are usually represented numerically as test scores. The administration of a test, therefore, produces a distribution of test scores that can be used to examine both the performance of the group and the performance of individual test takers. The test scores may be represented in a raw score distribution, in which a test taker's score is easily identifiable, or in a frequency distribution, in which the scores are grouped by frequency rather than by test taker. Frequency distributions may be in tables or graphs and are useful for getting an initial picture of the performance of the group, including a sense of the overall shape of the score distribution. Most distributions can be classified either as symmetric or skewed.

Descriptive statistics provide more detailed information about the performance of the group. Descriptive statistics include the three measures of central tendency, the **mode**, the **median**, and the **mean**, and the three measures of variability, the **range**, the **variance**, and the **standard deviation**. The relationship between these measures is affected by the frequency with which different scores occur. For example, when scores demonstrate the pattern of the **normal distribution**, the mode, median, and mean are equal.

Many psychological tests transform raw scores to a type of norm-referenced score. **Standard scores** provide information about relative performance on an interval scale of measurement. The most popular standard scores are *z*-**scores** and **T-scores**. Both are **linear transformations**, which change only the unit of measurement, not the scale of measurement or the relationship between scores. Percentile-based scores are also used to describe relative performance. **Percentile rank**, for example, is a popular score since its interpretation does not require understanding the concept of variability. Percentile rank and its companion transformations, such as stanine, are **nonlinear** or **area transformations**, which change the scale of measurement and relationship between scores. When interval-level test scores are converted to percentile ranks, the scale of measurement becomes ordinal. The relationship between standard scores and percentiles is affected by the overall shape of the distribution. When scores are normally distributed, we can convert *z*-scores to percentiles directly through the *z*-score or normal distribution table.

Sometimes in testing we are interested in the relationship between performance on two measures. This relationship can be represented visually in a **scatterplot** or mathematically as a correlation coefficient. A **correlation** indicates the degree of linear relationship between scores on two variables and usually is interpreted as a variance proportion called the **coefficient of determination**. When a reasonable degree of relationship exists, we can use **linear regression** to predict scores on one variable from scores on the other.

QUESTIONS

A local school administers a state-developed reading test as part of the promotion decision process. The following is a summary sheet for one class indicating the students' scores on the third grade reading test (top score = 70) and teacher rating of their fourth grade reading performance (top score = 7).

5.1 Convert each set of scores to a frequency table. Graph each distribution and identify its shape.

Student	Reading Test	Fourth Grade Performance
1	40	3
2	60	5
3	30	3
4	50	7
5	40	5
6	40	3
7	30	2
8	30	4
9	30	4
10	60	7
11	60	7
12	50	7
13	40	5
14	30	3
15	50	4
16	30	5
17	50	5
18	40	4
19	30	3
20	40	4

5.2 Calculate the three measures of central tendency and the three measures of variability for each distribution. In each case, how is the shape of the distribution reflected in these descriptive statistics?

5.3 Calculate the z-scores and T-scores for students 17, 18, and 19 on the reading test. Using the format of the example in this chapter, compare these scores to illustrate the principles of linear transformation.

5.4 Convert the reading test scores to percentile ranks using the using the PR_{mp} approach. Following the format of the example in this chapter, compare the performance of students 17, 18, and 19 to illustrate the principles of nonlinear transformation.

5.5 Make a scatterplot of the relationship between the two sets of scores. Now calculate the correlation between these scores. How is the value of the correlation reflected in the shape of the scatterplot?

5.6 Using linear regression, predict fourth grade performance from scores on the reading test. How is the value of the correlation reflected in the pattern of predicted scores?

Reliability

CHAPTER OUTLINE

CHAPTER GOALS AND OBJECTIVES

After completing this chapter you should be able to:

- Define reliability and explain its importance in testing.
- Explain the relevance of true score and error score to reliability analysis.
- Describe the factors producing measurement error in reliability analysis.
- Describe the features of test–retest, alternate-form, and internal consistency analysis.
- Calculate and interpret test–retest, alternate-form, split-half, and other internal consistency coefficients.
- Calculate and interpret the standard error of measurement for a reliability analysis.
- Use the standard error to construct and interpret confidence intervals.
- Use reliability information to evaluate difference scores and composite or average scores.
- Use shortcut tables to estimate test reliability.
- Use the Spearman–Brown prophesy formula to develop strategies for improving reliability.

LOGIC OF RELIABILITY ANALYSIS

As mentioned in Chapter 1, a good test must be reliable. In the language of testing, *reliable* is used in much the same way as it is in everyday conversation. Reliable tests, like reliable people, are dependable. Reliable tests can be depended on to generate scores that are realistic estimates of test takers' actual knowledge or characteristics. How do we know the scores are realistic estimates? Because analysis of test-taker performance indicates that people perform consistently on the test unless knowledge or characteristics change. In fact, common synonyms for reliability are *consistency* and *stability*.

There are three types of reliability analyses, each focusing on a different type of consistent performance. A reliable test is one on which people would earn similar scores if they were (1) tested on two different days (test–retest reliability), (2) tested with two different versions (alternate-form reliability), or (3) tested with different subsets of questions from the test (internal consistency or homogeneity). In all cases, reliability is represented statistically as a correlation called the *reliability coefficient*.

Test reliability is important because if people's scores *do* change between testings or across versions of the test, we would like to conclude that the differences reflect real changes in their knowledge or characteristics. Suppose a student retakes an exam to demonstrate improvement in mastery of coursework. If the test is not reliable, what can be concluded from comparing the two scores? Imagine a diagnostic test used to determine whether or not to terminate treatment. How can a change in score be interpreted as an indication of improvement if the test is not reliable?

Note the use of the phrase "similar scores" in the preceding descriptions of reliable tests. People are not expected to earn exactly the same scores on each testing. Instead, a reliable test is defined as one on which test takers will fall in the same positions *relative to* each other. This means that, without a true change in the person's knowledge or characteristics, an individual scoring 1 standard deviation above the mean on one testing should score 1 standard deviation above the mean on the second testing. The person's absolute score can change (e.g., scoring 2 points higher on the second testing) and the test can still be reliable—as long as the scores of the other test takers change by an equivalent amount. Why? Because if everyone's scores show similar change, the *relationship* between people's scores remains the same.

Although change in absolute scores does not necessarily affect reliability, it still may be important. Consider the following case. Several years ago, a colleague noticed a pattern in the scores on two versions of a brief test of neuropsychological functioning. Test takers usually earned higher scores on Form 2 than Form 1. This difference had important diagnostic implications. When pre- and posttreatment scores were compared, individuals tested first with Form 1 tended to show more improvement than individuals tested first with Form 2. We conducted a series of alternate-form reliability studies in which new patients were given both forms of the test upon admission. An interesting pattern emerged. Patients tended to fall in the same positions relative to each other on the two forms. Individuals with the lowest scores on Form 1 also had the lowest scores on Form 2. The alternate-form reliability coefficient was in fact quite high! Although Form 2 scores were higher than the Form 1 scores, they differed by a relatively consistent amount. Yet the difference between forms in absolute scores complicated assessment of improvement over time. The problem was eliminated by developing a new scoring system to equate scores on the two forms.

Theory Behind Reliability Analysis

Although students cringe when instructors discuss the theory behind a statistical analysis, knowing something about the underlying theory often helps you to understand the real point of the analysis. The actual calculation of a reliability coefficient is simple—in most cases we use the correlation formula presented in Chapter 5. And most students can memorize a sentence to plug the coefficient into for interpreting the correlation. The difficult part is understanding enough about what you are doing to apply the results of your analysis. Such understanding requires an appreciation of the basic assumptions of reliability analysis.

Reliability analyses assume that test scores reflect the influence of two factors:

1. Stable characteristics of the individual (called the *true* characteristics of the individual)
2. Chance features of the individual or the situation (called *random measurement error*)

If tests were perfect measurement instruments, like rulers, an individual would perform similarly on all tests of a particular attribute until that attribute changed. After all, when we measure height repeatedly, even using different rulers, we get the same number until the person actually grows. But tests are not perfect measurement instruments. Performance on tests also is influenced by random events that happen to occur during a particular testing. Have you ever tried to concentrate on a test while the groundskeeper operated a weed-eater outside your classroom? Or taken a test on a day when you were coming down with the flu? Or made a series of extremely lucky guesses on a difficult exam? On these occasions, your test score reflected not only what you knew (true characteristics), but also the testing environment, your illness, and your good luck (chance events).

The relationship between these components is represented mathematically as

$$X = T + E$$

in which

X = a person's test score (**raw score**)

T = the person's stable characteristics or knowledge (**true score**)

E = chance events (**error score**)

Remember that the events in question are chance events, ones that may occur during one testing but not necessarily during a second testing. The effect of these events is called *random measurement error* because their presence is unpredictable; they are represented by the E in the equation. Note also that T does not specify *which* stable characteristics or knowledge the test taps—that is the focus of validity analysis.

The equation provides one way to mathematically define a reliable test. In a reliable test, the value of E should be close to 0 and the value of T should be close to the actual test score, X. In other words, most of the test score should result from measurement of true characteristics (T). We can also use the equation to determine the proportion or percent of a test score reflecting each factor:

$$\frac{T}{X} = \text{proportion of test score reflecting person's true (stable) knowledge or characteristics}$$

$$\frac{E}{X} = \text{proportion of test score reflecting random error (chance events)}$$

Now a reliable test can be mathematically defined as one in which $T/X >$ E/X. In other words, a large percentage of the overall test score reflects true knowledge and characteristics, and a small percentage reflects the effects of random error. Although it might seem that T/X will always be greater than E/X, remember that chance events can either raise a test score, as in the case of lucky guesses, or lower a test score, as in the case of the weed-eater. In the first case, the value of E is positive; in the second case, it is negative because it *lowers* your overall test score.

But the reliability of a test is actually based on the performance of a group of people. This means reliability analysis cannot tell us the proportion of an *individual's* test score that is due to either true characteristics or error. Instead, reliability analysis identifies the roles of true score and error score in the performance of the overall group. Specifically, reliability analysis determines the extent to which differences among people in test scores reflect differences in their true scores. Differences among people in test scores are represented by test score variance; differences among people in true scores are represented by true score variance.

We can use a variation of the equation $X = T + E$ to indicate how true characteristics and random error contribute to the performance of the group: $\sigma_X^2 = \sigma_T^2 + \sigma_E^2$. This can be translated as follows: Differences between people in test scores (*test score variance*, or σ_X^2) reflect differences between them in actual knowledge or characteristics (*true score variance*, σ_T^2) plus differences in the effects of chance factors (*error score variance*, σ_E^2). We can use this new equation to define the proportion of test score variance due to true score differences (σ_T^2/σ_X^2) and the proportion of test score variance due to random error (σ_E^2/σ_X^2). These proportions enable us to generate an even more precise mathematical definition of a reliable test: A reliable test is one in which a greater proportion of test score variance is attributable to differences in true score, i.e., actual differences in test takers' knowledge or characteristics. This can be represented as

$$\frac{\sigma_T^2}{\sigma_X^2} > \frac{\sigma_E^2}{\sigma_X^2}$$

The reliable differences between people in test scores are the differences due to true knowledge or characteristics. This means that the reliability of a test is mathematically defined as

$$\frac{\sigma_T^2}{\sigma_X^2}$$

Measuring Reliability

Now comes the problem: The reliability of a test is equal to σ_T^2/σ_X^2. But we cannot actually measure true score because all testing involves some measurement error. So how can we calculate a measure of reliability? To answer this question, think back to the basic premise of reliability theory. Theoretically, people should perform similarly, relative to each other, on any test of a given attribute unless they change somehow between measurements. There is a statistic specifically designed to assess the degree to which people perform similarly on two measures—the Pearson correlation coefficient presented in Chapter 5. In its simplest form, a reliability analysis correlates performance on two interval scale measures and uses that correlation to indicate the extent of true score differences. Although we use the same formula to calculate the correlation coefficient, in reliability analysis it is called a *reliability coefficient* (r_{XX}) and it is interpreted as

$$r_{XX} = \frac{\sigma_T^2}{\sigma_X^2}$$

Basically, we define the reliability coefficient as the proportion or percent of test score variance due to true score differences. If there is relatively little error, the ratio of true score variance to test score variance approaches 1.0 (a perfect correlation, implying perfect reliability). If there is a relatively large amount of error, the ratio of true score variance to test score variance approaches 0 (no correlation, implying no reliability).

Let's take an example. A test developer administers a new personality test to the same group of people at the beginning and the end of a week. The correlation between their scores is .8. According to our previous discussion of correlation, this is a moderately high correlation—the highest possible value is 1.0. It indicates that people performed similarly, relative to each other, on the two administrations of the test. Since people performed similarly on the two administrations, the test appears reasonably reliable.

Remember, however, that the reliability coefficient is defined as a *variance* proportion. We define the reliability coefficient as true score variance divided by total test score variance. This proportion can be used to generate a more precise statement about test reliability. Returning to our example, the reliability coefficient of .8 indicates that 80% of the variance in test scores is true score variance. In more concrete terms, 80% of the differences among people in performance on the test (test score variance, σ_X^2) is attributable to differences among people in stable knowledge or characteristics (true score variance, σ_T^2).

If 80% of the test variance reflects true score differences, what accounts for the other 20%? The remaining 20% of test score variance, $1 - r$, is the variance due to random error. This must be the case since test score variance has only these two components. See if you can follow the logic as outlined next:

$$\text{If} \quad X = T + E$$
$$\text{Then} \quad \sigma_X^2 = \sigma_T^2 + \sigma_E^2$$
$$\text{If} \quad r = \frac{\sigma_T^2}{\sigma_X^2}$$
$$\text{Then} \quad 1 - r = \frac{\sigma_E^2}{\sigma_X^2}$$

Factors Affecting Test Reliability

As should be clear from the preceding sections, the reliability of a test is affected by any factor that introduces error into the measurement process. However, reliability is also affected by other variables such as test length and test score variability. The factors that can affect test reliability can be grouped into several categories: factors producing inconsistent performance, sampling factors, and statistical factors. Table 6.1 introduces the potential sources of error for each type of reliability analysis.

Events Producing Inconsistent Performance
One reason for a low reliability coefficient is that test takers do not perform consistently relative to each other on the test under study. A simple explanation for inconsistent performance is actual change in the knowledge or characteristics of certain test takers. *Real (true score) change* is possible any time a reliability analysis involves two test administrations that occur at different times—the test–retest and some alternate-form reliability scenarios. Often we want to separate two test administrations by several weeks or months to reduce the

TABLE 6.1   Factors Affecting Test Reliability

Factors	Test–Retest	Alternate Form	Internal Consistency
Events producing inconsistency			
True score change	×	×[1]	
Error score change			
Chance differences in test takers	×	×	×
Chance differences in test administration	×	×[1]	
Chance differences in test scoring	×	×[1]	
Chance differences in responses to test items	×	×	×
Sampling factors			
Test length	×	×	×
Item representativeness	×	×	×
Statistical factors			
Range restriction	×	×	×
Range extension	×	×	×

[1]Only if the two forms are administered separately.

likelihood of carry-over effects, i.e., test takers remembering test elements from the first administration. Test developers must weigh the need for time between administrations to reduce carry-over against the possibility of true score change in the interval between testings.

On the other hand, inconsistent performance could reflect changes in error score, i.e., the effects of random error. Changes in error score could result from *chance differences in test takers*, a factor over which test developers unfortunately have no control. Chance differences are produced by events such as illness, inability to concentrate, guessing, misreading test questions, or remembering questions from a previous administration (carry-over). Chance differences in test takers can occur in all reliability scenarios. If you are ill during one administration of a test, but not the other, you will not perform consistently relative to others on the two administrations, and thereby threaten the test's test–retest reliability. If you misread questions on one form of a test, but not on the other, you will not perform consistently relative to others on the two forms. This event threatens the test's alternate-form reliability. If you answer the easy questions on a test by thinking about them, but guess on the hard ones, you may not perform consistently relative to others on the different test items. After all, only the easy items are really measuring what you know! This event threatens the test's internal consistency or homogeneity.

Test-taker performance may also change because the conditions of test administration or the criteria for scoring change. *Chance differences in test administration* and *chance differences in test scoring* directly threaten test reliability. Inconsistency in administration and/or scoring procedures may result from lack of specific information about administration/scoring, from chance events such as the weed-eater outside your classroom, or from human error. Remember that scoring is more consistent for objective test items, such as true/false or multiple choice, than for subjective and projective items like short answers and sentence completion.

A final source of random error is item sampling. People may perform inconsistently on tests because of *chance differences in responses to test items*. If the test items within a test vary greatly in level of difficulty or readability, test takers may guess on some items but not on others. This behavior can alter where people fall relative to each other on different subsets of items and thus lower the internal consistency of the test. A similar event could occur when the items on two different forms of the test vary in difficulty or readability. Guessing within one form, but not the other, introduces randomness into the measurement process, lowering the potential alternate-form reliability.

Sampling Factors

Tests evaluate only a sample of the test takers' knowledge or characteristics. The adequacy of the sampling procedure used to develop the test will influence the reliability of the test. One obvious consideration is *test length*. As a general rule, reliability increases as test length increases. Longer tests provide a larger sample of knowledge or characteristics and, all else being equal, a larger sample is likely to be a more representative sample. Of course, test developers must weigh the higher reliability of longer tests against the threat to reliability posed by fatigue and loss of concentration.

A second concern is the *representativeness of the test items*. Perhaps you have taken a test that you felt did not adequately sample the material covered in class. You may even have remarked that your score on the test was not an accurate reflection of what you knew. And you may have been right. The items on a test represent a sample of items from the set of all possible items. The most reliable tests are those that include a representative sample from this set of possible test items. Why does this affect reliability? Because items drawn from the obscure aspects of a domain tend to be more difficult. This increases the likelihood of guessing, which introduces random error into the measurement process.

Statistical Factors

The range and degree of variability of test scores also affect test reliability. Actually, test score range and variability affect the value of any correlation coefficient. When the range of test scores is *restricted*, the correlation calculated between the scores decreases. A distribution of test scores with a more *extended* range typically produces a higher correlation coefficient. The scatterplot in Figure 6.1 can be used to illustrate the effect of range restriction on correlation. Scores on both variables range from 0 to 100, and the relationship between scores on the two variables is fairly linear. In other words, the scatterplot depicts variables with a high positive correlation. Now consider only those scores within the boxed insert, scores ranging from 80 to 100. The relationship no longer appears very linear. The correlation between scores within this restricted range will be much lower than the correlation for the complete set of scores. Why? When the range of scores is restricted, the variability of scores usually decreases. Remember that correlation measures the degree to which changes on one variable are paralleled by changes on the other. With restricted ranges the variability is so small that there isn't much "change" to evaluate.

There is a second, more subtle point about range restriction and reliability: At a given level of measurement error, test scores with a greater range will show more variability and therefore produce a higher reliability coefficient. Conversely, test scores with a restricted range will show less variability and therefore produce a lower reliability coefficient. Remember that reliability is conceptualized as the proportion of true score variance. If the variability of test scores increases and the error variance remains the same, test reliability will increase. Why? Because test score variance has only two components—true score variance and error variance. If test score variance increases and error variance remains the same, the increase *must* occur in true score variance.

FIGURE 6.1 Correlations between sets of scores with different ranges

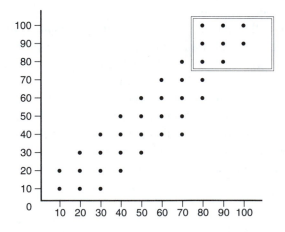

The range of test scores is often extended when test scores earned by people at different ability levels are pooled for analysis. Although this may seem like a good idea, there is a hidden cost. For example, consider an ability test being developed for use at ages 5, 10, and 15. Instead of calculating test–retest reliability separately at each age, all scores are combined for a single reliability analysis. Since ability level increases with age, the range of scores is extended, the variance increases, and a high reliability coefficient is obtained. However, this overall reliability coefficient is actually an inflated estimate of the test's reliability when it is used to compare children *within* each age group to each other.

TYPES OF RELIABILITY ANALYSES

Using Two Sets of Scores

There are two types of reliability analyses using two sets of scores: test–retest and alternate-form. Each addresses a different issue in reliability and involves a different testing scenario. In fact, it is possible that a particular test will be evaluated both ways, depending on its design and purpose. If the test is designed to be administered more than once, its test–retest reliability is important. If the test is designed in two equivalent forms, its alternate-form reliability is important.

In both cases, reliability analysis using two sets of scores requires calculation of the Pearson correlation coefficient. Although there are many versions of this correlation formula (see Chapter 5), the examples in this section will use the means and standard deviations formula:

$$r_{XX} = \frac{(\sum X_1 X_2) - (\overline{X}_1)(\overline{X}_2)}{(\sigma_{X_1})(\sigma_{X_2})}$$

in which

$$
\begin{array}{ll}
X_1 = \text{scores in one set} & X_2 = \text{scores in other set} \\
\sum X_1 Y_2 = \text{sum of each } X_1 \text{ score times its corresponding } X_2 \text{ score} \\
\overline{X}_1 = \text{mean of the } X \text{ scores} & \overline{X}_2 = \text{mean of the } Y \text{ scores} \\
\sigma_{X_1} = \text{st dev of the } X \text{ scores} & \sigma_{X_2} = \text{st dev of the } Y \text{ scores}
\end{array}
$$

Two notes bear repeating at this point: First, this short-cut formula uses the *uncorrected* standard deviation value (σ) for each distribution. Second, the coefficient computed through this formula should be identical to the one computed through the longer raw score formula. This means that the statistics within the formula, $\overline{X}_1, \overline{X}_2, \sigma_{X_1}$, and σ_{X_2}, must *not be* rounded off. Plan to work with numbers up to at least four decimal places.

Test–Retest Reliability

Test–retest reliability is an index of the stability of test scores. It is used to evaluate the error associated with administering a test at two different times. Tests used for testing and retesting typically are designed to measure relatively enduring characteristics. These could be physical characteristics, such as color blindness or brain damage, or psychological characteristics we believe are relatively stable, such as intelligence or learning disability. Because we have theoretical and research support for viewing these features as stable, changes in scores can be interpreted as random measurement error.

There are several applications of test–retest reliability. First, it can be used to support generalizations about test takers over time. If a test has a high 1-year test–retest reliability coefficient, a measure taken a year ago can still be used to describe a test taker today. The interval over which we can generalize depends on the interval used in evaluating the test. IQ score is a good example. If an IQ test has a high 1-year test–retest coefficient, an IQ score from last year can be used again this year. It's true that, if you took the test again, you might answer more questions correctly. But since IQ is a norm-referenced score, it indicates where you fall *relative to others*. If the test has good test–retest reliability, your position relative to others should be about the same.

Test–retest reliability can also be used to support research hypotheses. If a test has a high 1-year test–retest reliability coefficient, we can infer that the characteristic being measured is relatively stable. A researcher interested in demonstrating the stability of a characteristic can use a high test–retest reliability coefficient as one piece of evidence to support the stability hypothesis. Conversely, we would question the stability of a characteristic if researchers were unable to obtain high test–retest coefficients for tests of that attribute.

The procedure for determining test–retest reliability is fairly simple. A test is administered to a group of people and then readministered after an appropriate interval. The length of the interval is determined by beliefs about the stability of the characteristic. In general, characteristics are most stable over short intervals, meaning that the majority of studies use intervals of a few weeks to a few months. The two sets of scores are then correlated as illustrated in Table 6.2.

In the example, the test–retest reliability coefficient is .97. The coefficient indicates a high level of stability of scores over the two administrations. Although examination of Table 6.2 indicates that many people's scores do change, test takers maintain the same relative positions on the two administrations. In terms of proportions of variance, the coefficient indicates that the 97% of test

TABLE 6.2   Calculation of Test–Retest Reliability

General Description

A test is administered twice to the same group of people.

Differences in performance across the testings are viewed as a reflection of measurement error.

Most appropriate for studying long-term stability of a measure.

Formula

$$R_{X1X2} = \frac{(\sum X_1 X_2 / N) - (\overline{X}_1)(\overline{X}_2)}{(\sigma_{X1})(\sigma_{X2})}$$

in which X_1 = the first testing

X_2 = the second testing

Example

A 20-question multiple-choice test of spatial aptitude is administered to 10 students in October and again the following April.

Person	A	B	C	D	E	F	G	H	I	J	$\overline{X}$	σ
Oct	18	16	5	13	15	16	12	5	8	10	11.8	4.4226
Apr	18	18	6	16	17	16	14	5	7	11	12.8	4.8744
$X_1 X_2$	324	288	30	208	255	256	168	25	56	110	$\sum X_1 X_2 = 1720$	

$N = 10$ (number of people in the group)

$$r_{XX} = \frac{(1720/10) - (11.8)(12.8)}{(4.4226)(4.8744)} = \frac{172 - 151.04}{21.557521} = .97228 = .97$$

score variance reflects true score variance. Simply put, 97% of the differences among people in their scores on this test are due to differences among them in actual knowledge or characteristics. Only 3% $(1 - r)$ of the differences among people in their scores reflects measurement error.

Accurate interpretation of the error proportion requires that we consider the factors that can produce measurement error in a test–retest scenario. First, chance variables might affect performance during one testing but not the other, such as differences in test-taker mood or differences in the test administration. Second, changes in true score due to learning or maturation between the

---

PRACTICE BOX 6.1   Test–Retest Reliability

The following scores represent the number of questions correct on 10 math calculation problems. The same 10 problems were given on Monday and again on Wednesday of the same week. Calculate and interpret the test–retest reliability coefficient for this quiz.

Person	A	B	C	D	E	F	G	H	I	J	$\overline{X}$	σ
Mon	9	6	5	3	5	6	2	5	8	6	5.5	1.9621
Wed	9	8	6	6	7	6	4	5	7	8	6.6	1.4283

Check your answer against the answer at the end of the book. Reread sections as needed.

---

two testings are also included in the error variance. Any factor producing inconsistency in performance is part of the error variance (see Table 6.1). True score change, therefore, is part of the error component unless every test taker changes by the same amount. Finally, random changes due to retesting are part of the error component. Because the same test is administered twice, test takers may perform better on the second testing because of practice or remembering items from the first administration. Carry-over due to practice or memory produces inconsistency in performance since the extent of these effects varies from person to person.

In summary, test–retest reliability analysis assesses the stability of scores over time. It is most relevant to tests of characteristics that are viewed as relatively stable on the basis of current theory and data. The coefficient reflects the similarity of scores over time and is interpreted as a measure of the extent of true score differences. Since this is a reliability analysis, it cannot identify the factors underlying true score differences. The coefficient indicates the *degree* to which test score differences reflect true differences, but does not explain the *nature* of these true score differences. Changes in test scores are viewed as the result of measurement error. The interpretation and use of test–retest reliability coefficients require careful consideration of the appropriateness of the analysis for the characteristic in question and the factors associated with measurement error. Remember also to consider the testing scenario when interpreting test–retest coefficients. For example, if the two test administrations are closely spaced, the test–retest coefficient is more likely to be influenced by test takers' ability to remember test questions over time.

Alternate-form Reliability

Alternate- or parallel-form reliability is an index of the similarity of test items across two different forms. It is used to evaluate the extent to which the two different forms measure the same knowledge or characteristics. Alternate forms theoretically are separate tests measuring the same knowledge or characteristics (the same domain) with different test items. These test items are viewed as drawn from the larger population of all possible test items tapping this domain. If the two sets of test items are equally representative samples of this larger theoretical pool, people should perform similarly on both sets. Differences in performance on the two forms are interpreted as measurement error resulting from the selection of particular test items.

Alternate-form reliability has one obvious application: ensuring that different forms of a test are in fact equivalent. It is often desirable to have different forms of a test, because retesting people with a different version of a test minimizes the carry-over effects previously discussed. But alternate-form reliability is important for a second, more theoretical reason. Although all tests include only a subset of all possible test items, test scores typically are used to make inferences about test takers' knowledge and characteristics, not simply to describe their performance on a particular set of items. It is important to know whether we can make accurate generalizations from performance on one sample of items to the broader domain that the sample supposedly represents. Achieving a high alternate-form reliability coefficient demonstrates that performance is not tied to one particular set of test items.

The procedure for determining alternate-form reliability is straightforward. Two equivalent forms of a test are developed by selecting questions of similar form, content, and level of difficulty. The two forms are administered to a group of people in one of two ways. The forms may be administered at the same time, one following the other, or after a relatively short time interval. The choice of administration format depends both on practical considerations, such as test length, and measurement issues, such as interest in the stability of scores over time. The two sets of scores are correlated as illustrated in Table 6.3.

In the sample problem, the coefficient indicates a high level of equivalence between the forms ($r_{XX} = .96$). Scores on the first form of the test are very similar to scores on the second form. More precisely, test takers maintain the same positions relative to each other on the two forms. In terms of proportions of variance, the coefficient indicates that 96% of the differences among people in test scores are due to differences among them in actual knowledge or characteristics. Only 4% $(1-r)$ of the differences among people in their scores reflect errors in measurement. As in all reliability analyses, the coefficient can only detect random changes in scores, and it cannot identify the particular knowledge or characteristics tapped by the test items.

TABLE 6.3 Calculation of Alternate-form Reliability

General Description

Two equivalent forms of a test are administered at the same time to a group of people.

Order of administration is counterbalanced so that half receive Form A first and half receive Form B first.

Since the forms are equivalent, differences in performance across the testings are viewed as a reflection of measurement error.

Most appropriate for studying item sampling.

Formula

$$r_{X_A X_B} = \frac{(\sum X_A X_B / N) - (\overline{X}_A)(\overline{X}_B)}{(\sigma_{X_A})(\sigma_{X_B})}$$

in which X_A = Form A of the test

X_B = Form B of the test

Example

Two forms of a 20-item true/false self-concept test are administered to 10 people. Higher scores indicate more positive self-concepts.

Person	A	B	C	D	E	F	G	H	I	J	$\overline{X}$	σ
Form A	16	12	14	10	9	11	13	9	16	12	12.2	2.4413
Form B	15	12	15	10	10	12	14	9	16	13	12.6	2.2891
$X_A X_B$	240	144	210	100	90	132	182	81	256	156	$\sum X_A X_B = 1591$	

$N = 10$ (number of people in the group)

$$r_{XX} = \frac{(1591/10) - (12.2)(12.6)}{(2.4413)(2.2891)} = \frac{159.1 - 153.72}{5.5883798} = .9627 = .96$$

What factors are producing the measurement error? Because of the design of this particular example, inconsistency in performance can be attributed to item sampling. Since the two forms were administered together, we can eliminate differences due to true score change and administration. The order of administration of forms was counterbalanced so that half the group received Form A first and half received Form B first. Counterbalancing controls for chance differences in test takers, such as fatigue, practice, or changes in moti-

---

PRACTICE BOX 6.2   Alternate-form Reliability

The following table presents scores on two forms of a 10-item test of gender stereotypy. The numbers indicate the number of items marked *true*. Higher numbers indicate a greater degree of gender stereotypy. Calculate and interpret the alternate-form reliability coefficient.

Person	A	B	C	D	E	F	G	H	I	J	$\overline{X}$	σ
Form A	5	8	4	7	6	3	4	6	8	5	5.6	1.6248
Form B	4	8	6	8	7	3	3	6	7	4	5.6	1.8547

Compare your answer to the answer at the end of the book. Reread sections as needed.

---

vation. Finally, since objective (true/false) items were used, chance differences in scoring the two forms are unlikely.

In summary, alternate-form reliability analysis determines the similarity of performance on different item samples. Along with evaluation of characteristics such as item difficulty, it is an important procedure in the development of equivalent forms of a test. The analysis also determines the appropriateness of making generalizations about test takers from their performance on a particular set of items. The coefficient indicates the extent of similarity in performance and is interpreted as a measure of extent of true score differences. As a reliability analysis, the procedure does not examine the *nature* of those true score differences. Interpretation of error variance depends on the design of the test and the reliability study. Designs similar to the example in Table 6.3 control for a variety of possible sources of error. Sources of error variance in other designs are identified in Table 6.1 (see page 184).

Using One Set of Scores

Some tests do not have alternate forms and are administered only once. Yet the reliability of these tests is still important. We would like to be able to infer that differences among people in test scores reflect true differences in their knowledge or characteristics and, therefore, to infer that their scores on this test are generally accurate reflections of what they know or what they are like. In other words, we would like to be able to generalize from their performance on this test to their performance on other measures of the same domain. This particular approach to estimating a test's reliability is called the **internal consistency** or *homogeneity* approach. If a test is internally consistent, all test items are in fact tapping the same area of knowledge or personal characteristics. Likewise, the items can be thought of as homogeneous, all drawn from the same domain.

Split-half Reliability

The **split-half reliability** procedure treats the administration of a single test like the simultaneous administration of two alternate forms. The test is administered to a group of people and the test items are then split into two half-tests. Total scores on the items in each half-test are computed for each person, and the two distributions of half-test scores are compared using the traditional correlation formula.

There are many ways to divide a test into two halves. The most common technique is to divide the test into odd-numbered and even-numbered items. After completing the test, each individual's total score is broken down into two partial scores—one representing performance on odd-numbered questions, the other representing performance on the even-numbered questions. We now have two sets of scores earned by a single group of people that can be correlated just as we did in the test–retest and alternate-form scenarios.

In essence, we have divided a single test to create two separate "forms" of a test, each one supposedly assessing the same domain. The logic of split-half analysis, therefore, parallels the logic of alternate-form reliability. If these items are equally representative of a particular domain, people should perform similarly on them. Such similarity will be reflected in the correlation between scores on the two half-tests. The split-half procedure is illustrated in Part I of Table 6.4. Note that these test items are scored as correct or incorrect. However, the items could be true/false or yes/no (checklist) format. Split-half analysis usually uses some type of dichotomous (two-category) scoring.

The reliability coefficient in Table 6.4 is moderately high: 87% of the differences among people in performance reflects differences in true charac- teristics or knowledge and 13% reflects errors in measurement. Since there is only one administration and the test was split by alternating items, these measurement errors can only reflect differences in test content. The coefficient implies that people's scores on the odd items are similar to their scores on the even items.

However, the coefficient has been computed using scores between 1 and 3. The real test had 6 questions. Remember that longer tests typically are more reliable than shorter tests. It is likely, then, that the split-half coefficient is an *underestimate* of the actual reliability of this test. Fortunately, there is a formula for determining the effect of test length on reliability. The **Spearman–Brown prophesy formula** can be used to estimate the reliability of the complete 6-item

TABLE 6.4 Calculation of Split-half Reliability

General Description

Technique for estimating the overall reliability of a test based on a single administration.

Requires splitting the test into two half-tests, usually the odd versus the even items. Since questions in the two half-tests cover the same material, differences in performance on the two halves are viewed as reflecting errors in measurement.

Most appropriate for studying item sampling.

Formula

$$r_{X_O X_E} = \frac{(\sum X_O X_E / N) - (\overline{X}_O)(\overline{X}_E)}{(\sigma_{xO})(\sigma_{xE})}$$

in which X_O = the odd-numbered items

$\quad\quad\quad X_E$ = the even-numbered items

Example

A class of five people took a six-question quiz. Y indicates questions that were answered correctly; N indicates questions that were answered incorrectly.

Question	1	2	3	4	5	6	Total Score
Joe	Y	Y	Y	Y	N	Y	5
Sam	Y	N	N	Y	N	Y	3
Sue	Y	Y	N	Y	Y	Y	5
Peg	N	Y	N	N	Y	N	2
Gil	N	Y	N	N	Y	Y	3

$\overline{X} = 3.6, \ \sigma = 1.2.$

I. Calculating the split-half coefficient

First create two new distributions, the total score each person received on the odd questions and the total score each person received on the even questions. Then use these distributions as you would any set of distributions, calculating the mean and standard deviation of each and the sum of the cross products.

Student	Joe	Sam	Sue	Peg	Gil	$\overline{X}$	σ
Odds	2	1	2	1	1	1.4	.4899
Evens	3	2	3	1	2	2.2	.7483
$X_1 X_2$	6	2	6	1	2	$\sum X_1 X_2 = 17$	

$N = 5$ (number of people in the group)

$$r_{XX} = \frac{(17/5) - (1.4)(2.2)}{(.4899)(.7483)} = \frac{3.4 - 3.08}{.3665922} = .8729 = .87$$

II. Correcting the split-half coefficient

Use the Spearman–Brown prophesy formula with $N = 2$ to estimate the reliability of the overall test from the split-half coefficient.

$$\text{new } r_{XX} = \frac{(2)(.8729)}{1 + (2 - 1)(.8729)} = \frac{1.7457}{1 + .8729} = .9321 = .93$$

test from the split-half coefficient:

$$\text{new } r_{XX} = \frac{(N)(\text{current } r_{XX})}{1 + (N - 1)(\text{current } r_{XX})}$$

in which N is the factor by which test length is increased. In split-half studies, N always equals 2. Why? Because the split-half procedure determines reliability from half-tests, and the Spearman–Brown formula estimates the reliability of the complete test, which is 2 times as long as the half-tests. In our example, the half-tests analyzed in the split-half procedure had 3 items each. The formula is being used to estimate the reliability of a 6-item test. Part II of Table 6.4 illustrates use of the Spearman–Brown formula in split-half studies. The corrected or adjusted split-half coefficient is always greater than the uncorrected coefficient (.92 versus .87) and typically is the coefficient we report at the end of our analysis.

The split-half technique just described contains an important assumption about the two half-tests: It assumes that the variances of the two half-tests are about equal. If the two variances differ significantly, it is inappropriate to use the traditional Pearson correlation formula. An alternative formula (Guttman, 1945) does not make this assumption and should be used when half-tests have unequal variances:

$$r_{OE} = 2\left(1 - \frac{\sigma_O^2 + \sigma_E^2}{\sigma_X^2}\right)$$

In summary, the split-half procedure is used to determine the reliability of a test administered only once. Each person's total test score is transformed into two half-test scores, usually total score on the odd-numbered items and total score on the even-numbered items. If performance on the two half-tests is similar, as indicated by the reliability coefficient, the items are judged as drawn from the same domain. Performance on the test can then be generalized to predict performance on other measures of the same domain. Inconsistency in performance on the two half-tests is interpreted as error due to differences in test items. Because total test score is split into two half-test scores, the split-half coefficient usually is an underestimate of the reliability of the whole test. The coefficient should be corrected using the Spearman–Brown prophesy formula before making statements about the overall test reliability.

Other Internal Consistency Coefficients

Although the split-half coefficient traditionally is identified as a measure of internal consistency, it is not necessarily the best measure. An internally consistent test is homogeneous—all items are drawn from the same domain and therefore measure the same test-taker characteristics. In split-half analysis,

---

PRACTICE BOX 6.3   Split-half Reliability

A group of six job applicants was given a 10-sentence test of shorthand skill. Y indicates correct coding of the sentence; N indicates errors in coding the sentence. Calculate and interpret the split-half reliability coefficient. Check your answer with the answer at the end of the book. Reread sections as needed.

Person	1	2	3	4	5	6	7	8	9	10	Total
A	Y	N	Y	Y	N	Y	Y	Y	Y	Y	8
B	Y	N	N	Y	N	Y	Y	N	Y	Y	6
C	Y	Y	N	Y	Y	Y	N	Y	Y	N	7
D	N	Y	N	N	Y	N	Y	N	Y	Y	5
E	Y	Y	Y	Y	Y	Y	N	Y	Y	Y	9
F	N	Y	N	N	Y	Y	Y	Y	Y	Y	7

---

we compare test takers' performance on two subsets of test items. In essence, we determine whether or not the two *subsets* of items are drawn from the same domain. The best estimate of a test's internal consistency would compare performance on each item to performance on all other items. Rather than focusing on one pair of half-tests, it would take *all* possible split halves into consideration—a much more rigorous process.

One method would be to generate all possible split halves of the test, calculate the split-half coefficient for each, and determine the average of those coefficients. Fortunately, it is not necessary to go to such extremes to generate a better measure of internal consistency. Cronbach's **coefficient alpha** (Cronbach, 1951) can be computed from the individual test item variances and can be used to estimate the average split-half coefficient:

$$r_{XX} = \alpha = \frac{k}{k-1}\left(1 - \frac{\sum \sigma_i^2}{\sigma_X^2}\right)$$

in which

k = the number of test questions

σ_X^2 = the test variance

σ_i^2 = the variance on a specific test item (one calculated for each test item)

$\sum \sigma_i^2$ = the sum of all test item variances

Because Cronbach's coefficient alpha is based on the variances of individual test items, it is useful for determining the reliability of tests with items worth varying numbers of points, such as essay tests. The alpha coefficient is interpreted like a split-half coefficient: r = the proportion of test score variance due to true score differences; $1 - r$ = the proportion of test score variance due to random error.[1]

In all internal consistency analyses, the source of error is differences in test items. The error factor indicates the degree to which test items are heterogeneous, rather than homogeneous. Lack of homogeneity implies that all test items are not necessarily tapping the same knowledge or characteristics (i.e., they are not drawn from the same domain). Table 6.5 illustrates the calculation of Cronbach's alpha.

When test items are scored dichotomously (0 or 1), each item will have a fractional variance. It is easier to calculate alpha for these tests using one of the **Kuder–Richardson** formulas (Kuder & Richardson, 1937; Richardson & Kuder, 1939), such as the *KR-20*:

$$r_{XX} = \text{KR-20} = \frac{k}{k-1}\left(\frac{\sigma_X^2 - \sum p_i q_i}{\sigma_X^2}\right)$$

in which

k = the number of test questions

σ_X^2 = the test variance

p_i = the proportion of test takers answering an item correctly (one p value for each item)

q_i = the proportion of test takers answering an item incorrectly (equal to $1 - p$, one value for each item)

$\sum p_i q_i$ = the sum of each item's p value times its corresponding q value

The KR-20 formula can be calculated for any type of test using dichotomously scored items, including tests of personality, interests, and attitudes. Table 6.6 illustrates calculation of the KR-20.

When items are scored dichotomously *and* are of approximately equal difficulty, coefficient alpha can be determined by a second Kuder–Richardson

---

[1]Coefficient alpha can also be interpreted as the expected correlation between this test and another k-item test covering the same domain.

TABLE 6.5 Calculation of Coefficient Alpha

General Description
Technique for estimating the reliability of a single test.
Estimates average correlation from all possible divisions of the test into two half-tests.
Differences in performance viewed as measurement error.
Most appropriate for studying item sampling.

Formula

$$r_{XX} = \alpha = \frac{k}{k-1}\left(1 - \frac{\sum \sigma_i^2}{\sigma_X^2}\right)$$

in which

$$k = \text{the number of test questions}$$
$$\sigma_X^2 = \text{the total test variance}$$
$$\sigma_i^2 = \text{each test item variance}$$

Example
A class of six people took a five-question essay test. Each essay was worth 5 points. The entries indicate the points earned by each person on each of the questions.

Question	1	2	3	4	5	Total Score
Joe	3	4	4	3	5	19
Sam	4	3	4	3	3	17
Sue	2	3	3	2	3	13
Peg	4	4	5	3	4	20
Gil	3	2	4	3	3	15
Dot	3	2	3	2	3	13

$\overline{X} = 16.1667$

$\sigma^2 = 7.4722$

$\sigma = 2.7335$

$k = 5$

$N = 6$

$\sigma_i^2 = $ .4722   .6667   .4722   .2222   .5833

$$\alpha = \frac{5}{4}\left(1 - \frac{.4722 + .6667 + .4722 + .2222 + .5833}{7.4722}\right)$$

$$= (1.25)\left(1 - \frac{2.4166}{7.4722}\right) = (1.25)(1 - .3234) = .84575 = .85$$

PRACTICE BOX 6.4   Calculating Cronbach's Alpha

A group of 10 students completed a five-question essay exam. Entries indicate the number of points earned on each question. Calculate and interpret Cronbach's alpha. Check your answer against the answer at the end of the book. Reread sections as needed.

Person	1	2	3	4	5	6	7	8	9	10
1	8	6	7	5	6	5	7	7	6	6
2	7	6	6	6	7	5	7	8	5	7
3	8	7	8	6	7	6	6	7	6	7
4	6	5	6	4	5	6	5	7	5	6
5	7	6	6	6	7	6	7	8	5	5

---

formula, *KR-21*:

$$r_{XX} = \text{KR-21} = 1 - \left(\frac{\overline{X}(k - \overline{X})}{k(\sigma^2)} \right)$$

in which

k = the number of test questions

$\overline{X}$ = the mean number of questions correct

σ^2 = the test variance

Because the KR-21 formula requires items of approximately equal difficulty, it can be calculated *only* for tests whose items are scored as correct or incorrect. Table 6.7 illustrates the calculation of the KR-21.

In summary, Cronbach's alpha was developed to eliminate a major disadvantage to the split-half approach. In split-half analysis, the test is divided into two half-tests and analyzed as though the halves were alternate forms. Because there are a variety of ways to divide a test in half, it is possible that the split-half coefficients may vary for different divisions of the test. Cronbach's alpha estimates the average split-half correlation from all possible divisions of the test. The two Kuder–Richardson formulas may be used to calculate alpha if the test meets the requirements previously described.

The alpha approach generates a more conservative estimate of a test's internal consistency because it compares performance on each item to per-

TABLE 6.6 Calculation of KR-20

General Description

Technique for estimating Cronbach's alpha when test items are scored dichotomously (e.g., right or wrong).

Formula

$$r_{XX} = \text{KR-20} = \frac{k}{k-1} \left(\frac{\sigma_X^2 - \sum p_i q_i}{\sigma_X^2} \right)$$

in which

k = the number of test questions

σ_X^2 = the test variance

p_i = the proportion of test takers correct on item

q_i = the proportion of test takers incorrect on item

Example

A class of five people took a six-question quiz. Y indicates questions that were answered correctly; N indicates questions that were answered incorrectly.

Question	1	2	3	4	5	6	Total Score	
A	Y	Y	Y	Y	N	Y	5	$\overline{X} = 2.8$
B	Y	N	N	Y	N	Y	3	$\sigma^2 = 1.76$
C	Y	N	N	Y	N	N	2	$\sigma = 1.3266$
D	N	Y	N	N	N	N	1	$k = 6$
E	N	Y	N	N	Y	Y	3	$N = 5$
p_i	= .6	.6	.2	.6	.2	.6		
q_i	= .4	.4	.8	.4	.8	.4		
$(p)(q)$	= .24	.24	.16	.24	.16	.24	$\sum(p)(q) = 1.28$	

$$\text{KR-20} = \frac{6}{5} \left(\frac{(1.76) - 1.28}{(1.76)} \right) = (1.2) \frac{.48}{1.76}$$
$$= (1.2)(.2727) = .3273 = .33$$

PRACTICE BOX 6.5   Calculating KR-20

A group of six job applicants was given a 10-sentence "honesty" test. An A indicates an acceptable response; a U indicates an unacceptable response. Calculate and interpret the KR-20 reliability coefficient. Check your answer against the answer at the end of the book. Reread sections as needed.

Person	1	2	3	4	5	6	7	8	9	10	Total
A	A	A	A	U	A	A	A	U	A	A	8
B	U	U	U	A	U	U	U	A	U	A	3
C	A	A	U	U	A	A	U	U	A	U	5
D	U	U	U	A	U	U	A	U	U	A	3
E	A	A	A	A	A	A	U	A	A	A	9
F	U	A	A	U	A	A	A	U	A	U	6

formance on all other items. The decision between a split-half or an alpha analysis should be based on the characteristics of the test domain. If a test covers a *heterogeneous* domain, such as a cumulative final in Introductory Psychology, the split-half approach may be the better choice. In this case, it is not reasonable to expect performance on each item to predict performance on all other items. On the other hand, a test of a *narrow* domain, such as an attitude test or a test of a single personality trait, should be evaluated using the alpha approach. Likewise, each subscale of a multidimensional test, such as an IQ test or the MMPI-2, should be evaluated using alpha. Since each subscale is designed to measure a specific domain, it is reasonable to expect consistent performance across all items.

TABLE 6.7   Calculation of KR-21

General Description

Technique for estimating Cronbach's alpha when test items are scored dichotomously (e.g., right or wrong) and are of approximately equal difficulty.

Formula

$$r_{XX} = \text{KR-21} = 1 - \left(\frac{\overline{X}(k - \overline{X})}{k(\sigma^2)} \right)$$

in which

k = the number of test questions

$\overline{X}$ = the mean number of questions correct

σ^2 = the test variance

Example

A group of 10 people was given an 8-point true/false test on environmental issues. Entries indicate the number of correct answers for each person.

Person	A	B	C	D	E	F	G	H	I	J	$\overline{X}$	σ
Grade	8	6	2	3	7	6	2	3	8	6	5.1	2.2561

$k = 8$, $\sigma^2 = 5.09$

$$\text{KR-21} = 1 - \left(\frac{5.1(8 - 5.1)}{8(5.09)} \right) = 1 - \left(\frac{14.79}{40.72} \right) = 1 - .3632 = .6367 = .64$$

PRACTICE BOX 6.6   Calculating KR-21

A group of 10 students was given a 20-question history exam. Calculate and interpret the KR-21 reliability coefficient. Check your answer against the answer at the end of the book. Reread sections as needed.

Person	A	B	C	D	E	F	G	H	I	J
Grade	12	18	18	15	17	13	15	8	10	8

APPLYING RELIABILITY INFORMATION

How can we use reliability information? Obviously, when we select a test, such as picking a standardized achievement test to use in a school system, we would consider the test's reliability before making our choice. And, when we design a test, such as a classroom test, we should use information about its reliability as input for further development of the test. But reliability has other practical applications.

The primary reason for conducting a reliability analysis to determine the extent of measurement error in a test. The presence of measurement error leads us to two conclusions about test scores. First, test scores should always be viewed as *estimates* of an individual's knowledge or characteristics. A test taker might earn a different score if tested on a different day or with a different set of questions and that change could result purely from chance variation. Second, decisions based on test scores should always take into consideration the possibility of such chance variation. The analyses discussed in this section are designed to use test reliability to determine the extent of possible chance variation in a test taker's score.

Standard Error of Measurement

Every set of test scores has a **standard error of measurement** (SEM or S_M). The SEM is an index of the average amount of error in test scores. In practical terms, SEM uses the reliability coefficient to determine the average number of points by which test scores and true scores differ. Technically, SEM is defined as (1) the standard deviation of the error scores, or (2) the standard deviation of test scores around true scores. These actually are two different ways of saying the same thing. The standard deviation is a measure of the average amount of difference between the mean and the other scores in that distribution. In this case we are working with the distribution of error scores. Since the difference between a test score and its underlying true score *is* its error score ($X - T = E$), the standard deviation of the error scores (σ_E) *is* the average difference between test scores and true scores (σ_{X-T}). This is why we can interpret SEM as the average number of points by which true scores and test scores differ.

To illustrate the concept of SEM, imagine that a woman with an actual IQ of 120 is tested repeatedly with the same intelligence test. It should be obvious that she will not earn a score of 120 every time. Her performance will be affected by random events, such as how she feels that day, her ability to concentrate, and the testing conditions. Just as we expect close to 50 heads on the majority of sets of 100 coin tosses, we expect most of her scores to be close to 120—her true score. If only chance factors affect her performance, scores far above or far below 120 should occur less frequently. If we graphed her likely performance on these repeated testings, we would expect to find a relatively normal distribution with a mean of 120. The distribution should be relatively normal because we are dealing with changes due only to chance or random events. The SEM corresponds to the standard deviation of that expected distribution of test scores. It is the average number of points by which her set of possible test scores differ from her actual (true) IQ score.

But when we calculate the SEM of a test, we do not have repeated testing of a single person whose true score is known. Instead, we have a distribution of test scores generated by a group of people. In this case, the calculation of SEM derives from reliability theory. According to that model, every test score has two components, T or true score and E or error score. If we could determine these test score components, we could actually calculate the average number of points by which people's test scores differ from their true scores. Although we cannot determine either true score or error score, we can use the relationship between error variance $(1 - r)$ and test variance (σ_X^2) to estimate the average amount of error in test scores. Since error variance and test variance are in squared units, we need to take the square root of each to calculate an estimate in raw score (points on the test) units. The SEM or S_M of a test is calculated as

$$\text{SEM or } S_M = (\sigma_X)\sqrt{1 - r_{XX}}$$

SEM is an extremely useful statistic. Knowing a test's reliability is important, but reliability is a variance proportion. It does not translate information about true score and error score into a scale that reflects raw score points. And it cannot be used to make inferences about the performance of *individual* test takers. A reliability coefficient of .8 means that 20% $(1 - r)$ of the differences in the performance of a group (variance in test scores) reflects random error (error variance). It does *not* mean that 20% of an individual's test score reflects random error.

Table 6.8 presents the standard errors for the tests analyzed in Tables 6.2 through 6.7. In each case, SEM represents the average number of test score points attributable to random error. The value of SEM is determined by two characteristics of the test: its reliability and its standard deviation. Larger SEMs occur with low reliability coefficients and large standard deviations. The interpretation of SEM must be made in the context of these variables and the raw score scale. For example, a SEM of 5 points is not much on a test with a top score of 100 points, but is quite significant for a test with a top score of 25 points. Similarly, we would be concerned about a test with a top score of 10 points and an SEM of just .2 if the test standard deviation were .2! Think about it.

TABLE 6.8   Standard Error of Measurement

Formula

$$SEM \text{ or } S_M = (\sigma_X)\sqrt{1 - r_{XX}}$$

Problem Type (Table)	r_{XX}	$1 - r_{XX}$	σ_X	S_M
Test–retest (6.2)	.97	.03		
October administration			4.4226	0.76619
April administration			4.8744	0.84427
Alternate form (6.3)	.96	.04		
Form A			2.4413	0.48826
Form B			2.2891	0.45782
Split-half (6.4)	.92	.08	1.2	0.33941
Cronbach's alpha (6.5)	.85	.15	2.7335	1.05868
KR-20 (6.6)	.62	.38	1.3266	0.81777
KR-21 (6.7)	.64	.36	2.2561	1.35366

PRACTICE BOX 6.7   Standard Error of Measurement

Using your answers from Practice Boxes 6.1 through 6.6, calculate and interpret the SEM for each test evaluated. Check your answers against those at the end of the book and reread sections as needed.

SEM indicates the average amount by which test scores and true scores differ. It does not tell us the amount of error in any one person's test score. Consider a test with an SEM of 4. For the group of people tested, the *average* true score/test score difference is estimated as 4 points. It is likely that some test scores differ from true scores by much more than 4 points, while others differ by much less than 4 points. In fact, the average true score/test score difference can be 4 points even if not a single one of the differences was 4 points! Remember that the mean does not have to be an actual score in a distribution. But don't despair—we *can* use SEM as part of another analysis to draw some conclusions about individual test scores.

Confidence Intervals

SEM is necessary for the construction of **confidence intervals**. Because all test scores include measurement error and only estimate true score, it is useful to convert individual test scores to ranges within which the true score is likely to fall. These ranges are called confidence intervals. The most frequently used interval is the 95% confidence interval. It indicates the range of scores within which a person's score is expected to fall 95% of the time. For example, if a person were tested 20 times, we expect 19 of the scores (95% of 20) to fall within the 95% confidence interval. Only one test score is expected to fall outside this range (5% of 20). We assume that if 95% of test scores falls within this range, it is likely that the person's true score also falls within this range.

To illustrate the concept of confidence interval, let's return to the repeated testing of a woman with an IQ of 120. We have already established that her test scores would be normally distributed with a mean of 120. We attribute this to effects of chance events that introduce error into some of her test scores. Figure 6.2 presents a hypothetical graph of these scores. The standard deviation of this distribution, or the average number of points by which her true score and her actual test scores differ, is the SEM. Since the distribution is relatively normal, predictable percentages of scores fall between the mean (120) and different standard deviation cutoffs. Remember, for example, that approximately 34% of scores for a normally distributed variable fall between $\overline{X}$ and $+1\sigma$, with a corresponding 34% between $\overline{X}$ and -1σ (see Figure 5.4 on page 147).

We can take this logic one step further. If the SEM is the distribution's standard deviation, then 34% of her scores falls between 120 and +1 SEM ($\overline{X}$ and $+1\sigma$) and another 34% between 120 and -1 SEM ($\overline{X}$ and -1σ). Taken together, 68% of her scores falls in the interval defined by 120 ±1 SEM. In

FIGURE 6.2 Hypothetical distribution of test scores for a woman whose true IQ = 120

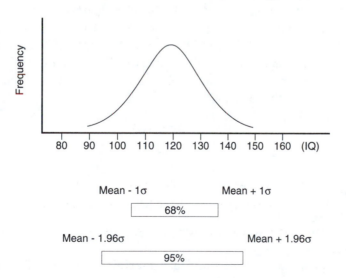

other words, we are "confident" that when she is tested repeatedly, 68% of her scores will fall in this interval. This interval is referred to as the "68% confidence interval."

To obtain the 95% confidence interval, we need to determine the number of standard deviations encompassing 95% of her test scores. For a normally distributed variable, 95% of the scores falls in the interval defined by $X \pm 1.96\sigma$ (see Figure 5.4). The 95% interval, therefore, would be 120 ±1.96 SEM.

We can apply this technique to construct a confidence interval that converts a test score to a range within which the person's true score is likely to fall. In essence, we use the person's test score and the SEM of the test to infer what would happen if the person were tested repeatedly. We assume that repeated testing of this person would produce a set of normally distributed scores, just like our example. The individual's test score (X) represents our current estimate of the mean of this hypothetical distribution. SEM represents our estimate of the standard deviation of these hypothetical test scores. Following the logic of our previous example, 68% of the person's scores should fall in the interval $X \pm 1$ SEM. If we are using test score as an estimate of true score, we would expect the true score to fall in this range 68% of the time. Another way of stating this relationship is to say that we are 68% confident that the person's true score lies in this range. And, since 95% of the scores should fall between $X + 1.96$ SEM and $X - 1.96$ SEM, we are 95% confident that the person's true score falls in this second larger interval.

Although it may not be immediately obvious, we have been using z-scores to construct these confidence intervals. The interval $\overline{X} \pm 1\sigma$ lies between $z = +1.0$ and $z = -1.0$. A score of $\overline{X} + 1\sigma$ is equivalent to a z-score of 1.0; a score of $\overline{X} - 1\sigma$ is equivalent to a z-score of -1.0. Likewise, the interval $\overline{X} \pm 1.96\sigma$ lies between $z = +1.96$ and $z = -1.96$. The only difference between these z-score intervals and our confidence intervals is the use of the current test score (X) as our estimate of the mean. The general formula for constructing a confidence interval, therefore, is

$$X \pm (z\text{-score})(s_M)$$

in which

$$X + (z\text{-score})(s_M) = \text{the upper limit of the interval}$$
$$X - (z\text{-score})(s_M) = \text{the lower limit of the interval}$$

Consult the z-score table to identify the scores to use for other sizes of confidence intervals.

Table 6.9 presents the 95% confidence intervals for a score of 6 on each of the tests analyzed in this chapter. In each case, the interval represents the range within which we expect the true score to fall 95% of the time, given the current

TABLE 6.9   Confidence Intervals

Formula for 95% Interval

$X \pm (1.96)(s_M)$

Problem Type (Table)	s_M	95% Interval for $X = 6$
Test–retest (6.2)		
October administration	0.76619	6 ± 1.5014
April administration	0.84427	6 ± 1.6542
Alternate form (6.3)		
Form A	0.48826	6 ± 0.9565
Form B	0.45782	6 ± 0.8973
Split-half (6.4)	0.33941	6 ± 0.6652
Cronbach's alpha (6.5)	1.05868	6 ± 2.0747
KR-20 (6.6)	0.81777	6 ± 1.6033
KR-21 (6.7)	1.35366	6 ± 2.6531

PRACTICE BOX 6.8   Confidence Intervals

Using your answers from Practice Box 6.7, calculate and interpret 68% and 95% confidence intervals for the mean of each test evaluated. Check your answers against those at the end of the book and reread sections as needed.

---

reliability of the test. Note that the size of the confidence interval increases as s_M, the extent of error in test scores, increases. All other things being equal, the higher the reliability is, the narrower the confidence interval and the greater our faith that differences among scores reflect true score differences.

Evaluating the Difference between Two Scores

Since all test scores reflect some measurement error, we must be careful when we compare test scores. For example, suppose a person took the SAT and received a total score (verbal + math) of 980. The person then enrolls in a cram course designed to increase SAT scores, retakes the SAT, and receives a total score of 1100. Clearly, the test score has improved. But why? Does this change reflect chance variation? Is the change great enough to conclude that actual level of knowledge has increased? Remember, test scores are best interpreted as representing a *range* within which one's true score lies. What if the ranges corresponding to these two SAT scores overlap? Can we then still say that they differ by a meaningful amount?

The reliability of a difference is not simply the average of the two tests' reliabilities. In fact, the reliability of the difference between two test scores is generally *lower* than the reliabilities of the two tests used. It is further adjusted by taking into account the correlation between the two tests in question. If we are comparing scores from these two tests, it is likely that the two tests are similar in some way and that the correlation between them is greater than 0. This adjustment lowers our estimate of the reliability of the difference.

If the reliability of a difference is *less* than the reliability of the tests in question, the SEM of a difference between two scores should be *greater* than the SEM of either test. To evaluate the difference between two test scores, begin by determining the SEM of the difference. SEM of a difference can be estimated by the formula

$$\text{SEM}_{\text{dif}} = \sqrt{(\text{SEM test}_1)^2 + (\text{SEM test}_2)^2}$$

Basically, the SEM of a difference is the standard deviation of the set of possible difference scores that could occur on a set of tests. The SEM of a difference, therefore, indicates the average amount by which test scores can be expected to differ on the basis of chance. The important question is how likely it is that a *particular* difference score will occur by chance. Assuming again that these difference scores would be normally distributed, we can use z-scores and percentages from the normal curve to evaluate specific score differences. If the SEM_{dif} is the standard deviation of the possible difference scores, an observed score difference of $+1(\text{SEM}_{\text{dif}})$ equals a z-score of $+1.0$. Based on the properties of the normal distribution, 68% of the difference score will fall between $+1(\text{SEM}_{\text{dif}})$ and $-1(\text{SEM}_{\text{dif}})$, or z-scores of $+1$ and -1. On 100 testings, we would expect score differences less than or equal to 1 SEM_{dif} to occur 68 times. By chance alone a score increase or decrease of more than 1 SEM_{dif} is expected less than 32 times. In other words, a difference of more than ± 1 SEM_{dif} would occur by chance less than 32% of the time. Such a difference is more likely to reflect a change in true score than simply chance variation.

This procedure is akin to performing a significance test on the difference between two scores to see if the difference is likely or unlikely on the basis of chance. For example, assuming normally distributed test performance, 95% of difference scores would be expected to occur between the difference score $+1.96$ $(\text{SEM}_{\text{dif}})$ and the difference score $-1.96(\text{SEM}_{\text{dif}})$. Observed score differences outside this range can be called *statistically significant* since they occur by chance less than 5% of the time (the most common criterion for significance in psychological research).

Table 6.10 illustrates the use of these procedures to evaluate a student's performance on a retake on an exam. The student's score on the retake is 9 points above the original score. A difference of 9 points will occur by chance less than 32% of the time ($9 > 6.4$), but more than 5% of the time ($9 < 12.544$). We would not, then, call the change a statistically significant difference. But

TABLE 6.10   Evaluating the Difference between Two Scores

A student receives a score of 63 on a unit exam and a score of 72 on a retake using an alternative form of the exam.

Observed score difference $= 72 - 63 = 9$ points

SEM form 1 $= 4$ points,   SEM form 2 $= 5$ points

$\mathrm{SEM_{dif}} = \sqrt{4^2 + 5^2} = \sqrt{16 + 25} = \sqrt{41} = 6.4$ points

Cutoff for 68% interval ($z = \pm 1.00$):
    ($\pm 1.0)(6.4) =$ score difference of ± 6.4 points

Cutoff for 95% interval ($z = \pm 1.96$):
    ($\pm 1.96)(6.4) =$ score difference of ± 12.544 points

PRACTICE BOX 6.9   Evaluating Score Differences

     Using information from your test–retest analysis in Practice Box 6.2, evaluate the difference between Person A's scores on the two test administrations (scores = 5 and 4). Do the same for Person C's scores on the two forms analyzed in Practice Box 6.3 (scores = 4 and 6). Compare your answers to the answers at the end of the book. Reread sections as needed.

---

it is still less likely to be a chance difference (less than 32% likelihood) than a true score difference (more than 68% likelihood).

Evaluating Composite or Average Scores

In certain contexts, a person is evaluated not by a single test score, but on the basis of a series of tests. This is often the case in classroom testing, where final grades are based on the student's total (composite) or average score. Since *all* the test grades going into this final calculation involve some measurement error, the student's total or average score might best be viewed as defining a range within which true level of performance lies. In other words, it might be a good idea to calculate a confidence interval around a student's total or average score before deciding on a final grade.

    To do this, you must calculate the SEM of the total or average score. The formula for the SEM of a total or average score is

$$\mathrm{SEM}_{T/A} = \frac{\sigma_X}{\sqrt{N}}$$

TABLE 6.11   Evaluating a Composite or Average Score

A student receives the following five grades: 76, 74, 78, 83, 84

$$X = 79$$
$$\sigma_X = 3.8987$$
$$N = 5$$
$$\text{SEM}_{ave} = \frac{3.899}{\sqrt{5}} = 1.744$$

95% C.I. = 79 ±(1.96)(1.744) = 79 ± 3.418 = 75.582 to 82.418

PRACTICE BOX 6.10   Evaluating Composite Scores

Construct a confidence interval for the average of each of the following sets of scores. Compare your answers to the answers at the end of the book. Reread sections as needed.

1.   72, 78, 80, 81, 76
2.   77, 80, 85, 82, 80
3.   88, 86, 90, 92, 89

---

in which

$$N = \text{the number of scores being considered}$$
$$\sigma_X = \text{the standard deviation of these scores}$$

Once you have the SEM of the total or average score, it can be used to form a confidence interval to represent that score as a range. The procedure is illustrated in Table 6.11. Based on these test scores, our best estimate (the 95% confidence interval) is that this student's true average lies between 75.58 and 82.42. Now the student can be compared with other students who have averages of 79 or 80 to see what grade seems most appropriate.

A final point: It is generally the case that the SEM of a total or average score is *less* than the SEMs of the individual test scores going into the calculation. Why? Because we have repeated measurements, and with each additional measurement, our accuracy improves. This also means that the reliability of a total or average score is generally *greater* than the reliability of the individual scores generating that total or average. This is why people are more confident when decisions are based on several tests.

STANDARDS FOR RELIABILITY

It is important to ask whether or not the reliability of a particular test is good enough. Although it is not possible to give precise requirements for the reliability of different kinds of tests, guidelines do exist. Table 6.12 presents the range and the median coefficients calculated for several types of psychological and educational tests.

Estimating Reliability

Every time I teach my testing course, students ask whether or not instructors and classroom teachers really evaluate the reliability of their tests. Clearly, many do not, some because they do not know the procedures, others because the procedures may take a lot of time. It is possible, however, to estimate the reliability and/or the SEM of a test on the basis of parameters like the number of items, the test mean, and the test standard deviation. Test reliability can be estimated from the information in Table 6.13 once you have calculated the test mean and standard deviation. SEM can be estimated from the information in Table 6.14. Although direct determination of reliability is the best approach, having *some* reliability information is better than having none at all!

Improving Reliability

Once you have determined the reliability of a test, you may decide it is not at the level you need. One way to improve the reliability of a test is to make the

**TABLE 6.12   Evaluating Reliability According to
                Test Domain**

Type of Test	Low	Median	High
Achievement test batteries	.66	.92	.98
Scholastic ability tests	.56	.90	.97
Aptitude test batteries	.26	.88	.96
Objective personality tests	.46	.85	.97
Interest inventories	.42	.84	.93
Attitude scales	.47	.79	.98

From G. C. Helmstadter, *Principles of Psychological Measurement*, ©1964, p. 85. Adapted by permission of Prentice Hall, Englewood Cliffs, New Jersey.

TABLE 6.13   Estimated Reliabilities of Tests

I. Approximate reliability of easy tests (average = 70% to 90% correct)

Number of items (n)	20	30	40	50	60	70	80	90	100
If st. dev. = .10(n)	.21	.48	.62	.69	.75	.78	.81	.83	.85
If st. dev. = .15(n)	.68	.80	.84	.88	.90	.91	.92	.93	.94
If st. dev. = .20(n)	.84	.90	.92	.94	.95	.96	.96	.97	.97

II. Approximate reliability of hard tests (average = 50% to 70% correct)

Number of items (n)	20	30	40	50	60	70	80	90	100
If st. dev. = .10(n)	—	.21	.41	.53	.61	.66	.71	.74	.77
If st. dev. = .15(n)	.49	.67	.75	.80	.84	.86	.88	.89	.90
If st. dev. = .20(n)	.74	.83	.87	.90	.92	.93	.94	.94	.95

From Paul B. Diederich, *Short-cut Statistics for Teacher-made Tests*, 1973, p. 10. Reprinted by permission of Educational Testing Service, the copyright owner.

TABLE 6.14   Estimated Standard Errors of Tests

No. of Items	SEM	Exceptions: Regardless of Length, SEM =
< 24	2	0 when the score is 0 or 100%
24–27	3	1 when 1 or 2 points from 0 or 100%
48–89	4	2 when 3 to 7 points from 0 or 100%
90–109	5	3 when 8 to 15 points from 0 or 100%
110–129	6	
130–150	7	

From Paul B. Diederich, *Short-cut Statistics for Teacher-made Tests*, 1973, p. 5. Reprinted by permission of Educational Testing Service, the copyright owner.

test longer. All else being equal, shorter tests have lower reliabilities because they are smaller samples of behavior and are more likely to be affected by measurement error. The Spearman–Brown prophesy formula indicates how much the reliability of a test would be increased by lengthening the test, assuming that the new items are just as good (or bad) as the original items.

$$\text{new } r_{XX} = \frac{(N)(\text{current } r_{XX})}{1 + (N-1)(\text{current } r_{XX})}$$

in which N is the factor by which test length is increased. This is the same formula used to correct the split-half coefficient. In that case, $N = 2$ because we are determining the reliability of a test twice as long as the two half-tests analyzed in the split-half calculations. However, the formula can be used to determine the effect of tripling or even quadrupling the number of test items.

The Spearman–Brown formula can also be used to indicate how much a test should be lengthened to reach a desired level of reliability, given its current reliability. This calculation is easier if the formula is transformed as follows:

$$N = \frac{(\text{desired } r_{XX})(1 - \text{current } r_{XX})}{(\text{current } r_{XX})(1 - \text{desired } r_{XX})}$$

This second version of the formula can be used in two ways:

1. To indicate the factor by which the length of a single test must be increased to reach a particular level of reliability
2. To indicate the number of tests of a given length and reliability needed for the *overall* score (based on all these tests) to have the desired level of reliability

In many cases, we cannot throw out scores and retest people with longer tests to improve the reliability of our measures. However, we can give several tests and base the final evaluation of the person on a composite or average score representing performance on multiple measures. Recall from the preceding section that the reliability of composite or average scores is greater than the reliability of the individual measures making up that composite. The Spearman–Brown prophesy formula enables you to determine how many tests of a given level of reliability you need so that the reliability of the composite or average score represents the desired level.

SUMMARY AND KEY CONCEPTS

A reliable test is one on which people perform consistently relative to each other. Such consistency implies that the test is a dependable measure of test taker knowledge or characteristics. Although reliability analysis cannot identify the specific knowledge or characteristics tapped by the test, the analysis can indicate whether the test can produce a consistent measure.

All test scores are defined as having a **true score** and an **error score** component. The focus of reliability analyses is the degree to which test scores reflect true score, true knowledge and characteristics, rather than the effects of random measurement error. The test is administered in such a way as to minimize the likelihood that knowledge or characteristics would change during the measurement process. If we take more than one measure of an unchanged property, either through retesting or by using multiple sets of test items, we expect people to perform consistently on these measures. The presence of consistent performance implies that the test is reliable. The degree to which performance varies indicates the extent of measurement error.

Some reliability analyses involve comparing two sets of scores earned by the same group of people, such as scores on two administrations of the same test, **test–retest reliability,** or scores on two different forms of a test, **alternate- or parallel-form reliability**. In addition, it is possible to determine the **internal consistency** or homogeneity of a single test. One approach is to create two sets of scores from the test and calculate its **split-half reliability**. Because this technique restricts the range of test scores, split-half coefficients should be adjusted using the **Spearman–Brown prophesy formula**. Alternatively, we can calculate the reliability of a test from its original score distribution. In this case, we choose between **coefficient alpha** and one of the **Kuder–Richardson** formulas, according to the nature of the test items. The decision between the split-half and the alpha approach should be based on the characteristics of the test domain.

The meaning of a reliability coefficient and the sources of measurement error vary according to the type of reliability analysis conducted. There is no single reliability for a test. Any test can be evaluated several different ways, each way providing its own estimate of a particular type of reliability. Furthermore, there is no single criterion for a "good" reliability coefficient. Different types of tests typically generate different levels of reliability.

All reliability analyses generate a reliability coefficient, r_{XX}, which indicates the proportion of true score variance or the proportion of test score variance attributable to true score differences. The remaining proportion of variance, the error score variance, reflects the proportion of differences due to measurement error. Once the reliability coefficient has been calculated, it can be used to determine the **standard error of measurement**, SEM or s_M, an estimate of the average amount of error in test scores. SEM in turn can be used to calculate **confidence intervals** indicating a range within which true scores are likely to fall. Test scores are best viewed as estimates of knowledge and characteristics and are more accurate estimates when converted to ranges. Similar procedures can be used to evaluate the degree of difference between two scores and the range within which a true average is likely to fall.

QUESTIONS

6.1 Using basic algebra, and the equation $\sigma_X^2 = \sigma_T^2 + \sigma_E^2$, prove that $1 - r_{XX} = \sigma_E^2 / \sigma_X^2$.

Questions 2 through 8 use the following data. A group of 15 people was tested on two equivalent forms of a 10-item test. Forms A and B were administered in May (rows labeled A1 and B). Form A was administered a second time in June (row labeled A2).

Person

	A	B	C	D	E	F	G	H	I	J	K	L	M	N	O
A1	8	4	9	6	4	9	6	4	7	6	8	5	4	7	4
B	8	5	8	5	4	9	6	4	8	7	8	4	5	8	4
A2	9	4	8	6	4	8	7	5	7	6	9	6	5	7	4

Summary statistics

$$A1: \quad \overline{X} = 6.067, \quad \sigma = 1.8061$$

$$B: \quad \overline{X} = 6.2, \quad \sigma = 1.7963$$

$$A2: \quad \overline{X} = 6.33, \quad \sigma = 1.6599$$

6.2 Calculate and interpret the test–retest reliability coefficient for Form A. To what can we attribute the error score variance?

6.3 Calculate and interpret s_M for each administration of Form A. Explain why S_M is different for the two administrations.

6.4 Using the values from Question 2, determine the 95% confidence interval for a score of 8 on each administration of Form A. Interpret each interval.

6.5 Explain how the test developer can lengthen the test to increase its reliability to .95.

6.6 Calculate and interpret the alternate-form reliability coefficient for Forms A and B using the A1 administration. To what can we attribute the error score variance in this case?

6.7 Calculate and interpret S_M for Form B. Use S_M to determine the 95% confidence interval for a score of 8 on Form B. Interpret the interval.

6.8   Use S_M to determine whether or not the difference between a score of 8 and a score of 5 is statistically significant.

Questions 9 through 11 use the following data. The tables present performance, by item, on two 6-point quizzes. Entries marked * indicate correct performance on the item.

Quiz 1   **Student**

Question No.	A	B	C	D	E	F	G	H	I	J
1	*	*	*	*	*	*	*	N	*	*
2	*	N	*	N	*	N	*	N	*	*
3	N	N	*	*	N	*	N	*	*	*
4	*	*	*	N	*	*	*	N	*	N
5	*	N	*	N	*	*	*	*	*	N
6	*	N	*	*	N	*	N	*	*	*
Grade:	5	2	6	3	4	5	4	3	6	4

Quiz 2   **Student**

Question No.	A	B	C	D	E	F	G	H	I	J
1	*	N	*	*	*	*	*	*	N	*
2	*	N	*	*	N	*	*	N	*	*
3	*	N	*	*	N	*	N	N	*	*
4	*	N	N	N	N	N	N	N	*	N
5	*	*	*	N	*	*	*	*	*	*
6	*	*	*	N	N	*	N	N	*	*
Grade :	6	2	5	3	2	5	3	2	5	5

Summary statistics

$$\text{Quiz 1:} \quad \overline{X} = 4.2, \quad \sigma = 1.24899$$
$$\text{Quiz 2:} \quad \overline{X} = 3.8, \quad \sigma = 1.46969$$

6.9   Calculate the split-half coefficient and the adjusted split-half coefficient for Quiz 1. Which one is a better estimate of the test's reliability? Why?

6.10   Calculate and interpret s_M for Quiz 1.

6.11   Calculate and interpret the appropriate internal consistency coefficient for Quiz 2. Justify your choice of analysis.

CHAPTER **7**

Validity Analysis

CHAPTER OUTLINE

CHAPTER GOALS AND OBJECTIVES

After completing this chapter you should be able to:

*   Define validity and explain its importance in testing.
*   Explain the relationship between a test's reliability and its validity.
*   Explain how validity is linked to the components of true score.
*   Differentiate between systematic and random measurement error.
*   Define criterion validity, content validity, and construct validity and explain when each of these is used.
*   Differentiate between predictive and concurrent validity studies.
*   Calculate and interpret a criterion validity coefficient.
*   Calculate a regression equation from correlational data and use it to generate predicted criterion scores.
*   Calculate and interpret the standard error of estimate.
*   Use the standard error to construct and interpret confidence intervals for predicted criterion scores.
*   Conduct a selection efficiency analysis and evaluate specific selection strategies.
*   Describe the process of conducting a content validity analysis.
*   Differentiate between content validity and face validity.
*   Describe the process of conducting a construct validity analysis.

LOGIC OF VALIDITY ANALYSIS

There are many parallels between validity and reliability. Both are characteristics of a good test. Both assess the degree to which test scores are accurate measures of knowledge or characteristics. Both are terms that actually identify a set of related concepts and procedures rather than a single type of assessment. Just as any test may be evaluated by more than one reliability procedure, a test may be evaluated by multiple validity procedures. Finally, both terms in testing mean much the same as they do in everyday conversation. A reliable test, like a reliable person, can be depended on to operate in a consistent manner. A valid test, like a valid point in a discussion, is appropriate to the issue at hand. All validity analyses address the same basic question: Does the test measure knowledge and characteristics that are appropriate to its purpose?

There are three types of validity analysis, each answering this question in a slightly different way. A valid test is one that (1) predicts future performance on appropriate variables (criterion validity), (2) measures an appropriate domain (content validity), or (3) measures appropriate characteristics of test takers (construct validity). Generally, validity is determined by the relationship between test scores and some other variable, referred to as the *validation measure*. However, unlike reliability analysis, no one procedure or statistic is used for all validity analyses.

Relationship Between Reliability and Validity

Reliability analysis indicates the ability of a test to produce consistent scores (i.e., measures of stable characteristics). Validity analysis indicates *which* stable characteristics test scores measure. There are important conceptual and statistical relationships between these processes. It is theoretically possible to develop a test that is reliable without being valid. Such a test would provide a consistent measure of differences between test takers, but would be measuring something irrelevant to the purpose of the test. In essence, the test would produce consistent scores that did not correlate with any variable that is relevant to test purpose. On the other hand, if a test is not reliable, its potential validity is limited. If the test cannot produce a consistent measure, it is unlikely that test scores will be highly correlated with other relevant variables.

Imagine using a yardstick to measure intelligence. A yardstick *is* a reliable measuring tool. Individuals evaluated with this instrument will receive approximately the same scores every time they are measured. But the scores generated by this technique will not correlate well with other variables known to measure intellect. In other words, the scores will not correlate with variables relevant to our purpose. The procedure is reliable, but not valid.

Now imagine using a rubber yardstick to measure height. A rubber yardstick is *not* a reliable measuring instrument. Because it is flexible, individuals will not necessarily receive similar scores every time they are measured. The scores generated by the process should be relevant to our purpose (measuring height). But because the scores include so much measurement error, it is unlikely they will correlate highly with other measures of height. The unreliability of the procedure limits its validity. In general, reliability is viewed as "necessary but not sufficient" for validity. All valid tests are reliable, but a reliable test may or may not be valid. Because it is a prerequisite for validity, reliability studies typically precede validity studies in the process of test analysis.

The impact of test reliability on its potential validity is not merely theoretical. It is *mathematical*. Let's use r_{XY} to represent the relationship between test scores and scores on validation measure. There is an upper limit, statistically, on the validity coefficient r_{XY}, our measure of test validity:

$$r_{XY\,MAX} = \sqrt{(r_{XX})(r_{YY})}$$

in which

$r_{XY\,MAX}$ = the maximum possible validity coefficient

r_{XX} = the reliability of the test under analysis (X)

r_{YY} = the reliability of the validation measure (Y)

Although the equation looks formidable, it's not too hard to understand if you examine it piece by piece. Remember, our goal is to illustrate how test reliability mathematically affects test validity. As the reliability of our test, r_{XX}, increases, the highest possible value of the validity coefficient, r_{XY}, also increases. Even though fractional numbers get smaller when subjected to the square-root operation, a larger starting fraction means a larger end product. Test reliability, therefore, has a direct mathematical influence on test validity.

But the equation actually tells us even more than that. Validity *also* is influenced by the reliability of the validation measure, r_{YY}. When we say that reliability is a "necessary but not sufficient" condition for validity, we refer not only to the reliability of the test being analyzed, but also to the reliability of the measure to which test scores are compared. Unless *both* measures are reliable, it is unlikely that the test will emerge as valid when its scores are compared to scores on the validation measure.

Theory behind Validity Analysis

In the discussion of reliability (Chapter 6), test scores were broken down into two theoretical components: T, the true characteristics of the person tested, and E, random measurement error. Two points from that discussion bear repeating here. First, the true score component, T, reflects factors producing stability in test scores, while the error component, E, reflects factors producing instability in test scores. Anything about test takers that contributes to consistency of test scores is an element of true score. Anything about the test, the testing scenario, or the test takers that produces inconsistency in test scores is an element of error score. Second, reliability analysis cannot identify *which* true characteristics produce the consistent performance. Although we can make inferences about the factors producing measurement error, we cannot make inferences about the factors producing true score. Reliability analysis only determines the degree to which the test scores reflect true score differences.

In validity analysis, we take that next step. Validity analysis focuses specifically on the variables producing true score differences. The analysis is used to determine the extent to which true score is determined by characteristics relevant to the purpose of the test. Theoretically, true score has two components:

1. Stable characteristics of the individual relevant to the purpose of the test
2. Stable characteristics of the individual irrelevant to the purpose of the test

If tests were perfect measurement instruments, the *only* stable characteristics measured would be those that the test was designed to measure. A person's test score would be determined by the individual's relevant characteristics and random measurement error. But tests are not perfect measurement instruments. Performance on tests reflects the influence of many stable characteristics of the individual which vary in their relevance to test purpose. Have you ever had difficulty answering a test question because you did not understand the vocabulary or the structure of the question? Or been asked questions about material that was never covered in any of your classes? On these occasions, your test score reflected not only your level of knowledge, but also your reading comprehension skill and your educational experience.

The relationship between these components is represented mathematically as

$$T = R + I$$

in which

T = a person's true score

R = the person's relevant characteristics or knowledge (measure of test-relevant characteristics)

I = the person's irrelevant characteristics or knowledge (measure of test-irrelevant characteristics)

The irrelevant characteristics measured by the test are stable characteristics that will be measured every time the test is administered. The effect of these characteristics is called *systematic measurement error* because its presence is unavoidable, given the nature of the test. It is an error component of true score, in contrast to random measurement error, an error component of overall test score. Considering both error components together, a test score (X) can be represented as:

$$X = R + I + E$$

in which

R = stable relevant characteristics

I = systematic measurement error, or the effect of stable characteristics irrelevant to the test's purpose

E = random measurement error, or the effect of chance events

Validity, like reliability, is determined by analyzing the performance of groups of people. Theoretically, the procedure examines the contributions of these components to test variance. The test score equation, therefore, should be rewritten as

$$\sigma_X^2 = \sigma_R^2 + \sigma_I^2 + \sigma_E^2$$

in which

σ_X^2 = test score variance

σ_R^2 = variance due to relevant stable characteristics **(relevant score variance)**

σ_I^2 = variance due to stable characteristics irrelevant to test purpose **(systematic error variance)**

σ_E^2 = variance due to chance factors (error score variance)[1]

A *reliable* test is one in which $\sigma_R^2 + \sigma_I^2$, the variance due to stable or true score differences (regardless of relevance), is greater than σ_E^2, the variance due to random measurement error. A *valid* test is one in which $\sigma_R^2 > \sigma_I^2$. In other words, the test scores tell us more about stable differences among people in relevant characteristics than about stable differences in irrelevant characteristics. Theoretically, the validity of a test is defined as σ_R^2/σ_X^2, the proportion of test variance due to variance in relevant characteristics. The goal of validity analysis is to identify and measure these different sources of variance.

To summarize, the differences among people in test scores, reflected in the variance of test scores, can come from several sources. Some of the differences reflect random measurement error, an issue we can investigate through reliability analysis. Some of the differences reflect real differences in the characteristics our test is supposed to measure, an issue we can investigate through validity analysis. The remaining differences are the result of neither random measurement error nor differences in test-relevant characteristics. In essence, we can divide or partition the total variability of test scores into three components:

1. The proportion of variance due to random measurement error, determined by the reliability of the test
2. The proportion due to measurement of relevant characteristics, determined by the relationship between test scores and another variable, i.e., validity
3. The proportion due to measurement of other factors and thus not explainable by either of our analyses

---

[1]As was the case with reliability, this is a representation of the *theoretical* relationship between component variances and total variance. Mathematically, total variance is not the simple sum of the component variances.

CRITERION VALIDITY

Criterion validity is the ability of a test to predict performance on another measure. It is described in terms similar to those used in linear regression: The test is referred to as the *predictor*, labeled X, and the validation measure as the *criterion*, labeled Y. Criterion validity is important whenever a test is used to make decisions by predicting future performance. In such instances, it is necessary to determine the degree to which differences in test scores (σ_X^2) reflect differences in characteristics relevant to the prediction process (σ_R^2).

For example, SAT score is often used to select students for admission to colleges and universities. In these instances, SAT is used to predict the likelihood of succeeding in college. The question "Is it reasonable to use SAT in admission decisions?" is a criterion validity question. If SAT predicts a relevant criterion measure, such as grade-point average (GPA), the test is criterion valid.

Designs for Criterion Validity Studies

Although all criterion validity studies examine the relationship between a predictor and a criterion, there are two different designs for criterion validity studies. The difference between them basically reflects the time at which criterion data are collected. In *predictive validity* studies, predictor and criterion scores are obtained at different times. For example, suppose we are developing a test to predict success in a particular job. To determine the predictive validity of the test, job applicants would take the test (predictor scores), enter the job, and later be evaluated as to performance (criterion scores). Scores on the test would not be used to decide which people to hire. Performance ratings would then be correlated with prior test scores to see if test scores accurately predict future job performance. In essence, predictive validity studies require a guinea-pig group, all of whom are evaluated both on the test and a future criterion measure.

However, the predictive validity approach presents certain practical and possibly ethical problems. Because predictive validity studies require a guinea-pig group, people are admitted to programs, given jobs, and so on without regard to their scores on the predictor, even if their scores suggest a low probability of success. Concurrent validity studies provide a technique for determining criterion validity that avoids these problems. In *concurrent validity* studies, we determine the correlation between test scores and a *current* criterion measure. For example, if we want to know if SAT predicts college GPA, we don't necessarily let everyone who takes the SAT enter college. Instead, we use other criteria to select our students and then correlate SAT and GPA for those people who have been admitted.

However, there are also disadvantages to concurrent validity studies. The first is a statistical problem. The potential size of a correlation is affected by the potential variability of both the predictor and criterion measures. If we use data only on a preselected set of people, such as those attending college, we may limit the variability of our measures. Those attending college are likely to have higher SATs than the total population of people who take the SAT; the range of their SAT scores is likely to be smaller than the range of SAT scores among the population as a whole. Range restriction affects the potential variability of a measure and can therefore reduce the size of the correlation. Practically, this statistical problem implies that correlations determined through concurrent validity studies may *underestimate* the true relationship between a predictor and a criterion. Fortunately, other statistical techniques can be used in concurrent validity studies to estimate what the correlation would be if there were no range restriction on the predictor.

Second, validity studies seek to determine if a predictor is useful as a way to make decisions. Since concurrent validity studies focus on preselected people, they do not provide much data about people who perform poorly on the predictor and may not necessarily be helpful in determining the validity of using the predictor to make decisions.

You may have noticed in the preceding paragraphs references to the "predictive validity" or the "concurrent validity" of a test. Because there are two ways to conduct a criterion validity study, we often refer to the criterion validity of a test with a term that reflects the way the study was conducted. Hence, the criterion validity of a test determined by a predictive validity study may be called the test's *predictive validity*. Likewise, the criterion validity of a test based on a concurrent validity study may be called the test's *concurrent validity*. Despite the different labels, we know that in both cases we are referring to the criterion validity of a test.

Criterion Validity Coefficient

Criterion validity can be represented statistically by a correlation called the *criterion validity coefficient* (r_{XY}). In our SAT example, X, the predictor, would equal SAT scores, and Y, the criterion, would equal some measure of college success, such as freshman GPA. Our goal is to calculate r_{XY}, the same Pearson correlation discussed in Chapter 5, and use it to estimate the test's criterion validity. A reasonable question at this point is how r_{XY} can serve as an index of test validity.

The coefficient r_{XY} indicates the relationship between scores on two variables, X and Y. In this case, the two variables are the test X, or predictor, and the validation measure Y, or criterion. As stated in Chapter 5 (p. 160), this measure of relationship is *also* an index of predictive ability. If the correlation between two different measures, such as SAT and freshman GPA, is high, we can make fairly accurate GPA predictions from SAT scores through procedures like linear regression. In other words, r_{XY}, the correlation between SAT and GPA, is a measure of the ability of the test to predict the validation measure.

As in all correlational analyses, we interpret the correlation as a variance proportion. Theoretically, the proportion of interest in criterion validity is σ_R^2/σ_X^2, the proportion of test score variance due to variance in relevant characteristics. Mathematically, we estimate this proportion as r_{XY}^2. See if you can follow the logic here as to why r_{XY}^2 can be used to estimate σ_R^2/σ_X^2.

In criterion validity analysis, the characteristics measured by the test that *do* predict criterion scores are defined as the valid or relevant characteristics. Therefore, any measure of the test's ability to predict criterion scores is also an index of the test's ability to measure valid or relevant characteristics. If SAT is a good predictor of GPA, SAT must be measuring characteristics of people that are relevant to college GPA. Taking this one step further, the *extent* to which a test measures relevant characteristics, σ_R^2/σ_X^2, can be estimated by the proportion of variance in criterion scores (Y) predicted by test scores (X). In other words, the degree to which SAT is a good predictor of GPA can be estimated by the proportion of variance in GPA predicted by SAT scores.

Now we need to identify a statistic that indicates the proportion of variance in criterion scores predicted by test scores. As indicated in Chapter 5 (see p. 159), the square of the coefficient (r_{XY}^2), the coefficient of determination, indicates the proportion of variance in one variable (Y) predicted by scores on the other variable (X). In our example, r_{XY}^2 would indicate the proportion of variance in GPA predicted by SAT scores. Using the terminology of criterion validity, the square of an XY correlation indicates the proportion of variance in criterion scores (Y) predicted by test scores (X). In criterion validity analysis, the square of the validity coefficient (r_{XY}^2) becomes a quantitative index of validity. In essence,

$$r_{XY}^2 = \frac{\sigma_R^2}{\sigma_X^2}$$

Using the Coefficient

Regardless of which design is used, predictive or concurrent, the data collected can be used to calculate the criterion validity coefficient (r_{XY}), which in turn indicates the relationship between predictor and criterion scores. The square of the correlation (r_{XY}^2) indicates the extent to which test scores predict criterion scores and thus the proportion of test score variance due to differences between test takers in relevant characteristics. Conversely, $1 - r_{XY}^2$ indicates the proportion of test score variance due to test-taker differences in characteristics *irrelevant* to test purpose. This latter measure reflects the extent to which criterion score variance is not predictable from scores on the test and represents the proportion of systematic error variance.

Consider the following scenario. The president of a small corporation is unhappy with the performance of people at the middle-management level. The president believes this performance results from lack of information about decision-making skill in candidates for these positions. The problem is referred to the personnel officer: Can we improve our personnel decisions if we include decision-making skill in our evaluation of candidates for middle-management positions? The personnel officer identifies a reliable test of decision-making skill that the company could adopt. A predictive validity study is conducted in which all individuals newly hired or promoted to middle-management positions complete the test. At the end of their first year as middle managers, each individual is evaluated by an appropriate superior. The personnel officer now has the data necessary for a criterion validity analysis. Here is research question: Do scores on the test of decision-making skill predict later job performance?

Table 7.1 presents the calculation of the criterion validity coefficient between score on the test of decision-making skill (the predictor) and supervisor rating of job performance (the criterion). There is a high positive correlation ($r_{XY} = .86$) between performance on the test and supervisor rating—people with high test scores are likely also to receive high supervisor ratings. Squaring the coefficient indicates that 74% of the variance in their supervisor ratings is

TABLE 7.1   Calculating a Criterion Validity Coefficient

Example

A personnel officer administers a test of decision-making skill to new middle-management employees at a small corporation. After 1 year, each employee is rated by an appropriate supervisor as to level of job performance on a 4-point scale.

Person	A	B	C	D	E	F	G	H	I	J	$\overline{X}$	σ
Test Score	2.0	5.5	4.5	4.0	3.0	6.0	2.5	3.0	3.5	4.0	3.8	1.2083
Job Performance	1.0	3.0	3.0	2.0	2.5	3.5	1.5	1.5	2.0	1.5	2.15	0.7762

$$\sum XY = 89.75, \ N = 10.$$

$$r_{XY} = \frac{(89.75/10) - (3.8)(2.15)}{(1.2083)(0.7762)} = .8583 = .86$$

$$r_{XY}^2 = (.8583)^2 = .7366 = .74$$

predictable from their decision-making test scores. Another way to say this is that 74% of the differences among people in job performance ratings are predictable from their scores on this test of decision-making skill. The second conclusion we can draw is that 26% of the variance in job performance ratings $(1 - r_{XY}^2)$ is not predictable from scores on this test of decision-making skill and thus must reflect stable test-taker characteristics not measured by the test. Remember what these variance proportions *really* mean: If we were to use these decision-making test scores to predict job performance ratings through linear regression, we would expect the variance of distribution of predicted scores to equal 74% of the variance of the actual job performance scores.

Evaluating Coefficients

Should the personnel officer recommend this test to the president? Certainly. The test appears to be a valid predictor of how supervisors rate middle managers in this company. If test scores predict 74% of the variance in supervisor ratings, we can also conclude that 74% of test score variance is due to differences between test takers in characteristics that are relevant to supervisor-rated job performance.

Note two points: First, we are referring to *this* group of people, not people in general. On the basis of a single study with such a small sample we cannot generalize beyond the one group we studied. Second, we cannot say that differences in job performance are predictable from decision-making skill. We have only one measure of decision-making skill—performance on this test—and one measure of job performance—supervisor rating. Different measures could produce different results. Our conclusions, therefore, must be specific to the measures we used. Would personnel decisions be improved by including this test in the evaluation process? Probably. Almost ¾ of the differences in job performance ratings are accounted for by performance on the test. That's quite a lot, considering all the possible factors that could influence performance on the job.

As our example demonstrates, evaluating a criterion validity coefficient requires consideration of many factors. The sample used in a criterion validity study must be representative of the other people to whom we plan to generalize our findings. Furthermore, the sample must be of adequate size for us to have confidence in our results. The test and criterion measure must be reliable, and the criterion itself must be a valid measure of test-taker characteristics. Finally, when a criterion validity coefficient is lower than expected, we should check for the presence of range restriction on both the predictor and criterion measures. Range restriction lowers the variability of scores, which in turn may lead to a low coefficient.

PRACTICE BOX 7.1   Calculating the Criterion Validity Coefficient

---

Sample Problem: A psychologist administers a neuropsychological screening test to newly admitted patients with head injuries. Higher scores indicate superior skills. Each patient is then rated by the ward nursing staff on a 5-point scale of behavioral competence (higher scores again indicate superior skills). The data are as follows:

Person	A	B	C	D	E	F	G	H	I	J	$\overline{X}$	σ
Test Score	8	6	3	4	6	5	3	4	7	4	5	1.6125
Behavioral Rating	5	4	2	4	4	3	2	3	4	3	3.4	0.9165

1. Calculate the criterion validity coefficient for predicting behavior rating from screening test score.
2. Interpret the statistic. Is the screening test a valid predictor of behavioral rating?

   Compare your answers to the answers at the end of the book. Reread sections as needed.

Applying Criterion Validity Coefficients

If a test is a valid predictor of performance on a criterion, test scores can be used to make decisions about test takers. One frequent use of criterion-valid tests is selection of people from a larger pool. Selection requires determining a cutoff score on the predictor associated with a desired level of future performance on the criterion. For example, if SAT is a valid predictor of college GPA, admissions officers can determine a SAT cutoff score to use in admission decisions. Several steps are required to select an appropriate score. First, college personnel must decide the minimal GPA they would like entering students to achieve. Next, they must determine the SAT score that predicts that future GPA. The procedure requires an unusual linear regression technique.

Predicting Criterion Scores
Chapter 5 discussed using linear regression to predict scores on one variable from scores on the other using the basic equation

$$Y' = a + bX$$

in which

Y' = a person's predicted criterion score

X = the person's score on the predictor

b = the slope of the regression line, calculated as $b = (r)\sigma_Y/\sigma_X$

a = the Y-intercept of the regression line, calculated as $a = \overline{Y} - (\overline{b})X$

After determining the slope and intercept of the regression line, the equation was used to calculate criterion scores from scores on a predictor. In criterion validity studies we may want to calculate *predictor* scores from criterion scores. In other words, we may already have selected an acceptable level of criterion performance (Y'). Now we want to determine the predictor score (X) associated with that particular criterion score.

In the sample problem about job performance, X is the person's score on the test of decision-making skill and Y is supervisor rating of job performance at 1 year. Assume that the company decides to use the test in evaluation of candidates for middle-management positions. Management wants to use the test to identify candidates likely to receive a 1-year supervisor rating of 2.0 or better. Table 7.2 illustrates how linear regression is used to determine the test score that predicts a supervisor rating of 2.0. According to Table 7.2, a score of approximately 3.5 on the decision-making skill test predicts a supervisor rating at 1 year of 2.0. The company is likely to select individuals who will receive 1-year ratings of at least 2.0 if it requires applicants to score 3.5 or higher on the test of decision-making skill.

There is one problem, however, with this technique. Linear regression assumes a *perfect* correlation between the predictor and criterion. In other words, the scores determined by the regression equation represent the values of X and Y when $r_{XY} = 1.0$. The procedure does not take prediction error into account. Consider the data in Table 7.3. The linear regression equation has been used to predict a Y-score for each value of X. Table 7.3 demonstrates several important aspects of this process. First, the distribution of Y'-scores has a mean of 2.15, the same as the mean for the actual Y-scores, and a variance of .4457. Second, the variance of the predicted scores is in fact 74% of the variance of the actual Y-scores. (Remember that if $r_{XY} = .86$, the coefficient of determination $r_{XY}^2 = .74$.) Also, note that a test score of 3.5 actually predicts a criterion score of 1.98425, not 2.0. The calculation in Table 7.2 indicated that a criterion score of 2.0 requires a predictor score of 3.5285, which is not the same as a score of 3.5. Finally, since linear regression calculates the value for each X assuming a perfect correlation ($r_{XY} = 1.0$), all individuals earning a particular X-score receive the same Y'-score. The difference between the actual XY relationships and the predicted relationships (XY') is represented graphically in Figure 7.1. Because the predicted relationship is linear, the XY'

TABLE 7.2   Using Linear Regression to Predict Criterion Scores

X = scores on test of decision-making skill (predictor)

Y = supervisor ratings of job performance (criterion)

$\sigma_X = 1.2083,$ $\overline{X} = 3.8,$ $r = .86$
$\sigma_Y = 0.7762,$ $\overline{Y} = 2.15$

Therefore,

$$b = (.86)\frac{.7762}{1.2083} = (.86)(.6424) = .5525$$
$$a = (2.15) - (.5525)(3.8) = 2.15 - 2.0995 = .0505$$

And the regression equation becomes

$$Y' = .0505 + .5525X$$

For a predicted supervisor rating of 2.0, the equation becomes

$$2.0 = .0505 + .5525X$$

Solving for X, the score on the decision-making skill test is

$$1.9495 = .5525X, \qquad X = 3.5285$$

TABLE 7.3   Calculating Predicted Y-scores (Y') through Linear Regression

X = score on test of decision-making skill

Y = supervisor rating of job performance

Using the linear regression equation; $Y' = .0505 + .5525X.$

X	Y'
2.0	1.1555
2.5	1.43175
3.0	1.708
3.5	1.98425
4.0	2.2605
4.5	2.53675
5.5	3.08925
6.0	3.3655

$$X_{Y'} = 2.15$$
$$\sigma^2_{Y'} = .4457$$

FIGURE 7.1   Actual and predicted *XY* relationships

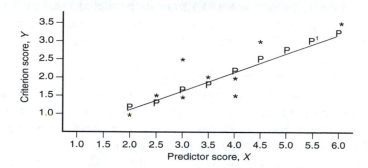

> *X* = score on test of decision-making skill (predictor)
> *Y* = supervisor rating of job performance (criterion)
>
> ★ = relationship of *X* to actual criterion (*Y*) score
> P = relationship of *X* to predicted criterion (*Y'*) score
>
> ¹ Both the *XY* and *XY'* pair lie at this point.

PRACTICE BOX 7.2   Predicting Criterion Scores

On the basis of prior experience, nursing staff indicate that patients with behavioral competence ratings below 4 require intensive supervision.

1. Applying linear regression to the data in Practice Box 7.1, determine the score on the screening test associated with a behavior rating of 4.
2. Should the staff plan to monitor all patients with screening scores below this point? Why or why not?

Compare your answers to the answers at the end of the book. Reread sections as needed.

---

pairs fall on a straight line. Since the correlation between decision-making test score and supervisor ratings is not perfect ($r_{XY} = .86$), applicants with test scores of 3.5 will not necessarily earn ratings of 2.0 at their 1-year evaluations. An additional statistic is needed to adjust for prediction error.

Standard Error of Estimate

In reliability analysis we were able to estimate the amount of measurement error in a set of scores by calculating SEM or s_M, the average amount by which actual test scores differ from underlying true scores. In criterion validity analysis, we can calculate a similar statistic, the **standard error of estimate** (s_E), to represent the average amount of prediction error. Standard error of estimate is the average number of points by which predicted criterion scores differ from actual criterion scores.

One way to determine s_E is to use the information from a criterion validity analysis to predict criterion scores. After we determine the regression equation, we can calculate a predicted criterion score (Y') for each test score (X). We can then subtract each criterion score (Y) from its predicted value (Y') to create a distribution of prediction errors called *residuals*. The standard deviation of that distribution would be s_E, the standard error of estimate. This process is illustrated in Table 7.4.

After the actual and predicted criterion scores are compared to determine the residuals ($Y - Y'$), the standard deviation of the residuals is calculated using the traditional standard deviation formula. This standard deviation is the standard error of estimate, s_E. In this example $s_E = .4$ point. On the average, *predicted* criterion scores differ from *actual* criterion scores by $\frac{4}{10}$ of a point.

Although the preceding analysis is useful for understanding what s_E actually represents, it is an impractical calculation technique. There is a simpler

TABLE 7.4   Determining the Standard Error of Estimate through Linear Regression

Person	X	Y	Y'	$Y - Y'$	$(Y - Y')^2$
A	2.0	1.0	1.1555	−0.1555	.0241803
B	5.5	3.0	3.08925	−0.08925	.0079656
C	4.5	3.0	2.53675	0.46325	.2146006
D	4.0	2.0	2.2605	−0.2065	.0678603
E	3.0	2.5	1.708	0.792	.627264
F	6.0	3.5	3.3655	0.1345	.0180903
G	2.5	1.5	1.43175	0.06825	.0046581
H	3.0	1.5	1.708	−0.208	.043264
I	3.5	2.0	1.9845	0.0155	.0002403
J	4.0	1.5	2.2605	−0.7605	.5783603

$$X_{Y'} = 2.15, \qquad \sigma^2_{Y'} = .4457$$

To calculate the standard deviation of the prediction errors or residuals $(Y - Y')$:

$$\sum(Y - Y') = 0.05375, \qquad \sum(Y - Y')^2 = 1.5864838, \qquad N = 10$$

$$\sigma^2_{Y-Y'} = \frac{1.5864838 - (.05375)^2/10}{10} = .1586, \qquad \sigma_{Y-Y'} = .3982 = .4$$

TABLE 7.5 Estimating the Standard Error of Estimate from r_{XY}

$r_{XY} = .86,$ $\sigma_Y = 0.7762$

$s_E = .7762\sqrt{1 - (.86)^2} = .7762\sqrt{1 - .74}$

$.7762\sqrt{.26} = .3958 = .4$

TABLE 7.6 Comparing the Two Types of Standard Errors

	Standard Error of:	
Dimension	**Measurement**	**Estimate**
Application	Reliability analysis	Criterion validity analysis
Focus	Test score–true score difference	Actual–predicted criterion score difference
Type of error measured	Measurement error (random error)	Prediction error (systematic error)
Error variance formula	$1 - r_{XX}$	$1 - r_{XY}^2$
Standard error formula	$\sigma_X\sqrt{1 - r_{XX}}$ or $\sigma_Y\sqrt{1 - r_{XX}}$	$\sigma_Y\sqrt{1 - r_{XY}^2}$
Symbol	s_M or SEM	s_E

way to determine s_E. Standard error of estimate can be approximated by the formula

$$s_E = \sigma_Y\sqrt{1 - r_{XY}^2}$$

Table 7.5 illustrates this alternative calculation of s_E for the sample problem on job performance. On the average, supervisor ratings predicted from scores on the test are expected to differ from actual supervisor ratings by .4 point. The $\frac{4}{10}$ point also represents the standard deviation of the distribution of prediction errors and in fact is equivalent to the standard error calculated through linear regression.

Like SEM, s_E indicates the *average* amount of error. Some predictions will be off by more than .4 point, others by less than .4 point. Knowing that there is error in prediction makes decisions based on linear regression less attractive. If selection of people is based on predicted criterion score, the error in prediction may lead to the rejection of some good candidates. It is useful,

---

PRACTICE BOX 7.3   Standard Error of Estimate

---

1. Using the data from Practice Box 7.1, calculate the standard error of estimate for predicting behavior rating from the screening test score using the approximation formula.
2. Interpret the statistic. What does it reveal about the predictor–criterion relationship?

    Compare your answers to the answers at the end of the book. Reread sections as needed.

---

therefore, to think of test scores as predicting a *range* of possible criterion scores, rather than a single specific score. In reliability analysis, SEM is used to construct confidence intervals representing a range within which the true score is likely to fall. In criterion validity analysis, s_E is used to construct similar confidence intervals for predicted criterion score.

Before leaving the topic of standard error, it may be useful to examine the two types of standard error together. Table 7.6 compares the formula for s_E to the formula for s_M. Both use the square root of the error variance and a standard deviation. In reliability analysis, the error term is $1 - r_{XX}$; in criterion validity analysis, it is $1 - r_{XY}^2$. In reliability analysis, each administration of a test has its own s_M based on the standard deviation of the test scores generated during that administration. In criterion validity analysis, we always predict performance on the criterion scores. The only prediction error to be measured, therefore, relates to criterion scores. The formula for s_E always uses σ_Y, the *criterion* standard deviation.

Establishing Confidence Intervals

In the absence of a perfect XY relationship, there is always some error in the prediction process. It is best, then, to represent predicted criterion scores as ranges rather than single values. Construction of a predicted criterion score confidence interval requires assumptions similar to those made in constructing a true score confidence interval. Reliability analysis assumes that repeated testing of any individual generates a normal distribution of test scores. The mean of this hypothetical distribution is the individual's true score; the standard deviation is the standard error of measurement, s_M. Since the distribution is assumed to be normal, z-scores can be used to locate intervals encompassing specific percentages of scores.

Criterion validity analysis assumes that repeated evaluation of a person with a given predictor score generates a normal distribution of criterion scores.

We estimate the mean of this hypothetical distribution to be the predicted criterion score calculated through linear regression. The standard error of estimate, s_E, serves as its standard deviation. Because the distribution is assumed to be normal, specific percentages of scores will fall within different intervals represented by z-scores (i.e., multiples of the standard deviation, s_E). Table 7.7 illustrates the calculation of confidence intervals for the sample problem. The hypothetical distribution of criterion scores generated by a predictor score of 3.5 has a mean of 1.98425 (Y') and a standard deviation of .4 (s_E). It is expected that 68% of the criterion scores will fall between z-scores of ±1.0, equal to the mean $(Y') \pm 1.0 s_E$, and 95% of the scores will fall between z-scores of ±1.96 ($Y' \pm 1.96 s_E$). Therefore, 68% of the time a decision-making score of 3.5 will predict a supervisor rating between 1.6 and 2.4; 95% of the time a decision-making score of 3.5 will predict a rating between 1.2 and 2.8. Note that this is an interval around Y', the *predicted* criterion score. Confidence intervals use information about the accuracy of prediction to convert a single predicted score to a predicted score range.

Confidence intervals provide an additional mechanism to improve decisions about cut off scores. Rather than selecting a predictor score based on a single solution of the regression equation, we can compare the outcome of selecting any of several predictor scores. For each, we can construct confidence intervals to determine the range of likely criterion scores for each possible cutoff score. We can then decide which cut off score we prefer. Table 7.8 uses data from the sample problem to illustrate a comparison of the criterion ranges predicted by different test scores.

Table 7.8 puts the selection of a cutoff score in a new light. With a cutoff score of 3.5, 68% of the expected supervisor ratings should fall between 1.6 and 2.4 and 95% between 1.2 and 2.8. Using a cutoff of 3.5 implies that 32% of expected ratings will be outside the 1.6 to 2.4 range and 5% outside the 1.2 to 2.8 range. Since these predictions are based on assuming a normal (symmetric) distribution, the company should expect about 16% (one-half of

TABLE 7.7   Calculating Confidence Intervals in Criterion Validity

X = score on test of decision-making skill = 3.5

Y' = predicted supervisor rating at 1 year = 1.98425

Computing the 68% confidence interval:

$$Y' \pm (1.0)(.4) = 1.9845 \pm .4 = 1.58425 - 2.38425$$

or between 1.6 and 2.4.

Computing the 95% confidence interval:

$$Y' \pm (1.96)(.4) = 1.98425 \pm 0.784 = 1.20025 - 2.76825$$

or between 1.2 and 2.8.

TABLE 7.8   Comparing Confidence
            Intervals in Criterion
            Validity

X = score on test of decision-making skill

Y' = predicted supervisor rating at 1 year

68% CI = $Y' \pm (1.0)(.4) = Y' \pm .4$

95% CI = $Y' \pm (1.96)(.4) = Y' \pm .784$

X	Y'	68% CI	95% CI
2.5	1.43175	1.0–1.8	0.7–2.2
3.0	1.708	1.3–2.1	0.9–2.5
3.5	1.98425	1.6–2.4	1.2–2.8
4.0	2.2605	1.9–2.7	1.5–3.0
4.5	2.53675	2.1–2.9	1.8–3.3

32%) of the ratings to fall below 1.6, 2.5% of which will be below 1.2 (one-half of 5%). If the company is serious about selecting individuals who are likely to earn ratings of 2.0 or above, it might consider raising the cutoff to 4.0 or even 4.5.

The construction of confidence intervals represents the final step in a lengthy process of analysis. Confidence intervals apply criterion validity information directly to score predictions and illustrate the likely outcomes of different decisions. Comparison of these intervals enables decision makers to evaluate different possible scenarios. However, selection decisions sometimes must be tempered by practical considerations. Suppose a college sets a modest SAT cutoff based on a validity analysis. What happens if most applicants meet the cutoff requirement? Has the administration considered the number of people it will be able to accept? Alternatively, what would happen if a cutoff were selected and hardly anyone earned that cutoff score? If our fictitious corporation needed five new managers and had only eight applicants, should selection policy be reconsidered? These questions require use of a different type of analysis that can make projections based on different selection strategies.

Selection Efficiency Analysis

The goal of a criterion validity study is to determine whether a test is useful for decision making. Although the criterion validity coefficient demonstrates how well the test predicts some outcome, it does not necessarily indicate the usefulness of the predictor for specific decision-making situations. For example, suppose a school system using a procedure to identify academically gifted children learns of a new test for identifying giftedness. Even if the test

> **PRACTICE BOX 7.4   Confidence Intervals**
>
> 1. Using the screening score obtained in Practice Box 7.2, calculate the predicted behavioral rating score.
> 2. Calculate the 68% and 95% confidence intervals for the predicted score. Based on your interpretation of these intervals, which patients should be monitored closely? Perform additional calculations as needed.
>
>   Compare your answers to the answers at the end of the book. Reread sections as needed.

proves criterion valid (i.e., predicts grades of children in the gifted program in this school system), the test might not improve on the current selection process. It is possible that the number of children selected would be more than the system could handle or that the performance of children selected through the new procedure is no better than the performance of current participants.

Furthermore, in many applied settings criterion validity coefficients are rather small. For example, in personnel selection research, obtained criterion validity coefficients rarely exceed .4. Table 7.9 presents average criterion validity coefficients for predicting success in clerical jobs based on an analysis of studies including over 140,000 individuals. It would appear that none of these types of tests can effectively predict either performance in job training or level of job performance. However, the criterion validity coefficient determines the *overall* usefulness of a test for decision making. It is also important to determine whether *specific* predictor cutoff scores can accurately classify people in terms of their general level of criterion performance.

The *selection efficiency approach* is designed to evaluate the accuracy of decisions generated by use of specific cut-off scores. Selection efficiency studies present a different approach to criterion validity analysis. The criterion validity coefficient analyzes the relationship between each predictor and criterion score, operating at the interval (or ratio) level of measurement. In contrast, selection efficiency studies determine the proportion of people who fall into different categories defined by combinations of predictor and criterion scores—an analysis of nominal data. Like validity coefficient studies, selection efficiency studies can use data collected through either a predictive or concurrent validity design.

To understand what happens in a selection efficiency study, think about the four possible outcomes when a decision is made:

1. A person could be accepted on the basis of predictor score and perform well on the criterion (an accurate prediction or **hit**, called a *true positive*).

TABLE 7.9 Average Criterion Validity Coefficients for Predicting Success in Clerical Jobs

Test	Job Proficiency Criteria[1]	Training Criteria[2]
General mental ability	.24	.43
Verbal ability	.19	.39
Quantitative ability	.24	.43
Reasoning ability	.21	.22
Perceptual speed	.22	.22
Spatial/mechanical aptitude	.14	.21
Clerical aptitude	.25	.38

[1]For example, performance ratings.
[2]For example, training course grades.
From F. L. Schmidt, J. E. Hunter, and K. Pearlman (1981). Task differences as moderators of aptitude test validity in selection: A red herring. *Journal of Applied Psychology*, 66, 166–185. Reprinted by permission of the American Psychological Association.

2. A person could be accepted on the basis of predictor score and perform poorly on the criterion (an inaccurate prediction or **miss**, called a *false positive*).

3. A person could be rejected on the basis of predictor score and *potentially* have performed well on the criterion (an inaccurate prediction or miss, called a *false negative*).

4. A person could be rejected on the basis of predictor score and *potentially* have performed poorly on the criterion (an accurate prediction or hit, called a *true negative*).

The relationships among these four categories are presented in Table 7.10. If a group of people is evaluated on a predictor test and a criterion measure, a proportion of people will fall into each of these categories. The validity of a test can be determined by comparing proportions of accurate and inaccurate predictions. In general, a test can be useful if it produces a high proportion of accurate decisions.

Factors Affecting Selection Decisions

Selection efficiency studies begin with identification of a desired level of criterion performance, usually referred to as *successful* performance on the criterion. Two variables determine the degree to which a test can improve the quality of decisions: the base rate and the selection rate. The **base rate** is the overall proportion of people in the group under study who are successful

TABLE 7.10   Types of Selection Decisions

Predictor Performance	Criterion Performance	
	Unsuccessful	Successful
Selected	false positive (FP)	true positive (TP)
Not Selected	true negative (TN)	false negative (FN)

Key

Positive refers to people who should succeed.

Negative refers to people who should not succeed.

True refers to an accurate prediction or hit.

False refers to an inaccurate prediction or miss.

Calculations

$$\text{FP rate} = \frac{\text{number of people selected but unsuccessful}}{\text{total number of people}}$$

$$\text{TP rate} = \frac{\text{number of people selected and successful}}{\text{total number of people}}$$

$$\text{TN rate} = \frac{\text{number of people not selected and unsuccessful}}{\text{total number of people}}$$

$$\text{FN rate} = \frac{\text{number of people not selected but successful}}{\text{total number of people}}$$

Note: FP rate + TP rate + TN rate + FN rate = 1.0.

on the criterion, regardless of scores on the predictor test. The **selection rate** is the ratio of people to be selected to people applying. If 100 people apply and 10 will be selected, the selection rate is 10%. Table 7.11 locates these additional measures in the selection efficiency table.

The base rate greatly influences the outcomes of decisions. If 95% of the people under consideration are likely to succeed, there is not much point to using a test for decision making. At that base rate, random selection will lead to selecting a potentially successful group. However, a high base rate presents an even more complicated scenario. Using the language of selection efficiency studies, the base rate equals the proportion of true positives (TPs) plus the proportion of false negatives (FNs). A high base rate indicates that the criterion characteristic is fairly common, even among those who are not selected. Whether selection is random or involves a predictor test, a high base rate implies that many of those who are not selected could in fact have succeeded. In other words, high base rates are associated with many TPs, correct decisions, *and* many FNs, incorrect decisions (see Table 7.11).

TABLE 7.11   Other Variables in Selection Efficiency Studies

	Criterion Performance		
Predictor Performance	Unsuccessful	Successful	
Selected	false positive	true positive	selection ratio (SR)
Not Selected	true negative	false negative	
		base rate (BR)	

$$SR = \frac{\text{number of people selected}}{\text{total number of people}} = FP \text{ rate} + TP \text{ rate}$$

$$BR = \frac{\text{number of people successful}}{\text{total number of people}} = TP \text{ rate} + FN \text{ rate}$$

On the other hand, if only 30% of the people typically succeed, there is room for improvement in the selection process. However, very low base rates present another potential problem. Low base rates imply that the criterion characteristic is rare. In an effort to select more people with the characteristic (TPs), the total number of people selected will increase. But the group of people selected also includes individuals *without* the characteristic—the false positives (FPs). Low base rates, by leading to the selection of more people, increase the rate of FP decision errors. In general, tests are most likely to be useful with moderate base rates (e.g., 50%).

The selection rate indicates the degree to which it is feasible to use a test for making decisions. If only 12 people apply for 10 jobs, there is not much point to using a test for selecting from the pool of candidates. With so few applicants, it will be difficult to turn anyone away. Alternatively, if 100 people apply for 10 jobs, it is certainly advantageous to develop a procedure to select the best individuals from the applicant pool. When the selection rate is small, even tests with low criterion validity coefficients can improve the decision-making process. However, the usefulness of a predictor test is affected by the *overall* accuracy of decisions. When the selection rate is high, most people will be selected, including people who are unlikely to be successful (FPs). When the selection rate is low, most people will be rejected, including people who could have succeeded (FNs). Extreme selection rates, like extreme base rates, can lead to increases in certain types of decision errors.

Evaluating Selection Strategies

Selection efficiency studies are used to determine the practical implications of using a test to select certain people from a larger group. There are two critical issues in a selection efficiency study. First, will selection on the basis of test score generate an acceptable number of people? Second, will it produce a larger group of people who are successful than random selection, if no selection procedure is currently in use, or the current selection procedure? In other words, selection efficiency studies focus on how use of the test affects the selection rate and the likelihood of selecting successful people.

The sample data presented in Table 7.1 can be adapted to illustrate a selection efficiency study. Recall that a corporation has obtained decision-making test scores and 1-year performance ratings for a group of middle-level managers. The test is under consideration as a screening device to select people likely to receive supervisor ratings of at least 2.0. This becomes our operational definition of "success" on the criterion. Earlier regression analysis suggested the strategy of selecting candidates with test scores of at least 3.5. This becomes our operational definition of "success" on the predictor, called the *cut off* or *cutting score*. Using this information, we can define some selection decision categories:

1. People with test scores of at least 3.5 and performance ratings of at least 2.0 (true positives)
2. People with test scores of at least 3.5 and performance ratings below 2.0 (false positives)
3. People with test scores below 3.5 and performance ratings of at least 2.0 (false negatives)
4. People with test scores below 3.5 and performance ratings below 2.0 (true negatives)

Table 7.12 presents the number of people in each category, based on the original information in Table 7.1. Note that the entries indicate the number of people in each category (a nominal measurement), that each person fits only into one category, and that all people are included in the table. The sum of the numbers in all the boxes should equal the total number of people studied ($N = 10$). The base rate (BR) is the proportion of people who are successful on the criterion regardless of their scores on the predictor. Since 6 out of 10 had performance ratings of 2.0 or better, the base rate is $\frac{6}{10}$, or 60%.

The selection rate (SR) is the proportion of people who will be selected *given a particular score on the predictor test*. In this case the company will select 6 people or 60% of the available candidates. The company now must address the first important issue in selection efficiency studies: If we use this test as planned, will we select a reasonable number of people? On the basis of the pilot data, the company will select 60% of the candidates. Management must determine

TABLE 7.12 Sample Selection Efficiency Problem

Predictor = score on test of decision making

Criterion = supervisor rating of job performance
Success on criterion = rating of at least 2.0

Score on predictor to be selected = at least 3.5
("success" on predictor)

Decision-making Test Score	Supervisor Rating		
	Rating < 2.0	Rating > or = 2.0	
Test score > or = 3.5	1	5	SR
Test score < 3.5	3	1	
		BR	

$$\text{Base rate (BR)} = \frac{5+1}{10} = 60\%$$

$$\text{Selection ratio (SR)} = \frac{1+5}{10} = 60\%$$

whether or not that translates into enough people or too many people, given the number of positions typically available. It is possible that a different predictor score might be better, given the practical constraint of number of positions.

The second issue is whether using the test as planned selects a greater proportion of successful people than either random selection or the current procedure, if one exists. According to this study, using the test will select a group of 6 people, 5 of whom are predicted to be successful. The rate of success in the selected group, called the *positive hit rate* (PHR), is $\frac{5}{6}$, or 83%. This looks pretty good. The base rate for successful performance on the criterion was 60%. We would expect 60% of the total group to succeed on the criterion; in other words, by random selection we should obtain a group in which 60% of the people are likely to succeed. By using scores on the *test* to select people, 83% of the people in the group we select are likely to succeed.

To evaluate the selection strategy more completely, we can compare its pattern of results to those generated either by random selection or the current selection procedure. Let's assume the company has no regular selection procedure; we then would compare the proposed selection process to random selection of people. We begin by creating a table of decisions based on a random selection strategy. Table 7.13 illustrates this process. The number of people expected to fall into each category by chance is determined using the base rate and selection rate generated in the selection study. In practical terms,

---

PRACTICE BOX 7.5   Creating a Selection Efficiency Table

---

1. Using the data from Practice Box 7.1, create a selection efficiency table in which:
   a. People with test scores of at least 7 are selected for minimal monitoring.
   b. People with behavioral competence ratings of at least 4 are considered competent.
2. Calculate the base rate and selection ratio. Interpret each statistic.
3. Calculate the positive hit rate and compare it to the base rate. Does the strategy look good? Explain.

   Compare your answers to the answers at the end of the book. Reread sections as needed.

---

this means we use the row and column totals from the selection efficiency table (Table 7.12) in our calculations. The expected number for each category is determined by the formula

$$\text{number expected by chance} = \frac{\text{row total} \times \text{column total}}{\text{total number of people}}$$

The data in Table 7.13 can be used to determine the positive hit rate expected when people are randomly selected. According to Table 7.13, random selection will generate 3.6 successful people out of a selected group of 6. The positive hit rate using random selection is 3.6/6 or 60%, the same proportion as the base rate itself! In fact, if our goal is only to compose positive hit rates using random selection or the proposed test, we don't even need to create this additional table. The base rate *defines* the positive hit rate using random selection. However, the table of random selection outcomes tells us much more. It presents the actual patterns of hits and misses. Comparing this table to the selection strategy table (see Table 7.12) clearly illustrates how the test increases prediction accuracy (the TP and TN boxes) and decreases prediction error (the FP and FN boxes).

There are other selection efficiency statistics that reflect the specific rates of inaccurate predictions (FP and FN) associated with a selection procedure. In some circumstances these rates greatly influence the usefulness of a predictor test. For example, assume that a test is being used in a prison prerelease program to decide which inmates to parole. A false positive in this scenario is an inmate who is released but does not "succeed" in the outside world. Since the inmate's "lack of success" may place other people in danger, it would be important to set the cutoff score at a point that minimizes the false positive rate. A general index of prediction success is the *total hit rate* (THR), the

TABLE 7.13 Decisions Generated through Random Selection

1. Determine the row and column totals using the data from the selection study (see Table 7.10).
2. Determine the randomly generated number for each box through the formula

$$\frac{\text{row total} \times \text{column total}}{\text{total number of people}}$$

Decision-making Test Score	Supervisor Rating		
	Rating < 2.0	Rating > or = 2.0	
Test score > or = 3.5	2.4 (FP)	3.6 (TP)	6
Test score < 3.5	1.6 (TN)	2.4 (FN)	4
	4	6	10

$$FP = \frac{6 \times 4}{10} = \frac{24}{10} = 2.4 \qquad\qquad TP = \frac{6 \times 6}{10} = \frac{36}{10} = 3.6$$

$$TN = \frac{4 \times 4}{10} = \frac{16}{10} = 1.6 \qquad\qquad FN = \frac{6 \times 4}{10} = \frac{24}{10} = 2.4$$

overall proportion of correct predictions, including both predictions of success and lack of success. The total hit rate, therefore, equals the proportion of true positives plus the proportion of true negatives. It is calculated by adding the number of true positives to the number of true negatives and dividing by the total number of people. In the preceding example (see Table 7.12), the total hit rate equals 5 (number of true positives) + 3 (number of true negatives) divided by 10, or .8. According to this analysis, 80% of our predictions in this case will be accurate. Inaccurate predictions, including both predictions of success and of failure, occur only 20% of the time.

In the sample problem the results of the two criterion validity analyses concur. In both cases the test is revealed as a valid way to predict 1-year supervisor ratings of job performance. This doesn't always happen. Sometimes the selection efficiency approach indicates that a predictor has value even though the criterion validity coefficient is rather low. The results may differ because the two types of criterion validity analysis deal with two different levels of measurement. The coefficient approach considers the value of every single predictor score and its relationship to a corresponding criterion score. It is an interval level of analysis, a precise type of analysis. The selection efficiency approach considers how different ranges of predictor scores are related to different ranges of criterion scores. It is a nominal level of analysis that does not

---

PRACTICE BOX 7.6   Evaluating a Selection Procedure

---

1. Using the information from the selection table developed in Practice Box 7.5, determine the number of people expected by chance in each decision category.
2. Calculate the positive hit for the chance scenario and compare it to the rate using the selection strategy. Does the strategy still look good? Explain.
3. Now calculate the false negative rates for both the chance scenario and the selection strategy. How do these statistics affect your conclusions about the value of the selection strategy? Explain.

   Compare your answers to the answers at the end of the book. Reread sections as needed.

---

examine the pairwise relationships between scores. It takes a more global approach. In the sample problem, the relationship between predictor and criterion was so strong that it emerged even in the more stringent, interval-level analysis.

Sometimes the reverse is true. A test may be able to predict criterion scores quite well, but it may not prove useful as a selection tool. Why? Check back through the section on factors affecting selection decisions. See if you can use the two selection efficiency variables described in that section to explain this set of events.

CONTENT VALIDITY

Any test includes only a sample of test items drawn from the set of all possible test items. **Content validity** is important whenever a test is used to make inferences about the broader domain of knowledge and/or skills represented by a sample of items. It is necessary to determine if differences among people in test scores (σ_X^2) are attributable to differences in their domain-relevant knowledge and/or skills (σ_R^2).

Achievement tests are the classic examples. An achievement test is designed to assess knowledge and/or skills within a particular domain. Although each test includes a finite number of items, scores on the tests are typically used to make inferences about mastery of the domain—not just mastery of the items. To be content valid, the test must provide an accurate estimate of the test taker's mastery of that domain. Test developers, therefore, are confronted with the task of selecting sets of test questions that adequately represent the underlying domain. Differences in test scores must reflect differences in domain-appropriate characteristics.

Imagine the construction of a college algebra test. The test provides a measure of student performance on a set of college algebra items. But the real variable of interest is students' knowledge of college algebra, not students' performance on this particular set of test questions. In other words, we would like to be able to use scores on this test to make inferences about mastery of college algebra. The validity of these inferences is determined by the extent to which the test items are a good sample of the total pool of possible test items.

Although content validity most often is associated with achievement tests, it sometimes is an issue for other types of tests. A test of spatial aptitude contains a sample of items representing a broader domain. A vocational interest test may sample reactions to different settings and activities. Basically, content validity is important for all maximal performance tests and for those typical performance tests designed to sample content and behavioral domains.

Process of Content Validation

Determining content validity usually is a qualitative process in which test items are compared to a detailed description of the test domain. Unfortunately, there is no single statistical measure of content validity. Instead, content validity is a judgment derived from the weight of evidence accumulated through the comparison process. Do not assume, however, that a haphazard comparison is sufficient to demonstrate content validity. The comparison process must adhere to certain guidelines and must be executed by individuals considered experts in the domain under study. If the test is judged *appropriate*, we infer that differences in test scores (σ_X^2) reflect differences in domain-relevant characteristics (σ_R^2).

Content validation begins with an analysis of the domain. The test developer must, as clearly as possible, specify the knowledge and skills that the test is designed to cover. In some cases, an analysis of the domain (i.e., a test plan) is written before the test items are selected. As discussed in Chapter 2, the construction of content-referenced tests *requires* specification of the content domain before generating test items. Whether written before or after item selection, the two most common techniques for analyzing a content domain are construction of a content or skills test plan and a set of behavioral objectives (see Chapter 2).

A detailed analysis of the domain requires more than simply outlining the nature of the domain. The analysis should include information about the centrality or importance of different topics and skills. In a content-valid test, elements of greater importance will receive more emphasis, usually in the form of more items or more points being devoted to that element. Furthermore, the analysis should include sufficient information about the importance of different skills and behaviors to determine the most appropriate types of test questions. The content validity of the test is also influenced by the form of the test items used to measure the domain.

Table 7.14 presents a possible analysis of the content domain *criterion validity* as presented in this chapter. The chart lists the different topics comprising the domain and uses the number of pages as a measure of the relative emphasis given to each one. According to the chart, a content-valid test would assign more points to questions regarding standard error of estimate than to questions about criterion validity designs. The analysis also includes specific information about how these topics are presented. On the basis of the chart, a valid test would stress skills such as recognition of terminology and calculation and interpretation of statistics. Questions requiring extensive evaluation of the usefulness of different statistics or the viability of their underlying assumptions would be inappropriate—these topics are drawn from a domain that extends to a much deeper level of analysis.

Once the analysis is complete, the content and structure of the test must be compared to the content and structure of the domain. Three issues must be addressed. First, is the content of the test items appropriate to the domain? Each test item must be related directly to an element of the domain. For example, a college algebra achievement test could contain questions about multiplication of fractions, but should not contain questions on the calculation of derivatives and integrals. Although multiplication of numerical fractions (e.g., $\frac{1}{2} \times \frac{3}{4}$) may be "too simple" for the college algebra domain, multiplication of algebraic fractions (e.g., $1/a \times 3/b$) is not. In the domain of college algebra, students learn to apply earlier multiplication skills to algebraic expressions. Questions on multiplication of algebraic fractions sample their application skills and therefore are appropriate. On the other hand, calculations of derivatives and integrals belong to the domain of calculus. These operations are outside the boundaries of college algebra, and furthermore are part of a domain that is *above* college algebra in the hierarchy of mathematical topics. Although the test can sample application of lower level skills (e.g., multiplication), it cannot sample skills that are beyond the level of college algebra.

Second, is the form of the questions appropriate? Questions can be written different ways to tap different behaviors and skills. For example, a question on multiplication of fractions could be written to tap simple knowledge of the rules, ability to interpret the rules, or ability to apply the rules to the solution of a specific word problem. The form of each question should be justifiable given the information in the domain analysis.

Third, is the item sample representative of the larger domain? A content-valid test has an overall structure that parallels the structure of the domain. Central elements of the domain, elements of greater importance, should receive more emphasis within the test. In other words, items representing important aspects of the domain should contribute more to total test score than items representing secondary aspects of the domain.

TABLE 7.14 Analysis of a Content Domain: The Criterion Validity Portion of Chapter 7

Topic	No. of Pages[1]	Focus[2]
Criterion validity designs	1.5	Identifies each Lists advantages and disadvantages Gives example of each
Criterion validity coefficient	4	Defines r_{XY} and r_{XY}^2 Gives example of each Interprets statistics
Predicting criterion scores	3	Reviews regression equation Gives example Interprets statistics Limitation of technique
Standard error of estimate	2	Defines s_E, residuals Calculation from regression (example) Approximation technique (example) Compares to s_M
Confidence intervals	3	Reviews logic of procedure Demonstrates calculation (example) Demonstrates application (example)
Selection efficiency approach	2	Describes rationale for technique Gives examples of its use Compares to coefficient approach Identifies types of decisions made
Factors affecting selection decisions	4	Defines base rate, selection ratio Describes impacts of each (examples)
Evaluating selection strategies	2.5	Describes basic logic of process Calculation of proportions (actual and expected by chance) Gives example Compares to coefficient approach

[1]Used as a measure of the relative emphasis given to each topic.
[2]Used to represent level of analysis and extent of detail presented on each topic.

Content Validity versus Face Validity

Content validity frequently is confused with **face validity**. A test has face validity when the items look like they measure what they are supposed to measure. In face validity, the judgment about item appropriateness is made by the test taker, rather than an expert in the domain. Face validity is determined by a superficial examination of test items and is based on the presence of obvious relationships between items and the domain. Content validity is determined by an in-depth analysis of the exam by someone who is knowledgeable about the content domain. It is based on clear relationships among item content, format, and distribution and the structure of the domain.

However, face validity may be an important influence on test-taker behavior. When items do not appear relevant to test purpose, test takers may become angry or discouraged and may not perform as well as they should. Perhaps you have taken an exam that you thought did not cover the assigned material and felt your ability to concentrate change as you considered the "unfairness" of the test. On the other hand, items that are obviously relevant to the purpose of the test may threaten the validity of test score data by introducing response sets (see Chapter 4). Consider an "honesty" test used as part of a job application process with true/false questions like "Big companies expect employees to pilfer office supplies." How many people would mark this statement "true"? In essence, test developers must create a delicate balance among three elements: the need for test takers to believe the test is valid, the need for accurate test data, and the need for content-valid items.

Other Approaches to Content Validation

The most common process of content validation is systematic comparison of a test to a domain by expert judges. Although such a process evaluates the nature of the item sample, the central issue in content validity, it does not produce a quantitative measure. Psychologists and educators have suggested a variety of techniques to supplement the evaluation process and provide some statistical measures relevant to content validity.

Two proposals use reliability coefficients to support conclusions regarding content validity. (Since these are reliability coefficients, they are not appropriate as actual *measures* of content validity.) Brown (1983) suggests the development of standard rating scales (see Chapter 4) for judges to use in the evaluation process. For example, scales could be developed to rate elements such as representativeness of item sample, appropriateness of item content, and appropriateness of item format. A series of judges would use the scales to rate a particular test. The ratings could be compared statistically to determine degree of agreement, which in turn would be used as an estimate of interrater reliability. A high degree of interrater reliability would imply consensus regarding the test's degree of content validity. Decisions about test items could be made by considering the extent to which a set of judges views the items as content-valid.

Cronbach (1971) proposes evaluating content validity by correlating scores on two independently constructed forms of a test. Two separate teams could be given the same analysis of a content domain and independently generate items to sample that domain. The two resulting tests would be administered to a group of people and the scores correlated as in an alternate form reliability analysis. A high correlation between the forms would imply that both sets of items are tapping the same content domain and therefore that each set of items has content validity.

Brown (1983) suggests two additional techniques common to construct validity analysis: (1) the use of a pretest–posttest design and (2) correlating scores of tests designed to measure the same domain. In the first scenario, a test is administered to a group of people who have no background in the test domain. The group is then exposed to the domain and posttested with the original test. A significant increase in test scores implies that the test covers material relevant to that domain. In the second scenario, scores on a test are correlated with scores on other tests theoretically measuring the same domain. The key to effective use of this technique is to ensure that the tests do measure the same domain both in terms of content and structure. Tests designed to cover similar topics (e.g., European history) may in fact be drawn from differently structured domains.

CONSTRUCT VALIDITY

Construct validity is another question about whether a test measures what it is intended to measure. In this case, the focus is a psychological construct, such as intelligence, aggression, or extroversion. Many of these attributes are referred to as *personality dimensions* or *personality traits*. In fact, the majority of construct validity studies focus on tests of personality.

To understand better the need for construct validation studies, consider the attribute *intelligence*, one which has been the subject of debate for over a century. Why so much disagreement? Isn't it simple to develop a test to determine level of intelligence? Not necessarily. Intelligence is not a physical characteristic, like height, that can be measured directly. Because it is a construct, psychologists must identify behaviors that reflect intelligence and develop tests of these behaviors. But to be certain that the tests really measure the desired characteristics, psychologists must reverse the process and examine the relationship between scores on the tests and other independent measures. Without additional data to confirm that the tests measure intelligence, it is impossible to know what the tests really measure.

Process of Construct Validation

There is no single statistic to determine the construct validity of a test. Like content validity, it is a judgment based on the weight of evidence collected from a variety of procedures. In general, these procedures compare performance on the construct test to other measures of behavior and personality. The measures selected are ones with predictable relationships to scores on the test. Selection of measures requires producing a detailed analysis of the construct, a process referred to in Chapter 2 as construct explication. Basically, the test developer compiles a list of specific attributes and behaviors that demonstrate the presence of the construct and specific attributes and behaviors inconsistent with its presence. In addition, the test developer may gather information about other tests of the construct being studied and tests of related constructs. All these items provide possible measures to be correlated with scores on the test.

Table 7.15 illustrates a possible analysis of the construct *anxiety*. First, the table lists behaviors related to the presence of anxiety. Measures of these variables should show positive correlations with scores on a test of anxiety. Next, the table lists behaviors inconsistent with the presence of anxiety. Measures of these variables should show negative correlations with scores on a test of anxiety. The table also includes other constructs related to anxiety. Measures of these constructs may also show positive correlations with test scores. The analysis enables us to make predictions for validating the test: Performance on the test should be related in specific ways to performance on other measures. The next step is to test these hypotheses through a variety of techniques.

TABLE 7.15   Possible Analysis of the Construct "Anxiety"

Measures indicating presence of construct

Physiological: increased heart rate, respiration, blood pressure, GSR (galvanic
              skin response)

Behavioral: pacing, nail-biting, fidgeting, lack of eye contact

Measures associated with absence of construct

Rapid decision making
Assertiveness
Life satisfaction
Self-confidence
Health

Related constructs

Depression
Fear
Stress

Construct Validation Techniques

A simple construct validation procedure is to correlate scores on the test with scores on another established test measuring the same construct. Referred to as a *congruent validity measure*, the resulting correlation coefficient indicates the extent to which scores on the test being analyzed predict scores on established tests. For example, scores on a new test designed to measure anxiety should have a high positive correlation with scores on existing measures of the construct. A related technique, calculating a *convergent validity measure*, correlates scores on the test under study with scores on tests of related constructs. If research demonstrates a relationship between anxiety and depression, scores on the new test should correlate positively with measures of depression.

Construct validity can also be supported by patterns of *criterion-validity* coefficients. A test of a particular construct should predict the presence of behaviors related to that construct. Test scores can be correlated with the instance of behaviors implied by the construct. For example, scores on a test of anxiety should predict the extent of eye contact during an interview. It is even possible to use experimental manipulations to examine relationships between scores on the test and different situations. For example, people with high and low scores on a test of anxiety should react differently to spending half an hour in a crowded waiting room.

In addition, scores on the new test can be correlated with scores on tests of unrelated constructs, especially those linked to behaviors inconsistent with the behaviors implied by the construct under study. Called a *discriminant* or *divergent validity measure*, the expected correlation would be near 0 or even negative depending on the constructs being compared. A test of extroversion, for example, might be expected to show no correlation with an intelligence test. But when scores are compared to scores on a test of anxiety, a negative correlation should occur.

Factor analysis is a statistical procedure that can be used to study the internal structure of a construct test. Basically, factor analysis is a sophisticated correlation technique that looks for the relationships between performances on sets of test items. The pattern of item correlations is used to identify the number of different factors or characteristics measured by the test. In construct validation, factor analysis can be used to determine whether the pattern of test scores is consistent with the construct under study. If the test covers a single, specific construct, a small set of factors should emerge. These factors should relate to the different behaviors exemplifying the construct under study. A test of anxiety might produce two factors: one factor covering questions about physiological reactions and the second covering questions about behaviors.

Table 7.16 presents a possible plan for evaluating the construct validity of a new test of anxiety. The plan describes the types of procedures to use, the

TABLE 7.16   Possible Plan for Validating a New Test of Anxiety

Congruent validity
Correlate scores on new test of anxiety with scores on established tests of
   anxiety; expect high positive correlations.

Convergent validity
Correlate scores on new test of anxiety with scores on established tests of
   related constructs such as depression, fear, and stress; expect high positive
   correlations.

Criterion validity
Correlate scores on new test of anxiety with physiological and behavioral
   measures characteristic of anxiety; expect high positive correlations.

Experimental manipulation
Place test takers in anxiety-producing situation; compare behavioral and
   physiological measures for people with high scores on the new test of
   anxiety to behavioral and physiological measures for people with low scores
   on the new test of anxiety; expect behavioral and physiological measures to
   increase more for people with high test scores.

Discriminant or divergent validity
Correlate scores on new test of anxiety with scores on tests of constructs
   inconsistent with the presence of anxiety; expect high negative correlations.

Factor analysis
Factor analyze scores on new test of anxiety; expect emergence of small
   number of factors.

variables and constructs to study, and the hypothesized relationships between
test scores and these other measures. The construct validation plan provides
the test developer with a specific set of hypotheses to evaluate and a coherent
strategy for the evaluation process. The construct validity of the test depends
on the extent to which these hypotheses are supported.

SUMMARY AND KEY CONCEPTS

The traditional validity question is whether a test measures what it was intended to measure. A valid test measures characteristics that are relevant to
its purpose. Determining test validity becomes important only after the test
has demonstrated reliability. If a test cannot produce a consistent measure
of performance, the question of *what* the test measures is moot. In fact, the
validity of a test is limited statistically by its reliability.

   Validity analysis focuses on the *true score* component of test scores,
the component measuring stable test-taker characteristics. Validity analysis
partitions true score into two factors: a measure of test-relevant characteristics

and a measure of test-irrelevant characteristics. Since these are components of true score, both types of characteristics are measured every time the test is administered. The latter component, however, is a source of measurement error. And because these test-irrelevant characteristics are stable attributes of test takers, present on every administration of the test, they are referred to as sources of systematic measurement error. Theoretically, the validity of a test equals the proportion of **relevant test score variance**, the proportion of test score variance due to variance in relevant characteristics. Validity is undermined by the extent of **systematic error variance**, the proportion of test score variance due to variance in irrelevant characteristics. However, unlike the case of test reliability, there is no single statistical measure of test validity.

There are three types of validity analysis, each appropriate for a different question about test performance. In **criterion validity** analysis, the purpose of a test is to predict performance on some other variable. The test is called the *predictor* and the other variable the *criterion*. We assume that if a test successfully predicts performance on the criterion measure it must be measuring criterion-valid characteristics of test takers. Criterion validity can be represented statistically with a criterion validity coefficient, which in turn can be used to predict criterion scores through linear regression. The degree of error in prediction is called the **standard error of estimate** or s_E. The standard error of estimate equals the standard deviation of the residuals and can be used to determine confidence intervals for predicted criterion scores.

Alternatively, criterion validity can be examined through the selection efficiency approach using nominal data. Selection efficiency studies determine the probability of four types of decisions based on predictor score: **hits**, including true positives and true negative and **misses**, including false positives and false negatives. Important statistics in selection efficiency studies include the **base rate**, the **selection rate**, the positive hit rate, and the total hit rate. Both types of criterion validity analysis can be performed on data collected through either predictive validity or concurrent validity studies.

In **content validity** analysis, the purpose of a test is to represent performance on a particular domain. Since any test represents only a sample of possible items, it is important to know whether we can generalize from performance on these items and draw conclusions about the overall domain. There is no statistical measure of content validity. Instead, it is a judgment based on comparison of the structure of the test to the structure of the domain. Unlike **face validity**, in which a test taker evaluates the appropriateness of test items, content validity requires the use of experts.

In **construct validity**, the purpose of a test is to measure a hypothetical construct, a dimension or attribute on which people may vary. Construct validation requires determining the relationship between scores on the test and other measures that are either theoretically related to the construct or theoretically distinct from the construct. The process begins with construct explication, a detailed analysis of the nature of the construct. Although there is no single statistical measure of construct validity, a variety of statistical procedures can be used in the validation process, including congruent validity measures, convergent validity measures, criterion validity coefficients, experimental manipulations, discriminant or divergent validity measures, and factor analysis. Construct validity is inferred from the weight of evidence accumulated through the validation process.

QUESTIONS

7.1 In your own words, explain the difference between random measurement error and systematic measurement error. Why does one affect test reliability and the other test validity?

7.2 Explain how you can tell which type(s) of validity are important in a particular testing scenario.

Questions 3 through 10 use the following data. A psychologist is developing a test of assertiveness. The chart presents the scores of 20 subjects on the personality test along with a behavioral measure of the number of times each person acted assertively in an experimental manipulation.

Person	Personality Test	Behavioral Measure
1	40	2
2	60	5
3	40	2
4	50	4
5	70	5
6	40	2
7	60	4
8	50	3
9	30	0
10	50	3
11	60	4
12	20	0
13	40	2
14	30	1
15	50	4
16	30	2
17	50	4
18	60	3
19	40	3
20	60	3

Summary statistics:

Personality test:	$\overline{X} = 46.5,$	$\sigma = 12.7574$
Behavioral measure:	$\overline{X} = 2.8$	$\sigma = 1.4$

7.3 Calculate and interpret the criterion validity coefficient and s_E.

7.4 Using linear regression, determine the test score associated with four instances of assertiveness in the experimental manipulation.

7.5 Using the regression equation, determine the number of assertive behaviors expected from someone with a test score of 60.

7.6 Calculate the 95% confidence interval for the predicted behavioral measure in Question 5. If you measured a person with a test score of 60 repeatedly, how often (approximately) would you expect the person to demonstrate less than three instances of assertive behavior?

7.7 The psychologist is interested in using this test to identify highly assertive individuals. The psychologist operationally defines "highly assertive" as the presence of four or more assertive actions in the experimental setting. Using the preceding data, what is the base rate for high assertiveness in the sampled tested?

7.8 What are the results of using a test score of 50 to select highly assertive people?

7.9 What is the lowest cut-off score the psychologist can use to select a group in which at least two-thirds of the people are highly assertive?

7.10 After all these criterion validity calculations, explain why this research is a good example of a construct validity analysis.

Item Analysis

CHAPTER OUTLINE

CHAPTER GOALS AND OBJECTIVES

After completing this chapter you should be able to:

- Explain how item characteristics can affect test reliability and validity.
- Calculate and interpret item difficulty values.
- Determine optimal item difficulty values for norm-referenced and criterion-referenced ability tests.

- Describe how item difficulty values affect patterns of ability test scores.
- Determine percent endorsement statistics for items on typical performance tests.
- Calculate and interpret item discrimination indexes for ability tests, personality and interest tests, and attitude scales.
- Calculate and interpret item-total correlations.
- Use item-discrimination data to construct personality, attitude, and interest test scales.
- Use item-discrimination data to estimate item difficulty.
- Use item-discrimination data to estimate a criterion validity coefficient.
- Calculate and interpret distractor power values.
- Describe the relationships among different item statistics.
- Construct and interpret discrimination by difficulty graphs.
- Construct and interpret item characteristic curves.

$\mathbf{T}$he term *item analysis* refers to a group of statistics that can be calculated for individual test items. There are a variety of item statistics that can be computed and a variety of calculation techniques. The three most commonly used statistics are item difficulty, item discrimination, and distractor power. Although these statistics are usually discussed in regard to multiple-choice ability tests, two of them, item difficulty and item discrimination, can be adapted to the analysis of short-answer and essay questions and are also used on personality, interest, and attitude tests.

The preceding two chapters stressed the importance of evaluating the reliability and validity of tests and presented several techniques for test analysis. Chapter 6 discussed how random events can affect the reliability of test results by introducing error into the measurement process. Chapter 7 discussed how measurement of stable but irrelevant characteristics of test takers threatens test validity. This chapter focuses on how the characteristics of test items affect the overall quality of a test, particularly the test's reliability and validity.

LOGIC OF ITEM ANALYSIS

Consider a 30-item test containing 10 items on which all test takers are incorrect. It is easy to illustrate how the presence of these difficult items threatens both the reliability and validity of the test. If all test takers are incorrect on 10 out of 30 items, the distribution of scores on this test is likely to be similar to the distribution of scores on a 20-item test. The presence of so many difficult items in essence reduces test length by one-third. Reducing the number of items on which test takers can differ reduces the potential variability of test scores. In Chapter 6, test length and the variability of test scores were identified as factors influencing test reliability. In fact, the increase in reliability to be expected by increasing the length of a test can be estimated by the Spearman–Brown prophesy formula. Conversely, when test length decreases, reliability decreases as well. A test with a large proportion of difficult items generates scores with properties similar to a shorter test, including lower reliability.

How does the presence of these 10 very difficult items affect the validity of the test? Chapter 7 presented several important relationships between the reliability and the validity of a test. For example, reliability was discussed as a "necessary but not sufficient condition" for test validity. Furthermore, the reliability of a test was identified as a factor placing actual statistical limits on that test's potential validity. If the presence of a large proportion of difficult items is likely to reduce test reliability, it also is likely to reduce the test's validity.

In short, item statistics such as item difficulty can help explain *why* a test shows a certain level of reliability and validity. Item analysis is particularly useful when tests are unreliable or fail to demonstrate predicted relationships with criterion measures. The test may include poorly worded questions that elicit guessing or questions not measuring the appropriate construct or content domain. The reliability and validity of the test can be improved by removing or rewriting these items.

Table 8.1 presents fictitious data from a 20-item multiple-choice test administered to a 30-person biology class. These data will be used to illustrate item-analysis procedures throughout the chapter.

TABLE 8.1   Sample Test for Item Analysis

The following charts present data on a 20-question, four-alternative, multiple-choice test taken by 30 biology students. The first chart shows the answers for the 10 students with the highest test grades (top 10), the second chart the answers for the 10 students with the middle 10 grades (middle 10), and the third chart the answers for 10 students with the lowest grades (bottom 10).

In each chart, the top row lists the total grade for each student in that group (maximum correct = 20). The left-hand column in each chart lists the question numbers (1 to 20), followed by the correct answer in parentheses. Questions answered correctly are marked with a *. The remaining entries indicate the incorrect alternatives each student selected for each question.

I. Top 10 students in the class

Question Number	Correct Answer	Total Number of Questions Correct									
		19	18	18	17	17	16	16	16	16	16
1	(A)	*	*	*	*	*	*	*	*	*	*
2	(C)	*	B	*	*	*	*	*	A	*	*
3	(D)	*	*	*	*	*	*	*	*	B	*
4	(B)	*	*	*	*	*	A	A	*	*	D
5	(C)	*	*	*	*	B	*	*	*	*	B
6	(B)	C	*	*	*	*	*	*	*	*	*
7	(A)	*	*	*	B	B	*	D	*	*	*
8	(D)	*	*	*	*	*	*	*	B	C	*
9	(A)	*	*	*	B	*	*	*	*	*	C
10	(C)	*	A	B	*	*	*	*	*	*	*
11	(B)	*	*	*	*	*	C	A	C	*	*
12	(A)	*	*	*	*	*	*	*	B	*	*
13	(D)	*	*	*	*	*	*	B	*	*	*
14	(C)	*	*	*	A	*	*	*	*	A	*
15	(B)	*	*	C	*	*	*	*	*	*	*
16	(A)	*	*	*	*	*	B	*	*	C	*
17	(D)	*	*	*	*	*	*	*	*	*	*
18	(C)	*	*	*	*	A	D	*	*	*	*
19	(D)	*	*	*	*	*	*	*	*	*	A
20	(B)	*	*	*	*	*	*	*	*	*	*

Table 8.1 continued on page 263

ITEM-DIFFICULTY ANALYSIS

Item-difficulty analysis is appropriate for maximal performance tests—achievement and aptitude tests—because the analysis requires that test items be scored as correct or incorrect. It is not appropriate for typical performance tests, such as personality tests or interest inventories. The most common measure of item difficulty is the percentage of test takers who answer the item correctly. Referred to as the **item-difficulty index**, it is represented by the symbol p and calculated as follows:

$$p = \frac{\text{number of persons answering item correctly}}{N}$$

in which

p = item difficulty for a particular test item

N = the total number of people taking the test

II. Middle 10 students in the class

Question Number	Correct Answer	Total Number of Questions Correct									
		15	15	15	15	14	14	14	13	13	12
1	(A)	*	*	*	*	*	*	*	*	*	*
2	(C)	B	B	*	*	D	*	*	A	*	D
3	(D)	*	*	A	*	*	*	*	*	B	*
4	(B)	*	A	*	A	C	A	*	D	D	D
5	(C)	*	*	*	*	*	*	B	*	*	B
6	(B)	C	*	D	*	*	*	*	*	*	*
7	(A)	*	*	*	D	B	*	B	C	*	*
8	(D)	*	*	*	*	*	*	*	B	C	*
9	(A)	*	*	*	*	*	B	*	*	*	C
10	(C)	*	A	B	*	*	*	*	*	*	*
11	(B)	A	C	*	*	A	C	C	*	C	A
12	(A)	*	*	*	*	*	*	*	B	*	*
13	(D)	*	*	*	B	*	*	*	*	*	*
14	(C)	*	*	*	*	A	*	*	*	A	*
15	(B)	A	*	C	C	*	*	*	*	*	A
16	(A)	*	*	*	*	B	B	D	C	B	*
17	(D)	C	B	C	A	*	B	C	B	A	*
18	(C)	*	*	*	*	*	D	A	*	*	D
19	(D)	*	*	*	*	*	*	*	*	*	A
20	(B)	*	*	*	*	*	*	*	*	*	*

Table 8.1 continued on page 264

The calculation of p may seem somewhat familiar. It is a component of the Kuder–Richardson 20 formula for calculating an internal consistency reliability coefficient, along with its counterpart q, the proportion of people incorrect on the item.

Several points are worth noting before going further. First, p is a *proportion* that varies between 0.0 and 1.0. It cannot be negative since it is based on the number of people who answer correctly. Second, p is based on the number of people *correct* on the item. A high p value, such as .9, means that most people answered the item correctly. An item with a high p value is actually a rather easy item. On the other hand, a low p value, such as .2, means that most people answered the item incorrectly. Difficult items, therefore, have p values closer to 0.0.

Third, calculation of p requires answers to test items to be categorized as correct or incorrect. On alternate choice items, such as multiple choice or true false, test-taker responses naturally fall into these dichotomous categories. On a free-response item, such as a short-answer or essay question, test-taker responses are likely to fall into several categories representing the number of

III. Bottom 10 students in the class

Question Number	Correct Answer	Total Number of Questions Correct									
		11	11	11	10	10	10	9	9	9	8
1	(A)	*	B	*	C	*	*	*	C	C	D
2	(C)	*	*	A	*	A	D	D	*	D	A
3	(D)	*	*	*	B	*	C	C	A	*	*
4	(B)	C	*	*	*	*	*	*	D	*	*
5	(C)	A	B	A	A	B	A	A	B	A	A
6	(B)	*	*	*	*	*	*	*	*	*	*
7	(A)	D	D	*	B	D	C	B	D	*	B
8	(D)	*	A	B	C	*	*	A	*	B	C
9	(A)	*	*	*	*	C	B	*	C	D	D
10	(C)	B	*	*	*	*	*	D	A	*	B
11	(B)	*	C	*	D	*	*	*	*	A	A
12	(A)	C	*	C	*	*	*	C	B	B	C
13	(D)	*	*	*	*	A	C	*	B	C	*
14	(C)	B	D	*	A	D	A	D	A	A	*
15	(B)	A	*	D	D	C	*	*	*	*	*
16	(A)	C	*	B	C	D	C	B	*	B	C
17	(D)	A	A	A	*	*	*	*	*	*	B
18	(C)	*	*	*	*	B	B	B	A	D	A
19	(D)	*	C	C	A	*	B	*	*	*	*
20	(B)	*	C	D	*	A	*	A	*	*	*

points earned on the item. It is possible, however, to dichotomize performance on free-response items. The test developer can select a criterion to classify a test taker's response as correct or incorrect. For example, on a 5-point short-answer question, the test developer might decide that persons earning at least 4 points will be counted as correct, while those earning less than 4 points will be counted as incorrect. The criterion can then be used to transform the existing scores to the dichotomous categories needed for an item-difficulty analysis.

Finally, no test item can be said to have a single p value. Item difficulty, like test reliability, can be calculated every time a test is administered. An item's difficulty index is specific to the test data under study. It is possible that a test item will vary in level of difficulty across different types of test takers. For example, a test item covering an aspect of third grade math might have a low p value when used with second graders, but a high p value when used with fourth graders.

Table 8.2 illustrates the calculation of item difficulty using the 20-item multiple-choice test presented in Table 8.1. Most items have p values in the .6 to .8 range. Items 7 and 16 stand out as the most difficult items ($p = .5$); item 6 is the easiest item ($p = .9$). But how are these values to be interpreted?

TABLE 8.2 Calculating Item
Difficulty

Item	Number of People Correct	p^1
1	25	.83
2	17	.57
3	23	.77
4	18	.60
5	16	.53
6	27	.90
7	15	.50
8	20	.67
9	21	.70
10	22	.73
11	16	.53
12	22	.73
13	24	.80
14	18	.60
15	21	.70
16	15	.50
17	18	.60
18	19	.63
19	24	.80
20	26	.87

$$^1 p = \frac{\text{number of people correct}}{\text{total number of people}}$$

Based on the item-difficulty analysis, are these questions any good or should they be revised?

Interpreting the Item-difficulty Statistic

Interpretation of p values is more complicated than might be expected. Since an item's p value equals the proportion of people correct, it is determined by the responses of test takers to the item. In other words, p is a *behavioral* measure of item difficulty. Item-difficulty analysis operationally defines a difficult item as one that few people answer correctly. It is up to the test developer to determine *why* so few people answer the item correctly. Although it is tempting to infer that an item with a low p value taps a difficult concept, the item-difficulty analysis confounds test-taker responses and test-taker knowledge. Does an item p value of .4 mean that most test takers have not learned the information or that the item is poorly written? For a multiple-choice question, a distractor power analysis (see p. 285) can help determine whether the problem lies in poor wording of alternatives. But by itself, the item-difficulty statistic cannot be used to determine the conceptual difficulty of the information assessed by the question.

The answer to the question "Are these good items?" depends on the nature of the test and the types of items. For example, norm-referenced tests are designed to sort test takers into groups relative to each other. As noted in Chapter 3 (p. 63), norm-referenced ability tests must include some difficult items, items that will challenge the most knowledgeable or skillful test takers. We would expect, therefore, a norm-referenced test to include some items with low (.2 to .3) p values.

Furthermore, to sort test takers effectively, a norm-referenced test must produce a varied distribution of test scores. In general, the variability of test scores is maximized when p values average around .5, sometimes referred to as the *optimal item difficulty* for norm-referenced tests. Although item-difficulty values between .5 and .7 are considered adequate for norm-referenced tests, test scores generate the greatest variability when the p values of *all* items are around .5. When a test will be used to make fine discriminations among test takers, items with p values near .5 are preferred over items with more extreme values.

In contrast, criterion-referenced tests are used to determine whether test takers meet some standard of performance (Chapter 3). For example, a high school minimum competency test is designed to determine whether test takers have acquired some minimal level of knowledge and skills. Screening tests, such as professional licensing exams, are used in a parallel way to identify highly knowledgeable test takers. On tests like these, test takers receive scores of either pass or fail depending on whether or not they reach the preselected criterion. In these instances, tests should be composed of items whose difficulty level corresponds to that criterion point. A competency exam aimed at identifying students in trouble might be designed to identify the bottom 20% of test takers. The test is not meant to be difficult. In fact, it is designed so that 80% of test takers will pass. The optimal item-difficulty value, therefore, would be .8 (80% of the people answering the item correctly). A licensing exam designed to identify the *top* 20% of test takers should have items with p values near .2. In this case, only 20% of test takers should pass the test. The most effective items, therefore, are those that only 20% of test takers answer correctly. In general, the optimum item-difficulty value for a criterion-referenced test equals the proportion of test takers expected to pass the test.

On norm-referenced tests, the test developer must also consider the types of test items used. On alternate choice test items, such as multiple choice and true/false, test takers can answer correctly by guessing. Analysis of p values for tests including alternate choice items should consider the effect of guessing on item difficulty. For example, a multiple-choice item with four alternatives could be answered correctly 25% of the time by guessing. On a true/false item with only two alternatives, test takers can guess correctly 50% of the time. For these types of items, the optimal item-difficulty value can be corrected to account for the probability of a random but correct guess.

Previously, we said that the optimal item difficulty on norm-referenced tests was $p = .5$, halfway between no one answering correctly ($p = 0$) and everyone answering correctly ($p = 1.0$). If we were to consider the effects of possible random guessing, we would correct this value based on the probability of a correct guess. The midpoint p value *corrected for guessing* is halfway between the probability of a correct guess and everyone answering correctly ($p = 1.0$). To convert this to the optimal p value, *corrected for guessing*, the midpoint value is added to the probability of a correct guess. The following formulas are used:

$$\left(\begin{array}{c} \text{midpoint } p, \\ \text{corrected for guessing} \end{array} \right) = \frac{1.0 - (\text{probability of correct guess})}{2}$$

$$\left(\begin{array}{c} \text{optimal } p, \\ \text{corrected for guessing} \end{array} \right) = \text{corrected midpoint } p + \text{probability of correct guess}$$

For example, test takers have a 25% chance of guessing correctly on a multiple-choice item with four alternatives. Using the preceding formulas,

$$\left(\begin{array}{c} \text{midpoint } p, \\ \text{corrected for guessing} \end{array} \right) = \frac{1.00 - (.25)}{2} = \frac{.75}{2} = .375$$

$$\left(\begin{array}{c} \text{optimal } p, \\ \text{corrected for guessing} \end{array} \right) = .375 + .25 = .625$$

Considering the preceding discussion, the pattern of item difficulty in Table 8.2 is appropriate. Since a classroom test is likely to be used in assigning grades, it should be evaluated according to the principles of norm-referenced testing. Since the test is composed of four-alternative multiple-choice questions, optimal item difficulty should take into account the probability of guessing correctly. Taken together, these statements imply that the test will be most effective if item difficulties range from .5 to .7, with an optimal value of .625. Examining the data in Table 8.2, 60% of the items ($N = 12$) have p values between .50 and .70. There are no items with p values below .50 and only three items have values above .80. The p values are distributed in a relatively normal manner with an average item difficulty of .678. On the basis of the item-difficulty analysis, the test is likely to be useful for sorting students into a variety of grading categories.

Effects of Item Difficulty on Test Scores

Item-difficulty values affect the pattern of test scores, specifically, the test mean, the standard deviation, and the relationship between scores. Items with p values of 0.0 lower test means and score ranges because everyone loses points on those items. The standard deviation in turn will reflect the lowered test range. Items with p values of 0.0 reduce the variability of test scores by reducing the number of points test takers can earn and by reducing the ability of the test to measure differences among test takers. As mentioned earlier, the presence of many items at the 0.0 level limits the potential reliability and therefore validity of the test.

On the other hand, items with p values of 1.0 raise test means because everyone gains points on these items. However, since *everyone* gains points, the difference between the highest and lowest scores and the test standard deviation will decrease. Like items with p values of 0.0, the presence of many items at the 1.0 level reduce the variability of scores and limit the test's potential reliability and validity.

In fact, items at the 0.0 and 1.0 level contribute nothing to the test's ability to measure differences among people. When tests are used to sort people into categories, such as classroom tests used to assign grades, these items might as well be dropped. Dropping a single item that no one gets correct changes all scores by a constant amount. It is a linear transformation of the original scores that changes the mean but does nothing to change the relationship between scores. If the distribution of original and transformed scores were converted to z-scores, any person in the group would receive the same z-score in both distributions. And although students might balk at the notion of dropping an item on which everyone is correct, the end result is the same—except that the mean would *decrease* rather than increase. In the process of test development, however, it typically is better to rewrite items than to drop them. If the quality of an item can be improved and the item therefore retained, the length of the test is preserved. Anytime a test is shortened by dropping items, its potential reliability and validity suffer.

Use of Percent Endorsement

At the beginning of this section, we noted that item-difficulty analysis is not appropriate for typical performance tests—tests of personality, attitudes, or interests. It is possible, however, to use the same calculation procedure in a slightly different way on these tests. Chapter 4 discussed the development of personality, attitude, and interest tests—tests used to determine whether a future test taker displays a particular characteristic or a particular pattern

PRACTICE BOX 8.1   Calculating Item Difficulty

The following two charts describe the performance of 20 students on a 15-item statistics quiz (three-alternative multiple choice). Correct answers = *; incorrect answers = letter (A, B, or C).

Question Number	Correct Answer	Total Number of Questions Correct									
		15	14	14	13	13	13	12	12	12	12
1	(A)	*	*	*	*	*	*	*	*	*	*
2	(C)	*	*	*	*	*	*	*	A	*	*
3	(C)	*	*	*	*	*	*	*	*	B	*
4	(B)	*	*	*	A	*	A	*	*	*	C
5	(C)	*	*	*	*	*	*	B	*	*	B
6	(B)	*	*	*	*	*	*	*	*	*	*
7	(A)	*	*	*	*	B	*	B	*	*	*
8	(B)	*	*	*	*	*	*	*	C	C	*
9	(A)	*	*	*	*	*	B	*	*	*	C
10	(C)	*	A	B	*	*	*	*	*	*	*
11	(B)	*	*	*	*	A	*	C	*	*	*
12	(A)	*	*	*	*	*	*	*	B	*	*
13	(A)	*	*	*	B	*	*	*	*	*	*
14	(C)	*	*	*	*	*	*	*	*	A	*
15	(B)	*	*	*	*	*	*	*	*	*	*

Question Number	Correct Answer	Total Number of Questions Correct									
		11	11	11	11	10	10	10	9	9	9
1	(A)	*	*	B	*	*	*	*	*	*	C
2	(C)	B	B	*	*	*	*	*	A	*	*
3	(C)	*	*	*	*	A	*	A	B	B	*
4	(B)	*	A	*	A	*	A	*	*	*	C
5	(C)	*	*	*	*	*	*	B	*	A	B
6	(B)	C	*	A	*	*	*	*	*	*	A
7	(A)	*	*	*	B	B	C	B	*	*	*
8	(B)	*	*	*	*	*	*	*	A	C	*
9	(A)	*	*	*	*	*	B	*	*	C	C
10	(C)	*	A	B	*	B	*	*	A	*	A
11	(B)	A	*	*	C	A	*	C	*	C	*
12	(A)	*	*	*	*	*	B	*	B	*	*
13	(A)	*	C	*	B	*	*	*	*	*	*
14	(C)	B	*	*	*	A	A	*	A	A	*
15	(B)	*	*	C	*	*	*	A	*	*	*

1. Using the information in the two charts, calculate the item-difficulty (p) value for each of the 15 items.
2. If this quiz will be part of the final grading process, what would be the optimal item-difficulty value?
3. Evaluate the items according to your criterion for optimal difficulty. Which are adequate? Too difficult? Too easy?

Compare your answers to the answers at the end of the book. Reread sections as needed.

of interests. When items for these tests are selected *empirically* (see p. 103), we need to know how items are answered by different types of people in our standardization group. We do so by calculating **percent endorsement** statistics for each test item. Percent endorsement indicates the percentage of people who select a specific answer to an item. Its calculation is identical to the item-difficulty index:

$$\% \text{ endorsement} = \frac{\text{number of people selecting an answer}}{\text{total number of people}}$$

For example, suppose we are developing a true/false test of extroversion including the following item: "I enjoy starting conversations with new people." We administer the test to a standardization sample including 100 introverted and 100 extroverted people—identified as such by some other criterion measures. If all extroverted people selected "true" and all the introverted people selected "false," the percent endorsement index would be 100/200 or .5. If the index is *greater than* .5, however, more than 50% (or 100) of the people must have selected "true," meaning that people of both types selected must have selected "true." Similarly, if the statistic is *less than* .5, less than 50% of the people selected "true," meaning that people of both types must have selected "false."

It is possible, however, for the percent endorsement to equal .5 even when *both* types of people answer "true." The statistic simply tells us that half (50%) of the people answered "true." It does not identify *which* people these were. We can examine the item further by calculating percent endorsement statistics separately for each type of person:

1. Percent of extroverted people selecting "true" =
$$\frac{\text{number of extroverted people selecting true}}{100}.$$

2. Percent of introverted people selecting "true" =
$$\frac{\text{number of introverted people selecting true}}{100}.$$

We now know the percentage of each type of person, extroverted and introverted, who selected "true" for this item. By simple subtraction, we also can determine the percentage who selected "false." If 80% of extroverts selected "true," then 20% of them must have selected "false." Similarly, if 30% of introverts selected "true," then 70% of them must have selected "false." When we move on to our item-discrimination analysis, we can determine if the item discriminates between extroverts and introverts—in other words, if these two types of people answer this item in different ways.

Although *conceptually* different from the item-difficulty index, the percent endorsement index is its typical performance analog. It is a critical element of empirical scale construction and can be used both on objective and projective tests. In projective test development, we calculate the percentage of each type of person who *generates*—rather than selects—a particular answer for each item. The percent endorsement statistics for a projective item can then be used to determine whether the item discriminates among different types of people.

ITEM-DISCRIMINATION ANALYSIS

Item-discrimination analysis is appropriate for almost any type of test. Basically, item-discrimination analysis indicates the extent to which different types of people answer an item in different ways. On a maximal performance (ability) test, the analysis determines whether an item discriminates between people who do well on the test and people who do not. A "good" item is one on which most people with high test scores are correct and most people with low test scores are incorrect. On a typical performance test, the analysis determines whether an item discriminates between people possessing a characteristic and people lacking that characteristic. A test designed to identify depression should be composed of items answered one way by depressed people and another way by people who are not depressed. A scale designed to compare your interests to those of successful architects should contain items that discriminate between people whose interests are and are not similar to the architects studied.

On a more theoretical level, item-discrimination analysis approaches each individual item as a separate measure of the characteristic being tested. The usefulness of an item depends on its ability to measure whatever the test as a whole is measuring. It is possible that some test items measure attributes unrelated to the purpose of the test, a situation that clearly would reduce the test's validity. Item-discrimination analysis can be used to determine which items best measure the construct or content under study. In theory, if the item measures the same property or properties as the overall test does, then people who perform well on the test should also perform well on the item.

Measures of Item Discrimination

There are a variety of procedures to evaluate item discrimination. This section discusses two different approaches: the item-discrimination index and the item-total correlation. Calculation of the item-discrimination index requires that performance on each item to be scored dichotomously, such as correct/incorrect or true/false. As was the case with the item-difficulty index, the item-discrimination index can be calculated for ability tests using short-answer and essay questions *only if* answers are rescored as correct and incorrect. In contrast, the item-total correlation can be used with either alternate choice or free-response ability test items, even if the latter items are not treated dichotomously.

Both item-discrimination measures are determined from the performance of a specific group of test takers. Item discrimination, like item difficulty, is a behavioral measure that can be computed anytime a test is administered. A test item does not have a single discrimination index or item-total correlation. In fact, it is possible that an item will vary in discriminating power across different groups of test takers. For example, items designed to identify the presence of depression might produce poor discrimination values when given to people with antisocial personality but generate adequate statistics when given to a nonclinical group of people.

Item-discrimination Index

One way to think about item discrimination is to ask if different types of people select or produce different answers to an item. This practical orientation to item discrimination is the basis of the **item-discrimination index**. The discrimination index, D, is a proportion obtained by comparing the performance of two subgroups of test takers. The two subgroups together can represent the entire set of test takers—a common procedure in classroom testing—or only a portion of the total group. In the latter case, called the *extreme groups method*, the calculation of D usually compares either the test takers in the top and bottom third of a group or the test takers in the top and bottom quarter. Extreme groups are used most often on standardized ability tests and tests of personality, interests, and attitudes. The use of thirds or quarters is the test developer's choice, as long as the choice does not produce extreme groups with very few members. Once the subgroups have been identified, we calculate the proportion of people selecting or producing each answer on each item *separately* for each subgroup. The pairs of proportions are subtracted to determine a D value for each item.

Use in Maximal Performance Testing. When we calculate the item-discrimination index for ability tests, we compare people who performed well on the test to people who performed poorly. This approach is possible because items on ability tests have correct and incorrect answers. Let's illustrate the process by considering the items on a classroom test. We begin by determining each person's total score; then we divide the people into two groups: those with scores in a top-score group and those with scores in a bottom-score group. (Remember, classroom tests may use either the total group or the extreme groups method.) Next, we calculate the proportion of people who are correct on each test item and subtract to determine the D value. Our process can be represented with the following formula:

$$D = p_T - p_B$$

in which

D = the item-discrimination index for a given test item

$$p_T = \frac{\text{the proportion of people in the top group who are correct on the item, calculated as number of people in the group who are correct on the item}}{\text{number of people in the group}}$$

$$p_B = \frac{\text{the proportion of people in the bottom group who are correct on the item, calculated as number of people in the group who are correct on the item}}{\text{number of people in the group}}$$

If the item is more difficult for people in the bottom group than people in the top group, the D value approaches 1.0. If the item is equally difficult for people in both groups, the D value is 0.0. There is, however, a third possibility: If the item is more difficult for people in the *top* group, the D value approaches -1.0. Unlike the item-difficulty statistic, p, the item-discrimination index *can* be negative. The best ability test items have positive D values. These items are answered correctly primarily by people possessing the characteristics being tested. The poorest ability items have negative D values. The majority of people who pass these items have low overall test scores. Items whose D values are 0.0 contribute nothing to the measurement of differences among test takers. Generally, a D value of .3 or better indicates good discrimination.

The discrimination index may appear to focus only on the ability of an item to distinguish among people with different types of scores. But it also addresses the more theoretical issue of what test items measure. If the test and the item measure the same characteristics of test takers, people who perform poorly on the test should also perform poorly on the item. An item with a positive D value fits this criterion; it is answered correctly more often by people who perform well on the test. The closer the value is to 1.0, the more likely it is that the item measures the same characteristics as does the overall test. It follows, then, that the pattern of D values influences test validity. Tests whose items produce positive D values are composed of items that are measuring the same characteristics. Tests containing many items with negative D values include items that do not measure the same characteristics as the overall test does.

Table 8.3 illustrates the calculation of D values using the extreme groups method and the 20-item test presented earlier. The results of the item-discrimination analysis also indicate that the test is successful at sorting test takers into groups. Of the 20 items, 16 or 80% have D values of at least .3. Two items, items 4 and 6, have negative D values. Note that item 6 also was identified as the easiest item in the difficulty analysis, with 90% of the group passing the item. Two other items (10 and 11) barely discriminate between high and low scorers, and one item (5) is passed *only* by students in the top group. The D values are distributed in a relatively normal fashion with an average of .355. The questions appear to represent a coherent test of the content area. Overall, the individual items appear to be measuring the same attributes as the total itself.

Use in Typical Performance Testing.   The same procedure can be used to determine item-discrimination indexes for personality, attitude, or interest test items. Let's return to our hypothetical true/false test of extroversion, discussed in the item-difficulty section. We had administered our items to a pool of 100 extroverts and 100 introverts and were using the empirical method to select good items for our final test. Our goal was to determine if the item "I enjoy starting conversations with new people" discriminated

TABLE 8.3   Calculating the Item-discrimination Index

Item	Number Correct in Top 10	p_T	Number Correct in Bottom 10	p_B	D^1
1	10	1.0	5	.5	.5
2	8	.8	4	.4	.4
3	9	.9	6	.6	.3
4	7	.7	8	.8	-.1
5	8	.8	0	0	.8
6	9	.9	10	1.0	-.1
7	7	.7	2	.2	.5
8	8	.8	4	.4	.4
9	8	.8	5	.5	.3
10	8	.8	6	.6	.2
11	7	.7	6	.6	.1
12	9	.9	4	.4	.5
13	9	.9	6	.6	.3
14	8	.8	2	.2	.6
15	9	.9	6	.6	.3
16	8	.8	2	.2	.6
17	10	1.0	6	.6	.4
18	8	.8	4	.4	.4
19	9	.9	6	.6	.3
20	10	1.0	6	.6	.4

$^1 D = p_T - p_B$

PRACTICE BOX 8.2   Calculating the Item-discrimination Index

---

1. Using the sample test data in Practice Box 8.1, calculate the item-discrimination index for each item. Use the top 7 and bottom 7 students to create your extreme groups.
2. Evaluate the item-discrimination values. Which items discriminate well and which do not?

Compare your answers to the answers at the end of the book. Reread sections as needed.

---

between extroverts and introverts in our standardization sample. We calculated, separately, the proportion of extroverts selecting "true" and the proportion of introverts selecting "true." These two proportions are analogous to the p_T and p_B calculated in the ability test example. Since they reflect the performance of extroverts and introverts, we could label them p_E (proportion of "trues" among extroverts) and p_I (proportion of "trues" among introverts). We now can compare these proportions by calculating a D value as follows:

$$D = p_E - p_I$$

in which

D = the item-discrimination index for the test item

p_E = the proportion of extroverts who answered "true"

p_I = the proportion of introverts who answered "true"

Let's consider some possible outcomes at this point:

1. $D = 0$. In this case, the item *fails* to discriminate between introverts and extroverts. A D value of 0 can only occur if the same percentage of people in each group selected "true" as their answer to the item.
2. $D = 1.0$. In this case, the item discriminates *perfectly*. A D value of 1.0 means that all extroverts answered "true" and no introverts answered "true." Furthermore, this outcome makes sense conceptually since the item in question seems related theoretically to extroversion.
3. $D = -1.0$. In this case, the item *also* discriminates perfectly. All introverts have answered "true" and no extroverts answered "true." Although this outcome may not be what we expected, it indicates that the item achieves our stated goal: It discriminates between people who are introverts and extroverts.

In reality, D values rarely equal 0, 1.0, or -1.0. They are more likely to fall between 0 and 1.0 or between 0 and -1.0. The point of this discussion is to highlight an important difference between the interpretation of D in maximal versus typical performance testing. Whereas good items in maximal performance tests have high, positive D values, good items in typical performance tests can have high, positive or low, negative D values. At either extreme, the D statistic indicates that the item discriminates among different types of people.

In Chapter 4, we also discussed the Likert method of attitude scale construction and alluded to how item-discrimination analysis fits into the process (see p. 116). Now that we have covered calculation of the D statistic, we can describe the way item discrimination could be used to select items for Likert scales. Although experienced psychologists use the more complicated item-total correlation procedure, students can use the extreme group method, based simply on D values, to produce some good scales.

Our Likert scale example concerned attitudes toward capital punishment and included the items "Murderers don't deserve to live" and "The Bible says 'Thou shalt not kill'" (see p. 116). A large group of people rates the pool of statements on a 5-point scale. When the ratings of all the items are scored and totaled, people with high scores have unfavorable attitudes, whereas people with low scores have favorable attitudes. (Remember that Likert scoring of unfavorable attitude statements is reversed.) We can now identify two groups of people with extreme scores, usually the upper 25% to 33% and the lower 25% to 33%, whose item performance can be contrasted. Next, we need to calculate two percent endorsement statistics, one for each extreme group, to calculate D values.

Because Likert scoring of unfavorable attitude statements is reversed, in all cases a score of 1 or 2 now indicates endorsement or a favorable attitude (see p. 116). For this reason, we can evaluate *any* statement, favorable or unfavorable, by examining the proportion of people in each group who receive scores of 1 or 2. Following the logic in our extroversion test example, the procedure would be

$$D = p_F - p_U$$

in which

D = the item-discrimination index for the test item

p_F = the proportion of people with favorable attitudes (*low* total scores), with 1's or 2's on the statement

p_U = the proportion of people with unfavorable attitudes (*high* total scores), with 1's or 2's on the statement

If the item does discriminate, D should be high and positive. In other words, more people with favorable attitudes should earn 1's and 2's, compared to people with unfavorable attitudes.

Item-total Correlation

Although the item-discrimination index is a useful statistic, it is somewhat difficult to interpret. Although we can specify which types of D values are good, a basic question remains: How high (or low) a D value is "good enough"? The primary advantage of calculating the **item-total correlation** is its statistical properties. As a correlation coefficient, it can be converted to a variance statement indicating the ability of a test item to predict overall test score. It can even be tested for statistical significance. The item-total correlation approach clearly focuses on the issue of what test items measure. If the test and the item measure the same attributes, performance on the item should be correlated with total test score.

Performance on each item is described by a separate item-total correlation. The two variables being correlated are the distribution of scores on an individual test item and the distribution scores on the total test. As with all correlations, scores are treated as pairs. Each test taker has a score on the item under study and a companion total score on the test. When working with item types that generate a variety of scores on each item (free response, projective, Likert), the two variables can be correlated using the traditional Pearson correlation formula:

$$r_{XY} = \frac{(\sum XY/N) - (\overline{X})(\overline{Y})}{(\sigma_X)(\sigma_Y)}$$

in which

X = scores on the item being analyzed

Y = total scores on the test

$\overline{X}$ = the mean for scores on the item being analyzed

$\overline{Y}$ = the mean of total test scores

σ_X = the standard deviation of scores on the item being analyzed

σ_Y = the standard deviation of total test scores

When working with items scored dichotomously (alternate choice, certain objective personality or interest items) we must switch to a different calculation formula. When item performance is dichotomous (e.g., correct/incorrect, true/false), the appropriate correlation is *point-biserial correlation*. The formula for the point-biserial correlation for item 1 on a test is

$$r_{PB} = \left(\frac{\overline{X}_1 - \overline{X}}{\sigma_X}\right)\sqrt{\frac{p}{1-p}}$$

in which

$\overline{X}$ = the mean on the test for all persons

$\overline{X}_1$ = the mean on the test for only those persons correct on item 1

σ_X = the standard deviation on the test

p = the proportion of people correct on item 1

Regardless of the formula used, the item-total correlation is interpreted in the same way as any XY coefficient. The closer the correlation is to 1.0, the more likely it is that the item and the overall test measure the same characteristic. On an ability test, for example, correlations close to +1.0 indicate that people with high test scores are correct on the item. Ability test items with *negative* correlations are answered correctly primarily by people with low test scores. The square of the correlation indicates the proportion of test score variance predictable from performance on the item. An item-total correlation of .3 indicates that performance on the item accounts for 9% of test score variance. Negative values, like negative reliability coefficients, cannot be converted to variance proportions.

Table 8.4 on pages 279–281 presents calculation of the point-biserial correlation for three items from the sample test. On the basis of the discrimination index analysis, item 1 was judged as good ($D = .5$), item 5 as excellent ($D = .8$), and item 11 as poor ($D = .1$). The pattern of item-total correlations confirms these evaluations. Item 1 generates a correlation of .6, indicating ability to predict 36% of the variance in total test scores. Item 5 produces a correlation of .73 and is able to predict 53% of test score variance. Item 11, with the lowest positive D value, correlates only .13 with total test score, predicting a dismal 1.7% of test score variance.

There is one important caution regarding use of the item-total correlation procedure. With very short tests, each item makes a major contribution to total test score. As a result, most items will show positive item-total correlations. In fact, the correlation is likely to overestimate item discrimination. One way to compensate for this when analyzing short tests is to remove the item under study from the calculation of total score. For example, to determine the item-total correlation for item 1 on a 5-point quiz, calculate the test mean and test standard deviation using only items 2 to 5. For item 2, base total score calculations on items 1, 3, 4, and 5, and so on.

Shortcuts Using Item-discrimination Data

The particular nature of item-discrimination data makes them useful for estimating other statistical properties of test items and test performance. Item-discrimination data can be used to derive an estimate of p, the item-difficulty

TABLE 8.4   Calculating the Item-total Correlation

Using the data from Table 8.1, for the group as a whole:

$$\overline{X} = 13.567 \qquad \sigma_X = 3.084$$

I. Calculating the point-biserial correlation for item 1

p_1 = proportion of people correct on item 1 = 25/30 = .83
X_1 = mean score for people correct on item 1 = 14.4
(based on scores listed in the following chart)

Total Scores for People Correct On Item 1

X	$f(X)$
19	1
18	2
17	2
16	5
15	4
14	3
13	2
12	1
11	2
10	2
9	1
8	0

$$\sum = 25 = \text{number of persons correct on item 1}$$

$$r_{PB} = \left[\frac{14.4 - 13.567}{3.084} \right] \sqrt{\frac{.83}{1 - .83}} = .2701\sqrt{4.88}$$

$$r_{PB} = (.2701)(2.2096) = .5968 = .60$$

statistic, and r_{XY}, the criterion validity correlation between performance on the test and performance on a criterion measure.

Combining Discrimination and Difficulty Calculations

In many settings, the use of computerized test scoring makes quick work of item-difficulty and item-discrimination analyses. But in other settings, such as classroom testing, the time costs of conducting the analyses seem to outweigh the benefits. It is possible to reduce the time needed to conduct the analyses by combining the calculation of item discrimination and item difficulty.

The calculation of D requires determining the proportion of people correct on an item in two subgroups of test takers. If each subgroup contains *half*

TABLE 8.4   *(Continued)*

II. Calculating the point-biserial correlation for item 5

p_5 = proportion of people correct on item 5 = 16/30 = .53

X_5 = mean score for people correct on item 5 = 15.688
(based on scores listed in the following chart)

Total Scores for People Correct On Item 5

X	$f(X)$
19	1
18	2
17	2
16	3
15	4
14	2
13	2
12	0
11	0
10	0
9	0
8	0

$$\sum = 16 = \text{number of persons correct on item 5}$$

$$r_{PB} = \left[\frac{15.688 - 13.567}{3.084} \right] \sqrt{\frac{.53}{1 - .53}} = .6877\sqrt{1.1277}$$

$$= (.6877)(1.062) = .7303 = .73$$

the test takers, the item-difficulty index actually equals the average of the D values. The item-difficulty index can be calculated as

$$p = \frac{p_T + p_B}{2}$$

If extreme groups are used, the item-difficulty index can be *estimated* by the average of these two proportions. In this approach, the test developer selects equal-size extreme groups, calculates the proportion of people correct in each group, and uses these proportions to determine both item discrimination and item difficulty. The item-difficulty estimate is calculated using the preceding formula.

Table 8.5 on page 282 illustrates this latter procedure for calculating item difficulty and compares the estimated difficulty values with those obtained from analysis of *all* test takers. For these data, the estimated values are relatively

TABLE 8.4   *(Continued)*

III. Calculating the point-biserial correlation for item 11

p_{11} = proportion of people correct on item 11 = 16/30 = .53

X_{11} = mean score for people correct on item 11 = 13.938
(based on scores listed in the following chart)

Total Scores for People Correct on Item 11

X	$f(X)$
19	1
18	2
17	1
16	3
15	2
14	0
13	1
12	0
11	2
10	2
9	2
8	0

$$\sum = \overline{16} = \text{number of persons correct on item 11}$$

$$r_{PB} = \left(\frac{13.938 - 13.567}{3.084}\right)\sqrt{\frac{.53}{1 - .53}} = .1203\sqrt{1.1277}$$
$$= (.1203)(1.062) = .1277 = .13$$

PRACTICE BOX 8.3   Calculating the Item-total Correlation

1. Using the sample test data in Practice Box 8.1, calculate the item-total correlation for items 4, 7, and 10.
2. Evaluate the item-total correlations. How do the results of this analysis compare with the item-discrimination index analysis?

Compare your answers to the answers at the end of the book. Reread sections as needed.

---

close to the actual values. The average estimated item difficulty is .6675, compared to the actual average of .678. However, the two procedures do not necessarily produce such similar values. The estimated p value is based on

TABLE 8.5   Using Extreme Groups to Estimate Item Difficulty

Item	p_T	p_B	Estimated p[1]	Actual p[2]
1	1.0	.5	.75	.83
2	.8	.4	.60	.57
3	.9	.6	.75	.77
4	.7	.8	.75	.60
5	.8	0	.40	.53
6	.9	1.0	.95	.90
7	.7	.2	.45	.50
8	.8	.4	.60	.67
9	.8	.5	.65	.70
10	.8	.6	.70	.73
11	.7	.6	.65	.53
12	.9	.4	.65	.73
13	.9	.6	.75	.80
14	.8	.2	.50	.60
15	.9	.6	.75	.70
16	.8	.2	.50	.50
17	1.0	.6	.80	.60
18	.8	.4	.60	.63
19	.9	.6	.75	.80
20	1.0	.6	.80	.87

[1] Estimated $p = \dfrac{p_T + p_B}{2}$

[2] From Table 8.2.

PRACTICE BOX 8.4   Estimating Item Difficulty

1. Using the data from Practice Box 8.2, estimate the item-difficulty index for each item.
2. Compare the estimated values to the actual values. Are they similar? Why or why not?

Compare your answers to the answers at the end of the book. Reread sections as needed.

---

the performance of a smaller number of people who in addition have scores at the extreme ends of the test score distribution. Estimated p values more closely approximate actual values when working with a large group of test takers whose scores are distributed in a relatively normal manner.

Estimating Criterion Validity Coefficients

Although it is extremely useful to know how well a test predicts other measures, calculating criterion validity coefficients can be a lengthy process. Item-discrimination data can be used to estimate the criterion validity coefficient between a test and a criterion measure. The procedure requires determining the percentage of people in the top half of the distribution on *both* the predictor test and the criterion measure. Using Table 8.6, the percentage is translated into the approximate correlation between scores on the two variables.

Using the sample test data as an example, suppose the instructor is interested in the ability of scores on our sample test (Table 8.1) to predict students' overall averages at the end of the course. At the end of the course, the instructor records each student's test grade and final average side by side, as illustrated in Table 8.7. The instructor calculates the medians for each distribution and uses them to determine which students are above the median on both measures. (If the distributions are roughly normal, the mean may be used instead of the median.) The number of students in the top group on both measures is then converted to a percentage and compared to the entries in Table 8.6. The data in Table 8.7 indicate that 40% of test takers fall in the top half of both distributions. According to Table 8.6, the approximate correlation between test scores

TABLE 8.6   Approximate XY Correlation Based on Item Discrimination

1. Find the percentage of people who stood in the *top half* of the distribution on *both* measures.

2. Use the following table to look up the correlation associated with that percentage.

%	r	%	r	%	r	%	r
45	.95	35	.60	25	.00	15	−.60
44	.93	34	.55	24	−.07	14	−.65
43	.91	33	.49	23	−.13	13	−.69
42	.88	32	.43	22	−.19	12	−.73
41	.85	31	.37	21	−.25	11	−.77
40	.81	30	.31	20	−.31	10	−.81
39	.77	29	.25	19	−.37	9	−.85
38	.73	28	.19	18	−.43	8	−.88
37	.69	27	.13	17	−.49	7	−.91
36	.65	26	.07	16	−.55	6	−.93

From Paul B. Diederich, *Short-cut Statistics for Teacher-made Tests*, 1973, p. 10. Reprinted by permission of Educational Testing Service, the copyright owner.

TABLE 8.7   Estimating a Criterion Validity Correlation

Student	X	X > Md?	Y	Y > Md?	Above on Both?
A	19	Yes	91	Yes	Yes
B	18	Yes	87	Yes	Yes
C	18	Yes	90	Yes	Yes
D	17	Yes	85	Yes	Yes
E	17	Yes	80	Yes	Yes
F	16	Yes	83	Yes	Yes
G	16	Yes	78	Yes	Yes
H	16	Yes	87	Yes	Yes
I	16	Yes	76	Yes	Yes
J	16	Yes	71	No	No
K	15	Yes	80	Yes	Yes
L	15	Yes	73	Yes	Yes
M	15	Yes	73	Yes	Yes
N	15	Yes	70	No	No
O	14	No	71	No	No
P	14	No	68	No	No
Q	14	No	75	Yes	No
R	13	No	77	No	No
S	13	No	68	No	No
T	12	No	70	No	No
U	11	No	68	No	No
V	11	No	65	No	No
W	11	No	70	No	No
X	10	No	63	No	No
Y	10	No	72	Yes	No
Z	10	No	68	No	No
AA	9	No	60	No	No
BB	9	No	56	No	No
CC	9	No	60	No	No
DD	8	No	53	No	No

$$Md^1 = 14.33 \qquad Md = 71.5$$

Number of people above the median on both measures = 12
Percentage of people above median on both = 12/30 = 40%

X = score on predictor test

Y = final average in the course

[1]Median calculated through interpolation.

and final averages is .81. Scores on the test appear to be valid predictors of final averages, predicting 66% (r_{XY}^2) of the variance in final averages.

With the estimation process, it is possible to determine quickly the predictive power of a test. The procedure can be applied to any type of criterion validity analysis: the ability of a pretest to predict an overall performance

---

PRACTICE BOX 8.5　Estimating the Criterion Validity Coefficient

The following chart provides some additional information about these students. At the beginning of the course, each student completed a math aptitude pretest. The pretest scores are listed along with the students' scores on the 15-item quiz.

Person	1	2	3	4	5	6	7	8	9	10
Pretest	86	92	83	94	82	78	80	85	72	82
Quiz	15	14	14	13	13	13	12	12	12	12

Person	11	12	13	14	15	16	17	18	19	20
Pretest	76	78	72	70	72	68	66	68	57	58
Quiz	11	11	11	11	10	10	10	9	9	9

1. Using Table 8.6, estimate the criterion validity coefficient between these two variables.
2. How good is the pretest at predicting grades on the quiz?

Compare your answers to the answers at the end of the book. Reread sections as needed.

---

measure, the ability of a test to predict a behavioral measure, or the ability of a test to predict scores on another related test.

DISTRACTOR POWER ANALYSIS

Tests of achievement and aptitude, whether norm or criterion referenced, often use a multiple-choice format. In a multiple-choice question, an incorrect alternative is called a **distractor**. Distractor power analysis evaluates the percentage of people selecting each incorrect alternative to determine if the distractors are useful. Perhaps you have read multiple-choice questions containing one or two obviously wrong alternatives. Even if you didn't know the material covered by the question, you could eliminate these alternatives and thus increase the probability of correctly guessing the right answer. The presence of these poorly written distractors detracts from the overall quality of the test because people can earn higher scores just by guessing. The test's ability to identify people who know the material and people who do not is reduced. Furthermore, the ability to eliminate one or two alternatives may encourage people to guess more often. Guessing reduces test reliability and therefore limits the test's potential validity. Distractor power analysis identifies alternatives in need of revision and therefore can facilitate the development of a more reliable and valid test.

Expected and Actual Distractor Power

A well-written multiple-choice question has two characteristics. First, people who possess the knowledge or skills being tested select the correct answer. Second, people who lack the knowledge or skills tested select randomly from the available choices. If people in this latter group approach the item randomly, an equal proportion should select each alternative. Some of these people will guess correctly. The remaining people, those who are incorrect on the item, should be equally distributed across the different distractors.

The number of people expected to pick each distractor by random choice is the *expected distractor power* or "expected pull" and is calculated as follows:

$$\text{expected distractor power} = \frac{\text{number of people incorrect on item}}{\text{number of distractors}}$$

The number of people selecting each distractor is the *actual distractor power* or "actual pull." It is compared to the expected power to judge the adequacy of the distractors. Distractors that are never selected or are selected less often than expected should be examined closely and probably be rewritten. It is possible that these distractors are obvious wrong answers. Distractors that are selected much more frequently than expected also need rewriting. In fact, these distractors may be so similar to the correct answer that even people who know the information select them.

Interpreting Distractor Values

Distractor values must be interpreted in light of information about item difficulty. Both the expected and actual distractor power depend on the number of people incorrect on the item. When an item is very difficult (low p value), a large number of people will be distributed across the item distractors. It is relatively easy to spot discrepancies between the expected and actual distractor values. In fact, it is possible that the difficulty of the item results from the presence of one or two very attractive distractors—wrong answers easily confused with the correct answer. When an item is very easy (high p value), the number of people available to select each distractor is small. The numbers may be so small in this case that it is difficult to evaluate the distractors at all.

TABLE 8.8   Analyzing Distractor Power

Using the test data from Table 8.1 (* is correct answer):

Item	Number of People Correct	Number of People Incorrect	Number Expected to Choose Each Distractor	Number Who Chose			
				A	**B**	**C**	**D**
1	25	5	1.67	*	1	3	1
2	17	13	4.33	5	3	*	5
3	23	7	2.33	2	3	2	*
4	18	12	4	5	*	2	5
5	16	14	4.67	7	7	*	0
6	27	3	1	0	*	2	1
7	15	15	5	*	7	2	6
8	20	10	3.33	2	4	4	*
9	21	9	3	*	3	4	2
10	22	8	2.67	3	4	*	1
11	16	14	4.67	6	*	7	1
12	22	8	2.67	*	4	4	0
13	24	6	2	1	3	2	*
14	18	12	4	8	1	*	3
15	21	9	3	3	*	4	2
16	15	15	5	*	7	6	2
17	18	12	4	5	4	3	*
18	19	11	3.67	4	3	*	4
19	24	6	2	3	1	2	*
20	26	4	1.33	2	*	1	1

$$\text{Expected number} = \frac{\text{number of people incorrect}}{3}$$

Table 8.8 presents the analysis of distractors for the sample test. Three items, 1, 6, and 20, are very easy items with 5 or fewer people out of 30 incorrect. With less than 2 people expected to select each distractor, it is difficult to evaluate their adequacy. Two additional items, 5 and 12, contain one distractor chosen by none of the test takers. These distractors should be rewritten. In their current form, test takers respond to these items as though each had only three alternatives. The test, therefore, contains items on which the probability of a correct guess varies. On items 5 and 12, the probability of a correct guess is 33% (1 out of 3) rather than 25% (1 out of 4). The group of people correct on these items is also likely to include people without the knowledge tested by the items. Items with this pattern usually contain a distractor that is obviously incorrect. Similar problems may exist for items 7, 10, 11, and 16. Each contains a distractor selected by only 1 or 2 people, with the remaining people distributed fairly evenly across the other two distractors.

PRACTICE BOX 8.6   Calculating Distractor Power

1. Using the data from Practice Box 8.1, calculate the expected and actual distractor power for each question in the sample quiz.
2. Evaluate the distractors. Which are adequate, too powerful, or not powerful enough?

Compare your answers to the answers at the end of the book. Reread sections as needed.

Item 14 presents another potential problem. On this item, 8 of the 12 people who are incorrect select the same distractor. Distractor A is selected twice as often as we would expect by chance; it definitely should be rewritten. The attractiveness of this distractor suggests that it is being confused somehow with the correct answer. It is possible that some people who know the material being tested are being misled by the wording of the distractor.

It is important to remember that distractor power analysis does not indicate *why* a particular distractor is powerful or not. A distractor may be picked frequently because it is poorly worded and easily misinterpreted by test takers. Alternatively, test takers may select a distractor because they have not mastered the information or skills needed to discriminate between the distractor and the correct answer. It is up to the test developer to determine whether and how to edit item distractors.

INTERACTIONS AMONG ITEM CHARACTERISTICS

It should be clear from the preceding discussions that item difficulty, item discrimination, and distractor power are not independent features of test items. Each characteristic in some way influences the qualities of the others. For example, an item's level of difficulty directly influences its discriminating power. When everyone chooses the correct answer ($p = 1.0$) or an incorrect answer ($p = 0.0$), the item-discrimination value will be 0. Items with extreme p values are less able to discriminate between test takers than items with moderate values. In fact, the potential discriminating power of an item is greatest when $p = .5$. Only when half the test takers are correct on an item and none of them are in the bottom group is it possible for the discrimination index, D, to equal 1.0.

However, item difficulty itself may be influenced by the quality of item distractors. The difficulty of multiple-choice items is directly related to the quality of their distractors. Most often test takers can identify totally implausible distractors. Once these are eliminated, the probability of guessing correctly increases and the item automatically becomes easier. On the other hand, the presence of distractors that are very similar to the correct answer can produce an extremely difficult item.

Finally, the quality of an item's distractors affects its ability to discriminate. Since distractors affect item difficulty, which limits discriminating power, distractors indirectly affect item discrimination. When analysis indicates a negative D value or item-total correlation, distractors should be examined closely. In these circumstances it is possible that knowledgeable test takers are being misled by the wording of a particular distractor.

GRAPHING ITEM CHARACTERISTICS

Sometimes a picture can be worth a thousand words. The same is true for a graph. One of the simplest ways to summarize information about test items is by graphing item characteristics. Two graphing procedures are discussed here: the discrimination by difficulty graph and the item characteristic curve.

Discrimination by Difficulty Graph

The relationship between item discrimination and item difficulty can be represented in a ***discrimination by difficulty graph***. The graph is useful for quick identification of good test items and items in need of study. Item-discrimination values, either D values or item-total correlations, are listed along the horizontal axis, with item difficulty values on the vertical axis. Each item is graphed at the point where its discrimination and difficulty values meet. A section of the graph can be marked to indicate optimal item statistics. Items falling within that section represent the best test items.

Figure 8.1 plots the item discrimination (D) and item difficulty (p) values for the sample test items. Lines have been drawn to indicate the optimal item difficulty range ($p = .5$ to $.7$) and the criterion for adequate discrimination ($D = .3$). According to the graph, the poorest test items are 6 and 10. Both are easy items that do not discriminate. Items 4 and 11 have adequate item difficulty but poor discrimination. Five items (1, 3, 13, 19, 20) discriminate well but are rather easy. The best items are items 2, 5, 7, 8, 9, and 14 through 18.

Item Characteristic Curves

A discrimination by difficulty graph includes information about all the items on a test. It is extremely useful for comparing the performance of the group on

FIGURE 8.1   Graphing item discrimination by difficulty

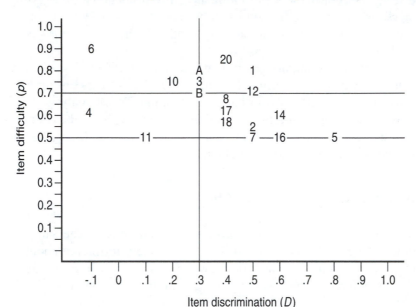

Each item is represented by its question number. The letters A and B represent the locations of two or more questions: A = 13, and 19; B = 9 and 15.

PRACTICE BOX 8.7   Graphing Discrimination-difficulty Relationships

1. Using the information from Practice Boxes 8.1 (item difficulty) and 8.2 (item-discrimination index), make a discrimination by difficulty graph of performance on the quiz items.
2. Identify the areas within the graph as "optimal ranges," "too difficult," "too easy," and "poor discrimination."

Compare your answers to the answers at the end of the book. Reread sections as needed.

---

various items. In contrast, an **item characteristic curve** is a graph drawn for an individual test item and represents the likelihood of a correct response as a function of total test score. Total test score is indicated on the horizontal axis, with proportion of test takers correct on the vertical axis. Points indicating the percentage of people correct in each test score category are plotted, and a line is drawn to represent the item curve. The resulting curve is useful for determining how well test items discriminate at different levels of performance.

Different types of tests require items with different curve characteristics. A perfect item for a norm-referenced test should show a relatively straight line with a positive slope. As total test score increases, the proportion of people correct increases. Such an item would discriminate well at all levels of performance, a necessary feature for items on a test designed to sort test takers into a variety of categories. However, an item with these characteristics would be inappropriate for a test designed to identify dyslexia. In this case, test items must discriminate well at the lower end of the test score distribution. Individuals with average or better reading skill probably will be correct on most items.

Creation of an item characteristic curve begins with defining the total score categories. With very large samples it is possible to have a separate category for each test score. With smaller samples it is advisable to establish ranges including several total scores. After the categories are defined, the proportion of people correct is determined *separately* for each score category and plotted on the item graph. Figure 8.2 presents the item characteristic curves for three items selected from the sample data set.

Because the group tested was small ($N = 30$), total test scores have been grouped into three-score ranges: 8 to 10, 11 to 13, 14 to 16, and 17 to 19 points. The curve for item 2 indicates good discrimination at all levels of test score. In fact, its curve represents a classic pattern: as total test score increases, the proportion of people passing the item increases. The item 2 curve is almost a straight line and has a positive slope. This is the pattern obtained by graphing correlations that are close to 1.0. Since the two variables being graphed are performance on the item and total score, we can infer from the graph that the item-total correlation for item 2 is relatively close to 1.0.

The curve for item 1 indicates good discrimination ability at the lower end of the test score distribution. However, the item does not discriminate among different groups of high-scoring test takers. The item 3 curve reveals a rather bizarre pattern of performance. Ignoring the group of test takers with the lowest scores, the curve resembles the item 2 curve. But for some reason, the largest percentage of test takers correct on this item are in the lowest-scoring group. Although all three items have different relationships to total score, item 3 clearly is a candidate for revision or elimination.

The graphs of these three items actually summarize much of the information from prior item-difficulty and item-discrimination analyses. Item 1 was a relatively easy item with excellent discrimination ($p = .83$, $D = .5$). Item 2 was a moderately difficult item with excellent discrimination ($p = .57$, $D = .5$),

FIGURE 8.2   Graphing item characteristic curves

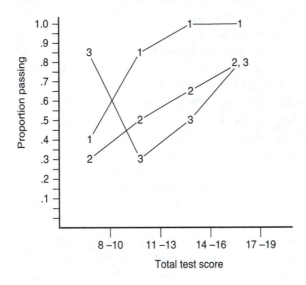

Curves are based on the following numbers and percentages of people passing each item:

Item	8–10 (N = 7)		11–13 (N = 6)		14–16 (N = 12)		17–19 (N = 5)	
	N	%	N	%	N	%	N	%
1	3	.43	5	.83	12	1.0	5	1.0
2	2	.29	3	.50	8	.67	4	.80
3	6	.86	2	.33	6	.50	4	.80

PRACTICE BOX 8.8   Graphing Item Characteristic Curves

1. Using the information from Practice Box 8.1, graph the item characteristic curve for items 4, 7, and 10.
2. Evaluate the performance of these items in view of the fact that this quiz will be part of the process of assigning final grades.

Compare your answers to the answers at the end of the book. Reread sections as needed.

while item 3 was a relatively easy item with adequate discrimination power ($p = .77$, $D = .3$). For those who prefer pictures to lists of statistics, item characteristic curves can provide a useful adjunct to item analysis tables.

SUMMARY AND KEY CONCEPTS

The purpose of item analysis is to determine which test items are useful and appropriate and which items require revision or elimination. For maximal performance tests, we focus on item difficulty and item discrimination. Both measures can be used with norm- and criterion-referenced tests, although optimal item difficulty is determined differently in the two cases. Item analysis is particularly important when ability tests demonstrate low reliability or validity. For example, the values of the **item-difficulty index** within an ability test may explain its lack of reliability. Because reliability is sensitive to test length and the variability of test scores, a test's reliability is likely to decrease as the number of extreme (high or low) item-difficulty values within it increases. Item-discrimination information may help explain an ability test's lack of validity. Items with poor discrimination indexes are not measuring what the overall test itself is measuring. A test with many such items is unlikely to be very valid.

For typical performance testing, the relevant statistics are **percent endorsement** and item discrimination. Both are important in the selection of items by empirical process. Percent endorsement of an answer to an item can be calculated separately for different types of people and the results used to identify items that discriminate among those types.

Two measures of item discrimination are used for both maximal and typical performance tests: the **item-discrimination index**, D, and the **item-total correlation**, r_{XY}. When test items are scored dichotomously, the item-total correlation is calculated using the formula for r_{PB}, the point-biserial correlation. The item-discrimination index is simple to compute but somewhat difficult to interpret. The item-total correlation requires more calculation time but can be translated directly into a variance statement. Item-discrimination characteristics can also be represented graphically in discrimination by difficulty plots and by using **item characteristic curves**.

If multiple-choice questions are used, analysis of individual **distractors** can help to identify poorly written items. This analysis requires calculating the expected distractor power and actual distractor power for each wrong answer. Comparison of these values may help explain an item's poor difficulty and/or discrimination statistics.

Several general points are worth repeating here. First, all item statistics are behavioral measures based on the performance of a specific group of test takers. No item has a single p or D value or item-total correlation. Second, although each type of item analysis addresses a separate conceptual issue, item analysis measures are not independent. The difficulty of an item affects its ability to discriminate. The plausibility of distractors affects the item's difficulty. Third, item analysis identifies test questions with certain statistical properties, such as many people correct or mostly high-scoring people correct. It cannot, however, explain why these particular values occur. It is up to the test developer to determine why an item is so difficult, why a distractor is so attractive, or why an item fails to discriminate.

QUESTIONS

8.1 How do the item-difficulty index and the percent-endorsement index differ? How is each index used?

8.2 Why is item-total correlation a more powerful measure of item-discrimination than the item-discrimination index?

8.3 How are item-difficulty, item-discrimination and distractor power interrelated? How is guessing reflected in these three statistics?

Questions 4 through 6 use the data on page 295. The charts present data on a 15-question multiple-choice test administered in a 20-student college statistics class. Chart 1 shows the answers given by the 10 students with the highest grades on the test (top 10), and chart 2 shows the answers given by the 10 students with the lowest grades (bottom 10). The top row in each chart lists the total grade for each student in that group. The left-hand column lists the question numbers (1 to 20) followed by the correct answer in parentheses. Correct answers are marked with a *. The remaining entries indicate the incorrect answer each student selected for each question.

Chart 1: Top 10

Question No./Answer	Number Correct									
	14	13	13	13	12	12	12	12	12	12
1 (A)	*	*	*	*	*	*	*	*	*	*
2 (C)	*	B	*	*	*	*	*	A	*	*
3 (D)	*	*	*	*	*	*	*	*	B	*
4 (B)	*	*	*	A	*	A	*	*	*	D
5 (C)	*	*	*	*	*	*	B	*	*	B
6 (B)	A	*	*	*	*	A	A	*	*	*
7 (A)	*	*	*	D	B	*	*	*	*	*
8 (D)	*	*	*	*	*	*	*	B	C	*
9 (A)	*	*	*	*	*	B	*	*	*	C
10 (C)	*	A	B	*	*	*	*	*	*	*
11 (B)	*	*	*	*	A	*	C	*	C	*
12 (A)	*	*	*	*	*	*	*	B	*	*
13 (D)	*	*	*	*	*	*	*	*	*	*
14 (C)	*	*	*	*	A	*	*	*	*	*
15 (B)	*	*	C	*	*	*	*	*	*	*

Chart 2: Bottom 10

Question No./Answer	Number Correct									
	11	11	11	10	10	10	10	9	9	8
1 (A)	*	*	*	*	*	*	*	C	C	C
2 (C)	*	*	A	*	A	*	D	*	D	A
3 (D)	*	*	*	B	*	C	*	*	*	*
4 (B)	C	*	*	*	*	*	*	D	*	*
5 (C)	*	B	A	A	B	*	A	B	A	A
6 (B)	*	*	*	*	*	*	*	*	*	*
7 (A)	D	*	*	B	D	*	B	D	*	B
8 (D)	*	A	B	*	*	*	*	*	B	*
9 (A)	*	*	*	*	C	B	*	C	*	D
10 (C)	*	*	*	*	*	A	*	*	*	*
11 (B)	*	C	*	D	*	*	*	*	*	A
12 (A)	C	*	C	*	*	*	C	B	*	C
13 (D)	*	*	*	*	*	C	*	*	C	*
14 (C)	*	D	*	A	*	A	D	*	A	*
15 (B)	A	*	*	*	C	*	*	*	*	*

8.4 Prepare an item-analysis chart including the item-difficulty index and the item-discrimination index for each item.

8.5   Plot the relationship between item difficulty and item discrimination in a $p \times D$ graph. Identify the five best test items.

8.6   Conduct a distractor power analysis for the remaining 10 items. Present the results in a summary table identifying expected and actual distractor power. Discuss how the results of this analysis can be used to develop strategies for rewriting test items.

Questions 7 through 10 use the following graph of student performance on four items from a final exam:

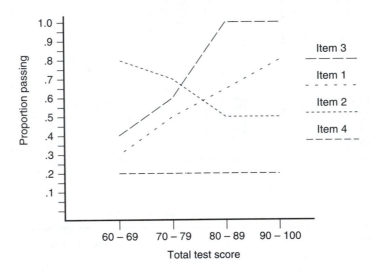

8.7   Which item discriminates at all levels of test performance?

8.8   Which item fails to discriminate at all levels?

8.9   Which item discriminates only at lower levels of performance?

8.10 Which item shows an inverse or negative pattern of discrimination?

PART

III

PRINCIPLES OF TEST USE

OVERVIEW

The final four chapters are "application chapters" that describe the use of tests in different types of settings. The focus of these chapters is the roles of tests in different settings, rather than the characteristics of the tests themselves. Each chapter will identify the ways tests are used to gather data and make decisions and describe several popular tests to illustrate these processes. This approach to discussing test use enables us to contrast the ways a single test, such as an intelligence test, can be is used in different scenarios.

Chapter 9, Testing in Educational Settings, describes how tests are used to evaluate student ability. Separate sections discuss the routine assessment of ability and the testing necessary to identify special needs students. A discussion of test bias identifies the strategies for investigating this issue and the impact of test bias research on the use of tests for educational decisions.

Chapters 10 and 11 detail the use of tests in clinical and counseling settings. Chapter 10 focuses on psychological and neuropsychological assessment—diagnostic testing designed to identify the nature and extent of personality and organic dysfunction. Chapter 11 focuses on testing for career guidance and for counseling individuals with personal and/or adjustment problems.

The final chapter, Testing in Business and Industry, discusses how tests are used in matters of personnel as well as in studies of organizational, human factors, and marketing issues. The use of tests in both the selection of new employees and the evaluation of current employees is described, along with legal issues surrounding the use of tests in employment decisions.

Testing in Educational Settings

CHAPTER OUTLINE

SUMMARY AND KEY CONCEPTS
QUESTIONS

CHAPTER GOALS AND OBJECTIVES

After completing this chapter you should be able to:

- Describe the ways classroom tests and standardized tests are used in educational settings.
- Describe the features and uses of tests of aptitude, achievement, skills, processes, and behavioral functioning.
- Distinguish between the process and goals of (1) routine ability assessment and (2) assessment to identify special needs.
- Identify the test-relevant characteristics of special needs students.
- Contrast the separate test and integrated battery approaches to identifying students with special needs.
- Explain the importance of construct, content, and criterion validity in educational testing.
- Define test bias and the types of statistical data necessary to demonstrate test bias.

Let's begin with a simple word association test: What do you think of when I say the word "school"? Chances are, if you generated more than one response, the word "tests" was on your list. Tests are a major element of all educational settings, from the lowly kindergarten to the doctoral-granting graduate program. In this chapter, we explore the why, who, and what of testing in educational settings: Why are tests used in educational settings? Who administers these tests? And what types of tests do they use?

USES OF TESTS IN EDUCATIONAL SETTINGS

Tests are used in a variety of ways in educational settings. Probably most familiar to you is the use of tests in the process of assigning grades. In this case, a test is used to represent your current level of knowledge and/or skill, a process referred to as a **summative evaluation** (Bloom, Hastings, & Madaus, 1971). However, tests can also be used to provide feedback about student progress or teaching effectiveness, a process referred to as **formative evaluation** (Bloom, Hastings, & Madaus, 1971). For example, an instructor can examine a new approach to teaching a concept by administering a test and comparing the progress of students using this technique to the progress of previous students exposed to a different instructional approach.

A third use of tests is in the assessment of student abilities. For example, tests are an important part of decisions about grade-level or ability-group placements. Tests are also used to identify students with special educational needs, such as students with learning problems and academically gifted students.

Finally, tests may be used to provide feedback about the performance of a teacher or the quality of a school. This third use of test data is part of a recent national movement in educational reform. In February 1990, after a summit meeting with then President George Bush, the governors of all 50 states established a set of six national educational goals. Goal 3 called for ensuring that students leaving grades 4, 8, and 12 have demonstrated competency in challenging subject matter (SRCD, 1992). The panel convened to develop procedures for addressing this goal issued several recommendations, including the development of a national assessment of educational programs and the compilation of international data comparing student achievement (APA, 1991a). Data from existing standardized achievement tests are now routinely used as part of a "national report card" on the adequacy of U.S. schools.

Before going any further, we should acknowledge that tests also can be used within schools during the process of counseling. Many school systems provide counselors, even at the primary levels, who may administer psychological tests as part of either vocational (career) or personal counseling. Since Chapter 11 covers the use of tests in counseling, this chapter will focus on the use of tests for educational decisions.

Types of Tests Used

Both classroom tests and standardized tests are used in educational settings. The classroom test is typically written and administered by a teacher and is designed to cover a specific content domain within the curriculum. Classroom tests are used in summative or formative evaluation. At the precollege level, most classroom tests are criterion referenced, whereas classroom tests at the college level and beyond may be either norm or criterion referenced (see p. 39). Classroom tests may use any of the item formats discussed in Chapter 3 and in fact often favor free-response items such as fill-in-the-blank, short answer, and essay.

In contrast to the classroom test, a **standardized test** is designed by professionals with expertise in test construction. Standardized tests are developed over a period of years and pretested on large samples of people. Standardized tests have specific requirements for their administration and scoring; most standardized tests are designed to generate norm-referenced scores that compare test takers' performance to a norm group tested during the standardization process. Standardized tests may use alternate-choice or free-response items, and many favor the multiple-choice format. In general, standardized tests cover a broader content domain than classroom tests.

Rather than being used for assigning grades, standardized tests are used for assessing student abilities, identifying students with special academic needs, and providing feedback about the quality of instruction in a particular class, school, or school system. The standardized tests used most often include intelligence tests, academic achievement tests, and tests of specific abilities. Standardized tests may be designed for individual or group administration.

Our discussion of tests in educational settings will focus on the use of standardized tests. This is not meant to diminish the importance of teacher-written tests. Because of their central role in the rating of students, classroom tests should be held to the same criteria for adequacy as standardized tests. They should be reliable and valid measures, designed to tap specific content and/or skill domains. However, because teachers typically write their own classroom tests, they have the opportunity to devise and revise these tests to ensure their adequacy. On the other hand, standardized tests are *selected* by school personnel, not created by them. Those who use standardized tests do not have the option of revising them and therefore must ensure that the tests chosen are (1) psychometrically sound and (2) appropriate to their assessment goals.

Role of School Psychologists

Although classroom teachers often administer group standardized tests, standardized tests requiring individual administration are usually given by school psychologists. A school psychologist may have either a master's or doctoral-level degree and has been trained to assess academic, behavioral, and emotional characteristics and to develop plans for meeting an individual's particular needs within the school setting (Wise, 1989).

Table 9.1 ranks the 10 tests used most frequently by school psychologists who responded to a recent survey of members of the National Association of School Psychologists (Goh, Teslow, & Fuller, 1981). Note that the majority are tests of either intelligence or achievement. The list also includes a test of perceptual functioning, the Bender, and tests assessing personality (sentence completions) and patterns of behavior (adaptive behavior scales).

TABLE 9.1   Tests Used Most Frequently by
School Psychologists

Rank	Test
1	Wechsler Intelligence Scale for Children
2	Wide Range Achievement Test
3	Stanford-Binet Intelligence Scale
4	Bender-Gestalt Test
5	Peabody Picture Vocabulary Test
6	Wechsler Adult Intelligence Scale
7	Goodenough Draw-A-Man Test
8	Sentence completions
9	Adaptive behavior scales
10	Peabody Individual Achievement Test

Adapted from Goh, Teslow, & Fuller (1981).

Other Components of Educational Decisions

Although testing is an important aspect of making educational decisions, it is only part of the data-gathering process. Educational decisions traditionally are made on the basis of several types of objective and subjective data, including test results, grades, teacher evaluations and/or recommendations, and student interviews with school or counseling psychologists. The quality of a decision is a direct function of the quality of the information used. Educational institutions are particularly sensitive to this, and oversight agencies, including the federal government, have strict policies about the information to be gathered before a decision is made. When tests are used, school personnel must be able to demonstrate that they are both reliable and valid to the issue under study.

ROUTINE ASSESSMENT OF ABILITIES

Assessment of student abilities is a routine part of educational testing. Most of us have taken a standardized intelligence test and probably several standardized achievement tests during our precollege years. We may not even realize that we have taken these tests; routine assessments typically use group tests that are administered by classroom teachers during regular class time. The two types of tests used most often in routine assessment are aptitude and achievement tests.

Measuring Student Aptitude

An aptitude test is designed to predict a student's ability to learn new information and skills. Aptitude tests are contrasted with achievement tests, which focus on how much students already have learned. In addition to being reliable, aptitude tests must demonstrate adequate criterion validity—their primary purpose is to predict future performance. Most standardized aptitude tests produce norm-referenced scores that compare your performance to that of your age-mates.

As discussed in Chapter 2 (see p. 33), the distinction between aptitude and achievement tests is somewhat hazy. In many cases our prediction about a student's future learning is based on an assessment of current knowledge and skills. Consider the Scholastic Aptitude Test (SAT), which is designed to predict success in college. The items on the SAT cover a variety of math and language skills that are acquired during earlier grades. Its classification as an aptitude test is based on (1) its ability to predict success in college and (2) its use of items that are not directly taken from school curricula. For example, the SAT assesses your reading comprehension by asking questions about unfamiliar text passages. You must apply the reading skills you acquired in school to understanding this new information. In other words, an aptitude test can require you to *use* existing knowledge or skills, but it should be designed to require use of that knowledge and skill in new ways.

The aptitude tests used most frequently in routine assessment are intelligence tests. Intelligence tests focus primarily on general learning and problem-solving skills and include both familiar and novel types of questions. Most intelligence tests are designed to produce norm-referenced scores. Before illustrating the use of intelligence tests used in routine ability assessments, let's take a moment to describe their most popular design features.

Design of Intelligence Tests

From the turn of the century to the 1930s, the dominant intelligence test was the Stanford–Binet, an American version of Binet's original intelligence test (e.g., Terman, 1916, 1937[1]). The Binet test was the first standardized general intelligence test, designed to predict school success by (1) measuring primarily verbal skills and (2) translating performance on test items into a single measure of intellectual functioning (Binet & Simon, 1905). This overall measure of intelligence is sometimes referred to as *g* or *g*-factor (e.g., Spearman, 1927).

Beginning in the 1930s, Wechsler revolutionized the design of intelligence tests by measuring two components of intelligence: verbal skills and

[1]The original test developed by Binet and Simon was adapted for use in this country by Louis Terman of Stanford University in 1916. From that point onward, the test has been called the Stanford–Binet.

nonverbal or performance skills (Wechsler, 1939, 1949, 1967). The assessment of separate domains reflected the influence of factor analytic research, which implied that overall intelligence (*g*) could be broken down into several separate abilities (e.g., *s*-factors, Spearman, 1927). In the Wechsler system, verbal intelligence reflects ability to understand and use language, whereas nonverbal intelligence reflects ability to work with other types of symbols, such as pictures or geometric shapes. Although Wechsler tests still included an overall measure of intelligence—a full scale IQ—the splitting of intelligence or *g*-factor into components became a traditional feature of intelligence tests.

Wechsler was also responsible for two innovations in the scoring of intelligence tests: the point scale and the use of standard scores called *deviation IQs*. In a *point scale*, items are grouped into subtests on the basis of content, each item is worth a specific number of points, and points are earned for each correct answer. This is contrasted with the Binet test's *age scale*, in which items are grouped according to the age at which most people answer them correctly. An age cluster can contain items of varying content, as long as the items are linked to the same age group. The test taker must answer a certain number of items correctly in each age cluster to receive credit for that cluster. If the criterion number of correct answers is not produced, no credit is given for that test section.

Deviation IQ is a standard score determined by comparing your raw score to the raw score mean and standard deviation for your age-mates in the standardization sample. Because it is a standard score, the scale of measurement is interval. This is an important advantage for a scoring system; with an interval scale, a 10-point score difference means the same thing at any point along the scale (see p. 17). Deviation IQ is contrasted with the *ratio IQ* scoring used in the early Binet tests (MA/CA × 100). As noted in Chapter 3 (see p. 83), this ratio procedure produces a quotient that is not a true interval measure, making it difficult to compare different IQ scores.

Many modern intelligence tests—even the current Stanford–Binet—incorporate the design features pioneered by Wechsler. Items are often grouped into subtests measuring different aspects of intelligence, and performance is represented on an interval scale using some type of standard score. In addition, most intelligence tests use a point scale rather than an age scale.

Group Intelligence Tests

Routine ability assessment typically uses group tests with the preceding design features. For the vast majority of people, the scores simply become part of an ongoing student record. Most of us are relatively average in ability, and our intelligence test scores are in line with our academic progress and other measures of our academic ability. However, group tests can also identify individuals who score lower than expected or show particular discrepancies in their scores on different subtests so that they can be referred for additional evaluation.

Otis–Lennon School Ability Test.   An excellent example of this type of test is the Otis-Lennon School Ability Test[2] or OSLAT (Otis & Lennon, 1990). Now in its sixth edition, the OLSAT is designed to measure thinking and reasoning ability in students from kindergarten to twelfth grade for the purposes of (1) assessing ability to cope with school tasks, (2) suggesting possible school placements, and (3) evaluating school achievement relative to student potential (Otis & Lennon, 1990). Its various subtests are organized into measures of two aspects of intellectual functioning, verbal ability and nonverbal ability. The classification of subtests is presented in Table 9.2. Note that the verbal/nonverbal distinction parallels Wechsler's classic distinction between using language and using other types of symbols. It is not a verbal/math nor a verbal/spatial distinction.

Rather than producing IQ scores, the new edition of the OLSAT generates *school ability indexes* (SAIs) for the verbal subtests, the nonverbal subtests, and for overall performance. These are standard scores with a mean of 100 and a standard deviation of 16. In fact, they are indistinguishable from IQ scores when they are written in a student's folder. The change of name is designed to reduce misinterpretation and misuse of scores by emphasizing the test's focus on school-related abilities. The validity data presented in the test manual indicate that the test does measure abilities relevant to school achievement.

The OLSAT is a good illustration of a problem common to group tests. Although the verbal, nonverbal, and total SAIs show good internal consistency, little is known about their test–retest reliability. In fact, the reported standard error of measurement is derived from internal consistency data. In Chapter 6, standard error of measurement was identified as the average difference between test scores and true scores, based on the reliability of a test (p. 204). It is based on the concept of repeated testing and the assumption that repeated testing will eventually reveal a range within which true ability lies. When standard error of measurement is calculated from other types of reliability data, such as the internal consistency data used in the OLSAT, the meaning of standard error becomes unclear.

Cognitive Abilities Test.   Another popular group test is the Cognitive Abilities Test[3] (CogAT), also designed for grades K–12 (Thorndike & Hagen, 1986).

[2]The OLSAT is descended from one of the earliest group intelligence tests, the Otis Group Intelligence Scale, an early adaptation of the early Binet test for group administration. Its previous edition was called the Otis–Lennon Mental Ability Test.

[3]The CogAT is an extension of the Lorge–Thorndike Intelligence Test, another early group test based on the Binet test.

TABLE 9.2   Organization of the Otis–Lennon School Ability Test

Subscale	Ability Area	Subtest[a]
Verbal	Verbal comprehension	Antonyms
		Sentence completion
		Sentence arrangement
		Following directions
	Verbal reasoning	Verbal analogies
		Verbal classification
		Arithmetic reasoning
		Aural reasoning
		Logical selection
		Word/letter matrix
		Inference
Nonverbal	Pictorial reasoning[b]	Picture classification
		Picture series
		Picture analogies
	Quantitative reasoning[c]	Number series
		Number matrix
		Numeric inference
	Figural reasoning	Figural analogies
		Pattern matrix
		Figural classification
		Figural series

[a]Not all subtests are used at all grade levels.
[b]Pictorial reasoning is assessed for grade K only.
[c]Quantitative reasoning assessment begins at grade 3.
Adapted from Otis & Lennon (1990).

The CogAT assesses reasoning and problem-solving skill in three areas: verbal, nonverbal, and quantitative. The classification of subtests for the primary battery (grades K–3) and multilevel edition (grades 3–12) is presented in Table 9.3. Unlike the OLSAT, the CogAT distinguishes between spatial/perceptual (nonverbal) ability and mathematical (quantitative) ability. The nonverbal subtests focus on geometric/spatial problems, whereas the quantitative focus on numerical/quantitative problems.

Like the OLSAT, the CogAT does not produce IQ scores. Raw scores on the verbal, quantitative, and nonverbal subtests are converted into *standard age scores* (SASs) with means of 100 and standard deviations of 16. Internal consistency coefficients for the various scales average in the .90s, and CogAT scores are good predictors of school performance—especially the verbal and quantitative scores. Again, little information is provided on test–retest reliability.

TABLE 9.3   Organization of the Cognitive Abilities Test

Ability area	Subtests
Verbal	Verbal classification[a,b] Sentence completion Verbal analogies Vocabulary[a]
Nonverbal	Figure classification[a,b] Figure analogies Figure analysis Matrices[a]
Quantitative	Quantitative relations Number series Equation building Quantitative concepts[a] Relational concepts[a]

[a]Only subtests used in the K–3 version.
[b]Subtests used in both K–3 and 3–12 version.
Adapted from Thorndike & Hagen (1986).

Question of Construct Validity

Although the preceding tests have been described as group *intelligence* tests, there is some concern about the use of this label. Critics charge that referring to these as intelligence tests leads to inaccurate generalizations about student ability. It is quite possible, critics charge, for a student to receive a below-average score on these tests but still to function effectively outside of school. In fact, the term "6-hour retarded child" was coined to describe students who are "mentally retarded" only while they are in school (e.g., Heward & Orlansky, 1988).

These criticisms raise questions about the construct validity of group intelligence tests. Intelligence is a complex, multifaceted property, and it appears that only certain facets—those specifically related to school success—are measured by the group tests administered in schools. Furthermore, most group intelligence tests tap abilities similar to those measured by group achievement tests. In discussing the Otis–Lennon, one reviewer notes, "Although validity data are presented to suggest the OLSAT measures similar abilities to other group-administered achievement tests, it is unclear what unique aspects are captured by the OLSAT" (Swerdlik, 1992, p. 639).

Although these tests are still referred to as intelligence tests, test developers have become sensitive to these criticisms. The Otis–Lennon is now called a test of "school ability" rather than a test of "mental ability." In addition, neither the OLSAT nor the CogAT uses the term "intelligence quotients" to describe their scores. In some classification systems, these tests are identified as multifactor aptitude tests rather than intelligence tests (e.g., Slavin, 1991), an effort to portray them as assessments of school-related aptitudes rather than as tests of all aspects of intelligence.

Measuring Student Achievement

In contrast to aptitude tests, achievement tests focus on knowledge and skills that are part of an academic curriculum. The purpose of an achievement test is to identify a student's mastery of a particular knowledge or skill domain. Like aptitude tests, most achievement tests produce norm-referenced scores.

Group Achievement Tests

Routine assessment of student abilities typically uses group achievement tests. In addition to providing information about individual students' progress and identifying students who should be referred for more in-depth evaluation, group achievement tests have become an important part of assessing the effectiveness of individual teachers, schools, and school systems. There are several popular group achievement tests, including the California Achievement Test, the Iowa Test of Basic Skills, the Stanford Achievement Test, and the Metropolitan Achievement Test. We will use two of them to illustrate the design of this type of test.

California Achievement Test.   The California Achievement Test or CAT is designed to measure basic skill areas that are commonly found in state-mandated curricula for grades K–12 (CTB/McGraw-Hill, 1985). Subtests are included for achievement in reading, language, vocabulary, spelling, mathematics, and study/reference skills, although the areas assessed and subtests used vary according to grade level. Additional subtests are available for science and social studies. The CAT uses multiple-choice items at all levels.

In addition to providing norm-referenced scores (e.g., percentile ranks) comparing students to a national standardization sample, the CAT provides criterion-referenced scores indicating how students have performed relative to a set of *category objectives*. These objectives represent specific skills and concepts identified as of central importance at each grade level. The identification of objectives was based on an analysis of the required curriculum in a national sample of school districts. Criterion-referenced scores indicate whether the student demonstrates "mastery," "partial mastery," or "nonmastery" of each category objective.

Analysis of CAT scores indicates good internal consistency coefficients, although again there are few data on test–retest reliability. Extensive data are provided on content validity and on the relationship of CAT scores to other measures of achievement and school aptitude.

Iowa Test of Basic Skills.   The Iowa Test of Basic Skills (ITBS) is designed to measure achievement in reading, vocabulary, language, spelling, math, and study/reference skills for grades K–9, although the subtests again vary according to grade (Hieronymous & Hoover, 1985). Supplemental tests are available for listening skills, social studies, science, and writing. All subtests use multiple choice items except the writing skills test which involves assessment of an actual writing sample.

Internal consistency coefficients for the various subtests fall in the .80s to .90s range. However, reliability coefficients for the writing sample, based on scoring of samples by different raters, range from about .4 to .7. The ITBS demonstrates adequate correlations with other achievement tests and tests of school aptitude such as the CogAT.

Question of Content Validity

A standardized achievement test is only useful if it covers the skills and concepts taught within a particular school system. Our primary concern in selecting achievement tests, therefore, is their content validity relative to the school curriculum. Test developers are making an increased effort to assist schools in selecting content-valid tests. For example, the CAT provides a detailed description of the objectives the test is designed to measure so that potential users can decide if it is a valid measure of their curricula.

Table 9.4 presents an example of a content validity analysis of the coverage of third grade topics by four group achievement tests. Note that the amount of time (i.e., number of questions) devoted to measuring each area varies across the four tests, as does the total time needed to administer the test. Analyses such as this are necessary to determine whether a particular achievement test is appropriate for use in a given school system.

IDENTIFICATION OF SPECIAL NEEDS

Recent federal legislation has mandated that schools provide mechanisms for identifying children with special educational needs and for meeting those needs in the least restrictive way possible. The two critical laws relative to psychological testing are Public Law (PL) 94-142, the Education for All Handicapped Children Act, and Public Law (PL) 95-561, the Gifted and Talented Children's Educational Act (Heward & Orlansky, 1988).

TABLE 9.4   Coverage of Third Grade Content Areas in Four Popular Group Achievement Tests

Area	% Testing Time			
	California Achievement Test	Iowa Tests of Basic Skills	Metropolitan Achievement Tests	Stanford Achievement Test
Language arts	**49.4%**	**44.6%**	**42.0%**	**42.0%**
Reading comprehension	20.8%	17.2%	21.0%	10.9%
Vocabulary	6.0	6.1	0.0	7.8
Language	18.4	16.4	21.0	17.1
Spelling	4.2	4.9	0.0	6.2
Mathematics	**35.7**	**28.6**	**21.0**	**28.0**
Arithmetic fundamentals	14.9	18.4	21.0	17.1
Arithmetic reasoning	20.8	10.2	0.0	10.9
Other knowledge areas	**0.0**	**0.0**	**36.8**	**18.6**
Social studies	0.0[a]	0.0[a]	18.4	9.3
Science	0.0[a]	0.0[a]	18.4	9.3
Other skill areas	**14.9**	**26.6**	**0.0**	**10.9**
Reference/ study skills	14.9	26.6	0.0	0.0
Listening comprehension	0.0	0.0[a]	0.0	10.9
Total working time (minutes)	168	224	190	320

[a]Optional subtests are available.
Note that these proportions change as the tests are revised.
Adapted from J. S. Ahman & M. D. Glock (1981). *Evaluating Student Progress: Principles of Tests and Measures.* Boston: Allyn & Bacon.

Passed in 1975, PL 94-142 states that all handicapped children must receive a free and appropriate public education that provides the services they need at no cost to parents. Schools are required to (1) identify and screen these children using reliable and valid procedures, (2) evaluate the results of these assessments using a multidisciplinary team, (3) develop written individualized programs for their educational needs, and (4) provide the educational services to meet these needs in the least restrictive environment possible (i.e., within a regular classroom whenever it is feasible). The legislation further states that no educational placement may be based on the results of a single assessment procedure (Hallahan & Kauffman, 1988).

Although academically gifted and talented students are not specifically covered under PL 94-142, subsequent legislation encourages school systems to evaluate and provide services for these students. PL 95-561, passed in 1978, provides financial incentives for states and local school systems to develop programs for identifying and educating academically gifted and talented students. Even though schools are not *required* to serve this population, a recent national survey revealed that 47 states have appointed either a consultant or a director for gifted programs (Sisk, 1984).

Types of Special Needs

Special needs students are often referred to as exceptional students. An **exceptionality** is an intellectual, behavioral, emotional, or physical characteristic that may affect a student's educational progress (Heward & Orlansky, 1988). Exceptional students include students with mental retardation, learning disability, giftedness, and other behavioral, emotional, and physical conditions that affect their educational needs. Before discussing the use of tests to evaluate these students, we need to identify the legal and/or traditional definitions of each exceptionality.

Giftedness

Any discussion of giftedness must begin by noting the variety of terminology used in this area. Some school systems identify children as academically gifted, meaning that their academic performance is significantly above the level expected on the basis of age. Other school systems identify children as gifted or talented, meaning that they possess either unusual academic ability or talents in specific areas. Specific talents may include traditional academic domains, such as math, or performance domains such as art, music, or dance.

To simplify our discussion, we will focus on academically gifted students. Traditionally, an individual must perform in the top 3% to 5% of the age-group distribution to be considered gifted (Marland, 1971). The criteria used most often to identify giftedness are intelligence test score, score on achievement tests, and teacher nomination, which is usually supported by school grades (Renzulli & Delacourt, 1986).

If we think in terms of normally distributed scores, an intelligence or achievement test score at the 93rd percentile is 1.5 standard deviations above the mean. If gifted students are in the top 3% to 5% of their age groups, we would expect their scores to fall above the 93rd percentile—more than 1.5

standard deviations above the mean. However, since schools serve the students in their own districts, many school systems use local norms rather than national norms to set cutoff scores. The qualifying score, therefore, may vary according to school district. In one district the top 5% of students may be identified by an IQ score that *nationally* falls at the 85th percentile, whereas in another district the top 5% may be defined by the score that falls nationwide at the 95th percentile.

Mental Retardation

The most widely used definition of mental retardation is the one developed by the American Association on Mental Deficiency (AAMD). The AAMD statement identifies mental retardation as (1) significantly subaverage intellectual functioning and (2) a subnormal level of adaptive behavior (H. J. Grossman, 1983). *Adaptive behavior* refers to ability to function at an age-appropriate level and to cope with demands in an age-appropriate way. Included within the construct of adaptive behavior are such skills as self-care, interacting with peers, and communicating with others.

Subaverage intellectual functioning is operationally defined as a score that is more than two standard deviations below the mean on a standardized intelligence test, usually translating to a score of 70 or less. No specific cutoff score is required to identify an individual as having a subnormal level of adaptive behavior. In fact, some psychologists (e.g., Zigler, Balla, & Hodapp, 1984) contend that identification of mental retardation should be based solely on intelligence because adaptive behavior is too difficult to define and measure. Research on identification of mental retardation indicates that 25 states do not require an assessment of adaptive behavior (Payne, Patton, & Patton, 1986).

Learning Disabilities

Although as many as 40 different definitions have been proposed for the term learning disability (e.g., Bennett & Ragosta, 1984), PL 94-142 provides a very specific definition of this set of problems. A specific learning disability is (1) a problem in a psychological process involved in understanding or using language that (2) does not result primarily from a physical handicap, from mental retardation, or from environmental, cultural, or economic disadvantage (Heward & Orlansky, 1988).

Because mental retardation must be ruled out as the source of the performance deficit, intelligence tests are routinely used in the identification of learning disability. An individual must have at least average intelligence to be a candidate for the learning disability diagnosis. Because the individual must also demonstrate problems in the understanding or use of language, achievement tests are used to identify the current level of language skills. In fact, learning disability is often referred to as an "IQ-achievement discrepancy," meaning that the individual is performing at a lower level than would be expected on the basis of intelligence test score (e.g., Hallahan & Kauffman, 1988).

Because PL 94-142 requires schools to develop educational programs to meet students' specific learning needs, students with learning disabilities must be given tests that identify the nature of their learning problems. These may include tests of specific skill deficits in areas such as math and reading and tests of process deficits. A *process deficit* is a problem in attention, perception, or memory that interferes with the ability to understand or use information. Because the federal legislation refers to learning disability as a problem in a language-related *process*, process tests have become an important assessment tool.

Behavioral and Emotional Problems

Although students with behavioral and/or emotional problems are specifically covered by PL 94-142, we once again find a variety of labels and definitions used in discussions of this population. Some systems identify these children as emotionally disturbed/behaviorally disordered (ED/BD), others use the term behaviorally and/or emotionally handicapped (BEH), and the law itself identifies these individuals as "seriously emotionally disturbed" (Hallahan & Kauffman, 1988). The federal statute is based on Bower's (1969) definition of emotional disturbance and includes individuals with inappropriate behaviors, feelings, and patterns of social interaction that (1) exist over a long period of time and (2) cannot be explained by intellectual, social, or physical/health factors.

The screening process for identifying individuals with behavioral/emotional problems usually involves interviews with parents and teachers, administration of at least one behavior rating scale, and direct classroom observation (Simpson, 1981). Individuals under evaluation may also be seen by a clinical or counseling psychologist, who in turn may administer additional objective or projective personality tests.

Separate Test Approach

When routine assessment indicates a possible learning problem, students are referred for additional testing with individually administered tests. Individual tests typically tap a wider range of abilities and contents, providing more sensitive measures of aptitude and achievement. For many years, the identification of students with special academic needs involved the administration of a series of separate tests. In most cases, students were given an individual intelligence test and an individual achievement test. Then, depending on the characteristics identified, students were given additional screening tests to assess (1) the presence of specific skill deficits, such as problems in math or reading skill, (2) the presence of processing deficits, such as problems in language processing or visual–motor integration, and (3) the presence of behavioral problems, such as behavior disorders or problems in adaptive behavior.

Today, more educational institutions are using integrated test batteries that assess many of these characteristics with a single instrument. These batteries are long, containing many different subscales, but have the advantage of providing direct comparisons of ability and achievement using subtests that are normed on a single standardization sample. In this section, we will highlight some of the tests used in a separate test approach. We should note, however, that some school systems use a combined approach. For example, a school system may use both an individual intelligence test and a test battery that itself contains a measure of academic ability.

Individual Intelligence Tests

Intelligence tests are particularly important in identification of gifted, mentally retarded, and learning disabled students. In all three cases, the special need requires the presence of particular intelligence test characteristics. We will use the two most popular tests, the Wechsler series and the Stanford–Binet, as examples. Our discussion will highlight the important features of each test without going into extensive detail about individual subtests. Students interested in more specific information about individual intelligence tests should consult additional sources, such as Anastasi (1988) and Kaplan & Saccuzzo (1993).

The Wechsler Tests.   The Wechsler series includes three separate tests designed for different age ranges: the Wechsler Preschool and Primary Scale of Intelligence (WPPSI), for ages 4 to $6\frac{1}{2}$, the Wechsler Intelligence Scale for Children (WISC), for ages 6 to 16 years, and the Wechsler Adult Intelligence Scale (WAIS), for ages 16 and above. All three tests have been revised recently, and our discussion will focus on their most recent forms.

The first Wechsler test was the Wechsler–Bellevue, the forerunner of the modern WAIS, a reflection of Wechsler's concern about the lack of valid tests for assessing adult intelligence (Wechsler, 1939). His subsequent two tests were developed as downward extensions of his adult test (Wechsler, 1949, 1967). All Wechsler tests include a series of subtests that are combined into three measures of intellectual functioning: a verbal IQ, a performance IQ, and a full-scale IQ (Wechsler 1981, 1989, 1991). Verbal subtests require understanding and use of language, whereas performance subtests require performing an action, such as arranging a set of pictures in order or assembling a puzzle.

The specific subtests comprising each scale for each test are presented in Table 9.5. Note the consistency in the verbal subtests across the three age groups, although the performance subtests vary somewhat according to age.

TABLE 9.5   Subtests of the WAIS–R, the WISC–III, and the WPPSI–R

Verbal Subtests	WAIS–R	WISC–III	WPPSI–R
Information	×	×	×
Comprehension	×	×	×
Arithmetic	×	×	×
Similarities	×	×	×
Vocabulary	×	×	×
Digit span	×	×[a]	—
Sentences	—	—	×[a,b]
Performance Subtests	**WAIS–R**	**WISC–III**	**WPPSI–R**
Picture completion	×	×	×
Block design	×	×	×
Picture arrangement	×	×	—
Object assembly	×	×	—
Geometric design	—	—	×[c]
Digit symbol	×	—	—
Coding	—	×[b]	—
Animal house	—	—	×[b]
Mazes	—	×[a]	—
Symbol search	—	×[a]	—
Animal house retest	—	—	×[a]

[a]These are supplementary subtests that are not used unless there are problems in the administration of the other subtests.
[b]These subtests are designed to be analogues of the subtests used with older individuals that are more appropriate for younger children.
[c]The geometric design subtest replaces both the picture arrangement and object assembly subtests.
Adapted from Wechsler (1981, 1989, 1991).

Consistency of subtests is a great advantage if individuals will be assessed repeatedly at different ages.

All scores reported for Wechsler tests are standard scores called *deviation IQs*. Test takers receive points for each correct answer (a point scale approach), which are totaled to determine the raw score for each subtest. Subtest raw scores are converted to standard or scaled scores with a mean of 10 and a standard deviation of 3. The verbal, performance, and full-scale IQs are determined by adding the raw scores on the appropriate subtests and converting the total to a standard score with a mean of 100 and a standard deviation of 15. All scores are norm referenced, comparing test takers to age-mates in the standardization group.

There are a few differences across the three Wechsler tests in the calculation of the verbal, performance, and full-scale IQs. As indicated in Table 9.5, the WAIS–R uses six subtests to determine verbal IQ, whereas the WISC–III and WPPSI–R use only five. Also, the WPPSI–R bases performance IQ on only four subtests, rather than the five subtests used in the WAIS–R and WISC–III.

Because of their design, the Wechsler tests provide an excellent opportunity to compare verbal and nonverbal functioning. Such a comparison can be useful in the identification of mental retardation and learning disability. For example, if an individual is mentally retarded, we would expect both verbal and performance IQs to be affected because mental retardation tends to be a global impairment. On the other hand, we expect an individual with a learning disability to have more difficulty in verbal areas because learning disability is an impairment in language-related processes. We would therefore expect to see a lower verbal than performance IQ.

We must be careful, however, about reading too much into a comparison of these scores. Although the Wechsler tests are generally reliable and valid measures, even the most recent revisions show group differences in score patterns. For example, comparison of the verbal and performance IQs of gifted children from four ethnic groups indicated that each group had a characteristic verbal/performance pattern (Saccuzzo, Johnson, & Russell, 1992). Although verbal/performance scores were equivalent for Hispanic-American children, as a group, African-American and white children showed higher verbal IQs, and Filipino children showed higher performance IQs.

The split-half coefficients for Wechsler tests are above .9, although the test–retest reliability coefficients vary as a function of both test-taker age and the time between testings (Wechsler, 1981, 1989, 1991). In addition, the standard error of measurement for the verbal and full-scale IQs is approximately 3 points, whereas the standard error of measurement for the performance IQ is closer to 4 points. Standard error of measurement estimates the test score-true score difference (see p. 204); the different standard errors indicate that performance IQs are more likely to be over- or underestimates of ability. Validity studies, focusing on the relationship between Wechsler scores and scores on other intelligence tests, reveal acceptable patterns of correlations.

There are several frequent criticisms, however, of Wechsler tests. First, factor analytic studies indicate that the Wechsler subtests may in fact tap three aspects of intelligence—verbal ability, performance ability, and memory function—rather than a verbal/performance contrast (e.g., Silverstein, 1982). Second, critics charge that adherence to the old two-factor model of intelligence does not keep pace with current research and theory in cognitive psychology. The Wechsler tests provide no information on such aspects of intelligence as metacognition, organizational skills, or executive processes (e.g., Sternberg, 1988). This lack of attention to processing issues leads to the third criticism of the Wechsler tests: They are not particularly valuable for diagnosing specific educational problems and planning appropriate treatments. As you will see later in this chapter, tests that measure specific *process* deficits are often more useful for identifying special needs children.

The final criticism of the Wechsler tests relates to the persistent patterns of group score differences. Even though the Wechsler tests have been standardized on heterogeneous groups, including individuals of different races, ethnic groups, ages, and geographic regions, average full-scale IQs and verbal/performance IQ patterns still vary along ethnic, racial, and socioeconomic lines. Although Wechsler tests do predict school achievement for all subgroups, white, middle-class children still earn the highest scores on Wechsler tests. These score patterns have been the subject of much debate: Why are they present? What do they mean? And, even though the test does predict performance for all groups, should it continue to be used if it produces score differences? We will return to this issue later in our discussion of test bias.

The Stanford–Binet.   With the development of the Wechsler tests, the popularity of the Stanford–Binet declined. Recent revisions of the Stanford–Binet, however, have incorporated many of the design features of the Wechsler tests. Like the Wechsler tests, the newer versions of the Stanford–Binet group items into subtests on the basis of their content and represent performance in standard scores (deviation IQs). Furthermore, the most recent revision goes beyond the Wechsler tests in its attention to current views on the nature of intellectual abilities.

The newest edition of the Stanford–Binet is the fourth edition (Thorndike, Hagen, & Sattler, 1986). Unlike earlier versions, the new Stanford–Binet adopts a multidimensional view of intelligence. It is composed of 15 subtests assessing four broad areas of intellectual functioning: verbal reasoning, abstract/visual reasoning, quantitative reasoning, and short-term memory. Note the splitting of nonverbal aspects into two subscales (abstract/visual and quantitative) and the inclusion of a process measure (short-term memory). Suitable for ages 2 through adulthood, the Stanford–Binet generates four area scores and an overall measure of intellectual ability.

The use of a separate short-term memory score reflects current views on how information processing differences contribute to differences in intellectual functioning (e.g., Sternberg, 1988) and is supported by factor analytic research on intelligence test scores (e.g., Silverstein, 1982). Memory ability appears to capture an aspect of individual differences in performance (i.e., test score variance) that is separate from either verbal or nonverbal ability.

The decision to include measures of the other three abilities reflects the influence of a popular view of intelligence as composed of crystallized and fluid abilities (e.g., Horn & Cattell, 1966). Theoretically, *crystallized abilities*, such as verbal and quantitative reasoning, develop as a result of learning, whereas *fluid abilities*, such as abstract reasoning, reflect the basic processing capacities of the individual. By providing measures of both crystallized and fluid abilities, the modern Stanford–Binet provides measures of aptitudes related to *specific* experiences, such as exposure to mathematics, and measures related more to general experience, such as exposure to problem-solving tasks. The relationship between these different aspects of intelligence, the four Stanford–Binet area scores, and the 15 Stanford–Binet subtests is presented in Table 9.6. Items within each subtest are arranged in order of difficulty according to the principle of **age differentiation**, a long-standing tradition in Binet tests. The goal of this process is to construct a scale in which the number of items answered correctly increases as age increases. The order of items is based on the proportion of different-aged children who answer them correctly using a "$\frac{2}{3}-\frac{3}{4}$ rule." For example, if less than two-thirds of 5 year olds answer an item correctly, it must be too difficult for this age group. If at least two-thirds of 6 year olds can answer it correctly, the item discriminates between or *differentiates* 5 and 6 year olds. We would therefore also expect most 7 year olds to answer it correctly. To make sure the item also differentiates between 6 and 7 year olds, we compare the proportion who answer it correctly at these two ages. If more than three-quarters of 7 year olds answer correctly, the item is classified as a 6 year old.

Instead of using a point scale like the Wechsler tests, all 15 subtests of the Stanford–Binet use an adaptive testing format based on basal and ceiling

TABLE 9.6   Classifying the Subtests of the Modern Stanford–Binet

Aspects of Intelligence	Areas	Subtests
Crystallized abilities	Verbal reasoning	Vocabulary Comprehension Absurdities Verbal relations
	Quantitative reasoning	Quantitative Number series Equation building
Fluid abilities	Abstract/visual reasoning	Pattern analysis Copying Matrices Paper folding and cutting
Memory abilities	Short-term memory skill	Bead memory Memory for sentences Memory for digits Memory for objects

Adapted from Thorndike, Hagen, & Sattler (1986).

ages. The **basal age** is the age at which the child typically answers at least two items of equal difficulty correctly. Examiners usually begin with items coded for the child's chronological age. If a basal is not reached, the examiner goes backward and administers easier items. Once a basal age is established, the examiner continues with more difficult items until the child reaches a **ceiling age**, the point at which the child typically misses at least three out of four consecutive items at the same age level. All individuals who fail three out of four items at a given level receive the same ceiling age, regardless of whether they were correct on two, three, or four items at the preceding level. Unlike the Wechsler tests, the Stanford–Binet does not award points based on the number of *items* answered correctly. Instead, points are awarded on the basis of the age groups successfully passed.

Rather than using the ratio IQ formula characteristic of earlier versions (MA/CA × 100), the modern Stanford–Binet adopts the deviation IQ approach introduced by the Wechsler tests. A test taker's raw scores are converted to standard scores based on the raw score mean and standard deviation of age mates in the norm group. On the individual subtests, raw scores are converted to standard age scores that have a mean of 50 and a standard deviation of 8. The four area scores are determined by combining raw scores from the relevant subtests (see Table 9.6); the composite score is based on raw scores across all subtests. Both area and composite scores have a mean of 100 and a standard deviation of 16.

Current research indicates that the Stanford–Binet is both a reliable and valid measure. The internal consistency coefficients for the area scores and the composite score are over .9, and the subtest coefficients average close to .9 (Thorndike, Hagen, & Sattler, 1986). Scores show reasonable test–retest reliability over a 16-week interval and correlate well with other measures of intelligence (e.g., Wechsler scores).

The two most often cited criticisms of the Stanford–Binet are its administration format and its possible cultural bias. Many psychologists avoid using the Stanford–Binet because it is so difficult to administer. Examiners must establish a basal and ceiling age for each of the 15 subtests and must estimate where to begin each subtest on the basis of the test taker's age. The basal/ceiling approach also complicates the calculation of internal consistency coefficients for the individual subtests, which may be responsible in part for their lower reliabilities. Because test taker's do not attempt all items, the calculation of internal consistency assumes that (1) all items below the basal age are answered correctly, and (2) all items above the ceiling age are answered incorrectly.

In terms of cultural bias, the current version of the Stanford–Binet still produces different patterns of scores for different racial, ethnic, and socioeconomic groups (Spruill, 1987). These group differences persist in spite of the use of a standardization sample of more than 5000 people chosen to represent the geographic, ethnic group, age, and gender distributions in the 1980 census. As was the case with Wechsler tests, these group differences imply possible problems when test scores are used to make educational decisions about minority children.

Individual Achievement Tests

Additional achievement test information is used most often in identification of academic giftedness and learning disability. Gifted children are traditionally viewed as high achievers as well as students of high aptitude, and most school systems consider scores on both types of tests when qualifying students for admission to gifted programs. In the case of learning disability, we look for *inconsistency* in intelligence/achievement data, rather than consistency. Learning disability is often defined as an "IQ/achievement discrepancy," meaning that students are not performing (achieving) at a level consistent with their aptitude (intelligence).

The Wide Range Achievement Test—Revised (WRAT—R) is a good example of a traditional individual achievement test. The WRAT—R measures reading, spelling, and arithmetic skills for individuals aged 5 to adult (Jastak & Jastak, 1984). The total number of correct answers determines the raw score on each scale (a point scale approach), which can be converted both to a grade equivalent score and a standard score. The standard scores look like IQ scores, with means of 100 and standard deviations of 16, and are even described in the manual as "deviation quotients." Because it is likely that unsophisticated users will confuse these with IQ scores, many school systems choose to report the grade equivalent scores. Unfortunately, this presents its own problems, because grade equivalent scores are not interval scores. They are percentile-based scores (see p. 82), which complicates interpretation of score differences and score changes.

Overall, the WRAT—R subscales have adequate test–retest reliability and internal consistency. Correlations between WRAT—R scores and other tests of achievement indicate adequate content validity. However, two previous criticisms continue to be raised about the new edition. First, the WRAT—R is a rather brief test, basing its assessment of achievement on a relatively small sample of knowledge and skill. Second, scores on the various subtests of the WRAT—R are correlated, implying that the test is a measure of global achievement rather than a set of measures of achievement in separate academic areas (e.g., Reinehr, 1984). In fact, many school systems routinely use the achievement section of one of the test batteries to be described later instead of using the WRAT—R.

Diagnostic Tests

In some circumstances, such as suspected learning disability, we need more information about the precise nature of an individual's learning problems. In these cases, we turn to diagnostic tests. A *diagnostic test* is designed to identify the specific problems an individual displays within a particular domain. Diagnostic tests are available for such diverse domains as math and reading skill, information processing, and behavioral functioning.

Tests of Skill Deficits.   Some diagnostic tests focus on identifying skill-based problems. For example, the Woodcock Reading Mastery Tests—Revised (WRMT—R) is a set of tests designed to diagnose reading problems from kindergarten through college (Woodcock, 1987). The WRMT—R evaluates such skills as letter identification, word identification, word comprehension, and passage comprehension. Both norm- and criterion-referenced scores are produced to assist in identifying the precise nature of a student's reading problems. The Gray Oral Reading Tests—Revised (GORT—R) is designed to identify reading problems in a read-aloud task (Wiederholt & Bryant, 1986). The GORT—R produces scores on reading speed, reading accuracy, reading comprehension, overall reading ability, and reading miscues—different types of errors made during the read-aloud task.

Compare the abilities measured by these tests to the abilities measured by intelligence and achievement tests. An intelligence test may measure a variety of verbal skills, but it is unlikely to produce scores for a specific academic area such as reading. An achievement test may measure an academic area like reading, but it does not break down the reading process into a set of component skills, each to be measured separately.

A similar contrast exists when diagnostic math tests, such as the KeyMath—Revised (Connolly, 1988), are compared to intelligence and achievement tests. The KeyMath—Revised assesses three areas of mathematics: basic concepts, operations, and applications. In the area of operations, separate subtests are provided for measuring skills in addition, subtraction, multiplication, and division. This is the type of detailed information we need to pinpoint the source of a student's math problems.

Tests of Process Deficits.   Even if we know that an individual lacks a specific academic skill, a diagnostic skill test does not tell us *why*. The goal of process tests is to uncover the underlying problems that might interfere with the acquisition of a particular skill. For example, a reading skill problem might involve an inability to translate the sight of a letter into a sound or an inability to see the difference between two letters.

Two good examples of process tests are the Illinois Test of Psycholinguistic Ability (ITPA) and the Bender Visual Motor Gestalt Test (Bender). The revised ITPA, designed for ages 4 to 8, consists of 12 subtests measuring aspects of the acquisition and use of language (Paraskevopoulos & Kirk, 1969). Whereas a reading skill test might focus on the ability to read words aloud or to understand the meaning of words, the ITPA focuses on *processes* that are necessary for reading, such as the ability to reproduce a visual or auditory pattern from memory and the ability to form associations between visual or auditory stimuli.

The Bender Visual Motor Gestalt Test, for ages 3 to adults, consists of nine geometric designs on separate cards that are presented sequentially for test takers to copy (Koppitz, 1975). It is used to investigate the ability to organize components of a visual stimulus into a whole or pattern, referred to as a Gestalt. The focus of the Bender on visual–motor processing makes it useful for identifying conditions such as learning disability and brain damage.

Tests of Behavioral Functioning. In the case of suspected behavioral/emotional handicap or mental retardation, the assessment typically includes some evaluation of student behavior. The Child Behavior Checklist and the American Association of Mental Deficiency (AAMD) Adaptive Behavior Scale will be used to contrast the focus of such assessments.

The Child Behavior Checklist is used to assess social competencies and behavior problems for ages 4 to 16 (Achenbach & Edelbrock, 1983). It is completed by the student's parents based on their observations over a 6-month period. Social competence measures reflect the extent and quality of the student's interactions with peers, the student's involvement in out-of-class activities, and the student's performance in school. The behavior problem scales include measures of internalizing behaviors, such as depression and social withdrawal, and measures of externalizing behaviors, such as aggression and delinquency.

The AAMD Adaptive Behavior Scales assesses a wide variety of physical and behavioral features known to vary among individuals with mental retardation (AAMD, 1981). A section on physical development assesses sensory and motor functions such as vision and control of hands; a similar section on language development examines expressive and comprehension skills. Several additional sections cover behaviors important to self-sufficiency, such as routine behaviors (eating, toileting, and dressing/undressing), shopping and handling money, and social skills. The final section, which includes some overlap with the CBC, is devoted to behavior problems, including antisocial behavior, withdrawal, and stereotyped or odd patterns of behavior.

Integrated Battery Approach

The separate test approach described in the preceding sections dictates that students be evaluated with a set of tests. But the use of separate tests can present interpretive problems. Consider the following scenario: A student takes the WISC—III to measure school-related aptitude, followed by the WRAT—R to measure achievement. The WISC—III assesses verbal and performance skills;

however, the three aspects of achievement measured by the WRAT (reading, spelling and arithmetic) all fall within the domain of verbal skills. When we compare performance on these two tests, we in essence are comparing aptitude and achievement in only one intellectual domain. Furthermore, these two tests were normed on different groups of people. Is drawing conclusions from a comparison of scores based on different standardization samples really the best approach?

The integrated battery approach to assessment is designed to address these issues. In educational testing, an integrated battery is a set of tests that measure both aptitude and achievement. The advantage of an integrated battery is that the component tests reflect the same perspective on cognition and learning and were standardized on the same norm group. Both of these features can simplify the comparison of ability level to achievement level in each domain. We will consider two popular batteries: the Woodcock–Johnson and the Kaufman Assessment Battery for Children.

Woodcock–Johnson Psycho-Educational Battery

The Woodcock–Johnson (WJ) is a set of individually administered tests covering four broad domains: academic aptitude, academic achievement, school/nonschool interests, and independent behavior (Woodcock & Johnson, 1978; Bruininks et al., 1984). The first three parts were standardized on a single sample of students in regular classes; the final part was standardized using a separate sample that included severely handicapped individuals in special classes. The measures within each domain are presented in Tables 9.7 and 9.8. As you can see, the battery provides a package useful both for routine assessment of students and for identifying the characteristics of special needs students. It is the first standardized individual test to report ability and achievement measures based on the same sample of people. It is also the first instrument to incorporate information about interest in academic versus nonacademic areas—data that may be useful in addressing motivational issues. The addition of scales on adaptive (independent) behavior and behavior problems makes it possible to address almost any aspect of exceptionality with this single test battery. Finally, the subtests in the achievement section (Part II) do provide some information on specific skill deficits.

The Woodcock–Johnson demonstrates reliability and validity coefficients comparable to other popular standardized tests. Its drawbacks are primarily its length, and therefore its cost to administer, and its extremely complex scoring procedures. In addition, some concern has been expressed about the ability of Part I (aptitude) scores to predict Part II (achievement) for children with severe cases of learning disabilities, mental retardation, and behavioral problems (e.g., Hager, 1986). With most other populations, however, the Woodcock–Johnson is psychometrically sound.

TABLE 9.7   Organization of the Woodcock–Johnson, Parts I–III

Part I: Tests of Cognitive Ability

Cognitive Factors	Scholastic Aptitudes
Verbal ability	Reading aptitude
Reasoning ability	Mathematics aptitude
Perceptual speed	Written language aptitude
Memory	Knowledge aptitude

Note: The four cognitive factors and four scholastic aptitudes are determined by performance on a subset of 12 subtests. The same subtest may be used in more than one factor and aptitude calculation.

Part II: Tests of Achievement

Area	Subtests
Reading	Letter–word identification, word attack, passage comprehension
Mathematics	Calculation, applied problems
Written language	Dictation, proofing
Knowledge	Science, social studies, humanities

Part III: Tests of Interest Level

Area	Subtests
Scholastic	Reading, mathematics, written language interest
Nonscholastic	Physical interest, social interest

Adapted from R. W. Woodcock (1987).

Kaufman Assessment Battery for Children

Although the Woodcock–Johnson contains a variety of aptitude and achievement measures, it does not address the issue of processing deficits. The Kaufman Assessment Battery for Children or K-ABC is designed to assess processing issues for ages $2\frac{1}{2}$ to $12\frac{1}{2}$ (Kaufman & Kaufman, 1983). Unlike the Wechsler tests or the Stanford–Binet, the K-ABC is based on a view of intelligence as involving sequential versus simultaneous processing of information (e.g., Das, Kirby, & Jarman, 1979). In sequential processing, we must form associations between the elements of a series, such as the sounds we string together when we read the word "rabbit." In simultaneous processing, we must synthesize elements into a coherent whole, such as recognizing a dot-to-dot pattern as the shape of a rabbit.

TABLE 9.8   Organization of the Woodcock–Johnson, Part IV

Part IV: Scales of Independent Behavior

Broad Independence Scale

Area	Subtests
Motor skills	Gross motor, fine motor
Social interaction and communication	Social interaction, language comprehension, language expression
Personal independence	Eating/meal preparation, toileting, dressing, self-care, domestic skills
Community independence	Time/punctuality, money, work skills, home/community orientation

Problem Behaviors Scale

Hurtful to self	Unusual/repetitive habits
Hurtful to others	Socially offensive behavior
Destructive to property	Withdrawal behaviors
Disruptive behavior	Uncooperativeness

Note: Each category of problem behavior is rated in terms of presence, frequency of occurrence, and severity.
Adapted from Bruininks et al. (1984).

The various mental processing subtests and achievement subtests are presented in Table 9.9. Six of the mental processing subtests may be administered nonverbally to assess the intellectual skill of children with communication impairments or who are non-English speakers. The six achievement subtests assess factual information; the distinction between processing and achievement subtests is designed to parallel the difference between fluid and crystallized intelligence (see p. 318).

Like the Woodcock–Johnson, the intelligence and achievement measures were standardized on the same sample. In contrast to the Woodcock–Johnson, the standardization sample included severely handicapped (nonmainstreamed) individuals, a procedure that enhanced the predictive relationships between intelligence/achievement scores. The K-ABC shows levels of reliability and validity comparable to other standardized tests. Furthermore, intelligence scores show smaller racial/ethnic differences than either the Wechsler or Binet tests (Naglieri, 1984; Nolan, Watlington, & Willson, 1989).

Although the K-ABC may be less biased against minorities, it appears to be less useful for identifying individuals at the extreme ends of the intelligence distribution. For example, it appears to underestimate the score of gifted chil-

TABLE 9.9   Organization of the Kaufman ABC

Mental Processing Subtests		
Mental processing composite	Sequential processing	Hand movements[a] Number recall Word order
	Simultaneous processing	Magic window Face recognition[a] Gestalt closure Triangles[a] Matrix analogies[a] Spatial memory[a] Photo series[a]

Achievement

Expressive vocabulary
Faces and places
Arithmetic
Riddles
Reading/decoding
Reading/understanding

[a]These six subtests are used to determine a nonverbal scale score.
Adapted from Kaufman & Kaufman (1983).

dren (McCallum, Karnes, & Oehler-Stinnett, 1985) and to fail to discriminate between preschoolers in the lower IQ range (Bloom et al., 1988). Finally, the distinction between simultaneous and sequential processing has been challenged. Critics (e.g., Sternberg, 1984) charge that the K-ABC subtests are poor representations of the processing distinction—possibly the result of selecting subtests using a logical strategy rather than an empirical procedure—and that the distinction itself is inaccurate (e.g., Herbert, 1982).

PROBLEM OF TEST BIAS

Because tests are used to make educational decisions, such as placement in special classes, the existence of test bias has direct impact on people's lives. The most prevalent concern has been about bias against minority group members in standardized intelligence tests. As the use of tests for educational decisions increased, so did the challenges to the validity of test scores for educational placements. The result has been an increase in the regulation of test use by legislation and by the courts. In this section, we will try to identify the issues surrounding test bias and summarize the current state of affairs regarding the use of tests for educational decisions.

Defining Test Bias

Because psychological tests are designed to assess individual differences, we expect to find variability in people's performance. Test bias cannot be claimed simply because people differ in test scores. Furthermore, we acknowledge that test scores only estimate a person's true characteristics—that's why we conduct studies of reliability and validity. Test bias cannot be claimed, therefore, just because test scores are not totally accurate measures. Test bias is a claim about the *relative* accuracy or inaccuracy of test scores. Test bias exists when test scores vary systematically in their accuracy according to the type of person being tested. A test is biased if it represents individual differences for some groups of people more accurately than it represents individual differences for other groups.

Note the use of the word *systematic* in the definition of test bias. It implies that a biased test has problems of validity (see p. 224). In essence, a biased test is measuring characteristics of people that are not relevant to its purpose.

For example, some psychologists contend that traditional intelligence tests are not valid measures of the intelligence of minority children. These critics contend that the scores of minority children reflect their knowledge of white, middle-class culture, rather than their intellectual ability. As a result, the differences between them in test scores do not indicate their relative levels of intellectual ability. Instead, score differences reflect their relative familiarity with mainstream culture.

Other psychologists counter this argument with a significant piece of data: Although group differences in scores do exist, traditional intelligence tests *are* good predictors of school performance—even for minority children. In other words, these are not only true score differences but also *relevant* true score differences.

To resolve the debate, we must determine what these group score differences mean. Are they evidence of test bias or of real group differences in ability? From a statistical standpoint, test bias is indicated by the presence of **differential validity**—evidence that a test measures different things for different groups of people. To demonstrate differential validity, researchers must demonstrate that the meaning of test scores varies according to the type of people being tested.

One final introductory point: It is important to separate the issue of test bias from concerns about fairness (e.g., Murphy & Davidshofer, 1988). Bias is an empirical concept, tied to patterns of test scores, that can be investigated through statistical procedures. If a test is biased against a particular group, it cannot be used to make fair decisions. However, we can also view the decisions made using an unbiased test as unfair. *Fairness* refers to our sense of what is right or just—not the statistical properties of test scores. Although we can analyze scores to determine if tests are biased, we must analyze our feelings and beliefs to determine if the decisions we make are fair.

Assessing Test Bias

Bias exists when a test shows differential validity according to the type of person tested. The bias may involve problems either in the measurement of characteristics (construct or content validity) or in the prediction of criterion measures (criterion validity). Before we discuss the research on test bias, we will explore the different ways to investigate and demonstrate differential validity.

Measurement Bias

If a test is a more accurate measure of the domain for one type of person than for another, the test has a problem of ***measurement bias*** (construct or content validity). For example, the claim that traditional IQ tests do not accurately measure the intelligence of minority individuals is an assertion about measurement bias. Questions about measurement bias require analysis of a test's construct and/or content validity.

Investigating bias in the measurement of a construct is difficult. Since we don't know peoples' true scores on the domain of the test, we cannot simply compare their test scores to their true scores. Instead, we use an adaptation of the strategies for studying construct validity—convergent and divergent validity studies (see p. 254). The difference between this research and general research on construct validity is that test bias studies analyze relationships *separately* for different groups of people.

In a convergent validity study, we correlate test scores with measures of other related characteristics. For example, we could correlate intelligence test scores with measures of reasoning ability, such as scores on a test of problem solving. If our concern is bias against minorities, we calculate these correlations separately for minority and nonminority individuals. To demonstrate differential validity—our statistical definition of test bias—we need to show that the correlations vary according to group membership. For example, a high correlation between IQ scores and problem-solving scores for white children and a low correlation for minority children indicate that the test is measuring different things for different groups. If the test shows low correlations for *both* groups, we might question the validity of the test as a measure of ability to reason, but we could not conclude that it was biased against minorities.

In a divergent validity study, we correlate test scores with measures of characteristics that are not relevant to the test domain. For example, we could correlate intelligence test scores with measures of socioeconomic status, such as family income. To demonstrate differential validity, we need to show that the correlations vary according to racial/ethnic group (e.g., white versus minority). As in the convergent validity study, a high correlation between test scores and socioeconomic status for *both* groups indicates an overall problem with test validity, not a problem of test bias.

If our concern is bias in test content, we can examine the performance of different groups on individual test items. To demonstrate differential validity, we need to show that the difficulty of test items varies systematically according to type of person tested. This type of pattern is referred to statistically as a group *X* item interaction (Murphy & Davidshofer, 1988). In an interaction, performance on one variable is influenced by another variable. In a group *X* item interaction, the performance on a test item (one variable) is influenced by membership in a particular group (the other variable).

To investigate this interaction, we calculate the average item difficulty *separately* for different groups of people. If 60% of white children are correct on an item, but only 30% of minority children are correct, the item shows a group *X* item interaction. Performance on the item is dependent upon racial/ethnic group membership, an indication of bias in content. Although we expect *individuals* to differ in performance on test items, we do not expect *groups* to differ in performance on specific items.

It is within this context that critics raise the issue of "opportunity to learn." Because we use tests to measure individual differences, we want test scores to reflect true differences in knowledge and skill. If a test includes many items that are drawn from a particular subculture, some test takers have not had the opportunity to acquire the information or skills covered by the test. Our measure of individual differences in knowledge or skill becomes contaminated by differences in experiences.

Prediction Bias

In addition to bias in the measurement of characteristics, a test may show prediction bias. A test demonstrates *prediction bias* if its ability to predict performance varies according to group membership. Prediction bias may be investigated either by examining group differences in criterion validity coefficients, in linear regression (prediction) equations, or in selection studies.

The simplest demonstration of prediction is the existence of different criterion validity coefficients for different groups of people. For example, we could calculate the criterion validity coefficient for intelligence test scores and school grades separately for different racial/ethnic groups. If the correlation is significantly higher for one group than for another, we have evidence of differential validity. We can further demonstrate this prediction bias by comparing the standard errors of estimate (s_E). The standard error of estimate is our estimate of prediction error—the average number of points by which predicted scores and actual scores differ (see p. 233). If the extent to which a test over- or underpredicts performance varies across groups, the test shows differential validity in prediction.

An alternative strategy is to use linear regression ($Y' = a + bX$) to predict performance on a criterion measure, Y', from test score, X (see p. 231). Again, we calculate the separate regression equations for the groups being compared. If the regression equations differ, there is a possible problem of test bias. Different regression equations indicate that individuals with the same test score (X) will not receive the same predicted criterion score (Y').

Figure 9.1 indicates a clear case of bias in prediction. The two regression lines have different slopes, indicated by their different slants within the graph. Remember that the slope of a regression line (b) is affected by the correlation between X and Y ($b = r(\sigma_Y/\sigma_X)$). When the regression lines have different slopes, the criterion validity coefficients are likely to differ, an indication of bias in prediction.

However, even when the slopes of the lines are the same, regression equations can differ in intercept (a). The impact of different intercepts is seen

FIGURE 9.1   Hypothetical regression data indicating bias in prediction

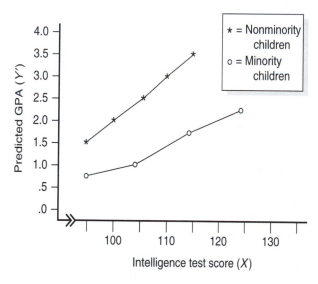

most clearly in selection studies. In selection studies, we look for the test score that is associated with a desired level of criterion performance (see p. 239). If the intercepts for two groups differ, we will end up using different test scores to select people who meet our criterion cutoff. Figure 9.2 illustrates this problem with hypothetical data about intelligence test scores and school performance.

Assume our goal is to identify high-achieving children for a special academic program. We set as our selection criterion a predicted grade point average of 3.5. According to Figure 9.1, nonminority children with IQ scores of 115 are likely to earn GPAs of 3.5. However, minority children with IQ scores of 115 are likely to earn a GPA of only 3.0. To select minority children likely to receive GPAs of 3.5, we would need to use a cutting score on IQ of 120.

The problem results from the different regression equations for predicting school grades from IQ. Although the slope or slant of the lines is the same, implying similar criterion validity coefficients, the Y-intercepts are different ($a = -8.0$ versus -8.5). The difference in intercept is due to the different average IQ scores ($\overline{X}$) for the two groups. The average IQ score for minority students

FIGURE 9.2   Hypothetical regression data indicating bias in selection

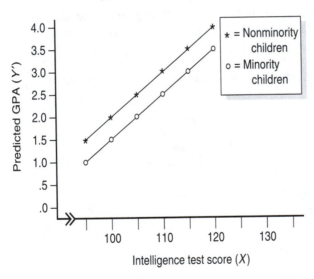

Regression equations:

For nonminority children: $Y' = .1(X) - 8$

For minority children: $Y' = .1(X) - 8.5$

is *lower* than the average score for nonminority students. As a result, a given IQ score will always predict a lower criterion score for minority students.

Outcomes of Research on Test Bias

What happens when racial/ethnic group score differences are analyzed using the preceding procedures? In general, the research does not indicate that the differences are due to content bias. For example, we have identified some test items with a group X item interaction. However, when we remove these items from standardized tests, minority children still earn lower test scores than nonminority children (e.g., Flaugher, 1978; Scheuneman, 1987). In addition, although some items appear to show group X item interactions, it is not clear that the differences are more than what we would expect by chance (e.g., Wild et al., 1989). In other words, the differences are too small to be statistically significant in most cases.

The majority of research also does not indicate that the differences result in inaccurate predictions for members of racial/ethnic minorities. In spite of the group differences in average scores, studies of the relationship between test scores and measures of achievement indicate few differences in criterion validity coefficients, standard errors of estimate, or the slopes of regression equations (e.g., Hartlage & Steele, 1977; Lunemann, 1974; Valencia & Lopez, 1992). However, these regression equations often *do* show different intercepts (e.g., Linn, 1982), and the differences can result in different predictions about school performance (e.g., Joseph, 1977; Mercer, 1979; Williams, 1971). As mentioned before, this presents problems when test scores are used for selection decisions.

Although empirical studies do not reveal an extensive test bias problem, various lawsuits have set limits on the use of intelligence tests for educational decisions. In reality the limitations arise more from concerns about fairness than demonstrations of bias. The two most important cases are *Diana* v. *State Board of Education*, filed in 1970, and *Larry P.* v. *Wilson Riles*, filed in 1979 (Kaplan & Saccuzzo; 1993). Both were class action suits, brought in California, challenging the use of IQ scores for the placement of minority children in classes for the retarded. The Diana case involved Mexican-American children who were tested by a non-Spanish-speaking examiner using tests that were not standardized on bilingual children. The Larry P. case involved African-American children whose initially low IQ scores increased when they were retested by African-American examiners. The Diana case was settled out of court, with the state agreeing to use special testing procedures for nonnative English speakers. The case of Larry P., however, led to a court decision banning the use of standardized IQ tests in California as a means of determining mental retardation. In 1986, the court extended the IQ testing ban to cover *all* educational decisions except placement in programs for the gifted.

Questions about the use of standardized tests with minority children are far from resolved. Although court decisions in other states, such as Illinois and Georgia, have not prohibited the use of IQ tests with minority children, many psychologists and educators are exploring other assessment strategies. One relatively recent approach to the problem is the development of multicultural assessment techniques such as the SOMPA (Mercer, 1979). An acronym for the System of Multicultural Pluralistic Assessment, the SOMPA is not a test; it is a compilation of measures, including a medical exam, an assessment of an individual's sociocultural and socioeconomic status, and a traditional intelligence test in which the person's performance is compared to others in the same social and cultural groups. Although reactions to this approach are mixed (e.g., Brown, 1979; Clarizio, 1979; Taylor, Sternberg, & Partenio, 1986), it may yet prove to be a useful way to cope with the issue of cultural diversity.

SUMMARY AND KEY CONCEPTS

The two types of tests used in educational settings are the classroom test and the **standardized test**. Classroom tests are written and administered by classroom teachers and may be used for **summative** or **formative evaluation**. Standardized group tests may be given by classroom teachers, but individual tests are usually administered by a school psychologist. Standardized tests are used for routine assessment of student abilities, for decisions about grade-level or ability placements, for identification of special needs students, and for feedback about the effectiveness of a teacher, school, or school system.

The standardized tests typically used in routine ability assessment are group intelligence tests and group achievement tests. If the results signal the possible presence of an **exceptionality**, students are referred for individual testing. One approach is to administer a series of separate tests, including (1) tests of intelligence and achievement, (2) diagnostic tests designed to identify skill deficits or process deficits, and (3) measures of behavioral functioning, such as tests of adaptive behavior. An alternative approach is to administer an integrated test battery that includes a series of tests covering these various domains.

Intelligence tests may use a point scale, in which points are awarded for each item correct, or an age scale, in which items are arranged according to **age differentiation**, requiring the establishment of a **basal** and **ceiling age**. In contrast to the ratio IQ calculated for early tests, most current tests use some form of standard scores such as a **deviation IQ**. Most intelligence tests provide an overall score, measuring general intelligence or g-factor, and a set of subscale measures, such as scores tapping verbal and nonverbal abilities.

In all cases, tests must demonstrate reliability and validity appropriate to their use. A primary concern is the presence of test bias, a systematic variation in the accuracy of test scores. Statistically, test bias exists when tests show evidence of **differential validity**. Tests may demonstrate measurement bias, a problem of content or construct validity, or prediction bias, a problem of criterion validity.

QUESTIONS

9.1 List five different ways that tests may be used in educational settings.

9.2 Explain why an intelligence test can be called an "aptitude test" if it covers skills you acquired in school.

9.3 Define g-factor. Describe three different ways that intelligence tests break g-factor into components.

9.4 Describe the difference between a point scale and an age scale. How does this difference affect the administration of an intelligence test?

9.5 Why do many psychologists prefer scores like deviation IQ to scores like grade or age equivalents?

9.6 Why do some psychologists and educators challenge the construct validity of group intelligence tests?

9.7 Describe the relevance of PL 94-142 and PL 95-561 to psychological testing.

9.8 Describe the difference in focus among (a) achievement tests, (b) skill tests, and (c) process tests.

9.9 What are the advantages of an integrated battery approach compared to a separate test approach.

9.10 Define test bias. Describe a technique to identify (a) content bias, (b) construct bias, and (c) prediction bias.

Testing in Clinical Settings

CHAPTER OUTLINE

CHAPTER GOALS AND OBJECTIVES

After completing this chapter you should be able to:

- Describe the role of testing, interview, and observation in clinical assessment.
- Explain how clinicians use intelligence tests in psychological assessment, including the processes of pattern and content analysis and the role of behavioral observation.
- Describe the different design features of popular objective personality tests and their advantages and drawbacks.
- Describe the different design features of popular projective personality tests and their advantages and drawbacks.
- Describe the design of other types of projective techniques and their roles in clinical assessment.
- Contrast the psychometric and clinical approaches to the use of tests in psychological assessment.
- Contrast the process and goals of psychological assessment with the process and goals of neuropsychological assessment.
- Explain how clinicians use intelligence tests in neuropsychological assessment.
- Contrast the use of specific tasks with the use of test batteries in neuropsychological assessment.
- Describe the design of popular neuropsychological tests, including their advantages and drawbacks.

Historically, a clinical setting was a facility for the study and treatment of disease, such as a hospital or a nursing home. A clinician was a physician— someone involved in the study and treatment of illness. Today, our concept of clinical has been broadened to encompass a wider variety of settings, professionals, and problems. Modern clinical settings include research facilities and private practice offices. Clinicians may be physicians, psychologists—we even have clinical social workers. Clinicians study and treat both physical and mental illnesses. In this chapter, we will discuss the ways psychological tests are used in these settings to explore both physical and psychological problems.

USES OF TESTS IN CLINICAL SETTINGS

The professionals who identify themselves as clinicians work in such settings as hospitals, community clinics, mental health centers, counseling centers, and private practice. Not all these professionals use psychological tests—after all, a radiologist who treats patients is a clinician. The clinicians most likely to make use of psychological tests are psychologists, psychiatrists, and clinical or psychiatric social workers. The tests are used in the process of diagnosis, in the planning of treatment, and in evaluation of the course of treatment.

Clinical Psychology versus Other Fields

The type of clinician best prepared to select, administer, and interpret psychological tests is a clinical psychologist. A clinical psychologist typically has completed a master's or doctoral degree and has been trained extensively in psychological theory and practice and in the design and use of psychological tests.

Students are often confused about the difference between clinical psychologists and psychiatrists. A chapter like this is a good place to emphasize one basic difference between them: A psychiatrist is a physician who has completed the same medical school program as all other physicians. It is the subsequent residency in psychiatry that distinguishes this physician from a surgeon or an ophthamologist. However, that residency is quite different from graduate training in clinical psychology. Of necessity, psychiatric residencies emphasize *medical* procedures for the diagnosis and treatment of psychological problems. Significantly less time is devoted to psychological testing. Although clinical psychology has a historical link to psychiatry, the training and expertise of professionals in these two disciplines can differ radically.

Likewise, clinical or psychiatric social workers receive less extensive training in psychological theory and testing. In fact, much of the testing that clinical psychologists do is with clients referred for assessment by psychiatrists and social workers (Lubin et al., 1986b). In a survey of clinical psychologists working in mental health centers, up to two-thirds of their assessments were requested either by psychiatrists or by social workers (Lubin et al., 1986a). Because psychological testing is primarily the provence of psychologists, our discussion of testing in clinical settings will focus on the use of tests by clinical psychologists. When we use the word clinician, we are referring to clinical psychologists.

Testing by Clinical Psychologists

We often think of clinical psychologists as therapists. However, without diagnostic tools, it would be difficult to develop a reasonable treatment plan.

According to surveys of members of the American Psychological Association's Division 12 (Clinical Psychology), clinicians report spending about one-third of their time administering and evaluating the results of psychological tests (e.g., Wade & Baker, 1977).

Table 10.1 lists the 30 tests used most frequently by Division 12 members (Lubin, Larsen, & Matarazzo, 1984). The top five tests include an intelligence

TABLE 10.1 Tests Used Most Frequently by Clinical Psychologists

Rank	Test
1	Wechsler Adult Intelligence Scale
2	Minnesota Multiphasic Personality Inventory
3	Bender Visual Motor Gestalt Test
4	Rorschach Inkblot Test
5	Thematic Apperception Test
6	Wechsler Intelligence Scale for Children—Revised
7.5	Peabody Picture Vocabulary Test
7.5	Sentence Completion Tests (all kinds)
9	House–Tree–Person Test
10	Draw-a-Person Test
11	Wechsler Memory Scale
12	Rotter Sentence Completion Test
13	Memory for Designs
14	Vineland Social Maturity Scale
15	Stanford–Binet Intelligence Scale
16	Strong Vocational Interest Blank—Men
17.5	Bender Visual Retention Test
17.5	Edwards Personal Preference Schedule
19	Strong Vocational Interest Blank—Women
20.5	Children's Apperception Test
20.5	Progressive Matrices
22	Kuder Preference Record
23	Porteus Mazes
24	Full Range Picture Vocabulary Test
25	Differential Aptitude Tests
26	Gray Oral Reading Test
27	Wechsler–Bellevue Intelligence Scale
28	Cattell Infant Intelligence Scale
29	Goldstein–Scheerer Tests of Abstract and Concrete Thinking
30	Blacky Pictures

From B. Lubin, R. M. Larsen, & J. D. Matarazzo (1984). "Patterns of Psychological Test Usage in the United States: 1935–1982," *American Psychologist*, *39*, 451–454. Granted permission to reprint from American Psychological Association (copyright, 1984).

test (the Wechsler), three personality tests (two of which are projective tests), and a test of visual–motor integration that is useful for identifying brain damage (the Bender). Table 10.2 categorizes the more familiar tests from this list in terms of purpose and design.

There is some variation in the rankings of tests according to the setting in which a clinician works. For example, clinical psychologists in veterans administration hospitals use projective tests less frequently than clinicians in private practice or mental health centers (Lubin et al., 1986a, 1986b). However, the top three tests across all three settings are the MMPI, the Wechsler, and the Bender.

The pattern makes a lot of sense, given what clinical psychologists do. Clinical psychologists typically work with individuals who are experiencing psychological and/or neuropsychological (brain-behavior) problems. Psychological tests are a central component to the process of identifying the nature and extent of these problems and planning an effective treatment program.

You may also have heard of clinical psychologists conducting mental status exams for the courts to determine if defendants (1) understand why they are involved in a court proceeding and (2) can participate effectively in their own defense. The administration of psychological tests, including intelligence and personality tests, is a key component of mental status evaluations.

TABLE 10.2 Categorizing the Design of Tests Frequently Used in Clinical Settings

Purpose/Format	Examples
Personality Objective Norm referenced Normative	Minnesota Multiphasic Personality Inventory Sixteen Personality Factor Questionnaire California Psychological Inventory
Personality Objective Norm referenced Ipsative	Edwards Personal Preference Schedule
Personality Projective Norm referenced Normative	Rorschach Inkblot Test Thematic Apperception Test House–Tree–Person Test Draw-a-Person Test Sentence-completion tests
Brain function Free response Norm referenced Normative	Bender Visual–Motor Gestalt Wechsler Memory Scale

Other Components of Clinical Assessment

Testing is not the only data-gathering process used by clinical psychologists. In fact, the decision to use tests and the selection of tests to administer usually follow some initial appraisal of an individual's functioning. In addition to administering tests, clinicians assess client characteristics through observation and interviews. In other words, there are other more subjective elements to clinical assessment, and decisions are made on the basis of both objective and subjective data. The fact that clinical judgments are based on both types of data underscores the importance of ensuring that clinicians be well trained and experienced.

The stereotype of the clinical psychologist watching and analyzing you, like all stereotypes, contains an element of truth. Clinicians tend to observe behavior during all client contacts, including interviews and the administration of tests. Clinicians may use a variety of interview techniques, each with its own particular purpose. Three common types are the life history interview, the diagnostic interview, and the stress interview (e.g., Aiken, 1991).

The goal of a *life history* interview is to obtain background information about the client, the client's family, and various events in the client's life (e.g., education and employment). These interviews are fairly structured, covering a specific set of topics. The goal of a *diagnostic* or clinical interview is to obtain information about the client's problems, the effects of these problems on the client's life, and the events that might be influencing these problems (e.g., interpersonal relationships or coping strategies). These interviews are less structured, with successive questions determined by the client's previous responses.

In a *stress* interview, the clinician seeks information about the impact of stress on client mood, thought, and behavior. The clinician purposely confronts or challenges the client by asking more sensitive questions and/or questioning the client's answers. The success of stress interviews depends greatly on the clinician's interviewing skills.

Although assessment through testing, observation, and interview is an important feature of clinical settings, there is a lot of variability in assessment activities across different clinical settings. Psychologists at mental health centers and in private practice typically engage in less assessment than hospital-based psychologists (Lubin et al., 1986a, 1986b). Furthermore, almost half the psychologists at mental health centers reported spending less time in all forms of assessment—and more time in treatment—than they did 10 years ago.

PSYCHOLOGICAL ASSESSMENT

Testing by clinicians occurs most often in the context of psychological assessment—an evaluation of an individual's cognitive and emotional functioning. These assessments primarily use intelligence and personality tests. Their goal is to generate an accurate picture of an individual's problems, to identify the interpersonal and environmental factors contributing to these problems, and to decide on an effective course of treatment. Tests are important because they provide a more standardized procedure for gathering and interpreting relevant data, compared to techniques like observation and interview. In some cases, the problems identified are serious psychological disturbances, referred to as forms of **psychopathology** or clinical syndromes. In other cases, the problems identified may be less serious problems of adjustment, but they are no less important.

Intelligence Tests

Perhaps you were surprised to see in Table 10.1 that the test administered most often by clinical psychologists was an intelligence test. We already know that intelligence tests provide objective, norm-referenced information about level of intelligence (see Chapter 9). In this section, we will discuss how intelligence tests in addition can be used *diagnostically* to suggest hypotheses about emotional and personality characteristics. We will not repeat a discussion of the design and scoring of the Wechsler tests and the Stanford–Binet; if you need to refresh your memory, reread the appropriate sections of Chapter 9.

Interpreting Intelligence Test Scores

When clinical psychologists administer intelligence tests, they choose individual tests like the Wechsler tests or the Stanford–Binet. Individual tests provide more comprehensive and sensitive measures; remember that they also are the format of choice for diagnostic evaluations in school settings. In clinical settings, however, we focus on slightly different aspects of intelligence tests. Although we are interested in clients' level of intellectual functioning, we are also interested in analyzing the patterns of test scores and the answers to specific test items.

Pattern Analysis.   *Pattern analysis* is a procedure in which we compare the scores on different subscales of an intelligence test and try to interpret the meaning of score differences. The process is based on two assumptions:

(1) psychological disturbance does not necessarily affect all intellectual functions equally, and (2) different disorders are characterized by different score patterns. Actually, we have already discussed one specific pattern analysis. Chapter 9 noted that we expect a learning disabled individual to show lower scores on verbal subtests than on nonverbal subtests (see p. 317).

The concept of pattern was introduced in early discussions of the WAIS (e.g., Wechsler, 1958). One reason why Wechsler tests are so popular among clinicians is that their scoring system was designed to simplify direct comparison of subtest scores. All Wechsler subtests are converted to the same standard score scale. To give you an idea of what pattern analysis involves, some common interpretations of Wechsler score patterns are presented in Table 10.3. For example, individuals with thought disorders, such as schizophrenia, might show low scores on the comprehension subtest. Why? Because the subtest assesses understanding of cultural standards, and individuals with schizophrenia may not have logical ideas or may be unable to explain their ideas logically.

There are many other types of pattern analysis that clinicians may consider. For example, in *scatter analysis*, we examine the degree to which subtest scores differ. We may even calculate a scatter index representing the variability of subtest scores (Anastasi, 1988). The underlying assumption is that normal individuals show less scatter than individuals with psychopathology. Scatter analysis can focus on comparison of subtest scores or only on scores within a subtest (Groth-Marnat, 1990). In *deterioration analysis*, we compare performance on

TABLE 10.3 Sample Interpretations of WAIS—R Subtest Patterns

Subtest Patterns	Possible Personality Characteristics
Low digit span, arithmetic, and coding	Anxiety (the "anxiety triad")
High information, vocabulary	Compulsivity, intellectualization
Low comprehension	Antisocial tendencies, thought disorder
Low picture completion	Impulsiveness
Low picture arrangement	Poor rapport, interpersonal problems

Adapted from Groth-Marnat (1990).

two types of subtests: those that theoretically are resistant to the effects of pathology and those that theoretically decline in the presence of pathology (Anastasi, 1988). We can also conduct an *intrasubtest analysis*, examining the patterns of correct responses and errors within a subtest (Groth-Marnat, 1990). Since items are arranged in order of increasing difficulty, we would expect test takers to pass initial items and begin slowly to fail more difficult items. An inconsistent pattern of passing and failing items might suggest the presence of pathology.

Although pattern analysis is very popular, research has produced inconsistent and contradictory findings on its diagnostic value (e.g., Frank, 1970; Matarazzo, 1972). For example, although a pair of scores may differ by a significant amount, the difference may occur frequently (e.g., Field, 1960). A verbal/performance IQ difference of at least 15 points is statistically significant, but in fact occurred in 25% of the WISC—R and 20% of the WAIS—R standardization samples (F. M. Grossman, 1983; Kaufman, 1976). Are all these people suffering from some psychological disturbance?

To some extent, the problem is due to the fact that the same score pattern may be associated with some very different characteristics. For example, according to Table 10.3 a low score on the comprehension subtest could signal the presence of a psychotic disorder like schizophrenia or a personality disorder like antisocial personality. Although clinicians may use pattern analysis to formulate and evaluate hypotheses, they tend to avoid drawing specific conclusions from this single procedure.

Content Analysis. Clinicians may also examine the *content* of a client's answers to intelligence test items for clues to possible psychological problems. Many individual intelligence tests use free-response items that require test takers to generate, rather than select, an answer. These responses may suggest the presence of particular thought or personality characteristics.

Consider Wechsler's (1958) example of possible definitions for the word *sentence* in a vocabulary subtest. An individual defining a sentence as a group of words is likely to differ in experiences or personality from an individual defining sentence as a penalty imposed by a judge. Logical but unusual associations might indicate certain personality characteristics; bizarre associations to vocabulary items might indicate a thought disorder such as schizophrenia.

The form of responses may also have diagnostic implications. Drawing lines through the walls of mazes might imply impulsivity. Generating overly long, elaborate responses might suggest compulsivity, whereas very short, cautious responses might suggest paranoia (Groth-Marnat, 1990).

As was the case with pattern analysis, content analysis is not a well-validated technique. It is even more difficult to study empirically because the responses to be analyzed are idiosyncratic—particular to the individuals being tested (Anastasi, 1988). Content analysis is best used to suggest characteristics to be investigated by additional assessments.

Observing Behavior during Intelligence Testing

An individual intelligence test is an intimate and challenging situation. The intimacy results from the one-on-one nature of individual testing; the challenge results from the fact that intelligence tests are *power* tests (see p. 34) including at least some items that are too difficult for the average person. The administration of an individual intelligence test, therefore, provides an opportunity to observe how clients react to both cognitive and interpersonal demands.

Because intelligence tests assess reasoning and problem-solving skill, clinicians can draw inferences about cognitive characteristics such as attention, memory, and judgment. Tests including verbal tasks, such as the Wechsler tests, provide additional information about communication skills and style of speech. Responses can also reveal elements of cognitive style, such as being reflective or impulsive in problem solving.

Aspects of personality and emotional functioning can also be observed. Clinicians may note a client's reaction to being tested, including such features as cooperativeness, motivation to perform well, and anxiety about making mistakes. Clinicians can make inferences about reactions to frustration, such as when a client cannot answer a question or is confronted with a timed task.

The observational data gathered during intelligence testing can be useful for identifying characteristics that should be explored in more depth, confirming initial impressions or the results of other assessments, and raising questions about inconsistencies in performance across different assessments. Like the data gathered from pattern and content analysis, observational data become part of a larger pool of data from which clinicians can develop their hypotheses.

Objective Personality Tests

A key element of psychological assessment is the administration of objective personality tests. Note in Table 10.1 that after the Wechsler adult test, the most frequently used test is the MMPI. The popularity of objective tests is a direct result of their design. Compared to other personality assessments, objective personality tests have the highest degree of standardization of administration and scoring—two important characteristics of a good test. As a result, these tests tend to be more reliable and valid than other personality assessments.

The two most popular tests in this category are the MMPI and the Edwards Personal Preference Schedule. We already have discussed some of the design features of these two tests in Chapter 4; in fact, these tests were used specifically to contrast different approaches to the design of personality tests. In this section, we will focus on the use of these tests in diagnosis and treatment planning.

Minnesota Multiphasic Personality Inventory

The MMPI is one of the first tests designed to discriminate between normal and pathological individuals. Both the original and revised versions (MMPI and MMPI—2) were developed through empirical scale construction using criterion groups of normal and previously diagnosed individuals (Hathaway & McKinley, 1940, 1943, 1989). The current 567 true/false statements are used to generate scores on four validity scales and ten clinical scales, each tied to a particular personality attribute. The various validity scales were described in detail in Chapter 4 (see p. 102). Table 10.4 presents a description of each clinical scale.

Raw scores on each scale are converted to T-scores with means of 50 and standard deviations of 10. In general, scores of 45 to 57 are considered within normal limits; scores of 65 or more are considered high scores since they are 1.5 standard deviations above the mean, and they are likely to suggest serious problems (Meyer, 1993). When clinicians use the MMPI—2, they construct profile codes based on the high scores individuals earn on the various clinical scales. The profile codes are written numerically, using the numbers assigned

TABLE 10.4 Clinical Scales of the MMPI—2

Scale Number/Name	Symbol	Meaning of High Score
1 Hypochondriasis	Hs	Many physical concerns/complaints
2 Depression	D	Distress, depression, withdrawal
3 Hysteria	Hy	Naivete, use of neurotic defenses
4 Psychpathic deviate	Pd	Antisocial, rebellious, hostile
5 Masculinity–femininity	Mf[a]	Nontraditional sex-role interests
6 Paranoia	Pa	Suspicious, hostile, externalizing
7 Psychasthenia	Pt	Anxiety, inferiority, obsessiveness
8 Schizophrenia	Sc	Confusion, bizarre ideas, alienation
9 Mania	Ma	High energy, distractible, grandiose
0 Social introversion	Si[a]	Shyness, social discomfort

[a]These scales were *logically*, not empirically, derived.
Adapted from Hathaway & McKinley (1989).

to each scale, with the scales listed in order from highest to lowest score. Codes may include one, two, or three elevated scales.

Considerable research has been devoted to linking profile codes with different types of psychological problems. For example, scales 1, 2, and 3 have been referred to as the "neurotic triad," and individuals with high scores on these scales typically show some type of anxiety (neurotic) disorder. Individuals with high scores on the 6 and 8 scales are likely to exhibit features of paranoid schizophrenia (Meyers, 1993).

The MMPI—2 has added a number of supplemental scales (Hathaway & McKinley, 1989). Additional content scales are designed to measure such attributes as health concerns, Type A personality, cynicism, low self-esteem, family problems, and attitudes predictive of work performance. Three additional validity scales are available: a supplemental F-scale, including items not keyed to the original scale, and two scales to identify possible response styles—a scale to check on random responding and a scale to measure acquiescence. As mentioned in Chapter 3, the original MMPI only had validity scales for identification or response *sets*.

From a psychometric point of view, the MMPI—2, like its predecessor, is a good instrument. Split-half coefficients run in the .70s, and median test–retest coefficients are in the .80s. Although it has only recently been published, the validity of MMPI—2 scores is already documented in several hundred studies.

There are, however, several criticisms of the MMPI—2. First, many of the items are scored on more than one scale; the answer to a single item may add points to several different scales. The resulting scales, therefore, are not statistically independent. This raises certain problems for analyzing the scales and also leads some people to question their diagnostic value. Second, critics are concerned about the design of two of the validity scales. The L-scale, designed to identify people presenting themselves in an overly idealistic/perfectionistic way, is composed of 15 items. For *all* 15 items, points are added to the scale only if test takers mark them "false." A similar problem exists with the K-scale, designed to identify people who might be "faking good." Of the 30 items, *29* add points to the K-scale only if they are marked "false." From a test design standpoint, it would be preferable to construct these scales using both true and false responses (Kaplan & Saccuzzo, 1993). The addition of the new response style scales provides a mechanism to somewhat address this problem.

A final concern raised about the MMPI—2 is the influence of demographic characteristics (e.g., Butcher et al., 1990). Research indicates that elevated scores on some scales may reflect characteristics such as age, race, and socioeconomic status, rather than the presence of a psychological disorder. For example, elderly individuals often score higher on the social introversion scale (Meyer, 1993). It is necessary, therefore, that clinicians consider demographic variables when constructing score profiles.

Edwards Personal Preference Schedule

As described in Chapter 4, the EPPS represents a very different approach to personality assessment. First, the EPPS uses forced-choice items that generate ipsative, rather than normative, scores. Second, the statements used in EPPS items were selected using a theoretical strategy, rather than the empirical process used in the MMPI. Specifically, statements were written to tap 15 basic needs drawn from Murray's (1938) model of human needs. Third, the tendency of test takers to "fake good" was presumably controlled by equating each pair of statements for social desirability (Edwards, 1959).

The EPPS is a 225-item test composed of 210 paired statements, 15 of which are repeated at random locations to check for response bias. Why 210 pairs? The test is constructed using statements to measure 15 different needs. A statement for each need is paired twice with one statement for each of the other 14 needs. This requires a total of $[15(15-1)]$ pairs, or 210 statements.

The 15 needs measured by the EPPS are described in Table 10.5. Because the items are forced choice, each need score is ipsative, expressing the strength of that need relative to the other 14. This means that two individuals who have the same *ipsative* score on nurturance in fact could differ in the absolute strength of that need. Raw scores are converted into percentile ranks based on the performance of a standardization sample. Separate norms are available for high school and college/adult groups. However, because the percentile ranks are derived from ipsative scores, it is difficult to use them to compare different people. Differences in percentile ranks actually refer to differences *within* each test taker in need strength.

Split-half and test–retest coefficients for the need scales range from the .50s to the .80s. Specific need scales generally produce moderate but statistically significant correlations with similar scales in other tests (Drummond, 1984). Criticisms of the EPPS focus on such factors as the lack of large-scale validity studies and the conversion of ipsative raw scores to normative percentiles (Kaplan & Saccuzzo, 1993). In addition, several studies question whether the forced-choice format really controls the social desirability response set (Feldman & Corah, 1960; Wiggins, 1966).

Clearly, the EPPS differs from the MMPI in more than just item format and scoring. The personality dimensions assessed by the EPPS are more like the dimensions we expect to find in normal individuals. In fact, the EPPS is used more often to explore an individual's personality structure than to diagnosis psychopathology. It typically is used by clinical psychologists who are working with less severely disturbed clients. Other frequent users of the EPPS are counselors, who also use it to explore personality structure, and psychology professors, who often use it as a teaching tool in courses on personality theory or measurement (Drummond, 1984).

**TABLE 10.5   Needs Measured by the Edwards Personal Preference
Schedule**

Need	Description
Achievement	Need to excel, to accomplish something difficult, to rival or surpass others
Deference	Need to support, admire, or emulate a superior, to conform to what is expected
Order	Need to achieve organization, balance, tidiness, precision
Exhibition	Need to make an impression, to be seen and heard by others
Autonomy	Need to be independent, to break confinement, to resist coercion/restriction
Affiliation	Need to form friendships and join groups, to cooperate, to love
Intraception	Need to analyze feelings and motives of oneself and others
Succorance	Need to be dependent, to seek aid, protection or help
Dominance	Need to influence or control others, to be regarded as a leader
Abasement	Need to submit passively to injury, blame, or criticism, to surrender, to be resigned
Nurturance	Need to help, aid, or protect others, to express sympathy
Change	Need to experience variety, to avoid routine and sameness
Endurance	Need to persevere, to persist, to be strong, to have stamina
Heterosexuality	Need to form erotic relationships, to engage in sexual activity
Aggression	Need to overcome opposition forcefully, to oppose, to fight

Adapted from Murray (1938) and Edwards (1959).

Projective Personality Tests

Projective personality tests play a different but no less important role in clinical assessment. In Table 10.1, note that two of the top five tests are projective instruments, the Rorschach Inkblot Test and the Thematic Apperception Test. Projective tests are among the most controversial assessment procedures. Their focus, purpose, and design are very different from other types of tests.

Projective tests were developed specifically for use in psychological assessment by clinicians. We rarely find them used by other types of professionals or in other testing scenarios. They are typically individually administered tests, and considerable time is taken in graduate programs to cover their administration. Projective tests as a group have a number of distinctive features. All projective tests use a relatively unstructured free-response task in which test takers can produce an almost infinite variety of possible answers. The choice of an unstructured task is deliberate. As discussed in Chapter 4 (see p. 107), projective tests are designed to reveal unconscious or hidden aspects of personality and thought. This focus is designed to complement the design of objective tests, in which test takers directly self-report on their personal characteristics (e.g., Anastasi, 1988).

This underlying assumption about projective tests is frequently challenged by critics. Because projective tests are designed to elicit information below the threshold of conscious awareness, it is difficult to evaluate the validity of these tests. Validity studies often end up comparing the results of one projective with the results of another (e.g., Little & Shneidman, 1959) when the validity of the second procedure itself may be questionable.

However, projective tests remain popular. In part, this reflects the fact that projective tests take a more global approach to personality assessment. Clinicians see this, too, as complementing objective tests, which tend to break personality down into a set of dimensions that are measured separately. The goal of projective testing is to produce a more integrated picture of test-taker personality, rather than to assess individual differences on specific dimensions. Perhaps now you can see why clinicians are not particularly concerned about the variety of answers test takers can produce to projective test items. If these tests were designed to compare individuals on specific dimensions, we would need items for which the answers can be neatly categorized. In projective testing, we are more concerned about developing a unique profile of each person tested.

None of the preceding discussion is meant to imply that projective tests cannot or are not scored. However, instead of the objective scoring rules used on tests like the MMPI, projective tests are likely to be scored using subjective rules—guidelines for the interpretation and classification of answers. This is the second controversial aspect of projective testing. Critics charge that it is difficult to evaluate the adequacy of projective tests because they do not necessarily score test-taker responses numerically. Without a set of scores to analyze, it is difficult to determine the reliability of the scoring procedure or the validity of the scores it produces. There are quantitative scoring systems for some projective tests, although the use of these systems varies widely among clinicians. Studies of reliability and validity have been conducted when these systems are used, but it is difficult to generalize from these studies to the typical, more qualitative analysis of projective tests favored by clinicians.

Rorschach Inkblot Test

Like the MMPI in its category, the Rorschach Inkblot Test is a prototype for projective tests (Rorschach, 1921). The Rorschach is composed of 10 symmetric inkblots: 5 black, white, and gray; 2 that also include touches of red; and 3 that include several other colors. Each is printed on a separate card and handed one at a time to the test taker. Test takers are simply asked to describe what the image on the card might be. No other instructions are given. After completing all the cards, the examiner readministers each one, systematically questioning test takers about their responses. During this second phase, test takers can clarify or expand on their previous descriptions.

In addition to recording the description of each card verbatim, the examiner may note the way each card is held, the time taken to respond to each card, facial expressions and other nonverbal behaviors—basically anything that might reveal some characteristic of the test taker. Although these additional data are not specifically scored, they become part of the pool of projective information considered during diagnosis.

You may recall from Chapter 4 that there are a variety of procedures for scoring Rorschach responses (see p. 113). The scoring dimensions of the system taught in most clinical psychology graduate programs, the Exner system (e.g., Exner, 1974, 1978), are described in Table 10.6. Note that we consider much more than just *what* the test taker sees in the inkblot. Our focus is on the way the test taker organizes the information in the inkblot to construct a response.

TABLE 10.6   Exner Dimensions for Scoring Rorschach Responses

Dimension	Description
Location	The part of the inkblot associated with each element of the test taker's description
Determinant	How the test taker responds to the form, color, and shading of the inkblot, including whether the test taker perceives movement within the pattern
Form quality	Extent to which the test taker's description is a reasonable match to the actual features of the inkblot
Content	What the test taker actually perceives when describing the inkblot
Popularity	Extent to which the responses given are common among people in general or original

Adapted from Exner (1986).

The Exner system has been referred to as a psychometric or "signs" system of Rorschach scoring (e.g., Lerner & Lerner, 1986). The task of describing an inkblot becomes a problem-solving task, and dimensions of personality are revealed in the way the individual copes with that task. The link between responses and personality was empirically determined during the development of the scoring system. Studies indicated that certain responses were *signs* of particular personality characteristics because they occurred more often in certain subgroups of people. Thus, the scoring system uses a comparison of answers in different criterion groups to link Rorschach responses to diagnostic categories. To illustrate in an overly simplified way, if only depressed individuals see a dead turtle in a particular card, the presence of that description is linked to the presence of depression.

When we use this system to score Rorschach responses, our key concerns are the reliability and criterion validity of the test. In other words, scores on the test must be reliable predictors of membership in different criterion groups. In fact, scores generated by the Exner system are (1) reliable over time, (2) good at identifying a number of specific personality characteristics, such as emotional immaturity and intense anger, and (3) good at differentiating between a variety of disorders, such as borderline personality and schizophrenia (e.g., Exner, 1978).

Although this approach to scoring is similar to what Rorschach himself envisioned (see p. 112), some psychologists see it as omitting an important aspect of projective testing—the development of an integrated picture of each test taker's unique personality. They contrast the Exner approach with a more "conceptual" approach that links Rorschach responses to underlying personality processes (e.g., Lerner & Lerner, 1986). In essence, these clinicians advocate interpreting, rather than scoring, Rorschach responses. Their goal in studying an individual's answers is to reconstruct the processes used to generate the answers and then to use that information in light of personality theory to draw diagnostic inferences. In this approach, we are more concerned about the *construct* validity of the test—its ability to identify key aspects of personality and thinking.

There are even proposals for systems to score the Rorschach using this more conceptual approach (e.g., Blatt & Berman, 1984). The focus is on creating composite variables, such as "thought organization," that integrate scores generated by the more traditional scoring system. Rather than replacing the traditional system, this alternative approach to scoring is proposed as a second stage or "higher-order" analysis.

At this point, you might well ask, "What's the point of giving this test?" True, there is still extensive controversy about how to use the Rorschach, but administration and scoring are much more standardized today than ever before. And in spite of all the controversy about how to score and use the test, the Rorschach is emerging as a reliable and valid instrument. A recent analysis of the combined statistical data in 39 Rorschach papers, published during the 1970s, indicated an overall internal consistency coefficient of .83 (Parker, 1983). Other studies using the Kuder–Richardson procedure generate an average coefficient of .77 (e.g., Wagner et al., 1986). In light of these data, the Rorschach likely will remain one of the most popular clinical tests.

Thematic Apperception Test

The contrast between the Thematic Apperception Test (TAT) and the Rorschach parallels the contrast between the Edwards and the MMPI. Both the TAT and the Edwards reflect a theoretical approach to scale construction, whereas the Rorschach and the MMPI use an empirical approach based on the contrasted performance of criterion groups. In fact, the TAT and the Edwards are designed to tap dimensions of personality drawn from the same theory—Murray's (1938) theory of needs. Like the Edwards, the TAT was not developed specifically as a diagnostic instrument; it was designed to explore personality issues in both clinical and nonclinical groups. In contrast, the MMPI and the Rorschach were designed to identify clinical disorders.

The TAT is designed to assess the strength of different needs as they are reflected in stories (Murray, 1943). The TAT stimuli consist of 19 cards with drawings of people in ambiguous situations, plus a blank white card. Some cards are designed to be used only with particular types of people, such as adult males, adult females, boys, or girls. Test takers are asked to tell a story about each picture, including the events leading up to the scene on the card and the outcome of the scene on the card. For the blank card, test takers are asked to imagine a picture, describe it, and then tell a story about it. In addition to recording the story verbatim, the examiner records the time taken to respond to each card. The test is projective in that each card can elicit a wide variety of stories, and we assume that the story told by a test taker reflects issues that are important to that person. Furthermore, the time taken to respond to a card may imply something about areas or issues that are particularly sensitive.

Rather than being scored in the traditional psychometric sense, TAT stories are analyzed on several dimensions. First, the examiner identifies the hero of the story, the protagonist or the central figure. It is assumed that the test taker identifies with this character and projects onto the hero many personal needs and problems. Second, the actual content of the story is analyzed in terms of the needs expressed and the environmental forces that affect satisfaction of those needs—referred to as *press*. The needs examined are similar to those assessed by the Edwards, which also uses Murray's (1938) model. A list of Murray's complete set of needs is given in Table 10.7.

When analyzing the content of TAT stories, clinicians pay attention to the intensity, duration, and frequency of each need and press. They attempt to

TABLE 10.7   Needs Explored by the TAT

Needs Also Assessed in the Edwards[a]

Achievement	Autonomy	Abasement
Deference	Affiliation	Nurturance
Order	Succorance	Heterosexuality
Exhibition	Dominance	Aggression

Additional Needs	Description
Blame avoidance	To be well behaved, to obey, to avoid blame or punishment
Counteraction	To defend one's honor by taking action, to refuse to admit defeat, to retaliate
Defendance	To defend oneself against blame, to offer explanations or excuses, to justify actions
Harm avoidance	To avoid pain or injury, to take precautions, to escape from dangerous situations
Inferiority avoidance	To avoid humiliation or embarrassment, to fear failure
Play	To enjoy oneself, to relax, to have fun, to avoid tension
Rejection	To be aloof and indifferent, to ignore or snub others
Sentience	To seek out sensuous experience, to enjoy sensation
Understanding	To analyze experience, to synthesize ideas, to engage in abstraction

[a]Needs described in Table 10.5.
Adapted from Murray (1938).

create a picture of the relative importance of each element in the test taker's life. For example, the presence of several stories revolving around achievement or accomplishment implies that this particular need is strong. Frequent descriptions of how authority figures react to the hero's actions imply that the judgments of others are a significant *press* in the test taker's life.

Unfortunately, administration and interpretation of the TAT are not well standardized. In practice, most clinicians administer 6 to 10 cards, but there is considerable variability in the cards used and their order of presentation (Ryan, 1985). Over the years, a large amount of normative information has been compiled on the frequent types of responses to each card (e.g., Henry, 1956). However, many clinicians prefer to use their own experiences with TAT stories when analyzing their content. The same is true for scoring systems. A variety of scoring systems has been proposed, including systems focusing on achievement issues (McClelland et al., 1953), on gender identity (May, 1966), on assessment of defenses (Cramer, 1983), and on ego development (Sutton & Swensen, 1983). However, most of these systems are complex and difficult to learn and do not provide the type of whole-person picture clinicians seek from TAT responses. In fact, qualitative methods are used much more frequently than quantitative methods (e.g., Westen, 1991).

Because the TAT is rarely scored numerically, it is difficult to draw conclusions about its reliability. Agreement among clinicians in TAT interpretations varies widely (e.g., Harrison & Rotter, 1945), and the median test–retest correlation when stories *are* scored quantitatively is only about .30 (e.g., Kraiger, Hakel, & Cornelius, 1984). Given the preference for qualitative scoring, it is also difficult to study its criterion validity. Most clinicians are more concerned about the construct and content validity of the TAT, noting that it does elicit much data relevant to needs, conflicts, and environmental influences. When used as part of a larger battery of tests and accompanied by detailed interviews and observations, clinicians view the TAT as useful for formulating hypotheses about the structure and dynamics of personality (Ryan, 1985).

There are several different special adaptations of the TAT. In addition to Murray's original test, there are two forms for children, one using animal characters and one using human characters (Bellak, 1954; Bellak & Hurvich, 1966). There are also two forms designed for older adults (Bellak & Bellak, 1973; Wolk & Wolk, 1971). The goal in developing these adaptations was to create stimulus cards likely to elicit identification with the characters by different groups of people, thereby facilitating projective responses. However, none of these alternative TATs appears to improve significantly on the information obtained through the traditional test (e.g., Anastasi, 1988), and Murray's original test is still the preferred technique.

Other Types of Projective Tasks

In addition to using complex projective tests, clinicians may choose to include other types of projective tasks in their assessment batteries. They are often used as screening tests to aid clinicians in developing initial hypotheses about client characteristics and problems. These other tasks are smaller in scope and easier to administer than tests like the Rorschach or the TAT. The popularity of these techniques is evident from examining Table 10.1. Although none are included in the top five assessments, we find three of these other techniques in the next set of five: sentence-completion tests and two types of drawing tasks.

Sentence-completion and drawing tasks provide a good contrast with other projective assessments. Sentence completion uses verbal stimuli to elicit verbal responses, in contrast to the picture-stimulus/verbal-response design of the Rorschach and the TAT. Drawing tasks combine verbal instructions with a psychomotor task. By using a variety of projective techniques, clinicians provide individuals with many different ways to express themselves. Some of us may respond more to verbal tasks, others of us to pictures, and still others of us to the opportunity to draw.

Sentence-completion Tasks

Sentence-completion tasks have become very popular in clinical assessment. They are simple to administer and take little time. Test takers are presented with a series of sentence stems, such as "My mother..." or "I hate...," which they complete in their own words. Although some people view these as self-report tasks, most clinicians see sentence completion as a projective technique. Test takers are confronted with ambiguous stimuli, and the way they respond to these stimuli is likely to reveal their personal issues.

There are two approaches to using sentence-completion tasks. In one approach, clinicians write their own sentence stems to tap specific aspects of personality or functioning. The goal is to elicit responses that are relevant to issues that have been identified as important through other assessments. This ability to tailor the task to each individual is one reason why sentence-completion tasks are so popular. However, the responses to clinician-constructed stems must be evaluated qualitatively within the context of the clinician's prior experiences and other data on the test taker.

The second approach makes use of standardized sentence-completion tests, such as the Rotter Incomplete Sentences Blank (Rotter & Rafferty, 1950) or the Incomplete Sentences Task (Lanyon & Lanyon, 1980). These instruments are designed to be scored, and test-taker scores are compared to normative data collected during their standardization. The Rotter test consists of 40 sentence stems selected for their relevance to clinical issues, a theoretical approach to test construction. Test takers are instructed to make a complete sentence from each stem that expresses their true feelings.

Answers are compared to sample answers in the manual and scored on a 7-point scale reflecting emotional adjustment (7) to maladjustment (1). Scoring is based on both the length and content of answers. For example, short, concrete answers with neutral to positive content receive high scores. Long answers with depressed or anxious content receive low scores. The scores on the 40 stems can be summed to provide an overall index of adjustment. Because the manual includes a good sample of completion answers, scoring is relatively objective and straightforward. However, little reliability or validity data are available.

The Incomplete Sentences Task (IST) reflects a more empirical approach to test construction. The three dimensions assessed—hostility, anxiety, and dependence—were selected for their special relevance to the adjustment of secondary school and college students (Lanyon & Lanyon, 1980). The stems were selected by a contrasted-groups approach comparing the answers of students rated high or low on each dimension by their teachers. Two forms are available, one for grades 7 to 12, the other for college years. Each completion is scored on a 3-point scale (0, 1, 2) by comparison to sample answers in the manual. Answers are grouped by personality dimension and totaled; total raw scores are converted to percentile ranks based on performance of students in the standardization samples.

In contrast to the Rotter, several studies have been undertaken to evaluate the reliability and validity of the IST. Initial data indicate that the scoring of the IST is reliable and that it is useful in assessing individual differences on the three personality dimensions (Cundick, 1985; Dush, 1985).

Drawing Tasks

Drawing tasks have been used in a variety of ways in psychological assessment. One early application of drawing tasks was the assessment of intelligence (e.g., Goodenough, 1926). There are predictable developmental changes in the detail of children's human figure drawings. As children get older, they incorporate more detail into their drawings and represent the arrangement and proportion of body parts in more realistic ways. A scoring system was developed to translate the level of detail and accuracy in a drawing into an IQ score.

Today, drawing tasks are used primarily as projective techniques. These tasks are sometimes referred to as *expressive techniques* because they provide test takers with relatively unstructured opportunities for self-expression (e.g., Anastasi, 1988). From a diagnostic standpoint, the construction of the drawings—the elements included, their relative locations and proportions—are believed to reflect emotional conflicts and needs.[1]

The two most popular tests, as indicated in Table 10.1, are the Draw-a-Person Test (Machover, 1949, 1971) and the House–Tree–Person Technique (Buck, 1948, 1981). In the Draw-a-Person Test (DAP), the test taker is given a blank, unlined sheet of paper and a pencil and instructed to draw a person. After completing the drawing, the test taker is given new materials and asked to draw a figure of the opposite sex from the first one. During the drawing process, the examiner takes notes on the order of drawing elements, the comments made by the test taker, and the test taker's nonverbal behavior during the task. The examiner may follow the drawings with a series of questions designed to elicit information about the figures, such as whom they represent and their ages and genders (Machover, 1949, 1971).

[1]In addition to their diagnostic value, the process of creating a drawing and expressing those emotions is viewed as therapeutic, as a means to at least partly relieve tensions and emotional blocks. The area of art therapy is an outgrowth of research on the effects of the drawing process on emotional distress.

DAP scoring is qualitative. Attention is paid to the size of the figures, the level of detail in each, their body proportions, the sequence of drawing body elements, the inclusion of clothing, and the position of each figure and body part. The goal is to construct a primarily psychoanalytic description of personality based on the analysis of the figure. Although an interpretive guide is presented in the manual, there are no norms and no reported reliability and validity data. Attempts by other psychologists to validate the test have been unsuccessful (e.g., Klopfer & Taulbee, 1976).

The House–Tree–Person Technique (HTP) is a somewhat more complex drawing task. The three objects drawn are assumed to be symbolic of aspects of the test taker's life (Buck, 1948). The house is symbolic of home and family life, the tree is symbolic of the test taker's relationship to the environment, and the person is symbolic of the test taker's interpersonal relationships. Test takers are assumed to project their feelings about these elements into their drawings.

In its revised form (Buck, 1981), the drawing task has two phases, each including a drawing and a structured interview stage. In the first phase, the test taker is given blank, unlined paper and a pencil and asked to draw a house. This is followed by two other sheets of paper with instructions to draw (1) a tree and (2) a person. The drawing stage is followed by a series of 60 questions designed to elicit information about the meaning of each figure. In the second phase, test takers draw the same three figures again on separate pages using a set of eight or more crayons. This second drawing stage is also followed by a series of questions.

During the drawing tasks, the examiner notes the time taken to respond, the order in which parts are sketched, and the test taker's comments and nonverbal behavior. During the postdrawing interviews, examiners may deviate from the question list to follow up on points that appear diagnostically relevant.

Drawings are quantitatively and qualitatively scored. The quantitative analysis compares test takers' drawings to those produced by a norm group of 140 adults representing a variety of levels of intelligence. Points are earned for different features of each figure and are converted to an overall IQ score. Qualitative analysis is based on comparison to a similarly small norm group (150 adults) representing a variety of clinical syndromes.

Although the HTP technique was developed through more empirical procedures, it has not emerged as a psychometrically sound test. The norm samples are extremely small, and the sample for qualitative analysis does not include a group of normal individuals (Killian, 1984). Few reliability and validity data are provided, with the exception of demonstrations that performance on the task does reflect both intellectual and personality factors (Buck, 1981). For example, the IQ scores generated by the HTP do show moderate correlations with other measures of intelligence, such as the Wechsler tests and the Stanford–Binet.

Although drawing tasks remain very popular, they are the psychometrically weakest type of projective technique. Many psychologists caution against overinterpreting figure drawings and advise using them instead as part of a diagnostic interview during the initial screening of a client (e.g., Anastasi, 1988; Kaplan & Saccuzzo, 1993). Until more reliability and validity data are available, these techniques are better viewed as investigative tools than as psychological tests.

Issues in Psychological Assessment

As you read through the preceding sections, you may have noticed less concern with traditional psychometric indexes of test adequacy, such as test–retest reliability and criterion validity, than we see in other testing scenarios. For example, in our discussion of testing in educational settings, we referred to specific cutoff points needed on certain tests to justify educational placements. We discussed how the courts have restricted the use of certain tests because of their failure to demonstrate statistically significant relationships with important criteria. You may also have noted that clinical assessment relies more on subjective information and interpretation of responses than does testing in other settings.

Clinical psychologists themselves have different perspectives on the purpose of testing and therefore on the need for tests to demonstrate the statistical properties usually used to identify a test as a "good" test. For example, testing in clinical settings can be viewed from a psychometric or a clinical perspective (Lerner & Lerner, 1986). The psychometric perspective is more concerned about testing as a measurement process. The emphasis is on creating standardized administration and scoring procedures and demonstrating that tests are reliable and valid measures. The examiner is seen as a potential source of measurement error, as someone who can introduce bias and subjectivity into the measurement process, and efforts are made to reduce the role of the examiner to that of a recorder of data. In essence, the data collected by an examiner during testing should be equivalent to the data collected by a machine such as a computer.

The clinical perspective is very different. From this perspective, the test administrator is a critical element of the data-gathering process (Lerner & Lerner, 1986). It is the examiner's skill, judgment, and intuition that enable us to understand the person being tested. The test itself is simply a tool that, when used by a skillful psychologist, can provide useful information for diagnosis and treatment planning. In this perspective, it is difficult to talk meaningfully about the general statistical properties of a test. When used by different clinicians, who differ in their training and expertise, tests are likely to produce different results.

Probably the most realistic position on clinical testing is somewhere between these two extremes. The issues being addressed in clinical assessment are complex and elusive. Examiner skill is likely to be of more importance in clinical assessment than in the assessment of math skills. We might expect more variation in administration and more interpretation of responses. However, the quality of a decision is influenced by the accuracy of the data being considered. Although tests for clinical assessment may not need to be held to the rigorous psychometric standards used in educational decisions, some demonstrations of reliability and validity are necessary. No test will be useful if it cannot accurately represent what it is designed to measure.

NEUROPSYCHOLOGICAL ASSESSMENT

Neuropsychology is a specialization within psychology and medicine that studies the relationship between behavior and the brain. In clinical neuropsychology, we examine the impact of brain injury, brain disease, or abnormal brain development on cognitive and behavioral functioning. As a multidisciplinary area, clinical neuropsychology involves both medical and psychological testing. Psychological tests typically are administered by clinical psychologists with additional training in neuropsychology.

The majority of neuropsychological testing occurs in medical settings, such as veteran's administration hospitals and medical centers. However, neuropsychological tests may also be given to individuals seeking outpatient treatment when patterns of behavior suggest a problem in brain function. Although you may think of neuropsychological testing as important primarily in cases of stroke or Alzheimer's disease, neuropsychological tests are also important in the diagnosis of problems such as learning disability, mental retardation, and attention deficit disorder, a syndrome sometimes associated with hyperactive behavior.

Intelligence Tests

Once again, intelligence tests like the Wechslers can provide useful information. In the simplest scenario, intelligence tests can be part of the diagnostic battery used to identify individuals with specific cognitive deficits. This procedure was discussed in Chapter 9 relative to identifying learning disability and mental retardation (see p. 315). If particular score patterns are observed, test takers can be referred for additional evaluation to determine whether these patterns reflect neurological problems or learning failures that might be tied to experience.

Similarly, current intelligence test scores can be compared to earlier scores to see if changes in ability have occurred. For example, evaluation of an individual with Alzheimer's disease—a progressive degeneration of brain functions—might involve repeated administration of an intelligence test to track the nature and extent of cognitive decline.

Considerable research has been conducted on using Wechsler tests to identify different cognitive deficits. For example, some psychologists suggest that individuals with a learning disability show low scores on the arithmetic, coding, information, and digit span subtests (e.g., Kaufman, 1979). Other psychologists propose that learning disability also is characterized by higher scores on performance subtests that do not require sequential actions, such as object assembly, block design, and picture completion. Spatial subtests that require sequencing, such as digit span, digit symbol, and picture arrangement, are usually more difficult (Bannatyne, 1974).

However, as often happens with pattern analysis, other studies challenge these proposals. For example, the difference between scores on sequencing/nonsequencing performance subtests is not present for all learning disabled individuals (Kavale & Forness, 1984). In addition, the pattern is not unique to learning disability. A similar pattern has been observed in the test scores of delinquents (Groff & Hubble, 1981) and emotionally handicapped children (Thompson, 1981). Once again, it is clear that diagnostic decisions must be based on data from a variety of assessments.

Neuropsychological Tests

As the field of neuropsychology grew, so did the collection of tests designed specifically to assess brain damage. The majority of these tests focus on spatial perception and memory, two cognitive abilities believed to be greatly affected by brain functioning (Anastasi, 1988). Neuropsychological tests can be grouped into two broad categories: tests of specific tasks and neuropsychological test batteries. All tests in both categories require individual administration.

Tests of Specific Tasks

Tests of specific tasks focus on a single cognitive function that is likely to be affected by brain impairment. The development of these tests dates to the post-World War I era, when observations of injured soldiers (e.g., Goldstein & Scheerer, 1941) and children who had experienced birth traumas or serious infectious diseases (e.g., Werner & Strauss, 1941) identified a number of specific cognitive problems. The most common characteristics were impairments in perception, abstract thinking, and memory.

According to Table 10.1, the two most popular tests in this category are the Bender Visual Motor Gestalt and the Wechsler Memory Scale. They provide an excellent contrast between tests focusing on perceptual issues and tests focusing on memory abilities.

Bender Visual Motor Gestalt.   The Bender was discussed briefly in Chapter 9 as a test useful in assessing learning disability. What we did not specify is that its use in these assessments derives from proposals that learning disability reflects an impairment in central nervous system functions (e.g., Sattler, 1988).

The Bender consists of nine simple line drawings presented one at a time on separate cards. The drawings include a variety of elements, such as dots, circles, and angles, that are combined into patterns or figures. The designs were selected specifically to tap different Gestalt laws of perception—processes for integrating elements into a whole unit or *Gestalt* (Wertheimer, 1923). Simulated Bender drawings are presented in Figure 10.1. Note that each design contains elements in particular orientations relative to each other. Some touch, others overlap, and still others are contained within a larger shape.

When developed in 1938, the Bender was proposed as an index of perceptual-motor maturation (Bender, 1938). However, for many years, there was no systematic scoring procedure for performance on these designs. Even today, there are a variety of scoring procedures, including procedures for using performance to diagnose emotional and psychological disorders (e.g., Hutt,

FIGURE 10.1   Simulated Bender drawings

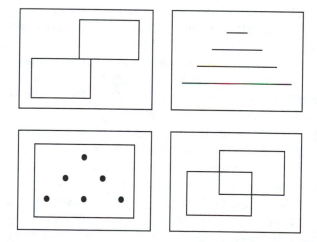

1985). In this aspect, the Bender is similar to the Rorschach and the TAT, two other tests that can be scored and interpreted using several different systems.

In general, the most widely accepted use of the Bender is for diagnosis of brain dysfunction (Groth-Marnat, 1990). Norms and scoring systems are available for children (e.g., Koppitz, 1975) and for adults (e.g., Lacks, 1984). Clinicians look for such features as simplifying a figure by omitting elements, rotating a figure or the elements within it, and replacing a straight or curved line with the other type.

Test–retest reliabilities vary greatly according to scoring system, age of test taker, and time between testings; coefficients for the Koppitz and Lacks systems typically are in the .90s. Although the results of validity studies are mixed, the Bender appears to be able to discriminate brain-damaged from nonbrain-damaged individuals and to provide a good index of perceptual-motor development (e.g., Koppitz, 1975; Lacks, 1984). However, correlations with scores on intelligence and achievement tests are low to moderate, indicating that the Bender should not be used as an overall measure of either aptitude or achievement.

Wechsler Memory Scale.   As its name implies, the Wechsler Memory Scale (WMS) is a test of short- and long-term memory deficits (Wechsler, 1945). Wechsler's goal in developing the test was to produce a measure of memory ability that was *not* highly correlated with intelligence (Heiby, 1984). A second form of the test was developed for use in retesting clients (Stone & Wechsler, 1946), and a revised form tied to current information-processing concepts is in development (see Russell, 1975).

Each form of the WMS consists of seven subtests, described in Table 10.8. The test is extremely easy for normal people and does not capture individual differences in normal memory skills. Several of the subtests were borrowed from other tests. For example, the digit strings in the memory span subtest for Form I were taken from the original WAIS digit span; the Form II digit strings were taken from an early version of the Army Alpha, the first group intelligence test for adults (Heiby, 1984). Although this may seem odd if the goal is to produce a test that is not correlated with IQ, this particular subtest taps basic processing skills rather than level of intelligence. Scores on the digit span subtest are not significant predictors of IQ scores for normal individuals.

The WMS is designed for ages 20 to 64. The test is scored by summing performance on the subtests, weighting the sum by adding a constant based on test-taker age, and converting the weighted sum to a memory quotient (MQ) with a mean of 100. There are no norms for performance on individual subtests, no norms for determining how much below the mean an MQ must be to suggest impairment in brain functions, and no internal consistency data. In light of these statements, you might wonder why clinicians bother to administer this test! In fact, the popularity of the WMS is due to the absence of

TABLE 10.8   Subtests of the Wechsler Memory Scale

Subtest	Description[a]
Personal and current information	Questions on name, date of birth, important recent events (e.g., the current president)
Orientation	Questions about time and place
Mental control	Tracking questions (e.g., counting by 3's)
Logical memory	Oral questions on two paragraphs read by the examiner
Memory span	Reciting strings of digits forward and backward
Visual reproduction	Drawing simple geometric figures from memory after studying each for 10 seconds
Associate learning	Paired words (i.e., paired associates) to be learned in three trials

[a]On all but the first 2 subtests, Form II uses different but equivalent items. For example, mental control on Form II uses counting by 4s, logical memory uses different paragraphs, and visual reproduction uses different drawings.

Adapted from Wechsler (1945) and Stone & Wechsler (1946).

other tests specifically designed to measure memory functions and to several significant validity studies. For example, scores on the WMS do decline in normal individuals with increasing age, and scores on the WMS do correlate with IQ scores for individuals with mental retardation and other forms of brain damage (Prigatano, 1978). It appears, therefore, that the WMS can be useful in identifying individuals with declining and impaired memory functions.

However, the technical data on the WMS raise an important point relative to the evaluation of neuropsychological tests. In many cases, the reliability of these tests is difficult to determine. We cannot use normal individuals in reliability studies because the tests are too easy for them. On the other hand, it is difficult to conduct reliability studies with brain-damaged individuals. People who have actual neurological problems are likely to deteriorate further over time—or to show improvement if they are involved in a productive type of treatment. As a result, many psychologists infer about reliability from validity data. Since a test cannot be valid unless it is reliable, they conclude that a test producing a valid measure in fact must have adequate reliability.

Test Batteries

The trend in neuropsychological assessment has mirrored the trend in other areas. Initially, assessment plans focused on the use of a separate series of tests, each measuring a different aspect of brain function. Over time, test batteries emerged, enabling clinicians to assess a variety of functions with an integrated set of tests. The fact that neuropsychological batteries are not found on the list of frequently used tests in Table 10.1 probably reflects the small number of clinical psychologists who are trained to use these complicated tests.

Unlike the test batteries used in educational settings, neuropsychological test batteries are not always normed on a single group of people. In some cases, the batteries have evolved over time, with additional tests added at later dates. However, the batteries still have an important advantage over the use of individual tests: Each battery represents a particular point of view about brain functions, and the tests within a battery are organized to assess functions corresponding to those views.

Halstead–Reitan.　The Halstead–Reitan Neuropsychological Battery is a series of tests designed to use performance on tasks to identify deficits within different brain areas (Reitan, 1969). You probably have heard about studies of brain localization and lateralization in other psychology classes. The Halstead–Reitan is designed to test abilities that are believed to be (1) localized within certain brain lobes or (2) lateralized within certain brain hemispheres.

Development of the battery began in the late 1930s, and additional assessments were added over a period of years. Drawing on research about brain–behavior relationships, the battery was designed to include tasks that are known to involve certain brain areas (Reitan & Wolfson, 1985). For example, we know that control of motor movements is localized in the frontal lobe. We also know that motor control of the body is lateralized; therefore, the right frontal lobe of the brain controls motor movements on the left side of the body. An individual who cannot perform motor tasks with the left hand is likely to have damage to the right frontal lobe.

Different versions are available for testing young children, teens, and adults. The basic battery consists of five tests, presented in Table 10.9. Other physical and sensory tests are sometimes added, such as a strength-of-grip test and a test of response to sensory information that is presented only to one side of the body (e.g., the left ear). In addition, test takers may also be asked to complete an intelligence test, such as the Wechsler, and a personality test, such as the MMPI. Total testing time, therefore, can be up to 12 hours, which is divided over a number of sessions.

Scores on each test are used to determine an impairment index, and the total number of tests for which impairment is seen determines an overall impairment index. Validity studies indicate that the battery is able to identify conditions such as tumors within different hemispheres of the brain and within different brain lobes (e.g., Reitan, 1967).

Luria–Nebraska.　In contrast to the views of Halstead and Reitan, Luria viewed the brain as an integrated system in which many areas together controlled patterns of behavior (e.g., Luria, 1973). Luria's original assessment

TABLE 10.9   Basic Tests in the Halstead–Reitan Adult Battery

Test	Purpose
Category test	Assesses learning and concept formation skills through a series of discrimination learning tasks in which test takers must figure out or "abstract" the principle used to group geometric shapes into categories.
Tactual performance test	Assesses psychomotor and memory abilities by requiring test takers to put differently shaped blocks into holes on a board. Three trials: using preferred hand only, nonpreferred hand only, and both hands. Followed by request for test taker to draw a diagram from memory of the board with the blocks in their proper positions.
Speech sounds perception test	Assesses auditory–visual coordination and language skill by requiring test takers to identify the nonsense words presented to them on tape from written multiple-choice lists. All words use "ee" as the vowel sound but vary in first or last consonant.
Rhythm test	Assesses nonlanguage auditory perception by requiring test takers to discriminate between same and different pairs of rhythmic beats presented on tape.
Finger-tapping test	Assesses motor speed and hand preference by requiring a test taker to tap each index finger as fast as possible for a series of 10-second trials, alternating hands on successive trials.

Adapted from Reitan (1969).

method was very subjective and did not use a standardized procedure. It was not, therefore, well received in this country. However, a psychologist at the University of Nebraska, C. J. Golden, subsequently standardized his procedures, producing a test known as the Luria–Nebraska Neuropsychological Battery[2] (Golden, Purisch, & Hammeke, 1985).

Designed for ages 15 through adult, the Luria–Nebraska includes 11 clinical scales, described in Table 10.10. Although the Luria contains more scales than the Halstead, testing time typically is only about $2\frac{1}{2}$ hours. Each item is scored 0 to 2, where 0 equals normal performance. Raw scores on each test are converted to T-scores, which are evaluated relative to expected performance based on age and educational level to determine the extent of impairment.

[2]This is similar to what happened when Louis Terman adapted the Binet test for use in this country. It did not become the Terman–Binet. Since Terman worked at Stanford University, the test became known as the *Stanford*–Binet.

TABLE 10.10   Subtests of the Luria–Nebraska Battery

Test	Purpose
Motor scale	Assesses performance of motor movements with the hands, arms, face, and mouth. Some are imitative, others are verbal instructions.
Rhythm scale	Assesses production of sound patterns, such as short melodies, and perception of sound qualities and patterns.
Tactile scale	Assesses processing of tactile information when blindfolded, such as letters traced on the back of the hand.
Visual processes scale	Assesses visual object recognition skill with line/perspective drawings, etc.
Receptive speech scale	Assesses understanding of spoken language, from speech sounds to complex sentences.
Expressive speech scale	Assesses ability to speak, using speech sounds, words, phrases, etc.
Writing scale	Assesses writing skills, including copying, spelling, and spontaneous writing.
Reading scale	Assesses reading skills, including letters, symbols, words, sentences, and stories.
Arithmetic scale	Assesses reading/writing numerals and simple/complex arithmetic operations.
Memory scale	Assesses immediate and delayed memory for pictures, rhythms, words, word–picture pairs.
Intellectual processes scale	Assesses general intellectual skills using tasks similar to traditional IQ tests.
Intermediate memory scale[a]	Assesses recent and incidental memory by asking for descriptions of earlier activities during the assessment.

[a]Available only for Form II.
Adapted from Golden, Purisch, & Hammeke (1985).

Although Luria had a more holistic view of brain activity, the Luria–Nebraska is designed to identify areas within the brain that are not functioning properly. The process for doing this, however, differs from the Halstead procedure. Since Luria saw many areas as influencing each task, the key to identifying possible areas of brain damage is *comparison* of the various subtest scores. Scores on tests designed to tap either right or left hemisphere activities are compared to identify damage within hemispheres. Scores on tests designed to tap activity in different lobes are compared in a parallel way.

As a relatively new test, the psychometric properties of the Luria–Nebraska are still under evaluation. Reviews of research indicate that reliability coefficients range from .54 to 1.0, depending on the type of coefficient computed, and that the summary scores on the Luria correlate at the .70 range or better with scores on the Halstead–Reitan (e.g., Franzen, 1985).

Issues in Neuropsychological Assessment

Neuropsychological assessment has become an important specialty area, due in part to the explosion of information about brain–behavior relationships in the last two decades. Even today, data from these assessments are often used as part of larger research projects on neurological functioning. Two points about these assessments are important to note.

First, neuropsychological assessment is a truly interdisciplinary enterprise. In this section we have focused on how tests of behavior can be used to make inferences about brain functions. However, a variety of other techniques is available to study brain activity, and these are often used along with tests of behavior. The most common of these are imaging procedures—techniques that generate pictures of brain structure or brain function (e.g., Andreasen, 1988). For example, an individual with a possible neurological deficit may receive a computerized tomography (CT) scan in which multiple x-rays are used to create pictures of brain sections. A more sophisticated technique magnetic resonance imaging (MRI) uses magnetic fields and radio waves to produce computer-enhanced images of brain structure. Brain function can be mapped using a PET or positron emission tomography scan in which radioactively tagged sugars are tracked as they are absorbed by active brain areas.

Second, neuropsychological assessments are complex and specialized procedures. The typical clinical psychology graduate program does not include extensive training in neuropsychology. Clinicians interested in neuropsychology often receive additional training at the postgraduate level. In fact, the field has grown so rapidly that psychologists now may specialize *within* neuropsychology in such areas as the evaluation of children, the evaluation of adults, or the geriatric evaluation. Students interested in more information about this area should consult the following references: Albert, 1981; Heaton & Pendleton, 1981; Satz & Fletcher, 1981.

SUMMARY AND KEY CONCEPTS

In contrast to earlier notions, a clinical setting today is any place in which physical and/or psychological problems are studied. Although psychiatrists and social workers are also employed in these settings, clinical psychologists are the professionals most likely to administer psychological tests. Tests are used both for identifying problems (diagnosis) and for planning effective treatments. In addition to using tests, clinicians evaluate their clients through observation and interview.

The two types of assessments performed most often are psychological assessment and neuropsychological assessment. The goal of psychological assessment is to produce an accurate picture of the individual, the individual's problems, and the environmental factors contributing to those problems. The problems identified may be forms of **psychopathology** or less severe problems of adjustment.

Clinicians use both intelligence and personality tests in psychological assessment. Intelligence test data may be subjected to various forms of pattern analysis and content analysis in an effort to develop hypotheses about client functioning. Many clinicians use traditional objective and projective personality tests and other projective techniques such as sentence-completion or drawing tasks. Unlike educational testing, with its emphasis on the psychometric properties of tests, clinical testing may focus more on qualitative analysis of test-taker responses. Tests are seen as part of a larger data-gathering process in which clinicians formulate and evaluate hypotheses about client functioning.

Neuropsychology is a multidisciplinary area dealing with brain–behavior relationships. Clinical psychologists perform neuropsychological assessments to identify behaviors associated with brain impairment. Intelligence tests can be used both to investigate overall level of cognitive functioning and to suggest possible types of neurological impairment. In addition, assessment may involve tests of perception, memory tests, and test batteries that are useful for identifying the specific brain areas that are likely to be damaged.

QUESTIONS

10.1   List and describe three different types of intelligence test data useful in evaluating psychological functioning.

10.2   How does the information generated by the MMPI differ from the information generated by the EPPS? How might each test be used?

10.3   Why do clinical psychologists like projective tests? What criticisms have been raised about these tests?

10.4   Describe the difference between a psychometric and a conceptual approach to scoring the Rorschach.

10.5 Explain what clinicians look at when they analyze TAT stories.

10.6 At what point in a psychological evaluation would sentence completion and drawing tasks be most useful? Why?

10.7 List and describe two ways to use intelligence tests in neuropsychological assessment.

10.8 Why is it difficult to evaluate the test–retest reliability of neuropsychological tests?

10.9 How is the design of neuropsychological test batteries similar to and different from the design of test batteries used in educational settings?

10.10 Compare and contrast the views of Halstead and Luria on brain organization. How are these views reflected in their respective test batteries?

CHAPTER 11

Testing in Counseling Settings

CHAPTER OUTLINE

CHAPTER GOALS AND OBJECTIVES

After completing this chapter you should be able to:

- Describe the difference between counseling settings and clinical settings and the ways tests are used in each.

- Describe the different design features of interest tests and their advantages and drawbacks.
- Explain why it can be difficult to provide career guidance based solely on interest test data.
- Identify the different types of ability tests useful in career guidance and explain how each type is used.
- Describe the difference in focus of personality tests used in counseling versus personality tests used in clinical assessment.
- Describe the different design features of the personality tests used in personal counseling and their advantages and drawbacks.
- Explain the concerns about these personality tests and the ways to use them effectively.
- Describe how other scales, such as attitude scales, can be useful in personal counseling.

W̲hy a separate chapter on the use of tests in counseling settings? Don't counselors use the same tests as clinicians? Not necessarily. Many students find it difficult to distinguish between clinical and counseling settings because clinicians and counselors do engage in some similar practices; both types of people may be trained to use some of the same therapeutic approaches, psychological tests, and other assessment techniques. However, since they differ in the focus of their training and their assessment and treatment goals, we often find different tests used in clinical and counseling settings. To underscore the importance of distinguishing between these settings, we will discuss the nature of counseling activities as well as the psychological tests used.

USES OF TESTS IN COUNSELING SETTINGS

Counseling is found within schools, colleges, and universities, in government and social service agencies, and in prisons, hospitals, and private practice offices (Wise, 1989). The majority of counseling occurs in educational settings and in private practice (Watkins et al., 1986). The testing component of counseling may involve the administration of interest tests, ability tests, and personality tests.

Nature of Counseling Activities

The focus of counseling is to identify people's abilities, personality characteristics, and patterns of interests and to assist people in making choices and changes to improve their sense of well-being and life-styles (Pietrofesa, Hoffman, & Splete, 1984). One way to understand better the specific uses and contributions of counseling is to contrast the fields of counseling and clinical psychology.

Counseling versus Clinical Psychology

Although these two fields do overlap, there are several important distinctions between them. Table 11.1 presents some of these contrasts based on the writings of Anastasi (1979) and Wise (1989). Unlike clinical psychology, with its historical roots in the medicine model, counseling psychology evolved from the vocational guidance movement. It is more focused, therefore, on assisting people with making decisions about their futures. The decisions may involve vocational (career) issues or personal issues such as substance abuse or marital/family discord. Although counseling psychologists are often involved in therapeutic activities, they are less likely to treat individuals with serious psychopathology.

Comparison of the employment of counseling and clinical psychologists identifies additional differences between the fields (Watkins et al., 1986). 31.1%

TABLE 11.1 Distinctions between Clinical and Counseling Psychology

Clinical Psychology	Counseling Psychology
Evolved from medical model with an emphasis on research and treatment (scientist–practitioner model).	Evolved from the vocational guidance movement with an emphasis on assessment and placement decisions.
More concerned with identifying problems in personality functioning.	More concerned with identifying patterns of personality and interest (more emphasis on strengths).
Seeks to identify causes of problems; interest in exploring the past.	More concerned with present and future functioning.
Seeks to remedy problems by changing aspects of personality and behavior.	Seeks to solve problems using individual's strengths without making major personality changes.
Likely to work with people whose problems are disabling and prevent them from living normal lives.	Likely to work with people whose problems are disruptive but who function adequately overall.

Adapted from Anastasi (1979) and Wise (1989).

of clinical psychologists were employed in private practice whereas 31.7% of counseling psychologists worked in university settings. Unlike the counseling psychologists at universities, who worked primarily in counseling centers, the clinical psychologists at universities typically held academic positions in psychology departments. Furthermore, clinical psychologists were almost three times more likely to be employed in hospitals (15% versus 5.4%).

Other People Who Engage in Counseling

A wide variety of people identify themselves as "counselors" or their activities as "counseling." There also are a number of different counseling specialties, including substance abuse counseling, marriage and family counseling, and vocational counseling. But in many states, the terms "counselor" and "counseling" are not legally regulated terms, and people do not need certain specific credentials to use these labels.

A counseling psychologist typically has a master's or doctoral degree in counseling psychology, which may be offered either through a psychology or an education department. Other individuals who may use the term counseling include social workers who have specialized in psychiatric social work, people with master's degrees in education who specialized in either school or nonschool counseling, and people with bachelor's degrees who have received additional training in substance abuse, marriage, or family counseling. To keep things simple, our discussion will focus on counseling psychologists—the group of people with the most extensive training in psychological assessment and treatment.

Tests Used by Counseling Psychologists

Because of their focus on vocational and personal problems, counseling psychologists tend to use psychological tests that assess people's abilities, personalities, and interests. Tables 11.2 and 11.3 present the tests used most often by two groups of counseling psychologists. The data in Table 11.2 are based on the responses of 700 members of APA's Division 17 (Counseling). The majority worked in university academic departments or counseling centers (56.3%); approximately 20% were in private practice, with the remainder employed in mental health clinics, medical settings, public schools, and consultation firms.

The top three tests are an interest inventory, a personality inventory, and an intelligence test, underscoring the previous point about the focus of counseling activities. A comparison of these ranks to the data from clinical psychologists in Table 10.1 reinforces the distinction between the two fields. In terms of personality testing, counseling psychologists are less likely to use projective tests such as the Rorschach and the TAT. Furthermore, counseling psychologists are more likely to use objective tests such as the Sixteen Personality Factor Question-

TABLE 11.2   Tests Used Most Often by
              Counseling Psychologists in
              University and Private Practice
              Settings

Rank	Test
1	Strong–Campbell Interest Inventory
2	Minnesota Multiphasic Personality Inventory
3	Wechsler Adult Intelligence Scale
4	Sentence-completion blanks
5	Bender–Gestalt
6	Thematic Apperception Test
7	Sixteen Personality Factor Questionnaire
8	California Psychological Inventory
9	Wechsler Intelligence Scale for Children
10	Edwards Personal Preference Schedule

Adapted from Watkins, Campbell, & McGregor (1988).

naire and the California Psychological Inventory. These are tests that focus on the *structure* of personality, rather than the identification of clinical syndromes.

The data in Table 11.3 were generated by counselors in college and university counseling services and private counseling agencies. The individuals responding to the survey included not only counseling psychologists but also other types of professionals involved in counseling activities. Note that this group was even *less* likely to use personality tests, whether objective or projective, and focused primarily on assessment of interests and abilities.

A final point about the tests used in counseling settings: Most of these tests are paper-and-pencil, self-report tests that do not require administration by an examiner. Tables 11.4 and 11.5 summarize the design and administration requirements for the most popular tests.

How Tests Are Used in Counseling

Tests are used in counseling settings primarily to help psychologists better understand each client, to promote the client's self-awareness, as an aid to planning treatment, and to help client's make choices and solve problems (Goldman, 1971). The information that counseling psychologists most often seek through testing includes vocational and career-related information, evidence of possible psychopathology, and measures of clients' intellectual functioning (Fee, Elkins,

TABLE 11.3   Tests Used Most Often by
             Counselors in Counseling Services
             and Agencies

Rank	Test
1	Strong–Campbell Interest Inventory
2	Kuder Occupational Interest Survey
3	Edwards Personal Preference Schedule
4	Nelson–Denny Reading Test
5	Sixteen Personality Factor Questionnaire
6	Holland Self-Directed Search
7	Wechsler Adult Intelligence Scale
8	American College Testing Assessment
9	Survey of Habits and Attitudes
10	Minnesota Multiphasic Personality Inventory

Adapted from Zytowski & Warman (1982).

& Boyd, 1982). Tests also can be used for research, such as comparison of the effectiveness of different therapeutic approaches.

One significant difference between the use of tests in counseling and clinical settings is the role of the client. In clinical settings, test results are not necessarily shared directly with clients. Instead, clinicians use these results to make decisions about the course of treatment. In counseling settings, test results are likely to be discussed with clients. Since a primary goal of counseling is to aid clients in developing self-awareness and making choices, the client is viewed as the *primary user* of test results (AERA/APA, 1985). The clinical psychologist can be seen as a *gatekeeper*, whereas the counseling psychologist is more like a *facilitator* (Wise, 1989).

Counseling psychologists also frequently use clinical interview and behavioral observation to learn more about their clients (Fee, Elkins, & Boyd, 1982). However, as in many other scenarios, tests provide a mechanism to obtain objective data using standardized procedures and to provide the individual difference information needed to assist client's with decision making. Counseling psychologists may also use a testing session as a standardized observational setting in which the behavior of clients can be noted and compared (Goodman, 1971). For example, the behavior of clients during an intelligence test can provide indications of their levels of self-confidence or anxiety or the extent to which they are reflective or impulsive.

TABLE 11.4 Categorizing the Design of Tests Frequently Used in Counseling Settings

Purpose/Format	Examples
Aptitude Free response Norm referenced	Wechsler Adult Intelligence Scale Wechsler Intelligence Scale for Children
Personality Objective Norm referenced Normative	Minnesota Multiphasic Personality Inventory Sixteen Personality Factor Questionnaire California Psychological Inventory
Personality Objective Norm referenced Ipsative	Edwards Personal Preference Schedule
Personality Projective Norm referenced Normative	Thematic Apperception Test Sentence-completion tests
Interest Objective Norm referenced Normative	Strong–Campbell Interest Inventory[a]
Interest Objective Norm referenced Ipsative	Kuder Occupational Interest Survey

[a]One set of SCII scales report ipsative rather than normative scores.

VOCATIONAL COUNSELING

Historically, vocational guidance was the primary concern of counseling psychology. According to current data from surveys of counseling psychologists, assisting clients with vocational decisions is still a central element of counseling interactions. Most vocational counseling occurs in high schools, in college or university counseling centers, or in private practice settings. In this section we will discuss the two types of tests used most often for vocational counseling: interest tests and ability tests.

TABLE 11.5   Categorizing the Administration Format of Popular Counseling Tests

Tests Requiring Administration by an Examiner

Wechsler Adult Intelligence Scale—Revised (WAIS—R)
Wechsler Intelligence Scale for Children—R (WISC—R)
Thematic Apperception Test (TAT)
Bender–Gestalt

Self-Report Tests[a]

Minnesota Multiphasic Personality Inventory (MMPI)
Sixteen Personality Factor Questionnaire (16PF)
California Psychological Inventory (CPI)
Sentence-completion tests
Strong–Campbell Interest Inventory (SCII)
Edwards Personal Preference Schedule (EPPS)
Kuder Occupational Interest Survey (KOIS)

[a]These paper-and-pencil tests may be administered individually or to groups.

Interest Tests

Interest tests fall into the category of objective tests described in Chapter 4. The use of interest tests for vocational counseling reflects a belief that the people who are likely to be happy and successful in a particular career share certain common interests. In fact, research on different criterion groups—each composed of people who have worked in a specific field for several years and who report enjoying that work—indicates that common interests do exist. The case for interest–career relationships, however, should not be overstated. Differences do exist, especially when subgroups of people such as men and women are compared. For an interest test to provide useful career guidance, the test must be carefully normed and must demonstrate valid relationships with other measures of occupational choice.

Types of Interest Tests

Like other objective tests (e.g., personality tests), interest tests can use either independent items or forced-choice items. Tests using independent items generate normative measures, whereas tests using forced-choice items generate ipsative measures (see pp. 95–96). The scales used to represent patterns of interests typically are produced either through a criterion-group strategy or a combined theoretical/criterion group strategy (see pp. 103–105). The tests discussed in this section have been selected because they are (1) frequently used in counseling settings and (2) good examples of different approaches to test construction, test administration, and test scoring.

Strong–Campbell Interest Inventory.　The Strong–Campbell Interest Inventory (SCII) is a new version of a test first developed in the 1930s. The original test, called the Strong Vocational Interest Blank (SVIB), was designed to match the interests and values of test takers with those of criterion groups selected from a broad range of business and professional occupations. The SVIB was developed using a criterion-group strategy; the responses of individuals who were happy in their careers determined the relationship between the answers to test items and the occupational scales.

Although the SVIB demonstrated impressive reliability and validity (Strong & Campbell, 1966), it was severely criticized on two specific grounds. First, there were separate SVIB forms for men and women, and their interests were compared to different occupational groups. For example, a man could produce a profile that identified "pilot" as a possible career, whereas a woman could only generate a profile matching the career "stewardess." Second, the SVIB was criticized for being a test without a theoretical orientation. In our discussion of the criterion-group strategy, we noted that empirically derived scales are not necessarily theoretically coherent (see p. 105). In other words, it may be difficult to explain *why* certain patterns of interests are linked to satisfaction in specific careers. Even in the presence of statistical validity data, the lack of theoretical relationships between the interest profiles and occupations led many psychologists to question the meaning of the scales.

The SCII was designed to remedy these problems. The separate forms for men and women were combined, and a series of *theme scales* was added to identify personality patterns relevant to career choice (Hansen & Campbell, 1985). The SCII contains 325 items presented in seven parts, six of which use independent items. The first five parts list different occupations, school subjects, day-to-day activities, recreation/leisure activities, and types of people, each to be rated as "like," "dislike," or "indifferent." A sixth section requires test takers to mark a set of self-descriptive statements, such as being able to make friends easily, as either "yes," "no" or "?" (cannot say). The remaining section uses a forced-choice format in which test takers express a preference for one of two paired statements, such as reading a book or watching television.

The SCII provides a set of validity scores and three different sets of norm-referenced T-scores (see p. 84). The validity scores are designed to identify profiles containing (1) many omitted items, (2) many infrequent (unusual) responses, and (3) unusual percentages of "like," "dislike," or "indifferent" responses. Test takers who omit many items and/or rate many items with "indifferent" may not provide enough data to construct a valid profile. On the other hand, too many "like," "dislike," or unusual responses could indicate the presence of a response bias.

Analysis of interests begins with the identification of dominant occupational themes based on Holland's model of occupational themes (Holland, 1966, 1985a). The six themes identified in Holland's model and used in the SCII are realistic, investigative, artistic, social, enterprising, and conventional. According to extensive research by Holland and others, these six themes not only describe different types of people, but also identify the environments in which they are likely to be happy. For example, a person whose interests match the "investigative" theme would be likely to enjoy a career in science or math, whereas a person whose interests match the "enterprising" theme would be more likely to enjoy a career in law or business. Through the use of forced-choice items, the SCII is able to rank order the strength of these themes on the basis of test-taker responses. A person can then be described with a series of codes that indicates the relative dominance of each theme.

Because the items are forced choice, test takers cannot earn the same *raw scores* on all occupational themes. The item format dictates that the selection of one theme statement adds points to its scale at the expense of other scales. Therefore, each occupational theme must be associated with a different raw score, and the sum of those raw scores equals the total number of items presented (or forced choices made). However, when the occupational themes scores are converted to T-scores, the frame of reference changes. Each raw score is now being compared to the raw scores earned by members of the standardization sample. If a test taker's raw scores for the "realistic" and investigative" themes equal the raw score means for the standardization sample, the test taker will receive T-scores of 50 on both occupational themes. This means that a test taker can receive the same *T-score* for several different occupational themes. The T-scores indicate where test takers' raw scores are on the occupational themes relative to the standardization sample.

The 23 basic interest scores are reported in clusters according to occupational theme (see Table 11.6). For example, military activities and mechanical activities are reported under the "realistic" theme, whereas teaching and athletics are reported under the "social" theme. The interest T-scores are normative (absolute) scores that compare a test taker's interests to those of a general norm group. They indicate whether a test taker's interest in, for example, art or athletics is average, above average, or below average—compared to people in general. A T-score of 60 on the art scale is one standard deviation above the mean (50 + 10) and is higher than 84% of the scores generated by the norm group. These T-scores are also accompanied by phrases such as "very high," "moderately high," "high," and "average."

The final set of scales is the 207 occupational scales that compare test takers' answers to those produced by different criterion groups. To identify

TABLE 11.6 Categorizing SCII Basic Interest Scales According to General Occupational Themes

Theme	Interest Scales
Realistic	Agriculture Nature Adventure Military activities Mechanical activities
Investigative	Science Mathematics Medical science Medical service
Artistic	Music/dramatics Art Writing
Social	Teaching Social service Athletics Domestic arts Religious activities
Enterprising	Public speaking Law/politics Merchandising Sales Business management
Conventional	Office practices

Adapted from Hansen & Campbell (1985).

items and responses characteristic of each criterion group, the answers of each group were compared to the answers selected by a general group of people. Test-taker performance is reported as normative T-scores based on comparison to each criterion group and is clustered according to occupational themes. A T-score of 60 on the "mathematician" scale is one standard deviation above the mean and is higher than 84% of the scores generated by mathematicians in the standardization sample. The scores are accompanied by phrases such as "very similar," "similar," and "moderately similar."

The 207 scales include 101 occupations normed on both men and women (202 scales total), 4 scales (e.g., dental hygienist) normed only on women, and one scale (agribusiness manager) normed only on men. Because the interests of men and women in a given career do differ, separate criterion groups are used whenever possible. However, each test taker's scores are compared to *both* the male and female criterion groups. The 5 scales normed only on one gender represent occupations in which there are not enough members of the other gender to select a valid sample.

The excellent psychometric properties of the SCII contribute to its enormous popularity. The test–retest reliabilities for SCII scales fall in the .8 to .9 range, and the scales both discriminate among the interests of different occupational groups (concurrent validity) and predict later job satisfaction (predictive validity). One limitation of the SCII is its focus on occupations in business and the professions. Counseling psychologists who want to assess interests relative to "blue collar" and unskilled occupations can turn to the Career Assessment Inventory (Johansson, 1976), a test whose design and format closely resemble the SCII.

Kuder Occupational Interest Survey.   The Kuder Occupational Interest Survey (KOIS) differs from the SCII in several important ways (Kuder 1979; Zytowski, 1985). In terms of design, the KOIS is composed entirely of forced-choice items, each of which presents a set of three activities, or a triad. Scores on the KOIS scales are all ipsative, indicating the relative strength of particular interests. Also, Kuder did not select items for the occupational scales by comparing the responses of criterion groups to the responses of a general group of people. Instead, the actual responses of criterion groups were used to link items to occupational scales.

The other two differences involve the domains covered by the KOIS. The KOIS includes a set of scales designed to match patterns of interests with possible college majors. These scales were determined by administering items to college seniors who were majoring in different disciplines. Also, the KOIS taps interests in a wider range of occupations than the SCII, including skilled and semiskilled activities.

The KOIS is composed of 100 forced-choice triads. For each item, test takers select the "most preferred" and "least preferred" activity, a procedure that generates a relative ranking of the three activities. Although the nature of KOIS scores differs from most SCII scores (ipsative rather than normative), the KOIS does produce a similar set of scales. The four experimental scales are used to evaluate the validity of a profile. They were determined by asking groups of men and women to answer the items truthfully (the M and W scales) and then asking them to answer the items while deliberately trying to create the "best impression" (the MBI and WBI scales). Comparison of test-taker scores on these scales is used to determine the presence of a possible social desirability bias. The M and W scales can also be used to determine if a

test taker's answers are more similar to those of men or women—information provided in the SCII by examining the occupational scales scores.

The KOIS includes 10 *vocational interest estimates* representing critical interest areas. According to the manual for the newest edition (Zytowski, 1985), these 10 areas are very similar to the SCII's occupational themes (see Table 11.7). The 126 occupational scale scores are reported as correlations indicating the similarity between a test taker's responses and the responses of people in each criterion group. Higher scores indicate more similar interests. Separate coefficients are reported for male and female criterion groups. Rather than categorizing occupational scores by interest areas, they are listed in order from strongest to weakest, a pattern in keeping with the test's ipsative nature.

A unique feature of the KOIS is the set of college major scales. Scores on these scales indicate the extent to which a test taker's interests are similar to those of college seniors majoring in various academic disciplines. Because some disciplines include mostly male or female majors, some scales were normed on only one gender. This creates some interpretive problems. For example, the "home economics education" scale is normed only on women. Since we know that men and women in the same field often have different interests, it is difficult to know what to recommend when a male test taker's interests are identified as similar to the interests of female home economics majors.

The KOIS demonstrates good test–retest reliability, with coefficients in the .9 range. Concurrent validity studies indicate that the KOIS occupational

TABLE 11.7   Relationship between KOIS and SCII Theme Categories

SCII Occupational Themes	KOIS Vocational Interest Estimates
Realistic	Outdoor Mechanical
Investigative	Scientific
Artistic	Artistic Musical Literary
Social	Social service
Enterprising	Persuasive
Conventional	Clerical Computational

Adapted from Zytowski (1985).

scales differentiate between groups. There is less research on the test's predictive validity, but the existing research suggests that scores are good predictors of actual career selection and satisfaction. Although there are many similarities between the SCII and the KOIS, the KOIS is a good choice if we are interested in (1) ideas about possible college majors, (2) a wider range of career options, and (3) information about the relative strengths of different interests.

Holland's Self-Directed Search.   Yes, Holland himself did develop an interest test—the Self-Directed Search (Holland, 1985b). Now that the other two popular tests have linked their scales to his model, is there any reason even to consider using another interest test? Some psychologists say yes, because of the SDS's unique design. Although the SCII and the KOIS are self-administered, both tests require scoring and interpretation by a trained examiner. As its name implies, the SDS is designed to be self-administered, self-scored, and self-interpreted. In addition, the SDS requires test takers to rate both their interests and their abilities, a feature unique to this test.

The test taker begins by completing the Self-Assessment Booklet. The 228 items include six 11-item activity lists, six 11-item lists of competencies, six 14-item lists of occupations, and two 6-item sets of self-estimates. The repeated use of the number six occurs because all activities, competencies, and occupations are organized around Holland's six occupational themes. The test taker then calculates summary scores for each of these occupational themes and uses the highest three scores to find a three-letter self-descriptive code. For example, a test taker whose three highest scores were *r*ealistic, *i*nvestigative, and *e*nterprising would be described with the code R-I-E. The code is used with the Occupations Finder, a second booklet, to identify the occupations whose codes match the test taker's.

As a relative newcomer, the SDS does not have the research history of the other two tests. Initial studies indicate good test–retest reliability for the summary scores. The few available validity studies indicate moderate relationships between SDS scores and other measures of vocational goals.

Issues in the Use of Interest Tests

You may have noticed in the preceding discussions that the reliability of interest tests is often more impressive and well documented than their validity. Furthermore, high test–retest reliability coefficients typically are obtained when people are retested over a relatively short interval (e.g., several months). These reliability and validity problems highlight some important issues in the use of interest tests.

The reliability problem is tied somewhat to the age at which interest tests are given. Interest tests are most likely to be administered to high school or

college students. After all, it is at these ages that individuals need guidance regarding possible career choices. However, interests are not necessarily stable over the course of a person's life and are particularly likely to change during the high school and college years. For example, the test–retest reliability for a 17 to 18 year old on the SCII is .8 when the individual is retested 1 year later, but drops to .7 when retested 2 to 5 years later and to .65 when retested 6 to 10 years later (Campbell, 1971). Even if we assume that career satisfaction is tied to the match between the career and personality (e.g., Holland, 1985a; Super, 1957), we may not know whether test takers are mature and self-aware.

One possible solution is to accompany interest testing with a test of vocational maturity. The most popular one is the Career Maturity Inventory (CMI), formerly called the Vocational Maturity Inventory (Crites, 1973, 1974). In addition to generating scores for vocational maturity, the CMI provides scores on relevant constructs such as attitude, knowledge of self, problem solving, and ability to look ahead toward the future.

The validity problem is due in part to the fact that interest tests measure interests, not abilities. Even the SDS, which collects information about areas of competence, provides only subjective self-report data about ability levels. To be successful in a career requires the presence of job-relevant skills. The presence of interests matching a criterion group may be important, but without the necessary abilities you may not even have an opportunity to *enter* the career you desire. Interest tests may predict job aspirations or even actual career choices, but it is difficult to predict job success solely on the basis of interest data. For this reason, vocational counseling often includes the administration of ability tests.

Ability Tests

In contrast to interest tests, which are designed to tap typical performance dimensions, ability tests are norm-referenced tests of maximal performance. They may use alternate-choice items, free-response items, or a combination of the two item types. Some ability tests used in vocational counseling, such as intelligence tests and academic achievement tests, are administered as part of evaluating educational progress and making educational placement decisions. When vocational counseling occurs in school settings, counselors are able to use this existing data as part of the guidance process. Ability tests are most likely to be administered as part of vocational counseling when (1) the counseling occurs in agency or private practice settings, meaning that counselors do not necessarily have access to ability data, (2) the ability data available are not current or up to date, or (3) the counselor is interested in obtaining information on specific job-relevant aptitudes.

Types of Ability Tests

The ability tests used most often in vocational counseling are intelligence tests, achievement tests, academic aptitude tests, and specific ability tests. Each of these tests is used in a different way. For example, intelligence tests are used to assess a person's overall level of functioning, whereas achievement tests are used to represent an individual's current level of knowledge and skills in specific curricular areas. Academic aptitude tests are designed to predict likelihood of success in settings such as college or graduate school. Specific ability tests are used to assess skill areas that are not part of the traditional academic curriculum, such as ability to interpret mechanical drawings. All four types of tests can be useful for making predictions about a person's likelihood of success in different careers.

Intelligence Tests. We have already discussed the design and scoring of intelligence tests in Chapters 9 and 10. Rather than repeat the points previously made, we will consider the following two questions:

1. What can intelligence tests tell us that is useful for career-related decisions?
2. When would we administer an intelligence test as part of vocational counseling?

Intelligence tests have two uses in vocational counseling. First, intelligence tests are designed to predict likelihood of success in traditional academic settings. Many modern careers require additional education beyond the high school level, and individuals with higher intelligence test scores are better candidates for such training. Individuals interested in business or professional careers will need to obtain graduate degrees and must therefore be comfortable and successful in educational settings.

Second, many modern intelligence tests provide a variety of scores to describe overall level of functioning. For example, the Wechsler tests generate measures on 12 different subtests, which are then combined to produce separate scores for verbal, performance, and overall (full-scale) IQ. Examining an individual's scores on the different subtests and on the verbal/performance composites is a useful strategy to develop initial hypotheses about patterns of strengths and weakness and make decisions about which additional tests to administer.

In which circumstances would we administer an intelligence test as part of vocational counseling? Intelligence tests are routinely administered to children at some point during their grade school years. Because of this trend, vocational counseling at the junior high and high schools levels rarely includes intelligence testing. However, when *adults* seek vocational counseling, such as in a college, agency, or private practice setting, counselors are less likely to have access to intelligence test data and may decide to administer an intelligence test. This point is underscored by the data in Tables 11.2 and 11.3—the Wechsler Adult Intelligence Scale is the intelligence test most likely to be administered in a counseling setting.

Even if we have access to intelligence test data, we may choose to administer an intelligence test if (1) the data were gathered at a much earlier age or (2) a group test was used. Intelligence test scores show only moderate stability over time, and scores obtained before the age of 10 are not particularly good predictors of scores at 15 or 25. In addition, although group test scores show adequate correlations with scores on individual tests, individual intelligence tests tap a much wider range of abilities.

Academic Achievement Tests.   Achievement tests are the most common standardized measures of performance in traditional curricular areas. Since we have already discussed the design of achievement tests, our present concern is the role of achievement tests in vocational counseling.

Counselors use academic achievement information the same way educators use these tests: Comparison of intelligence and achievement measures helps counselors evaluate level of achievement relative to the individual's level of aptitude. A high intelligence test score may imply that an individual is a good candidate for a career that requires college or graduate work, such as a business or professional career. But aptitude alone is not enough to succeed. By evaluating achievement in the context of aptitude, counselors can better predict if an individual is likely to succeed in a more demanding or challenging career.

When aptitude and achievement measures agree, a counselor can direct the individual to appropriate clusters of careers. The difficult issue is deciding the meaning of an aptitude/achievement discrepancy. Aptitude and achievement scores can differ for a variety of reasons. The presence of learning disability was noted in Chapter 9 as one source of an aptitude/achievement discrepancy. However, motivational issues, personal problems, and personal circumstances—such as having to work to help support one's family—also may result in lower than expected school achievement. Counselors must determine whether or not an individual who has not performed well in high school or college is likely to continue to have difficulties at the next educational level.

Vocational counselors at the high school and college level are likely to have access to academic achievement data, such as scores on the California Achievement Test (CAT). However, in contrast to the practice with intelligence tests, counselors are unlikely to administer achievement tests when adults seek vocational guidance. These tests typically are normed only through the high school level. Counselors instead are likely to request earlier test data and transcripts of prior school performance.

It might seem that intelligence test scores and measures of achievement would provide enough information for counselors to advise people about reasonable career choices. However, it is extremely difficult to make decisions about career success based solely on these two types of tests. For individuals considering college or graduate school, scores on entrance exams are likely to be better predictors of later success. And because many careers require particular *types* of ability, such as spatial or mechanical reasoning skills, counselors typically expand their pool of data by considering additional ability measures.

Entrance Exams.   Although it may not be obvious, entrance exams such as the Scholastic Aptitude Test (SAT) and the Graduate Record Exam (GRE) are similar to intelligence tests. Both types of tests are designed to predict school success. Intelligence tests are designed to measure aptitude in areas that are relevant to success in primary and secondary school. Entrance exams are designed to measure aptitude in areas that are relevant to success in higher education. They differ, however, in test domain. Intelligence tests tap a variety of reasoning and problem-solving skills, whereas entrance tests traditionally focus on verbal and quantitative reasoning. Because most vocational counseling occurs at the high school level or beyond, these other ability tests typically may be useful in career counseling than either intelligence or achievement tests.

Most colleges, graduate schools, and professional schools (e.g., law schools and medical schools) require students to take entrance exams. Counselors routinely recommend that individuals interested in these programs take the appropriate tests and use those test results when assisting people with school and career choices. The two most popular tests for predicting college success are the Scholastic Aptitude Test (SAT) and the American College Test (ACT); the two tests used most often for graduate school decisions are the Graduate Record Exam (GRE) and the Miller Analogies Test (MAT).

You may already know quite a bit about the SAT—it is the leading college ability test in the United States, given annually to over 1.5 million students. The SAT is designed to predict the potential for high school seniors to succeed in college. Using five-option multiple-choice items, the SAT produces two primary scores: a verbal score (SAT-V) and a math score (SAT-M) (Donlon, 1984). SAT-V represents performance on items covering sentence completion, antonyms, analogies, and reading comprehension; SAT-M covers items on arithmetic, algebra, and geometry. Other sections are available to test achievement in areas such as English and Biology.

Performance is represented as T-scores, with means of 500 and standard deviations of 100, and as percentile ranks. The norm group for these comparisons is the set of test takers in the original 1941 standardization sample. An SAT-V of 500 means that your raw score was equal to the average score of test takers in the 1941 sample. This use of a standard norm group simplifies the comparison of scores earned by people in different years. SAT scores are *normative*, not ipsative. If an individual earns an SAT-V of 600 and an SAT-M of 550, we can conclude that this person is more above average in verbal than in mathematical ability. We cannot necessarily conclude that the person is stronger in verbal than mathematical ability. In fact, the person could have earned the same raw scores on both subtests; the different T-scores reflect where those raw scores fell within the distribution of scores in the standardization sample.

The SAT is one of the most reliable standardized tests ever developed, with internal consistency, alternate form, and test–retest reliabilities in the .80s to .90s range. The SAT-V and SAT-M scores correlate with each other at about the .60 level, possibly because the math test includes a large number of word problems (Wallace, 1972). The criterion validity data, however, are more variable. Coefficients range from the .10s to the .60s, depending on the college and the major to which scores are compared. Remember, though, that colleges do not admit everyone who takes the SAT. As a result, data are only available on a subset of SAT examinees, and that subset shows less variability than the total pool of test takers. When variability on a measure is restricted, its potential correlations with other measures decreases. However, when SAT scores are combined with high school grades, the two together produce a multiple correlation of approximately .65 (Donlon, 1984). This means that, together, high school grades and SAT scores can predict over 40% ($.65^2$) of the variance in freshman college GPAs, a very impressive statistic.

Despite its immense popularity, the SAT is not without critics. SAT scores have been decreasing, with current SAT-V and SAT-M scores each averaging about 20 points lower now than in previous decades. Although some attribute this to a more heterogeneous pool of test takers and a lowering of high school standards, others say the problem is the test procedure itself (e.g., Morgan, 1984). SAT scores do not correlate well with the number of English or math classes a student has completed. If we assume that students who take more English and math classes will be better prepared for college, these results imply that the SAT is not capturing differences in preparedness for college (Singh, 1986). SAT also tends to be a weaker predictor for students in the middle score ranges, who in fact are likely to need the most assistance with career and educational plans.

The most common alternative to the SAT is the American College Test, or ACT. The ACT produces a composite score and separate content scores in English, math, social studies, and science. Scores are presented on a 36-point scale with a mean of 16 and a standard deviation of 5. Although the ACT covers a wider domain than the SAT, scores on the two tests are highly correlated (e.g., Pugh & Sassenrath, 1968). Compared to the SAT, however, the ACT is not as reliable a measure. Although the internal consistency for the composite score is in the .90s, the content scores show correlations in only the .70s to .80s range. In addition, the content of the ACT is tied more directly to school curricula, and critics view it as an inferior measure of general academic ability (e.g., Anastasi, 1988).

If an individual is considering graduate education, counselors turn instead to tests such as the Graduate Record Exam (GRE) and Miller Analogies Test (MAT). The GRE is the college-level equivalent of the SAT, designed to predict the graduate school success of college seniors (ETS, 1993). The GRE General Test includes measures of verbal and quantitative ability (GRE-V and GRE-M), and an analytic score (GRE-A) introduced in 1977 as a measure of logical reasoning ability. The verbal items are the same types used on the SAT. The quantitative items include SAT-type items and additional items covering quantitative comparison and interpretation of data. Analytic items include syllogisms, interpretations of logical diagrams, and abstraction of rules from sets of statements, an item type also popular on the law school admissions test.

The GRE also includes a set of achievement subtests, referred to as the GRE Subject Tests (ETS, 1993). Subject tests are available for most of the major areas of concentration at the college and graduate school levels, and new ones are added as new fields of concentration emerge. An individual interested in graduate work in anthropology would take the anthropology subject test, whereas an individual interested in psychology would take the psychology subject test. Be forewarned if you have not studied the area extensively at the undergraduate level: The subject tests are designed to tap the information that is traditionally covered in college major programs. All items are multiple-choice.

Scores are reported as T-scores with means of 500 and standard deviations of 100 and are referenced to the 1952 standardization group of test takers. A T-score of 500 on the GRE-V means you earned a raw score equal to the average raw score of test takers in the 1952 group. Three sets of percentile ranks are presented in the annual *Guide to Use of the Graduate Record Examinations Program* (e.g., ETS, 1993). One set provides the percentile ranks for T-scores based on *all* test takers during the previous 3 years. Two other sets are based on T-scores over the past 3 years for the individuals who are most similar to the typical graduate school applicant—college seniors and recent college graduates not yet enrolled in graduate school. The first of these applicant-pool tables covers the group as a whole, whereas the second breaks down the group according to the fields test takers plan to study. A given General Test score, therefore, corresponds to different percentile ranks depending on the reference group used.

Interpretation of the Subject Test T-scores is more complex. Although it is a bit difficult to follow, it is a wonderful illustration of a creative scaling approach. The test developers reasoned that it was important to link performance on the aptitude (General) and achievement (Subject) tests. Although the overall average SAT-V and SAT-M are 500, the average SAT-V and SAT-M do vary when we compare test takers in different disciplines. The strategy was to use regression equations to determine T-scores on the Subject Tests based on the average General Test T-scores for test takers in that field. These regression equations use *two* X-scores (SAT-V and SAT-M) to predict score on the subject test (Y'). For example, psychology majors in the 1952 standardization sample earned an average SAT-V of 527 and an average SAT-M of 495 (ETS, 1977). A score of 500 on the psychology test is the predicted score (Y') for psychology majors in the 1952 sample who earned an SAT-V of 527 (X_1) and an SAT-M of 495 (X_2), the average scores for psychology students on the two General Test subtests (ETS, 1977). The regression equation is generated by using these values to solve for two weights, b_1 and b_2, that are multiplied by X_1 and X_2 respectively to produce Y^1. The average score on the Psychology Subject Test is therefore directly tied to the average scores of psychology students on the General Test.

Like the SAT, the GRE is an extremely reliable test, with internal consistency coefficients in the .90s. Although some critics charge that the use of multiple-choice items reduces the test to a measure of rote memory, the items are quite complex and in fact require the analysis, synthesis, and evaluation of information. The most frequently raised concern is its predictive validity. The problem again results from restriction of variability: Criterion validity studies can only include those individuals who take the exam and are then accepted in graduate programs. In these studies, a composite of GRE verbal and math scores is significantly better than undergraduate GPA in predicting graduate school GPA, performance on department graduate exams, faculty ratings, and likelihood of completing a graduate program (e.g., Conrad, Trismen, and Miller, 1977). As was the case with the SAT, the best predictions are produced when undergraduate GPA and GRE scores are used together in a prediction equation (Anastasi, 1988).

Unlike the GRE, the Miller Analogies Test (MAT) is a strictly verbal test (Psychological Corporation, 1988). The test includes 100 analogy problems of sharply contrasting difficulty. Table 11.8 contains some analogies of the type found on the MAT. For each item, pairs of words are used to present two relationships, one of which is incomplete. The test taker must deduce the relationship in the completed pair and use that information to create a similar relationship in the other pair. The score is the total number of analogies completed correctly in 50 minutes.

The MAT is not a "pure" test of logical reasoning skill. Performance is influenced by your familiarity with both construction of analogies and the content of those analogies. For example, if you do not know the order of the letters of the Greek alphabet—as I didn't when I took the MAT—you will not be able to complete an analogy that uses Greek letters to reflect the order of events in a series. The MAT is an adequate but not psychometrically spectacular test, and many graduate programs do not use the test. Split-half reliability studies indicate coefficients in the .80s; correlations between the MAT and GRE scores are in the same range. Although the MAT alone is

TABLE 11.8   Items Similar to the Type Found on the Miller Analogies Test

(1) Sunrise : day :: sunset :
   a. evening
   b. night
   c. darkness
   d. moon

(2) Knob : door :: _____ : lid
   a. top
   b. label
   c. can
   d. can opener

(3) Saw : ten :: was :
   a. twenty
   b. tool
   c. net
   d. none

not a particularly powerful predictor of graduate school success, it is useful for discriminating between applicants who show high levels of verbal ability (Kaplan & Saccuzzo, 1993).

Specific Ability Tests.   All the preceding tests are in some way tied to school curricula and/or performance in a classroom setting. Specific ability tests are designed to tap performance in domains that are *not* part of a regular school curriculum. These tests may be administered to teen-aged or adult clients when a counselor feels that assessment of job-relevant skills will be useful to the guidance process. The most common approach in vocational counseling is to administer a multiple-aptitude test battery, a set of tests designed to tap different skill areas. The most popular multiple-aptitude batteries are the Armed Services Vocational Aptitude Battery (ASVAB), the General Aptitude Test Battery (GATB), and the Differential Aptitude Tests (DAT). Because the ASVAB and GATB are used more often in employment screening, we will discuss them in detail in Chapter 12. Our discussion here will focus on the DAT.

Prior to the development of the multiple-aptitude batteries, counselors interested in measures of specific abilities commonly administered several separate tests—similar to what educators might do in the assessment of special needs children (see p. 314). As we have said before, it is difficult to interpret sets of scores obtained from tests because they are designed for different purposes and standardized on different samples. Developed in the 1940s, the

DAT was one of the first multiple-aptitude batteries—a set of aptitude tests standardized on a single sample.

The current DAT is designed primarily for use with grades 8 to 12 (Bennett, Seashore, & Wesman, 1982). The eight tests, described in Table 11.9, were selected because of their relevance to academic and occupational choices. The battery generates a percentile band for each test plus a combined score for the verbal reasoning and numerical ability tests that correlates highly with other measures of academic aptitude (Pennock-Roman, 1985). The percentile bands are 90% confidence intervals based on the test taker's percentile rank ±1.5 standard errors.

Separate norms are used for evaluating male and female test takers. The authors recommend that students compare their scores to male norms if they are interested in male-dominated careers and to female norms if they are interested in female-dominated careers. It is extremely important that counselors help students understand the implications of their scores so that they can make reasonable career choices. Five of the tests show large sex differences: males earn higher scores on the mechanical reasoning and space relations test, whereas females earn higher scores on the language usage, spelling, and clerical speed/accuracy test. A female student with a low score on mechanical reasoning might be

TABLE 11.9   Organization of the Differential Aptitude Tests

Test	Item Type(s)	Purpose
Verbal reasoning	Verbal analogies	Assess ability to reason with words and understand ideas expressed in words
Numerical ability	Computational problems	Assess basic skills in arithmetic and algebra
Abstract reasoning	Abstract design series	Assess nonverbal reasoning, attention to detail, relational thinking
Clerical speed and accuracy	Letter/number combinations	Assess speed and accuracy of comparing letter strings and number strings
Mechanical reasoning	Pictures of devices/tools	Assess understanding of mechanical principles and laws of physics
Space relations	Unfolded figure patterns	Assess ability to determine shape, size, and orientation of an object from a pattern
Spelling	Correct/incorrect words	Assess ability to recognize correct spellings on sight
Language usage	Sentences	Assess ability to identify errors in grammar, punctuation, capitalization

Adapted from Bennett, Seashore, & Wesman (1982).

discouraged about pursuing certain careers. However, scores on the more specialized aptitude tests, such as mechanical reasoning, are likely to change if students receive additional experience and training (Pennock-Roman, 1985).

A unique feature of the DAT is the availability of an optional career planning questionnaire that assesses test-taker interest in activities and occupations. If a test taker also completes this questionnaire, an analysis of occupational choices relative to interests and abilities can be reported along with DAT scores. An mentioned earlier, an integrated assessment of abilities and interests is an extremely valuable approach to vocational counseling.

A common criticism of multiple-aptitude batteries is that they do not really measure separate or distinct aptitude areas. If the test is measuring separate aptitudes, scores on the various scales should show small correlations. If these different scales measure aptitudes that are required for job success, each scale should show high correlations with measures of job performance or performance during job training. In many cases, multiple-aptitude batteries fail on both accounts.

In the DAT, the spelling, clerical, mechanical reasoning, and space relations tests have the lowest correlations with other scales (Bennett, Seashore, and Wesman, 1982). These scales do appear to be measuring relatively distinct abilities. However, validity research indicates that the best predictor of achievement, even in specialized training courses such as industrial arts, is the verbal/numerical composite. This is attributed to the fact that the items on the specialized ability scales require specific types of knowledge and experiences. You are unlikely to score well on the mechanical reasoning test if you have not either taken physics or spent time working with tools. The verbal/numerical composite, however, is likely to capture individual differences that are not linked to the presence of specialized knowledge.

Overall, the DAT is the most psychometrically sound of the multiple-aptitude tests currently available. Its scales are internally consistent, with reliability coefficients in the high .80s to low .90s. It provides a good predictor of performance in job training—the verbal/numerical composite—and its specialized aptitude scales for the most part appear to measure separate aptitude areas. These features, combined with the availability of an integrated aptitude/interest assessment, make it the most popular aptitude battery for vocational counseling.

Issues in the Use of Ability Tests

The key point in a discussion of ability tests is to emphasize the importance of collecting and evaluating appropriate data. When working with junior high or high school students, measures such as intelligence test and achievement test scores can provide useful information about the feasibility of different career paths. As the age of the individual increases, these measures become less useful than measures like grades, scores on specific ability tests, and scores on entrance exams.

Specific ability tests are most useful for counseling noncollege-bound students. The areas covered by these tests are more relevant to predicting success in skilled jobs than in business or professional careers. In fact, scores on these tests can help identify students whose interests would be best served by entering a technical school or a vocational training program.

For those considering college and/or graduate school, GPAs and scores on entrance exams are the most important counseling data. Most colleges and graduate schools develop their own cutoffs for measures like undergraduate GPA and SAT/GRE/MAT scores, and these cutoffs may vary within a school according to program. Counselors should consult published data about recommended scores when discussing options with their clients.

Two points are raised in discussions of why entrance exams are so influential in selection decisions (e.g., Kaplan & Saccuzzo, 1993). First, many colleges and graduate schools see grades as inflated. Their claim is based on the fact that high school and undergraduate GPAs are rising at the same time as SAT scores are declining. In addition to higher average GPAs, the *range* of GPAs is narrowing, reducing the variability of this measure and thus its ability to capture individual differences between students. Second, amendments to the federal Freedom of Information Act, passed in the 1970s, and the Family Educational Rights and Privacy Act, passed in 1974, give students the right to inspect their files, including their letters of recommendation. Although this right is restricted to students who actually enroll in a college or graduate program, there is concern that faculty may write less candid letters because they know that someday the students might read them.

PERSONAL COUNSELING

The goal of personal counseling is to assist people in making choices and changes to improve their sense of well-being and life-styles (Pietrofesa, Hoffman, & Splete, 1984). In addition to exploring career-related issues, counseling may focus on personal issues such as improving interpersonal relationships or increasing self-awareness. Most personal counseling occurs in college or university counseling centers, in agencies, or in private practice settings. Although counseling psychologists also use techniques such as clinical interview, tests are an important part of this process. Tests provide an opportunity to obtain standardized individual difference information that can be useful both for treatment planning and promoting clients' understanding of themselves.

In contrast to the diagnostic orientation of clinical psychologists, counseling psychologists are likely to help clients explore the structure of their personalities and seek ways to improve their lives by building on personality strengths (see Table 11.1). Counseling psychologists, therefore, are more likely than clinical psychologists to use objective personality tests and attitude scales.

Personality Tests

According to Tables 11.2 and 11.3, the personality tests used most frequently are the MMPI, the TAT, the Sixteen Personality Factor Questionnaire, the California Psychological Inventory, and the Edwards. We will not discuss the MMPI, the Edwards, and the TAT again; these tests were described in Chapter 10. Instead, we will focus on the other two tests and a third test, the Myers–Briggs, that has been identified as useful in counseling scenarios (Lowman, 1991). In addition to being popular tests, the three tests represents different approaches to test construction. One uses the criterion-group approach, one uses the factor-analytic approach, and one uses the theoretical approach.

California Psychological Inventory

The California Psychological Inventory (CPI) was originally developed in the 1970s and has become one of the most popular tests using a criterion-group approach (Gough, 1975, 1987). The CPI consists of 462 true/false items, over one-third of which are similar to items on the MMPI. However, the CPI is designed to evaluate the structure of personality in normal individuals, rather than to identify the presence of clinical syndromes.

The CPI generates scores on three validity scales and 17 personality scales. Four of the 17 personality scales were developed through the logical content strategy in which items were subjectively grouped and the scales checked for internal consistency. The remaining 13 were developed using criterion groups contrasted in terms of dimensions such as course grades, social class membership, and participation in extracurricular activities. The scales are grouped into four broad categories based primarily on conceptual similarity, as shown in Table 11.10. A new interpretive model has been developed that focuses on three broad themes identified in subsequent factor analysis of the 20 scales (Gough, 1987): (1) introversion–extroversion, (2) favoring/following versus doubting/rejecting conventional norms, and (3) self-realization and sense of integration.

Test–retest reliability of CPI scales ranges from .57 to .77, which is comparable to scale reliabilities for the MMPI. Reviews of research (e.g., Megargee, 1972) indicate adequate validity compared to similar tests and identify the class 1 (interpersonal effectiveness) and class 2 (internal controls) scales as particularly important in capturing the extent of individual differences in personality. From a psychometric standpoint, the CPI is the "normal personality" analog of the MMPI, making it one of the most popular objective personality tests.

TABLE 11.10   Scales of the CPI

Class 1: Interpersonal effectiveness

Dominance   Self-acceptance
Capacity for status   Independence
Sociability   Empathy
Social presence

Class 2: Internal controls

Responsibility   Good impression[a]
Socialization   Well-being[a]
Self-control   Communality[a]
Tolerance

Class 3: Cognitive and intellectual functioning

Achievement via conformance
Achievement via independence
Intellectual efficiency

Class 4: Thinking and behavior

Psychological mindedness
Flexibility
Femininity–masculinity

---

[a]These are validity scales corresponding to "fake good," "fake bad," and frequency of popular responses.
Adapted from Gough (1975).

Sixteen Personality Factor Questionnaire

The Sixteen Personality Factor Questionnaire (16PF) is designed to measure basic personality dimensions or traits and is a monument to the use of factor analysis in test construction (Cattell, 1949; Cattell, Eber, & Tatsuoka, 1970). In contrast to the criterion-group strategy, factor analysis examines the patterns of correlations between scores on different items to identify the items most similar to each other and most unlike each other (see p. 104). Through factor analysis, Cattell hoped to identify the smallest number of terms necessary to capture the extent of individual differences in personality.

Cattell began with a list of more than 4000 adjectives used to describe people in dictionaries and psychological/psychiatric literature. The list was reduced to 171 items by eliminating obvious synonyms, and college students were asked to rate their friends using each of the 171 terms. The resulting data were factor analyzed to identify the distinct concepts or factors represented by these terms. Cattell repeated the rating and factor analysis procedures until the

TABLE 11.11   Source Traits Measured by the 16PF

Dimension	Sample Descriptors
Cool–warm	Reserved, formal versus outgoing, kindly
Concrete–abstract thinking	Less intelligent versus more intelligent, bright
Affected by feelings– emotionally stable	Easily annoyed versus calm, mature
Submissive–dominant	Easily led, accommodating versus assertive
Sober–enthusiastic	Restrained, prudent versus spontaneous
Expedient–conscientious	Self-indulgent versus rule-bound, staid
Shy–bold	Hesitant, intimated versus venturesome
Tough–tender minded	Realistic versus sensitive, intuitive
Trusting–suspicious	Accepting conditions versus skeptical
Practical–imaginative	Steady versus absorbed in thought
Forthright–shrewd	Unpretentious, open versus calculating
Self-assured– apprehensive	Secure, self-satisfied versus insecure, self-blaming
Conservative– experimenting	Respecting traditional ideas versus critical, liberal
Group oriented– self-sufficient	Listens to others versus prefers own decisions
Undisciplined self-conflict– following self-image	Lax, careless of social rules versus socially precise, compulsive
Relaxed–tense	Composed, unfrustrated versus has high drive, frustrated

Adapted from Cattell, Ebert, & Tatsuoka (1970).

data were reduced to a set of 16 factors he called *source traits*. The 16 source traits are listed in Table 11.11.

Nine sets of norms are available for the 16PF, including men only, women only, and combined men/women at three different age ranges (adults, college students, and high school students). Age corrections are available for scales on which performance changes with age. The demographic characteristics of the standardization group (e.g., geographic region and race) reflect data provided by the U.S. Census Bureau. Alternate forms are available for individuals at various levels of literacy, as is an oral (tape recorded) form for nonreaders and the visually handicapped. A "motivational distortion" key is also available to check on possible response bias.

Although the short-term test–retest coefficients for the various scales average around .8, the longer-term coefficients, the split-half coefficients, and the alternate-form coefficients are significantly lower. In addition, many psychologists question whether the personality factors identified by the 16PF really are the basic or "source traits" of personality. For example, in spite of the use of factor analysis to construct scales, the various scale scores are somewhat correlated. A set of four "second-order" factor scores has been developed through factor analysis of the original 16 dimensions, which can be used instead. In general, psychologists see the MMPI as significantly more useful for evaluating personality dimensions.

Myers–Briggs Type Indicator

Although it is not listed in Tables 11.2 and 11.3 as one of the frequently used tests, the Myers–Briggs Type Indicator (MBTI) deserves special mention in a chapter on counseling (Myers, 1977). The MBTI is a personality test that can be useful in predicting vocational preference when used along with interest and ability tests (Lowman, 1991). Furthermore, the MBTI represents a different approach to test construction than either the CPI or the 16PF. The MBTI is a theoretically constructed test (see p. 103) based on Carl Jung's theory of personality types. A *personality type* is a category defined by a cluster of personality and behavioral characteristics. Psychologists who emphasize personality types frequently are contrasted with those who emphasize personality traits. A *personality trait* is a dimension of personality. Traits predispose people to respond to stimuli in particular ways, but trait psychologists do not see these dimensions as (1) occurring in clusters or (2) defining categories of people (types).

Basically, Jung proposed that people differ in the extent to which they favor specific modalities or ways of learning about the world (Myers, 1976). The modalities we prefer define a category or personality type that characterizes our thoughts, feelings, and behaviors. The MBTI uses forced-choice items to determine personality type within this model by determining where people fall on four basic dimensions representing Jungian modalities: introversion–extroversion, sensing–intuition, thinking–feeling, and judgment–perception. Because of the forced-choice format, the MBTI generates ipsative (relative) measures that identify the dominant modalities in order of strength. For example, an ESFP is a person whose predominant modes are extroversion (E), sensation (S), feeling (F), and perception (P). These modality preferences are viewed as important determinants of our interests, values, and motivation.

The MBTI has been normed on over 2000 individuals in grades 4 through 12 and shows split-half reliabilities in the .7 to .8 range. Although many psychologists dislike the rigidity implied by viewing people as possessing personality "types," the MBTI has acquired a small but faithful following in the world of counseling. It is particularly relevant to the study of personality during the junior high and high school years and, therefore, can be a useful adjunct test in both personal and vocational counseling.

Issues in the Use of Personality Tests

The tests discussed in this section represent a variety of approaches to assessing the personalities of ordinary people, yet in no case has an "ideal" test been constructed. In fact, many psychologists question whether it is possible to develop good measures of normal personality. All personality tests must be developed through one or more scale construction processes, and each process has its flaws. We may dislike the theoretical approach because it requires us to agree with a particular orientation, such as Jung's view of people as falling into different personality types. We may favor the use of empirical procedures because their emphasis on scientific method seems likely to produce a superior product. But even empirically developed tests have problems. For example, many psychologists question the criterion group data used to develop the CPI scales because some of the criterion groups were created by having friends rate the group members, a not particularly objective procedure.

Furthermore, it appears extremely difficult to develop tests that measure separate or distinct dimensions of normal personality. Despite its use of criterion groups, the personality scales on the CPI do correlate with each other. Even the 16PF, developed through factor analysis, does not generate statistically distinct personality scales. If we cannot produce independent scales, maybe personality *does* occur in categories or "types." And back into the circle we go.

We can improve the counseling process by using a variety of types of information in the quest to understand our clients, including several different tests and other techniques, such as interview. And we can increase the likelihood that testing provides useful data by carefully matching the properties of the test to the counseling scenario itself. We can make sure that the test provides data on the dimensions we want to explore and that the test was standardized on people similar to those we are evaluating. For example, if we want to measure both dimensions of normal personality and identify possible psychological disorders, we can administer the 16PF along with the Clinical Analysis Questionnaire, which adds 12 new factors designed to assess clinical syndromes (Delhees & Cattell, 1971). If we are working with junior high or high school clients, we can consider using downward extensions of popular tests, such as the Personality Inventory for Children (Wirt & Lachar, 1981), a CPI-like test for ages 6 to 16. By making sure we use tests in appropriate and responsible ways, even less than ideal tests can contribute to the counseling process.

Attitude and Other Scales

Other types of tests can also be useful in counseling settings. Remember that our goal is to help an individual develop self-awareness and the skills to make decisions and solve personal problems. Scales that measure aspects either of personality or life-style can identify characteristics and events that may contribute to an individual's problems.

Probably the best example of such a scale is the Social Readjustment Rating Scale (SRRS), designed to explore the extent of stress an individual has experienced (Holmes & Rahe, 1967). The SRRS lists 43 stressful events, such as getting married and changing jobs. These events were rated as to amount and intensity of readjustment required by a standardization sample. The most stressful event—death of a spouse—was given a rating of 100 *life change units*. Each other event was assigned points by comparing its rated stressfulness to death of a spouse. For example, death of a spouse was rated twice as stressful as getting married; getting married thus was assigned 50 "life change units." When it is administered, individuals mark the events that have occurred within a specific interval, usually the past 6 or 12 months. The events marked generate a total life stress score for that period of time.

In addition to research applications, such as investigating the role of stress in child abuse and in illness, the SRRS is useful for helping clients recognize the extent to which stress is contributing to their personal circumstances. Other psychologists have developed alternative questionnaires that are specifically suited to different subgroups of people. The College Schedule of Recent Experiences (Marx, Garrity, & Bowers, 1975) lists 47 events that frequently occur during college years, such as change in major, change in dating, and trouble with parents. Each is given a stress rating, and the total score is based on the stress score for each event times the number of times the event has occurred.

Personality and attitude scales can be used to help clients recognize the extent to which personal characteristics contribute to their problems or patterns of behavior. Although personality tests such as the CPI explore a variety of characteristics, many specific personality and attitude dimensions are not covered by these tests. Scales are available for such characteristics as shyness, self-esteem, powerlessness, trust in people, embarrassability, authoritarianism, and sex roles (e.g., Robinson, Shaver, & Wrightsman, 1991).

Issues in the Use of Scales

Attitude, life events, and personality scales can be useful in the course of personal counseling. They can help underscore points about an individual's life or personality that are revealed by other assessments and bring to light new information that is not provided by other measures. However, the scales in this category vary enormously in their reliability and validity. Although some, such as the Tennessee Self-Concept Scale (Roid & Fitts, 1988), are backed by decades of published technical research, others are recent developments with small standardization samples and little psychometric information. The key to using scales effectively is to ensure that the scales selected are reasonable measures of their stated domains. Even in an area like counseling, there is no substitute for reading technical manuals and published research.

SUMMARY AND KEY CONCEPTS

In contrast to clinical settings, professionals in counseling settings focus on the identification of abilities, personality characteristics, and interests to help people improve their sense of well-being and make life-style decisions. Although many types of professionals engage in counseling, a counseling psychologist is specifically trained both in psychological assessment and in a variety of treatment approaches.

The two primary activities in counseling settings are vocational or career counseling and personal counseling. Interest tests are an important component of career counseling; there are good tests available for both normative and ipsative assessment, for suggesting possible careers and college majors, and for individuals interested in technical or skilled jobs. Because success in a career involves both interest in that type of work and particular abilities, vocational counseling may also involve administration of ability tests. The ability tests most useful in career counseling include intelligence tests, achievement tests, entrance exams, and specific ability tests, the most popular of which are multiple-aptitude test batteries.

In personal counseling, tests are used to explore the structure of personality both for increasing client self-awareness and for planning the course of treatment. In contrast to the tests used in clinical settings, these tests focus on typical personality dimensions rather than clinical syndromes. Some tests, such as the CPI and the 16PF, focus on the analysis of personality traits— particular patterns of responding to environmental events. For example, the 16PF identifies where individuals fall on a series of dimensions called source traits. Other tests, such as the Myers–Briggs, classify individuals into groups known as personality types.

Scales that measure individual attitudes, personal qualities, or life events can complement or expand on the information provided by personality tests. However, in some cases these scales are neither as reliable nor as valid as the tests used for overall personality assessment. In counseling, as in all other scenarios, the effective use of psychological tests depends on the user's ability to identify good measurement instruments.

QUESTIONS

11.1   List four ways in which tests could be used in counseling settings.

11.2   Describe how the interest scores produced by the Strong–Campbell differ from the interest scores produced by the Kuder.

11.3   What explanations have been proposed for the low test–retest reliability and predictive validity of interest tests?

11.4   Describe the circumstances in which intelligence and achievement test scores would contribute to the process of career counseling.

11.5   Explain why colleges and graduate programs continue to emphasize entrance exams in their selection processes.

11.6   What is the advantage gained by using a multiple-aptitude battery rather than a series of separate aptitude tests?

11.7   Contrast the design of the CPI with the design of the 16PF. What are the advantages and limitations of each design approach?

11.8   How does the purpose of the Myers–Briggs differ from other tests such as the CPI and the 16PF?

11.9   Why might a professional decide to use other types of scales in addition to personality tests?

11.10   What factors should be considered before deciding to use additional personality, attitude, or life events scales?

CHAPTER 12

Testing in Business and Industry

CHAPTER OUTLINE

CHAPTER GOALS AND OBJECTIVES

After completing this chapter you should be able to:

- List and describe the ways tests are used in business and industry.
- Identify the types of reliability and validity important for different testing scenarios.
- Contrast the use of tests with the use of interviews in employee selection and describe the advantages and limitations of each technique.
- Describe the use of ability tests, work sample tests, and integrity tests in the selection of employees and the issues raised by each type of test.
- Discuss the problems associated with validating selection tests.
- Describe the use of productivity measures, personnel measures, and evaluation scales in the assessment of job performance and the issues surrounding the use of each measure.
- Describe federal regulation of selection and performance testing and the impact of these regulations.
- Describe the use of human factors studies, organizational studies, and marketing studies in the evaluation of business activities.

The final scenario to consider in our discussion of test use is the world of business and industry. Many businesses and corporations employ psychologists to screen job applicants, to evaluate employees, or to assess the effectiveness of company operations. In terms of training, these psychologists are most likely to have either a master's or doctoral degree in industrial/organizational (I/O) psychology, an applied field focused on the application of psychological research to the world of work. Industrial/organizational psychologists comprise about 7% of the membership of the American Psychological Association (Stapp & Fulcher, 1983). This chapter will focus on the ways psychologists and others use tests in the workplace and the issues surrounding the use of tests.

USES OF TESTS IN BUSINESS AND INDUSTRY

When psychological tests are used in the workplace, our primary concern is the selection or construction of tests that are reliable and valid for the task at hand. This seemingly simple statement has wide-ranging implications. For example, if a single test will be used repeatedly to evaluate employees, the test must possess adequate test–retest reliability. On the other hand, if a test with two forms will be used to screen applicants, such that some will receive one form and some will receive the other, the two forms must have alternate-form reliability. If a multidimensional test will be used, generating scores on several different subscales, the scales must be internally consistent.

In terms of validity, a primary concern is criterion validity. In many business applications, tests are used to predict the future performance of test takers. The prediction may relate to a job applicant's likelihood of success in the job (a hiring decision) or an employee's likelihood of success in a new position (a promotion decision). Construct and content validity are important when tests are used to measure variables such as employee attitudes about the workplace or consumer attitudes about products and programs. In this section, we will examine the specific ways tests are used and the factors to consider in each scenario.

Selection of New Employees

At some point, nearly every business is faced with the task of selecting new employees. In a small business, the selection process is likely to be conducted by the owner. In larger businesses and corporations, the process typically is coordinated by the personnel officer, who may be an I/O psychologist or a psychologist hired on a contract basis. The ideal scenario is a multistage process in which the business (1) identifies the specific tasks to be performed by the new employees using the process of job analysis (see p. 49), (2) develops a description of the job based on the job analysis, (3) recruits applicants, (4) evaluates the applicants, and (5) selects the new employees based on the evaluation data (Wise, 1989).

Job applicants routinely are required to complete application forms, submit letters of reference, and be interviewed. The use of psychological tests, such as ability tests, is more variable. Research indicates a recent decline in the use of testing for applicant screening. In a survey of members of the American Society of Personnel Administrators (Tenopyr, 1981), approximately 75% of the respondents indicated that they did less employee testing than they had done 5 years earlier. Only 60% of companies with 25,000 or more employees used at least one psychological test, and only 39% of companies with fewer than 100 employees used a psychological test. The decline has been attributed to the increased regulation of test use by professional societies, lawmakers, and the courts and to business' general distrust of paper-and-pencil tests.

Evaluation of Current Employees

Evaluation of job performance by current employees serves several important functions. Assessment of job performance is a necessary component of decisions about raises and promotions. It also can provide feedback to employees, communicating information about employer expectations and employee performance relative to these expectations. In addition, job performance evaluations may provide valuable input to the process of job analysis (Wise, 1989). For example, the results of an employee evaluation may lead a business to revise its definition of the tasks comprising a given job. An evaluation might indicate that the job is poorly defined or includes too many tasks, making it difficult for employees to be successful.

Performance evaluation may be a formalized, ongoing process that occurs at periodic intervals or a more informal, occasional event. Many businesses evaluate their employees on a regular basis and compile the results of these performance evaluations in each employee's personnel file. Regardless of the procedure and mechanism used, all individuals can be expected to be evaluated at some point during their employment. In its ideal form, performance evaluation centers around the tasks identified in the job analysis written when applicants were recruited. Measures are selected or constructed for each job task and are considered together for decisions about the adequacy of job performance. Performance evaluations typically focus on rating scales.

Evaluation of Programs and Products

Psychological tests are also used to evaluate aspects of the workplace itself or to evaluate the goods and services provided by a business. Evaluation of the workplace involves two separate issues. *Human factors research* assesses the impact of the work environment on employee behavior and seeks to identify ways to improve employee performance by modifying that environment (McCormick & Sanders, 1982). For example, psychological tests could be used to determine how the redesign of a console affects an individual's ability to operate a machine or how workers are affected by variables such as lighting, noise, and temperature. Because we know that behavior, such as a worker's level of productivity, is influenced by attitudes, human factors research also examines how changes to the environment affect employee satisfaction. Human factors research, therefore, could investigate how the addition of an employee lounge on each floor affects employee's morale. Human factors studies may use observational techniques, experimental manipulations incorporating skills tests, and attitude scales.

Evaluation of the workplace also involves *organizational research*. The employees of a business or industry constitute a group of people working within a hierarchical structure. Their attitudes and behavior are affected by both the characteristics of that structure and the dynamics that emerge as employees interact with each other (Siegel & Lane, 1982). In organizational research, we examine issues such as supervisor–worker relationships, opportunities for workers to be involved in business decisions, and conflict resolution processes. The goal is to identify aspects of organizational structure and dynamics that contribute to productivity and satisfaction and organizational elements that need to be changed. Organizational studies may involve observational research, interviews, and the administration of attitude scales.

In contrast to research evaluating the characteristics of the workplace, *marketing research* is used to determine the success or likely future success of a product or service. Rather than focusing on workers, marketing research targets consumers, usually through attitude scales and product field testing (Schiffman & Kanuck, 1983). Data generated through marketing studies may be used to revise the design of a product or the delivery of a service or as the basis for later advertising campaigns.

PROCEDURES FOR SELECTING NEW EMPLOYEES

Although the use of testing in employee selection has declined, it is estimated that about two-thirds of companies in the United States use some form of written test in the selection process (Friedman & Williams, 1982). The administration of a test, however, does not necessarily indicate its importance in the decision process. In fact, when tests are used, their role in the process is extremely variable (Tenopyr, 1981). Written tests are more common and more emphasized for office positions and positions involving specific skills than for production and sales jobs. Applicants for clerical positions represent the most heavily tested group, followed by applicants for skilled positions such as electrician or mechanic. In contrast, screening for management positions relies heavily on credentials, interviews, and letters of reference. The use of testing also varies as a function of employer. Public sector jobs, such as civil service jobs, jobs with state, county, and local government, and jobs within the military, routinely require psychological testing (Friedman & Williams, 1982).

Selection Testing versus Employment Interviews

Psychological testing and employment interviews are common but very different approaches to the selection of new employees. It is useful, therefore, to reflect on the relative merits of each technique. The popularity of interview reflects its simplicity, its flexibility, and its ability to provide information not available through testing. It is unfortunate, however, that the current trend is for companies to rely more on interview and less on testing. Testing is an objective assessment procedure using standardized content, standardized ad-

ministration, and standardized scoring. Tests are an efficient and effective way
to obtain the same information, under the same conditions, about all applicants
for a job. Good published tests are available for employment screening with
reliability coefficients at or above .8 and validity coefficients at or above .6.
On the other hand, interview is a subjective technique in which both content
and administration may vary. In fact, this flexibility was just cited as one
of the strengths of the interview process. It is, however, a two-edged sword.
Research on employment interviews identifies some serious reliability and validity problems that occur most often when interviewers *do* vary the content
and administration of questions. As a result, most psychologists recommend
the use of structured employment interviews.

In *structured interviews*, a predetermined set of questions is posed to all
applicants in a specific order. *Unstructured interviews* are more like clinical
interviews (see p. 342), using broad, open-ended questions whose content and
sequence is determined largely by the applicant's earlier answers. One obvious
difference is the nature of the information gathered. Structured interviews
lead to the collection of comparable data on all applicants that facilitates the
process of evaluating individual differences. Structured interviews are also more
likely to lead to potential agreement among different interviewers, a measure
of interview reliability, and accurate predictions about future performance, a
measure of interview validity (Wiesner & Cronshaw, 1988). Research indicates
that both the reliability and validity of structured interviews are twice that of
unstructured interviews (Harris, 1989).

Even when a structured format is used, interviews are open to a variety
of sources of potential bias that threaten their reliability and validity. People
tend to form first impressions rapidly in interpersonal encounters, and first
impressions exert a powerful influence over our processing of later information (e.g., Lyman, Hatlelid, & MacCundy, 1981). We tend to focus more on
information that confirms our impression and to discount information that runs
counter to it. Interviewers often form a quick first impression based on an
obvious or outstanding characteristic of an applicant and may compound the
problem by making inappropriate inferences from those features. For example,
an applicant's personal appearance may be used as the basis for inferences
about level of intelligence (Gilmore, Beehr, & Love, 1986). In a similar way,
interviewers may make quick judgments about a person's characteristics on
the basis of gender, ethnic group, social class, or cultural heritage (Sattler,
1993). Finally, interviews are particularly susceptible to the "halo effect," in
which a single, general impression leads an interviewer to form a favorable or
unfavorable attitude early in the interview process (Cooper, 1981).

Although interview is prone to the classic problems of subjective assessment techniques, it can be a valuable source of information during the
screening process. When interviewers are trained to focus on evaluation of

specific applicant characteristics, the reliability and validity of judgments improve (Dougherty, Ebert, & Callender, 1986). Furthermore, when interviewers use a structured format, validity coefficients often are close to .7 (Harris, 1989).

On the other hand, research comparing the use of standardized tests, interviews, biographical information, letters of reference, and work samples clearly identifies standardized tests as a superior technique (e.g., Reilly & Chao, 1982). According to a report by the National Academy of Sciences (Wigdor & Garner, 1982), although each technique has merits, none of the alternatives to standardized tests is as informative, fair, and psychometrically sound.

Types of Tests

The tests used to select employees may be written or performance based. The two types represent a distinction between the use of signs and the use of samples (Wernimont & Campbell, 1968). An applicant's score on a clerical test is viewed as a *sign* or indicator of potential success in the job. The inference is based on theoretical and research support for a relationship between the abilities tested and the tasks comprising the job. However, an applicant's performance on a series of clerical tasks provides an actual *sample* of job-relevant behaviors. As the old maxim in psychology states, "Nothing predicts behavior like behavior." Research on performance-based or **work sample tests** suggests that they are often better predictors than written ability tests (e.g., Reilly & Chao, 1982).

Integrity tests address a separate issue in employee selection. Integrity tests are designed to predict a candidate's likely level of honesty and trustworthiness. Over the past few decades, employers have become increasingly concerned with these issues. In some cases, employees may be placed in positions where they have access to sensitive or confidential information. Employers naturally want to ensure that the individuals selected for these jobs can be trusted. In other cases, the concern is based more on economics. Businesses have become increasingly concerned about protecting themselves from all types of employee theft, ranging from pilfering of office supplies to embezzlement. As the use of integrity tests has increased, questions have been raised about the validity of these tests as predictors of employee behavior patterns.

Ability Tests

The ability tests used in employee selection fall into several categories: general ability or intelligence tests, aptitude test batteries, and tests of specific aptitudes. Research on popular tests in each category indicates that employers are most likely to use tests of specific aptitudes and that these tests are most likely to make accurate and useful predictions about an applicant's potential job performance.

General Ability Tests.   The general ability or intelligence tests used tend to be paper-and-pencil, relatively short, group tests such as the Wonderlic Personnel Test. The Wonderlic is a 50-item multiple-choice test of mental ability normed on a sample of 50,000 individuals 20 to 65 years old. The Wonderlic includes verbal, mathematical, pictorial, and analytic items and is available in five different forms. Alternate form and split-half reliabilities typically exceed .9, and scores correlate with performance in a variety of jobs (Dodrill & Warner, 1988; Murphy, 1984a).

Multiple-aptitude Batteries.   Three popular multiple-aptitude batteries used in employment testing are the Armed Services Vocational Aptitude Battery (ASVAB), the General Aptitude Test Battery (GATB), and the Differential Aptitude Tests (DAT). Designed for the Department of Defense, the ASVAB is used in both educational and military settings. The 10 subtests are grouped into three academic composites—academic ability, verbal, and math—and four occupational composites: mechanical and crafts, business and clerical, electronics and electrical, and health, social, and technology. Data from the 1980 revision indicate that the internal consistency coefficients for composite scores average close to .9 and that the test is a valid predictor of performance during job training.

The problem with the ASVAB lies in the relationship between the composite scores. Since each composite score is designed to measure a different type of aptitude, we would expect to find very small correlations between the composite scores. In fact, the average correlation between composite scores is .86. The high correlations reflect the fact that the same subtest may be part of several different composite scores. For example, the score on the Arithmetic Reasoning subtest is used in computation of five of the seven composite scores. This parallels the problem discussed in Chapter 10 (see p. 348): The scoring of items on more than one subscale leads to the creation of scales that are not independent. The high correlation between composite scores makes it difficult to view these as measures of distinct aptitudes. The ASVAB composites are more like multiple measures of overall level of aptitude (Murphy, 1984b).

It is possible, however, to develop batteries that do measure multiple aptitudes. The General Aptitude Test Battery or GATB includes 12 separate tests that yield a score on general mental ability and scores on eight different factors: verbal, numerical, and spatial aptitudes, form perception, clerical perception, motor coordination, manual dexterity, and finger dexterity. In contrast to the ASVAB, the average intercorrelation between these nine scores is only .24. Furthermore, the correlations between the motor tests, like finger dexterity, and the intellectual tests, like verbal aptitude, are close to 0. We can explain this in part by noting the use of the word *factors* to describe the subscales at the beginning of the paragraph. The GATB scales were developed through a factor analytic procedure. As discussed in Chapter 4 (see p. 104), factor analysis is designed to generate a set of subscales that are as independent (uncorrelated) as possible.

The GATB has been used routinely by the Department of Labor and state employment services. However, on July 10, 1990, the Department of Labor (DOL) announced that it would discontinue using the GATB because it appeared to be a discriminatory test. African-American and Hispanic-American test takers typically score lower on the test than nonminority individuals, a possible indication of differential validity (see p. 328). Because of the group score differences, the DOL had been using separate scoring criteria for minority and nonminority groups, a procedure endorsed in a 1989 report by the National Academy of Sciences reviewing research on the GATB (APA, 1990a). Norm-referenced scores for minority group members were generated by comparing the performance of minority applicants to the performance of others within their specific ethnic groups. However, the Academy report did raise questions about the merits of these score adjustments, and provisions within the pending Civil Rights Act, subsequently passed in 1991, prohibited the use of score adjustments. The Department of Labor felt that it had no alternative but to suspend use of the GATB until the test could be revised and thoroughly researched.

Both the ASVAB and GATB are hindered by psychometric problems—the ASVAB in the independence of composite scores, the GATB in the prediction of performance for minority group members. A third test, the Differential Aptitude Tests (DAT), is a possible alternative for applicant screening. As discussed in Chapter 11 (see p. 394), the DAT was designed for educational and vocational counseling with high school students, and includes eight tests designed to tap aptitudes that are relevant to academic or occupational choices. However, the DAT has been criticized as a tool for employee selection because few studies are available on the relationship between DAT scores and measures of actual job performance (Bennett, Seashore, & Wesman, 1982). Until additional criterion validity studies are conducted, it is unlikely that the DAT will fill the gap created by reduced use of the other two tests.

Tests of Specific Aptitudes.   Unlike the multiple-aptitude batteries, tests for specific aptitudes are generally valid and useful predictors of future job performance. This should not be surprising since each test focuses on specific skill areas whose direct relevance to a job can easily be determined. Since we identified clerical and skilled technical jobs as the two cases in which written tests are likely to be used, we will illustrate this category using the Minnesota Clerical Test and the Bennett Mechanical Comprehension Test.

The Minnesota Clerical Test (MCT) is designed to measure perceptual speed and accuracy. It falls into the category of speed tests described in Chapter 2 (see p. 34). All items are short and straightforward, and individual differences are reflected in the number of items answered correctly within a strict time limit. Its two subtests, number comparison and name comparison, are composed of pairs of numbers or names that must be identified as the same or different. In both subtests, the "different" items vary in only a minor detail such as a single digit or a single letter in the spelling of a name. Test–retest reliability usually is at least .7, and scores correlate well with later ratings of job performance by supervisors. However, the source of these criterion validity relationships is uncertain. The test may be a good predictor because it is tapping a cognitive difference in speed of mental operations, not because it presents tasks similar to what clerical workers actually do (Murphy & Davidshofer, 1988).

The Bennett Mechanical Comprehension Test is designed to measure mechanical knowledge and mechanical reasoning. Using pictorial multiple-choice items varying in level of difficulty, test takers are required to answer questions about the operation of machines, tools, and vehicles and to solve problems by applying the principles of physics and mechanics. In addition to generating internal consistency coefficients in the .8 to .9 range, the test is an excellent predictor both of performance in job training courses and later job performance (Ghiselli, 1966).

Work Sample Tests

The use of work samples in employee selection is a long-standing tradition. For example, an advertising company looking for a graphic designer invariably requires each candidate to bring a portfolio of previous work. **Work sample tests** represent an effort to standardize the collection of work samples. All applicants are required to perform the same tasks under the same conditions, facilitating the collection of comparable data and the assessment of individual differences in ability. Because the work samples are obtained during application for a job, it is reasonable to assume that candidates are motivated to do their best. Work sample tests, therefore, should be viewed as tests of maximal performance.

Work sample tests range from performance of simple tasks to performance in complex scenarios. A candidate for a typing position might be required to type a 400-word letter, whereas a candidate for a pilot's job might be required to navigate a route via a flight simulator. The key to designing or selecting a valid work sample test is to select tasks that are actual elements of the job itself. This requires writing a detailed job analysis that identifies the components of the job and selecting a representative sample of these tasks for the work sample test. In essence, the criterion validity of these tests is a function of their content validity (Asher & Sciarrino, 1974). If the tasks measured in the work sample test are a representative sample of the job tasks (content validity), performance on the work sample test is likely to predict future job performance (criterion validity).

It is easy to see how we could develop a work sample test for a skill-based job. It may be more difficult to imagine designing a work sample job for a managerial position. In fact, samples of management behaviors can be obtained through a variety of techniques and are useful predictors of performance as a manager (Cascio, 1982). A popular technique is the *in-basket test* (Frederickson, 1961), a simulation task in which each candidate is asked to respond to a collection of memos, letters, notes, and other materials in a manager's in-basket. Each applicant must actually do whatever is necessary to handle the tasks defined by the contents of the basket—write letters and memos, set up an agenda of meetings, and the like. Responses can be scored in terms of the priorities each applicant sets, based on the order of handling tasks, responses to critical incidents or issues, and overall effectiveness in accomplishing the designated tasks.

Integrity Tests

Employers understandably are concerned about the honesty and trustworthiness of potential employees. Until recently, these concerns could only be addressed through on-the-job surveillance, subjective judgments, or use of a polygraph (lie detector) test. Video surveillance is an expensive procedure and can offend employees and produce a hostile work environment. Lesser forms of surveillance, such as requiring supervisor approval for purchases paid by check, are less effective and often annoying to customers. Subjective judgments based on application forms, letters of reference, or interviews typically are neither reliable nor valid. The problems with these approaches have led many employers to turn to more "scientific" techniques, such as polygraph or integrity tests.

A polygraph test involves comparison of physiological responses, such as heart rate and respiration, when applicants answer control questions and questions of integrity. For example, an applicant's physiological responses to questions about name, age, and address (control questions) could be compared to questions about stealing, lying, and cheating (integrity questions). Polygraph tests are extremely controversial and in fact are banned in several states.[1]

[1]The following states, plus the District of Columbia, prohibit the use of polygraph exams in applicant screening: Alaska, Connecticut, Delaware, Maine, Massachusetts, Minnesota, New Jersey, New York, Rhode Island, West Virginia, and Wisconsin. In the following states, an employer may request but not *require* a polygraph exam when screening applicants: California, Hawaii, Idaho, Illinois, Iowa, Maryland, Michigan, Montana, Nebraska, Nevada, Oregon, Pennsylvania, Virginia, and Washington (Bright & Hollon, 1985).

The problem with polygraph tests is their level of accuracy in identifying instances of lying. Empirical studies of polygraph data indicate that the accuracy of judgments based on physiological responses frequently is at the chance level (e.g., Lykken, 1979). Furthermore, polygraph tests generate a relatively high proportion of false positives—people identified as lying when they are telling the truth (Ben-Shakar, Lieblich, & Bar-Hillel, 1982). Concern about the unreliability of polygraph tests led to passage of the Employee Polygraph Protection Act in 1988, which prohibits private employers from requiring or requesting polygraph exams. Security firms and firms that manufacture controlled substances are exempted from the prohibition. Although a subsequent polygraph law in Massachusetts included written exams in their definition of "lie detector tests," the federal statute does not ban the use of oral or written tests (Sackett, Burris, & Callahan, 1989).

Contrary to what you may suspect, integrity tests appear to be both a reliable and valid approach to the issue of applicant honesty (e.g., APA, 1991a). Integrity tests can be grouped into two broad categories: overt integrity tests and personality-oriented measures (Sackett & Harris, 1984). The overt integrity tests are designed specifically to measure issues relevant to integrity. They typically have sections devoted to attitudes about theft and dishonesty and sections soliciting admissions about theft and dishonesty. Examples of overt integrity tests include the Reid Report (Brooks & Arnold, 1989), the Stanton Survey (Harris & Gentry, 1992), and the London House Personnel Selection Inventory (London House, 1991).

The personality-oriented tests are not designed specifically to measure honesty. Instead, they focus on a variety of counterproductive tendencies, including such constructs as dependability, conscientiousness, and nonconformity. Examples of this type include the Hogan Personnel Selection Series (Hogan & Hogan, 1985), the London House Employment Productivity Index (Terris, 1986), and the PDI Employment Inventory (Paajanen, 1986). Although these tests may be used by employers who are concerned about theft, our discussion will focus on the more overt tests of integrity.

Internal consistency coefficients for overt integrity tests typically are .85 or higher, with test–retest coefficients ranging from the .60s to the .90s (e.g., Sackett, Burris, & Callahan, 1989). The most compelling data in favor of integrity tests is their correlations with criterion measures such as on-the-job theft and disciplinary action. This is particularly important because of concerns about response bias in integrity testing. It is obviously in an applicants' best interests to present themselves in a favorable light. In fact, scores on integrity tests do correlate with measures of social desirability, such as the MMPI validity scales and the Edwards Social Desirability Scale (Sackett, Burris, & Callahan, 1989). However, the correlations between integrity test scores and criterion measures are based on studies of groups of people. Although they indicate that the tests are good predictors in general, their validity for predicting the behavior of an individual applicant is less clear.

Regulation of Selection Procedures

Employee selection procedures are regulated in a variety of ways: by legislation, by court decisions, and by the rules set down by professional societies. Chapter 1 described activities by the American Psychological Association, the American Education Research Association, and state licensing boards (see p. 24). In this section, we will focus on regulation at the federal level.

The Equal Employment Opportunity Commission (EEOC), created by Title VII of the 1964 Civil Rights Act, developed guidelines defining fair employee selection procedures in 1970 that were revised and published in 1978 (EEOC, 1978). These guidelines are used by all employers in the public sector and can also be imposed on private businesses that receive government funds. Furthermore, many private businesses voluntarily agree to follow these guidelines as a gesture of good faith in hiring practices.

The guidelines state explicitly that procedures used to screen potential employees must be valid. "Procedures" is broadly defined to include interviews, psychological tests, and even tests using physical standards such as height, weight, or strength (Hogan & Quigley, 1986). The "validity" to be demonstrated may be criterion or content validity, and the guidelines even define the procedures to be used to demonstrate validity. For example, demonstration of criterion validity requires an initial job analysis, the selection of a representative sample, the selection of criterion measures, and the presence of a statistically significant (at the .05 level) predictor–criterion relationship (EEOC, 1978). Recent reviews of federal court cases in which the validity of screening tests has been challenged indicate that the courts take these guidelines seriously. The screening tests successfully defended have been written tests focusing on specific job-related tasks for which there are several different validity studies using large samples of people (e.g., Thompson & Thompson, 1982).

As an outgrowth of the Civil Rights Act, the basic intent of the EEOC guidelines is to prohibit discrimination in hiring practices. A major focus is the identification of selection procedures that might have "adverse impact" on a particular racial, ethnic, religious, or gender group. The guidelines set a statistical criterion for defining adverse impact, known as the *rule of four-fifths* (EEOC, 1978). Stated simply, the rule identifies a procedure as discriminatory if the selection rate for any racial, ethnic, or gender group is less than four-fifths (80%) of the highest rate of selection for any other group. For example, assume that both white and African-American individuals apply for a job. Applicants in both groups are given a screening test with a specific cutoff score to be used for hiring decisions. According to EEOC guidelines, the selection rate using this cutoff score must be determined separately for each group, and the rates compared according to the four-fifths rule. The lower selection rate must be at least 80% of the higher rate for the procedure to be fair. If the selection rate for whites is 60%, the selection rate for African-Americans must be at least 80% of the white rate, or 48% (80% of .60, or .80 × .60). If the selection rate for African-Americans is only 40%, the procedure has adverse impact and is discriminatory. If an African-American who was not hired challenged the decision, the employer would be required to demonstrate that there are extenuating circumstances preventing adherence to the four-fifths rule.

Although EEOC guidelines place the burden of proof on employers, a recent Supreme Court action (*Wards Cove Packing Company* v. *Antonio*, 1989) shifted that burden to *employees*. Minority employees of Wards Cove Packing, primarily nonskilled Eskimos and Filipinos, charged that the company's selection procedure was biased against them, preventing them from obtaining more desirable, higher-paying jobs. After losing in the lower courts, the employees brought their case to the Supreme Court. The Court refused to hear the case, noting that the employees had not demonstrated the procedure to be invalid. In response to this decision, Congress included a provision in the 1991 Civil Rights Acts that returned the burden of proof in selection testing to employers.

Although we have already discussed many of the legislative and court actions relative to employee testing, we have not addressed the issue of affirmative action in the workplace. Because tests are often used for hiring decisions, affirmative action decisions affect the way tests can be used in these areas. One aspect of affirmative action is aggressive recruiting of minority applicants. The four-fifths rule contained in the EEOC guidelines (EEOC, 1978) indirectly creates some problems for aggressive recruiting. A company that successfully recruits a large number of minority applicants may end up hiring a smaller percentage of minority workers than a company that begins with a small minority pool. The problem arises because the number of jobs available is independent of the size of the pool, but the *percentage* of people hired changes to reflect the size of the pool. Because EEOC guidelines require the percentage of minorities selected to reach a specific level relative to the hiring of other groups, the guidelines can discourage a company from working to develop a large minority pool. The EEOC recognizes this problem and can authorize exceptions to the four-fifths rule in specific cases.

A second aspect of affirmative action is the establishment of hiring goals or quotas for minority workers. In a 1985 case, *U.S.* v. *City of Buffalo*, the Supreme Court addressed the use of hiring goals for minority groups who were underrepresented at a workplace because of a previously used discriminatory selection procedure. Hiring goals were approved as a *temporary* measure while the employer developed a new, valid selection procedure.

A third aspect of affirmative action is the use of different selection criteria for different racial, ethnic, or gender groups. Although this issue is thought of most often in relationship to educational decisions, it is also an element of hiring decisions. One reason for using different cutoff scores might be the presence of differential validity data (see p. 421) indicating that the predictor scores linked to successful job performance vary across groups. On the other hand, companies may decide to use different cutoff scores for minority and majority groups to increase the number of minority workers hired.

In the past, it has been permissible to use different cutoff scores to increase minority presence as a redress for past discrimination. Furthermore, the EEOC focus on valid selection procedures made it *necessary* to use different cutoff scores if differential validity in fact existed. This was the basis for the Department of Labor's use of separate scoring procedures for different minority groups on the GATB. Both of these actions, however, appear to be illegal under the 1991 Civil Rights Act. Although the law reaffirms a commitment to affirmative action, Section 9 on the use of test scores states that it is illegal to use different cutoff scores on the basis of race, ethnic group, religion, or gender. It further identifies adjusting or altering scores on the basis of group membership as illegal. Although the provision is designed to prevent discrimination against minority group members, it may in some cases reduce the number of minority individuals hired by preventing score adjustments that favor minority groups. It may also reduce the use of tests in employment decisions, as seen in the Department of Labor's decision to discontinue using the GATB.

Conducting Validity Studies

To be both psychometrically sound and legal, the tests used in employee selection must be valid for the selection process. Since the focus is predicting likelihood of future success, the test's criterion validity is a key element. Most criterion validity studies for business and industry use a concurrent validity design (see p. 225). In the concurrent design, we test a representative sample of current employees on the test under consideration and correlate their scores on the test with a separate measure of job performance. A predictive validity design would dictate that all applicants be tested and *hired*—a clearly impractical event—with data on job performance to be collected at a later time.

The use of concurrent designs, however, presents a different but no less important problem. For a validity study to be useful, we need to compare people with a variety of scores on both the predictor test and the criterion measure. Since the criterion measure is job performance, we may not generate a wide range of criterion scores by testing only people who are currently employed—people who perform poorly at the job probably either have quit or been fired. If our goal is to calculate a criterion validity coefficient, this procedure may lead to restriction of variability on the criterion measure, a factor that can statistically limit the size of the correlation and jeopardize our validity study. If our goal is to conduct a selection efficiency study, we may not be able to identify a group of people who (1) did well on the test but (2) did poorly on the job. The lack of these false positives similarly jeopardizes the results of our analysis.

The increasing use of work sample tests reflects concern over the concurrent validity design problem. In a work sample test, all applicants are evaluated based on a job-relevant sample of behavior. Then, we can compare their work samples to the work samples generated by current successful employees. In essence, we are creating a criterion-referenced procedure using the performance of current successful employees as the standard to which applicants are compared. If samples of current work correlate well with future job performance, the work sample test is a valid technique for candidate screening. Work samples are most likely to predict future performance accurately in skill-based jobs (Asher & Sciarrino, 1974; Reilly & Chao, 1982).

PROCEDURES FOR EVALUATING CURRENT EMPLOYEES

Evaluation of job performance is important in decisions about raises and promotions and can also provide feedback to employees and provide input to the process of job analysis (Wise, 1989). Performance evaluation may be a formal, ongoing process or a more informal, occasional event. Ideally, employees are evaluated on the tasks identified in the job analysis written during recruitment, using specific measures for each job task.

Evaluation Procedures

Theoretically, three types of information could be used to evaluate the performance of an employee (Murphy & Davidshofer, 1988). In reality, the usefulness of each measure varies according to the nature of the job. A *productivity measure* is a direct measure of worker accomplishment. In its simplest form, productivity can be defined as the total of the number of times a particular task is performed. The postal service could count the number of letters sorted by each postal worker within a specific period of time, whereas an automobile plant could count the number of parts installed by each worker on an assembly line. A *personnel measure* focuses on information recorded by supervisors or managers in employee personnel records. Personnel measures include absenteeism, lateness, and days off due to illness or accidents. A *judgmental measure* is a scale used by peers or a supervisor to evaluate employee performance. Evaluation scales can be designed to assess the performance of a single employee or a group of employees and use either a rating or ranking procedure.

Productivity Measures

Although productivity measures seem most appropriate for industry, they can be applied to a variety of businesses. For example, a telephone company supervisor could total the number of calls an operator fields in a given day. A real estate company could tally the total dollars worth of transactions completed by each salesperson in the preceding year. However, there are three problems with the use of productivity measures (e.g., Guion, 1965).

First, a productivity measure requires that we define a unit of behavior to be counted. Although we can count calls answered or dollars generated by sales, it is difficult to define countable units for managerial and professional positions. Second, the item we count must be a valid and useful measure of job performance. Imagine a hospital administrator who uses a count of the number of operations performed to evaluate the surgical staff! The number of units produced is not necessarily a good measure of an employee's effectiveness.

Third, a productivity measure requires that we select an item on which employees are likely to vary and an item on which variations are directly attributable to employee behavior. If the measure is to be useful, it must discriminate between employees doing well on the job and employees who are not. In other words, it must provide individual difference information. In some jobs, employees cannot vary much on count measures because their activities are constrained by other variables. The number of calls a telephone operator can answer is determined by the capacity of the machinery that feeds the calls to the operator's station. Other times, the variations between employees in productivity measures are due to factors other than employee competence. A real estate agent may sell fewer houses because of problems with traffic, road construction, or clients who want to see many houses and spend a lot of time at each property.

Personnel Measures

Personnel measures are used frequently in performance evaluations, but present serious problems to objective measurement of job performance. Personnel measures often show low levels of test–retest reliability (e.g., Hammer & Landau, 1981). The number of times an employee is late or absent is likely to vary considerably depending on the time when the measure is taken and the length of the interval over which data are collected. As we have said repeatedly, an unreliable measure cannot be a valid or useful way to assess individual differences in performance.

Part of the problem with personnel measures is the operational definition of the characteristics to be measured. Absenteeism is a classic example. Recent reviews indicate as many as 40 different indexes of absenteeism, including number of absences, frequency of absences, timing of absences, voluntary absences, and involuntary (illness) absences (e.g., Landy & Farr, 1983). Furthermore, most employees differ little on dimensions such as absenteeism and lateness. When there is little variability on a measure, it is not surprising that it generates low reliability coefficients.

Evaluation Scales

Perhaps because of the problems characterizing the other two measures, evaluation scales have become the most popular technique for evaluation of job performance. Evaluation scales may require a ranking or rating process; rating is the most frequently used format. Regardless of scale format, the most useful data are generated when employees are evaluated using a separate scale for each task comprising the job and for each important employee characteristic (e.g., communication skills).

Ranking Scales.   **Ranking scales** are comparative scales (see p. 122) that evaluate the members of a group by comparing each person's performance to the performance of the other group members. The simplest type is a *full ranking scale* in which the employees being evaluated are listed in order from "best" to "worst." A series of full ranking scales could be used in which each scale represents a different job performance dimension. Employees could be ranked one time on productivity, another time on initiative, and a third time on interpersonal skills. The process is illustrated in Table 12.1.

Full ranking may require the evaluator to make very fine discriminations between people and therefore can result in arbitrary and unreliable classifications. Furthermore, full ranking can be difficult to use when evaluating a large group—imagine ranking a set of 20 shift workers in terms of job performance!

A simple alternative to full ranking is a *forced distribution scale*. A forced distribution scale presents a series of categories and requires the evaluator to identify a fixed number of people in each. For example, a forced distribution scale could require identification of employees in the top, middle, or bottom thirds on a performance dimension. By using a series of forced distribution scales, employers can identify people who are in the upper, middle, and lower groups on a variety of job-relevant dimensions. Table 12.2 presents a sample forced distribution ranking task.

Forced distribution scales do not require evaluators to make fine discriminations among people and are particularly useful with large groups. In

TABLE 12.1 Sample Full Ranking Task

Instructions: Please list the 6 employees on your shift in order from best (1) to worst (6) on each dimension listed.

Productivity	Initiative	Dependability
1.	1.	1.
2.	2.	2.
3.	3.	3.
4.	4.	4.
5.	5.	5.
6.	6.	6.

TABLE 12.2 Sample Forced Distribution Ranking Task

Instructions: For each dimension listed, please identify the 2 employees on your shift who fall into each category.

Category 1 = top third of your shift group
Category 2 = middle third of your shift group
Category 3 = bottom third of your shift group

Employee	Productivity	Initiative	Dependability
Bill Murray	____	____	____
Robin Williams	____	____	____
Jerry Seinfeld	____	____	____
Roseanne Arnold	____	____	____
John Belushi	____	____	____
Gilda Radner	____	____	____

addition, forced distribution scales also address the leniency and severity problems common in performance evaluation (see p. 123) by requiring the people being rated to be distributed across all rating categories.

A *paired comparison scale* presents the names of people to be evaluated as pairs, requiring the evaluator to identify the person performing best within each pair. A series of items can be generated so that the various pairs are evaluated separately for different elements of the job. The advantage of pair comparison scales is the simplicity of the judgment process. Each pair requires

TABLE 12.3   Sample Paired Comparison Task

Instructions: For each pair of employees on your shift, circle the name of the employee whose performance is better.

Which employee is more *productive*?

Murray or Williams	Williams or Radner
Murray or Seinfeld	Seinfeld or Arnold
Murray or Arnold	Seinfeld or Belushi
Murray or Belushi	Seinfeld or Radner
Murray or Radner	Arnold or Belushi
Williams or Seinfeld	Arnold or Radner
Williams or Arnold	Belushi or Radner
Williams or Belushi	

Which employee shows more *initiative*?

Murray or Williams	Williams or Radner
Murray or Seinfeld	Seinfeld or Arnold
Murray or Arnold	Seinfeld or Belushi
Murray or Belushi	Seinfeld or Radner
Murray or Radner	Arnold or Belushi
Williams or Seinfeld	Arnold or Radner
Williams or Arnold	Belushi or Radner
Williams or Belushi	

Which employee is more *dependable*?

Murray or Williams	Williams or Radner
Murray or Seinfeld	Seinfeld or Arnold
Murray or Arnold	Seinfeld or Belushi
Murray or Belushi	Seinfeld or Radner
Murray or Radner	Arnold or Belushi
Williams or Seinfeld	Arnold or Radner
Williams or Arnold	Belushi or Radner
Williams or Belushi	

only comparison of the relative performance of two people, producing a highly reliable measure. A paired comparison procedure is illustrated in Table 12.3.

The problem, however, is that the total number of pairs to be compared is $N(N-1)/2$, in which N equals the number of people being evaluated. For a group of 5 employees, a relatively small group, the number of pairs to be evaluated is $5(5-1)/2$ or 10 pairs. But as the size of the group increases, the number of comparisons jumps radically. For a group of 10 people, the number of comparisons is 45!

The trade-off in choice of ranking scales is between precision of measurement and decision-making effort. Forced distribution scales are easy to use, but do not provide very precise information about individual differences. Paired comparison scales may require a lot of time and effort, but provide much more information about the relative performance of each employee.

Rating Scales.   Unlike ranking scales, **rating scales** are standard scales that represent the performance of each employee independently (see p. 118). One reason for their popularity is that rating scales can be used with either a single employee or a group of employees. *Continuous scales* represent a performance dimension like "productivity" with a line, a set of boxes, or a series of numbers (e.g., 1 to 5). The end points are typically anchored with terms such as "excellent" and "poor," and sometimes other points along the dimension are identified as "average," "above average," or "below average." The evaluator marks the line, boxes, or numbers to indicate where an employee falls on that particular dimension. A set of continuous scales is presented in Table 12.4.

Continuous scales appear simple to use, but they often produce unreliable judgments or ratings with low validity. The problem is operationally defining the dimension being rated and the meaning of the anchor points. Because continuous scales traditionally use general terms like "initiative" (dimension) and "high" (anchor), ratings are influenced by the rater's interpretation of the terms used (Murphy & Davidshofer, 1988).

The alternative to continuous scales is *behavioral scales*, such as behaviorally anchored rating scales (BARS) and behavioral observation scales (BOS). In both cases, employee performance is compared to actual descriptions of job-relevant behaviors. Even characteristics like "communication skills" can be rated using behavioral statements such as "The supervisor explains each job requirement to new employees during their first day of work."

The difference between the BARS and BOS approach is the type of rating to be made. As illustrated in Table 12.5, each item in a BARS system presents the rater with a series of statements describing poor to superior performance. The rater must identify the particular statement from the set that

TABLE 12.4   Set of Continuous Rating Scales

Instructions: Please mark the box indicating the employee's performance on each dimension listed.

Employee: Bill Murray

Productivity:

low   high

Initiative:

low   high

Dependability:

low   high

best characterizes the employee's behavior. The sample BOS system in Table 12.6 presents a series of statements describing different levels of performance. The rater must indicate how often each behavior occurs. The scale may use numbers to represent patterns such as "never," "a few times," "half the time," "often," and "all of the time" or may require an actual count of the number of times the behavior has occurred.

Although behavioral scales are designed to reduce the ambiguity of the rating task, research does not indicate that they produce better or even different evaluations than continuous scales (e.g., Landy & Farr, 1980). Given the time and effort needed to construct behavioral scales, most performance evaluation is conducting using simple graphic or numerical scales.

Issues in the Use of Scales.   Inevitably, the ranking or rating of an employee's performance is a subjective process, and rater's judgments are prone to the same errors and biases regardless of scale format. Furthermore, it is difficult to determine the validity of these job performance measures. Although we can study their reliability by requiring raters to evaluate employees repeatedly, studies of the validity of these measures requires that we correlate ranking/rating scores with other measures of job performance. Because productivity measures and personnel data are likely to focus on other aspects of job performance, we are left with the task of comparing one ranking/rating system to another.

TABLE 12.5 Hypothetical Behaviorally Anchored Rating Scale

Instructions: Please mark the statement that best describes your employee.

Employee: Bill Murray

Dependability	Points
Attends all meetings and completes assigned work on time.	5
Attends meetings and completes work although is occasionally late.	4
Attends meetings and completes work but is late about half the time.	3
Rarely attends meetings and frequently is late in completing work.	2
Rarely attends meetings or completes assigned work.	1

TABLE 12.6   Hypothetical Behavioral Observation Scale

Instructions: Rate how often each of the listed behaviors has occurred during
the past month using the following scale:
   5 = all the time
   4 = most of the time
   3 = about half the time
   2 = a few times
   1 = never

Employee: Bill Murray

Event	Frequency
Arrives on time for meetings.	_____
Forgets to complete assigned work.	_____
Arrives late for a meeting.	_____
Turns assigned work in early.	_____
Fails to attend meetings.	_____
Turns assigned work in on time.	_____

Some researchers suggest that the validity of evaluation scales can be
determined indirectly by comparing the rankings or ratings generated by a
series of different raters (e.g., Bernardin, Alveres, & Cranny, 1976). A high
degree of agreement among raters could be used to support the validity of the
rating process. This is similar to using reliability data to make inferences about
the content validity of a test (see p. 251) and confuses the true meaning of
reliability and validity analyses. Although reliable ratings have the *capacity* to
be valid, the presence of reliability alone is not sufficient to indicate validity.
Despite these problems, evaluation scales, particularly those using rating scales,
are a commonplace element of performance evaluation.

Regulation of Evaluation Procedures

EEOC guidelines also apply to the evaluation of workers for promotions and
raises. In 1971, the Supreme Court affirmed these guidelines in *Griggs* v.
Duke Power, a discrimination lawsuit filed by a group of African-American
workers in North Carolina's Duke Steam Plant. The Court required Duke
Power to provide specific evidence that the test used for promotion decisions
was reliable and demonstrated a valid relationship with job activities.

The Court's emphasis on quantifiable validity data was underscored by the
1988 decision in *Watson* v. *Fort Worth Bank and Trust*. In this case, an African-

American employee charged that a promotion procedure was discriminatory because the proportion of minorities selected was significantly less than what would be expected on the basis of (1) the proportion of African-Americans in the Fort Worth community and (2) the proportion of African-Americans employed at the bank. In other words, the procedure used for promotion decisions selected significantly fewer minorities than would be expected by chance alone. Although this is not necessarily surprising—we expect a rigorous procedure to identify only the most competent people—the Court ruled that the selection ratios indicated adverse impact and that the procedure was discriminatory.

However, the courts do not always side with employees. In a 1979 case filed against Detroit Edison by the National Labor Relations Board, an employee denied promotion for a low test score was refused access to the test to check for a possible scoring error. The Supreme Court ruled that the company's desire to protect the test questions from possible distribution to other employees was reasonable.

PROCEDURES FOR EVALUATING PROGRAMS AND PRODUCTS

The preceding two sections described how psychological tests can be used to evaluate people—either potential employees or current employees. In this section, we examine how psychological tests are used to evaluate the workplace itself and the products provided by a business. Studies evaluating the workplace may focus on organizational issues or human factors issues. Studies of goods and services (business) products involve marketing research.

Organizational Studies

Except in cases of self-employment, the employees of a business or industry function as a group of people working within a hierarchical structure. Their attitudes and behavior are affected by both the characteristics of that structure and the dynamics that emerge as they interact (Siegel & Lane, 1982). In other words, a workplace is a social system in which people have specific roles and are expected to adhere to certain norms. Their job performance and their feelings about their jobs are affected by the way roles and norms are defined, the power structure created by the organization's hierarchy, and the general climate of the workplace (Muchinsky, 1987). Organizational studies may include observations, interviews, and the administration of attitude scales.

When assessing organizational issues, psychologists emphasize the importance of the fit between the person and the work environment (e.g., Pervin, 1968). When people work in jobs that match their interests, abilities, and goals and feel that they are treated fairly and with respect, they are likely to perform well, feel satisfied with their jobs, and experience low levels of stress. On the other hand, people who feel powerless, who dislike their jobs, or who feel that they are treated unfairly are likely to perform poorly, feel dissatisfied, and experience job stress.

When the fit between a person and a job is poor, we have two choices: replace the person or change something about the job. If our goal is to improve person–environment fit by modifying the workplace, it is important to develop techniques for assessing factors such as organizational climate, job satisfaction, and job-related stress. The results of these assessments can also be useful in evaluating how organizational characteristics contribute to job performance and work attitudes.

The Organizational Climate Questionnaire (Litwin & Stringer, 1968) is designed to assess employees' perceptions of organizational structure, standards, and reward policies. Each statement is rated on a 5-point scale from "strongly agree" to "strongly disagree." Statements address issues such as the extent to which jobs are clearly defined (structure), the extent to which people are accountable for their work (standards), and the extent to which people are given credit for their accomplishments (reward policies). The instrument is useful for exploring employee perceptions of the workplace itself and can be a point of departure for additional studies on the relationship of job performance and job satisfaction to organizational features.

The Maslach–Jackson Burnout Inventory (MJBI) is designed to measure the effects of workplace stress (Maslach & Jackson, 1981). Burnout is conceptualized as a consequence of severe and prolonged job stress in which employees become emotionally exhausted and develop negative, cynical attitudes about themselves and their jobs. The MJBI contains items such as "I feel emotionally drained from my work" and "I've become more callous toward people since I took this job." Measures of stress and burnout can be used along with measures of organizational climate to (1) identify individuals or groups of employees experiencing serious job-related problems and (2) explain how organizational features might contribute to these problems.

There are several popular measures of job satisfaction. The most frequently used and researched instrument is the Job Descriptive Index (JDI), designed to measure five aspects of the work environment: the work itself, supervision, pay, promotions, and co-workers (Smith, Kendall, & Hulin, 1969). The items on each scale are a series of words and phrases. Employees are instructed to mark each item "Y" (yes) if it describes their jobs, "N" (no) if it does not, and "?" (cannot say) if they cannot decide. Scores on the five sections are added to derive an overall job satisfaction score.

The inventory has adequate test–retest reliability (Schneider & Dachler, 1978), is equally valid for white, African American, and Hispanic-American workers (McCabe et al., 1980; Smith, Smith, & Rollo, 1974), and successfully measures several different facets of job satisfaction (Smith, Smith, & Rollo, 1974). In fact, the JDI *may* assess more aspects of job satisfaction than it was intended to measure, possibly because some scales include items tapping more than one element of a workplace dimension (Yeager, 1981). For example, the supervision scale contains the items "hard to please" and "up-to-date," which appear to tap, respectively, supervisor interpersonal skills and the quality of supervision.

A second popular instrument is the Minnesota Satisfaction Questionnaire (MSQ), assessing 20 different aspects of work and the workplace (Weiss et al., 1967). Each item is rated on a 5-point scale from "very dissatisfied" (1) to "very satisfied" (5). With 20 different scales, the MSQ permits assessment of several unique elements, such as creativity and independence as components of a job, and separate measurement of multidimensional elements such as job supervision.

One strategy in organizational research is to administer measures of job satisfaction, such as the JDI and the MSQ, along with measures of organizational climate. The job satisfaction scores can be used to define groups of "satisfied" and "unsatisfied" employees, whose scores on climate measures can be compared to identify aspects of organizational structure and policies contributing to different job satisfaction attitudes.

Human Factors Studies

Human factors[2] studies ask whether the design of physical equipment, facilities, and the work environment is suitable for human use (McCormick & Sanders, 1982). The first extensive human factors research was conducted during World War II when problems arose in operating and maintaining new types of military equipment (McCormick & Ilgen, 1985). Today, human factors research explores the design of such diverse entities as industrial equipment, buildings, consumer products, and systems for transportation, communication, and the delivery of health care services.

The impact of a design feature can be assessed using physiological, performance, or subjective criteria (McCormick & Ilgen, 1985). Physiological criteria include heart rate, blood pressure, muscle activity, and energy expenditure and are particularly relevant to the design of industrial equipment. For example, it is possible that the design of a piece of industrial equipment places unnecessary physical stress on a worker's arms during the operation of the equipment. A human factors study could be used to test the impact of

---

[2]In most other countries, human factors is referred to as *ergonomics* (McCormick & Ilgen, 1985).

redesigning the machinery on muscle activity. Performance criteria include measures such as the time taken to complete a task, productivity, and the quality of job performance. Subjective criteria include attitudes, such as job satisfaction, and judgments, such as ratings of design features. Performance and subjective criteria are relevant to evaluation both of workplace design (e.g., a machine console) and the design of systems for delivering services (e.g., a transportation system).

Psychological tests may be useful when studies include performance criteria and/or subjective criteria. For example, a study of a new computer keyboard design might require a group of computer operators to:

1. enter a data set within a specific time limit using an existing and a newly designed keyboard (a speed-based performance test), and
2. rate the design features of each keyboard on dimensions such as key location, key tension, and finger cramps after 15 minutes of continuous use (a judgmental rating task).

Similarly, a study of the effect of adding an employee lounge on each floor might include a measure of job satisfaction (an attitude scale) and a survey assessing preferences among a set of possible lounge locations (a judgmental rating task).

The data generated by a human factors study will only be as good as the measures. A key concern, therefore, is the construction or selection of measures that are reliable and valid for each scenario. When psychological tests will be part of a human factors study, their use in the research project should be preceded by a pilot study of the measures themselves.

Marketing Studies

Rather than focusing on employees, marketing research examines the behavior and attitudes of consumers and others (e.g., legislators) who may affect the exchange of goods and services. The goal of a marketing study is to gather and analyze data relative to the current success of a product or service or predict the likely future success of a planned product or service (Schiffman & Kanuck, 1983).

Marketing research involves collection of data through observational studies, surveys, and experimentation, usually in the form of field testing a product or service (Stanton & Futrell, 1987). Two types of psychological tests—attitude and rating scales—can be used in the survey and experimentation techniques. For example, a company planning to market a new educational toy might administer attitude and rating scales to the parents of preschool children. A personal example can illustrate this procedure.

Several years ago, while approaching a discount store with my young son, I was approached by a researcher to participate in a marketing study. First, I was asked to complete a survey about the value of toys designed to help children learn basic concepts (e.g., shape and color discrimination). The survey basically was an attitude scale, containing a series of items designed to identify the extent to which I was "pro" educational toys. When I completed the survey, the researcher took a moment to glance over my answers and then invited me and my child to field test a new toy in an adjacent trailer. After I watched my son spend about 15 minutes playing with the toy, I was asked to complete a questionnaire about the features of the toy and his interest in it. The questionnaire was a rating scale containing a variety of statements about the appropriateness of the toy for his age, its similarity to other currently marketed toys, its likely appeal to girls versus boys, and so on.

If we examine the interaction in detail, we can see how each component contributes to the marketing study. The initial attitude scale serves two important functions. First, the pattern of scores obtained would provide important data about the potential size of the market for educationally oriented toys. If many parents see toys as a valuable learning tool, then the potential market for these toys is large. Second, scores on the scale could be used to identify the specific individuals with positive attitudes about educational toys. These individuals, who comprise the potential market for this toy, would be good candidates for a field test of the toy. The ratings scales administered after the field test were designed to provide information about the features of the toy and its merits relative to other currently marketed items.

As we have said so many times before, the data generated by psychological tests are only useful if the measures themselves are accurate. It would be important, therefore, to assess the reliability and validity of the attitude and rating scales for marketing research *before* deciding to use them within a particular marketing study.

SUMMARY AND KEY CONCEPTS

Tests are used in a variety of ways by business and industry, often involving the expertise of a psychologist specializing in industrial/organizational psychology. In each workplace scenario, the tests selected or constructed must demonstrate reliability and validity that are appropriate to the event being measured.

The selection of new employees may involve an application form, letters of reference, interview, and testing. Although the use of testing in employee selection has declined recently, research comparing these selection procedures confirms that tests are the most psychometrically sound techniques. Selection testing may include general ability tests, multiaptitude batteries, specific ability tests, **work sample tests**, and **integrity tests**. As the popularity of work sample tests has increased, psychologists have developed creative ways to sample job-relevant behaviors, such as the in-basket test for managerial positions. Because of practical problems, the validation of selection procedures typically uses concurrent validity designs.

The performance of current employees can be determined using a productivity measure, a personnel measure, or a judgmental measure. Judgmental measures are the most popular approach and require construction of **ranking scales** or **rating scales**. Ranking scales, including the full ranking scale, the forced distribution scale, and the paired comparison scale, indicate the relative performance of each member of an employee group. Rating scales may be either continuous scales or behavioral scales and assess the performance of each employee independently.

Federal concerns about discrimination in hiring and promotion have lead to extensive regulation of tests used in these contexts. For example, guidelines issued by the Equal Employment Opportunity Commission (EEOC) include a statistical criterion—the rule of four-fifths—for determining whether a procedure adversely affects minority individuals. Supreme Court decisions and the passage of the 1991 Civil Rights Act have expanded these regulations, in some cases with unanticipated results.

In addition to evaluating employees, psychological tests are also used in research about the workplace itself and the goods and services produced by a company. Studies of the workplace include human factors research and organizational research. Human factors studies are concerned with issues of workplace design, whereas organizational studies focus on the impact of a company's structure and operations. On the other hand, studies about the goods and services produced are part of marketing research. Marketing studies often use attitude and/or rating scales.

QUESTIONS

12.1   The procedures used to select new employees must be reliable and valid. Why is it reasonable to be concerned about the *criterion* validity of a selection test, but to be concerned about the *content* validity of an interview?

12.2   Why does a structured employment interview produce more reliable and valid data than an unstructured employment interview?

12.3   What is the rule of four-fifths? Give an example of how it could affect the use of (a) a selection test and (b) a promotion test.

12.4   Why do most workplace validity studies use a concurrent validity design? What problems does this present to (a) criterion validity studies and (b) selection efficiency studies?

12.5   Describe the steps you would take to develop a valid work sample test for a particular job.

12.6   Are integrity tests a better technique for assessing honesty and trustworthiness than lie detectors? Explain.

12.7   Why do most psychologists prefer to use evaluation scales to assess job performance over productivity and personnel measures?

12.8   How does the information provided by ranking scales differ from the information provided by rating scales?

12.9   Describe how you might combine data from measures of climate, job-related stress, and job satisfaction to evaluate the impact of a company's organizational structure.

12.10 Describe how you might design a marketing study for a new word-processing software package.

Appendix A
Sources of Information About Tests

I. TEST INFORMATION AVAILABLE FROM PUBLISHERS

Publishers

American Association on Mental Deficiency
5201 Connecticut Ave., NW
Washington, DC 20015

American College Testing Program
P.O. Box 168
Iowa City, IA 52243

American Guidance Service
Publisher's Building
Circle Pines, MN 55014

American Orthopsychiatric Association, Inc.
1790 Broadway
New York, NY 10019

Consulting Psychologists Press
577 College Ave.
Palo Alto, CA 94306

Tests

AAMD Adaptive Behavior Scale

American College Tests

Kaufman Assessment Battery for Children
KeyMath Test
Peabody Picture Vocabulary Test
Woodcock Reading Mastery Test

Bender Visual Motor Gestalt

California Psychological Inventory
Maslach Burnout Inventory
Myers–Briggs Type Indicator
Strong–Campbell Interest Inventory

Publishers	Tests
CPS, Inc. P.O. Box 83 Larchmont, NY 10538	Senior Apperception Test
CTB/McGraw-Hill Del Monte Research Park Monterey, CA 93940	California Achievement Test Career Maturity Inventory
DLM Teaching Resources One DLM Park P.O. Box 4000 Allen, TX 75002	Woodcock–Johnson Psycho-Educational Battery
Educational Testing Service Princeton, NJ 08540	Graduate Record Exam Scholastic Aptitude Test
Evaluation Research Associates P.O. Box 6503 Teall Station Syracuse, NY 13217	Organizational Climate Index
Grune & Stratton 757 Third Ave. New York, NY 10017	Rorschach Inkblot Test
Houghton Mifflin 110 Tremont St. Boston, MA 02107	Cognitive Abilities Test Stanford–Binet Intelligence Scale

Institute for Personality and Ability
    Testing
1602 Coronado Dr.
Champaign, IL 68120
	Children's Personality Questionnaire
	Jr/Sr High School Personality
	    Questionnaire
	Sixteen Personality Factor Questionnaire

London House
1550 Northwest Highway
Park Ridge, IL 60068
	London House Personnel Selection
	    Inventory
	London House Employment Productivity
	    Index

National Computer Systems PAS Division P.O. Box 1416 Minneapolis, MN 55440	Hogan Personnel Selection Inventory

Publishers	Tests
Pinkerton Services Group 6100 Fairview Road Suite 900 Charlotte, NC 28210	Stanton Survey
Psychological Assessment Resources, Inc. P.O. Box 998 Odessa, FL 33556	Children's Apperception Test Gray Oral Reading Tests Holland Self-directed Search Thematic Apperception Test Wide Range Achievement Test
Psychological Corporation 757 Third Ave. New York, NY 10017	Bennett Mechanical Comprehension Test Differential Aptitude Test Edwards Personal Preference Schedule Holtzman Inkblot Test Miller Analogies Test Minnesota Clerical Test Otis–Lennon School Ability Test Rotter Incomplete Sentences Blank System of Multicultural Pluralistic 　Assessment Wechsler Adult Intelligence Scale–R Wechsler Intelligence Scale for Children Wechsler Memory Scale Wechsler Preschool and Primary Scale of 　Intelligence–R
Reid Psychological Systems 200 South Michigan Ave. Chicago, IL 60604	Reid Report
Reitan Neuropsychological Laboratories 1338 East Edison St. Tucson, AZ 85719	Halstead–Reitan Neuropsychological Test 　Battery
Research Psychologists Press Box 984 1110 Military St. Port Huron, MI 48061	Personality Research Form

Publishers	Tests
Riverside Publishing Co. 8420 Bryn Mawr Ave. Chicago, IL 60631	Iowa Test of Basic Skills
Science Research Associates 259 East Erie St. Chicago, IL 60611	Kuder Occupational Interest Survey Minnesota School Attitude Survey
Stoelting Co. 1350 South Kostner Ave. Chicago, IL 60623	Incomplete Sentences Task
Charles G. Thomas 301-327 East Lawrence Ave. Springfield, IL 62717	Machover Draw-a-Person Test
United State Employment Service North Capitol and H Streets N.W. Washington, DC 20401	General Aptitude Battery Test

United States Military Entrance
    Processing Command
Testing Directorate
2500 Green Bay Rd.
North Chicago, IL 60064
	Armed Services Vocational Aptitude
	    Battery

University of Illinois Press Box 5081 Station A Champaign, IL 61820	Illinois Test of Psycholinguistic Ability
University of Minnesota 2037 University Ave. S.E. Minneapolis, MN 55414	Minnesota Multiphasic Personality Inventory
University of Vermont Department of Psychiatry Burlington, VT 05405	Child Behavior Checklist
Vocational Psychology Research University of Minnesota Minneapolis, MN 55414	Minnesota Satisfaction Questionnaire

Publishers	Tests
Western Psychological Services 12031 Wilshire Blvd Los Angeles, CA 90025	House–Tree–Person Test Luria–Nebraska Neuropsychological Battery Tennessee Self-concept Scale
Wonderlic & Associates P.O. Box 8007 820 Frontage Rd. Northfield, IL 60093	Wonderlic Personnel Test

II. TEST INFORMATION AVAILABLE IN BOOKS/ARTICLES

Citation in References	Test
Harris, D. B. (1963)	Draw-a-Family
Smith, Kendall, & Hulin (1969)	Job Descriptive Index
Kent, G. H., & Rosanoff, A. J. (1910)	Kent–Rosanoff Free Association Test
Paajanen, G. E. (1986)	PDI Employment Inventory
Holmes, T. H. & Rahe, R. H. (1967)	Social Readjustment Scale
Woodworth, R. S. (1920)	Woodworth Personal Data Sheet

Appendix B

This table indicates the proportion of scores that fall between $z = 0$ and the specified z-score. For example, .3413 (34.13%) of scores falls between $z = 0$ and $z = 1.0$.

FIGURE B-1   Graph of the normal curve.

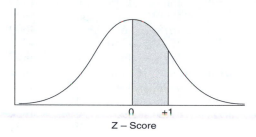

TABLE B.1   Normal Distribution or *z*-Score Table

X	.00	.01	.02	.03	.04	.05	.06	.07	.08	.09
0.0	.0000	.0040	.0080	.0120	.0160	.0199	.0239	.0279	.0319	.0359
0.1	.0398	.0438	.0478	.0517	.0557	.0596	.0636	.0675	.0714	.0753
0.2	.0793	.0832	.0871	.0910	.0948	.0987	.1026	.1064	.1103	.1141
0.3	.1179	.1217	.1255	.1293	.1331	.1368	.1406	.1443	.1480	.1517
0.4	.1554	.1591	.1628	.1664	.1700	.1736	.1772	.1808	.1844	.1879
0.5	.1915	.1950	.1985	.2019	.2054	.2088	.2123	.2157	.2190	.2224
0.6	.2257	.2291	.2324	.2357	.2389	.2422	.2454	.2486	.2517	.2549
0.7	.2580	.2611	.2642	.2673	.2704	.2734	.2764	.2794	.2823	.2852
0.8	.2881	.2910	.2939	.2967	.2995	.3023	.3051	.3078	.3106	.3133
0.9	.3159	.3186	.3212	.3238	.3264	.3289	.3315	.3340	.3365	.3389
1.0	.3413	.3438	.3461	.3485	.3508	.3531	.3554	.3577	.3599	.3621
1.1	.3643	.3665	.3686	.3708	.3729	.3749	.3770	.3790	.3810	.3830
1.2	.3849	.3869	.3888	.3907	.3925	.3944	.3962	.3980	.3997	.4015
1.3	.4032	.4049	.4066	.4082	.4099	.4115	.4131	.4147	.4162	.4177
1.4	.4192	.4207	.4222	.4236	.4251	.4265	.4279	.4292	.4306	.4319
1.5	.4332	.4345	.4357	.4370	.4382	.4394	.4406	.4418	.4429	.4441
1.6	.4452	.4463	.4474	.4484	.4495	.4505	.4515	.4525	.4535	.4545
1.7	.4554	.4564	.4573	.4582	.4591	.4599	.4608	.4616	.4625	.4633
1.8	.4641	.4649	.4656	.4664	.4671	.4678	.4686	.4693	.4699	.4706
1.9	.4713	.4719	.4726	.4732	.4738	.4744	.4750	.4756	.4761	.4767
2.0	.4772	.4778	.4783	.4788	.4793	.4798	.4803	.4808	.4812	.4817
2.1	.4821	.4826	.4830	.4834	.4838	.4842	.4846	.4850	.4854	.4857
2.2	.4861	.4864	.4868	.4871	.4875	.4878	.4881	.4884	.4887	.4890
2.3	.4893	.4896	.4898	.4901	.4904	.4906	.4909	.4911	.4913	.4916
2.4	.4918	.4920	.4922	.4925	.4927	.4929	.4931	.4932	.4934	.4936
2.5	.4938	.4940	.4941	.4943	.4945	.4946	.4948	.4949	.4951	.4952
2.6	.4953	.4955	.4956	.4957	.4959	.4960	.4961	.4962	.4963	.4964
2.7	.4965	.4966	.4967	.4968	.4969	.4970	.4971	.4972	.4973	.4974
2.8	.4974	.4975	.4976	.4977	.4977	.4978	.4979	.4979	.4980	.4981
2.9	.4981	.4982	.4982	.4983	.4984	.4984	.4985	.4985	.4986	.4986
3.0	.4987	.4987	.4987	.4988	.4988	.4989	.4989	.4989	.4990	.4990

Bernard W. Taylor III, *Introduction to Management Science,* 4th ed. Appendix A, page 704. © Allyn and Bacon, 1993.

GLOSSARY

achievement test: A type of maximal performance (ability) test designed to assess previous learning.

age differentiation: A test construction principle used in Binet tests. An item shows age differentiation if the proportion of people answering it correctly increases with age.

age-equivalent score: A type of **norm-referenced score** based on the raw score at the 50th percentile for a particular age. Any individual who earns this raw score, regardless of actual age, is identified as having scored at that age-equivalent. Used in the original Binet intelligence test (mental age).

alternate-choice item: A type of item used on maximal performance (ability) tests that presents a question and a set of possible answers. Test takers respond by selecting one of these answers. Common types include true/false, matching, and multiple choice.

alternate or parallel forms reliability: A measure of the similarity in test scores across two versions of a test. Used to estimate measurement error associated with using different sets of items drawn from the same domain. Represented mathematically as an XX correlation.

aptitude test: A type of maximal performance (ability) test designed to assess potential for learning new information or skills.

assessment: A procedure used to gather information about people.

attitude test: A typical performance test designed to measure personal beliefs and/or opinions.

basal age: A scoring component used in Binet tests. The age level at which a test taker passes all subtests by correctly answering a specific number of items.

base rate: The proportion of people in a group who are at or above a specific cutoff on a criterion measure (Y). Used in **criterion validity** selection studies to determine the rate of success on a criterion measure without regard to scores on a predictor.

ceiling age: A scoring component used in Binet tests. The age level at which a test taker fails all subtests by answering a specific number of items incorrectly.

coefficient alpha: A conservative measure of **internal consistency** that is important when test items are drawn from a small or focused domain. Estimates the average split-half coefficient for all possible splits of a test. Used as an estimate of measurement error associated with drawing different test items from the same domain. Interpreted as an XX correlation.

coefficient of determination: The proportion of variance in one variable (Y) that is predictable from the other (X). The proportion of variance accounted for by the XY relationship. Calculated as the square of an XY correlation.

comparative rating scale: A scale for rating the personality or behavior of individuals in a relative way. Requires the rater to consider an individual's characteristics relative to others within a specified group. Common formats include full ranking, forced distribution, and pair-comparison.

confidence interval: A range within which a particular score is likely to occur. Based on the **psychometric properties** of a test, specifically, what is known about measurement error. Used in **reliability** analysis to estimate a test taker's true score and in **validity** analysis to estimate the predicted criterion score associated with a particular test score.

construct: A hypothetical dimension or characteristic on which individuals differ. Its presence is inferred from individual differences in patterns of behavior. Common examples include intelligence, aggression, and self-concept.

construct explication: A written list of the behaviors, beliefs, and attitudes to be measured in a construct-based test. Used primarily in the development of **personality** and **attitude tests**.

construct validity: The extent to which a test measures the underlying attributes it is designed to assess. Determined through a series of procedures, including exploring the relationship between test scores and other measures and investigating the factor structure of a test.

content-referenced score: A type of **criterion-referenced scoring** using mastery of test content as the standard of performance. Commonly represented as percent correct.

content validity: The extent to which the actual content of a test is representative of the domain it is designed to cover. Determined by comparing the structure of the test to the structure of the domain.

correlation: A statistical measure of the relationship between scores on two variables, X and Y. Correlations can be positive or negative and can have values between -1 and $+1$.

criterion-referenced scoring: A procedure used to transform raw scores into measures that compare test takers' performance to a standard or criterion. Used only on **maximal performance tests**. Common examples include percent correct and pass/fail.

criterion validity: The extent to which scores on a test can predict performance on another related measure (a *criterion*). A type of **validity analysis** that often uses

linear regression. Also a component of **construct validity** analysis. Represented mathematically as an *XY* correlation.

deciles: Points that divide a frequency distribution into equal tenths (D1 to D10). Often computed as a transformation of **percentile rank** in which D1 contains scores up to the 10th percentile, D2 contains scores between the 10th and 20th percentile, and so on. A type of **norm-referenced score**.

descriptive statistics: Numbers used to summarize the features of a score distribution (a set of scores).

deviation IQ: A standard score measure used on modern intelligence tests. Deviation IQs are based on the raw score mean and standard deviation for a given age group. The **z-scores** for each age group are transformed to **T-scores** with means of 100 and standard deviations of 15.

differential validity: Evidence that a test measures different characteristics for different groups of people. An important component of research on test bias.

dissimulation: Responding to a test item in a way that conceals or distorts the test taker's actual characteristics. Also called response bias. Includes response set and response style.

distractor: An incorrect alternative on a multiple-choice item. Evaluating distractor power is a component of **item analysis**.

domain: The knowledge, skills, or characteristics measured by a test.

error score: A theoretical measure of the extent to which random events affect a test taker's score. According to **reliability** theory, all test scores have two components: a **true score** and an error score. A test cannot be reliable when differences between people in test scores primarily reflect the effects of random events.

examiner: A person who administers a test and records test taker responses. Used with individually administered tests.

exceptionality: An intellectual, behavioral, emotional, or physical characteristic that may affect a student's educational progress.

face validity: An obvious relationship between the content of test items and the domain they are designed to cover. A judgment about the **content validity** of a test made by a test taker after examining the test items.

forced-choice: An item type used on **typical performance tests** to generate an **ipsative score**. Presents two or more alternatives, each measuring a different characteristic; requires the test taker either to choose one alternative or to rank the set of alternatives. Used only on tests on more than one characteristic.

formative evaluation: The use of a test to provide feedback to test takers regarding their progress or to provide feedback to teachers regarding the effectiveness of instruction.

free-response item: A type of item used on maximal performance (ability) tests that presents a question without a set of possible answers. Test takers respond by constructing an answer. Common types include fill-in-the-blank, short answer, and essay.

grade-equivalent score: A type of **norm-referenced score** based on the raw score at the 50th percentile for a particular grade level. Any individual who earns this raw score, regardless of actual grade level, is identified as having scored at that grade equivalent.

halo effect: The tendency of raters to base their ratings on general impressions, resulting in fairly uniform, favorable ratings.

hit: A correct prediction. Includes true positives and true negatives. An element of the selection efficiency approach in **criterion validity** analysis.

independent item: An item type used on **typical performance tests** to generate a **normative score**. Used to determine the overall or absolute strength of test-taker characteristics. May be used on tests of a single characteristic or tests of several characteristics.

integrity test: A test designed to predict a test taker's level of honesty and trustworthiness. Often used in employee selection.

interest test: A typical performance test designed to identify patterns of likes and dislikes useful for making educational and career decisions.

internal consistency: The extent to which different test items can be viewed as drawn from the same domain. The internal consistency coefficient is used to determine whether or not all the items on a test are tapping the same test-taker characteristics. Common internal consistency measures include **split-half reliability**, **coefficient alpha**, and the **Kuder–Richardson** coefficients.

interval: A scale of measurement in which people or objects are ranked using an equal unit system. A difference of 1 unit or 2 units therefore is equivalent at any location along the scale. The scale of measurement used most often in testing.

ipsative score: A test score that represents the strength of a test-taker characteristic relative to the other characteristics tested. Used only in **typical performance tests** that assess more than one characteristic. May be transformed using **norm-referenced scoring**.

item analysis: A set of procedures for evaluating the properties of individual test items. Includes **item difficulty**, **percent endorsement**, and **item discrimination**.

item characteristic curve: A graph of test-taker performance on an item that indicates the proportion of people correct as a function of total score on the test. A representation of **item discrimination**.

item difficulty: A representation of how easy or hard an item is based on the proportion of people who answer the item correctly. Used on **maximal performance tests**.

item difficulty index: A ratio of the number of people answering an item correctly to the total number of people who took the test. The measure of **item difficulty**.

item discrimination: A measure of the extent to which an item identifies people with different characteristics. On a **maximal performance test**, evaluates item responses as a function of test takers' total scores. On a **typical performance test**, evaluates the item responses as a function of test-taker characteristics.

item discrimination index: A measure of **item discrimination** based on the responses of two subgroups of test takers. Compares the proportion of people in each group who selected a particular answer.

item-total correlation: A correlation between test takers' performance on a specific item and their total test scores. A measure of **item discrimination**.

Kuder–Richardson: A technique used to estimate the value of **coefficient alpha** when test items are scored dichotomously. A measure of **reliability**.

Likert scales: A technique for scoring an **attitude test**. Test takers indicate their degree of agreement or disagreement with each item using a several-point scale. The most common format is a 5-point scale ranging from "strongly agree" to "strongly disagree." Not all tests using Likert-style items generate true Likert scale scores.

linear regression: A statistical technique for predicting scores on one variable (Y) from scores on another (X). Defines the equation for the straight line that best represents the correlation between X and Y.

linear transformation: A procedure for changing raw scores to a new unit of measurement while preserving the relationships between scores. Common examples include **z-scores** and **T-scores**.

local norms: **Norm-referenced scoring** scales based on the performance of a subgroup of people, such as the students within a particular state or a particular school system.

mastery score: A type of **criterion-referenced scoring** in which successful completion of a unit is the standard of performance. A variation on the pass/fail system.

maximal performance test: A test designed to measure the upper limits of test-taker knowledge or skill. Also called an ability test. Includes **achievement** and **aptitude tests** and can be designed to measure **power** or **speed**.

mean: The arithmetic average of a set of scores. The mean does not have to occur as a score in the distribution. A measure of central tendency.

median: The point dividing a frequency distribution into two equal halves. The point in the distribution at the 50th percentile. The median does not have to occur as a score in the distribution. A measure of central tendency.

miss: An incorrect prediction. Includes false positives and false negatives. An element of the selection efficiency approach in **criterion validity** analysis.

mode: The most frequently occurring score in a frequency distribution. A distribution can be bimodal; however, when more than two scores are tied as most frequent, the mode typically is not reported. A measure of central tendency.

neuropsychology: The study of the relationship between behavior and the brain.

nominal: A scale of measurement in which people or objects are placed in categories according to their properties. When numbers are used in nominal measurement, they serve only as the category labels; they do not indicate the extent of a property.

nonlinear or area transformation: A procedure for changing raw scores to a new unit of measurement that also changes the relationship between scores. Common examples include **percentile rank** and **age- or grade-equivalent scores**.

norm group: The group of people to whom we compare test takers in **norm-referenced scoring**.

norm-referenced scoring: A procedure used to transform raw scores to new scores that indicate where each person falls in relationship to the others in a group. Used on both **maximal performance** and **typical performance tests**. Requires identifying a **norm group** or using a **standardization sample**. Common examples include **standard scores** and **percentile ranks**.

normal distribution or normal curve: A theoretical distribution generated by a mathematical rule. It is symmetric and unimodal, and the **mean**, **median**, and **mode** all have the same value. Because of its particular properties, there are direct relationships between *z*-scores and **percentile ranks**.

normative score: A test score that represents the absolute strength of a test-taker characteristic. Used in **typical performance** tests. May be transformed using **norm-referenced scoring**.

objective scoring: A scoring procedure in which a test takers' responses are awarded points by comparing them to lists of possible answers. Used primarily in alternate-choice ability tests and objective typical performance tests.

objective item: A type of typical performance test item presenting a question and a set of possible answers. Similar in format to alternate-choice ability test items. Commonly used on tests of personality, interests, and attitudes.

objective-referenced score: A type of **criterion-referenced scoring** using mastery of the test objectives as the standard of performance. Usually represented as the number or percent of objectives mastered.

operational definition: A statement that describes how a construct is measured. Because tests can be used to measure constructs, a score on a test can serve as an operational definition.

ordinal: A scale of measurement in which people or objects are ranked on a property or dimension. The numbers indicate the relative extent of the property being measured.

percent endorsement: A statistic used to evaluate items in **typical performance tests**. The proportion of test takers who select a particular answer to a test item. May be calculated separately for different subgroups of test takers.

percentile norms: A table used for translating raw scores into percentile ranks using the performance of a specified **norm group**.

percentile rank: A type of **norm-referenced score** using an **ordinal** scale. Indicates the proportion of scores that fall at or below a given score.

personality test: A typical performance test designed to measure individual dispositions and preferences.

power test: A type of maximal performance (ability) test that uses items of varying difficulty to determine the level of test-taker knowledge or skill.

projective hypothesis: The proposal that the interpretation of an ambiguous stimulus elicits projection and therefore can reveal latent or unconscious aspects of test-taker personality.

projective item: A type of personality test item using an ambiguous stimulus and/or response. Theoretically, the type of response constructed reflects the unique characteristics of the test taker. Used in inkblot tests, incomplete sentence tests, story tests, and drawing tasks.

psychometric properties: The measurement characteristics of a test, including its reliability, validity, and item statistics.

psychopathology: A psychological disorder. The study of psychological disorders.

quartiles: Points that divide a frequency distribution into equal fourths (Q1 to Q4). Often computed as a transformation of **percentile rank** in which Q1 contains scores up to the 25th percentile, Q2 contains scores between the 25th and 50th percentile, and so on. A type of **norm-referenced score**.

quotients: Mathematical formulas used to integrate **age-** or **grade-equivalent scores** with information about actual age or grade level. Used in the creation of early IQ scores (ratio IQs).

range: The difference between the highest and lowest scores in a score distribution. A measure of variability.

ranking scale: A scale used to evaluate the relative performance of the members of a group. Often used in evaluation of employees. Also called a **comparative rating scale**.

rating scale: A scale used to evaluate the performance of each member of a group independently. Often used in evaluation of employees. Also called a **standard rating scale**.

ratio: A scale of measurement containing both equal-interval units and a true zero point. A score of 10, therefore, is not only 5 units more than a score of 5—it is twice as much as a score of 5.

raw score: The original score earned on a test before any score transformations occur. Usually the total number of points earned.

relevant score variance: Theoretically, the test score variance attributable to differences among people in stable characteristics that are appropriate to test purpose. A component of **true score** variance. An element of **validity** theory.

reliability: The extent to which a test measures stable characteristics of test takers and therefore is free from random measurement error. A reliable test provides a relatively consistent measure of test-taker characteristics. Theoretically defined

as the ratio of true score variance to test score variance. Types include **alternate form**, **test–retest**, **split half**, and **internal consistency**.

scatterplot: A graph depicting the relationship between scores on two variables, X and Y.

selection rate: The proportion of people in a group who are at or above a specific cutoff on a predictor measure (X). In **criterion validity** selection studies, indicates the current rate of success on a predictor.

Spearman-Brown prophesy formula: A technique for predicting the increase in reliability due to increasing the number of items on a test or the number of tests used in a decision. Used to correct the **split-half reliability** coefficient.

speed test: A type of maximal performance (ability) test that determines the number of items a test taker can answer correctly within a specific time limit.

split-half reliability: A measure of the similarity in test scores across two subsets of test items. Requires dividing a single test into two half-tests and treating the half-tests as alternate or parallel forms. Estimates measurement error associated with using different items drawn from the same domain. Represented mathematically as an XX correlation. Because the value of the coefficient is affected by test length, the estimate of the complete test's reliability is the split-half coefficient after correction using the **Spearman–Brown prophesy formula**.

standard deviation: The average deviation of scores from the mean in unsquared (raw score) units. A measure of variability. Calculated as the square root of the **variance**.

standard error of estimate: The standard deviation of prediction errors; also, the standard deviation of predicted criterion scores around actual criterion scores. Used to estimate the average number of points by which actual and predicted criterion scores differ. Derived from a **criterion validity** coefficient. A component of constructing **confidence intervals**.

standard error of measurement: The standard deviation of **error scores**; also, the standard deviation of test scores around **true scores**. Used to estimate the average number of points by which test scores and true scores differ. Derived from a **reliability** coefficient. A component of constructing **confidence intervals**.

standard rating scale: A scale for evaluating behavior or personality independently for each person under study. Common formats include continuous scales, BARS, and BOS.

standard score: A type of **norm-referenced score** using an **interval** scale. Indicates a score's location relative to the **mean** in **standard deviation** units.

standardization sample: The group of people used in the test development phase to develop **norm-referenced scoring**.

standardized test: A test designed by individuals with expertise in test construction. Standardized tests have specific requirements for administration and scoring and have been studied psychometrically during their development.

subjective scoring: A scoring procedure in which test takers' responses are evaluated by comparing them to a set of scoring guidelines. Used primarily in free-response ability tests and projective personality tests.

summative evaluation: The use of a test to summarize a test taker's level of knowledge or skill, such as the use of a test in assigning final grades.

systematic error variance: Theoretically, the test score variance attributable to differences among people in stable characteristics that are irrelevant to test purpose. A component of **true score** variance. An element of **validity** theory.

tailored testing: A feature of computer-assisted testing in which a branching program selects the items to present next based on test-taker performance on the current item set. Can be used to mirror the basal/ceiling procedure in individual testing.

task or job analysis: A written outline of the specific components of a task or job that are to be measured by a test. Used in the construction of scales for evaluating behavioral domains such as effective teaching.

test: A type of assessment procedure that uses systematic procedures to obtain information and convert that information to numbers or scores.

test battery: A set of two or more tests used in combination to evaluate an individual.

test plan: A written outline of the knowledge or skills to be measured by a test (content objectives) and the behaviors required to demonstrate the presence of each element of knowledge or skill (behavioral objectives). Used in **maximal performance tests**.

test–retest reliability: A measure of the stability in test scores over time. Used to estimate measurement error caused by administering a test at two different times. Represented mathematically as an *XX* correlation.

Thurstone scales: A technique for scoring an **attitude test** that uses scaled statements to represent different attitude strengths. Test takers mark the statements with which they agree; final score on the scale is the median scale value of the statements marked.

true score: A theoretical measure of a test taker's actual knowledge, skills, and characteristics. According to **reliability** theory, all test scores have two components: a true score and an **error score**. A test is reliable when differences among people in test scores reflect differences among them in true scores.

T-score: A type of **standard score**. Raw scores converted to a new scale usually with a mean of 50 and a standard deviation of 10. Typically calculated as a transformation of *z*-scores.

typical performance test: A test designed to measure usual or habitual thoughts, feelings, and behaviors. Common types include **personality**, **interest**, and **attitude tests**.

validity: The extent to which a test measures characteristics of test takers that are relevant to the domain and therefore is free from systematic measurement error. A valid test measures the characteristics it is supposed to measure. Types include **content**, **construct**, and **criterion validity**.

variable: A property or characteristic on which people are likely to differ.

variance: The average squared deviation of scores from the mean. A measure of variability. The basis for determining the **standard deviation**.

work sample test: A standardized test in which a job applicant is required to execute a set of job-related behaviors. Often used in employee selection.

z-score: The basic type of **standard score**. Raw scores are converted to a new scale with a mean of 0 and a standard deviation of 1. A linear transformation.

REFERENCES

AAMD: American Association of Mental Deficiency (1981). *AAMD Adaptive Behavior Scale.* Monterrey, CA: Publishers Test Service.

Achenbach, T. M., & Edelbrock, C. (1983). *Manual for the Child Behavior Checklist and the Revised Child Behavior Profile.* Burlington, VT: University Associates in Psychiatry.

AERA: American Education Research Association, American Psychological Association, & National Council on Measurement in Education (1985). *Standards for Educational and Psychological Testing.* Washington, DC: American Psychological Association.

Ahlgren, A. (1983). *Minnesota School Attitude Survey: Manual.* Chicago: Science Research Associates.

Aiken, L. R. (1982). Writing multiple-choice items to measure higher-order educational objectives. *Educational and Psychological Measurement, 42,* 803–806.

Aiken, L. R. (1987). Testing with multiple-choice items. *Journal of Research and Development in Education, 20,* 44–58.

Aiken, L. R. (1991). *Psychological Testing and Assessment.* Boston: Allyn & Bacon.

Albert, M. S. (1981). Geriatric neuropsychology. *Journal of Consulting and Clinical Psychology, 49,* 835–850.

Allison, D. E. (1984). The effect of item-difficulty sequence, intelligence, and sex on test performance, reliability, and item difficulty and discrimination. *Measurement and Evaluation in Guidance, 16,* 211–217.

Anastasi, A. (1979). *Fields of Applied Psychology,* 2nd ed. New York: McGraw-Hill.

Anastasi, A. (1988). *Psychological Testing,* 6th ed. New York: Macmillian, Inc.

Andreasen, N. C. (1988). Brain imaging: Applications in psychiatry. *Science, 239,* 1381–1388.

APA: American Psychological Association, Committee on Professional Standards & Committee on Psychological Tests (1986). *Guidelines for Computer-based Tests and Interpretations.* Washington, DC: American Psychological Association.

APA: American Psychological Association (1990a). Science directorate opposes Department of Labor's suspension of GATB. *Psychological Science Agenda, 3,* 5.

APA: American Psychological Association (1990b). New directions in educational testing. *Psychological Science Agenda, 3,* 14.

APA: American Psychological Association (1991a). APA Task Force releases final report on integrity testing. *Psychological Science Agenda, 4,* 1.

APA: American Psychological Association (1991b). A national exam in education? *Psychological Science Agenda, 4,* 2.

APA: American Psychological Association (1992). Ethical principles of psychologists and code of conduct. *American Psychologist, 47*, 1597–1611.

Asher, J. J., & Sciarrino, J. A. (1974). Realistic work sample tests: A review. *Personnel Psychology, 27*, 519–533.

Bannatyne, A. (1974). Diagnosis—a note on recategorization of the WISC scaled scores. *Journal of Learning Disabilities, 7*, 272–273.

Beck, S. J. (1937). *Introduction to the Rorschach Method: A Manual of Personality Study.* American Orthopsychiatric Association Monograph, 1.

Bellak, L. (1954). *The Thematic Apperception Test and the Children's Apperception Test in Clinical Use.* New York: Grune & Stratton.

Bellak, L. (1986). *The TAT, CAT, and SAT in Clinical Use*, 4th ed. New York: Grune & Stratton.

Bellak, L., & Bellak, S. S. (1973). *Manual: Senior Apperception Test (SAT).* Larchmont, NY: Consulting Psychologists Service.

Bellak, L., & Hurvich, M. S. (1966). A human modification of the Children's Apperception Test (CAT—H). In R. V. Kail, Jr., & J. W. Hagen (eds.), *Perspectives on the Development of Memory and Cognition.* Hillsdale, NJ: Erlbaum.

Bender, L. (1938). *A Visual Motor Gestalt Test and Its Clinical Uses.* Research Monograms No. 3. New York: American Orthopsychiatric Association.

Bennett, R. E., & Ragosta, M. (1984). *A Research Context for Studying Admission Tests and Handicapped Populations.* Princeton, NJ: Educational Testing Service.

Bennett, G. K., Seashore, H. G., & Wesman, A. G. (1982). *Administrator's Handbook, Differential Aptitude Tests, Forms V and W.* Cleveland, OH: The Psychological Corporation.

Ben-Shakar, G., Lieblich, I., & Bar-Hillel, M. (1982). An evaluation of polygraphers' judgments: A review from a decision theoretic perspective. *Journal of Applied Psychology, 61*, 701–713.

Berk, R. A. (ed.) (1984). *A Guide to Criterion-referenced Test Construction.* Baltimore, MD: Johns Hopkins University Press.

Bernardin, H. J., Alveres, K. M., & Cranny, C. J. (1976). A recomparison of behavioral expectation scales to summated scales. *Journal of Applied Psychology, 61*, 564–570.

Binet, A., & Simon, T. (1905). Methodes nouvelles pour le diagnostic du niveau intellectuel des anormaux. *L'Annee Psychologique, 11*, 191–244.

Blanz, F., & Ghiselli, E. (1972). The mixed standard scale: A new rating system. *Personnel Psychology, 25*, 185–199.

Blatt, S., & Berman, W. (1984). A methodology for use of the Rorschach in clinical research. *Journal of Personality Assessment, 48*, 226–239.

Block, J. H. (ed.) (1971). *Mastery Learning: Theory and Practice.* New York: Holt, Rinehart and Winston.

Block, J. H. (1978). *The Q-sort Method in Personality Assessment and Psychiatric Research.* Palo Alto, CA: Consulting Psychologists Press.

Bloom, A. S., Allard, A. M., Zelko, F. A., Brill, W. J., Topinka, C. W., & Pfohl, W. (1988). Differential validity of the K-ABC for lower functioning preschool children versus those of higher ability. *American Journal of Mental Retardation, 93*, 273–277.

Bloom, B. S. (ed.) (1956). *Taxonomy of Educational Objectives, Handbook I: Cognitive Domain.* New York: Longman, Green and Company.

Bloom, B. S., Hastings, J. T., & Madaus, C. F. (1971). *Handbook of Formative and Summative Evaluation of Student Learning*. New York: McGraw-Hill.

Bower, E. M. (1969). *Early Identification of Emotionally Handicapped Children in School*, 2nd ed. Springfield, IL: Charles C Thomas.

Bright, T. L., & Hollon, C. J. (1985). State regulation of the polygraph tests at the workplace. *Personnel*, 50–56.

Brooks, P., & Arnold, D. (1989). *Examiner's Manual for the Reid Report*, 3rd ed. Chicago: Reid Psychological Systems.

Brown, F. G. (1979). The SOMPA: A system of measuring potential abilities? *School Psychologist Digest, 8*, 37–46.

Brown, F. G. (1983). *Principles of Educational and Psychological Testing*, 3rd ed. New York: Holt, Rinehart and Winston.

Bruininks, R. H., Woodcock, R. W., Weatherman, R. F., & Hill, B. K. (1984). *Scales of Independent Behavior*. Allen, TX: DLM Teaching Resources.

Buck, J. N. (1948). The H-T-P technique, a qualitative and quantitative scoring manual. *Journal of Clinical Psychology, 4*, 317–396.

Buck, J. N. (1966). *The House–Tree–Person Technique: Revised Manual*. Beverly Hills, CA: Western Psychological Services.

Buck, J. N. (1981). *The House–Tree–Person Technique: Revised Manual*. Beverly Hills, CA: Western Psychological Services.

Buros, O. K. (ed.) (1970). *Personality Tests and Reviews*. Highland Park, NJ: Gryphon Press.

Buros, O. K. (ed.) (1974). *Tests in Print II*. Highland Park, NJ: Gryphon Press.

Buros, O. K. (ed.) (1975a). *Intelligence Tests and Reviews II*. Highland Park, NJ: Gryphon Press.

Buros, O. K. (ed.) (1975b). *Personality Tests and Reviews II*. Highland Park, NJ: Gryphon Press.

Buros, O. K. (ed.) (1975c). *Reading Tests and Reviews II*. Highland Park, NJ: Gryphon Press.

Buros, O. K. (ed.) (1975d). *Vocational Tests and Reviews II*. Highland Park, NJ: Gryphon Press.

Butcher, J., Graham, J., Williams, C., & Ben-Porath, Y. (1990). *Development and Use of the MMPI-2 Content Scales*. Minneapolis: University of Minnesota Press.

Campbell, D. P. (1971). *Handbook for the Strong Vocational Interest Blank*. Stanford, CA: Stanford University Press.

Campbell, D. P. (1974). *Manual for the SVIB–SCII Strong–Campbell Interest Inventory*, 2nd ed. Stanford, CA: Stanford University Press.

Carlson, S. B. (1985). *Creative Classroom Testing*. Princeton, NJ: Educational Testing Service.

Cascio, W. F. (1982). *Applied Psychology in Personnel Management*, 2nd ed. Reston, VA: Reston.

Cattell, J. B. (1890). Mental tests and measurements. *Mind, 15*, 373–380. Englewood Cliffs, NJ: Prentice Hall.

Cattell, R. B. (1949). *Manual for Forms A and B: Sixteen Personality Factors Questionnaire*. Champaign, IL: Institute for Personality and Ability Testing.

Cattell, R. B., Eber, H. W., & Tatsuoka, M. M. (1970). *Handbook for the Sixteen Personality Factor Questionnaire (16PF)*. Champaign, IL: Institute for Personality and Ability Testing.

Champney, H., & Marshall, H. (1939). Optimal refinement of the rating scale. *Journal of Applied Psychology, 23,* 323–331.

Clarizio, H. F. (1979). SOMPA—A symposium continued: Commentaries. *School Psychology Digest, 8,* 207–209.

Connolly, A. J. (1988). *KeyMath Diagnostic Arithmetic Test—Revised.* Circle Pines, MN: American Guidance Service.

Conoley, J. C., & Kramer, J. J. (eds.) (1989). *The Tenth Mental Measurements Yearbook.* Lincoln, NE: Buros Institute of Mental Measurements.

Conoley, J. C., & Kramer, J. J. (eds.) (1992). *The Eleventh Mental Measurements Yearbook.* Lincoln, NE: Buros Institute of Mental Measurements.

Conrad, L., Trismen, D., & Miller, R. (eds.) (1977). *Graduate Record Examinations Technical Manual.* Princeton, NJ: Educational Testing Service.

Cooper, W. H. (1981). Ubiquitous halo. *Psychological Bulletin, 90,* 218–244.

Cramer, P. (1983, August). *Defense Mechanisms: A Developmental Study.* Paper presented at the annual meeting of the American Psychological Association, Anaheim, CA.

Crites, J. O. (1973). *Career Maturity Inventory: Theory and Research Handbook and Administration and Use Manual.* Monterey, CA: CTB/McGraw-Hill.

Crites, J. O. (1974). The Career Maturity Inventory. In D. E. Super (ed.), *Measuring Vocational Maturity for Counseling and Evaluation.* Washington, DC: National Vocational Guidance Association.

Cronbach, L. J. (1946). Response sets and test validity. *Educational and Psychological Measurement, 6,* 475–494.

Cronbach, L. J. (1950). Further evidence on response sets and test design. *Educational and Psychological Measurement, 10,* 3–31.

Cronbach, L. J. (1951). Coefficient alpha and the internal structure of tests. *Psychometrika, 16,* 297–334.

Cronbach, L. J. (1971). Test validation. In R. L. Thorndike (ed.), *Educational Measurement,* 2nd ed. Washington, DC: American Council on Education.

Cronbach, L. J., & Meehl, P. E. (1955). Construct validity in psychological tests. *Psychological Bulletin, 58,* 281–302.

CTB/McGraw-Hill (1985). *California Achievement Tests.* Monterey: CA: Author.

Cundick, B. P. (1985). Review of the Incomplete Sentences Task. In J. V. Mitchell (ed.) *The Ninth Mental Measurements Yearbook.* Lincoln, NE: Buros Institute of Mental Measurements.

Das, J. P., Kirby, J. R., & Jarman, R. F. (1979). *Simultaneous and Sequential Cognitive Processes.* New York: Academic Press.

Delhees, K. H., & Cattell, R. B. (1971). *Manual for the Clinical Analysis Questionnaire* (CAQ). Champaign, IL: Institute for Personality and Ability Testing.

Dickinson, T. L., & Zellinger, P. M. (1980). A comparison of behaviorally anchored rating and mixed standard scale formats. *Journal of Applied Psychology, 65,* 147–154.

Diedrich, P. B. (1973). *Short-cut Statistics for Teacher-made Tests.* Princeton, NJ: Educational Testing Service.

Dodrill, C. B., & Warner, M. H. (1988). Further studies of the Wonderlic Personnel Test as a brief measure of intelligence. *Journal of Consulting and Clinical Psychology, 59,* 145–147.

Donlon, T. F. (ed.) (1984). *The College Board Technical Handbook for the Scholastic Aptitude Test.* New York: College Entrance Examination Board.

Dougherty, T. W., Ebert, R. J., & Callender, J. C. (1986). Policy capturing in the employment interview. *Journal of Applied Psychology, 71*, 9–15.

Drummond, R. J. (1984). Review of the Edwards Personal Preference Schedule. In D. J. Keyser & R. C. Sweetland (eds.) (1987). *Test Critiques Compendium.* Kansas City, MO: Test Corporation of America.

DuBois, P. H. (1966). A test-dominated society: China 115 B.C.–1905 A.D. In A. Anastasi (ed.), *Testing Problems in Perspective.* Washington, DC: American Council on Education.

DuBois, P. H. (1970). *A History of Psychological Testing.* Boston: Allyn & Bacon.

Dunn, I. M., & Dunn, L. M. (1981) *Peabody Picture Vocabulary Test—Revised.* Circle Pines, MN: American Guidance Service.

Dush, D. M. (1985). Review of the Incomplete Sentences Task. In J. V. Mitchell (ed.) *The Ninth Mental Measurements Yearbook.* Lincoln, NE: Buros Institute of Mental Measurements.

Ebel, R. L. (1962). Content standard test scores. *Educational and Psychological Measurement, 22*, 15–25.

Ebel, R. L. (1979). *Essentials of Educational Measurement*, 3rd ed. Englewood Cliffs, NJ: Prentice Hall.

Edwards, A. L. (1957). *Techniques of Attitude Scale Construction.* New York: Appleton-Century-Crofts.

Edwards, A. L. (1959). *Edwards Personal Preference Schedule.* New York: Psychological Corporation.

Edwards, A. L. (1970). *The Measurement of Personality Traits by Scales and Inventories.* New York: Holt, Rinehart and Winston.

Elwood, D. L. (1969). Automation of psychological testing. *American Psychologist, 24*, 287–288.

Equal Employment Opportunity Commission (1978). *Uniform Guidelines on Employee Selection Procedures.* Washington, DC: U.S. Government Printing.

ETS: Educational Testing Service (1973). *Making the Classroom Test: A Guide for Teachers.* Princeton, NJ: ETS.

ETS: Educational Testing Service (1977). *GRE Technical Manual.* Princeton, NJ: Educational Testing Service.

ETS: Educational Testing Service (1993). *Guide to the Use of the Graduate Record Examinations Program.* Princeton, NJ: ETS.

Exner, J. E. (1974). *The Rorschach: A Comprehensive System: Vol 1. Basic Foundations.* New York: John Wiley & Sons.

Exner, J. E. (1978). *The Rorschach: A Comprehensive System: Vol. 2. Current Research and Advanced Interpretations.* New York: John Wiley & Sons.

Exner, J. E. (1986). *The Rorschach: A Comprehensive System: Volume 1. Basic Foundations*, 2nd ed. New York: John Wiley & Sons.

Exner, J. E., & Exner, D. E. (1972). How clinicians use the Rorschach. *Journal of Personality Assessment, 36*, 403–408.

Exner, J. E., & Weiner, I. B. (1982). *The Rorschach: A Comprehensive System: Vol 3. Assessment of Children and Adolescents.* New York: John Wiley & Sons.

Fee, A. F., Elkins, G. R., & Boyd L. (1982). Testing and counseling psychologists: Current practices and implications for training. *Journal of Personality Assessment, 46*, 116–118.

Feldman, M. J., & Corah, N. L. (1960). Social desirability and the forced choice method. *Journal of Consulting Psychology, 24*, 480–482.

Feldman, S. E., & Sullivan, D. S. (1960). Factors mediating the effects of enhanced rapport on children's performance. *Journal of Consulting and Clinical Psychology, 36*, 302.

Ferguson, R. L., & Novick, M. R. (1973). *Implementation of a Bayesian System for Decision Analysis in a Program of Individually Prescribed Instruction* (ACT Research Report No. 60). Iowa City, IA: American College Testing Program.

Field, J. G. (1960). Two types of tables for use with Wechsler's Intelligence Scales. *Journal of Clinical Psychology, 16*, 3–6.

Flaugher, R. L. (1978). The many definitions of test bias. *American Psychologist, 33*, 671–679.

Frank, G. H. (1970). The measurement of personality from the Wechsler tests. In B. A. Mahrer (ed.), *Progress in Experimental Personality Research*. New York: Academic Press.

Frank, L. K. (1939). Projective methods for the study of personality. *Journal of Psychology, 8*, 343–389.

Franzen, M. D. (1985). Review of the Luria–Nebraska Neuropsychological Battery. In D. J. Keyser & R. C. Sweetland (eds.) (1987). *Test Critiques Compendium*. Kansas City, MO: Test Corporation of America.

Frederickson, N. (1961). In-basket tests and factors in administrative performance. In H. Guetzkow (ed.), *Simulation in Social Science: Reading*. Englewood Cliffs, NJ: Prentice Hall.

Friedman, T., & Williams, E. B. (1982). Current use of tests for employment. In A. Wigdor & W. Garner (eds.), *Ability testing: Uses, Consequences, and Controversies. Part II. Documentation Section*. Washington, DC: National Academy Press.

Fuchs, D., & Fuchs, L. S. (1986). Test procedure bias: A meta-analysis of examiner familiarity effects. *Review of Educational Research, 56*, 243–262.

Galton, R. (1869). *Hereditary Genius: An Inquiry into its Laws and Consequences*. London: Collins.

Gerow, J. R. (1980). Performance on achievement tests as a function of the order of item difficulty. *Teaching of Psychology, 7*, 93–94.

Ghiselli, E. E. (1966). *The Validity of Occupational Aptitude Tests*. New York: John Wiley & Sons.

Gilmore, D. C., Beehr, T. A., & Love, K. G. (1986). Effects of applicant sex, applicant physical attractiveness, type of job on interview decisions. *Journal of Occupational Psychology, 59*, 103–109.

Glaser, R. (1963). Instructional technology and the measurement of learning outcomes. *American Psychologist, 18*, 519–522.

Glass, G. V. (1978). Standards and criteria. *Journal of Educational Measurement, 15*, 237–261.

Goh, D. S., Teslow, C. J., & Fuller, G. B. (1981). The practice of psychological assessment among school psychologists. *Professional Psychology, 12*, 696–706.

Goldberg, P. A. (1965). A review of sentence completion methods in personality assessment. *Journal of Projective Techniques and Personality Assessment, 29*, 12–45.

Golden, C. J., Purisch, A. D., & Hammeke, T. A. (1985). *Luria–Nebraska Neuropsychological Battery: Forms I and II*. Los Angeles: Western Psychological Services.

Goldman, L. (1971). *Using Tests in Counseling*, 2nd ed. New York: Appleton-Century-Crofts.

Goldstein, K., & Scheerer, M. (1941). Abstract and concrete behavior: An experimental study with special tests. *Psychological Monographs, 53*(2), whole No. 230.

Goodenough, F. (1926). *Measurement of Intelligence by Drawings.* New York: World Book.

Gough, H. G. (1960). The adjective checklist as a personality assessment research technique. *Psychological Reports, 6,* 107–122.

Gough, H. G. (1975). *California Psychological Inventory, Revised Manual.* Palo Alto, CA: Consulting Psychologists Press.

Gough, H. G. (1987). *California Psychological Inventory: Administrator's Guide.* Palo Alto, CA: Consulting Psychologists Press.

Gough, H. G., & Heilbrun, A. B., Jr. (1983). *The Adjective Check List Manual,* rev. ed. Palo Alto, CA: Consulting Psychologists Press.

Groff, M., & Hubble, L. (1981). Recategorized WISC—R scores of juvenile delinquents. *Journal of Learning Disabilities, 14,* 515–516.

Grossman, F. M. (1983). Percentage of WAIS-R standardization sample obtaining verbal-performance discrepancies. *Journal of Consulting and Clinical Psychology, 51,* 641–642.

Grossman, H. J. (ed.) (1983). *Classification in Mental Retardation.* Washington, DC: American Association on Mental Deficiency.

Groth-Marnat, G. (1990). *Handbook of Psychological Assessment,* 2nd ed. New York: John Wiley & Sons.

Guilford, J. P. (1954). *Psychometric Methods,* 2nd ed. New York: McGraw-Hill.

Guion, R. M. (1965). *Personnel Testing.* New York: McGraw-Hill.

Guttman, L. (1945). A basis for analyzing test–retest reliability. *Psychometrika, 10,* 255–282.

Guttman, L. (1947). The Cornell technique for scale and intensity analysis. *Educational and Psychological Measurement, 7,* 247–280.

Hager, P. C. (1986). Review of the Woodcock–Johnson Psycho-Educational Battery. In D. J. Keyser & R. C. Sweetland (eds.) (1987). *Test Critiques Compendium.* Kansas City, MO: Test Corporation of America.

Hallahan, D. P., & Kauffman, J. M. (1988). *Exceptional Children: Introduction to Special Education,* 4th ed. Englewood Cliffs, NJ: Prentice Hall.

Hambleton, R. K., & Novick, M. R. (1973). Toward an integration of theory and method for criterion-referenced tests. *Journal of Educational Measurement, 10,* 159–170.

Hammer, T. H., & Landau, J. (1981). Methodological issues in the use of absence data. *Journal of Applied Psychology, 66,* 574–581.

Hansen, J. C., & Campbell, D. P. (1985). *Manual for the SVIB–SCII,* 4th ed. Stanford, CA: Stanford University Press.

Harris, D. B. (1963). *Children's Drawings as Measures of Intellectual Maturity.* New York: Harcourt, Brace, Jovanovich.

Harris, M. M. (1989). Reconsidering the employment interview: A review of recent literature and suggestions for future research. *Personnel Psychology, 42,* 691–726.

Harris, W. G., & Gentry, M. U. (1992). *Test Manual for the Stanton Survey: New Edition.* Charlotte, NC: Pinkerton Services Group.

Harrison, R., & Rotter, J. B. (1945). A note on the reliability of the Thematic Apperception Test. *Journal of Abnormal and Social Psychology, 40,* 97–99.

Hartlage, L. C., & Steele, C. T. (1977). WISC and WISC—R correlates of academic achievement. *Psychology in the School, 14,* 15–18.

Hathaway, S. R., & McKinley, J. C. (1940). A multiphasic personality schedule (Minnesota). I: Construction of the schedule. *Journal of Psychology, 10,* 249–254.

Hathaway, S. R., & McKinley, J. C. (1943). *Manual for the Minnesota Multiphasic Personality Inventory.* New York: Psychological Corporation.

Hathaway, S. R., & McKinley, J. C. (1989). *The Minnesota Multiphasic Personality Inventory II.* Minneapolis: University of Minnesota Press.

Haynes, J. P., & Peltier, J. (1985). Patterns of practice with the TAT in a juvenile forensic sample. *Journal of Clinical Psychology, 42,* 534–537.

Heaton, R. K., & Pendleton, M. G. (1981). Use of neuropsychological tests to predict adult patients' everyday functioning. *Journal of Consulting and Clinical Psychology, 49,* 807–821.

Heiby, E. M. (1984). Review of the Wechsler Memory Scale. In D. J. Keyser & R. C. Sweetland (eds.) (1987). *Test Critiques Compendium.* Kansas City, MO: Test Corporation of America.

Henry, W. E. (1956). *The Analysis of Fantasy: The Thematic Apperception Technique in the Study of Personality.* New York: John Wiley & Sons.

Herbert, W. (1982). Intelligence tests: Sizing up a newcomer. *Science News, 122,* 280–281.

Heward, W. L., & Orlansky, M. D. (1988). *Exceptional Children,* 3rd ed. Columbus, OH: Merrill Publishing Co.

Hieronymous, A. N., & Hoover, H. D. (1985). *Iowa Test of Basic Skills—Forms G and H.* Chicago: Riverside Publishing Co.

Hogan, J., & Hogan, R. (1985). *Hogan Personnel Selection Series.* Minneapolis, MN: National Computer Service.

Hogan, J., & Quigley, A. M. (1986). Physical standards for employment and the courts. *American Psychologist, 41,* 1193–1217.

Holland, J. L. (1966). *The Psychology of Vocational Choice.* Waltham, MA: Blaisdell.

Holland, J. L. (1973). *Making Vocational Choices: A Theory of Careers.* Englewood Cliffs, NJ: Prentice Hall.

Holland, J. L. (1985a). *Making Vocational Choices: A Theory of Vocational Personalities and Work Environments,* 2nd ed. Engelwood Cliffs, NJ: Prentice Hall.

Holland, J. L. (1985b). *Self-directed Search: Professional Manual—1985 Edition.* Odessa, FL: Psychological Assessment Resources, Inc.

Holmes, T. H., & Rahe, R. H. (1967). The social readjustment rating scale. *Journal of Psychosomatic Research, 11,* 213–218.

Holtzman, W. H., Thorpe, J. S., Swartz, J. D., & Herron, E. W. (1961). *Inkblot Perception and Personality.* Austin: University of Texas Press.

Horn, J. L., & Cattell, R. B. (1966). Refinement and test of the theory of fluid and crystallized intelligence. *Journal of Educational Psychology, 57,* 253–276.

Hutt, M. L. (1985). *The Hutt adaptation of the Bender–Gestalt Test,* 4th ed. New York: Grune & Stratton.

Jackson, D. N. (1967). *Personality Research Form Manual.* Goshen, NY: Research Psychologists Press.

Jastak, J. F., & Jastak, S. (1984). *Wide Range Achievement Test.* Wilmington, DL: Jastak Associates, Inc.

Johansson, C. B. (1976). *Manual for the Career Assessment Inventory.* Mineapolis, MN: National Computer Systems, Inc.

Johnson, D. F., & Mihal, W. L. (1973). The performance of blacks and whites in manual vs. computerized testing environments. *American Psychologist, 28,* 694–699.

Joseph, A. (1977). *Intelligence, IQ, and Race–When, How, and Why They Become Associated.* San Francisco: R & E Research Associates.

Jung, C. G. (1910). The association method. *American Journal of Psychology, 21,* 219–269.

Kaplan, R. M., & Saccuzzo, D. P. (1993). *Psychological Testing: Principles, Applications and Issues,* 3rd ed. Pacific Grove, CA: Brooks/Cole Publishing Co.

Kaufman, A. S. (1976). Verbal-performance IQ discrepancies on the WISC—R. *Journal of Consulting and Clinical Psychology, 44,* 739–744.

Kaufman, A. S. (1979). *Intelligent Testing with the WISC—R.* New York: John Wiley & Sons.

Kaufman, A. S., & Kaufman, N. L. (1983). *K-ABC: Kaufman Assessment Battery for Children.* Circle Pines, MN: American Guidance Service.

Kavale, K. A., & Forness, S. R. (1984). A meta-analysis of the validity of Wechsler Scale profiles and recategorizations: Patterns or parodies? *Learning Disability Quarterly, 7,* 136–156.

Kent, G. H., & Rosanoff, A. J. (1910). A study of association in insanity. *American Journal of Insanity, 67,* 37–96.

Keyser, D. J., & Sweetland, R. C. (eds.) (1984–1988). *Test Critiques, Vols. I–VII.* Kansas City, MO: Test Corporation of America.

Killian, G. A. (1984). Review of the House–Tree–Person technique. In D. J. Keyser & R. C. Sweetland (eds.) (1987). *Test Critiques Compendium.* Kansas City, MO: Test Corporation of America.

Klopfer, B. (1937). The present status of the theoretical development of the Rorschach method. *Rorschach Research Exchange, 1,* 142–147.

Klopfer, W. B., & Taulbee, E. S. (1976). Projective tests. *Annual Review of Psychology, 27,* 543–568.

Koppitz, E. M. (1975). *The Bender–Gestalt Test for Young Children: Vol. II. Research and Application, 1963–1975.* New York: Grune & Stratton.

Kraiger, K., Hakel, M. D., & Cornelius, E. T., III (1984). Exploring fantasies of TAT reliability. *Journal of Personality Assessment, 48,* 365–370.

Krathwohl, D. R., Bloom, B. S., & Masia, B. B. (1964). *Taxonomy of educational objectives, Handbook II: Affective domain.* New York: David McKay.

Kuder, G. F. (1979). *Manual, Kuder Occupational Interest Survey, 1979 revision.* Chicago: Science Research Associates.

Kuder, G. F., & Richardson, M. W. (1937). The theory of the estimation of reliability. *Psychometrika, 2,* 151–160.

Lacks, P. (1984). *Bender–Gestalt Screening for Brain Dysfunction.* New York: John Wiley & Sons.

Landy, F. J. (1985). *The Psychology of Work Behavior,* 3rd ed. Homewood, IL: Dorsey Press.

Landy, F. J., & Farr, J. L. (1980). Performance rating. *Psychological Bulletin, 87,* 72–107.

Landy, F. J., & Farr, J. L. (1983). *The Measurement of Work Performance: Methods, Theory, and Applications.* New York: Academic Press.

Lanyon, B. P., & Lanyon, R. I. (1980). *Incomplete Sentences Task: Manual.* Chicago: Stoelting.

Latham, G. P., & Wexley, K. (1977). Behavioral observation scales. *Journal of Applied Psychology, 30,* 255–268.

Latham, G. P., Fay, C. H., & Saari, L. M. (1979). The development of behavioral observation scales for appraising the performance of foremen. *Personnel Psychology, 32,* 299–316.

Latham, G. P., Saari, L. M., & Fay, C. (1980). BOS, BES, and baloney: Raising Kane with Bernardin. *Personnel Psychology*, *33*, 815–821.

Lerner, H., & Lerner, P. (1986). Review of the Rorschach Inkblot Test. In D. J. Keyser & R. C. Sweetland (eds.) (1987). *Test Critiques Compendium*. Kansas City, MO: Test Corporation of America.

Likert, R. (1932). A technique for the measurement of attitudes. *Archives of Psychology*, No. 40.

Linn, R. (1982). Ability testing: Individual differences, prediction, and differential prediction. In A. Wigdor & W. Garner (eds.), *Ability Testing: Uses, Consequences, and Controversies, Part II*. Washington, DC: National Academy Press.

Little, K. B., & Shneidman, E. S. (1959). Congruencies among interpretations of psychological test and anamnestic data. *Psychological Monographs*, *73*, 6, whole No. 476.

Litwin, G. H., & Stringer, Jr., R. A. (1968). *Motivation and Organizational Climate*. Cambridge, MA: Harvard University, Graduate School of Business.

London House, Inc. (1991). *Personnel Selection Inventory Information Guide*. Park Ridge, IL: London House.

Lowman, R. L. (1991). *The Clinical Practice of Career Assessment*. Washington, DC: American Psychological Association.

Lubin, B., Larsen, R. M., & Matarazzo, J. D. (1984). Patterns of psychological test usage in the United States: 1935–1982. *American Psychologist*, *39*, 451–454.

Lubin, B., Larsen, R. M., Matarazzo, J. D., & Seever, M. (1986a). Selected characteristics of psychologists and psychological assessment in five settings: 1959–1982. *Professional Psychology: Research and Practice 17*, 155–157.

Lubin, B., Larsen, R. M., Matarazzo, J. D., & Seever, M. (1986b). Psychological assessment services and psychological test usage in private practice and in military settings. *Psychotherapy in Private Practice*, *4*, 19–29.

Lunemann, A. (1974). The correlational validity of IQ as a function of ethnicity and desegregation. *Journal of School Psychology*, *12*, 263–268.

Luria, A. R. (1973). *The Working Brain*. New York: Basic Books.

Lykken, D. T. (1979). The detection of deception. *Psychological Bulletin*, *86*, 47–53.

Lyman, B., Hatlelid, D., & MacCundy, C. (1981). Stimulus–person cues in first-impression attraction. *Perceptual and Motor Skills*, *52*, 59–66.

McCabe, D. J., Dalessio, A., Briga, J., & Sasaki, J. (1980). The convergent and discriminant validities between the IOR and the JDI: English and Spanish forms. *Academy of Management Journal*, *23*, 778–786.

McCallum, R. S., Karnes, F. A., & Oehler-Stinnett, J. (1985). Construct validity of the K-ABC for gifted children. *Psychology in the Schools*, *22*, 254–259.

McClelland, D. C., Atkinson, J. W., Clark, R. A., & Lowell, E. L. (1953). *The Achievement Motive*. Englewood Cliffs, NJ: Prentice-Hall.

McCormick, E. J., & Ilgen, D. (1985). *Industrial and Organizational Psychology*, 8th ed. Englewood Cliffs, NJ: Prentice Hall.

McCormick, E. J., & Sanders, M. S. (1982). *Human Factors in Engineering and Design*, 5th ed. New York: McGraw-Hill.

Machover, K. (1949). *Personality Projection in the Drawing of a Human Figure*. Springfield, IL: Charles C Thomas.

Machover, K. (1971). *Personality Projection in the Drawing of the Human Figure*, 2nd ed. Springfield, IL: Charles C Thomas.

Marland, S. P. (1971). *Education of the Gifted and Talented*. Washington, DC: U.S. Office of Education.

Marx, M. B., Garrity, T. F., & Bowers, F. R. (1975). The influence of recent life history on the health of college freshmen. *Journal of Psychosomatic Research, 19,* 87–98.

Maslach, C., & Jackson, S. E. (1981). The measurement of experienced burnout. *Journal of Occupational Behavior, 2,* 99–113.

Matarazzo, J. D. (1972). *Wechsler's Measurement and Appraisal of Adult Intelligence*, 5th ed. Baltimore, MD: Williams & Wilkins.

May, R. (1966). Sex differences in fantasy patterns. *Journal of Projective Techniques and Personality Assessment, 30,* 576–586.

Megargee, E. (1972). *The California Psychological Inventory Handbook*. San Francisco, CA: Jossey-Bass, Inc.

Mercer, J. R. (1979). In defense of racially and culturally nondiscriminatory assessment. *School Psychology Digest, 8,* 89–115.

Meyer, R. G. (1993). *The Clinician's Handbook*, 3rd ed. Boston: Allyn & Bacon.

Miller, P. W., & Erickson, H. E. (1985). *Teacher-written Student Tests: A Guide for Planning, Creating, Administering, and Assessing*. Washington, DC: National Education Association.

Mitchell, J. V. (ed.) (1983). *Tests in Print III*. Lincoln: University of Nebraska Press.

Mitchell, J. V. (ed.) (1985). *The Ninth Mental Measurements Yearbook*. Lincoln, NE: Buros Institute of Mental Measurements.

Morgan, D. (1984). What do the SATs mean? SATs are getting in the way of education. *Current, 1,* 9–13.

Muchinsky, P. M. (1987). *Psychology Applied to Work: An Introduction to Industrial and Organizational Psychology*. Chicago: Dorsey Press.

Murphy, K. R. (1984a). Review of Wonderlic Personnel Test. In D. Keyser & R. Sweetland (eds.), *Test Critiques, Vol. 1.* Kansas City, MO: Test Corporation of America.

Murphy, K. R. (1984b). Review of Armed Services Vocational Aptitude Battery. In D. Keyser & R. Sweetland (eds.), *Test Critiques, Vol. 1.* Kansas City, MO: Test Corporation of America.

Murphy, K. R., & Davidshofer, C. O. (1988). *Psychological Testing: Principles and Applications*. Englewood Cliffs, NJ: Prentice Hall.

Murphy, K. R., Martin, C., & Garcia, M. (1982). Do behavioral observation scales measure observation? *Journal of Applied Psychology, 67,* 562–567.

Murray, H. A. (1938). *Explorations in Personality*. New York: Oxford University Press.

Murray, H. A. (1943). *Thematic Apperception Test Manual*. Cambridge, MA: Harvard University Press.

Myers, I. B. (1976). *Introduction to Type*. Palo Alto, CA: Consulting Psychologists Press.

Myers, I. B. (1977). *The Myers/Briggs Type Indicator: Supplementary Manual*. Palo Alto, CA: Consulting Psychologists Press.

Naglieri, J. A. (1984). Concurrent and predictive validity of the Kaufman Assessment Battery for children with a Navajo sample. *Journal of School Psychology, 22,* 373–380.

Nitko, A. J. (1983). *Educational Tests and Measurements*. New York: Harcourt Brace Jovanovich.

Nolan, R. F., Watlington, D. K., & Willson, V. L. (1989). Gifted and nongifted race and gender effects on item functioning on the Kaufman Assessment Battery for Children. *Journal of Clinical Psychology, 45,* 645–650.

Osgood, C. E., Suci, G. J., & Tannenbaum, P. H. (1957). *The Measurement of Meaning.* Urbana: University of Illinois Press.

Otis, A. S., & Lennon, R. T. (1990). *Technical Manual for the Otis–Lennon School Ability Test.* New York: The Psychological Corporation.

Paajanen, G. E. (1986, August). *Development and Validation of the PDI Employment Inventory.* Paper presented at the 94th Annual Convention of the American Psychological Association, Washington, DC.

Paraskevopoulos, J., & Kirk, S. (1969). *The Development and Psychometric Characteristics of the Revised Illinois Test of Psycholinguistic Ability.* Urbana: University of Illinois Press.

Parker, F. (1983). A meta-analysis of the reliability and validity of the Rorschach. *Journal of Personality Assessment, 42,* 227–231.

Payne, J. S., Patton, J. R., & Patton, F. E. (1986). Adaptive behavior. In J. R. Patton, J. S. Payne, & M. Beirne-Smith (eds.), *Mental Retardation,* 2nd ed. Columbus, OH: Merrill.

Pennock-Roman, M. (1985). Differential aptitude tests. In D. J. Keyser & R. C. Sweetland (eds.), *Test Critiques Compendium.* Kansas City, MO: Test Corporation of America.

Pervin, L. A. (1968). Performance and satisfaction as a function of individual–environment fit. *Psychological Bulletin, 69,* 56–68.

Peterson, C. J., & Thurstone, L. L. (1933). *Motion Pictures and the Social Attitudes of Children.* New York: Macmillan, Inc.

Petrie, B. M. (1969). Statistical analysis of attitude scale scores. *Research Quarterly* (AAHPER), *40,* 434–437.

Pietrofesa, J., Hoffman, A., & Splete, H. (1984). *Counseling: An Introduction.* Boston: Houghton Mifflin.

Popham, W. J. (1980). Domain specification strategies. In R. J. Berk (ed.), *Criterion-referenced Measurement.* Baltimore, MD: Johns Hopkins University Press.

Prigatano, G. (1978). Wechsler Memory Scale: A selective review of the literature. *Journal of Clinical Psychology, 34,* 816–832.

Psychological Corporation (1988). *Guide to the Miller Analogies Test.* New York: Psychological Corporation.

Pugh, R. C., & Sassenrath, J. M. (1968). Comparable scores for the CEEB Scholastic Aptitude Test and the American College Test Program. *Measurement and Evaluation in Guidance, 1,* 103–109.

Rahmlow, H. F., & Woodley, K. K. (1979). *Objectives-based Testing: A Guide to Effective Test Development.* Englewood Cliffs, NJ: Educational Technology Publications.

Rapaport, C., Gill, M., & Schafer, J. (1946). *Diagnostic Psychological Testing.* Chicago: Year Book Publishers.

Rapaport, C., Gill, M., & Schafer, J. (1968). *Diagnostic Psychological Testing,* revised ed. Chicago: Year Book Publishers.

Recase, M. D. (1977). Procedures for computerized testing. *Behavior Research, Methods and Instrumentation, 9,* 148–152.

Reilly, R. R., & Chao, G. T. (1982). Validity and fairness of some alternate employee selection procedures. *Personnel Psychology, 35,* 1–67.

Reinehr, R. C. (1984). Review of the Wide Range Achievement Test. In D. J. Keyser & R. C. Sweetland (eds.) (1987). *Test Critiques Compendium.* Kansas City, MO: Test Corporation of America.

Reitan, R. M. (1967). Neurological and physiological bases of psychopathology. *Annual Review of Psychology, 27,* 189–216.

Reitan, R. M. (1969). *Manual for Administration of Neuropsychological Test Batteries for Adults and Children.* Indianapolis, Ind.: Author.

Reitan, R. M., & Wolfson, D. (1985). *The Halstead-Reitan Neuropsychological Test Battery: Theory and Clinical Interpretation.* Tucson, AZ: Tucson Neuropsychological Press.

Renzulli, J. S., & Delacourt, M. A. (1986). The legacy and logic of research on identification of gifted persons. *Gifted Child Quarterly, 30,* 20–23.

Richardson, M. W., & Kuder, G. F. (1939). The calculation of test reliability coefficients based on the method of rational equivalence. *Journal of Educational Psychology, 30,* 681–687.

Ritzler, B. A., & Alter, B. (1986). Rorschach teaching in APA-approved clinical graduate programs: Ten years later. *Journal of Personality Assessment, 50,* 44–49.

Roback, H. B. (1968). Human figure drawings: Their utility in the clinical psychologist's armentarium for personality assessment. *Psychological Bulletin, 70,* 1–19.

Robinson, J. P., Shaver, P. R., & Wrightsman, L. S. (1991). *Measures of personality and social psychological attitudes.* San Diego, CA: Academic Press.

Roid, G. H., & Fitts, W. H. (1988). *Tennessee Self-concept Scale* (revised manual). Los Angeles, CA: Western Psychological Services.

Rorschach, H. (1921). *Psychodiagnostik* Bern: Bircher. (Hans Huber, verlag, trans., 1942).

Rosenfeld, P., Doherty, L. M., Vicino, S. M., Kantor, J., et al. (1989). Attitudes assessment in organizations: Testing three microcomputer based survey systems. *Journal of General Psychology, 116,* 145–154.

Rotter, J. B., & Rafferty, J. E. (1950). *Manual: The Rotter Incomplete Sentences Blank.* San Antonio, TX: Psychological Corporation.

Russell, E. (1975). A multiple scoring method for the assessment of complex memory functions. *Journal of Consulting and Clinical Psychology, 43,* 800–809.

Ryan, R. M. (1985). Review of the Thematic Apperception Test. In D. J. Keyser & R. C. Sweetland (eds.) (1987). *Test Critiques Compendium.* Kansas City, MO: Test Corporation of America.

Saccuzzo, D. P., Johnson, N. E., & Russell, G. (1992). Verbal and performance IQs for gifted African-American, Caucasian, Filipino and Hispanic children. *Psychological Assessment, 4,* 239–244.

Sackett, P. R., & Harris, M. M. (1984). Honesty testing for personnel selection: A review and critique. *Personnel Psychology, 37,* 221–245.

Sackett, P. R., Burris, L. R., & Callahan, C. (1989). Integrity testing for personnel selection: An update. *Personnel Psychology, 42,* 491–529.

Sattler, J. M. (1988). *Assessment of Children,* 3rd ed. San Diego, CA: Sattler.

Sattler, J. M. (1993). *Interviewing.* San Diego, CA: Sattler.

Satz, P., & Fletcher, J. M. (1981). Emergent trends in neuropsychology: An overview. *Journal of Consulting and Clinical Psychology, 34,* 172–176.

Sax, G. (1989). *Principles of Educational and Psychological Measurement,* 3rd ed. Belmont, CA: Wadsworth.

Scheuneman, J. D. (1987). An experimental, exploratory study of causes of bias in test items. *Journal of Educational Measurement, 24,* 97–118.

Schiffman, L. G., & Kanuck, L. K. (1983). *Consumer Behavior,* 2nd ed. Engelwood Cliffs, NJ: Prentice Hall.

Schneider, B., & Dachler, H. P. (1978). A note on the stability of the Job Descriptive Index. *Journal of Applied Psychology, 63,* 650–653.

Sellitz, C., Wrightsman, L. S., & Cook, S. W. (1976). *Research Methods in Social Relations,* 3rd ed. New York: Holt, Rinehart and Winston.

Shneidman, E. S. (ed.) (1951). *Thematic Test Analysis.* New York: Grune and Stratton.

Siegel, L., & Lane, I. M. (1982). *Personnel and Organizational Psychology.* Homewood, IL: Richard D. Irwin.

Silverstein, A. B. (1982). Factor structure of the Wechsler Adult Intelligence Scale—Revised. *Journal of Consulting and Clinical Psychology, 50,* 661–664.

Simpson, R. L. (1981). Screening and assessment strategies for behaviorally disordered adolescents. In G. Brown, R. L. McDowell, & J. Smith (eds.), *Educating Adolescents with Behavior Disorders.* Columbus, OH: Merrill.

Singh, L. (1986). Relationships of graduation requirements and course offerings to Scholastic Aptitude Test performance of seniors in high schools. *Journal of Educational Research, 80,* 5–9.

Sisk, D. A. (1984, October). *A National Survey of Gifted Programs.* Presented to the National Business Consortium for Gifted and Talented, Washington, DC.

Slavin, R. E. (1991). *Educational Psychology,* 3rd ed. Englewood Cliffs, NJ: Prentice Hall.

Smith, P., & Kendall, L. (1963). Retranslation of expectations: An approach to the construction of unambiguous anchors for rating scales. *Journal of Applied Psychology, 47,* 149–155.

Smith, P. C., Kendall, L. M., & Hulin, C. L. (1969). *The Measurement of Satisfaction in Work and Retirement.* Chicago: Rand McNally.

Smith, P. C., Smith, O. W., & Rollo, J. (1974). Factor structure for blacks and whites of the Job Descriptive Index and its discrimination of job satisfaction. *Journal of Applied Psychology, 59,* 99–100.

Society for Research in Child Development (1992). Testing in American Schools: Issues for research and policy. *Social Policy Report, 6,* 1–24.

Sparrow, S. S., Balla, D. A., & Cicchetti, D. V. (1984). *Vineland Adaptive Behavior Scales.* Circle Pines, MN: American Guidance Service.

Spearman, C. E. (1927). *The Abilities of Man.* New York: Macmillan, Inc.

Spruill, J. (1987). Review of the Stanford–Binet Intelligence Scale, 4th ed. In D. J. Keyser & R. C. Sweetland (eds.) (1987). *Test Critiques Compendium.* Kansas City, MO: Test Corporation of America.

Stanton, W. J., & Futrell, C. (1987). *Fundamentals of Marketing,* 8th ed. New York: McGraw-Hill.

Stapp, J., & Fulcher, R. (1983). The employment of APA members: 1982. *American Psychologist, 38,* 1298–1320.

Stephenson, W. (1953). *The Study of Behavior.* Chicago: University of Chicago Press.

Sternberg, R. J. (1984). The Kaufman Assessment Battery for Children: An information processing analysis and critique. *Journal of Special Education, 18,* 269–279.

Sternberg, R. J. (1988). *The Triarchic Mind: A Theory of Human Intelligence*. New York: Viking.

Stone, C., & Wechsler, D. (1946). *Wechsler Memory Scale Form II*. New York: The Psychological Corporation.

Strong, E. K. (1927). Vocational Interest Test. *Educational Record, 8,* 107–121.

Strong, E. K., Jr., & Campbell, D. P. (1966). *Manual for the Strong Vocational Interest Blank.* Stanford, CA: Stanford University Press.

Super, D. E. (1957). *The Psychology of Careers: An Introduction to Vocational Development.* New York: Harper & Row.

Sutton, P. M., & Swensen, C. H. (1983). The reliability and concurrent validity of alternative methods for assessing ego development. *Journal of Personality Assessment, 47,* 468–475.

Sweetland, R. C., & Keyser, D. J. (eds.) (1983). *Tests: A Comprehensive Reference for Assessment in Psychology, Education, and Business.* Kansas City, MO: Test Corporation of America.

Sweetland, R. C., & Keyser, D. J. (eds.) (1986). *Tests: A Comprehensive Reference for Assessment in Psychology, Education, and Business,* 2nd ed. Kansas City, MO: Test Corporation of America.

Swensen, C. H. (1957). Empirical evaluations of human figure drawings. *Psychological Bulletin, 54,* 431–466.

Swensen, C. H. (1968). Empirical evaluations of human figure drawings. *Psychological Bulletin, 70,* 20–44.

Swerdlik, M. E. (1992). Review of the Otis–Lennon School Ability Test, 6th ed. In J. C. Conoley & J. J. Kramer (eds.). *The Eleventh Mental Measurements Yearbook.* Lincoln, NE: Buros Institute of Mental Measurements.

Taylor, R. L., Sternberg, L., & Partenio, I. (1986). Performance of urban and rural children on the SOMPA: Preliminary investigation. *Perceptual and Motor Skills, 63,* 1219–1223.

Tenopyr, M. L. (1981). The realities of employment testing. *American Psychologist, 36,* 1120–1127.

Terman, L. M. (1916). *The Measurement of Intelligence.* Boston: Houghton Mifflin.

Terman, L. M., & Merrill, M. A. (1937). *Measuring Intelligence.* Boston: Houghton Mifflin.

Terris, W. (1986). *The Development and Validation of the EPI-3.* Technical Report. Park Ridge, IL: London House.

Thompson, D. E., & Thompson, T. A. (1982). Court standards for job analysis in test validation. *Personnel Psychology, 35,* 865–874.

Thompson, R. J. (1981). The diagnostic utility of Bannatyne's recategorized WISC—R scores with children referred to a developmental evaluation center. *Psychology in the Schools, 18,* 43–47.

Thorndike, R. L., & Hagen, E. P. (1986). *Technical manual for the Cognitive Abilities Test.* Chicago: Riverside Publishing Co.

Thorndike, R. L., Hagen, E. P., & Sattler, J. M. (1986) *Technical manual: Stanford–Binet Intelligence Scale,* 4th ed. Chicago: Riverside Publishing Co.

Thorndike, R. M., Cunningham, G. K., Thorndike, R. L., & Hagen, E. P. (1991). *Measurement and Evaluation in Psychology and Education,* 5th ed. New York: Macmillan, Inc.

Thurstone, L. L. (1925). A method of scaling psychological and educational tests. *Educational Psychology, 16,* 433–451.

Thurstone, L. L. (1947). The calibration of test items. *American Psychologist, 2*, 103–104.

Thurstone, L. L. (1959). *The Measurement of Values*. Chicago: University of Chicago Press.

Thurstone, L. L., & Chave, E. J. (1929). *The Measurement of Attitude*. Chicago: University of Chicago Press.

Torgerson, W. S. (1958). *Theory and Methods of Scaling*. New York: John Wiley & Sons.

Turner, J. E. (1986). *Air Traffic Controller*. Englewood Cliffs, N.J.: Prentice Hall.

Valencia, R. R., & Lopez, R. (1992). Assessment of racial and ethnic minority students: Problems and prospects. In M. Zeidner & R. Most (eds.), *Psychological Testing: An Inside View*. Palo Alto, CA: Consulting Psychologist Press.

Wade, T. C., & Baker, T. B. (1977). Opinions and use of psychological tests. *American Psychologist, 32*, 874–882.

Wagner, E. E., Alexander, R. A., Roos, G., & Adair, H. (1986). Optimum split-half reliabilities for the Rorschach: Projective techniques are more reliable than we think. *Journal of Personality Assessment, 50*, 107–112.

Wallace, W. L. (1972). Review of the SAT. In O. K. Buros (ed.), *The Seventh Mental Measurements Yearbook* (vol. 1). Highland Park, NJ: Gryphon Press.

Ward, T. K., et al. (1989). The effect of computerized tests on the performance and attitudes of college students. *Journal of Educational Computing Research, 5*, 327–333.

Watkins, C. E., Jr., Campbell, V. L., & McGregor, P. (1988). Counseling psychologists' uses of the opinions about psychological tests: A contemporary perspective. *Counseling Psychologist, 16*, 476–486.

Watkins, C. E., Jr., Lopez, F. G., Campbell, V. L., & Himmel, C. D. (1986). Counseling psychology and clinical psychology: Some preliminary comparative data. *American Psychologist, 41*, 581–582.

Wechsler, D. (1939). *The Measurement of Adult Intelligence*. Baltimore, MD: Williams & Wilkins.

Wechsler, D. (1945). *Wechsler Memory Scale*. New York: The Psychological Corporation.

Wechsler, D. (1949). *Manual for the Wechsler Intelligence Scale for Children*. New York: The Psychological Corporation.

Wechsler, D. (1958). *The Measurement and Appraisal of Adult Intelligence*, 4th ed. Baltimore, MD: Williams & Wilkins.

Wechsler, D. (1967). *Manual for the Wechsler Preschool and Primary Scale*. New York: The Psychological Corporation.

Wechsler, D. (1975). *Manual for the Wechsler Intelligence Scale for Children—Revised*. New York: The Psychological Corporation.

Wechsler, D. (1981). *Manual for the Wechsler Adult Intelligence Scale—Revised*. New York: The Psychological Corporation.

Wechsler, D. (1989). *Manual for the Wechsler Preschool and Primary Scale—Revised*. New York: The Psychological Corporation.

Wechsler, D. (1991). *Wechsler Intelligence Scale for Children—III Manual*. San Antonio, TX: The Psychological Corporation.

Weiss, D. J., & Davidson, N. L. (1981). Test theory and methods. *Annual Review of Psychology, 32*, 629–658.

Weiss, D. J., Dawis, R. V., England, G. W., & Lofquist, L. H. (1967). *Manual for the Minnesota Satisfaction Questionnaire* (Minnesota Studies on Vocational Rehabilitation, vol.

22). Minneapolis: University of Minnesota, Industrial Relations Center, Work Adjustment Project.

Werner, H., & Strauss, A. A. (1941). Pathology of figure–background relation in the child. *Journal of Abnormal and Social Psychology, 36*, 236–248.

Wernimont, P. F., & Campbell, J. P. (1968). Signs, samples, and criteria. *Journal of Applied Psychology, 52*, 372–376.

Wertheimer, M. (1923). Studies in the theory of Gestalt psychology. *Psychological Forsch, 41*, 301–350.

Wesman, A. G. (1972). Writing the test item. In R. L. Thorndike (ed.). *Educational Measurement*, 2nd ed. Washington, DC: American Council on Education.

Westen, D. (1991). Clinical assessment of object relations using the TAT. *Journal of Personality Assessment, 56*, 56–74.

Whipple, G. M. (1910). *Manual of Mental and Physical Tests*. Baltimore, MD: Warwick & York.

Wiederholt, J. L., & Bryant, B. R. (1986). *GORT—R (Gray Oral Reading Tests—Revised) Manual*. Austin, TX: PRO-ED.

Wiesner, W. H., & Cronshaw, S. F. (1988). A meta-analytic investigation of the impact of interview format and degree of structure on the validity of the employment interview. *Journal of Occupational Psychology, 61*, 275–290.

Wigdor, A. K., & Garner, W. R. (1982). *Ability testing: Its Uses, Consequences and Controversies. Part I: Report of the Committee, Part II: Documentation Section*. Washington, DC: National Academy Press.

Wiggins, N. (1966). Individual viewpoints of social desirability. *Psychological Bulletin, 66*, 68–77.

Wild, C. L., McPeek, W. M., Koffler, S. L., Braun, H. I., & Cowell, W. (1989). Concurrent validity of verbal item types for ethnic and gender subgroups. *GRE Publication Report 84–10p*. Princeton, NJ: Educational Testing Service.

Williams, R. L. (1971). Abuses and miscues in testing black children. *Counseling Psychologist, 2*, 62–77.

Wise, P. S. (1989). *The Use of Assessment Techniques by Applied Psychologists*. Belmont, CA: Wadsworth.

Wirt, R. D., & Lachar, D. (1981). The Personality Inventory for Children: Development and clinical applications. In P. McReynolds (ed.). *Advances in Psychological Assessment* (vol. 5). San Francisco: Jossey-Bass.

Witmer, J. M., Bornstein, A. V., & Dunham, R. M. (1971). The effects of verbal approval and disapproval upon the performance of third and fourth grade children on four subtests of the Wechsler Intelligence Scale for Children. *Journal of School Psychology, 9*, 347–356.

Wolk, R. L., & Wolk, R. B. (1971). *Manual: Gerontological Apperception Test*. New York: Human Sciences Press.

Womer, F. B. (1970). *What Is National Assessment?*. Ann Arbor, MI: National Assessment of Educational Progress.

Woodcock, R. W. (1987). *Woodcock Reading Mastery Tests—Revised*. Circle Pines, MN: American Guidance Service.

Woodcock, R. W., & Johnson, M. (1978). *Woodcock–Johnson Psycho-Educational Battery*. Allen, TX: DLM Teaching Resources.

Woodworth, R. S. (1920). *Personal Data Sheet*. Chicago: Stoelting.

Yeager, S. J. (1981). Dimensionality of the Job Descriptive Index. *Academy of Management Journal, 14,* 205–212.

Yerkes, R. M., Bridges, J. W., & Hardwick, R. S. (1915). *A Point Scale for Measuring Mental Ability*. Baltimore, MD: Warwick & York.

Zigler, E., Balla, D., & Hodapp, R. (1984). On the definition and classification of mental retardation. *American Journal of Mental Deficiency, 89,* 215–230.

Zytowski, D. G. (1985). *Kuder DD Manual Supplement*. Chicago: Science Research Associates.

Zytowski, D. G., & Warman, R. E. (1982). The changing use of tests in counseling. *Measurement and Evaluation in Guidance, 15,* 147–152.

Answers to Practice Problems

CHAPTER 5 PRACTICE BOXES

Practice Box 5.1: Frequency Distributions (Tables and Graphs)

Quiz 1		Quiz 2		Quiz 3		Quiz 4	
X	$f(X)$	X	$f(X)$	X	$f(X)$	X	$f(X)$
9	1	9	1	10	1	10	2
8	3	8	3	9	1	9	3
7	4	7	4	8	2	8	5
6	3	6	5	7	3	7	3
5	2	5	1	6	4	6	2
4	1	4	1	5	3		
3	1			4	1		

Quiz 1

Quiz 2

Quiz 3

Quiz 4

Practice Box 5.2: Measures of Central Tendency

	Quiz 1	Quiz 2	Quiz 3	Quiz 4
Mode	7	6	6	8
Median	Between 6.5 and 7.5	Between 6.5 and 7.5	Between 5.5 and 6.5	8
	$p_b = .5$ of 4 @ 7	$p_b = .5$ of 4 @ 7	$p_b = 3.5$ of 4 @ 6	
	$6.5 + .5/4(7.5 - 6.5)$	$6.5 + .5/4(7.5 - 6.5)$	$5.5 + .5/4(6.5 - 5.5)$	(interpolation
	$6.5 + .5/4(1)$	$6.5 + .5/4(1)$	$5.5 + 3.5/4(1)$	not necessary)
	$6.5 + .125 = 6.625$	$6.5 + .125 = 6.625$	$5.5 + .875 = 6.375$	
Mean	$96/15 = 6.4$	$100/15 = 6.667$	$99/15 = 6.6$	$120/15 = 8$

Practice Box 5.3: Measures of Variability

	Quiz 1	Quiz 2	Quiz 3	Quiz 4
Range	$9 - 3 = 6$	$9 - 4 = 5$	$10 - 4 = 6$	$10 - 6 = 4$
Var.	$\dfrac{652 - [(96)^2/15]}{15}$	$\dfrac{690 - [(100)^2/15]}{15}$	$\dfrac{691 - [(99)^2/15]}{15}$	$\dfrac{982 - [(120)^2/15]}{15}$
	$= 2.5067$	$= 1.5555$	$= 2.5067$	$= 1.4667$
St. dv.	$\sqrt{2.5067} = 1.5832$	$\sqrt{1.5555} = 1.2472$	$\sqrt{2.5067} = 1.5833$	$\sqrt{1.4667} = 1.2111$

Practice Box 5.4: Describing Distributions

Quizzes 1 and 2 are negatively skewed: the mean is less than the median in both cases. Quiz 3 is positively skewed: the mean is greater than the median. Quiz 4 is symmetrical and approximates the normal distribution: the mean, median, and mode are equal.

Practice Box 5.5: Calculating z-Scores

Quiz 1		Quiz 2		Quiz 3		Quiz 4	
X	z_X	X	z_X	X	z_X	X	z_X
9	1.6422	9	1.8706	10	2.1475	10	1.6514
8	1.0106	8	1.0688	9	1.5159	9	0.8257
7	0.3789	7	0.2669	8	0.8843	8	0
6	−0.2527	6	−0.5348	7	0.2527	7	−0.8257
5	−0.8843	5	−1.3366	6	−0.3789	6	−1.6514
4	−1.5159	4	−2.1384	5	−1.0106		
3	−2.1476			4	−1.6422		

Practice Box 5.6: Calculating Correlations

	Quiz 1 (X scores) and Quiz 3 (Y scores)				
	X	X^2	Y	Y^2	XY
A	8	64	8	64	64
B	4	16	6	36	24
C	3	9	4	16	12
D	6	36	7	49	42
E	8	64	8	64	64
F	9	81	10	100	90
G	6	36	5	25	30
H	7	49	6	36	42
I	5	25	6	36	30
J	7	49	5	25	35
K	6	36	5	25	30
L	7	49	7	49	49
M	8	64	9	81	72
N	7	49	7	49	49
O	5	25	6	36	30
Σ	96	652	99	691	663

1. Using "means and st. dev." formula:

$$r_{XY} = \frac{(663/15) - (6.4)(6.6)}{(1.5832)(1.5832)}$$

$$r_{XY} = \frac{44.2 - 42.24}{2.5065222}$$

$$r_{XY} = \frac{1.96}{2.506522}$$

$$r_{XY} = .78195 = .7819 = .78$$

See earlier boxes for means and standard deviations.

2. Using "raw score" formula:

$$r_{XY} = \frac{15(663) - (96)(99)}{\sqrt{[15(652) - (96)^2][15(691) - (99)^2]}} = \frac{9945 - 9504}{\sqrt{[564][564]}}$$

$$r_{XY} = \frac{441}{\sqrt{318,096}} = \frac{441}{564} = .7819 = .78$$

	X	**X²**	**Y**	**Y²**	**XY**
A	7	49	8	64	56
B	6	36	7	49	42
C	4	16	6	36	24
D	7	49	8	64	56
E	7	49	7	49	49
F	9	81	10	100	90
G	6	36	8	64	48
H	7	49	9	81	63
I	5	25	6	36	30
J	8	64	9	81	72
K	6	36	8	64	48
L	6	36	8	64	48
M	8	64	10	100	80
N	8	64	9	81	72
O	6	36	7	49	42
Σ	100	690	120	982	820

Quiz 2 (X scores) and Quiz 4 (Y scores)

1. Using "means and st. dev." formula:

$$r_{XY} = \frac{(820/15) - (6.6667)(8)}{(1.2472)(1.2111)}$$

$$r_{XY} = \frac{54.6667 - 53.3336}{1.5104839}$$

$$r_{XY} = \frac{1.333066}{1.5104839}$$

$$r_{XY} = .8825 = .88$$

See earlier boxes for means and standard deviations.

2. Using "raw score" formula:

$$r_{XY} = \frac{15(820) - (100)(120)}{\sqrt{[15(690) - (100)^2][15(982) - (120)^2]}} = \frac{12,300 - 12,000}{\sqrt{[350][330]}}$$

$$r_{XY} = \frac{300}{\sqrt{115,500}} = \frac{300}{339.8529} = .8827 = .88$$

Practice Box 5.7: Linear Regression

1. Predicting Quiz 3 scores from Quiz 1 scores

X = predictor = Quiz 1 scores; Y = criterion = Quiz 3 scores

$$b = .7819\left[\frac{1.5832}{1.5832}\right] = .7819, \qquad a = 6.6 - (.7819)(6.4) = 1.5958$$

The linear regression equation is $Y' = 1.5958 + .7819X$. Applying the linear regression equation to predict Quiz 3 scores and comparing those scores to the actual Quiz 3 scores:

X	Y'	Y
9	8.6329	10
8	7.851	9, 8, 8
7	7.0691	7, 7, 6, 5
6	6.2872	7, 5, 5
5	5.5053	6, 6
4	4.7234	6
3	3.9415	4

This stem-and-leaf chart lets you summarize a variety of XY relationships in a simple format. Next to each X score is the predicted Y score, Y', and all the actual Y scores are listed in descending order. The three actual pairs with $X = 8$ were 8/9, 8/8, 8/8.

2. Predicting Quiz 4 scores from Quiz 2 scores

$$X = \text{predictor} = \text{Quiz 2 scores;} \quad Y = \text{criterion} = \text{Quiz 4 scores}$$

$$b = .8825\left[\frac{1.2111}{1.2472}\right] = .85696, \quad a = 8 - (.85696)(6.6667) = 2.2869$$

The linear regression equation is $Y' = 2.2869 + .85696X$. Applying the linear regression equation to predict Quiz 4 scores and comparing those scores to the actual Quiz 2 scores:

X	Y'	Y
9	9.9995	10
8	9.1426	10, 9, 9
7	8.2856	9, 8, 8, 7
6	7.4287	8, 8, 8, 7, 7
5	6.5717	6
4	5.7147	6

Practice Box 5.8: Linear Transformations

	Quiz 1			Quiz 2	
X	z_X	T-score	X	z_X	T-score
9	1.6422	66.422 = 66	9	1.8706	68.706 = 69
8	1.0106	60.106 = 60	8	1.0688	60.688 = 61
7	0.3789	53.789 = 54	7	0.2669	52.669 = 53
6	-0.2527	47.473 = 47	6	-0.5348	44.652 = 45
5	-0.8843	41.157 = 41	5	-1.3366	36.634 = 36
4	-1.5159	34.841 = 35	4	-2.1384	28.616 = 29
3	-2.1475	28.525 = 29			

	Quiz 3			Quiz 4	
X	z_X	T-score	X	z_X	T-score
10	2.1475	71.475 = 71	10	1.6514	66.514 = 67
9	1.5159	65.159 = 65	9	0.8257	58.257 = 58
8	0.8843	58.843 = 59	8	0	50
7	0.2527	52.527 = 53	7	-0.8257	41.725 = 42
6	-0.3789	46.211 = 46	6	-1.6514	33.486 = 33
5	-1.0106	39.894 = 40			
4	-1.6422	33.578 = 34			

Comparing scores of 6, 7, and 8 in each distribution:

	Quiz 1		Quiz 2		Quiz 3		Quiz 4	
	z dif	T dif	z dif	T dif	z dif	T dif	z dif	T dif
6, 7	.6316	7	.8017	8	.6316	7	.8257	8
7, 8	.6317	6	.8019	8	.6316	6	.8257	8

Practice Box 5.9: Nonlinear Transformations

	Quiz 1					Quiz 2			
X	$f(X)$	$cf_B(X)$	cf-mp	PR	X	$f(X)$	$cf_B(X)$	cf-mp	PR
9	1	14	14.5	.9667	9	1	14	14.5	.9667
8	3	11	12.5	.8333	8	3	11	12.5	.8333
7	4	7	9.0	.60	7	4	7	9.0	.60
6	3	4	5.5	.3667	6	5	2	4.5	.30
5	2	2	3.0	.20	5	1	1	1.5	.10
4	1	1	1.5	.10	4	1	0	0.5	.0333
3	1	0	0.5	.0333					

	Quiz 3					Quiz 4			
X	$f(X)$	$cf_B(X)$	cf-mp	PR	X	$f(X)$	$cf_B(X)$	cf-mp	PR
10	1	14	14.5	.9667	10	2	13	14.0	.9333
9	1	13	13.5	.90	9	3	10	11.5	.7667
8	2	11	12.0	.80	8	5	5	7.5	.50
7	3	8	9.5	.6333	7	3	2	3.5	.2333
6	4	4	6.0	.40	6	2	0	1.0	.0667
5	3	1	2.5	.1667					
4	1	0	0.5	.0333					

Comparing scores of 6, 7, and 8 in each distribution:

	Quiz 1		Quiz 2		Quiz 3		Quiz 4	
	X dif	PR dif	X dif	PR dif	X dif	PR dif	X dif	PR dif
6, 7	1	.2333	1	.30	1	.2333	1	.1666
7, 8	1	.2333	1	.3333	1	.1667	1	.2667

Practice Box 5.10: Using the z-Score Table

Quiz 1

Raw Score	9	8	7	6	5	4	3
z-Score	1.6422	1.0106	.3789	−.2527	−.8843	−1.516	−2.1475
Calculated PR	.9667	.8333	.6000	.3667	.2000	.1000	.0333
Estimated PR	.9494	.84375	.64803	.4013	.18943	.06553	.01578

The estimated PRs are close to the calculated PRs at the high end of the score distribution (X = 9, 8). They differ more at the middle and most at the low end (X = 4, 3). This makes sense because the distribution is negatively skewed, meaning that its greatest deviation from the normal curve is at the low-score end of the distribution.

Quiz 2

Raw Score	9	8	7	6	5	4
z-Score	1.8706	1.0688	.2669	−.5348	−1.337	−2.138
Calculated PR	.9667	.8333	.6000	.3000	.1000	.0333
Estimated PR	.96926	.85769	.60642	.29806	.09012	.01618

Because this distribution shows less of a negative skew, the estimated PRs are good approximations of the calculated PRs until we reach the very end of the score distribution (X = 4).

Quiz 3

Raw Score	10	9	8	7	6	5	4
z-Score	2.1475	1.5159	.9943	0.2527	−.3789	−1.011	−1.6422
Calculated PR	.9667	.9000	.8000	.6333	.4000	.1667	.0333
Estimated PR	.98422	.93574	.83891	.59871	.35197	.15625	.05051

This distribution is positively skewed; therefore, the estimated PRs begin to diverge from the calculated PRs as you go *up* the raw score scale. They are better estimates in the low and middle sections.

Quiz 4 Raw Score	10	9	8	7	6
z-Score	1.6514	.8257	0	−.8257	−1.651
Calculated PR	.9333	.7667	.5000	.2333	.0667
Estimated PR	.95053	.79673	.5000	.20327	.04947

This distribution is symmetric and approximates the normal distribution. The estimated and calculated PRs differ by about the same amount all along the distribution.

CHAPTER 6 PRACTICE BOXES

Practice Box 6.1: Test–Retest Reliability

M = Monday testing,   W = Wednesday testing

$$r_{MW} = \frac{(385/10) - (5.5)(6.6)}{(1.9621)(1.4283)} = \frac{2.2}{2.8024674} = .78502 = .78$$

The test shows moderate test–retest reliability ($r = .78$). The coefficient indicates that people earn relatively similar scores on the two testings, implying that the test is measuring stable attributes of test takers. Because of this stability, we could use scores on either administration to estimate test-taker characteristics. The coefficient can be interpreted to mean that about 78.5% of the differences among people in test scores (i.e., test score variance) reflects true score differences (i.e., differences among people in actual knowledge and skills); about 21.5% of test score variance reflects the effects of random measurement error.

Practice Box 6.2: Alternate-form Reliability

A = form B of the test,   B = form B of the test

$$r_{AB} = \frac{(339/10) - (5.6)(5.6)}{(1.6248)(1.8547)} = \frac{2.54}{3.0135166} = .8429 = .84$$

The two forms show good alternate-form reliability ($r = .84$). The coefficient indicates that people earn similar scores on the two forms, implying that the forms are measuring similar attributes of test-takers. Because of this parallelism, we could use scores on either form to estimate test-taker characteristics.

The coefficient can be interpreted to mean that about 84% of the differences among people in test scores (i.e., test score variance) reflects true score differences (i.e., differences among people in knowledge and skills); about 16% of test score variance reflects measurement random error.

Practice Box 6.3: Split-half Reliability

O = score on odd-numbered items,   E = score on even-numbered items

	A	B	C	D	E	F	Mean	St. Dev.
Score on odd items	4	3	3	3	4	3	3.3333	.4714
Score on even items	4	3	4	2	5	4	3.6667	.9428
Odd score × even score	16	9	12	6	20	12	Sum = 75	

$$r_{OE} = \frac{(75/6) - (3.333)(3.667)}{(0.4714)(0.9428)} = \frac{.277889}{.444436} = .6253 = .63$$

$$r_{SB} = \frac{2(.6253)}{1 + .6253} = \frac{1.2506}{1.6253} = .76945 = .77$$

The test shows moderate split-half reliability ($r = .63$). The coefficient indicates that people earn relatively similar scores on the two half-tests, implying that the items on the two halves are measuring similar attributes of test takers. Because of this similarity, we can use overall score on the test as a measure of test-taker characteristics within this domain.

Since the split-half coefficient is calculated using half-tests, the coefficient in effect is an alternate-form coefficient for two 5-item tests. We can estimate the reliability of a single 10-item test from this coefficient using the Spearman–Brown prophesy formula. The reliability of a comparable 10-item test would be .77 and we use this second value as our "best estimate" of the reliability of the original test. Roughly 77% of test score variance reflects true score variance; the remaining 23% reflects random measurement error.

Practice Box 6.4: Calculating Cronbach's Alpha

Person	1	2	3	4	5	6	7	8	9	10
Score	36	30	33	27	32	28	32	37	27	31

Test mean = 31.3,   test variance = 10.81

Item	1	2	3	4	5
Item variance	.81	.84	.56	.65	.81

Σ(item variances) = 3.67,   no. of items = k = 5

$$r = \frac{5}{4}\left(1 - \frac{3.67}{10.81}\right) = (1.25)(1 - .3395) = .8256 = .83$$

According to the coefficient, people perform consistently across the different test items (r = .83); therefore, the test shows good internal consistency. About 82.5% of test score variance reflects true score differences; the remaining 17.5% reflects random measurement error.

Practice Box 6.5: Calculating KR-20

Items	1	2	3	4	5	6	7	8	9	10
p	.5000	.6667	.5000	.5000	.6667	.6667	.5000	.3333	.6667	.6667
q	.5000	.3333	.5000	.5000	.3333	.3333	.5000	.6667	.3333	.3333
$(p)(q)$	.2500	.2222	.2500	.2500	.2222	.2222	.2500	.2222	.2222	.2222

$$k = 10, \quad N = 6, \quad \Sigma(p)(q) = 2.3332, \quad \sigma^2 = 5.2222$$

$$r_{KR\text{-}20} = \frac{10}{9}\left(\frac{5.2222 - 2.3332}{5.2222}\right) = (1.1111)(.5532) = .6147$$

$$= .61$$

This is a moderate level of internal consistency. There does seem to be some consistency in how people answer the various questions. Therefore, the test items do appear to be tapping the same domain.

Practice Box 6.6: Calculating KR-21

$$\overline{X} = 13.4, \qquad \sigma = 3.63868, \qquad \sigma^2 = 13.24 \quad K = 20$$

$$r_{\text{KR-21}} = 1 - \left(\frac{13.4(20 - 13.24)}{20(13.24)} \right) = 1 - \frac{90.584}{264.8} = 1 - .3421$$

$$= 1 - .3421 = .6579 = .66$$

The test shows a moderate level of internal consistency. The relationship between the mean, the standard deviation and the number of items implies that the items are tapping the same domain elements.

Practice Box 6.7: Calculating SEM

Test in:	St. dev.[a]	r[b]	SEM
PB 6.1 (Mon.)	1.96	.785	.9088
PB 6.1 (Wed.)	1.43	.785	.6631
PB 6.2 (form A)	1.625	.843	.6439
PB 6.2 (form B)	1.855	.843	.7350
PB 6.3	1.291	.769	.6205
PB 6.4	3.2879	.826	1.3715
PB 6.5	2.2852	.615	1.4179
PB 6.6	3.6387	.657	2.1311

[a]In some problems, only the variance is listed. Calculation of SEM requires using the standard deviation, not the variance.

[b]Remember, the formula for SEM uses the square root of $(1 - r)$.

In each case, the SEM indicates the average number of points by which true scores differ from test scores (i.e., the average amount of error in test scores).

Practice Box 6.8: Calculating Confidence Intervals

Test in:	SEM	Mean	65% C.I.	95% C.I.[a]
PB 6.1 (Mon.)	.9088	5.5	5.5 ± .9088	5.5 ± 1.7812
PB 6.1 (Wed.)	.6631	6.6	6.6 ± .6631	6.6 ± 1.2997
PB 6.2 (form A)	.6439	5.6	5.6 ± .6439	5.6 ± 1.262
PB 6.2 (form B)	.7350	5.6	5.6 ± .7350	5.6 ± 1.4406
PB 6.3	.6205	7	7 ± .6205	7 ± 1.2162
PB 6.4	1.3715	31.3	31.3 ± 1.3715	31.3 ± 2.688
PB 6.5	1.4179	5.67	5.67 ± 1.4179	5.67 ± 2.779
PB 6.6	2.1311	13.4	13.4 ± 2.1311	13.4 ± 4.1769

[a]Uses SEM × 1.96

The 65% C.I. is the interval within which we are 65% sure that the *true test mean* lies; the 95% C.I. is the interval within which we are 95% sure the *true mean* lies.

Practice Box 6.9: Evaluating Score Differences

Person A's scores in Practice Box 6.1 (test–retest scenario):

$$X_M = 9, \quad X_W = 9, \quad \text{a score change of 0 points}$$

$$SEM_M = .9088, \ SEM_W = .6631; \quad \text{so } SEM_{dif} = 1.1249$$

$$(1.96)(1.1249) = 2.2048$$

The score difference is *less than* (1.96)(SEM_{dif}); therefore, it is not a statistically significant difference. In other words, there is more than a 5% likelihood that this change is the result of chance factors. Person C's scores in Practice Box 6.2 (alternate-form scenario):

$$X_A = 4, \ X_B = 6, \quad \text{a score change of 2 points}$$

$$SEM_A = .6439, \quad SEM_B = .7350; \quad SEM_{dif} = .9772$$

$$(1.96)(0.9772) = 1.9153$$

The score difference is *more than* $(1.96)(SEM_{dif})$; therefore, it *is* statistically significant. In other words, these is less than a 5% likelihood that this is a chance difference.

Practice Box 6.10: Evaluating Composite Scores

1. Mean = 77.4, st. dev. = 3.2, $N = 5$

$$SEM = \frac{3.2}{\sqrt{5}} = 1.4311,$$ 95% CI for the mean
$$= 77.4 \pm (1.96)(1.4311)$$
$$= 77.4 \pm 2.8049$$
$$= 74.5951 - 80.2049$$

2. Mean = 80.8, st. dev. = 2.6382, $N = 5$

$$SEM = \frac{2.6382}{\sqrt{5}} = 1.1798,$$ 95% CI for the mean
$$= 80.8 \pm (1.96)(1.1798)$$
$$= 80.8 \pm 2.3124$$
$$= 78.4876 - 83.1125$$

3. Mean = 89, st. dev. = 2, $N = 5$

$$SEM = \frac{2}{\sqrt{5}} = 0.8944,$$ 95% CI for the mean
$$= 89 \pm (1.96)(.8944)$$
$$= 89 \pm 1.753024$$
$$= 87.2469 - 90.7530$$

CHAPTER 7 PRACTICE BOXES

Practice Box 7.1: Calculating the Criterion Validity Coefficient

1. X = test score (predictor), Y = behavior rating (criterion)

$$r_{XY} = \frac{(183/10) - (5)(3.4)}{(1.6125)(0.9165)} = \frac{1.3}{1.4778563} = .87965 = .88$$

2. Since $r_{XY}^2 = .7738$, we can conclude that approximately 77% of the variance in the behavior ratings is predictable from score on the neuropsychological screening test. The remaining 23% of the variance in behavior ratings is accounted for by factors other than those measured by the screening test. The test is a valid predictor of behavioral ratings; coefficients of .6 or greater are considered good when using a single measure to predict a future behavior.

Practice Box 7.2: Predicting Criterion Scores

1. $b = .87965\left(\dfrac{0.9165}{1.6125}\right) = .87965(.56837) = .4999$

$a = 3.4 - (.4999)(5) = 3.4 - 2.4995 = .9005$
The regression equation is $Y' = .9005 + .4999(X)$.
To find the test score predicting a behavior rating of 4 ($Y' = 4$):

$$4 = .9005 + .4999(X), \quad \text{so} \quad 3.0995 = .4999(X), \quad \text{and} \quad X = 6.20024$$

2. The test is an adequate predictor, but the best predictions always involve more than one measure. The test certainly would be useful as part of a larger predictive scheme. If our goal is to be conservative in identifying patients needing more care, we should use a test score of 7 as our cutoff score. The equation indicates that even with a *perfect XY* relationship, people with scores of 6 may earn ratings slightly below 4, whereas those with scores of 7 are likely to earn ratings of *at least* 4.

Practice Box 7.3: Calculating Standard Error of Estimate

1. $s_E = .9165\sqrt{1 - (.87965)^2} = .9165(.4756) = .4359 = .44$

2. On the basis of the validity analysis, the average difference between actual behavior rating and predicted behavior rating is .44 points. On a 7-point scale, that's a relatively small standard error.

Practice Box 7.4: Establishing Confidence Intervals

1. Using the regression equation and a screening test score of 7, the predicted behavioral rating is

$$Y' = .9005 + .4999(7) = 4.3998$$

2. The 68% C.I. for this predicted behavioral rating is

$$4.3998 \pm .4359 = 4.8357 - 3.9639$$

We expect 68% of the behavioral ratings earned by people with screening test scores of 7 to fall in this range.

The 95% C.I. for this predicted behavioral rating is

$$4.3998 \pm (1.96)(.4359) = 5.2542 - 3.5454$$

We expect 95% of the behavioral ratings earned by people with screening test scores of 7 to fall in this range.

Practice Box 7.5: Creating a Selection Efficiency Table

Predictor (Test)	Criterion (Behavior Rating)		
	Not Competent ($Y < 4$)	Competent ($Y \geq 4$)	
No monitoring ($X \geq 7$)	0	2	2
Monitoring ($X < 7$)	5	3	8
	5	5	10

The base rate is the proportion of people who meet the criterion used to define behavioral competence. In this case, only 5 individuals out of 10 are rated as behaviorally competent (i.e., have behavior ratings of at least 4). The base rate, therefore, is 50%.

The selection ratio is the proportion of people who would be predicted to be competent (i.e., *selected*) on the basis of their screening test scores. In this case, only 2 individuals out of 10 earned high enough predictor scores to be selected as not requiring monitoring.

The positive hit rate is the proportion of people who are (1) selected on the basis of predictor scores and (2) judged competent on the criterion. Based on a predictor score of 7, we would select 2 people, both of whom are in fact judged competent. Our positive hit rate, therefore, is 2/2 or 100%! This looks like a great selection strategy—so far. We would expect only 50% of the group to be behaviorally competent (base rate = 50%); by using predictor scores of 7, *all* the people we select are behaviorally competent.

Practice Box 7.6: Evaluating a Selection Procedure

	Criterion (Behavior Rating)		
Predictor (Test)	Not Competent ($Y < 4$)	Competent ($Y \geq 4$)	
No monitoring ($X \geq 7$)	$\dfrac{5 \times 2}{10} = 1$	$\dfrac{5 \times 2}{10} = 1$	2
Monitoring ($X < 7$)	$\dfrac{5 \times 8}{10} = 4$	$\dfrac{5 \times 8}{10} = 4$	8
	5	5	10

2. and 3. The positive hit rate is the proportion of people who are (1) selected on the basis of predictor test scores *and* (2) identified as meeting the criterion. If only chance were operating, we would select 2 people who did not need monitoring, but only 1 would be likely to be behaviorally competent. Since the predictor and criterion *are* related, use of the predictor results in selection of 2 people, *both* of whom meet the criterion. The positive hit rate by chance alone is 1/2 or 50%; the *actual* positive hit rate is 2/2 or 100%!

The false negative rate is the proportion of people who are (1) rejected on the basis of predictor test scores, *but* (2) do meet the criterion. If only chance were operating, we would expect 4 people to be misclassified as likely to need monitoring. Because the predictor and criterion are related, only 3 people placed in the "needs monitoring group" actually earned behavior ratings of 4 or above (i.e., met the criterion). The false negative rate by chance alone is 4/10 or 40%; the *actual* false negative rate is 3/10 or 30%.

The plan looks good at first glance—the predictor and criterion are related and use of the predictor produces better decisions than expected by chance alone. Furthermore, the positive hit rate is 100%. However, there is a significant problem: the false negative rate is very high. Of the 5 people who earned acceptable behavior ratings, 3 would be misidentified as in need of monitoring if the plan were used. Perhaps the hospital should consider lowering the cutoff score on the screening test to 6 (rather than 7).

CHAPTER 8 PRACTICE BOXES

Practice Box 8.1: Calculating Item Difficulty

Item No.	1	2	3	4	5	6	7	8	9	10
p	.90	.80	.75	.65	.75	.85	.70	.80	.75	.65
Evaluation	E	E	A	A	A	E	A	E	A	A

Item No.	11	12	13	14	15
p	.65	.85	.85	.70	.90
Evaluation	A	E	E	A	E

A = adequate (.5–.75)
E = easy (> .75)
H = hard (< .5)

Practice Box 8.2: Calculating the Item Discrimination Index

Item No.	1	2	3	4	5	6	7	8	9	10
Top 7	1.0	1.0	1.0	.714	.857	1.0	.714	1.0	.857	.714
Bottom 7	.857	.857	.429	.571	.571	.857	.429	.714	.571	.571
D	.143	.143	.571	.143	.286	.143	.285	.286	.286	.143
Evaluation	P	P	E	P	A	P	A	A	A	P

Item No.	11	12	13	14	15
Top 7	.714	1.0	.857	1.0	1.0
Bottom 7	.429	.714	.857	.429	.857
D	.285	.286	0	.571	.143
Evaluation	A	A	P	E	P

A = adequate (≤ .2)
E = excellent (> .3)
P = poor (< .2)

Practice Box 8.3: Calculating Item-total Correlations

1. Calculate the overall test mean and standard deviation.
2. Identify the people who were correct on the relevant items.
3. Use these numbers to determine p, the proportion of people correct, on each item.
4. Create distributions of total scores only for these people.
5. Calculate the mean of each of these new distributions.

Overall test mean = 11.55, overall test st. dev. = 1.7168

Frequency distributions of scores for people who were *correct* on:

Item 4		Item 7		Item 10	
X	$f(X)$	X	$f(X)$	X	$f(X)$
15	1	15	1	15	1
14	2	14	2	14	0
13	1	13	2	13	3
12	3	12	3	12	4
11	2	11	3	11	2
10	2	10	0	10	2
9	2	9	3	9	1
No. people correct	13	No. people correct	14	No. people correct	13

$$p_4 = 13/20 \qquad p_7 = 14/20 \qquad p_{10} = 13/20$$
$$= .65 \qquad\qquad = .70 \qquad\qquad = .65$$
$$\overline{X}_4 = 11.6923 \qquad \overline{X}_7 = 11.7857 \qquad \overline{X}_{10} = 11.7692$$

$$r_{\text{pb-4}} = \left[\frac{11.6923 - 11.55}{1.7168} \right]\left[\frac{.65}{1 - .65} \right] = (.08289)(1.85714) = .1539$$

$$r_{\text{pb-7}} = \left[\frac{11.7857 - 11.55}{1.7168} \right]\left[\frac{.70}{1 - .70} \right] = (.13729)(2.3333) = .3203$$

$$r_{\text{pb-10}} = \left[\frac{11.7692 - 11.55}{1.7168} \right]\left[\frac{.65}{1 - .65} \right] = (.127679)(1.85714) = .2371$$

	Item 4	Item 7	Item 10
r_{pb}	.1539	.3203	.2371
D	.143	.285	.143

The values of r_{pb} are relatively close to the D values in two cases. The r_{pb} is a more stringent test of item discrimination, although the D statistic can serve as an estimate of the item-total correlation.

Practice Box 8.4: Estimating Item Difficulty

Item No.:	1	2	3	4	5	6	7	8	9	10	11	12	13	14	15
Top 7	1.0	1.0	1.0	.714	.857	1.0	.714	1.0	.857	.714	.714	1.0	.857	1.0	1.0
Bottom 7	.857	.857	.429	.571	.571	.857	.429	.714	.571	.571	.429	.714	.857	.429	.857
Estimated p	.929	.929	.715	.643	.714	.929	.572	.857	.714	.643	.572	.857	.857	.715	.929
Actual p	.90	.80	.75	.65	.75	.85	.70	.80	.75	.65	.65	.85	.85	.70	.90

The values estimated by D are generally close to the actual p values. Average estimated item difficulty from D is .7717. Actual average item difficulty, based on p, is .77.

Practice Box 8.5: Estimating the Criterion Validity Coefficient

Determining the medians on both measures:
1. Quiz grades

Top 10 scores are:	15 14 14 13 13 13 12 12 12 12
Bottom 10 scores:	11 11 11 11 10 10 10 9 9 9
Median score = 11.5	

2. Pretest grades

Top 10 scores are:	94 92 86 85 83 82 82 80 78 78
Bottom 10 scores:	76 72 72 72 70 68 68 66 58 57
Median score = 77	

Proportion of people above the median on both measures (Quiz > 11.5 *and* Pretest > 77) = 9/20 or .45. Estimated $r_{XY} = .95$ (from Table 8.6). The pretest is an excellent predictor of grades on the quiz. In terms of variance, 90% ($.95^2$) of the variance in quiz grades is predictable from grades on the pretest!

Practice Box 8.6: Calculating Distractor Power

Because there are two distractors for each item, the number of people expected to select each distractor, for any given item, is

$$\frac{\text{No. of people incorrect on that item}}{2}$$

The $\times$ for each item identifies the correct answer; the remaining alternatives are the distractors.

Item No.:	1	2	3	4	5	6	7	8	9	10	11	12	13	14	15
Expected no.	1.0	2.0	2.5	3.5	2.5	1.5	3.0	2.0	2.5	3.5	3.5	1.5	1.5	3.0	1.0
No. of A	$\times$	2	2	5	1	2	$\times$	1	$\times$	4	3	$\times$	$\times$	5	1
No. of B	1	2	3	$\times$	4	$\times$	5	$\times$	2	3	$\times$	3	2	1	$\times$
No. of C	1	$\times$	$\times$	2	$\times$	1	1	3	3	$\times$	4	0	1	$\times$	1

Items needing examination are 4, 5, 7, 12, and 14. In each case, one distractor is significantly more powerful than the other. Perhaps these distractors need to be rewritten.

Practice Box 8.7: Graphing Discrimination–Difficulty Relationships

The numbers within the graph are the actual item numbers, plotted according to their D and p values. Lines have been drawn within the graph to identify regions of (1) good versus poor discrimination and (2) different levels of item difficulty.

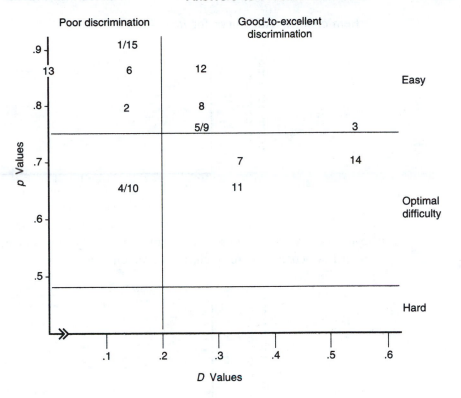

Practice Box 8.8: Graphing Item-characteristic Curves

Use the frequency data from Practice Box 8.3 to get started.

Total Score	Frequency	Number (Proportion) of People with Each Total Score Who Were:		
		Correct on Item 4	Correct on Item 7	Correct on Item 10
15	1	1 (1.0)	1 (1.0)	1 (1.0)
14	2	2 (1.0)	2 (1.0)	0 (0.0)
13	3	1 (.33)	2 (.67)	3 (1.0)
12	4	3 (.75)	3 (.75)	4 (1.0)
11	4	2 (.50)	3 (.75)	2 (.50)
10	3	2 (.67)	0 (0.0)	2 (.67)
9	3	2 (.67)	3 (1.0)	1 (.33)

Item characteristic curve for *Item 4*

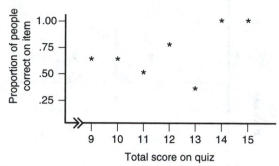

The curve is not too bad, considering the small number tested. However, those with middle scores are a bit less likely to be correct than those with low scores. There might be a problem here.

For Item 7

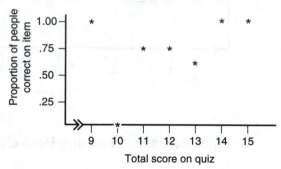

This curve does not look good. Although most high scorers are correct, so are the low scorers. And those in the middle are less often correct than those with low scores.

For Item 10

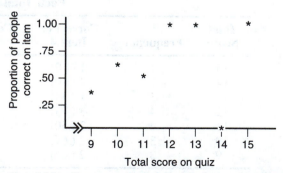

This is the "healthiest" curve. People with lower scores usually are wrong; high and mid scorers are more likely to be correct. But the item does not sort mid and high scorers well.

Name Index

Achenbach, T. M., 323
Ahlgren, A., 115
Ahman, J. S., 311
Aiken, L. R., 36n, 64, 71, 95, 342
Albert, M. S., 369
Alter, B., 113
Alveres, K. M., 429
Anastasi, A., 36n, 55, 107, 112, 113, 118, 315, 344, 345, 351, 356, 358, 360, 362, 375, 392, 393
Andreasen, N. C., 369
Arnold, D., 418
Asher, J. J., 417, 422

Baker, T. B., 340
Balla, D. A., 122, 313
Bannatyne, A., 362
Bar-Hillel, M., 418
Beehr, T. A., 412
Bellak, L., 110, 356
Bellak, S. S., 110, 356
Bender, L., 322, 323, 363
Bennett, G. K., 395, 396, 415
Bennett, R. E., 313
Ben-Shakar, G., 418
Berk, R. A., 87, 89
Berman, W., 353
Bernardin, H. J., 429
Binet, A., 8, 82, 304, 304n
Blatt, S., 353
Block, J. H., 89, 119
Bloom, A. S., 300, 301, 327
Bloom, B. S., 45–46
Bornstein, A. V., 54
Bower, E. M., 314
Bowers, F. R., 403
Boyd, L., 378
Bridges, J. W., 8
Brooks, P., 418
Brown, F. G., 40, 87, 122, 251, 252, 334
Bruininks, R. H., 324
Bryant, B. R., 322
Buck, J. N., 110, 112, 358, 359
Buros, O. K., 23
Burris, L. R., 418
Butcher, J., 104, 348

Callahan, C., 418
Callender, J. C., 413
Campbell, D. P., 97, 105, 381, 382, 383, 387

Campbell, J. P., 413
Campbell, V. L., 377
Carlson, S. B., 45
Cascio, W. F., 417
Cattell, James, 8
Cattell, R. B., 105, 318, 399–401, 402
Champney, H., 99
Chao, G. T., 413, 422
Chave, E. J., 115, 116
Cicchetti, D. V., 122
Clarizio, H. F., 334
Connolly, A. J., 322
Conoley, J. C., 23
Conrad, L., 393
Cook, S. W., 116, 117
Cooper, W. H., 412
Corah, N. L., 101, 349
Cornelius, E. T., III, 356
Cramer, P., 356
Cranny, C. J., 429
Crites, J. O., 387
Cronbach, L. J., 100, 197–98, 252
Cronshaw, S. F., 412
Cundick, B. P., 358

Dachler, H. P., 431
Das, J. P., 325
Davidshofer, C. O., 51, 120, 328, 330, 416, 422, 427
Davidson, N. L., 57
Delacourt, M. A., 312
Delhees, K. H., 402
Dickinson, T. L., 121
Diedrich, P. B., 213, 214, 283
Dodrill, C. B., 414
Donlon, T. F., 390, 391
Dougherty, T. W., 413
Drummond, R. J., 349
DuBois, P. H., 8
Dunham, R. M., 54
Dunn, I. M., 53, 67
Dunn, L. M., 53, 67
Dush, D. M., 358

Ebel, R. L., 64, 87
Eber, H. W., 105, 399, 400
Ebert, R. J., 413
Edelbrock, C., 323
Edwards, A. L., 98, 100, 103, 106, 349, 350
Elkins, G. R., 377, 378

497

Subject Index

Ability tests
  academic achievement tests and, 389–90
  achievement, 32–34, 35
  alternate-choice, 32, 33, 64–71
  aptitude, 32–34, 35
  basic issues, 62–64
  comparing alternate-choice with free-response, 75
  completion/fill-in-the-blank tests, 32, 33, 72–73
  difference between typical-performance tests and, 94
  entrance exams and, 390–94
  essay tests, 32, 33, 74, 75, 76
  factors to consider before writing, 64
  free-response, 32, 32n, 33, 71–74
  general, 414
  intelligence tests, 388–89
  issues in use of, 396–97
  matching tests, 32, 33, 66
  multiple-choice tests, 13, 32, 33, 66–71, 75, 76
  for selecting employees, 413–16
  short answer tests, 32, 33, 73
  specific, 394–96, 415–16
  true/false tests, 32, 33, 65
  vocational counseling and use of, 387–97
Academic achievement tests, vocational counseling and use of, 389
Achievement tests, 32–34, 35
  California Achievement Test (CAT), 309–10, 311, 389
  content and behavorial objectives and, 46–47
  content validity and, 310
  group, 309–10
  individual, to identify special needs, 321
  Iowa Test of Basic Skills (ITBS), 310, 311
  vocational counseling and use of academic, 389
Adaptive behavior, 313
Adaptive Behavior Scale, 323
Adjective Check List, 118
Administration procedures, standard, 12–13
  computer-assisted, 56–57
  group, 55–56
  individual, 53–55
  interrelatedness between purpose, format and, 52–53
Age differentiation, 319
Age-equivalent scores, 82–84, 85
Age scale, 305
Alternate-choice ability tests
  comparing free-response with, 75
  defining, 32, 33, 64–65
  matching tests, 32, 33, 66

multiple-choice tests, 13, 32, 33, 66–71, 75, 76
true/false tests, 32, 33, 65
Alternate-form reliability, 187, 191–93
Alzheimer's disease, 362
American Association of Mental Deficiency (AAMD), 121, 313
  Adaptive Behavior Scale, 323
American College Test (ACT), 13, 390, 391
American Education Research Association (AERA), 24, 379
American Psychological Association (APA), 8, 301, 379
  clinical psychology testing and, 340
  computer-assisted testing and, 56
  counseling psychology testing and, 376
  industrial/organizational psychologists in, 408
  integrity tests and, 418
  regulations on use of tests and, 24, 25–26
American Society of Personnel Administrators, 409
Aptitude tests, 32–34, 35
  Cognitive Abilities Test (CogAT), 306–8, 306n
  construct validity and, 308–9
  design of intelligence tests, 304–5
  group intelligence tests, 305–8
  measuring student aptitude, 304–9
  Otis–Lennon School Ability Test (OSLAT), 306, 306n, 307, 308–9
Area transformations, 163, 164, 168–71
Armed Services Vocational Aptitude Battery (ASVAB)
  employment testing and, 414, 415
  vocational counseling and use of, 394
Assessment, definition of, 5
Attitude scales
  defined, 114
  item formats, 114–15
  item selection and scale construction, 115–17
Attitude tests, 36, 36n
Audience, test, 12, 37–38

Basal age, 320
Basal level of performance, 54
Base rate, 240, 241–42
Behavioral and emotional problems, 314
Behavioral domains, 49–51
Behavioral functioning, tests of, 323
Behaviorally anchored rating scales (BARS), 120–21, 427–28
Behavioral objectives, 45–46
Behavioral observation scales (BOS), 121–22, 427–28
Behavioral scales, 427–28